# BUILDING
# A SUCCESSFUL MARRIAGE

# BUILDING A SUCCESSFUL MARRIAGE

## SEVENTH EDITION

Judson T. Landis

Professor Emeritus of Family Sociology
Research Associate, Institute of Human Development
University of California at Berkeley

Mary G. Landis

PRENTICE-HALL, INC., ENGLEWOOD CLIFFS, NEW JERSEY 07632

*Library of Congress Cataloging in Publication Data*

LANDIS, JUDSON T
    Building a successful marriage.

    Bibliography: p.
    Includes index.
    1. Marriage.  2. Family life education.  I. Landis,
Mary G., joint author.  II. Title.
HQ734.L25 1977      301.42      77–1662
ISBN  0–13–087007–2

Printed in the United States of America

10    9    8    7    6    5    4    3    2

PRENTICE-HALL INTERNATIONAL, INC., *London*
PRENTICE-HALL OF AUSTRALIA PTY. LIMITED, *Sydney*
PRENTICE-HALL OF CANADA, LTD., *Toronto*
PRENTICE-HALL OF INDIA PRIVATE LIMITED, *New Delhi*
PRENTICE-HALL OF SOUTHEAST ASIA PTE. LTD., *Singapore*

To
Judson and Sheron, Jeffrey, Brian, and Kevin

and to
Janet and Worth, Anne, Stephen, and David

# CONTENTS

chapter **8**

LOVE, *108*

chapter **9**

MARRIAGE UNDER SPECIAL CIRCUMSTANCES, *118*

chapter **10**

PREMARITAL SEXUAL RELATIONS, *136*

chapter **14**

ACHIEVING ADJUSTMENT IN MARRIAGE, 236

chapter **15**

SEXUAL ADJUSTMENT IN MARRIAGE, 266

chapter **19**

BUYING LIFE INSURANCE, *338*

chapter **20**

DIVORCE, *358*

chapter **21**

REMARRIAGE, *380*

chapter **22**

REPRODUCTION, *398*

chapter **23**

FAMILY PLANNING, *428*

chapter **24**

CHILDLESS MARRIAGES AND ADOPTION, *446*

# PREFACE

This book is written for people who are marrying in a time when marriage failure is frequent in the United States but also a time when there can be greater emotional fulfillment and happiness in marriage than in the past when man-woman relationships were more rigidly structured. University students are concerned with defining their own attitudes, values and needs, as these relate to their life choices. They are equally involved in trying to understand and assess the social institutions of which they are a part. We have found that as they look critically but hopefully at marriage they want facts. They are interested in the views and values of others, but they ask for empirical data. They want to know what research studies have discovered about courtship, marriage adjustment, and interpersonal relationships within families, that will serve as orientation points for them in considering their life choices.

Therefore, as we write of the varied aspects of courtship, mate selection, and marital adjustment, we draw from insights gained from study, research, and counseling with students and people in the successive stages of the family life cycle; our continuing frame of reference is research data from reliable studies.

Our emphasis is upon the dynamic aspects of relationships in each stage of the life cycle—during youthful dating and courtship, the first years of marriage and of parenthood, the middle and later years of marriage. This concept of the growth requirements made upon the individual by each succeeding stage of life leads to a redefining of many terms commonly used in discussions of marital adjustment. Thus, situations that might seem to be "problems" can be more accurately assessed as challenges to the individual to grow into the new life stages. For example, problems are not inherent in in-law relationships nor in the necessity to put aside dependence on parents to achieve a pair relationship with the spouse; such situations become problem areas of life only when individuals fail to make growth commensurate with their moving into a new stage of the life cycle. This concept of the growth requirements necessary for building a successful marriage is applied throughout the book.

The book draws from research studies providing a perspective on courtship, sex standards, and problems of adjustment in marriage such as: a study of courtship, dating, sexual attitudes and behavior, and engagements, as reported by more than 3000 students in 18 American colleges and universities; a study of the problems of adjustment in marriage, based on reports from 581 happily married couples, 155 troubled couples who were having counseling, and 164 divorced people. Responses from these three groups offered insights into the nature of crises or stress periods in marriage, the ways in which people face such crises in adjustment, and an evaluation of the long-term effects of their ways of reacting to the stress periods in their relationships.

This seventh edition is a comprehensive revision, although the basic viewpoint and purpose of the book remain the same as in previous editions. We have written a chapter on remarriage. Today one-fourth of all marriages are remarriages for one or both partners. We have enlarged our discussion of adjustment to divorce and have included a discussion of adjustment to widowhood. The dating and courtship processes of the widowed and divorced are discussed and compared. The adjustment of those in second marriages is examined as is the success and failure of the widowed and the divorced in remarriages.

All topics have been updated in treatment and new material based on current research has been added. Topics such as premarital intercourse, sexual adjustment in marriage, contraceptives, abortion, venereal disease, and living together before marriage are discussed from an objective viewpoint. All materials have been rewritten to eliminate sexism and greater attention has been given to changing sexual roles and new life styles. The many legal aspects of living together without formal marriage are considered. A consideration is given to what couples living together before marriage should learn about each other during such a relationship.

We wish to acknowledge the contribution of all who have taken part in our research studies: the different generations of college and university students who have responded concerning their maturation and dating; the engaged couples who have reported on their progress through courtship; the married couples, happy and unhappy—and the divorced people who have reported on their experiences in resolving or failing to resolve their differences, and on various phases of their courtships and approaches to marriage.

Our colleagues in different schools have helped us greatly through their comments and criticisms as they have used earlier editions of this book. We owe much also to the many thousands of students who have contributed to our knowledge and thinking by their discussions in our classes and their evaluations of the text and lecture materials.

Mary and I worked cooperatively in marriage and in the writing of the first six editions of this text. Our marriage of 43 years ended with her death and I found myself in a new stage of the life cycle—a stage that calls for growth to make the adjustments necessary after 43 years of living and working together with one person. One of my adjustments to my life situation was to remarry. Grace, my present wife (a sister of Mary's), and I have each gone through the period of adjustment to widowhood and are now adjusting to a new stage in life. Growth is necessary to understand a new spousal relationship, to appreciate our combined children and grandchildren, and to work cooperatively. In this seventh edition, Grace has been responsible for the editing, changing words and sentences to bring them into harmony with present-day expression, and rewriting all material to eliminate sexism. Together we are learning to live as a team in our new life situation. This experience is giving us insight into a new stage of marital adjustment, some of which is expressed in the chapter on remarriage added in this edition.

We want to acknowledge our debt to our children. All the way along we have learned from them. Living with them as children and seeing them grow into productive adulthood has been most challenging and rewarding. Now their children add new dimensions and meanings to our lives.

We hope this seventh edition will prove useful to the present generation of college students and others looking toward happy and successful marriages.

*Judson T. Landis*

# SUCCESSFUL MARRIAGE

Today marriage is being questioned critically by many people. One hears the statement that marriage is an outmoded institution, no longer serving a necessary function for men and women in our society. Such views are based upon a cluster of developments: (1) The availability of reliable contraceptives along with an increased awareness of worldwide problems arising from population growth. From these two related facts some people conclude that if couples choose not to reproduce, why marry? (2) An increase in sexual permissiveness that has the effect of making sexual experience more available outside of marriage than was true when moral standards and social attitudes were more rigid than they are today. Some people who formerly would have felt impelled to marry in order to satisfy sexual drives are freer to remain single. (3) Greater economic independence and freedom for women so that fewer women now feel they must marry in order to be economically secure.

All these developments have some relevance in any discussion of marriage as an institution today. However, the basic realities about marriage as an institutionalized relationship have not changed. Rather, some developments operate to give marriage more value for individuals than ever before. In our society, where change is the norm, individuals are subject to constant shifts in associations and in relationships. Geographical relocation because of vocational necessities or educational opportunities, rapid political and social changes that have the effect of disorienting many individuals and polarizing them from others—these and other factors characteristic of our society in the 1970s serve to alienate and isolate individuals. The individual becomes aware of a great need for one person with whom to share a continuous relationship on more than a temporary basis. This commitment to share the future together, to take the risks and enjoy together the rewards of the unpredictable years ahead is the basis of marriage. In marriage two people share their present life, their future, and their past. This element of commitment to a permanent union of lives distinguishes marriage from other relationships that may temporarily meet the needs of two people. The resulting personal confidence—even security—contributes to an ability and a willingness to work to create a successful marriage. Evidence that such commitment has basic value and meaning for individuals is the fact that despite a conflicting variety of viewpoints about marriage today, a very high percentage of people still choose to marry. This year approximately 4,000,000 people in the United States will marry. In 1975, 94 percent of men and 95 percent of women ages 45 to 54 were or had been married. The percentage of people who married has increased steadily since 1910 and now stands at an all-time high for both men and women. The average age at first marriage decreased for most of this century until the 1960s and 1970s when people, especially women, again started delaying marriage to a later age.

## SOCIAL IMPLICATIONS OF CHANGE IN STATUS

By marrying, individuals change status permanently, even if the marriage should later be broken. The couple become a new family unit. They now have legal, emotional, financial, and other responsibilities toward each other. They also have new obligations toward a larger kinship group, for by their marriage they unite two families who have not heretofore been "family connection" or related to each other. Thus, the marrying couple have changed not only their own status but have conferred a new status on other people as well.

Most people, when they marry, are concerned primarily with their own happiness as a pair. More realistically, we should say that, at marriage, each individual is hoping to be happy and to receive certain benefits from the marriage. The couple may develop more slowly within the deeper involvement of married living. Few people at the time of their wedding are in a state of mind to give much thought to the broader social implications of their marriage or to what society may have at stake in their union.

For many marrying couples, the wedding does mark the beginning of a partnership that enriches their lives, fulfills their hopes for happiness, and enables them to grow toward their greatest potential as persons. Such couples assess themselves as "happily married." That such a marriage also makes a positive contribution to society may remain outside of their thinking. For some other couples, marriage brings disappointment and disillusionment. They may remain married or they may divorce, but their union seems to result in deterioration rather than fulfillment.

In this book we are concerned with successful marriages and how they are created and maintained. What is a successful marriage? A variety of approaches may be made to that question. The most obvious test is whether the two remain married for a lifetime or end the marriage by divorce. Is a marriage a success if the two later regret marrying but remain married, or if only one of them regrets the marriage and they do not divorce? May success in marriage be judged by whether children are born and cooperatively reared even though the married pair consider themselves less than happily married? Is success to be measured in terms of how capable the two are in providing for their own security and accumulating material possessions to pass on to the next generation?

Further, at what *time* may the success or failure of a marriage be determined: during the honeymoon? the time before parenthood? the years of parenthood? or the later years after the children have left home?

By whatever standards success is judged, to what extent does a couple have control over the quality of their marriage?

A successful marriage becomes a union of personalities. Each one brings to the partnership qualities that enrich the life of the other as well as his or her own. Both experience some enhancement of personality, for they benefit from each other's attributes and capacities. They develop an interdependence so that pleasures and rewards are enlarged through sharing and disappointments are made easier. This union of personalities is not a sudden transformation that occurs at the wedding, nor is it an automatic accompaniment of being in love. It is achieved gradually through cooperation by people who are motivated to give of themselves and some of their individual freedom in exchange for the close affectional relationship marriage can provide.

Many things affect the quality of the relationship within a marriage. The personality traits of the husband and wife and their family backgrounds are major factors. Their conceptions of marriage, what it will require of them and what they hope to receive from it, will also significantly affect their happiness in marriage. Their attitudes toward marriage and their ability to cooperate unselfishly may be of more value to them over the years than will how much in love they were at first.

A successful marriage will provide a healthy emotional climate for any children who are born to the couple. Through children, marital happiness can be extended and perpetuated. Sociologists have discovered that, in our society, successful marriages run in families. Hence, the couple who marry, aware that they have committed themselves to living together in harmony, with respect for each other's individuality and tolerance for each other's faults, and who are able to create a permanently satisfactory relationship in the marriage, are setting a pattern for the successful marriages of their children.

How well people understand themselves and their own personality needs and how well they habitually get along with themselves and with others will be major factors in the success of their marriage. Marriage does not change basic personality. It will not work miracles and bring happiness to people who do not have the habit of happiness. Those who marry with a reasonably accurate evaluation of their own marriageability and an appreciation of the obligations of marriage as well as its privileges are likely to achieve greater success and happiness.

## MARRIAGE AS A DYNAMIC PROCESS

The relationship that exists between two people when they marry does not remain static. New understandings and new adjustments continue to be necessary at each stage of life, and each stage will have its own special requirements, pressures, and rewards. Quite universally, married couples are confronted with a series of situations that require them to rise to challenges in their relationship—to change, to bend, and to adjust. The engaged couple have not yet had to cope with being flexible and thinking of each other to the extent that is necessary in marriage. Nor has the married couple without children yet encountered many of the stresses that accompany parenthood. The middle-aged couple married to each other for many years may experience strain when their children leave home and they are confronted with the need to give new vitality and meaning to their interaction as a couple.

To be able to build relationships that survive and improve as two individuals go through the succeeding stages of life means that they continue to grow. The growth they make in any specific stage of life equips them to function more adequately in later stages. Their relationship will move inevitably toward either deterioration or new levels of understanding.

The ability to build a successful marriage is handicapped or enhanced by many background factors beyond each person's control. Nevertheless, growth potential in human personality is such that for most people absolute limits are not set.

## SOME FUNCTIONS OF MARRIAGE

Ideally, marriage satisfies certain personality needs that are difficult to satisfy outside marriage. Some years ago a group of men and women who were engaged or who had been married less than a year were asked by Anselm Strauss to list the needs they hoped to have satisfied in marriage (see Table 1-1).[1]

The specific needs these men and women listed are individual needs,

[1] Anselm Strauss, "A Study of Three Psychological Factors Affecting Choice of Mate" (Ph.D. diss., Chicago: University of Chicago Libraries, 1945). Summarized in Ernest W. Burgess and Harvey J. Locke, *The Family* (New York: American Book Company, 1960), pp. 365–69.

TABLE 1-1

Percentages of 373 men and women stating various personality needs that they hoped to have satisfied through marriage *

| Personality need | Men | Women |
|---|---|---|
| Someone to love me | 36.4% | 53.5% |
| Someone to confide in | 30.6 | 40.0 |
| Someone to show affection | 20.8 | 30.0 |
| Someone to respect my ideals | 26.0 | 26.0 |
| Someone to appreciate what I wish to achieve | 28.3 | 24.0 |
| Someone to understand my moods | 23.1 | 27.5 |
| Someone to help make my decisions | 15.0 | 32.5 |
| Someone to stimulate my ambition | 26.6 | 21.0 |
| Someone to look up to | 16.2 | 29.0 |
| Someone to give me self-confidence | 19.6 | 24.0 |
| Someone to back me in difficulty | 16.2 | 25.5 |
| Someone to appreciate me just as I am | 20.2 | 20.5 |
| Someone to admire my ability | 18.5 | 19.5 |
| Someone to make me feel important | 20.8 | 17.0 |
| Someone to relieve my loneliness | 18.5 | 18.5 |

* Anselm Strauss, "A Study of Three Psychological Factors Affecting Choice of Mate" (Ph.D. diss., Chicago: University of Chicago Libraries, 1945).

kinds of emotional support or response each one individually hoped to receive from the other. They did not list *pair* needs or *mutual* benefits hoped for from the marriage.

A somewhat different emphasis appears in the rating of values felt to be important to their marriage by couples married as long as ten years (see Table 1-2). These couples rated "communication with each other" as a most important value. They were in general happily married; the unhappy marriages or marriages in trouble were a very small minority, and few were divorced.[2] We also studied a group of 155 couples, who were going to counselors because they were having serious marriage problems, and a group of 164 divorced people, to learn how they would rate the values considered important to marital happiness.[3] In most instances these two groups agreed with the happily married group in listing the values in the order as shown in Table 1-2.

[2] Throughout this book reference will be made to findings of our research with 581 couples who had been married an average of seven years. At least one member of each pair had been a student in the Marriage and Family course at the University of California, Berkeley, in the 1950s. As students they had indicated willingness to cooperate in future studies of courtship and marriage. In 1966, 1041 of the former students were located, and they agreed to cooperate in research. Questionnaires were sent to each spouse, to be filled out independently and anonymously, sealed separately, and returned with the spouse's sealed questionnaire in one envelope. Questionnaires completed by both members of 581 couples are used as the basis for the findings reported in Table 1-2 and in later chapters of this book. The study is concerned with all the aspects of marital interaction dealt with in our earlier studies, but focuses especially upon ways in which this group of married couples approached solutions to differences they encountered in their marriages.

[3] Reference will be made to the "counseling" and the "divorced" groups throughout the text.

Clearly, the needs listed by the engaged or just-married group quoted by Strauss could be met only in marriages in which communication between partners is good. Other values rated by the married group as important to marital success, such as mutual emotional need, children, and sex, suggest the deeper involvement and awareness of each other that develops in successful marriages as time passes.

In many marriages, each partner either consciously or unconsciously seeks to give the other the love, understanding, and moral support that enable each of them to feel valued and accepted. In many marriages, enough of these needs are met so that each partner feels fairly well satisfied with the bargain, and such marriages may be called successful. In other marriages, one or the other may be entirely unaware of the personality needs of the mate and make no effort to meet them. The consciousness of these needs, nevertheless, impels people toward marriage, and in successful marriages, the two individuals meet most or many of these needs for each other.

## HOW SUCCESSFUL ARE MARRIAGES IN THE UNITED STATES?

This question can be answered in two ways—in terms of permanence and happiness. If we answer the question in terms of how many couples make permanent marriages, the picture we get of success is discouraging. The trend in divorce since 1900 has indicated an increasing instability in

TABLE 1-2  Values considered important in contributing to happiness in marriage, as reported by 581 husbands and wives

| Values in marriage | Important or very important | |
|---|---|---|
| | Husbands (N–581) | Wives (N–581) |
| Being able to communicate with each other | 97% | 99% |
| Being in love with each other | 94 | 95 |
| Emotional need for each other | 88 | 95 |
| Sexual relations | 92 | 91 |
| Children | 81 | 84 |
| Personality traits and/or habits of spouse | 81 | 78 |
| Shared recreational interests | 67 | 73 |
| Intellectual stimulation | 65 | 74 |
| Financial security | 67 | 69 |
| Shared cultural interests—music, art, etc. | 60 | 61 |
| Religion | 49 | 55 |
| Having an orderly home | 56 | 48 |
| In-laws | 43 | 53 |
| Good food | 32 | 28 |
| Association with relatives | 22 | 31 |
| Possessions | 24 | 17 |

marriages. The divorce rate doubled between 1963 and 1974. This year approximately two million couples will marry and one million couples will seek to end their marriages through separation, annulment, or divorce. It is doubtful whether the trend toward increasing marital instability will change in the near future, although it may level off to about the present rate. In 1975 the divorce rate showed the smallest increase of any year since 1967.

If we look at those couples who remained married, the picture we get of marriage success is more encouraging. Studies of happiness in marriage have been made over the past 40 years. These studies have found that approximately two-thirds of married people consider their marriages as happy or very happy. The National Opinion Research Center studied national samples of couples in 1973 and 1974 and found that 70 percent of men and women reported their marriages as "very happy." [4] There has been no report of a decrease of happiness in marriage for those who stay married. With the increased ease of obtaining a divorce and with public acceptance of the fact that many couples make unwise marriages, possibly more couples will attain very happy marriages through a second or third try. Those who fail in a first marriage have a higher failure rate in second and third marriages, but some do eventually find happiness. It is possible that in the future there will be more "very happy" marriages, since in the past many "unhappy marriages" continued for a lifetime while today people end unhappy marriages and try again.

## MARRIAGE AND THE FUTURE

At the present time there is much discussion concerning the future of marriage as an institution. Advance in contraceptive methods and an increased acceptance of abortion and sterilization have seemed to indicate to some that the basic function of marriage, reproduction, no longer exists and that traditional marriage as we have known it may soon become outmoded.

During the 1960s the "hippie generation" rejected traditional marriage. Groups rented houses and established communes. People rejected permanent pair relationships and substituted the *group* as a means of providing security and understanding. Children were cared for by the group. Some hippie communes were established in rural areas, showing a rejection of the urban culture as well as of the family. Back to the simple life in the country, all members worked to raise food, to build lodging, and to carry out communal activities. People did not have exclusive sexual relationships, consequently few permanent sexual relationships developed.

[4] Norval D. Glen, "The Contribution of Marriage to the Psychological Well-Being of Males and Females," *Journal of Marriage and the Family,* 37:3 (August 1975), 594–600.

In the 1970s the hippie culture has largely disappeared, although some of the rural communes of the 1960s still survive. New types of communes have developed which appeal to various types of people. These communes vary greatly in life styles. Some are true communes in that everything—sexual relations, money, child care, and work—is shared by all. At the other extreme are communes in which people share little more than a place to live with others of similar beliefs.

Studies of the communes have found that they do not remain an adequate or enduring substitute for the traditional family. Most communes have temporary members. Members try communal living but may soon move on to something else. Communal living becomes an experience for some in their quest for maturity, but it does not meet permanent needs for security and understanding. Couples who meet in a commune may soon leave to gain privacy and security in their new relationship.

As we have studied young people, we have seen nothing that would indicate that marriage as an institution will become outmoded. Rather, we interpret what we see as indicating that young people today, as never before, are seeking relationships which are enduring.

A study of 23,000 high school seniors in 1974 found that 81 percent believed in the "until-death-do-us-part" marriage contract. Studies of college students in the 1970s show that most plan to marry. A Gallup poll in 1976 found that although 70 percent of women reported they believed in women having jobs outside the home, 76 percent viewed marriage and children as the ideal life.

Questions were asked of men at the University of Michigan and at Dartmouth College in 1952, 1968, and 1974 on what activities in their lives they thought would give them the greatest satisfaction. We have given a summary of that study in Table 1-3. The men at both colleges and at all three periods of time rated family relationships as first in importance. More than twice as many men gave first importance to the family over career or occupation.[5]

Through the media, much attention has been given to a minority who have experimented with "new" life styles. Such a focus on this minority group has given an exaggerated view of marriage trends.

Those who believe traditional marriage is no longer necessary are ignoring the basic needs in human personality. The needs which people hope to have satisfied in marriage as indicated by the study summarized in Table 1-1 are the same today as they were when the study was made over 30 years ago. The values believed important in marriage relationships as summarized in Table 1-2 are fundamental in human personality. There has been no permanent change in basic personality needs. The disturbances and disillusionments in society show the need for lasting and understanding relationships as never before. Formal marriage has been and will continue to be the one institution that is essential in meet-

[5] Dean R. Hoge, "Changes in College Students' Value Patterns in the 1950's, 1960's and 1970's," *Sociology of Education*, 49:2 (April 1976), 155–63.

SUCCESSFUL MARRIAGE

TABLE 1-3

Percentages of Dartmouth and University of Michigan men reporting expected sources of life satisfaction, 1952, 1968, 1974. (Specific question, "What three things or activities in your life do you expect to give you the most satisfaction?")

| Expected sources of life satisfaction | Dartmouth | | | University of Michigan | | |
|---|---|---|---|---|---|---|
| | First rank | | | First rank | | |
| | 1952 (N–349) | 1968 (N–360) | 1974 (N–366) | 1952 (N–386) | 1968 (N–384) | 1974 (N–328) |
| Family relationships | 64% | 63% | 56% | 62% | 60% | 52% |
| Your career or occupation | 26 | 25 | 24 | 29 | 25 | 25 |
| Leisure-time activities | 6 | 3 | 6 | 4 | 7 | 12 |
| Religious beliefs or activities | 2 | 1 | 8 | 3 | 3 | 5 |
| Citizen participation and community affairs | 1 | 1 | 1 | — | 1 | 1 |
| Activities directed at national or international betterment | 1 | 7 | 4 | 2 | 5 | 4 |

ing the day-to-day, year-to-year needs of people for intimacy, security, and understanding while going through the life cycle.

## REVIEW QUESTIONS

1 What social factors and developments in our society operate to give meaning to the institution of marriage for individuals?

2 What percentage of people in the United States marry?

3 What is meant by saying that a young couple's attitudes toward marriage will have more to do with their happiness than the intensity of their love at the time of the wedding?

4 What is a successful marriage?

5 In marriage, each partner gives up some of his or her personal freedom. What does each gain in exchange?

6 What is meant by the statement that those who can build a good marriage are making a positive contribution to the world about them?

7 Successful marriages run in families. Why?

8 Why is the idea that marriage will mean complete happiness a handicap?

9 Discuss the statement that relationships in marriage do not remain static.

10 What are three different stages in life that require special growth in married couples?

11 Why is the affectional function of the family more important today than ever before?

12 What are some of the personality needs fulfilled in marriage?

13 Approximately what proportion of married couples report their marriages as happy or very happy today? Has this percentage changed in recent years?

14 Are there indications that the communal type of family will replace the traditional family in the future? Why or why not?

15 What evidence is there that young people today believe in traditional marriage? Why do you think this is true?

# SEXUAL DIFFERENCES AND ROLES: IMPLICATIONS FOR MARRIAGE

A significant element in marriage is the attitude each person has concerning his or her role in life. Today, in a time of shifting definitions, most essential is agreement between a couple on roles and acceptance of each other's definitions. The success of some marriages is jeopardized by rigid ideas about man's place or woman's place in life.

## STATUS OF WOMEN IN THE PAST

A few generations ago, higher education was not open to women. They had few opportunities to train for work other than household tasks and were therefore economically dependent on the men of their families. Until fairly recently, the legal rights of women as individuals in the United States were few. American mores favored the pattern advocated by the bachelor Paul: "If the woman would learn anything let her ask her husband at home." [1]

The accepted attitude toward women was expressed in a book published in 1881, *Decorum: A Practical Treatise on Etiquette and Dress of the Best American Society*. The author offered the following advice to gentlemen: "When addressing ladies, pay them the compliment of seeming to consider them capable of an equal understanding with gentlemen . . . they will appreciate the delicate compliment." In the same treatise the author said, "Young married ladies must never appear in any public place unattended by their husbands or by elder ladies. This rule must never be infringed." And, "Of late years ladies have taken to rowing; this can be managed in a quiet river or private pond but it is scarcely to be attempted in the . . . public parts of rivers unless superintended by a

[1] 1 Corinthians 14:35.

gentleman." He commented further, "Most women are naturally amiable, gentle and complying."

These attitudes were reflected and given force by laws. A member of the Supreme Court of that time referred in a written decision to the "natural and proper timidity and delicacy which belongs to the female sex." As late as 1961, in ruling on a case concerned with women's rights, Justice Harlan said, "Woman is regarded as the center of the home and family and therefore has her own special responsibilities." Today this is viewed as discrimination against women.

## EFFORTS TO END DISCRIMINATION

A battle for more equality and less discrimination between the sexes has been in process for many years. A constitutional amendment to establish equal rights for women was introduced (but not passed) in every session of Congress from 1923 to 1972. In the present decade there is a new and more widespread awareness of problems resulting from discrimination against various segments of our society, and this social awareness again is being reflected in law. In 1964 the United States Congress passed the Civil Rights Act, which included women with other minority groups to be protected against discrimination in employment. The act specified that persons of equal training, education, and experience shall have equal pay regardless of race, nationality, religion, or sex. But many women in professions and industry have found that discrimination is applied in many other ways than by a difference in pay to a man and a woman doing the same work. Arbitrary limits set upon the work a woman may do, the overtime she may work, and other limitations still discriminate against her.

By 1971 the movement to end all discrimination against women in any facet of life involved large groups of thoughtful and articulate men and women, many of them trained in the law. A constitutional amendment designed to achieve equality was passed by the United States House of Representatives in 1971, and by the Senate in 1972. Many states quickly ratified the proposed amendment. But as it was given more consideration, women's groups organized to defeat the amendment in states that had not ratified it. The women were convinced that the amendment would take away many rights that had protected them in the past. In 1975 only one state ratified the amendment and 16 states defeated it. As of 1977, 33 states have approved the amendment, and 3 more states are required before it can become law. President Carter is urging the necessary states to support the amendment.

Some people believe that no amendment is necessary, that the Fourteenth Amendment already provides for equality, and that the only solution is a long series of legal cases through which the courts will force states to abide by the requirements of the Constitution and the Civil Rights Act. Many such cases are already in the courts. A clear effect of court decisions is to free men also from some restrictions and requirements that arbitrary sex typing has always placed upon them as it has upon women.

In some ways women are their own worst enemies when it comes to bias against their own sex. Gallup found in a 1976 poll on the subject of biases that women prefer a male boss by a ratio of 6 to 1, and that the majority of women would prefer the professional services of male rather than female doctors, lawyers, and bankers. The poll also found that more men than women support the equal rights amendment and more men than women would vote for a woman for political office.

## BIOLOGICAL DIFFERENCES OR SOCIAL CONDITIONING?

Some groups involved in the push for male–female equality go so far as to argue that there are no real biological differences between the sexes other than the difference in reproductive systems. Their view is that any apparent differences in sexual, social, or psychological responses are a result of the contrast in conditioning that girls and boys receive in our culture.

Undeniably such contrasts do exist. One has only to observe children, teachers, and mothers in any nursery school or kindergarten to see that the adults put continuous pressure upon little girls and little boys to have the interests socially defined as appropriate to their sex, and to behave according to social definitions of "masculine" or "feminine" behavior. That is, little boys are "not supposed to cry," and little girls are "not supposed to be rough or noisy." Little girls are "supposed to be pretty" and little boys are "supposed to be strong and energetic." Paul Torrance, a psychologist interested in studying creativity, found that in the early grades little boys often say, "I'm not supposed to play with that," about such toys as a nurse's kit or a sewing kit, and little girls say the same about scientific toys. He noted that these definitions served to restrict the children's *ability* to use such toys creatively. He believes his studies show that the sex-role conditioning is very strongly established in children by the time they reach the fifth grade.[2]

Despite the sex-type conditioning that continues in our society, many long-established norms are being reassessed. Thoughtful people are making serious efforts to look at people as individual persons, each one unique, rather than as prototypes of a sex, a race, or an age group. The little children of today may as adults live in a world with far different definitions from those of their early conditioning. Diana Trilling, a social critic, commenting on changes occurring and on the fact that many differences are assigned to the sexes on bases other than biological, said, "Gone, or going, is the social-sexual differentiation between men

[2] Florence Howe, "Sexual Stereotypes Start Early," *Saturday Review*, 16 October 1971, p. 80.

and women in terms of dress and hair-style. The uni-sexual appearance of the sexes [is to be welcomed] if only for its criticism of a culture in which sexually differentiated styles of hair and dress, designed not by God but by man, were treated as if they were biological actualities. . . . Whatever reduces the false separations between men and women is bound to reduce their hostilities, and thus permit them a fuller expression of their human potentiality." She goes on to say that if men and women could be free of the wasteful effects of *culturally conditioned* sexual differences, perhaps people could reach a sounder knowledge of real distinctions between maleness and femaleness.[3]

It is not our purpose in this chapter to explore in depth current developments in a continuing struggle for equality for men and women in our society. Diversity of views on the subject will continue to cause division among women, among men, and between men and women for some time to come. What is essential for college students reading this book is some knowledge concerning biologically based sexual differences and some objectivity concerning their own attitudes and feelings on the subject. Feelings and attitudes about a man's or a woman's place and prerogatives are factors that will profoundly affect the relationship between a husband and wife in the United States in the 1970s.

## Some biological differences

The two sexes are biologically different. If a cell or cells from the body of an unborn child can be obtained at any time after conception, the cells can be identified through laboratory analysis of their biochemical structure as having come from a male or female individual. (Such cells sometimes are obtained for genetic tests in unusual cases, although the process is not undertaken for the sole purpose of knowing the sex of the fetus.)

For generations women have been called the "weaker sex." But careful study of children and adults in all phases of their growth and achievement has forced a redefining of terms. Studies show that in rate of development, both physical and mental, the female leads. In muscular strength, the male leads. The female has greater resistance to disease and death, and to emotional pressure, than the male. Also, the differences in body chemistry and hormonal functioning of the two sexes may account for behavioral dissimilarities.

## Mortality and morbidity

A woman sometimes says of her husband, "He doesn't get sick very often, but when he does, illness seems to hit him awfully hard!" A wife making that observation may believe she is describing only her individual hus-

---

[3] Diana Trilling, "Female Biology in a Male Culture," *Saturday Review*, 10 October 1970, p. 40.

band's reaction to illness. However, medical records show that, in general, although men are sick less often than women, when illness strikes them it does hit harder. The death rates for males are higher from the time of conception through every age. Biologists have discovered that at least 120 males are conceived to every 100 females, yet at birth the sex ratio has dropped to 105.5 males to 100 females. The great surplus of males conceived do not survive to be born. During the first four months of pregnancy, at least four times as many male as female fetuses die. The proportion of deaths gradually decreases until the eighth month of pregnancy, when the average is 55 males to 45 females. One-fourth more boys than girls die during the first year after birth. And vital statistics show that this ratio occurs quite consistently year after year. When conditions are improved and the total infant mortality rate is lowered, as it has been in the United States during this century, the proportion of male to female deaths becomes even higher. In other words, the greater resistance of the female enables her to profit more from a better environment than the male is able to do.

Accidents claim many lives at all ages, but boys between the ages of one and four are much more likely to get killed than are girls of those ages. The accident rate per 100,000 population is approximately 36 for boys and 27 for girls. Boys are more likely to chase a ball into the street or to ride a tricycle in front of a car than are girls. Table 2-1 summarizes the accidental death rate of males and females in the United States in 1968, at each stage in life showing a much higher death rate for males than for females.

As adults, more women than men have occasion to consult doctors, many of the occasions arising from conditions related to the reproductive processes. Although they may require more medical attention, women may still be in relatively good health. Men, on the other hand, less frequently need to consult doctors, but they are susceptible to the more serious diseases, and once ill, they are far more likely to succumb.

TABLE 2-1    Accidental death rate, U.S., 1968 (per 100,000 population)

| Ages | Male | Female |
|---|---|---|
| 1–4 | 35.9 | 26.9 |
| 5–14 | 27.8 | 12.6 |
| 15–19 | 100.5 | 28.9 |
| 20–24 | 129.2 | 24.9 |
| 25–29 | 94.1 | 20.3 |
| 30–34 | 78.5 | 18.8 |
| 35–44 | 74.7 | 22.2 |
| 45–54 | 82.1 | 26.3 |
| 55–64 | 98.5 | 35.4 |
| 65 and over | 180.7 | 125.7 |

Source: National Center for Health Statistics.

TABLE 2-2    Death rates from all causes by sex and age (United States, 1973) *

| Age period | Death rates per 1000 | |
| (years) | Males | Females |
|---|---|---|
| under 1 | 20.3 | 15.7 |
| 1–4 | 0.9 | 0.7 |
| 5–14 | 0.5 | 0.3 |
| 15–24 | 1.9 | 0.7 |
| 25–34 | 2.1 | 0.9 |
| 35–44 | 3.8 | 2.2 |
| 45–54 | 9.2 | 4.9 |
| 55–64 | 22.1 | 10.8 |
| 65–74 | 47.3 | 24.5 |
| 75–84 | 101.1 | 65.6 |
| 85 and over | 198.1 | 162.3 |

* Dept. of Health, Education and Welfare, Public Health Service; Annual Report, *Vital Statistics of the United States.*

Table 2-2 summarizes statistics on the death rates of males and females from all causes.

The higher mortality rate of males from the time of conception through the prenatal period, as well as during the first 12 months after birth, and the fact that they fall victim to almost all the major diseases in greater numbers than do females, force the conclusion that males have been equipped by nature with less ability than females to resist and survive illness and infection. The difference in the mortality rates of men and women is reflected in women's greater life expectancy. In 1975 the average life expectancy for white women was 76.7 and for white men 68.9. For nonwhite people, it was 71.3 for women and 62.9 for men.

### Differences in muscular strength and coordination

Although females show from the beginning a greater natural ability to withstand illness, males from early infancy show development of a different type of strength. Observers who have tested large numbers of infants and young children report that boys consistently show greater muscular strength than girls do in the preschool years. Girls during this time develop a finer motor coordination. They are able to do things that require use of fingers, such as buttoning clothing; boys can lift heavier objects and can throw and climb more easily.

Although some differences in play activities of preschool children are due to social conditioning, inherent biological differences between the sexes also account for some of the differences in interests and performance. Since the boy's larger muscles are growing and developing strength at a faster rate, it would seem natural for him to feel the need for pushing, lifting, climbing, or entering into any type of play activity that makes use of his muscular strength. The girl's finger dexterity is better, hence she enjoys activities like stringing beads or dressing dolls. In nursery schools it is observed that little girls like to tie and untie their shoes and usually learn to lace their shoes considerably earlier than do little boys. While a girl works at lacing her shoes, her brother may be busy lining up the chairs and pushing them along in imitation of a train. In institutions for blind and deaf children who have no contact with a normal social environment, some sexual differences in activities are as pronounced as with nonhandicapped children.

## Rate of growth

While the average little boy is developing muscular strength, his sister is growing at a faster rate. From infancy until middle adolescence, girls on the average show faster physical growth, with accompanying differences in emotional and mental development. At birth, the average male is slightly longer than the female. Between the ages of 6 and 11, girls grow faster than boys in both height and weight, so that by age 11 the girl has caught up with and passed the boy in size. The girl continues to be taller until about the fifteenth year, when the boy passes her in height. She passes the boy in weight at about the twelfth year and continues to outweigh him for some time.[4]

The most marked difference in rate of development is evident during the years of early adolescence. Girls of 12 and 13 are usually well into puberty, and their figures show signs of their growing toward physical maturity. The average boy enters puberty somewhat later than the girl does. Our study of 3189 college students showed that, of those who entered puberty between the ages of 10 and 16, the average age for women had been 12.5 and for men, 13.3 years. (The measure of puberty entrance was first menstruation in girls and the first seminal emissions in boys.) Most rapid growth comes for boys between the ages of 15 and 18.

## Differences in achievement

In many types of achievement males have the advantage in our culture. Studies done over a period of years in the past have shown that girls advanced more rapidly than boys and maintained higher scholastic averages throughout many of their school years, the boys catching up and beginning to surpass girls scholastically during late adolescence. An illustration of this was found in Terman's classic study of 1300 superior children. The careers of these gifted children were followed from their

[4] *Height and Weight of Children, United States,* Washington, D.C.: Vital and Health Statistics, U.S. Department of Health, Education and Welfare, Series 11, Number 104, 1970.

How they grow

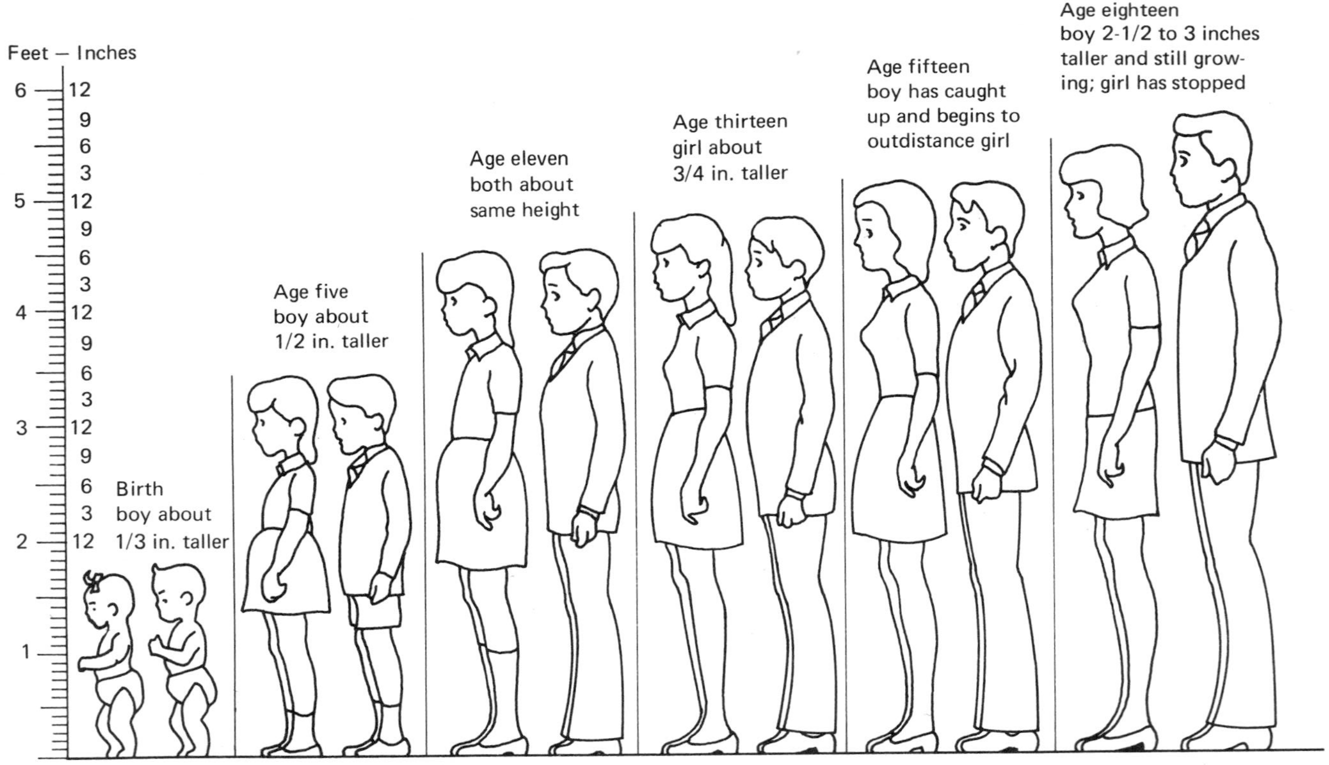

Feet — Inches

Age five
boy about
1/2 in. taller

Age eleven
both about
same height

Age thirteen
girl about
3/4 in. taller

Age fifteen
boy has caught
up and begins to
outdistance girl

Age eighteen
boy 2-1/2 to 3 inches
taller and still grow-
ing; girl has stopped

Birth
boy about
1/3 in. taller

FIG. 2-1  Adapted from Amran Scheinfeld, Women and Men (New York: Harcourt Brace Jovanovich, 1943), p. 54.

early childhood through many years of their adulthood. It was found that during adolescence the girls began to fall behind in relative achievement, and that three times as many boys as girls continued their high level of achievement. The history of this group showed far greater achievement among the men in proportion to their numbers than among the women.

In commenting on this finding, Terman said, "The woman who is a potential poet, novelist, lawyer, physician, or scientist usually gives up any professional ambition she may have had and devotes herself to home, husband, and children. The exclusive devotion of women to domestic pursuits robs the arts and sciences of a large fraction of the genius that might otherwise be dedicated to them. Data strongly suggest that this loss must be debited to motivational causes and to limitations of opportunities rather than to lack of ability."[5] Other researchers have attempted to explain past achievement difference in terms of "drive." They have theorized that man's drive to achieve is related to his sex drive, and hence not subject to the limitations placed upon woman by her sex. It must be recognized that although "drive" may be continuous in the male, women's "drive"—because of the recurring changes in hormonal balance and physical functioning that accompany menstruation and childbirth—fluctuates periodically.

Undoubtedly, the traditional concept of man as a doer, accomplishing great things in the world, continues to serve as a stimulus toward achievement for men. Conversely, the traditional concept of the place of women cannot but inhibit achievement in the lives of a great many women. This inhibiting influence may account for the intellectual lag in girls in adolescence. To conform to the roles expected by the group, the boy will do his best to excel, whereas the girl may not be motivated toward achievement except within certain well-defined feminine areas.

## Interdependence of roles

A consideration of sexual differences within our culture emphasizes that what rights or privileges one has because of one's sex, and one's obligations in marriage, are determined not entirely by the biological facts of nature or by cultural habits (tradition). Some role expectations and definitions are biologically based and relatively impervious to change. Others are based on folklore, custom, and tradition, and these change with time and circumstances.

The individual's role in life exists only in terms of interaction with other people. Any one person's role performance is partly a reflection and partly a determinant of the roles played in turn by the other persons with whom one interacts. Changes in the role definitions or role functioning of women are thus concomitant with role adjustments in

---

[5] Lewis M. Terman, "Psychological Approach to the Biography of Genius," *Science* 92 (4 October 1940), 293–301.

men. It is not simply a matter of women's conflicts and frustrations. Some people see the problem in those terms; they fear that if women dress like men or do "man's work," they may confuse their sons about who is mother and who is father and make them uncertain about their own masculinity. Similarly, it is implied that the man who does housework or bathes the baby is depriving his son of a needed masculine model. Does a child's perception of masculinity and femininity arise from clothing and work or is it based in a deeper identification? Couples marrying today need to have this perspective upon the question of role definitions and situations. Each must understand the pressures and requirements put upon the other by the fact that they are living in a time of readjustment and reassessment of many long-held definitions. Among college-educated people today can be found extremes of views, some people tending to retreat to the hoped-for safety of a rigid traditional definition of men's and women's places in life, others unwilling to accept any degree of traditionalism. In marriages that are successful today, both men and women must become able to recognize a broadened definition of masculinity and femininity; they must have flexibility in order to function in a wide variety of masculine–feminine patterns.

Many wives and husbands are too busy to give much thought to theories about "woman's place" or "man's place" in life or in the family. They are occupied with living and adjusting in the world in which they find themselves. Thus the man who, a few years ago, might have argued before he married that a woman's place is at home, may freely concede today that both of them must work to provide adequate support for the family, and that if a woman is to work she has a right to do whatever work she is capable of doing and should be paid as adequately for it as a man is paid. The same husband is also likely to agree that, under the circumstances, a husband must do a share of the housework and child rearing.

Modern advances in business, manufacturing, and production mean that the nature of the work to be done in the home has changed. Such tasks as canning foods, baking, and dressmaking are not considered a part of the work of the average homemaker, but rather are done by professionals or are done as hobbies by people—men or women—who hold income-producing jobs. Labor-saving equipment has shortened the time required for tasks that still must be done at home, and has helped also to break down traditionally established ideas of man's or woman's work. Boys and men who might never have thought of doing the family laundry when it had to be done by hand now in many families as readily load and start an automatic washing machine as they run a lawn mower. Nevertheless, it is true that in many families the division of labor still remains traditional—families in which a boy has never seen his father wash or dry dishes, shop for groceries, or cook a meal.

Many people approaching marriage are not aware of the significance role concepts assume in marriage. Attitudes and views concerning the role or function that each believes will be his or hers in marriage have implications for mate choice, and these attitudes profoundly affect the quality of the relationship two people are able to build in marriage.

Whether a rigidly defined traditional, or a more flexible, equalitarian role definition is the "best" depends on the two people in any marriage. However, Rainwater's study of husband–wife patterns in four widely differing cultures highlights certain elements in the traditional role pattern that are relevant for middle-class Americans.[6] The study was of family patterns in certain areas of poverty in England, Puerto Rico, Mexico, and the United States. The findings offer an only slightly exaggerated version of marital situations still found in traditionally oriented middle-class families in our society, as well as among the groups Rainwater studied.

We quote Rainwater: "In all these lower-class subcultures a pattern of highly segregated role relationships exists. Men and women do not have many joint relationships; the separation of men's and women's work is sharp, as is the separation of men's and women's play . . . the women do not have common activities with their husbands outside the home . . . the necessity for respect toward the husband reduces joint activities."

Further, Rainwater noted that the more generalized pattern of separateness in these marriages extended to sexual relations, with, consequently, a low value placed on mutuality. "The role segregation of which the pattern of sexual relationships seems a part, has as one consequence, a lack of communication between husbands and wives on any matter not clearly defined in terms of traditional expectations. It is difficult for such couples to cope with problems that require mutual accommodation or empathy. In these groups, husbands and wives tend to be fairly isolated from each other. They do not seem to be dependent on each other emotionally although each performs important services for the other." [7]

Echoes of these rigid traditional definitions are apparent in some middle-class American marriages in which life is highly compartmentalized. Some people find it easier to cope with the requirements of family living if they rigidly divide their authority and responsibilities and avoid the necessity for close cooperation and communication in too many areas of life. The question arises whether a rigid compartmentalization of life according to traditional lines may deprive today's educated young couples of some of the satisfactions hoped for in their marriages, such satisfactions as mutuality in decision making, in work interests, and in interaction with their children.

[6] Lee Rainwater, "Marital Sexuality in Four Cultures of Poverty," *Journal of Marriage and the Family* 26:4 (November 1964), 462.

[7] Ibid., p. 463.

A male graduate student in chemistry was applying for a second part-time job. He explained, "Anne's baby is due in two months so she will have to quit work. From now on, of course, she will not work any more. Her job will be the home and the family." Asked if he saw that his holding two jobs as well as carrying a heavy load of graduate studies might mean he could not give much of himself to being a husband and father, he answered, "What do you mean? As I see it, my part is the *financial* part. The *family* is Anne's job." Anne, who was present but had been silent until then, protested, "But I've told Jim that it seems to me the family should be ours, not just mine. I think we'll miss out on something valuable if we divide life up the way he thinks we must. I think that would mean Jim and the children would be the losers." It seems clear that this couple had not yet faced or recognized a serious divergence between their separate conceptions of what each one's family role was to be, nor of what effect their division of responsibility would have on each one's feelings about his or her contribution and, consequently, upon their relationship.

## ATTITUDES TOWARD ROLES

Although the trend toward greater equality in all aspects of life between men and women is accelerating in this decade, change will be uneven for some time because of traditionally held attitudes. Activists in the Women's Liberation movement refer to the fact that both sexes have been "programmed" all their lives to accept certain role definitions without question. Whatever the explanation, unmarried university students, when queried on such matters as the sharing of tasks or the allocation of responsibilities in their hypothetical future homes, are inclined to express traditional attitudes, and university women tend to express more traditional attitudes than the men express. Table 2-3 shows responses to our questions on this subject. A larger percentage of men

**TABLE 2-3** Percentages of 165 men and 300 women reporting household tasks performed by their fathers and those they thought a husband should do

| Household tasks | Father did | | Husbands should do | |
|---|---|---|---|---|
| | Men | Women | Men | Women |
| Repairs | 81.0% | 84.0% | 75.0% | 85.0% |
| Cooking | 30.0 | 29.0 | 28.0 | 13.0 |
| Setting table | 15.0 | 11.0 | 38.0 | 11.0 |
| Drying dishes | 47.0 | 32.0 | 61.0 | 53.0 |
| Washing dishes | 39.0 | 20.0 | 32.0 | 22.0 |
| Cleaning house | 16.0 | 13.0 | 23.0 | 12.0 |
| Laundry | 12.0 | 7.0 | 13.0 | 5.0 |
| Buying groceries | 53.0 | 43.0 | 67.0 | 44.0 |

thought the husband should help with seven of the eight tasks listed. In general, a slightly larger percentage of the men expressed the opinion that the husband should do more of the household tasks than they reported their fathers were in the habit of doing.

Another survey in 1971, with a national sample of young people aged 14 to 22, and which included people of both high school and college age, found that there is still a quite general traditionalism concerning roles among young people, especially in the younger age groups. Three out of five of those in this sample expressed the view that a woman's place is in the home. The percentages of those holding this view decreased with increased years of age and of education, the older college students being less traditional.[8]

Osmond and Martin studied sex-role attitudes of college students and found acceptance of the traditional division of tasks in the home. They concluded that attitudes will be slow to change in this area of living. They found the greatest difference in attitudes regarding roles of women outside the home. Men were less willing to accept women in supervisory, decision-making, and leadership roles. The women felt they should be as free to have these roles as were men.[9]

A study by Parelius of changing sex-role attitudes of college women found that although the women believed their careers to be as important as those of their husbands and expected to work most of their lives, they still did not change greatly in their views on marital and maternal roles. Few would sacrifice marriage and parenthood for occupational success, and few expressed the belief that a man would want to marry a feminist.[10]

An interesting comparison with the views students express about their future role intentions is found in the attitudes expressed by some husbands of working and of nonworking wives, a group now living in the reality of the students' anticipated "future." This study compared the attitudes of husbands whose wives had jobs with those whose wives were full-time homemakers.[11] The husbands of working wives expressed more equalitarian attitudes; more than twice as many of them believed a husband should help around the house "all the time." A majority of both groups of men believed that a wife's work should not interfere with the husband's work. Four-fifths of the husbands of nonworking wives believed a working wife would be less of a companion to her husband;

[8] Study of 2000 young people by The Research Guild, Inc. *Teaching Topics* (New York: Institute of Life Insurance) 21:1 (Fall 1971), 8.

[9] Marie Withers Osmond and Patricia Yancy Martin, "Sex and Sexism: A Comparison of Male and Female Sex-Role Attitudes," *Journal of Marriage and the Family* 37:4 (November 1975), 744–58.

[10] Ann P. Parelius, "Emerging Sex-Role Attitudes, Expectations, and Strains Among College Women," *Journal of Marriage and the Family* 37:1 (February 1975), 146–53.

[11] Leland J. Axelson, "The Marital Adjustment and Marital Role Definitions of Husbands of Working and Non-working Wives," *Journal of Marriage and the Family* 25:2 (May 1963), 189.

only one-fifth of the husbands of working wives agreed. Almost one-third of the husbands of working wives said it would not make them feel inadequate if the wife earned the higher salary of the two. In this group, apparently, the husband of the working wife does not see her working as a threat to his masculinity. It is possible that, among this group at least, a wife's working in the competitive world outside the home means that the husband and wife have more interests in common, a partial compensation in the husband's view for his being obliged to "help" more than he would if his wife did not work. Or, perhaps here a selective process operates in mate choice, so that the woman who will be a "working wife" is more likely to marry a man who holds the equalitarian views represented by these husbands.

Another point that may operate today as role lines become less rigid is that some men, now free to participate more fully in "homemaking" and child care, find pleasure and enjoyment in this part of life, satisfactions that they were denied in the past, but that women have been free to experience.

Like many of our other values in life, our feelings about what is "woman's place" or "man's place," and what the special prerogatives of each sex are, are likely to be more emotional than rational, and it is difficult to examine such attitudes objectively. Therefore, frustration and antagonism may arise in a marriage in which views on this matter are widely divergent. Often neither will be able to define personal attitudes clearly or to pin down the basis of certain antagonisms.

In the average marriage, the husband and wife must harmonize their feelings about roles. A couple who are cooperative and who can give each other recognition and respect for ability or achievement in whatever line have a better chance of happiness, regardless of how they work out the division of labor and authority.

A task of the courtship and dating years is to try to understand each other's attitudes, recognizing that attitudes toward roles in life and toward the ego needs of another person are not necessarily the same as the opinions one may express ahead of time when the discussion is more or less theoretical or academic.

A crucial point is how each member of a married pair feels about the part he or she plays in life, and especially whether each feels his or her contribution is respected and valued by the other. Some men who believe they want their wives to play a traditional role actually don't have a high regard for that role. In our society a higher value is placed upon work in a competitive world than upon homemaking, and this norm tends to be accepted by both men and women. Thus, homemaking is in some ways denigrated. One woman expressed her feelings this way, "My husband just thought of me as 'the little woman.' He didn't seem to think anything I did was of any real importance until I went out and got a paying job. He wanted me to stay home and be a housewife, but he certainly puts more value on what I'm doing now."

SEXUAL DIFFERENCES AND ROLES

FIG 2–2 "Oh, Bert, I think the novelty of housework has worn off." From *Ladies' Home Journal*, Mary Gibson.

## ROLE CONFLICTS FOR MEN

Men, like women, react in many different ways to the role requirements made of them today. Many men, like the husbands of working wives in Axelson's study, accept as logical and potentially rewarding the concept of equal husband–wife sharing in almost all aspects of family living.

Some others feel insecure and threatened in any but the traditionally accepted masculine role. Not all men could be as comfortable in a cooperative, equalitarian, and many-faceted role as a young engineer who answered the doorbell at dinnertime and stood on the porch talking with a colleague about plans for a business meeting while wearing a kitchen apron and holding his baby son tucked against his shoulder. But an ever-increasing percentage of young men are finding this complex role meaningful and satisfying.

Nevertheless, the overlapping of roles and blurring of lines of distinction between roles of men and women create certain frustrations for men. A contradictory factor in the situation is that changes in social expectations do not move at a uniform rate. For example, men today must be more flexible in accepting some obligations formerly considered to be feminine, yet they are still expected to be "masculine" as traditionally defined. Meeting both these expectations may involve strain or internal conflict. Is it evidence of strength (hence masculinity) for a man to take over baby tending and dishwashing because his job allows him more time and energy for these tasks than his wife's job allows her? The man who does undertake such responsibilities for reasons satisfactory to himself may at times be uncomfortably aware that, among his associates, ideas differ as to what constitutes masculinity and strength or weakness. He may encounter an emotional and irrational attitude among some other men, just as a woman sometimes encounters animosity or criticism from some other women regarding her role choice.

Today men have less freedom of choice about roles than women have. Whatever role a man has at home, in general he is still expected to make the living as well. But regardless of any hard economic necessities in a family, the woman is not as subjected to social censure if she remains at home and takes little or no responsibility for making the living. These disparate social attitudes and expectations are potentially tension producing for some men.

## INCONSISTENCIES CONCERNING ROLES

Clifford Kirkpatrick developed some theories on conflicts arising from inconsistencies in the attitudes of men and women concerning roles. His views are pertinent here. He recognized that cultural changes have opened a wide range of roles to women other than the traditionally accepted wife-and-mother role, and that men are confronted with the necessity for adjusting to life in a role far more complicated and different from the traditional role as dominant family head. Kirkpatrick's hypothesis is that both sexes are inconsistent: Women tend to want to have the privileges and rewards of several major roles, such as wife and mother, companion, and partner, while accepting the obligations of only one; and men are inclined to want their wives to accept the responsibilities of several roles, while they are willing to give them the privileges and rewards of only one or two. Kirkpatrick points out that unfairness results in cases of wives claiming and getting the privileges of more than one role without accepting the corresponding obligations, or accepting the obligations of several roles without receiving corresponding privileges. He suggests that some wives expect to be treated as though they were the mothers of a half-dozen well-brought-up children in a well-kept home, although they have no children and actually contribute little to the comfort, well-being, or economic success of their husbands. Other wives may rear children, carry the full load of homemaking, and in addition, earn almost as much as the husband does without receiving any special recognition from their husbands for their contribution.[12]

People naturally see situations in the light of their own personal desires, and in marriage it is easy to be concerned with only one's own needs and expectations without seeing the other side of the question. Those

[12] For a report of this research, see Clifford Kirkpatrick, "Inconsistencies in Marriage Roles and Marriage Conflict," *The International Journal of Ethics* 46 (1936), 444–60. Reprinted in Judson T. Landis and Mary G. Landis, *Readings in Marriage and the Family* (Englewood Cliffs, N.J.: Prentice-Hall, Inc., 1952), pp. 386–92.

who can recognize at the outset that they tend to be inconsistent in what they would require of their mates and in what they are willing to concede in return will have a better chance for success in marriage.

Couples contemplating marriage need to give thought to how well they understand each other and to what kinds of situations are tolerable or intolerable to each. A competitive attitude toward each other during courtship may indicate conflicting role expectations. Each married couple must work out the husband–wife pattern according to the capacities and the adaptability of the two and the circumstances of their lives. Whatever role patterns develop in any particular marriage, mutually supportive attitudes are essential to a good relationship.

## OUTLINE FOR SELF-STUDY: ROLE EXPECTATIONS

Think through the following outline, deciding on the answers to the questions. Then write a short analysis of your own attitudes toward the roles of men and women, with attention to what role definitions you think you will be able to live with comfortably in marriage.

### I ROLE SITUATIONS IN YOUR FAMILY BACKGROUND

1 How would you classify the interaction between your grandparents: Husband dominant? Wife dominant? Equal sharing in decisions and in dominance? Sharing in tasks? Sharing in interests? Does one of the pair "speak for" the two of them?

2 With the above questions in mind, what type of interaction seems most common among your aunts and uncles?

3 Apply the same questions to your own parents' interaction. Is one dominant? Does one make most of the decisions? Is one more likely than the other to "speak for" the two of them? Would you classify your family as a father-dominated or a mother-dominated family? An equalitarian type of family?

4 If you have married brothers and sisters, apply the same questions to their interaction with their spouses, as well as you can.

### II YOUR FEELINGS ABOUT THE ROLES OF MEN AND WOMEN IN MARRIAGE

1 As you think about your different married relatives, do you find that you approve in general of one type of husband–wife interaction pattern ("role solution")?

2 Which type of husband–wife interaction is especially distasteful to you? Just why do you find this type of interaction distasteful?

3 Among nonrelatives, what husband–wife role patterns do you find difficult to understand or appreciate?

### III EVALUATE YOUR REACTION TO THE FOLLOWING STATEMENTS

1 "In the sight of God there is equality between men and women but when it comes to governmental arrangements in the home the husband is

the head. God says he cannot answer prayers which come from a woman who doesn't take her God-given place in the home."—Billy Graham

2  I would vote for a woman for a public office such as senator or the vice-presidency. Qualifications other than sex of the candidate should be the criteria.

3  It is natural that men should dominate and women play a submissive role.

4  Women who compete in a man's world outside the home are unfeminine and less attractive than women who remain housewives.

5  I think the career-type of woman is more interesting and attractive than the home-type.

IV  IN MY ASSOCIATIONS WITH THE OTHER SEX I HAVE FOUND THAT:

1  I tend to be competitive toward the other sex.

2  I get along better when the male is definitely dominant and the female is submissive.

3  I am happier when I am dominant in the relationship.

4  I like to date those who let me make most of the decisions.

5  I am unhappy dating those who expect me to make many decisions.

6  I like to date people who are as intelligent or more intelligent than I am.

## REVIEW QUESTIONS

1  Discuss the implications of the constitutional amendment guaranteeing equal rights and responsibilities to women.

2  What benefits might result from the trend toward unisex styles in hair and dress?

3  Why do some groups oppose legislation designed to give women complete "equality" with men?

4  Which is the "weaker" sex as measured by morbidity and mortality? Cite statistics to support your answer.

5  Give some reasons for the greater life expectancy of women.

6  What are some of the observable differences in muscular strength and coordination of preschool boys and girls? Are these differences due to cultural conditioning?

7  How does the rate of growth differ in boys and girls?

8  What are the results of Terman's study of the achievements of gifted children?

9  Give some reasons that would help explain the greater achievement of the male in our society.

10  Why do girls tend to show a lag in intellectual development during late adolescence?

11  Summarize the findings of Rainwater's study of traditional roles among poverty groups in four cultures. How are these findings relevant to our consideration of roles in American marriage?

SEXUAL DIFFERENCES AND ROLES

12   In what ways does a rigidly traditional assignment of roles in marriage affect the degree of companionship in the marriage?

13   List some developments that have encouraged male participation in household tasks.

14   Summarize the findings of the study of student attitudes concerning the husband's participation in household tasks. How do you explain the greater willingness of men to say they will help with household tasks when they marry than of girls to say they think a husband should help?

15   Do you think a girl could be happy playing the subservient role during courtship and be unhappy in that role after she is married?

16   Explain why current social attitudes and expectations concerning roles may produce greater tension for men than for women.

17   What inconsistencies did Kirkpatrick find in the attitudes of men and women in his study of roles?

## PROJECTS AND ACTIVITIES

1   Repeat the study given on p. 22 with the class and have it summarized for class discussion.

2   *Panel discussion.* The married students in the class discuss changes in their conception of roles from the time they become engaged to the present. If there are too few married students in the class, single engaged students take part in the discussion, bringing out their attitudes about roles in marriage. What patterns do they anticipate in their future marriages?

3   *Panel discussion.* Invite some older couples from the community to come to class and discuss role situations in marriage.

4   *Sociodrama.* Write and present a skit that illustrates role patterns today. The scenes might show: a group of women talking about women's roles; a group of husbands discussing their common problems; a family scene that illustrates some possible problems involving several family members.

5   Report on examples of sex-role conditioning of children that you have observed among family and friends, or that you recall from your own growing up.

# DATING

Dating has special functions in a society with a family system based, as ours is, on free mate choice. This may be seen more clearly when we look at the situation in some countries where dating as we know it is rare or unknown, and yet in recent years the old system of arranged marriages has been in transition. Many young people in such countries as Japan, India, and others now feel they should have the right to choose their own mates as people in the Western world do. Some of their parents are inclined to agree and to relinquish a part of their authority when it comes to choosing mates for their children. But how is the young person to choose wisely as long as social custom limits free association among unmarried young people? Any freedom of choice under such circumstances can be even more of a hazard than it is under the dating system in the United States.

Clearly, no perfect system of mate selection has yet developed. Evidence of this in our own country is the rate of marital failure, and, in other countries, such customs as concubinage, which recognizes the failure of arranged marriages to meet all the needs of individuals.

However, dating serves functions other than the specific choice of a mate. Certain developmental tasks confront people during the dating years. These growth tasks are more likely to be achieved by people who: (1) understand what purposes or functions the dating stage of life potentially serves; and (2) assess the contribution of their own dating experiences both to their growth toward maturity and toward achieving life-time goals.

## DATING BEGINS EARLY

The dating period starts for many people when they are about 14, and is over by the time they reach 19 or 20. More than 28 percent of all the women in the United States marry before they are 20, and 50 percent marry when they are slightly over age 21. Fifty percent of the men marry by the time they are 23. These figures represent an average of all young people, based on census records. However, the bulk of the early marriages, which lower the average age at marriage, are not among the college-educated part of the population. College-educated people tend to marry somewhat later, but there is evidence that college students begin dating as early as the rest of the population. The current trend is for people to delay marriage until they are older, in contrast to the 1950s and 1960s when people married at younger ages. The trend to delay marriage is especially true of people who are college educated. This will give this group a longer period of time for the courtship years.

The average age at which 3189 college students reported having had their first date was 14.3 for boys and 14.2 for girls. Slightly more boys had first dated at the age of 11 or younger, and slightly more boys had not dated until they were 16 or older.[1] Since boys are somewhat older than girls when they marry, and since they begin dating at approximately the same age as girls do, the dating stage of life lasts slightly longer for boys than for girls.

[1] A study of attitudes, behavior, and background factors among 3189 students in 18 colleges and universities in 1967. The schools cooperating were Florida State University, Western Michigan State University, Kansas Wesleyan University, South Dakota State University, the universities of Connecticut, Alabama, Wisconsin, Dubuque, Hawaii, Utah, California (Berkeley), and the following colleges: Sacramento State, Mankato State, Chico State, Anderson, Flint Junior, American River Junior, and South Carolina State College for Women. The study repeats research which collected data from 3000 students between 1952 and 1955 in the following 11 schools: universities of Illinois, Nebraska, Louisiana, Minnesota (Duluth), Kansas, Stanford, Dubuque, California (Berkeley), New York (New Paltz), and from Whittier College and Fullerton Junior College.
In 1971 we repeated the study at the University of California (Berkeley) and at Sacramento State College with 68 men and 135 women. In some places in the text we will refer to the 1971 findings and compare them with the larger study in 1967.
For reports of the 1952–1955 research with 3000 students, see:

> Judson T. Landis, "Dating Maturation of Children from Happy and Unhappy Marriages," *Journal of Marriage and Family Living* 25:3 (August 1963), 351–53.
>
> —————, "Religiousness, Family Relationships, and Family Values in Protestant, Catholic, and Jewish Families," *Journal of Marriage and the Family* 22:4 (November 1960), 341–47.
>
> —————, "A Re-examination of the Role of the Father as an Index of Family Integration," *Journal of Marriage and Family Living* 24:2 (May 1962), 122–28.
>
> —————, "A Comparison of Children from Divorced and Non-divorced Unhappy Marriages," *The Family Life Coordinator* 11:3 (July 1962), 61–65.

References will be made both to data from the 1952 and the 1967 studies, and significant attitude or behavior changes revealed by the data from the two time periods will be reported. In 1967, 16 percent were freshmen, 30 percent sophomores, 25 percent juniors, 26 percent seniors, and 3 percent graduate students. Thirteen percent were married, 12 percent formally engaged, and 15 percent had an "understanding to be engaged." The 1952 sample showed approximately the same proportions in each category. Most students in both groups were enrolled in family sociology and marriage courses.

Data from our study of the dating experiences of 3189 college students show that two-thirds of these students had dated while they were in junior high school, 95 percent had dated while they were in senior high school, and 95 percent in college. As to the extent of the dating with different people, 14 percent of the women and 15 percent of the men had dated at least 15 different people during their high school years, and 26 percent of the women and 25 percent of the men had dated at least 15 different people while in college. The study also found that those from happy rather than unhappy homes began dating earlier, had dated more people in junior and senior high school rather than steadily dating one or a few persons, and were dating more frequently in college.[2]

The current trend on most campuses is toward a less formalized approach to dating. People associate together in casual companionship groups and become fairly well acquainted within this context. College students have always tended to meet prospective dates in settings such as classes, the library, exchange events of living groups, or in school or church activities. But asking for a first date was on a more formal basis than it is today.

There is now a broadening of opportunities that lead to pairing off. Barriers to a free mingling of the sexes are letting down in society, especially for people in the dating years. Schools formerly women's colleges or men's colleges are becoming coeducational, and living groups are coeducational on many campuses. Many new student groups have been organized around interests such as ecology, race relations, opposition to foreign involvement, and political activities. Participation by young people in interest groups gives impetus to less formal patterns in dating. People who become acquainted in informal situations and drift into pair relationships become steady couples according to the meaning of the term as used on campuses in the past. This process seems to reduce some of the tension and uncertainty that used to characterize dating. A young man does not have to be afraid to ask for a date by telephone or in person; by the time the two pair off they are likely to have associated within a group enough so that either one may suggest an activity without great risk of rejection.

Research indicates that over a period of time in this century dating has become not only less formal but also less exploitative, with the motivation for dating tending more toward a search for personal identity and for a friend with whom there can be a meaningful relationship. Dating motivated by a desire for prestige and status or as a specific search for a wife or husband seems to be decreasing.

These changes are reflected in studies of a decade of student dating

[2] Judson T. Landis, "Dating Maturation of Children from Happy and Unhappy Marriages," *Journal of Marriage and Family Living* 25:3 (August 1963), 351–53.

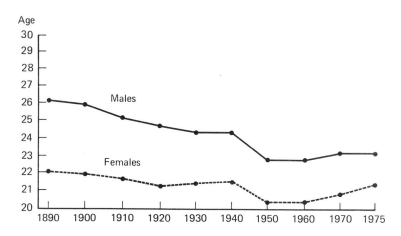

FIG. 3–1    Average age at first marriage, males and females, 1890 to 1975.

at Harvard reported by sociologist R. S. Vreeland.[3] A questionnaire asked the men to rank in order of personal importance a list of dating motives: recreation, finding a good listener, sexual intimacy, finding a wife, being seen with someone who would enhance reputation, finding a female friend.

In the 1960s sample over half the men gave first or second place to "recreation" as the chief function of their dating. In contrast, more than half the men in 1970 gave "finding a friend" as the most or second most important motive for their dating. When the responses giving "finding a good listener" were combined with "finding a friend," the results showed that companionship was the motivation for dating to a greater extent than it had been in the early 1960s. In the 1960s sample approximately 13 percent gave "finding a wife" as the most important function of dating; in 1970 approximately 6 percent gave this motivation. More than 75 percent of both groups ranked "prestige" or "being seen with someone who would enhance my reputation" as last or next to the last reason for dating.

In summarizing the results of the study of Harvard dating, Vreeland comments, "For today's male student, the most important dating motive is finding a friend who is female. The most essential characteristic in a good date is her ability to make conversation and the primary dating activity is sitting around the room talking. At the same time, the sexual component of dating cannot be ignored . . . sex was one of the important dating activities for a fifth of the Harvard seniors in 1970."

Among characteristics rated as "making no difference" were several that reflect departure from tradition-bound attitudes. Among these were for a girl to be "highly intelligent *and hide it*," or to be "older."

[3] Rebecca S. Vreeland, "Is It True What They Say About Harvard Boys?" *Psychology Today* 5:8 (January 1972), 65–68.

Evidence shows that similar motivations for dating are effective among people of younger ages. In a study of dating patterns among a group of high school students, the most important reason given for their steady dating was "being with someone I enjoy." [4] This study also found a difference in dating patterns between rural and urban youth. Urban students dated more different people, dated for "companionship," and had fewer serious thoughts of selecting a marriage partner. Rural youth dated later, dated fewer different people, and dated with more serious thoughts of finding a marriage partner.

Various studies have shown that about one-fifth of pre-college-age young people do not date. The experience of dating during the teen-age years would seem to contribute importantly to emotional and social maturing. It presents the young person with situations in which he or she learns to adjust to a variety of personalities, to talk freely about a variety of subjects with a friend of the other sex, and to give and receive affection and companionship. In our society, if dating is too long delayed it can be a handicap in developing the ability to establish and maintain enduring relationships.

## FACTORS THAT MOTIVATE TOWARD BEGINNING TO DATE

Among the very young, to begin to date represents growing up and becoming a part of the social world. The pressure of social custom and the influence of the peer group motivate toward early dating; developing biological impulses are not necessarily the motivating force. During the first dating experiences of some young people, physical responses or urges toward the other sex may be incidental or even absent. Data on the age at which the 3189 college students had begun dating show, for example, that those boys and girls who had reached puberty at age 12 or younger were more likely to have begun dating at 12 or younger than were those who reached puberty at later ages. However, the data show also that a considerable group (about 13 percent) began dating at 12 or younger although they did not reach puberty until age 15 or older, and another group (about 21 percent) did not begin to date until 16 years or older although they reached puberty at 12 or younger. The data show that boys and girls from happy homes who mature early physically are the ones who are most likely to start dating at 12 years or younger, and boys and girls from unhappy homes who mature late physically are more likely to start dating at 16 years or older. These data emphasize that social practice in a community, and the home environment are factors influencing the age at which young people begin to date; biological physical development is not the only factor.[5]

[4] James S. Wittman, Jr., "Dating Patterns of Rural and Urban Kentucky Teen-agers," *The Family Coordinator* 20:1 (January 1971), 63.

[5] Landis, see footnote p. 32.

FIG. 3–2 © 1956, United Features Syndicate, Inc..

## FUNCTIONS OF THE DATING STAGE

While much of dating today may not be a direct search for a wife or a husband, dating nevertheless tends to grow into courtship. Friendships grow into permanent relationships leading to marriage. The dating stage of life, before one is committed to any permanent relationship, serves important functions for the individual.

**Acquiring social competence.** When people first venture into the "couple world" they are occupied for a time with learning social skills. They are motivated to study people in social situations and to observe what is acceptable and what is unacceptable behavior. Much of life in today's world for adults involves rather continuous interaction with other people. In business and the professions, in work situations of all kinds, a person needs some measure of competence in social interaction. The dating years permit young people to test themselves in different situations and to learn finesse in social interaction at a time when crucial stakes are seldom involved in any one situation, and also when their contemporaries are all in the process of growing and testing. At this stage, people are not judged or held accountable for social errors to the extent that may be true later in life.

The young person in the early years of dating is more specifically concerned with learning how to get dates and to get along on dates than with any other phase of social experience. Because of this direct interest, there is motivation to learn a wide range of skills.

How to carry one's responsibility in conversation without overdoing it, to sense what others would like to talk about and draw them out, to balance listening and talking—these are skills important in all relationships throughout life. How to dress appropriately for different occasions, to ask for dates, to accept dates or invitations graciously or refuse with equal grace are skills learned by experience. The individual who makes progress in acquiring such skills during the dating years, becomes freer to achieve other important growth processes.

In the study of the 3189 college students, we found that only one-fourth of the students felt very confident in associating with the other sex, and more than half reported some difficulty. If these students typify

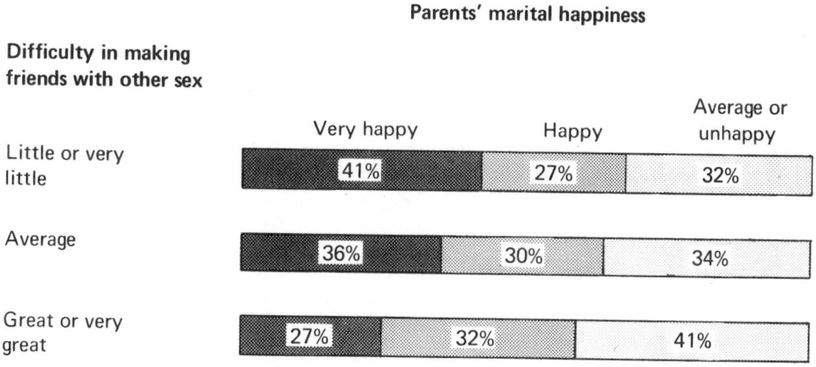

**Difficulty in making
friends with other sex**

|  | Very happy | Happy | Average or unhappy |
|---|---|---|---|
| Little or very little | 41% | 27% | 32% |
| Average | 36% | 30% | 34% |
| Great or very great | 27% | 32% | 41% |

FIG. 3–3  Difficulty in making friends with the other sex in early adolescence and parental marital happiness as given by 3189 students in 18 colleges in 1967.

college people, developing confidence in associating with the other sex is somewhat of a problem for the majority of young people.

**Developing self-understanding and an understanding of others.**  Until the dating years, most people are not much concerned with self-evaluation, nor have they much impetus to try to change their habits or personalities. But, whether cause or effect, dating is often accompanied by a growing awareness of many aspects of personality in oneself and in other people. The young adolescent may make little constructive progress here; this function of dating may not be achieved in early experiences. Even many older young people allow their dating to be more or less random activity, their goal being only to keep in the social group. But for many people, the dating years provide a special motivation to assess their own personality growth and needs. Setbacks or failures in heterosexual associations may jolt a person into objective self-study for the first time. As a result, he or she may begin to have self-understanding and begin to achieve a broader conception of personality and how it functions.

It is true that painful experiences may occur in the process. The young person is seeking personal identity. In association with people of the other sex, the individual is probing and testing personal motivations and self-definitions. Any defeat or rejection can only be painful. Nevertheless, through the social interaction of dating, one perceives contemporaries in the same process. And out of the experience can come a more assured self-definition and growth toward self-acceptance.

One can become able to consider specifically such questions as: What kinds of responses do I bring out in others? What specific traits or types of people bring out the best or the worst in me? *Why* do I react as I do in my association with others? A case may illustrate some of the kinds of things that can be learned through dating. A college senior tells her experience:

> I dated Stan all through our junior year. From the first my parents were not enthusiastic about Stan. I knew they would rather I dated boys of my own religion, and a few times when Stan came for me and had been drinking too much they were very upset. I felt that they didn't have a chance to see him at his best. I did think Stan drank too much, but on our campus other people were doing it, too, and I thought I just needed to grow up and develop a more sophisticated attitude about some things. Stan often told me that I was naive and teased me about being old-fashioned. I never quarreled with Stan, but sometimes when he was tired or irritated about something he would say cutting things that hurt me. He was always sweet and apologetic afterwards though, and it was easy to forgive him. I talked it over with my roommate, and she said that emotional upsets between people in love are to be expected, and that I should appreciate his apologizing—that some men wouldn't. In general, I knew that I was not so happy as I had always been, but I thought it was because my parents' negative attitude toward Stan made it hard for me to be as carefree as I usually am in my friendships.
>
> While Stan and I were apart during the summer vacation, I had some dates with Bill, whom I've known all my life. I was amazed at what a good time I had with him. He is considerate, and he never belittles me. We found that we think alike on so many things. Suddenly I realized that I felt like myself again, happy almost all the time, and comfortable with myself and my family and in my friendship with Bill. I could act as I felt and not have to worry about being naive or unsophisticated. When school started again this fall I decided not to date Stan any more. I've learned a few things about myself and I know now what some of the qualities are that I want in a man I date or might ever think of marrying.

**Discovering and testing conceptions of sex roles.** The average person tends to take for granted whatever type of masculine–feminine dominant-submission pattern existed in his or her own parental family. But after dating different people, it may be discovered that the pattern accepted for so long is not the most satisfactory for one's own relationships. Or one may discover that in no other pattern can one be comfortable. Marriage counselors' files hold many cases of married couples who seek counseling because of conflicts arising from differences in attitudes about roles. Typical of such cases is the strongly dominant girl married to a man who either rebels against any kind of feminine dominance or seems to accept it but reacts by losing his self-confidence and becoming less effective generally. Another type is seen in the case of a man who grew up in an equalitarian home where both parents were strong personalities who were able to live cooperatively, yet with considerable independence. This man married an extremely dependent girl whose security was threatened if she had to make independent decisions or act in any situation without the decisive reassurance of her husband. In their relationship the wife often felt let down or rejected, while the husband missed equalitarian companionship and felt her dependence as pressure.

There are unlimited gradations in the attitudes and feelings of different people about dominating or being dominated. Dating different people should help the young person become more aware of personal feelings, as well as more aware of the different ways in which other people react to situations that this individual finds satisfactory or unsatisfactory. One girl explained what she had learned in this area in these words:

"I think the first boy who made me see myself differently from the way I had before was Bob. Bob was definitely protective and possessive. He was the big, strong type who wanted to lash out at the world for criticizing women. He was so helpful I felt smothered."

Instead of feeling smothered, a girl with different attitudes and needs might have enjoyed Bob's attitudes. Before choosing a mate, the individual should assess his or her own feelings and attitudes about male–female roles and about dominating or being dominated.

**Assessing life values and goals.** It is important during the dating years that young people give thought to the values they live by, what they hope to accomplish in life, and what things matter most as they consider choosing their vocations. College students in general have similar values or they would not be attending college. However, wide differences exist among college people in specific, predominant values. The prime standard for some is making money; with others, position or status is of first importance; others are chiefly oriented to the purpose of having the "good life," or toward some type of service to mankind, with a very great range of possible definitions of the "good life" and of "service." Dating should help an individual to determine in some measure just what her or his own orientation is, how well it fits with that of the people found to be congenial, and to what extent personal adjustment could be made if the circumstances of life made change necessary. This may be illustrated in one way by the experience of people who date outside their own religion. Many college students discover for the first time, as they date, just how much their religion is their own and how much it is a previously unquestioned part of their family background.

**Examining habitual ways of meeting problems.** Most people by the late teens have already established fairly habitual ways of meeting problems in life. Some people learn while still very young to know and accept their own weaknesses, and they are able to act constructively when confronted with defeat or frustration. One shy nine-year-old boy said, "I used to be afraid of a lot of things, and when I'm afraid I get a stomachache. I used to think I was sick when I had a stomachache. But I found out that there are two kinds of stomachaches, the kind when you're really sick and the kind that just means you're afraid; and I can tell the difference. I'm still afraid sometimes, but not as much as I used to be; and when I get that kind of stomachache now I just go on doing whatever I have to do and pretty soon I feel O.K. again."

This boy at nine was making progress in objectivity and in coping with a personal weakness. Sometimes people many years older have not gone so far. When they meet frustrating situations or encounter difficult problems, they cannot face their feelings; they try such escapes as overeating, illness, blaming others for all their troubles, excessive drinking, taking drugs, or aggressive and antagonistic behavior toward those close to them—friends, wives, husbands, or roommates. Such ways of reacting to problems are quite easy to recognize in others, when one's judgment is not clouded by being in love. Therefore, during the casual dating stage of life, it is important to be alert to kinds of behavior that are likely to lead to poor mental health, not only in associates but in one's self. It is never too late to begin to change habit patterns. The person who can discover his or her tendencies toward poor mental health, and go on to change and improve, need not be handicapped by going beyond casual dating with another who has unconstructive ways of facing life and who is neither aware nor able to learn better ways.

**Assessing ego needs.** An assessment of one's own ego needs and one's ability to meet the needs of others is a task of the dating years.

In the young child, ego needs are all-encompassing; the child does not hesitate to express his feelings with such phrases as: "Watch me!" "Listen to me!" "Let *me* talk!" "Look what *I* can do!" But a part of maturing is becoming able to appreciate that others have the same needs and to receive pleasure and a sense of fulfillment through meeting the needs of others as well as having one's own needs met.

Most people have at some time dated a person who has not yet grown up enough to be aware in any sense of the needs of others. With such a person a relationship tends to be all one way. This person is happy and expansive, often very interesting, as long as he or she is the center of attention. The conversation is fascinating, as long as the subject remains close to personal interests, experiences, or feelings. But let the conversation drift to the interests of the other person, and this person becomes bored.

Like everyone else, such a person enjoys being praised, but it may never occur to him or her to praise others. One young man whose friend complained that he was too critical said, "Well, I don't go round passing out compliments. I don't praise someone unless I mean it. No one could say I'm insincere." This was a rationalized defense of his habitually indifferent or even disparaging attitudes toward others.

In order to build good relationships, it is necessary to look for the good and the worth in others and to give recognition freely. Satisfying relationships with friends, dates, and later in marriage cannot be one-way relationships. There must be giving as well as receiving, not merely occasionally, but most of the time.

The time when self-centered egotism can be observed in oneself and when one can become able to recognize it in others at the least cost is during casual dating before one is involved in a serious relationship. Lynne, a college freshman, said of two boys, "I listen to Bill's problems all the time, and I'm glad to do it. But it seems that if I start talking about my problems, somehow or other we are off the subject right away. With Jerry, it's just the opposite. I have to watch myself, because he always seems so interested in what I'm interested in that, first thing I know, we are talking about *me* all the time and I think afterwards that I must have sounded awfully self-centered and childish."

Our study of college students showed that both men and women felt the other sex to be self-centered. This may be because everyone is naturally somewhat self-centered. The dating years are the time when this trait becomes evident to others and, if one is alert, to oneself.

**Recognizing and evaluating possessiveness and jealousy.** Feelings of possessiveness and jealousy are natural, and most people have some measure of these feelings. But because they are "natural," insofar as they begin to show up early in life, many people have the mistaken idea that such feelings are acceptable or even desirable. Sometimes it is mistakenly believed that possessiveness or jealousy is proof of true love. The maturing person will work to overcome the tendency toward possessiveness and feelings of jealousy. In reality, possessiveness is never acceptable, except perhaps in small children, when it can be overlooked as normal for the age. The mother in the following situation was not unduly upset by her child's actions:

> A mother was sewing, her three-year-old son playing contentedly on the floor, when a neighbor dropped in. Almost as soon as the two women began to talk interestedly with each other, the child left his toys and climbed upon his mother's lap. He became very loving, and put his arms around her neck so closely that she could not see around him. The mother tried to turn him around in order to continue her conversation, but he put his hands on her cheeks and held her face toward his, saying, "Look at *me*, talk to me." The mother said, "Later, Tommy," and gave him a cookie, got a different book for him and settled him again on the floor where he appeared contented for a moment. Then he laid down his book and walked over to the caller, kicked her in the shin, and said, "Why don't you go home?"

In dating relationships, most people have acquired more finesse than this three-year-old. They are beyond shin kicking, but sometimes not far enough beyond. And the motivation for the possessive behavior they do show is identical with that of the three-year-old. They cannot willingly share any part of the attention of a loved one with others.

Usually, uncontrolled possessiveness accompanied by jealousy in an adult or a person in the late teens or twenties indicates insecurity and a lack of self-confidence. This lack is the basis for her or his inability to have confidence and trust in relationships with others. The jealous, possessive person tries to force loyalty and response. In personal relationships this person tends to be demanding rather than trusting. A fairly well-adjusted person is likely, after a time, to find that a relationship with a possessive person is an intolerable burden. In a friendship with such a person, one may begin to feel boxed in and overcontrolled. The time to find out whether this kind of possessive control is endurable is before one has reached such serious dating involvement as engagement.

Dating offers excellent opportunities for young people to study themselves and others for overly possessive attitudes and behavior. Possessive tendencies or urges to dominate, and some jealous feelings, may occur in everyone's life at times. But those who achieve maturity and build permanently happy and satisfying relationships work to overcome or control these tendencies in themselves and try to be realistic about the characteristics of others.

## SOME GROWTH TASKS PRESENT THEMSELVES AS PROBLEMS

The term "developmental tasks" refers to the challenges that confront people at each stage of life. During the dating years, some matters that arise as problems can be recognized as necessary and important learning tasks, stages in growth toward permanent and satisfying heterosexual relationships.

**Coming to terms with sex impulses.**  A developmental task that creates problems is the necessity for coming to terms with one's sexual nature and impulses within the context of dating activities.

The fact that sexual maturity is reached and sexual impulses become strong before people are ready for marriage creates problems that must be faced realistically. These may be viewed as falling largely within the following categories:

1   How far should one go with physical intimacies during dating?
2   How does one control the limits of physical intimacy?
3   How does one recognize and cope with exploitative behavior in dating situations?
4   What are desirable and workable standards?
5   How does one distinguish between physical attraction and love, or relate them?

**Who initiates lovemaking?**  It is usually assumed that the male initiates lovemaking, because of his stronger sex drive or because he thinks he is expected to do so. When we queried 465 university students, 84 percent of the men and 97 percent of the women said the man had initiated the lovemaking on the last date reported upon. An unexplained discrepancy was that 16 percent of the men said the woman had initiated the lovemaking, but only 3 percent of the women said they had started it. Does this indicate a breakdown in communication between people dating each other—the man interpreting as encouragement or invitation actions or words that a woman means otherwise? Does it represent a tendency for women to express the traditional viewpoint that "of course" it is the man who starts lovemaking? More than half the women (58 percent) reported that the man had tried to go farther than they wished.

**Drawing the line.**  Over a period of years we have asked students who is responsible for drawing the line in physical intimacy. The answers reflect a gradual trend toward equalitarian attitudes in man-woman relationships—a moving away from the older double standard of behavior. There has been a tendency for a larger percentage of each student generation to say that both are responsible, rather than to express the traditional view that it is the woman who must draw the line.

*NO WAY*

**Coping with the sexual element.**  It becomes necessary to distinguish between a sexual relationship and love. The younger and more inexperienced the individuals, the more they are inclined to confuse sexual drives and their satisfaction with love. During dating they can learn to accept their own sexuality and can decide how far to go toward satisfying sexual impulses.

Those who date different people will find widely varying standards. If the young people are to be comfortable in associations, they must know what they consider desirable and undesirable, right and wrong. This is not only true in deciding how far they will go in petting; they must also know their attitudes on such moral issues as honesty and loyalty, and such social habits as drinking.

Studies of college students show that a large percentage of young people still plan to wait to have sexual intercourse until after they are married. However, couples who have made that decision often find it a problem to keep lovemaking within the limits they have mutually agreed upon.

In more casual dating, both girls and boys need to know how to draw the line tactfully and effectively. This may be difficult, especially for a girl who is inexperienced with boys or lacking in confidence.

That "techniques" for controlling behavior are necessary indicates that, in a great many dating relationships, there is no clear understanding between the two about the actual nature of their relationship. One person may feel an involvement or a commitment that the other does not acknowledge. Listed below are some techniques offered by 200 college girls for controlling petting on dates:

1   Be honest—say no sincerely and politely.
2   Keep talking. Keep up an interesting conversation.
3   Avoid situations that are an easy setup for petting.
4   Plan dates thoroughly.
5   Double date or date in groups.
6   Let the boy know your attitude from the start.

7   Keep an early curfew.

8   Plan after-date activities.

9   Use reason; discuss your viewpoints.

10  Don't prompt petting by your actions.

11  Set a point beyond which you won't go.

12  Divert your date's attention.

13  Ask to be taken home.

14  Don't date fellows interested only in petting.

15  Refrain from long "good nights."

Most of these techniques would apply to dates before engagement, although some of the suggestions would be applicable after engagement also. Engaged couples who have a meeting of minds about wanting to draw the line do not need such techniques, since the girl would not have to take most of the responsibility for control.

Statements by the men and women in our study of engagements show a fairly high degree of agreement on setting the limits of intimacy. A summary of their statements is given in Table 3-1.[6]

**Recognizing exploitative behavior.**   In some dating relationships exploitative behavior may occur. Certain circumstances or conditions, such as differences in social class, differences in age, and traumas of certain courtship experiences, are conducive to an unfair or unjust utilization of

TABLE 3-1          Feelings of 122 engaged couples toward limiting intimacies

| Statement | Men | Women |
|---|---|---|
| We are in agreement that we want to save intercourse for marriage | 42% | 43% |
| After discussing it, we mutually agreed on a set limit | 53 | 68 |
| Fiancé(e) set the limit | 15 | 6 |
| I set the limit | 15 | 9 |
| We never discussed it, but there was mutual agreement | 22 | 19 |
| There is much conflict on how far we should go | 13 | 6 |
| Religion dictates action | — | 1 |

[6] Later references will be made to this study of engagements. Students in family sociology classes at the University of California, Berkeley, and at Chico State College in 1967 were asked to give questionnaires to engaged student couples they knew. The engaged couples were asked to fill in the questionnaires independently of each other and to mail them separately to the researcher. Of the 122 couples, 88 percent were formally engaged and 12 percent had an "understanding" of engagement. Only if both the man and woman returned a questionnaire were their responses included in the study. This study repeats a study done with 200 engaged couples at the University of California in 1957 but includes additional questions not asked in the former study.

an individual by one of the other sex. Exploitation usually indicates a one-sided emotional involvement. The exploited one is emotionally involved, but the other is seeking selfish gratification, or is motivated by other considerations.

Men from a higher *social class* are in a position to exploit women from lower social classes. College men sometimes use their position to exploit noncollege girls.

In a study of University of Florida students, Ehrmann found that when college men dated women of a lower social class they were more apt to have sexual intercourse if the girl would permit. On the other hand, if they were dating within their own social class, they did not try to go farther than the women thought was right.[7] If the women were from a higher social class, the men did not try to go so far as they did with women of their own social class. Ehrmann points out that a girl from a lower social class dating a boy from a higher class may permit or even encourage the boy in exploitative behavior if she wishes to marry him. There is a chance that she will win the gamble and he will marry her.[8] In cases of this type it would seem that a form of exploitation is reciprocal. Both are exploitative, but from dissimilar motives and with different considerations at stake.

**Age as a basis for exploitation.**   Older, experienced men may exploit girls for sex. Society protects girls until a certain age through laws on statutory rape. After the girl reaches the specified age, she is supposed to be worldly-wise enough to be able to protect herself from exploitation.

Exploitative behavior is carried on by women as well as by men. Boys have less legal protection from exploitation by older women, although such exploitation certainly occurs. Young women also exploit older men, as well as men their own age, by using physical charm to keep a man or men emotionally involved. The feminine exploiter may take advantage of the emotional involvement of men not only to have the convenience of their devotion, but to exploit them economically. Men tend to exploit for sexual gratification, women more often for prestige, status, or economic advantages.

It has been theorized that, in a disparate situation, the one with the greater emotional involvement will have the least control over the situation and will suffer the greatest distress over occurrences in the relationship—or, in other words, that the one most emotionally involved is the most exploitable.[9] An illustration of this type of exploitation is pro-

[7] Winston W. Ehrmann, "Student Cooperation in a Study of Dating Behavior," *Journal of Marriage and Family Living* 14:4 (November 1952), 322–26.

[8] Ehrmann, "Influence of Comparative Social Class of Companion Upon Premarital Heterosexual Behavior," *Journal of Marriage and Family Living* 17:1 (February 1955), 48–53.

[9] J. K. Skipper, Jr., and Gilbert Nass, "Dating Behavior: A Framework for Analysis and an Illustration," *Journal of Marriage and the Family* 28:4 (November 1966), 412–20.

vided by a study of young women training in a large city hospital nursing school, a situation in which there were few dating opportunities and the women tended to become exploitable by interns, doctors, and older medical students whose motives for dating were different from theirs. The authors of that study point out that, because the women in such a situation are interested in a serious relationship or marriage, they are susceptible to serious emotional involvement, whereas the men are either not yet ready to consider marriage or are already married and are motivated by a need for temporary gratification, emotional or sexual. Because of their unique position as students in a training situation that emphasizes their deference to the doctor and his authority and judgment, the women are especially exploitable in dates with medical personnel.

## FINDING SUITABLE DATES

The framework of young single adult social life is solidly based on pair relationships. The stage of dating should be a time of freedom to associate casually and a time of carefree social enjoyment. However, finding friends is a problem for a great many young people. Theoretically, on college campuses where there is a fairly equal numerical distribution of the sexes, no such problem should arise. Yet conditions in many colleges and universities make it difficult for the sexes to meet under circumstances that will lead to friendships and dates. Large numbers of students who commute, lack of housing facilities on campus so that many live in off-campus apartments, homes, or rooming houses—these conditions contribute to isolating many individual students who may find it extremely difficult to make meaningful friendships on campus. The situation is similar among young single people who live and work in cities; for them it is probably worse, since on college campuses the problem is at least recognized and some efforts are made to provide for social needs.

### Coeducational housing

The student union, snack bars, coffee houses, and church social centers all have facilities which make it possible for students to meet. On many campuses, student dormitories and other housing facilities have become coeducational, so the sexes mingle more freely and get acquainted on a casual basis.

Young single people who live in cities may also find it easier to get acquainted today than formerly because rooming houses are rented to both men and women. Sometimes single, working young people lease houses and live on a semi-communal basis. They share the household tasks, such as cooking, doing dishes, buying the groceries, and keeping the house in order, but each has a private room. In some houses, when a vacancy occurs, the occupants screen prospective tenants, thus hoping to maintain a congenial group.

On some campuses, experiments have been conducted with pairing couples for dates by computer. Sociologists at Iowa State University attempted to test the effectiveness of computer dating on their campus.[10] They paired 500 men and 500 women for a social event by means of a computer. The students filled out questionnaires, one just after the event and another six months later, stating how well satisfied they were with the computer choice. Interesting differences were revealed between the attitudes of the men and the women. In general, the women tended to want in a date qualities more in keeping with those that would meet social approval if the date became a permanent mate, qualities pertaining to occupational or professional plans. The men were more interested in the attractiveness of the women and showed less interest in any possible future from the encounter. The women reported less satisfaction with the computer choices than did the men. The six-month follow-up showed that the men did not lose enthusiasm for the computer-selected partners as rapidly as did the women. Immediately after the event, 50 percent of the men and 40 percent of the women thought they were matched quite successfully in their dates, with about 25 percent of both thinking the match was only "so-so"; 30 percent of the women and 22 percent of the men thought the choice very poor.

Another study of computer dating matched one group of student couples on the basis of similarity and another group on a random basis, with no attention to similarity. In a follow-up study both the men and women who had been matched for similarity in backgrounds and interests rated the dates slightly more successful than did those couples matched in the random sample. The men rated their first single date by computer higher than did the women.

The researchers in this study answered the question, "Is computer dating successful?" with the answer, "What are your expectations?" A majority of the males and females indicated that they found at least one satisfactory date among the three names with whom they were matched. The researchers concluded, "Computer dating is at least as efficient as blind dating, chance meetings on campus, and the other avenues that are commonly used." [11]

One implication of the interest in experiments in computer dating may be that there is some awareness today of the importance of background factors in mate choice and of compatibility on matters like values and goals in life. Rational attempts to find suitable dates may represent a response to evidence that poor mate choice accounts for a considerable proportion of failing marriages.

[10] Robert H. Coombs and William F. Kenkel, "Sex Differences in Dating Aspirations and Satisfactions with Computer-Selected Partners," *Journal of Marriage and the Family* 28:1 (February 1966), 62–66.

[11] Emily Strong, William Wallace, and Warner Wilson, "Three-Filter Date Selection by Computer," *The Family Coordinator* 18:2 (April 1968), 166–71; Emily Strong and Warner Wilson, "Three-Filter Date Selection by Computer—Phase II," *The Family Coordinator* 18:3 (July 1969), 256–59.

Whatever the approach to finding dates, one of the major growth tasks of the dating years is to become able to assess relationships accurately on the basis of their potential for permanently satisfactory relationships in life. The following chapter will explore this matter further.

## OUTLINE FOR SELF-STUDY: DATING

### I  BEING A GOOD DATE

1  What specific traits are you working on to improve yourself as a date? Can you see progress?

2  What criticisms do you think others might have of you as a date? Consider whether the criticisms are justified.

### II  LEARNING THROUGH DATING

1  What specific social skills did you acquire through dating in junior high school? In senior high school? In college? Which of your social techniques could still be improved?

2  What values and goals do you have that seem to differ from the values and goals of some people you have dated? Can you determine just how important these values are to you?

3  What role seems to be most natural for you? Dominant and decisive? Equalitarian and cooperative? Easily dominated? A combination of some of the above?

4  What roles have you had to play at times in dating that did not seem to fit you? Has the role that you feel most natural playing become more set as you have dated more people?

5  Can you think of one or more specific traits or ways of reacting to situations and people that you have discovered in yourself through dating experiences?

6  When you have had a bad day, how do you work off your negative feelings? Do you take it out on others? Do you relieve your feelings through activities such as reading, working, playing, or in other ways? Are you inclined to give vent to your feelings by slamming doors, brooding, drinking, overeating, speeding in a car, making those about you suffer?

7  How well do you know your own ego needs? Are your feelings often hurt? Do you often need to be complimented? Are you angry often? Have you established the habit of complimenting people for the good things they do or say, or for traits you see in them?

8  What type of people whom you date seem to give you a special sense of well-being? Does any type leave you feeling deflated or insecure? In this same way try to evaluate your effect on those you date.

9  Have you ever been possessive or jealous of those you have dated? Have you ever dated a person who was jealous or possessive? If you have a tendency toward jealousy or possessiveness, what steps are you taking to curb this tendency?

1   In your dating pattern, can you see progress toward becoming better prepared to make a wise choice of a mate?

2   Has your dating helped you toward a realistic understanding of what love is or may be?

## REVIEW QUESTIONS

1   How should thoughtful young people look upon dating?

2   What is the average age at first marriage for men and women in the United States today?

3   What determines the age at which young people begin to date? Explain.

4   What are some of the elementary skills that should be learned during the early years of dating?

5   What are some of the specific things to be learned about oneself and others through dating?

6   What does extreme jealousy or possessiveness often indicate?

7   What is the meaning of the term "developmental task"? How does it apply to dating?

8   What are some of the developmental tasks associated with sex and dating?

9   What are student beliefs about who should draw the line in petting?

10   What evidence is there that there may be poor communication between boys and girls in petting?

11   What techniques did college girls list as helpful in controlling the extent of intimacy during dating? If couples are engaged, should it be necessary for either to have to draw the line?

12   What is meant by exploitation? What are some common patterns of exploitation?

13   What are some advantages and disadvantages of "computer dating"?

14   Where do people meet at your school? Do commuting students find it difficult to meet possible dates at your school?

## PROJECTS AND ACTIVITIES

**Panel discussion.**   A group of students discuss the problem of poor communication between boys and girls on dates.

# DATING – DANGER SIGNALS

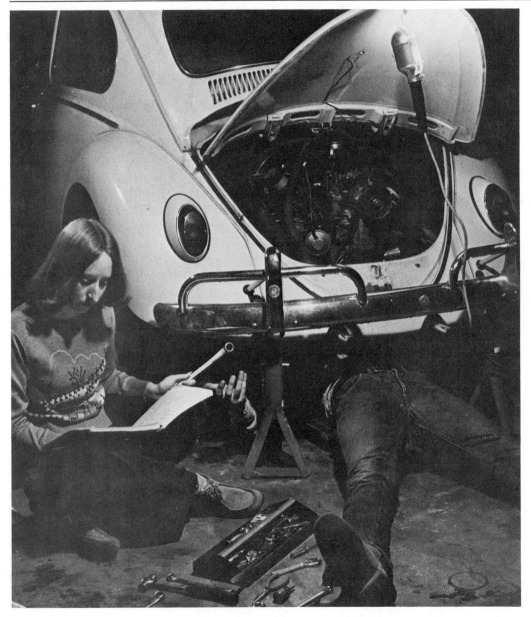

# 4

In many developing relationships, elements appear that indicate serious incompatibilities between the two people. Such elements are warning signals that may go unrecognized at first. If they are not recognized and the relationship is formalized through an engagement and marriage, later frustration is likely to result if the relationship remains intact, and trauma if the relationship must be broken.

During childhood, before the dating years, social relationships outside the family are usually temporary. Children at play may quarrel and be separated by their mothers, or they may shift friendships in what seems a mere whimsical reshuffling of alignments. However, some of such shifts are actually based on real personality conflicts or incompatibilities sensed by the children. In the adult world, relationships necessarily last longer. Marriage, parenthood, one's obligations in a job, and one's contacts with neighbors or with associates in community activities require more permanent commitments. Unworkable relationships can no longer be reshuffled as painlessly as they were in childhood.

Therefore, as people approach the age when their choices will involve permanent associations, they should develop insight into their relationships. They should assess accurately the meaning underlying the ways in which they react in a relationship with a specific person and the meaning of the responses they evoke from that person.

The elements in a relationship that predict trouble ahead we may call "danger signals." In most marriages that fail, especially those that fail early, there were danger signals which, if recognized by the couple during dating and courtship, would have warned them against trying to form a permanent relationship with each other. A later chapter considers reasons why engagements are broken; it only need be said here that many are broken because at least one member of the couple does recognize danger signals and concludes that the planned marriage could not be a happy one. Many dating couples recognize danger signals without so labeling them. They simply have a few dates and then "lose interest," going on to date others. Time is essential for recognizing danger signals. Couples who short-circuit the dating phase and marry after brief acquaintance block the possibility of such warnings becoming clear during courtship.

With maturity, emotional and chronological, one should be able to assess relationships with more understanding and confidence. Certain kinds of things in one's interaction with another person are significant as indicators of the quality of a permanent relationship with the person.

How can one recognize a danger signal, since in every friendship or love affair there will be some factors that are less than totally satisfactory?

## QUARRELING

Many people have romantic illusions about "lovers' quarrels." They tend to ignore the implications of the quarrels and dwell on the pleasure of making up afterwards. As this is written, the newspapers are publicizing a snarling battle in public between a young actress and her husband, the reports complete with pictures and the husband's statement afterwards, "It's such fun to make up with her!" The marriage is now only a few months old; one could safely predict that, by the time this book appears in print, the marriage of this couple with their quarreling and making up will have broken.

Quarreling during courtship has implications for any future marriage. In some cases, quarrels may mean that basic personality needs are not being met in the interaction. The quarreling may represent a battle each makes, perhaps unconsciously, in defense of needs unmet or denied by the other. In other cases, quarreling means that one of the pair habitually uses his or her close personal relationship as an outlet for neurotic pressures; a good permanent relationship with such a person is difficult, if not impossible.

It is true that a few quarrels may occur in potentially good relationships during the time when the pair are trying to develop an understanding of each other and are in the process of working out a relationship based on a healthy adaptation to normally occurring individual differences. But if, over a period of time, quarrels continue to occur, one should evaluate the quarrels with as much objectivity as possible. Do they have a *pattern*? That is, do certain types of events or situations tend to result in a quarrel?

> An engaged couple had several rather serious quarrels. In each case, the matter over which they quarreled seemed trivial. But each quarrel was emotionally packed and included sarcasm and bitterly critical verbal attacks made by the young man. Usually the woman could not understand what had started the trouble.

As time passed, however, and she became more thoroughly acquainted with her fiancé's life, she began to discover a pattern of events. He was a highly competitive man, employed in an organization in which the struggle for advancement was intense. She was employed by a different organization in which her position was secure and her abilities recognized. On a number of the occasions when they had quarreled, her fiancé had suffered what he considered to be a defeat at work: someone else had received greater recognition than he or had been advanced beyond him. At such times his emotional pressure built up to an explosive point. He tended to hold his feelings in check or block them off until, on a date, his fiancée happened to speak of some pleasant experience or development in her own job. This would spark a reaction of antagonism, which he would express more or less indirectly at first. He would take exception to some statement or comment she might make, and then go on to criticize her on some relatively unrelated matter, gathering steam as the conversation progressed. She reacted with shock and indignation at what seemed to her totally unreasonable attacks from him, and very shortly on such occasions they would be embroiled in a quarrel. She concluded that her fiancé quarreled with her as a substitute for attacking colleagues whom he resented as competitors. He transferred to her a mantle of competitiveness and he felt that she flaunted her job success to goad him. She herself began to wonder whether she was not reacting to their quarrels by actually becoming competitive toward him. At times she was aware of an impulse to do the thing he seemed to expect of her—to goad him by reminding him of her successes. At the same time she realized that there were subjects other than her job that she could not talk to him about without fearing that she would set off what she called a "ricochet" effect. She concluded that, whatever her own weaknesses in the relationship might be, she could not happily face a future in which she would have to live in fear of taking the brunt of anger or frustrations that arose in some other area of her husband's life. This man's basic lack of confidence in his own abilities and his unreasonable behavior under pressure were characteristics this woman felt that she never would be able to live with. The marriage would have had little chance for happiness, but she would probably not have realized that in time had she not taken the trouble to try to figure out the real basis for their "lovers' quarrels."

Thus, patterns of any quarrels that occur must be considered. Further, if in a dating relationship quarrels are fairly frequent or regular, even without a discernible pattern, it must be recognized that a marriage between these two will be characterized by quarreling. What may romantically be called "lovers' quarrels" before marriage will be called by no such romantic name when they become deadly "family quarrels."

## BREAKING LOVE AFFAIRS AND DOUBTS

Another danger signal often unrecognized is the uneven course some love affairs take. It is a danger signal if couples break up and then make up once or more during their dating. Even if they do not break up although they consider it, or if one, especially the girl, has doubts about their relationship, something is likely to be wrong. The best objective evidence that this is a danger signal comes from the research of Burgess and Wallin, who studied 1000 engaged couples and then followed them through into marriage.[1] The Burgess–Wallin research shows that those couples who had doubts about whether they should marry and whether their marriages would work out were more likely to break their engagements, and if they married in spite of their doubts, their marriages were more likely to end in divorce. In our study of 3189 college students, 240 men and 570 women who had broken engagements listed causes for the breakup of the engagement (Table 4-1).

All the findings indicate that the girl, her family, and her friends are more accurate in judging danger signals in relationships. That is, their doubts about the success of the relationship and their belief that the engagement should be broken are significant in forecasting the future of a relationship.

In one of our studies, 581 married couples described their feelings of confidence or uncertainty about the happiness of their marriages as they remembered their feelings to have been before the marriage.[2] They also rated their present happiness and satisfaction in the marriage. We found a very high association between premarital confidence in the future of the relationship and the later marital happiness. Most of those (96 percent) who had few doubts and felt very confident before marriage rated their marriage as happy or very happy. Only 4 percent of the ones who had no doubts ahead of time rated their marriages as average or unhappy. On the other hand, of those who were a "little uncertain," 28 percent reported their marriages as average or unhappy. Of the few who were "very uncertain" but married anyway, 50 percent said the marriage was average or unhappy.

**TABLE 4-1**

Causes of conflict (danger signals) during engagements which were broken, as reported by 240 men and 570 women in 18 colleges and universities in 1967 *

| Cause of conflict | Men (N–240) | Women (N–570) |
|---|---|---|
| Possessiveness | 21% | 31% |
| Jealousy | 22 | 25 |
| Disagreement about future | 20 | 24 |
| How far to go in sex | 15 | 26 |
| Conflict of personalities | 18 | 18 |
| Quarreling about many things | 16 | 15 |
| Irritability | 10 | 11 |
| Criticism | 9 | 11 |
| Dominance | 10 | 11 |
| Dislike of each other's friends | 10 | 7 |

* Landis; see footnote 1, page 32.

[1] Ernest W. Burgess and Paul Wallin, *Engagement and Marriage* (Chicago: J. B. Lippincott Company, 1953), pp. 561–67.

[2] Landis; see footnote 2, page 5.

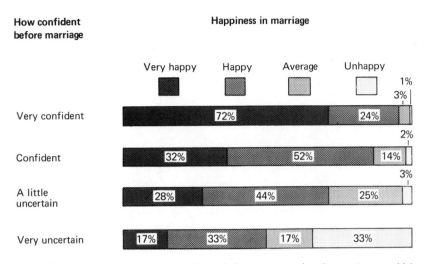

**How confident before marriage**

**Happiness in marriage**

| | Very happy | Happy | Average | Unhappy | |
|---|---|---|---|---|---|
| | ▓ | ▓ | ▓ | ▢ | 1% |
| Very confident | 72% | | 24% | | 3% |
| | | | | | 2% |
| Confident | 32% | 52% | 14% | | |
| | | | | | 3% |
| A little uncertain | 28% | 44% | 25% | | |
| Very uncertain | 17% | 33% | 17% | 33% | |

FIG. 4–1 Happiness in marriage and confidence before marriage that the marriage would be happy (581 husbands and wives reporting).

The evidence does not suggest that every minor doubt or hesitancy about the future is a danger signal. A certain measure of hesitancy is natural for thoughtful people who are making a lifetime decision. Individuals can test their doubts by comparing feelings about this matter with ways of approaching decisions on other matters. If they are not usually troubled by excessive uncertainty, if they usually have confidence in their ability to make wise choices, and if experience has proved that their judgment is usually sound, then uncertainty in this situation may be considered a danger signal. If there are personal doubts, and family and friends are also doubtful, there is likely to be a sound basis for their attitudes. On the other hand, if the hesitancy is the more or less normal caution that any person might take who is trying to make a serious decision, and there are no serious problems in the relationship, the uncertainty is probably not a danger signal but rather a cautious attitude.

## BASIC RESPECT FOR EACH OTHER

Happy and satisfying relationships depend on mutual respect. It is not unusual for couples to feel critical of each other before marriage, but to withhold the criticism until after marriage when each hopes to change the other. A strong desire to change the other person is a danger signal in a relationship. It means a less than complete acceptance of this person as he or she is, and it is likely that the two could not meet each other's needs without more changing than would be possible. Basic personality structure is fairly well set by the time of marriage; it will be difficult to change oneself much after that, and quite impossible to force change upon another person.

A young man as he approached marriage after a relatively long engagement began to realize that he was less confident and decisive in his actions than he had been before. He found himself hesitating about decisions and then worrying after making them and questioning whether the outcome would be right. After several sessions with a counselor, this man began to face some elements he had not recognized in his relationship with his fiancée. She habitually expressed or implied doubts about his choices or decisions when they were not in exact agreement with hers. She was quick to point out real or imagined mistakes he had made and she frequently urged him to change his viewpoints to coincide with hers, even on small matters not affecting their future. Eventually he broke the engagement, although with some sorrow. He said, "She meant a lot to me, but I had to face it that I couldn't suit her. I couldn't be myself comfortably without feeling that I was letting her down, and my constant efforts to suit her—along with so many of these efforts failing—were breaking down my self-confidence.

Had their engagement been short, this couple would probably have married before the man came to recognize the undermining effect of the girl's inability to accept him as he was.

A sincere respect for the mate's ideals and goals in life and for each other's moral standards is also necessary. In our society it is important for the wife to respect the man's choice of a vocation and have confidence in his ability to make a living. He in turn must respect her work and achievements whether in the home or in an outside vocation. Without such respect the relationship will have a deteriorating and undermining effect on the personality of one or both members of the couple.

In all cases, a wish to alter the course of life that the mate has chosen should be recognized as a warning signal for both a man and a woman. But many people are not realistic about what they see in each other's attitudes before marriage, or they believe that because they are in love all such matters are unimportant. Sometimes, before marriage, they will both avoid discussing the points that they sense would bring out disparaging attitudes toward each other's goals or values in life, because they are emotionally involved and want to brush aside all potential hindrances to their marriage. But an inability to accept completely the other person's goals in life and to respect those goals as worth mutual sacrifice is a danger signal that should warn two people away from marriage to each other.

## DOES A RELATIONSHIP BRING OUT THE BEST IN THE INDIVIDUAL?

A satisfying courtship should bring out the best in each partner. For the courtship period to be characterized by feelings of depression and moodiness in one who is usually fairly content and cheerful means there is danger ahead.

A girl came for counseling because she was worried about crying spells and sleepness nights after dates with her fiancé. She said she had always before been of even temperament and able to take circumstances in life with a fairly easy and cheerful acceptance. She said, "I love him with all my heart, but since we've been engaged, life seems to have become so much more complicated. I am irritable and cross, and critical of all my other associates as I have never been before. Maybe this only means that I'm growing up and thinking for myself instead of accepting so many things uncritically as I used to do. But I don't like myself this way."

The fact that she came for counseling showed that her feeling of regressing rather than growing toward being a better person was real. It indicated undesirable elements in her relationship with her fiancé.

## OTHER DANGER SIGNALS

There are other kinds of circumstances that may serve as indicators of the future quality of any relationship. Some of these are likely to be found in the points or subjects that a couple cannot discuss. Matters that both tactfully avoid discussing, or that either one "blocks" on, are the ones that should be given some serious, objective thought.

Differences about friends may be significant. Does he have friends she considers "beneath" him? How closely is he tied to them and how much do they mean in his life? If there is a strong difference over friends, can each drop old friends and make new ones that are acceptable to both? Or would that be impossible for one or the other? A difference over friends may indicate other basic differences in points of view and in goals in life. The woman who feels that her fiancé's friends are all of lower caliber than he is, that they tend to drag him down, probably does not know the man well enough. The man who usually feels uncomfortable around his wife's or fiancée's friends may hold values that differ from those of his wife and her friends. Differences over friends should be considered seriously during courtship and attention given to whether this reflects that other unrecognized differences exist. A comparison of the courtship histories of three groups of people shows observable differences in the patterns followed by those who make successful and unsuccessful marriages (Table 4-2).

## FAILURE TO RECOGNIZE DANGER SIGNALS

Danger signals do not always show up early in dating; time is essential. This is one reason why long acquaintance and long engagement tend to predict success in marriage. Among the people who fail to recognize danger signals in a relationship are those who rush toward marriage without allowing time to assess the implications of some of the elements in their relationship.

Some people in effect use haste as a way to avoid facing danger signals because they are compulsively determined to marry. There are various

TABLE 4-2

Approach to marriage, as reported by 1162 married people, 155 unhappily married people seeking help through marriage counseling, and 164 divorced people *

| Approach to marriage | Married group (N–1162) | Counseling group (N–155) | Divorced group (N–164) |
|---|---|---|---|
| Knew partner less than 1 year | 16% | 43% | 41% |
| Had "understanding" engagement | 63 | 42 | 64 |
| Had formal engagement | 88 | 37 | 57 |
| Contemplated breaking engagement | 29 | 44 | 50 |
| Broke engagement temporarily | 9 | 26 | 22 |
| Felt confident marriage would be happy | 90 | 83 | 71 |
| Both parents approved of marriage | 84 | 58 | 58 |
| Had premarital sexual relations with spouse | 38 | 73 | 58 |
| Wife was pregnant at time of marriage | 5 | 23 | 11 |
| Married in church wedding | 84 | 41 | 55 |

* The same 1967 questionnaire used with 581 couples (see footnote 2, page 5) was filled in by 155 couples who were unhappily married and going to a California Court of Conciliation for counseling, and by a third group of 164 divorced individuals who were members of the organization "Parents Without Partners." Comparative data from the three groups showed many kinds of differences characterizing the happily and the unhappily married.

kinds of circumstances or characteristics that motivate people toward blocking off danger signals and going ahead to marry.

A crisis or serious problem may arise in an individual's life and he or she hopes marriage will be a way out; so this person is motivated to ignore or misconstrue doubtful elements in a relationship. Divorce of one's parents, a death in the family, a difficult and unpleasant step-parent relationship, entering military service, finishing school and uncertainty about what to do next—any one of such situations may impel the individual toward compulsiveness about getting married. Some people, in such situations, do not want to look ahead and evaluate the chances for success in a marriage. Clinging to the idea of marriage per se, they cannot face objectively anything that might prevent or postpone a marriage.

Others may not see danger signals because they lack caution. They habitually make hasty decisions without weighing alternatives. They have a history of failures in situations because only when it is too late can they see that they overlooked important considerations when they made decisions.

Still others ignore clearly evident warnings in a relationship because of folk beliefs or unrealistic ideas about love and marriage. A surprisingly large number of Americans still believe that there is a "one and only" or a "soul mate" for each person. Holding such beliefs, they go blindly on to marry the one they fall in love with, despite all indications that the marriage will be incompatible.

## MARRYING IN SPITE OF DANGER SIGNALS

Sometimes, after a fairly long engagement, or after living together, people become aware of warning signals but decide to marry anyway. They have an advantage over those who have not recognized the danger signals. If they can face the realities in their relationship and in each other and decide they can live with the particular troublesome element in their marriage, they will be prepared, in some measure, for what is to come.

For example, a woman may recognize that her fiancé is emotionally tied to his mother, but she may decide that she can live with this situation because other qualities in her fiancé outweigh it. She will be better prepared to adjust after marriage because while she still had a choice she chose to accept a less-than-ideal situation. She has already decided the marriage is worth some sacrifice and adjustment. Her attitude, and consequently her problem in marriage, might have been far different had she found herself confronted after marriage with a mother–son closeness she had neither anticipated nor consciously chosen to accept or reject. However, people who want very much to marry are inclined to minimize future problems and to believe optimistically that after they are married some irritating circumstance will be easier to take than before marriage. Such a belief is likely to lead to disappointment. Irritating or problem elements in a relationship seldom disappear with marriage. In fact, they are likely to loom larger under the pressure of the close association that marriage involves.

## WHAT IS THE TOTAL RELATIONSHIP?

We have discussed different specific factors that may be danger signals. However, the *total relationship* is most important. How does it all add up? A thoughtful assessment sometimes shows that both partners are blinded by one satisfactory element; they allow this one factor to outweigh many other things in their relationship that should warn them not to marry each other. A strong sex attraction may dominate the association of a couple from the first date. If they engage in heavy petting and coitus, the relationship may include a mutual sexual satisfaction that holds them together in spite of conflicts in other areas. Such a couple, after marriage, may find that they have too meager a foundation for building a good marriage. Sex alone can not carry a marriage if the relationships are unrewarding and unsatisfactory in other facets of living.

> Sue and Jack met in college and, from the beginning, there was a strong sexual attachment which early led to heavy petting and coitus. Sue soon discovered that Jack was self-centered and emotionally immature. In addition, she learned that he came from a mixed-up, disorganized family; he was also of a different religious faith. She saw danger signals but felt guilty about having sexual intercourse before marriage and decided to marry Jack. They had not been married long before Sue could see the seriousness of the danger signals in their relationship. In addition,

she found that Jack had difficulty finishing what he started. She got a teaching job to support him in graduate school, but Jack changed his field of study and never seemed able to complete his course work. Finally, when Sue was teaching in another town, Jack started having sexual intercourse with other women. He defended his behavior as an acceptable way of life. He was willing for Sue to do the same. After six years of marriage and many separations, Sue finally decided to get a divorce. Even then she hesitated because she was afraid she could not find another sexual partner as satisfactory as Jack.

The error is to allow any single factor, whatever it may be, to prevent a sound evaluation of a total relationship.

This can be true positively as well as negatively. A single serious point of difference may not be enough to prevent success in a relationship that has other good elements that meet important needs of both people. Facing the one or two handicaps, and assessing them with respect to the whole relationship, has every advantage for the future. Doing so will help the couple to keep a sense of proportion later when the negative factors cause problems.

This discussion of danger signals has pointed out considerations for evaluating dating and courtship relationships. Such a discussion might seem to lead people to be too cautious about marrying. However, to look with thoughtful objectivity at all aspects of a relationship does not hurt one that is sound and conducive to the growth and well-being of two people. On the contrary, those who are realistic about marriage and about what is required for building a good marriage can face danger signals. They can assess their own capacities and the quality of their relationships, and when they marry it can be with confidence in the future.

## IN SUMMARY

This and the preceding chapter have discussed a wide range of purposes and tasks of the dating stage of life. We see dating customs in the United States not as random activity growing out of youthful freedom from responsibility, but as a time when unique growth possibilities are available for the individual. At this point in life one has a final opportunity to pause before making life choices that are not reversible without some measure of personal disaster. Progress through the dating years can be an intelligent advance toward mature conceptions of the potentialities of human relationships, and so serve as preparation for later successful marriage.

## REVIEW QUESTIONS

1  How do the social relationships of children differ from those of adults?

2  How does the resolution of conflicts differ between children and adults?

3  Would one be more conscious of danger signals in short or long acquaintances? Explain.

4  What may be some bases for quarreling in a relationship?

5   Should "lovers' quarrels" be considered danger signals? Discuss.

6   Is the man or the woman likely to be more accurate in judging danger signals?

7   Why is it to be expected that there will be some hesitation on the part of those who approach marriage rationally?

8   What does a strong desire to change the other person mean? What are the implications for marriage?

9   Give illustrations of the kinds of desired changes in the other person that should be considered "danger signals."

10   What are the advantages of seeing the danger signals before marriage for those couples who decide to marry in spite of them?

11   What are some of the motivations that underlie failure to see danger signals?

12   Will people who know about danger signals in relationships and what such warnings mean tend to be too cautious about getting married? Discuss.

# SOME WILL NOT MARRY

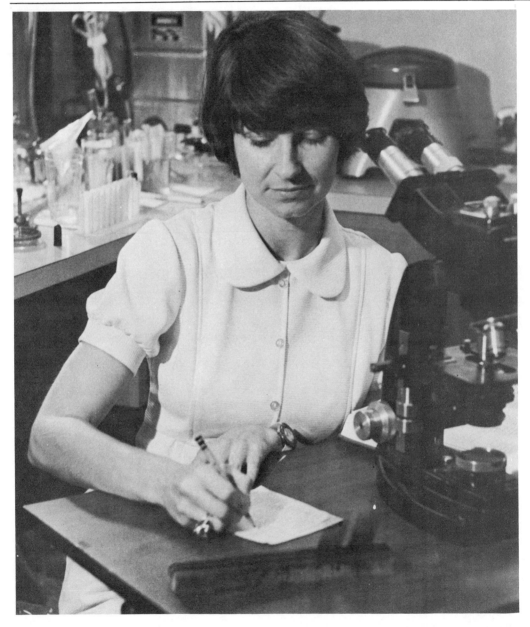

# 5

Dating, for most people, eventually leads to marriage. In the United States today, 96 percent of women and 94 percent of men aged 45–54 and over are married or have been married. These percentages have increased during the past seventy years.

Nevertheless, a certain percentage of the population does not marry. Some people pass through the years when most people are choosing mates, but for any of a number of reasons they do not develop relationships that lead to marriage.

## PRESSURE TOWARD MARRIAGE

Because most people do marry, the single person is usually aware of a strong pressure toward conformity. This pressure impels some into marriage before they are ready for it, or into marrying unsuitable mates when they might live more effectively as single persons.

If social attitudes about marriage and singleness were more realistic, many disastrous marriages would probably be prevented, and the proportion of those who remain single in the population would be much greater. Certainly the age at marriage would rise. Many who marry at a very young age are acting in unquestioning response to the idea that marriage is the universal goal—the thing to do—and proof that one is now an adult. They move obsessively toward marriage without knowing what it means or what it will require of them.

People other than the very young also react to the social attitudes exerting pressure toward marriage by marrying hastily, allowing no possibility for seeing danger signals in a relationship. Consciously or unconsciously, their feeling is that this might be the "only chance," and that any marriage is better than none. Typical of this compulsion toward marriage are the cases of girls on some campuses who become engaged in the spring of their senior year to whatever boy is a current possibility, rather than face leaving the campus as an unattached person. Pressures that lead to such reactions sometimes are contributed to by members of the parent generation whose daughters are aware that they are expected to find a husband before they leave school.

It would be well if social attitudes could be revised to accept single-ness more realistically, recognizing that all levels of satisfactory and unsatisfactory adjustment are achieved by people who remain single as well as by those who marry. There is some evidence that a trend is developing in this direction. The average age of women at first marriage increased from 20.3 in 1960 to 21.2 in 1975. Possibly some women are getting married at a later age because society is putting less pressure on them to marry. The widespread recognition that marriage failure rate is high among those who marry young may be causing more people to delay marriage.

## THE SEX RATIO AND MARRIAGE RATE

The sex ratio is such that, from a numerical point of view, most young people who want to marry should be able to find mates even though numerically males and females are not equal. In 1970, women 18 years old and older outnumbered men in the United States population by a little over four million, or 1067 women to 1000 men. At age 65 and over, there were 1300 women to 1000 men, and the ratio of women to men in our country continues to increase steadily. Some demographers predict that there will be 1403 women to 1000 men over age 65 in 1980.

Actually, for young people from 18 to 30, the numbers of both males and females available as marriage partners are approximately equal, since over-all population figures do not tell the whole story. A larger percentage of males than females of marrying age are unmarriageable for physical, mental, or emotional reasons, and men tend to date and marry women who are younger. The average man of 35 marries a woman six and one-half years younger, and there are more women in the age group from 25 to 29 than there are men in the age group from 30 to 34. Furthermore, there are more single women than single men working in cities, except in certain highly industrialized cities that attract more men than women.

## MEETING OTHERS, A PROBLEM FOR THE UNATTACHED

Conditions in cities, with their heterogeneous religions, occupations, and nationalities, make it difficult for those interested in finding dates or marriage partners to meet other interested people of similar backgrounds.

It is true that in both rural and urban settings women in certain occupations such as teaching, library work, and social work have fewer opportunities to meet eligible men than women have in some other occupations.

In many cities, social clubs are organized specifically for unmarried adults with few, if any, restrictions other than age and marital status placed upon membership. Naturally, such clubs provide opportunities for members to find mates, although the specific purpose of the group is usually announced as social rather than matrimonial.

For years, "introduction" services and organizations frankly announcing themselves as matrimonial agencies have flourished in the larger urban centers. Some of these have been exploitative of lonely people and unreliable in the information offered about marriage prospects to those who have paid their fees. That such organizations can exist emphasizes the fact that it is difficult within a city for unattached adults to find a marriage partner. With the increasing urbanization of our national population, the number of single people living in cities but having few social ties has increased.

## COMPUTER DATING AGENCIES

The first experiments in computer dating were on the East Coast; others followed throughout the country. By the late 1960s experiments had been successful enough to make computer dating agencies profitable commercial ventures in cities. Computer dating agencies vary widely in their aims, methods, reliability, and costs. Some, as the name implies, aim to help people find suitable dates—persons with similar backgrounds, interests, and other bases for congeniality. These are not specifically trying to function as matrimonial agencies. Other agencies place more emphasis on possible matrimonial prospects.

Some organizations make a fairly adequate effort to assess accurately each person who signs up with them and to see that potential dating pairs are actually as compatibly paired as is possible by computer. Others are unreliable, exploiting lonely individuals for profit. Methods of assessing candidates go all the way from a few superficial questions by mail to extensive tests requiring an interview and several hours of time at a central testing center. Costs vary from very small charges to fees of several hundred dollars. All the organizations advertise extensively, as an examination of the advertising section of any metropolitan newspaper will show.

The people who seek the services of computer dating agencies are of many types, just as are those found in the general population. One young woman who signed up with an agency in a western city reported that most of the men she met through the agency had signed up because they were looking for an easier way of meeting people than the usual ways available, or because they were introverted enough so that they found it especially difficult to make friends in a city. Another girl said of her experience with computer dating, "I haven't yet found anyone through this system that I want to marry. But neither did I find anyone when I was just on my own; and before I tried this system I wasn't meeting anyone new; I seldom had any dates at all. At least now I keep meeting new men who frankly admit they want to meet a girl like me."

Some others who tried computer dating complained that no matter how well the prospects appeared to fit requirements, too many of them turned out to have traits or ways that eluded the computer but made them unattractive for any further association. However, the same complaint is made in all dating situations. Much of the dating people do in general does not lead to marriage or even to extended friendships.

## SOME REASONS FOR FAILURE TO MARRY

Not all those who remain single do so because of the difficulty of meeting possible mates. Some people court and become engaged but avoid marriage itself. The capable single woman may hesitate to give up her job with its economic security to face the uncertainties of marriage; or the bachelor who has been fairly content while single may resist the added responsibility for another person that marriage brings. People may be unaware of their reasons for stopping short of marriage. The single person may rationalize concerning economic or personal independence without recognizing an underlying fear concerning ability to cope with a close relationship such as marriage. And no doubt many women find rational reasons for postponing marriage without recognizing that conditioned fearful attitudes toward sexual experience or childbirth are influencing their thinking.

Another factor contributing to some failures to marry is the slowness of some people to achieve emotional independence from their parents or siblings. This slowness or failure may be due to a combination of traits in parents and children. Sometimes the individual who lacks confidence in associating with the other sex, or who has undefined fears relating to sex or the responsibilities of marriage, may allow himself or herself to rely heavily on the security of established relationships within the parental family. Such a person may remain content enough with an already satisfactory association with parents or siblings to make no continuing efforts to cultivate heterosexual relationships outside the family. This person accepts as a substitute the relationships in which he or she feels adequate.

In another kind of family situation the parents dominate, making demands upon the son or daughter in such a way that the person never marries. From earliest childhood children of such parents are so impressed with their obligations to the parent that it is hard for them ever to break away and marry. In studying large families, Bossard and Boll found that the eldest child of large families, especially if the eldest is a girl, tends to stay single.[1] In some cases, this is because older children must take over many of the duties of the parents in caring for younger children. Some of these people are highly marriageable, but they pass the time for marrying before they are able to be free from the burdens they carry in their parental family.

Sometimes parents, disillusioned with their own marriage and finding many of their relationships inadequate, show attitudes that condition their children against marriage. Some of these believe they want their children to marry. They may express a desire for grandchildren and a wish to see their sons and daughters happily settled in homes of their own, yet they continue to exercise an emotional control that keeps their children tied and dependent. In other cases, a parent may use illness or grief or loneliness as a means of keeping a devoted son or daughter at his or her side and unmarried. That such tactics can be successful indicates that the child is overly submissive and already conditioned toward dependence.

A study by Spreitzer and Riley of people who had never married found that remaining single was associated with what they called "family pathology."[2] Men and women who had not married were more likely to come from homes with faulty parent-child relationships and homes disrupted by divorce or separation.

Certain types of faulty parent-child relationships may also contribute in some cases to the development of homosexuality rather than heterosexuality. In the past the social pressure toward marrying impelled many homosexuals into marriage. Today, with a better understanding of homosexuality, fewer such persons seek marriage as a cure or a "cover" for homosexuality. Accurate figures are not available on the prevalence of homosexuality, but a conservative estimate is that 5 percent of people are homosexuals in their feelings and desires. It is doubtful whether people who are completely homosexual in their orientation to sex should ever marry. People who, as they mature, come to doubt what their sexual orientation is might better delay marriage until they are older and are more sure.

[1] James H. S. Bossard and Eleanor Stoker Boll, *The Large Family System* (Philadelphia: University of Pennsylvania Press, 1956), p. 284.

[2] Elmer Spreitzer and Lawrence E. Riley, "Factors Associated With Singlehood," *Journal of Marriage and the Family* 36:3 (August 1974), 533–41.

Married people have a lower death rate at every period of life than do single people, or those whose marriages have been broken by death or divorce. The greatest difference in the death rate is found among people under the age of 45. Until recently, because of the higher death rate of married women in childbirth, single women in the age group from 20 to 24 had a lower death rate than married women, but this is no longer true. Among males aged 20 to 44, the death rate for the married is only about half that for the single. Deaths from almost all causes are lower among married men. The differences in the death rates are not so great among females, although married females have the lowest rates.

Tables 5-1a and 5-1b summarize the mortality ratios for white men and women for several different causes.[3] The widowed and the divorced

**TABLE 5-1a**  Standardized marital status—mortality ratios * for white women for selected causes of death: United States, 1959–1961

| Cause of death | Single (compared with married) | Married | Widowed | Divorced |
|---|---|---|---|---|
| All causes | 130 | 100 | 145 | 144 |
| Tuberculosis, all forms | 237 | 100 | 143 | 245 |
| Malignant neoplasm of digestive organs and peritoneum | 115 | 100 | 123 | 116 |
| Malignant neoplasm of respiratory system | 104 | 100 | 118 | 153 |
| Malignant neoplasm of breast | 146 | 100 | 111 | 114 |
| Malignant neoplasm of female genital organs | 114 | 100 | 118 | 165 |
| Leukemia and aleukemia | 106 | 100 | 110 | 107 |
| Diabetes mellitus | 66 | 100 | 111 | 90 |
| Vascular lesions affecting central nervous system | 128 | 100 | 147 | 135 |
| Arteriosclerotic heart disease, including coronary disease | 126 | 100 | 148 | 130 |
| Cirrhosis of liver | 84 | 100 | 131 | 264 |
| Motor vehicle accidents | 103 | 100 | 110 | 228 |
| All other accidents | 172 | 100 | 184 | 237 |
| Suicide | 116 | 100 | 166 | 319 |
| Homicide | 51 | 100 | 128 | 451 |

* The standardized mortality ratios are expressed, after adjustment for age by the indirect method, in terms of the corresponding cause-specific death rates for white married women. The second SMR for the single group is expressed in terms of the death rates for the ever married groups. Data refer to white women 15 years of age and over.

[3] *Marital Status, United States—Part A,* Vital and Health Statistics, Series 20, Number 8a (December 1970), Rockville, Md., U.S. Department of Health, Education and Welfare, pp. 37, 47.

TABLE 5-1b

Standardized marital status–mortality ratios * for white men for selected causes of death: United States, 1959–1961

| Cause of death | Single (compared with married) | Married | Widowed | Divorced |
|---|---|---|---|---|
| All causes | 148 | 100 | 154 | 223 |
| Tuberculosis, all forms | 382 | 100 | 217 | 667 |
| Malignant neoplasm of digestive organ and peritoneum | 125 | 100 | 126 | 155 |
| Malignant neoplasm of respiratory system | 116 | 100 | 126 | 213 |
| Malignant neoplasm of male genital organs | 95 | 100 | 123 | 137 |
| Leukemia and aleukemia | 119 | 100 | 108 | 121 |
| Diabetes mellitus | 146 | 100 | 141 | 192 |
| Vascular lesions affecting central nervous system | 137 | 100 | 150 | 181 |
| Arteriosclerotic heart disease, including coronary disease | 132 | 100 | 146 | 177 |
| Cirrhosis of liver | 257 | 100 | 242 | 622 |
| Motor vehicle accidents | 129 | 100 | 199 | 380 |
| All other accidents | 151 | 100 | 227 | 420 |
| Suicide | 153 | 100 | 239 | 408 |
| Homicide | 103 | 100 | 269 | 722 |

* The standardized mortality ratios are expressed, after adjustment for age by the indirect method, in terms of the corresponding cause-specific death rates for white married men. The second SMR for the single group is expressed in terms of the death rates for the ever married groups. Data refer to white men 15 years of age and over.

stand apart from the married in having the highest rates, and for most causes of death have higher rates than the single.

Marriage may contribute to longevity and mental balance because two people care for each other, but the larger factor is probably a selective process that may operate. Those who do not marry tend to include a large proportion of the handicapped. And among those who fail in marriage and return to a single state are found a higher proportion with emotional handicaps, as evidenced by the far higher suicide and death rate of the divorced and widowed. The crisis of becoming widowed or divorced is doubtless an added factor in the higher death rate of this group, especially among the men.

## LIVING A SINGLE LIFE

Many people who might live happy and successful lives as single people marry because they cannot ignore social attitudes that assume the married state to be the inevitable eventuality for all "normal" people. They know that to stay single is to remain deliberately in a special minority group. There will always be some people qualified for marriage but unable to find suitable mates, but also many people who are better suited for single than for married living. Any individual should be able to remain single by choice with no social stigma.

In this connection it may be conjectured that some of those who remain single permanently or who delay marriage until they are in their thirties or later may be more autonomous individuals than the average person. They are able to resist the pressure toward marriage resulting from general social attitudes about singleness and they postpone marriage until they find someone with whom they can have a permanently satisfactory relationship. Some implication of this notion may be found by examining the age at marriage of men who have achieved distinction in areas such as politics or in science. Many such men married at later ages than the marriage age among men in the general population.

Research has concentrated on the satisfactions and problems of marriage, whereas folklore and hearsay predominate in the thinking in regard to remaining single. A number of single women have given us their case histories. They have discussed their reasons for remaining single, and summarized what they consider to be the advantages and disadvantages of single living. Some professional women state candidly that they have put success in a career ahead of marriage for reasons that seem to them valid. One said, "I don't think I could have managed the double or triple life that married career women must lead. Either the marriage or the career would have suffered." Several research studies of singleness have shown that higher intelligence, education, and occupation are associated with singleness among women. This is not the case among men.[4] One study showed that female scientists and engineers were six times less likely to marry than were male scientists.[5]

## SOME DISADVANTAGES OF SINGLENESS

Some pleasant pursuits such as travel are less so without the companionship of marriage. But loneliness—a disadvantage mentioned often by the single—is also a specter in the lives of many married people. The absence of loneliness is not absolutely guaranteed by marriage. A woman who was once married but has now been divorced for many years said, "Sometimes I'm very lonely. But I look back and remember how desperately alone I used to feel during my marriage. The loneliness now is easy and peaceful compared to that."

Disadvantages other than loneliness weigh against the advantages of being single, and certain of the disadvantages loom larger for some single

[4] Spreitzer and Riley, "Factors Associated with Singlehood."

[5] Debora David, "Career Patterns and Values: A Study of Men and Women in Science and Engineering" (Columbia University: Bureau of Applied Social Research, Vol. 82, 1973).

people than for others. Even today, when women are freer than ever before to seek openly masculine companionship, to live alone or with friends independently, to establish their own social life, and to invite men as well as women to share their leisure hours, there is still the necessity to cope with life in a society organized on the basis of married couples.

Almost all adults feel the need for interaction and communication with members of the other sex. Today women are likely to accept and acknowledge their own sexuality as men have always done. Women who decide to remain single may find it easy to have sexual partners in their younger years but, as they become older, it may become increasingly difficult to find partners, although their desires for sexual satisfaction may remain high. Thus to remain single in our society is to cope with complex emotional and physical needs, desires, and frustrations. Single women also mention their regret that they have never had children. And, if single people live and work away from their families or kinship groups, they feel the lack of relationships that provide emotional security. As one said, "No one around here would know or care what happened to me, as long as I don't fail to show up for work. I don't really matter to anyone."

## SOME ADVANTAGES

However, many single women are aware of some advantages they have. Some feel that by not marrying they are freer to be themselves, to take their own lives seriously, and to develop their own life style more than would be possible if they married. Even with the trend toward male–female equality in our society, those freedoms still remain more secure for married men than for women.

Some advantages of being single are: Single living requires less of the individual in the day-to-day affairs of life. Sharing and cooperating in all phases of life does not come easily to all people. Probably the greatest problem of married people is in learning to succeed in cooperative living. The single person is free to live according to personal preferences. He or she can escape the necessity for changing and adjusting to the preferences of another person, or coping with conflicts in a relationship if change is not desired. There are also some material advantages. Two definitely cannot live as cheaply as one. The single person responsible for only himself or herself can plan for activities and expenditures that might be out of the question after marriage.

## SINGLENESS AND HAPPINESS IN LIFE

The National Opinion Research Center studied almost 4000 people in 1972, 1973, and 1974 in an attempt to find out the general happiness of people who were single or married. They asked the question, "Taken all together, how would you say things are these days—would you say that you are very happy, pretty happy, or not too happy?" The data were analyzed by age and marital status of respondents. The findings revealed that a larger percentage of married men and women from all age groups rated themselves as very happy than did the single people.[6] The study does not satisfactorily answer the question of whether better adjusted people are more likely to marry, or whether it is marriage that brings greater happiness and contentment in life. The study did find that married people who said they were very happy with life in general also rated their marriages as very happy.

## IN SUMMARY

Most people do marry. The type of social interaction practiced by people during their early adult lives, especially during the school and college years, tends to lead to marriage.

A certain proportion of people do not follow the usual dating pattern. If they wish to marry, these people will need to be objective about the facts of their lives: where they live, the type of job they hold, and the resulting opportunities or lack of them for finding a mate. They will also need to consider their personality make-up and attempt to determine whether they do really want to marry.

Marriage is not necessarily the desirable life for all. People should consider both singleness and marriage as they make choices that will affect their entire lives. However, to be "marriageable" is necessary even for those who remain permanently single, insofar as to be marriageable implies the ability to live effectively among others.

## REVIEW QUESTIONS

1  What percentage of people in the United States marry?

2  It takes greater effort to find an eligible mate in the city than in the country. Why?

3  Is the sex ratio on your campus favorable to the men or to the women?

4  What are some of the reasons why some people do not marry?

5  Which live longer, the married or the single? What are some of the probable explanations for this difference?

6  What are some of the advantages of living a single life?

[6] Norval D. Glenn, "The Contribution of Marriage to the Psychological Well-Being of Males and Females," *Journal of Marriage and the Family* 37:3 (August 1975) 594–600.

7   What are some of the disadvantages of living a single life?

8   Assess "computer dating" as you understand it.

9   Discuss the statement that some of those who marry late or remain permanently single may be more autonomous than the average person.

# MARRIAGEABILITY

Marriage is the way of life for the majority in our country, but concepts about marrying and marriage are widely held that verge on the superstitious. In spite of all evidence to the contrary, many people believe that at a given point in life one responds to an impulse or an irresistable attraction, marries, and, with luck, will live happily ever after.

Successful marriages have no such haphazard, unpredictable basis. The quality of a marriage depends not on luck but on the marriageability of the two people involved. Many traits and habit patterns combine to determine the marriageability of each individual.

## PERSONALITY TRAITS AND SUCCESSFUL MARRIAGE

The wedding does not change basic personality structure. If change occurs soon after the wedding, it is more likely to be that people revert to their real selves, and traits or tendencies that may have been suppressed or controlled or even temporarily dormant during courtship become evident again. It is true that a good marriage promotes growth in both partners, so that over a period of time, people do change in many ways. However, the growth changes that occur under the impact of a good marriage will be gradual and will require time, sometimes a lifetime. The changes will also tend to go in the directions and remain within the limits set long before marriage by the early developmental experiences of each person. For this reason, people choosing mates need to be alert to traits of marriageability or unmarriageability already developed in themselves and others, for such traits are significant indications concerning the potential quality of a marriage throughout its future.

Some people are definitely more marriageable than others. They would have a better than average probability of making a success of any marriage they might enter. Others would have difficulty no matter whom they married.

## TRAITS OF HAPPY AND UNHAPPY HUSBANDS AND WIVES

Professor Lewis M. Terman, a psychologist at Stanford University, did a pioneer study of personality as related to happiness and unhappiness of husbands and wives.[1] Although this study was done in the 1930s, continuing research tends to support most of his conclusions. We quote some of the findings from that original research. The happily married women were more likely to show these characteristics:

1  Have kindly attitudes toward others.

2  Expect kindly attitudes from others.

3  Do not easily take offense.

4  Not unduly concerned about the impressions they make upon others.

5  Do not look upon social relationships as rivalry situations.

6  Are cooperative.

7  Are not annoyed by advice from others.

8  Frequently have missionary and ministering attitudes.

9  Enjoy activities that bring educational and pleasurable opportunities to others.

10  Like to do things for the dependent or underprivileged.

11  Are methodical and painstaking in their work.

12  Are careful in regard to money.

13  Have expressed attitudes that imply self-assurance and a decidedly optimistic outlook upon life.

The unhappily married women showed a different set of personality characteristics. In general, they were as follows:

1  Characterized by emotional tenseness.

2  Inclined toward ups and downs of moods.

3  Give evidence of deep-seated inferiority feelings to which they react by aggressive attitudes rather than by timidity.

4  Are inclined to be irritable and dictatorial.

[1] Lewis M. Terman, *Psychological Factors in Marital Happiness* (New York: McGraw-Hill Book Company, 1938), pp. 142–66. Terman and his associates made a study of 792 couples from the middle and upper-middle classes living in urban and semi-urban California. The couples had been married varying lengths of time, from less than one year to more than 30 years, the average being 11 years. Approximately one-third (38 percent) were college graduates. Each spouse was asked to fill out a detailed questionnaire independently of the other. The study was anonymous; the chief purpose was to determine what psychological factors are associated with marital happiness. Data were collected in the early and middle 1930s. Various aspects of Terman's studies have been repeated in recent years and the repeat studies support his findings. We shall refer to the Terman study occasionally throughout this book.

**5** Have compensatory mechanisms resulting in restive striving, as evidenced by becoming active joiners, aggressive in business, and overanxious in social life.

**6** Strive for wide circle of acquaintances; are more concerned with being important than being liked.

**7** Are egocentric.

**8** Have little interest in benevolent and welfare activities unless these activities offer personal recognition.

**9** Like activities fraught with opportunities for romance.

**10** Are more inclined to be conciliatory in attitudes toward men than toward women.

**11** Are impatient and fitful workers.

**12** Dislike cautious or methodical people.

**13** Dislike types of work that require methodical and painstaking effort.

**14** In politics, religion, and social ethics are more often radical.

Terman found that happy husbands were inclined to have the following characteristics in contrast to unhappy husbands:

**1** Have even and stable emotional tone.

**2** Are cooperative.

**3** Show attitude toward women that reflects equalitarian ideals.

**4** Have benevolent attitude toward inferiors and the underprivileged.

**5** Tend to be unselfconscious and somewhat extroverted.

**6** Show superior initiative.

**7** Have a greater tendency to take responsibility.

**8** Show a greater willingness to give close attention to detail.

**9** Like methodical procedures and methodical people.

**10** Are saving and cautious in money matters.

**11** Have a favorable attitude toward religion.

**12** Strongly uphold the sex mores and other social conventions.

Unhappy husbands showed personality traits that were comparable to those of the unhappy wives, although not identical:

**1** Are inclined to be moody and somewhat neurotic.

**2** Are prone to feelings of social inferiority.

**3** Dislike being conspicuous in public.

**4** Are highly reactive to social opinion.

**5** Often compensate for a sense of social insecurity by domineering attitudes.

**6** Take pleasure in commanding roles over business dependents or women.

**7** Withdraw from playing inferior role or competing with superiors.

**8** Often compensate by daydreams and power fantasies.

**9** Are sporadic and irregular in their habits of work.

**10** Dislike detail and methodical attitude.

11  Dislike saving money.

12  Like to wager.

13  More often express irreligious attitudes.

14  More inclined to radicalism in sex morals and politics.

A study of the personality characteristics in the four classifications above suggests that the people who were unhappy in marriage had characteristics that would tend to make them unhappy in their associations, whether they were married or single. The marriage relationship is not so different from other personal relationships. One would not rationally choose friends who are uncooperative, selfish, moody, aggressive. People who show more positive attitudes, those who willingly share, and those who are dependable in the day-to-day affairs of life are more satisfactory friends. They are also more marriageable.

## HUSBAND–WIFE GRIEVANCES

In order to find what common grievances married people hold against their spouses, Terman asked the 792 couples to rank 57 common grievances according to their seriousness. The 28 most serious are given in Table 6-1.

It will be noticed that, although some of the grievances such as "nagging" or unfaithfulness or lack of affection may indicate basic disturbances in a marriage, most of the other complaints have little to do with conditions of the marriage; rather, they are almost entirely personality faults. Terman pointed out that this holds true for the first 20 items on the husbands' list, and for all but one of the first 20 on the wives' list. "A majority of the faults are of the kind commonly thought to be indicative of emotional instability, neurotic tendency, or marked introversion," he noted.[2]

Interestingly, among the first eight grievances, three are the same on both lists. The husbands put in third place and the wives in first place selfishness and being inconsiderate. One-third of the least happy husbands and wives, but only 3 percent of the more happy spouses, listed this complaint. Selfishness is not a trait that suddenly afflicts people after they marry. It was undoubtedly clearly evident in the person before marriage, to anyone who was not emotionally involved.

Complaining is in fourth place on both lists. Again, the person who has a complaining attitude toward life developed that attitude long before marriage. Chronic complainers usually do not recognize that they are complaining; the habit reflects an attitude toward life that may be traceable to some other personality difficulty.

One-third of the less happy husbands and wives said that the spouse was not affectionate enough. Failure to show affection may be due to

[2] Terman, *Psychological Factors in Marital Happiness*, p. 101.

TABLE 6-1

Rank order of marital grievances according to seriousness, as given by 792 husbands and 792 wives *

| | Order for husbands | | Order for wives |
|---|---|---|---|
| 1 | W. nags me | 1 | H. selfish and inconsiderate |
| 2 | W. not affectionate | 2 | H. unsuccessful in business |
| 3 | W. selfish and inconsiderate | 3 | H. is untruthful |
| 4 | W. complains too much | 4 | H. complains too much |
| 5 | W. interferes with hobbies | 5 | H. does not show his affection |
| 6 | W. slovenly in appearance | 6 | H. does not talk things over |
| 7 | W. is quick-tempered | 7 | H. harsh with children |
| 8 | W. interferes with my discipline | 8 | H. touchy |
| 9 | W. conceited | 9 | H. has no interest in children |
| 10 | W. is insincere | 10 | H. not interested in home |
| 11 | W.'s feelings too easily hurt | 11 | H. not affectionate |
| 12 | W. criticizes me | 12 | H. rude |
| 13 | W. narrow-minded | 13 | H. lacks ambition |
| 14 | W. neglects the children | 14 | H. nervous or impatient |
| 15 | W. a poor housekeeper | 15 | H. criticizes me |
| 16 | W. argumentative | 16 | H.'s poor management of income |
| 17 | W. has annoying habits | 17 | H. narrow-minded |
| 18 | W. untruthful | 18 | H. not faithful to me |
| 19 | W. interferes in my business | 19 | H. lazy |
| 20 | W. spoils the children | 20 | H. bored with my small talk |
| 21 | W.'s poor management of income | 21 | In-laws |
| 22 | In-laws | 22 | H. easily influenced by others |
| 23 | Insufficient income | 23 | H. tight with money |
| 24 | W. nervous or emotional | 24 | H. argumentative |
| 25 | W. easily influenced by others | 25 | H.'s insufficient income |
| 26 | W. jealous | 26 | H. has no backbone |
| 27 | W. lazy | 27 | H. dislikes to go out with me |
| 28 | W. gossips indiscreetly | 28 | H. pays attention to other women |

* From *Psychological Factors in Marital Happiness* by L. M. Terman, p. 99. Copyrighted 1938 by McGraw-Hill Book Company.

selfishness or thoughtlessness, or it may mean only that one comes from an undemonstrative family. Some families do not easily show affection; caresses between parents and children are rare, even though the family may be a "close" and happy one. The pattern of the parental family is often carried over into their own marriages by the children. A person brought up in a family where there were frequent demonstrations of affection may expect this outward demonstration of affection in marriage and feel the lack of it as deprivation.

Many of the other grievances listed are simply the outward indication of unhappy temperaments. *One of the most important characteristics of a marriageable person is the habit of happiness.* It would be impossible to overestimate the value of cultivating this trait in oneself and of seeking it in a marriage partner.

The findings of a study by Eleanor Luckey emphasize Terman's statement that a marriage depends on what goes into it, and that among the most important things going into it are the attitudes, preferences, aversions, habit patterns, and emotional response patterns, which give or deny to one the aptitude of compatibility.[3] Luckey studied married people who were satisfied or not satisfied with their marriages.[4] Those who rated their marriages as unsatisfactory characterized their mates as gloomy, bitter, complaining, and frequently angry, all traits of persons of unhappy temperament. The group satisfied with their marriages saw their mates as strong but not dominating, self-confident but not boastful or selfish, firm and fair, not sarcastic, and not too outspoken. They saw their mates as moderate rather than too intense or extreme, characterizing them in general as responsible, generous, cooperative, and conventional. The group not satisfied with their marriages saw their mates in general as having more extreme and intense qualities such as being either too dictatorial or too passive, impatient with others' mistakes, and as unkind, hardhearted, and slow to forgive. They felt their mates were skeptical and distrustful, blunt and aggressive.

## SOME OTHER CHARACTERICTICS IN MARRIAGEABILITY

The marriageable person has developed, or is in the process of developing, *adaptability.*

Young people who have been brought up in such a way that they find it easy to adjust to new situations and to many different kinds of people will fit more easily into marriage. Some people have rigid personalities; they find it difficult to change their ways, accept new ways, to make new friends, or to fit into any situation that is different from what they have always been used to. Since marriage requires many adjustments, the person who does not look upon change as a threat to her or his security will make a better marriage partner.

In comparing groups of divorced and happily married couples, Locke found that the happily married men and women rated higher on adaptability. He considered as more adaptable those who could "give in" in arguments, who were not dominating, who were slow to anger, and who were quick to get over anger.[5]

Burgess and Wallin concluded that some of the 1000 engaged couples they studied who had low marital-prediction scores still made happy marriages, possibly because of a high rating on general adaptability.[6]

[3] Ibid., pp. 110–11.

[4] Eleanor Braun Luckey, "Marital Satisfaction and Personality Correlates of Spouses," *Journal of Marriage and the Family* 26:2 (May 1964), 217–20.

[5] Harvey J. Locke, *Predicting Adjustment in Marriage* (New York: Holt, Rhinehart & Winston, Inc., 1951), p. 192.

[6] Ernest W. Burgess and Paul Wallin, *Engagement and Marriage* (Chicago: J. B. Lippincott Company, 1953) pp. 620–55.

These two investigators made a perceptive analysis of the components of adaptability. They concluded in their pioneer study of 1000 engaged couples that many of those who had low marital-prediction scores still made happy marriages, and this research has been supported by newer studies. They also pointed out that adaptability involves three elements: understanding, knowledge of the different kinds of responses appropriate to specific situations, and the ability to incorporate these responses into one's behavior.[7] In other words, the adaptable person can perceive not only "How would I feel in the other person's place?" but "How does the other person feel, and what is it in the situation that underlies the other's feeling?" Then, in addition to this understanding of another's feelings, the adaptable person has learned by experience and observation what kinds of responses or actions would be most helpful to the other person and to the quality of the relationship between the two of them. But knowledge is not enough; some people who know what actions or responses would be most helpful to the other person and to the relationship involved still cannot act according to their knowledge. Habit patterns are too strong for them. Adaptable people become able to *do* the things they know. Some people may know how not to "rub other people the wrong way," but they may still be too rigid and inflexible to act according to this knowledge. Such a person will say, "I know I'm stubborn, but that's the way I am. I can't help it." Or, "I criticize. I think people ought to be able to take honest criticism. Oh, I know the other person doesn't like it, and it does cause trouble between us, but I can't help it. I've always been this way."

A young husband described his experience:

I realize that it is much easier for me to criticize than to praise. It seems to come naturally to say, "The roast is a little overdone, isn't it?" when what is really going through my mind is that this is a darn good dinner. Sometimes when I've definitely made up my mind to compliment my wife on some special thing, because she deserves the compliment and I know how good it makes her feel for me to tell her so, I find myself coming out with something that sounds a lot more like a criticism than a compliment. She stayed up half the night recently to type a paper for me, and I wanted to say something about it the next day. I heard myself saying, "I guess late at night is not your best time for typing. I found some of the funniest mistakes when I proofread that paper this morning." Now, why couldn't I have said, "Thank you, Honey, for staying up and missing your sleep to type my paper last night. I appreciate it"? That was what I *meant*, but as usual what I *said* just hurt her feelings.

This man had developed insight enough to understand some of his wife's feelings and to know what was wrong with his own habitual responses to situations. He was struggling to become able to incorporate his

[7] Ibid., p. 635.

knowledge into his behavior. The ability to act and respond to situations flexibly is a most important part of the adaptable personality.

**Empathy.** To be able to perceive accurately the feelings and attitudes of others is empathy; the ability to empathize is extremely important in the adaptable, marriageable personality. The person who rates high in empathy can use perceptive understanding of the feelings of one's mate as a regulator of one's own responses and behavior in ways that add greatly to the success and happiness of the marriage. It must be said here that the empathic ability of the partners in a marriage also arms them with weapons that they may use against each other if they lack the will or the motivation to build a good marriage. A wife or a husband can hurt the mate far more seriously than any outsider ever could, simply because she or he knows so well the inner strengths and weaknesses of the mate. Spouses who are empathic know how to hurt as well as they know how to give emotional support and to build up the mate.

Empathy differs from sympathy in that sympathizing with another is "feeling for him or her" whether or not one can understand how the other feels; but empathizing is being sensitively aware of another's feelings, even if they are not the kind of feelings one might have oneself in the same situation. The small child who says unexpectedly to a guest, "You don't like me, do you?" or to the mother who is patiently helping the child get ready for school, "Why are you mad at me this morning, mother?" is probably putting into words the true feelings or attitudes the child has sensed in the other person at the moment. Some degree of empathy is part of everyone's natural endowment, but as people grow older, their empathy may decrease because their own anxieties and motivations or the pressure of their neurotic needs prevents the effective functioning of empathy. So there are people at an age for marrying who have trouble understanding others; their assessment of situations, actions, and feelings is more often erroneous than accurate. Their failure in empathy leads to misunderstandings and to strains growing out of mis-judging actions and misinterpreting words.

The most marriageable people are those whose own motivations and emotional tensions are not so dominant in their lives that their ability to empathize is weak or nonfunctioning. Moreover, the most marriageable people use their empathic ability positively as a basis for becoming more adaptable in their behavior in relationships with others. They are able to control their words and actions so that they do not say the thing that hurts or do the thing that is sure to rub the other person the wrong way and complicate a difficult situation. The person who is habitually tactless either lacks empathy or is not yet able to regulate personal responses and behavior toward the goal of building good interpersonal relationships.

**Evaluating the functioning of empathy in oneself and in others.** It is possible to recognize an individual's failure in empathic processes in several ways. There is the "tactless" person. Also, for example, the person has failed in empathy who in a group will drive through with his or her own ideas or plans, successfully overruling all objections from others, and then feel happy and satisfied with successful dominance without sensing that, even though others have outwardly agreed, it was not their choice. The person who gets his or her own way and then is all smiles and happiness, unaware that the one who has given in is not equally happy; the one who frequently expresses pronounced or forceful opinions before drawing out any views from anyone else, and then concludes that all are in agreement with him or her since no one offers any dissenting argument —these people are not empathic. Many situations that occur in everyday associations with people bring out the presence or absence of a perceptive understanding of other people's feelings.

The young person who is working to improve his or her own level of marriageability will need to try to be objective in observing his or her own interaction with other people. "Do I ride roughshod over other people's wishes or preferences?" "Do I tend to talk when I ought to listen?" "Do I usually get my own way?" "Do I make quick judgments of other people, and rate them without bothering to get to know them well?" Such questions as these may possibly be helpful. One does not create empathy in oneself; rather, one should allow it to begin to function, by working at understanding other people.

**Ability to work through problems.**   The ability to work through problems is another important point in marriageability.

Most problems that confront people in the normal course of events in life have the possibility of solution. The solution may not always be a satisfactory or happy one; nevertheless, it is possible for the average person to formulate some fairly satisfactory way of coming to terms with personal problems. The test of one's approach is whether the policy he or she follows in relation to problems results in bettering or worsening personal effectiveness as an individual functioning in a situation, in a group, or in interpersonal relationships. An illustration may clarify this point:

> Don, a college freshman whose parents were unable to help him financially, was invited to live with his aunt and uncle in a university city and attend school there. The aunt and uncle were anxious to help Don in every possible way; they provided him room and board, and also gave him an allowance to cover school expenses. However, they had no children of their own and their ideas about what the life of a college student should be like seemed very unrealistic to Don. They thought he should be in his room studying every weekday evening except Saturday, and on that night they thought he should be in by midnight. They checked up on his progress constantly, inquired into his assignments, and in general showed so much interest that Don felt overwhelmed by supervision.
>
> The situation soon became a serious problem to him. He was irritable and unhappy, and frequently frustrated because he controlled his impulses to blow up

and tell his aunt and uncle to leave him alone and let him handle his own affairs. He became aware of an inclination to let his studies slide and to spend more and more time fooling around with other students, enjoying himself all he could, partly from a feeling that he wasn't going to be in college long anyway since the situation at his uncle's was getting him down. When his midterm grades showed that his average was dangerously low, he realized that something must be done. He tried to face the problem objectively. He came up with this summary of possible alternatives: He might quit school and go home. He ruled that out as accepting unnecessary failure. If he stayed, he might try to adjust completely to his relatives' rigid ideas in order to avoid conflicts. He felt he could not do that. He might try to support himself in school and move out of their home. He knew that would hurt them and they would not understand his doing it. Moreover, he found that to support himself in school was not immediately possible anyway, although he concluded that by careful planning he could do so another year by carrying a lighter study load and working more. The only possible and reasonable alternative that he could see at the moment was to try to find some compromise with his relatives and continue the present arrangement. This he set out to do.

He was able to have some frank and friendly discussions with his aunt and uncle, trying to show them that he appreciated their help and seriously intended to make a success of his education; but at the same time he gave them exact information about what rules governed the activities and hours of other students on the campus, and he tried to get them to see why it was so difficult for him to live by a rigid set of rules that applied to none of his associates.

There was no quick and final solution, but Don was able to pinpoint the problem for himself and for his aunt and uncle. The trouble arose from a natural difference in viewpoints because of differences in age and experience; there was no difference in basic motives or intentions. After he had analyzed the problem so objectively, much of Don's frustration disappeared, and he could use patient persistence to build a better understanding with his relatives and to work out irritating details of policy.

Many people have never set up a positive system for facing problem situations in their lives. They do not assess a problem realistically and choose ways of acting that will bring constructive results. Instead, they give up easily and consider a situation hopeless, or they regress to some form of immature emotional behavior that may create new problems or cause the old ones to snowball into unmanageable proportions.

People who can face problems realistically and seek intelligent solutions are more likely to be successful in married living. The need for an established way of meeting problems constructively arises at times in every marriage. For example, for some couples early in their marriage, excessive control or dominance may come from one or both sets of parents-in-law. People who do not let problems overwhelm them or force them into irrational or destructive action can meet such in-law situations with some objectivity. They have learned through practice that there are positive ways of working out even the most difficult situations.

In such a problem as strained relationships with in-laws, the solution might be found in temporary acquiescence; in escape—putting distance between the in-laws and the couple; in frank and open discussion of the situations; in making greater efforts to understand and accept the motives underlying the problem behavior; even in limiting contacts with the in-laws, or in making changes in living arrangements or in financial plans. Whatever the eventual solution may be, however, those who have an habitual policy of facing problems constructively will find a good solution; they will not just go through random or destructive motions based on emotion, complicating their problems.

## FAMILY BACKGROUND AS PART OF MARRIAGEABILITY

Researchers who have investigated the background factors in the lives of people and related these factors to success in marriage have concluded that young people are usually conditioned early in life in ways that will make them good or bad risks in marriage. Although the studies were made in different parts of the country and many years ago, they produced many of the same conclusions as current research does concerning the background factors that make for happiness in marriage. Terman found the following ten circumstances most predictive of marital happiness.[8]

1 Superior happiness of parents.
2 Childhood happiness.
3 Lack of conflict with mother.
4 Home discipline that was firm, not harsh.
5 Strong attachment to mother.
6 Strong attachment to father.
7 Lack of conflict with father.
8 Parental frankness about matters of sex.
9 Infrequency and mildness of childhood punishment.
10 Premarital attitude free from disgust or aversion toward sex.

Terman believed that anyone who passes on all ten of these points is a distinctly better than average marital risk. Burgess and Cottrell found similar background factors to be important in predicting success in marriage.[9]

[8] Terman, *Psychological Factors in Marital Happiness*, pp. 110–11.

[9] Ernest W. Burgess and Leonard S. Cottrell, *Predicting Success or Failure in Marriage* (Englewood Cliffs, N. J.: Prentice-Hall, Inc., 1939). Burgess and Cottrell conducted a study of 526 middle-class couples living in and about Chicago. The couples had been married from one to six years, an average of three years. Approximately 60 percent had some education beyond high school. Married, separated, and divorced couples were included in the study. In most cases, the wife completed the questionnnaire. The chief purpose of the study was to determine the factors and personality traits predictive of success or failure in marriage. The data were collected during the early 1930s. Charles E. King later repeated the Burgess–Cottrell study with a group of 466 black couples and found the same relationships between premarital factors and marital adjustments. See King, "The Burgess–Cottrell Method of Measuring Marital Adjustment Applied to a Non-White Southern Urban Population," *Marriage and Family Living* 14:4 (November 1952), 280–85.

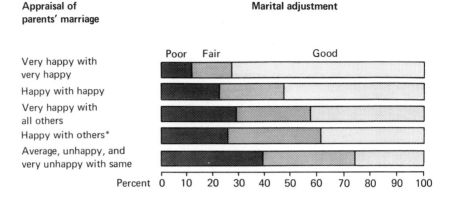

Appraisal of
parents' marriage

Marital adjustment

Poor  Fair          Good

Very happy with
very happy

Happy with happy

Very happy with
all others

Happy with others*

Average, unhappy, and
very unhappy with same

Percent  0   10   20   30   40   50   60   70   80   90   100

*Except with Very Happy

FIG. 6–1  Appraisal of the happiness of parents' marriage (combined ratings) and adjustment of their children in marriage. If both sets of parents had very happy marriages, the children have a much better chance for happiness in marriage. From Ernest W. Burgess and Leonard S. Cottrell, *Predicting Success or Failure in Marriage* (Englewood Cliffs, N.J.: Prentice-Hall, Inc., 1939).

The most significant factors are concerned with the happiness of the parents' marriage and the relationship of the child with his parents. People from homes where the parents had happy marriages, and from homes in which a satisfactory relationship existed between the parents and their children, have an advantage in developing traits of marriageability. People reared in homes in which the parents were unhappy, and in which there was constant parent–child friction, have some handicaps for successful marriage. The factors and conditions that researchers found to be significant in the family background in the earlier studies are found to be as true today as they were then. A recent study of marriage and remarriage by Riley and Spreitzer found that people who as children had lived in families of "high pathology" were more likely to fail not only in a first marriage but also in a second marriage. They define pathology as the disruption which had occurred in the parent marriage and the relationships of these children with their parents and siblings.[10] Our research, summarized in Table 6-2, gives many of the family background factors which differentiate the unhappily married from the happily married.

It is also true that divorce tends to run in families. Reports from approximately 2000 students at the University of California, Berkeley, concerning the marital records of their parents, grandparents, and aunts and uncles showed a significantly greater proportion of divorces in families

[10] Lawrence E. Riley and Elmer A. Spreitzer, "A Model for the Analysis of Lifetime Marriage Patterns," *Journal of Marriage and the Family* 36:1 (February 1974), 64–70.

TABLE 6-2

Family background, as reported by 1162 married people, 155 unhappily married people seeking help through marriage counseling, and 164 divorced people *

| Family background | Married group (N–1162) | Counseling group (N–155) | Divorced group (N–164) |
|---|---|---|---|
| Happiness of parents' marriage | | | |
| happy or very happy | 55% | 35% | 39% |
| Childhood—happy or very happy | 66 | 42 | 41 |
| Adolescence—happy or very happy | 55 | 37 | 36 |
| Relationship with father to age 15 | | | |
| close or very close | 42 | 42 | 23 |
| Relationship with mother to age 15 | | | |
| close or very close | 63 | 59 | 44 |
| Doubts about having a | | | |
| successful marriage | 24 | 41 | 42 |

* Landis; see footnotes, page 5.

whose grandparents had divorced than in families whose grandparents had remained married.[11]

The evidence shows, then, that people are conditioned by their family background in ways that affect their marriageability. Those reared in happy homes have an advantage in that their parents were able to give them an example of successful family living. Nevertheless, those reared in unhappy homes are not doomed to failure. Research in the past has been based almost entirely on success or failure among people who had had no formal preparation for marriage. Today young people can evaluate their own marriageability and overcome many of the effects of whatever handicaps they may have. With a rational approach to marriage, people can and do break cycles of unhappiness that may have run in their families. Those who have not had the background of happily married parents can be alert to danger signals that might warn of special problems ahead because of traits in themselves or in the persons they consider marrying. They can avoid rushing into marriage if doubts exist about a relationship. By such alertness, they can avoid repeating the mistakes their parents may have made.

Some support for the view that rational preparation for marriage does contribute to breaking cycles of marriage failure is appearing in

[11] Judson T. Landis, "The Pattern of Divorce in Three Generations," *Social Forces* 34:3 (March 1956), 213–16. In studying the dating and engagement histories of these 1977 students, it was found that a slightly higher percentage of the students who came from homes in which there had been divorce among both their parents and their grandparents went steady with, and became engaged to, people from homes broken by divorce. However, any tendency of children from divorced families to marry children from divorced families would not be sufficient to explain the high divorce rate among children of divorced parents.

findings of the study of 581 marriages, in which one or both members had taken a university course in preparation for marriage.[12] Their parents and grandparents, as groups, had had a higher than average rate of marriage failure. According to evidence from previous studies that revealed the statistical predictability of marriage failures in families, the present group of people could be expected to have had a failure rate at least twice as high as they have had, or will have. Figure 6-2 summarizes the research findings showing the trend toward marriage failure in successive family generations, which is in contrast to the experience of the 581 marriages in our research group. Only 55 percent of the parents of this group were rated as very happy or happy in marriage, 25 percent as average, and 20 percent as unhappy. The ratings by their children may be assumed to be accurate since 19 percent of the parent marriages ended in divorce. If trends revealed by other research were to occur with this group, the group could be expected to have an unusually high unhappiness and failure rate, but this is not the case. In the present group, 90 percent rate their marriages as happy or very happy, 8 percent as average, and only 2 percent as unhappy. If, with the passing of time, *all* who rate their marriages as average or unhappy should divorce (and this is unlikely), the failure rate would still be only half as high as the failure rate of their parents. These findings do not negate the significance of background factors in marriageability. They do emphasize the point that individuals are not absolutely bound by their background, either negatively or positively.

It follows that young people who have grown up in happy families, with parents who had good marriages, are not automatically assured of successful marriages. It is necessary for every couple, no matter what

[12] See footnote 2, page 5.

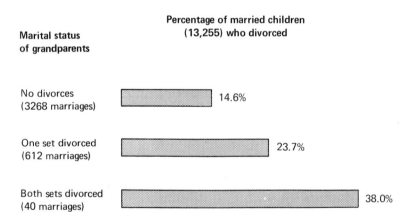

**Marital status of grandparents**

**Percentage of married children (13,255) who divorced**

No divorces (3268 marriages) — 14.6%

One set divorced (612 marriages) — 23.7%

Both sets divorced (40 marriages) — 38.0%

FIG. 6–2 Percentage of parents and aunts and uncles of 1977 college students who had divorced, and the marital status of the grandparents. From Judson T. Landis, "The Pattern of Divorce in Three Generations," *Social Forces* 34:3 (March 1956), 213–16.

their backgrounds, to approach marriage intelligently and to work at building happy and successful relationships within marriage. Important as background is, it can never guarantee happiness in marriage, nor can it doom one to unhappiness.

In this chapter we have discussed a number of different considerations that have to do with marriageability. The most important aspects of marriageability are related to personality and to one's habitual ways of meeting life situations. Habits and personality patterns are closely related to the family background and what is expected of the individual in the future but can, nevertheless, be modified.

## OUTLINE FOR SELF-STUDY: YOUR MARRIAGEABILITY

Think through the following outline, and decide upon your answers to the questions. Then write an assessment of your own marriageability as revealed by your study and thinking.

### I YOUR PERSONALITY TRAITS

1   Which of the personality traits found in the Terman study of happy husbands and wives do you have?

2   In general, do you have an outgoing and accepting attitude toward others? Are you often critical of other people?

3   Do you find it easy to work happily with others? When you work with others do you tend to feel either that you are pushed around or that you have a hard time getting them to cooperate with you or accept your leadership?

4   Do you find it easy to live with yourself? Do you tend to feel depressed when alone, or do you have a fairly sustained sense of well-being?

5   Are you cautious in making most decisions? Or do you act first and think later?

6   Can you accept things as they come in life, or do you often complain about circumstances or wish your life were different?

7   Do you lose your temper?

8   What kind of personality or self do other people reflect back to you? You can judge this by whether you usually feel liked, responded to, and accepted by others.

### II HANDLING PROBLEMS IN YOUR LIFE

1   How do you react to failure or disappointment? Would an outside observer say your habitual way of reacting is positive and mentally healthy? Will it lead to living harmoniously with others?

2   If some circumstances in life are difficult for you, or put you under pressure, can you make an objective evaluation of the problem situation and take positive rather than negative action? Think of a specific problem

you have had. How did you meet it? Did your course of action result in an improvement in your situation, or growth in yourself? What was constructive or what was destructive in the way you met that problem? Did you learn from it so that you could handle more constructively a similar problem that might arise?

### III ASSESS YOUR ADAPTABILITY AND EMPATHY

1   How do you fit into new situations? If your family once moved, what difficulty, if any, did you have fitting into a new community? When you first went to college, did you adjust readily to living away from home?

2   Do you make friends easily? How many friends have you kept for two or more years?

3   How do you rate in empathy? Can you size up situations and people as they really are, or does it sometimes seem that everyone is out of step except you? Do you have a reputation for being considerate of other people's feelings? Do other people seem to get annoyed with you for reasons that are unclear to you?

### IV ASSESS YOUR FAMILY BACKGROUND

1   How many happy marriages can you count among your grandparents, aunts and uncles, cousins, and brothers and sisters? How many divorces or unhappy marriages are there in your immediate background?

2   If there has been divorce or unhappines in your family, have you tried to figure out the causes of the failures? How have the failures affected your thinking about marriage? What are you doing in a positive way to prepare for success in your future marriage?

3   What are your relationships with your parents and brothers and sisters? Friendly and close? Indifferent? Antagonistic? Can you recognize what traits in yourself may contribute to the kinds of relationships you have with your family members? How will these traits affect your future relationship in marriage?

4   Do you know which of your family's values are a part of you that you will take into marriage? Making money? Service to others? Religious values? Participating in civic and community affairs? Having the respect of friends and associates? Material possessions? Keeping up with others in standard of living? Success in a vocation?

## REVIEW QUESTIONS

1   How much change in the personality traits of your spouse can you expect after marriage? Will annoying personality traits disappear after marriage if two people love each other?

2   What are some of the personality traits Terman found to be characteristic of happily married men and women? Of unhappily married men and women?

3   Why is it difficult to recognize undesirable personality traits during courtship?

4 What does Terman's study of husband–wife grievances reveal about personality traits?

5 Why is the habit of happiness important in marriageability?

6 Why is adaptability important in marriageability? What elements are involved in adaptability?

7 Define empathy. How might empathic ability be used destructively in a marriage?

8 What factors might prevent empathy from functioning effectively?

9 How can one recognize the failure to empathize in others? In oneself?

10 What is a good test of whether one is facing problems in life constructively?

11 What are some constructive steps in meeting a problem?

12 What family background factors seem to be important in predicting success or failure in marriage? Do research studies agree on this subject?

## PROJECTS AND ACTIVITIES

1 Make a list of ten personality traits that you find hard to tolerate in others. Now make a self-analysis and try to determine why this is so.

2 *Panel Discussion.* A group from the class discusses ways in which others meet their problems or handle their aggressive feelings.

3 Write a paper on your marriageability, taking into consideration personality traits and family background.

4 *Sociodrama.* Try writing and acting a skit that brings out some personality traits that would make for happiness or unhappiness in marriage.

# MATURITY FOR MARRIAGE

Chronologically there is no question about when people are old enough to marry. The age at which people may marry without parental consent is set by state laws. In the past most states set the age at 18 for women and 21 for men. The passage of the Twenty-Sixth Amendment in 1971 will probably define the legal age for both men and women, since it, in effect, defines people as legally adults at 18.

However, people of courtship age are interested in knowing whether there is a "best" age for marriage aside from legal age. Many variables must be taken into consideration; chronological age is but one of several related factors that cannot be considered independently in assessing readiness for marriage. To illustrate: Studies seem to show that college-educated people tend to have happier marriages than non-college-educated people, if divorce rates of college and non-college people are taken as a measure. College graduates marry at a later age than non-college graduates. Is it the age at marriage or some other factors that result in happier marriages among college graduates? Or are there selective factors that may differentiate college and non-college people and that also affect marital success? The question of what age is best emerges as less to the point than the question of what level of maturity is necessary before one is old enough to marry.

## EMOTIONAL MATURITY

A factor of the greatest importance in the success or failure of any marriage is the emotional maturity of the partners. Emotional maturity can be defined as the level of development of one's ability to see oneself and others objectively, to be able to discriminate between facts and feelings, and to act on the basis of facts in a situation rather than on feelings alone. The child of 10 is developing satisfactorily if this child is as mature as other children the same age. At each stage of life a certain degree of maturity is necessary if one is to function adequately at that stage. Problems arise when the emotional growth of people is arrested at immature stages. Problems are especially likely to be acute if one or both partners in a marriage have not achieved a level of maturity satisfactory for their situation.

Certain traits discussed in the preceding chapter, such as the ability to use empathy in constructive ways, are characteristic of mature adults. The maturity an individual has achieved may also be measured by the degree of flexibility or adaptability with which that person reacts in relationships with other people. The rigid, inflexible person, like a small child, clings to certainty, sameness, and habit. Growth toward understanding and cooperation in a close relationship such as marriage is handicapped by this type of immaturity.

## OBJECTIVITY

With growth into maturity it is necessary to develop the ability to get outside ourselves and see ourselves and our interests realistically, to look at external facts as separate from our feelings about them. Small children view most of the circumstances of their lives subjectively. They are self-centered. With increased maturity should come the ability to see things in their true relationships, the ability to stand aside, as it were, and judge events more impartially—to recognize that the world does not necessarily revolve about one's own life and experiences. Without objectivity, individuals will have distorted ideas about themselves, their needs, and what may be their rights. They will fail to evaluate their own motives. Few people can be completely objective, but people who are growing toward maturity adequate for marriage are able, through their experiences and observations in living, to be more objective than subjective in their attitudes and judgments. They perceive the relative importance of events as they relate to themselves and to other people, and can act according to fairly accurate perceptions.

## A REALISTIC CONCEPTION OF MARRIAGE

Mature people are able to see marriage realistically. They know that marriage is not an easy escape from reality and from personal problems, but rather a way of life that may bring new problems and that certainly will bring greater responsibility. They realize that marriage also has the potential for a happy fulfillment of personal needs. Mature people see marriage as most rewarding if the total relationship between the two is a mutual meeting of personality needs. They can accept as well the fact that marriage is not an entirely private matter between two people. It is an institution designed by a civilized society to protect its adult members, make secure the children born into that society, and guarantee the stability and continuity of the whole social group. The many legal and social regulations and prohibitions that affect marriage are evidence of society's stake in each marriage. People who are mature enough for marriage are aware of these larger implications of marriage, as well as its meaning in their own lives.

## MATURITY FOR MARRIAGE INCLUDES:

**A conception of love based on reality.**   An understanding of the nature of love may develop slowly while going through adolescence and early adulthood. All individuals may go through a process of experiencing different levels and types of love. They may know a type of love in junior high school, and possibly have several "loves" in high school. Each of these experiences will teach something about the nature of love. During this part of life, they will probably come to realize that they can love people with whom they could not possibly have an enduring relationship such as marriage. They will have learned that love must be supported by a broad foundation of common interests, common goals in life, acceptance of each other, and mutual respect; and that love, to grow and become more satisfying in marriage, must be based on a total relationship between two people. Mature people see "romantic love," as pictured in movies, plays, and fiction, for what it is—a form of fantasy that has little relationship to the type of love that can cement a permanent relationship.

**A philosophy to live by.**   Mature people are working to develop a philosophy that will be a guide through the future. They are coming to terms with the universe in moral philosophy, religious or ideological concepts, and in response to and functioning among other people. They have a measure of security concerning their philosophy of life because in finding that it is workable it enables them to cope with difficult circumstances or situations in life. Mature people test and evaluate their basic attitudes and will continue to do so throughout life, if maturing continues; but they have already experienced and matured enough to have made the major shifts and reshufflings in their philosophy that are characteristic of adolescence. At this point, directions are set, even if the exact course is not charted. Thus, they are ready to choose a marriage partner wisely, and those who choose other mature people do not have to make a blind choice.

**A reasonable evaluation of self.**  Mature people make a fairly accurate and objective evaluation of themselves. They see their strengths and weaknesses, and work to overcome the weaknesses. If there are weak points within their personalities that they cannot change, they accept them without regret or feelings of guilt. They build on their strengths and make the most of themselves in terms of their abilities. They recognize that there are activities they cannot do well, if at all, but they also know what they can do well. They accept without regret their inabilities and limitations, and appreciate and use their assets.

**An evaluation of family background.**  Before people are mature enough for marriage they need to be able to view and understand their own family background, the contribution it has made to their personalities, and the implications it may have for marriage. Since most research shows that one's chances for success in marriage are influenced by the success or failure of one's parents' marriage and by the emotional climate of the home, mature people can look at their family background and attempt to evaluate it objectively. If they see that marriage failure and unhappiness occurred in one or more generations in their immediate past, they may think constructively about the situation and try to avoid a repetition, just as they would face the fact of a family history of lung cancer or migraine, and try to live in such a way as to avoid becoming a victim so far as it might be within their control. If there has been conflict and unhappiness in their families, they do not accept it as inevitable for their own marriage. Rather, they attempt to determine how this family history has affected them, and they take positive action to overcome handicaps in their background. Mature people do not harshly blame their parents for their weaknesses and failures; they give them credit for the strengths and achievements that they can see in their parents' lives. Similarly, they do not take for granted that their own happiness is assured on the fact that their parents have had a satisfactory marriage. They try to understand the techniques of living that have contributed to the successful relationships in their families. Especially, they attempt to assess their own contribution to the emotional climate in which they have grown up, in order to be able to contribute positively to the happiness of their future marriage and family life.

## MATURE PEOPLE

**Meet problems constructively.**  Another trait that distinguishes mature people from the immature, at any age, is that mature people have learned how to meet problems in constructive ways. They are not easily thrown into confusion, discouragement, or disorganization by disappointments or frustrations. They are able to use past experiences as means of growth and establish more or less habitual policies that enable them to cope with emergencies and crises. This phase of maturity will significantly affect ability to build a successful marriage.

**Have an understanding of human motivations.**  Mature people have not only given thought to their own personality and family background but also have gained some understanding of human personality and how it functions. They have come to recognize types of behavior in themselves and others in relation to inner motivations. They can see aggressive and domineering behavior as indicative of feelings of insecurity; they see heavy drinking, the use of drugs, certain physical illnessess, moodiness, or clinging dependence as means sometimes used to escape from problems in life; they recognize jealousy as an expression of insecurity or an inability to cope with feelings of inadequacy; they know that gossip is motivated by a desire to build oneself up by pushing others down, which also represents self-doubt. These perceptions and understandings of the motivations that influence behavior should enable mature people to be charitable in their judgment of others, and also to be wiser in choosing a marriage partner. Sometimes behavior patterns that might for a time seem charming or desirable in a girl friend or boy friend—such as an adoring possessiveness—when understood, may constitute a warning about a personality or a relationship.

**Can think independently.**  Mature people have achieved some degree of independence in their thinking. They can profit by what they have been taught at home, but are able to think for themselves. If at one time while growing up they threw overboard much of what they had been taught, they are now past the stage of immature rebellion against authority and have integrated their ideas based on life experiences with attitudes derived from experience. Decisions can now be truly independent rather than mere overreactions in the form of either rebellion or dependency.

**Take responsibility for mistakes.**  Mature individuals have become able to accept responsibility for their own mistakes. They have grown beyond blaming others for their own weaknesses and refusing to recognize their own faults. When they make a mistake, they accept their actions and try to learn from the experience. Many people in their teens have developed to the extent that they rationally try to learn and do learn from their mistakes. A 17-year-old girl expressed an attitude that is predictive of the eventual achievement of a level of maturity adequate for successful marriage:

I think it's safer to try to learn from my mistakes than to try to dodge what happens. I've found out that if I try to duck responsibility for something and tell myself, "Oh, well, it wasn't my fault anyway," it seems that the same kind of thing happens again later, and it hits me harder the next time. I think it's easier to learn all you can from each experience so that you won't have to learn it later the hard way.

**Have a sense of proportion about present desires and future goals.** Young children want what they want when they want it. Mature individuals recognize their wants, but can also look ahead and make choices. They want a secure job, but are willing to take years of training to be ready for that job. They want money to spend, but are willing to work, learn, and enjoy the present while moving toward the future goal. They know what they want in the future in a marriage relationship and they keep a sense of proportion about the place of sex in the present framework of life. They would like to have a car now but, if necessary, will settle for whatever transportation they can have at present so that they can afford to get married next summer. Mature people do not deny their desires and wants, but are willing to plan and to wait and, if necessary, to make sacrifices today in order to carry out plans that they have decided will mean greater overall satisfaction in the future.

**Are ready to sacrifice for others.** Marriage is a cooperative venture involving two people who must make some sacrifices for the partnership and for each other. Maturing individuals begin to appreciate that much of life consists of exchanges. At one level, children give obedience in exchange for protection or for approval. At another level, workers give their time, energy, and ability in exchange for a material reward in the form of a paycheck. On the far deeper level of relationships within marriage and the family, people give of themselves; they give emotional support, acceptance, and cooperation as a part of a mutual exchange that adds up to a satisfying relationship. In material and practical matters, too, they recognize the necessity for giving. Mature parents, no matter how young, are willing to lose sleep to sit up with a sick child, to get up for the baby's two o'clock feeding when they are dead tired, and to give up buying things they want for themselves or for the house in order to provide for their children.

Some "adults" marry, never having reached this level of maturity. They cannot think first of the needs of a spouse or a baby and forget themselves. So the grocery money goes for new clothes or for a few rounds at a bar; the babies are slapped for crying, or children are left to their own resources while the parents attempt to escape back into the freedom they had before marriage. This type of immaturity, the inability to sacrifice for others or for the partnership, can be seen daily in our world. It accounts for much marital breakup and is responsible for many personality maladjustments in children. In contrast to such immaturity is this statement by a 19-year-old husband and father who, in discussing his job and financial budget, said:

> I think our biggest problem is to make my paycheck cover all the things we need. We've had so many unexpected expenses. We didn't plan to have a baby the first year, but we had a baby boy, and of course we're glad we've got him. . . . He wasn't very husky at first and we've had a lot of extra medical bills. Sometimes I get under pressure just trying to figure out which one of all the places to put each dollar, but it hasn't been too bad because so far we've managed to get along. I think sometimes about all the money we used to spend just fooling around going to shows and such things before we were married; it was a lot of fun, and it would be nice if we could go out together once in a while for an evening now, but there's no money for baby sitters or for shows. I don't waste much time thinking about it; I'm too busy supporting the three of us to waste time wishing we could do things we can't do. I'll tell you, you have a different feeling about your job when you've got two other people to take care of than you have when you're just working to earn money for a good time for yourself.

**Have outgrown immature sex attitudes.** For many reasons, people may have immature attitudes toward the place of sex in life. This is partly because of the way sex education of children is handled. Because of the negative attitudes held or expressed by many people, children often learn to think of sex as dirty and vulgar, or secret and shameful. Some people need many years after they have reached biological sexual maturity before they can appreciate sexuality as a positive force in personality, and sexual impulses and responses as a wholesome expression of love between two people. They may go to one extreme or the other in their sex attitudes— either denying their real feelings or overemphasizing sex in life while at the same time failing to recognize the value of sex in all its aspects as a factor in successful marriage.

People who are mature enough for marriage will be capable of considering whether their attitudes about sex are realistic and wholesome; they will try to change their attitudes if change is needed. To do so is not easy, but it can be done. Some people will need the help of a counselor, but those who are achieving maturity in other areas of life will take whatever steps are desirable in order to increase their growth toward maturity in sex attitudes.

FIG. 7–1 © 1957, United Features Syndicate, Inc..

**Can assess their own level of maturity.** Perhaps one of the more significant measures of progress toward maturity is the ability of people to be fairly objective in assessing their own level of maturity. Immature individuals are usually not aware of much need to grow or change. The less mature they are, the more readily they may plunge into marriage with little or no understanding of the obligations and responsibilities they are assuming, and with no thought about whether they are ready or willing to accept the obligations. Mature people will not be unduly fearful of assuming responsibility, but will face the fact that with marriage they *are* assuming new responsibilities. They will consider, before taking the step, whether they are ready for it. We quote from a self-evaluation written by a college girl:

> I'm in love with Ted, but I know I'm a long way from being ready to marry. I want to marry and have children some day, but right now I just couldn't face all that responsibility. It's a problem in some ways, because I think it would be nice to have children while I'm young—perhaps in the early twenties—so I'd have all the energy it takes to be a good mother—but when I see other girls my age with babies, I feel sorry for them. I still want to have fun before I get tied down to that. And another thing, I've been in love two or three times, but so far, it has not lasted. Each time after the affair has ended I have found someone else who turns out to be more nearly the type I'd like to marry some day. I'm still not sure enough about some things in my own personality or sure enough of my judgment of another's personality to make a choice that would be permanent. In the last year I've learned several things about myself. . . . Perhaps in another year or so I'll be more nearly ready to marry.

The young woman who made this self-evaluation had made more progress toward the maturity necessary for marriage than many others her age who do not know or are only vaguely aware that marriage will make requirements more rigorous than they are used to. She was achieving a realistic attitude toward love and marriage, and some objectivity about her own level of maturity.

## AGE AS A FACTOR IN READINESS FOR MARRIAGE

All the characteristics discussed in this chapter require time and experience for development. Some people mature more easily and quickly under the impact of life experiences, but most people need years—chronological maturity—in order to develop a sound readiness for marriage. For this reason, although it is difficult to isolate the age factor, evidence indicates that the more successful marriages are not the very youthful marriages.

Many of those who marry young would, a few years later, choose an entirely different kind of spouse from the one chosen at 18. Between the ages of 16 and 22, people's conception of a desirable spouse will change as much as, or more than, their ideas about a vocation. If the 16-year-old takes a job, he or she is more apt to drift into it, but the 22-year-old has given more serious thought to a vocation and can approach a special field with greater certainty and confidence. That may have some relationship to the fact that college graduates tend to have relatively fewer marriage failures than non-college people; many of them do not marry until after college—they have had four college years in an environment that exposes them to opportunities for growing toward at least certain kinds of maturity before they marry.

Studies made of the relationship between age at marriage and happiness in marriage are summarized in Table 7-1. All the studies show that the chances for happiness in marriage are less when men marry before the age of 20 and when women marry before the age of 18. Three of the studies show that men who married as they approached their thirties were more likely to find happiness in marriage than those who married at younger ages.

In our study of 409 older-generation couples, we found that it took longer for the men and women married under the age of 20 to reach good working arrangements in sexual relations, spending income, associating with mutual friends, in-law relationships, and social activities and recreation.[1] The couples who were 20 years old or over when they married

TABLE 7-1    Studies of the best age for marriage as judged by marital success and failure

|  | Poor | Good | Excellent |
|---|---|---|---|
| Burgess-Cottrell (526 marriages) | | | |
| Men | Under 22 | 22–27; 31 and over | 28–30 |
| Women | Under 19 | 19–27 | 28 and over |
| Terman (792 marriages) | | | |
| Men | Under 22 | 22 and over | 22 and over |
| Women | Under 20 | 20 and over | 20 and over |
| Landis (409 marriages) | | | |
| Men | Under 20 | 20–29 | 30 and over |
| Women | Under 20 | 25 and over | 20–24 |
| Landis (544 marriages) | | | |
| Men | Under 20 | 20 and over | 20 and over |
| Women | Under 18 | 18–21 | 22–27 |

[1] This study was an analysis of the experience of 409 couples to determine how long it takes to work out adjustments after marriage, and to discover what factors are associated with happiness in marriage. The couples had been married from 3 to 40

made the adjustments in less time than those under 20, and, in general, those who were married at 30 and over made the adjustments in less time than any other age group. The men who married at an early age had far greater difficulty than the women who married at an early age, and the men who married at 30 years and over had less difficulty than the women who married at 30 years and over. Only 47 percent of the men who married under 20 said the sex adjustment was satisfactory from the beginning of the marriage; 83 percent of the men who were 30 and over when they married said the sex adjustment was satisfactory from the beginning. In general, this is the pattern existing between age at marriage and adjustments that take place after marriage.

All the studies we have been quoting on age at marriage and happiness in marriage were done some years ago. The United States Census does not collect such data but it does collect data on age at marriage and success or failure as measured by divorce. We summarize the census studies as well as some of our studies on this subject. In one Bureau of the Census survey, women were asked how many times they had been married and their age at first marriage. For the women who had been married once, the median age at first marriage was 21.1 years; for those who had been married more than once, the median age at first marriage was 19.0 years. The report shows that the pattern has held constant for the past 35 years; that is, those remarrying were married for the first time when they were approximately two years younger than those married only once.[2]

An analysis of the United States statistical abstracts on age at first marriage and divorce among women found that 43 percent divorced if they had married under the age of 20, 33 percent if married at ages 20 to 24, 17 percent if married at ages 25 to 29. Only 7 percent of those who married between 45 and 49 years of age had divorced.[3]

Figure 7-2 summarizes our study of the divorce rate in 3000 marriages. All the couples in this study were the parents of college students, and

---

years, an average of 20 years, and all were still married. Each spouse was asked to fill out an anonymous questionnaire independently of the other. The couples were largely residents of the Middle West, Michigan, and Illinois; and they were of the middle or upper class economically. One-third of the participants were college graduates, and many of them were the parents of college students. Data were collected in 1945. For a summary of the study see: Judson T. Landis, "Length of Time Required to Achieve Adjustment in Marriage," *American Sociological Review* 11:6 (December 1946), 666–77.

[2] Bureau of the Census, *Current Population Reports, Population Characteristics,* Series P-20, No. 67 (2 May 1956), 3.

[3] P. Krishnan and Ashraf K. Kayani, "Estimates of Age Specific Divorce Rates for Females in the United States, 1960–1969," *Journal of Marriage and Family Living,* 36:1 (February 1974), 72–75.

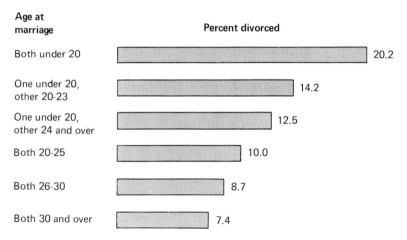

FIG. 7–2  Age at marriage and the divorce rate in 3000 marriages.

therefore would not represent a cross section of the population. As the age at marriage increased the divorce rate decreased in these families. If one spouse was under 20 and the other over 20 at marriage, the divorce rate was higher than if both were over 20 years old at marriage.

All these findings emphasize the fact that chronological age is related to the other kinds of maturity necessary to make a success of marriage. Certainly age at marriage is not the sole factor responsible for the higher proportion of failures among youthful marriages. Some other typical life circumstances and patterns and some individual characteristics tend to be present in cases of youthful marriages. One hypothesis is that more of those who marry early do so to escape unhappy home surroundings or to defy parental dominance than is true of those who marry later. To choose marriage as a hoped-for means of escape from pressures may represent immature judgment and lack of the experience in problem solving needed to make a success of marriage. Some who marry as an escape might not have the judgment to make a wiser choice even if they were much older, but many of them, if given time, would achieve a degree of maturity not present when they marry at a very early age. They would become able to find other more appropriate solutions or escapes than marriage.

Undoubtedly, some early marriages are handicapped at the outset because they are entered into hastily, after short acquaintance, often without due consideration of the realities that will have to be faced after marriage.

Many youthful marriages are forced by pregnancy; were it not for pregnancy, the couples would never have married each other. All studies made of this type of forced marriage show a high failure rate. Our analysis of the records of 1425 marriages of high school students in 75 California high schools revealed that, if both members of the couple were in high school at the time of the marriage, between 44 and 56 percent of the marriages were forced by pregnancy. Burchinal, in a similar study of high school marriages in Iowa, found that, if both were high school students, 87 percent were forced by pregnancy.[4] In our study of high school marriages that had taken place three years before the time of the study, one in five had already ended in annulment, divorce, or separation.

It is often believed that people who are older when they marry will have greater difficulty adjusting in marriage because they have become "set" in their ways. However, the studies on age for marriage do not bear this out. Older people will have learned many things that may give them advantages. They have had an opportunity to observe the successful and unsuccessful marriages of their acquaintances. Their observations are conducive to more realistic ideas of what marriage is than they may have had when younger.

The person who marries at a later age knows what it is to be a single adult, and has had time to decide whether he or she is willing to work at achieving a happy marriage.

Any one or more of these factors may operate to increase the probability of success in marriages not made at very young ages. Nevertheless, the crucial factor in marriage success or failure is the degree of maturity in all areas of life that has been reached by the two partners in a marriage. The studies showing the relationship between marriage success and age at marriage underline the fact that most people require years of experience before they develop the maturity adequate for marriage success.

The California legislature passed a law in 1970 requiring all couples in which one or both were under the age of 18 to have premarital counseling before they could marry. Teenagers had accounted for 40 percent of divorces in California. Of the women who married as teenagers, 80 percent had one child and 30 percent had two or more children when they divorced. There has been no follow-up study to determine the effectiveness of the counseling in preventing teenage marriages. Ohio also has such a law applying to teenagers. If all states had this law it might discourage such marriages.

[4] Lee G. Burchinal, "Research on Young Marriages: Implications for Family Life Education," *The Family Life Coordinator* 9:1–2 (September–December 1960). Also, Burchinal, "School Policies and School Age Marriages," *The Family Life Coordinator* 8:3 (March 1960), 43–48.

Much of the success of any marriage depends on the maturity of the two people involved. Study yourself on the following criteria. If you find it difficult to rate yourself, ask a friend or a member of your family to help you. Few people are mature on all points, so do not be discouraged if you find some immaturities in yourself.

**I HAVE YOU DEVELOPED A MEASURE OF OBJECTIVITY?**

1 Can you see yourself as you appear to other people?

2 Can you see others as most other people see them?

3 Can you discriminate between facts and feelings about yourself, other people, and things?

4 Do you act on the realities of a situation, in spite of your feelings?

**II HAVE YOU DEVELOPED A MEASURE OF MATURITY IN HANDLING FRUSTRATION?**

1 What was your pattern of behavior when your wishes were blocked at age five? Age ten? Age fifteen? Your present age? Can you see growth toward maturity in your changing pattern of behavior?

2 As you think of mistakes you have made in the past, can you think of specific things you have learned from your mistakes?

3 How many times during the past month have you blamed others for something that was partly your fault?

**III ARE YOU DEVELOPING THE CHARACTERISTICS OF A MATURE ADULT?**

1 Do you have a philosophy of life that enables you to meet unalterable situations with poise?

2 Do you practice a reasonable measure of self-discipline in getting your work done or meeting responsibilities and obligations?

3 Do you live in the present and plan for the future, leaving the past behind, except insofar as you can profit by having learned from experience?

4 Can you support yourself financially?

5 Have you had the experience of earning your own money and living within a fixed budget?

6 Have you developed a degree of other-centeredness? Do you find it easy to fit in with, and meet, the ego needs of others?

7 How many strong prejudices do you have? (Prejudice relates to matters like being a good or a poor student, being liberal or conservative in attitudes, and to social standing, as well as to race, politics, religion, modes of dress, and many other matters.) Do you have fewer than, more than, or about the same number of strong prejudices as you had five years ago?

1  Can you look at your family background and assess its contribution to your attitudes, views, and feelings about marriage?

2  Have your experiences with love and affection enabled you to grow in your understanding of love?

3  Do you see sex in marriage as a desirable and wholesome relationship designed to bring satisfaction and security to both partners?

4  Have you become emotionally weaned from your parents so that your spouse will have little reason to feel that you are too dependent on them?

5  Have you matured sufficiently to be able to think first of your responsibilities to others and sacrifice your personal needs when necessary?

## REVIEW QUESTIONS

1  Why is it difficult to isolate the age factor in determining success in marriage?

2  Define emotional maturity.

3  Why is objectivity important in developing maturity?

4  What is a mature conception of marriage?

5  How should the mature person view love? What may contribute to a person's ability to see love in this light?

6  Why is developing a philosophy of life a part of maturity?

7  How do mature people evaluate themselves and their family background?

8  What are some of the understandings the mature person has of human motivations?

9  Why do some people have difficulty in developing mature attitudes and feelings about sex?

10  Maturing people can assess their own maturity. Discuss.

11  Cite factors other than age that may explain the greater failure of youthful marriages.

12  Is there evidence to support the view that, as people grow older, they get "set" in their ways and cannot adjust in marriage?

## PROJECTS AND ACTIVITIES

1  Analyze your own emotional maturity. Then prepare two lists, one giving the ways in which you are quite mature, the other giving ways in which you still need to mature.

2   *Role playing.* Two couples discuss their future marriage, one couple taking the part of two 18-year-olds and the other couple the part of two 23-year-olds. Each couple brings out attitudes to represent the maturity of the age group they represent.

# LOVE

One may believe that love will be a transforming experience, recognizable as unique, different from any other emotional experience or feeling in the past. Yet such a person may find himself or herself responding to another or to several others with feelings that are hard to identify, feelings that are related to childhood and yet new in that a sexual element is more consciously present now than in earlier relationships.

Feelings may include some of what one feels for a brother or a sister, some of what one feels for a parent, and much of the kind of unromantic, affectionate attachment that lifelong friends have for each other.

In our society a variety of definitions and meanings are related to the concept of love, so that a vast confusion exists on the subject. Our society has been called a "love-oriented" and a "marriage-oriented" society, in that people are under pressure (whether conscious or not) to fall in love or to be in love with someone. In some ways being in love is viewed as evidence of normality, a way of conforming to the expectations of society. Are these attitudes about the necessity and inevitability of love merely superficial norms that have developed in a romantically inclined society, norms fostered by television and magazines?

Evidence that more basic elements in human personality and experience are involved is available to the thoughtful person. The infant needs to have love as much as he or she needs to have shelter and food. Babies who are touched lovingly and often and talked to by their parents grow and develop more satisfactorily than babies deprived of the touch and sounds of love. Young children, adolescents, and adults have this same need. People of any age who know they are loved experience a validation of themselves, a confirmation by another person of a satisfactory self-image, and like babies, need also the touch and the sounds of love.

This chapter is concerned with love that occurs between people who have reached the age for making lasting relationships outside their family of origin. People are often misled into becoming committed to relationships intended to be permanent because they fall in love with someone who seems to meet their needs, or who meets some needs for a time, but with whom an enduring relationship is not possible.

## BEGINNINGS OF LOVE

The beginning of love is response of one person to another person who gives acceptance, admiration, or respect, who reflects to the individual an image of oneself as one would like to be or hopes that one is. "This person finds me attractive, so I can believe that I am attractive," or "This person likes the same things I like—agrees with the way I feel about things, so my preferences and feelings are verified." One responds to this acceptance and agreement and approval with feelings of greater self-esteem, which are in turn reflected back to the other. So needs of both begin to be met. They begin to feel one level or one version of love. As they fall in love, they need physical closeness also, and sexual attraction and response contribute to their developing relationship.

Such love relationships are important in the experience of young people as they seek and test their own identity. The love serves a valuable purpose whether or not it leads to a permanent commitment such as marriage. In truth, many first (or even second or third) loves should not lead to marriage; they serve their purpose although elements necessary for a lasting love relationship may be lacking. How can young people assess a love? How can they be confident it could endure through the future in marriage? It may be useful to consider some of the things that love is not.

## SOME MISCONCEPTIONS OF LOVE

Love is not a one-sided attachment that reaches out with desire or frustration toward another person who does not share or respond. A love that clutches and clings and attempts to control the object of the emotion is not love as much as it is the expression of neurotic needs and pressures. People who have developed some measure of self-acceptance can more readily give acceptance and respect to another person. They have less need to cling in fear of losing the other's love, and far less need to control or dominate a loved one. If one dominates, demands, and requires, while the other does most of the giving, adjusting, and acquiescing, the relationship may meet some of the neurotic needs of one or even of both but this is a misconception of love.

Love is not an overwhelming, sudden emotional experience. It is not easily and quickly recognizable as unique, because a developing love includes so many familiar elements of experience. It grows out of the character and personality each has developed through life experiences thus far.

A love that can endure in marriage is not a violent and unpredictable emotion. It is not a paralyzing or disorganizing compulsion that holds two people together.

It is not exclusively sexual. Because sexual attraction and response provide an important element in most loves and in individual needs, one's assessment of a friendship or a relationship may be distorted by the sexual aspect so that one is confused about the extent to which other elements in the relationship are important.

How, then, can love be recognized? Above all, how can we know whether the feelings and responses that we interpret as love are the kind of love that will grow and last for a lifetime in marriage?

A young man said, after four years of marriage, "I wonder sometimes how Carol and I ever happened to get married at all, because the way we feel about each other now is so far beyond what we felt for each other when we were married. We have grown close to each other. We think together; where we differ, we can talk over our differences. We seem to have more need to understand each other than to win in our differences. As I look back it seems that the basis for our marriage had only the smallest beginning of a love."

The kind of love experience that can be the basis for an enduring lifetime relationship includes some specific components. The thoughtful person looking forward to a permanent commitment to the loved one can consider these factors and assess the potential durability of a relationship. In our culture, one must, in order to assess a love realistically, disregard or deny much of the kind of "love propaganda" to which all young people are exposed in movies, magazines, television, and commercial advertisements of products. All these media present definitions of love that are distorted and misleading.

## LOVE: MOTIVATION TOWARD COOPERATION

When two people love each other, they have a motivation that enables them to cope with problems and potential frustrations of living in partnership rather than as completely independent individuals. They are motivated to work at the cooperation that is an essential part of love.

The motivation to cooperate is strong in lovers for several reasons. The relationship with the loved one is a chosen relationship, chosen because the two find each other attractive and meet at least some of each other's needs. In this way it is different from love relationships with members of one's own family, which are thrust upon one without choice. When a person has chosen another and has committed himself to loving the chosen one, there is a strong urge to prove the rightness of the choice, to "make it work," even if doing so requires adjustment and cooperation that might be withheld or unwillingly given in other relationships. The rightness of one's own perceptions and judgments is at stake.

Perhaps a stronger motivation toward cooperation and adjustability is based on the fact that the love relationship brings security and reassurance to the individual. One feels deeply, whether consciously or not, that the emotional support that comes as a result of loving and being loved is worth working for and, if necessary, sacrificing to maintain. The emotionally healthy person becomes willing to adjust and change when necessary for the sake of such a cooperative relationship.

Cooperative adjustment may be lacking in relationships that are based on neurotic needs of one, and that do not have a potential for meeting enough of the needs of both to be permanent. In the neurotically based relationship, compliance is likely to be required, rather than cooperation offered: "If you love me, you will do what I want," and its counterpart, "If you loved me, you wouldn't ask anything of me." These attitudes mean in reality, "I can think *only* of my own wants and needs, and I'll use love as a means of coercion."

## COMPANIONSHIP AS A PART OF LOVE

In a love that is adequate for a lifetime of marriage, for the two to be congenial friends is more important than any other part of their relationship. This does not mean that they both have to like to fish or climb mountains or dance, or read the same books, although, if they like doing the same things, their friendship-love will be more rewarding. But it is essential that they share feelings about some values that matter most to them both. Based on their research, Burgess and Locke made the point that sharing in intellectual, religious, artistic, or altruistic interests means more to a relationship than a sharing in matters such as athletic interests or other general activities that might involve a smaller part of the whole personality.

A man and a woman who love each other should be friends in the same sense that any two people of the same sex are friends. This means they enjoy each other's company because of genuine congeniality, aside from sexual interest; they want to confide in each other, to talk things over, and to share amusement, ideas, disappointment, or grief. They tend to see life through each other's eyes. They are at ease and comfortable with each other, as are good friends.

Two people who are not at ease and comfortable with each other do not remain close friends. They seek other, more congenial company. But, because of mistaken ideas about what love is like, and also because sexual impulses may be a strongly operating force at the time, a couple who have no basis for companionable friendship may believe themselves to be in love, and marry. Many such couples do make lasting marriages. They work out some kind of adjustment that enables them to make a home and rear children. But missing from their relationship are some of the elements that could add joy and confidence to a relationship heavily weighted with duty and obligation. Certainly, duty and obligation have a place in any sustained relationship, but when love is based firmly in companionable friendship, such words have a different meaning.

## LOVE AT FIRST SIGHT

If love needs time to grow, if it grows upon cooperation and companionship, then what about "love at first sight"?

Of his lifelong love a man said:

> I fell in love at sight when I was 17. I dated other girls, even had other romances, but five years after I met her, and after we'd gone through college together, I married my first-sight love. Now, after 30 years of being married to her, the magic is still there. I think I kept my eyes open during our school years together. If I had found that my heart had fooled me about her, I would have fought off the spell, because above all I wanted a good marriage. But I was lucky. She turned out to be all that I dreamed she was the day I met her.

Another first-sight love:

> I fell in love at sight with a man I met last month on a bus. We're planning to be married soon but my parents are terribly opposed. They object to his age and they say I don't know anything about him or his past or future. I say that the instant he spoke to me I knew I loved him, and that's enough.

An objective outsider would recognize at once that the latter love has little chance to eventuate in the kind of successful marriage that grew out of the at-sight response in the first case. What was different about the two affairs, and what was similar? Were they both "love at first sight"?

Both included the one element that characterizes love at first sight: an immediate, strong attraction to another person. In some cases, this attraction may be almost entirely physical. Perhaps in the case of the girl and the man on the bus, the tone of his voice or the look in his eyes when he spoke to her evoked a response that was more intense than she had ever before experienced. In some such affairs, the attraction is mutual; both are aware almost from the moment of their meeting of a response to each other that exerts a compulsive pull toward physical intimacy.

In other cases, the immediate attraction may arise more predominantly from the fact that the two see in each other's appearance or manner, or in the circumstances under which they meet, the "ideal" they have been looking for in a mate. Chance may bring about their meeting at a moment in their lives when both are in an attitude of openness and readiness to embrace the embodied "ideal." This second factor, perhaps, operates in at-sight affairs more often than specific sexual attraction does.

What brings people to the point of emotional readiness to fall in love at sight is an interesting question. Sometimes there is a particular need at the moment to escape from certain problems in the circumstances of life or in one's own emotional life. Emotional or material complications may exert a strong pressure toward sudden falling in love. David Rioch, a psychiatrist, says that among his clients have been a number of people who fall suddenly in love when confronted with a crisis in life or with the necessity for making a major choice or decision. To quote him,

> When the time comes that one must "go on to the next thing" such as at the end of the college years or after the death of a parent or loved one, love offers an out that is not publicly disapproved; rather it is an out that society even approves and looks upon with sentimental fondness.[1]

At such a time, two people meet. It makes little difference whether the immediate mutual attraction is chiefly physical or whether it is a response to a conception of an ideal. In either event, the resulting flare-up is what is known as love at first sight. The urge is strong to make fast the bonds without delay. If such a couple marries at once, their marriage might accidentally be a compatible union. It has about the same chance for success as any other unpremeditated, wild plunge has for producing a happy outcome. But some couples so attracted to each other proceed cautiously and become well acquainted. They take time to discover each other's attitudes, beliefs, habits, and tastes. Some such couples scarcely know at what point in their association they pass the phase of rather superficial attraction and progress into a relationship enriched by the other elements necessary to real love. All their lives they may be staunch believers in love at first sight, because that is the way it seemed to happen to them. If, on becoming better acquainted with each other, they had discovered no sound basis of congeniality, the early attraction would have had little chance to survive.

The cases of love at first sight that do not end in happy marriage are probably far more numerous than those that do. They receive less attention, however, for when the affair turns out to be a passing thing, those involved forget that it was "love" and relegate it to its place with other short-lived infatuations.

## A LASTING LOVE: IN SUMMARY

Emotional change goes on throughout life. One either grows toward greater acceptance of self and of others or emotional deterioration may occur. Therefore, the men and women who love and are loved and accepted by another person can live and function in other relationships more effectively. They are freer to be themselves without defensiveness,

[1] David Rioch, director, Division of Neuro-Psychiatry, Walter Reed Medical Center. (Gimbel Lectures, Stanford Medical School, April 1957.)

can worry less about protecting their ego from hurt. They can be more outgoing and confident in relationships.

These emotional effects of love mean that people who love and are loved are not completely absorbed with love; they are more fully functioning personalities in all aspects of life. The all-absorbing "love" that puts people so completely in the clouds that they fail to make grades in school or lose their jobs lacks some of the essential ingredients love should have. Love promotes growth and increases awareness of meanings, needs, and opportunities in the world; it does not make people less effective or fully functioning.

To say that love means adjustability and cooperation is not to imply that if two people are truly in love all will be sweetness and agreement in every circumstance. Two people remain two individuals, with their personal faults and inclinations, no matter how much in love they are. But the motivations that function in the love relationship mean that, even under the pressure of difficult circumstances, the basic attitude toward each other is supportive rather than destructive. They can be generous in judging each other, can think the best instead of the worst. In short, they have a basis for getting together when there are differences. Their relationship can survive their individual peculiarities, even though these may cause some friction. That is to say, love is not necessarily blind. Rather, love that can survive the shocks and shifting requirements of a lifetime of two people together is not blind at all. It sees clearly, but can judge kindly and give acceptance and understanding instead of the unrelieved condemnation that might come, even justifiably, from others. Two who love each other may desire and enjoy the closest physical intimacy; a good relationship in sex enhances their association in other phases of living. It may hold a relatively small place in some loves—in others, a large place. Love depends for permanent survival on the knowledge and understanding two have of each other, their acceptance of each other as worth loving, their shared values and purposes, their respect for each other, and the trust and confidence that grows out of the total relationship that has been built between them.

## SOME QUESTIONS TO THINK ABOUT
## IN ORDER TO EVALUATE A LOVE

1 Are you comfortable and at ease with him or her? Able to be yourself without strain?

2 Since you have been in love, are you more inclined to live up to your best conception of yourself and your abilities?

3 Are you conscious of a continuing stable bond between the two of you, even when you have no feeling of love?

4 Does this person matter greatly to you, regardless of emotion or lack of emotion at the moment?

**5** Would you love him or her just as much even if the other were sick instead of well, or even if his or her physical appearance should be marred or disfigured?

**6** Is he or she physically attractive to you, so that you have no inclination to apologize or feel defensive about the other's physical characteristics?

**7** Are you proud to be seen together?

**8** How well do you agree on the things worth sacrificing for in life?

**9** Can you talk over points of disagreement and reach an understanding? (Have you known each other long enough and well enough so that you have discovered your inevitable points of disagreement?)

**10** Do your disagreements result in a better understanding of each other? (When disagreements result in tabling and blocking off the issue, or in the same one's always giving in, that is a danger signal.)

**11** Do you have confidence in his or her judgment? Do you respect his or her general mental ability?

**12** Do you confide in this person freely, with complete confidence that what you say will be understood, judged kindly, and never carelessly divulged no matter what the temptation?

**13** Are you happy and satisfied with the way he or she shows affection for you?

**14** As you look toward the future as realistically as you can, do you feel that the two of you have in your relationship the elements that will enable you to cooperate and if necessary sacrifice for your continuing union?

## REVIEW QUESTIONS

**1** What are some mistaken conceptions of love?

**2** How does love contribute to a positive self-image?

**3** How does love motivate people to cooperate?

**4** What basic needs fulfilled by love make it possible for those who love and are loved to be more fully functioning in their other associations?

**5** If two people love each other, will there ever be times when they disagree? Quarrel? Have emotional explosions? Ridicule each other?

**6** How important is companionship in love?

**7** What are some of the situations that may predispose an individual toward falling in love at sight?

**8** Do first-sight attractions usually end in successful marriage? Explain.

**9** What is meant by the statement that love is an ability or a capacity in the person who loves?

## PROJECTS AND ACTIVITIES

**1** From different sources, find as many definitions of love as you can and bring them to class. For a beginning see Burgess and Locke, *The Family* (New York: American Book Company, 1960), pp. 315–43.

2   Make a study of love stories in current magazines or in movies. In how many of the cases was it "love at first sight"? Evaluate the fictional loves on the basis of the concepts in this chapter.

# MARRIAGE UNDER
# SPECIAL CIRCUMSTANCES

According to the traditional American stereotype, two young people grow up, finish their education; the man gets a job so he can begin to support a family; they marry and spend the rest of their lives together. But today fewer and fewer marriages conform to this stereotype. Cultural changes in our society, inability to get jobs, and educational requirements that affect the marriage plans of a great many couples, mean that large numbers of marriages are made under special circumstances. These may require special adjustability if they are to be successful. People need to recognize what some of the problems are and to consider their ability to cope with them.

## MARRIAGE WHILE IN COLLEGE

Many students now in college are deciding whether to marry immediately or to postpone marriage until their education is completed. Before World War II, marriage while in college was rare. Student marriages were generally disapproved by parents and college administrators. Some colleges automatically dropped students who married before graduation. World War II and the Korean and Vietnam conflicts changed that situation. When men returned from service, they married and had children and yet continued their education.

College administrators came to see advantages in having married students on campus, and several studies made in midwestern colleges revealed that married students in the studies were making better grades than single students. Our study of 3000 students in 11 colleges showed that men who were married as college students had, when they were in high school, made lower grade averages than had men who were single as college students. But married men were making better grades in college than were single men. Married women students had, in high school, made about the same grade averages as women who were single in college, but married women were making much better grades in college than were single women. We analyzed grade averages by comparing grades made by married and single women of the same ages: 22 and under, 23 to 25, and 26 and over. In all age groups, married women had made higher grade averages than single women. Grade averages were higher with advancing age for both married and single women, but the married consistently made better grades. Grade averages for married men of 23 and older were higher than for single men, but married men of 22 and under had done no better than had single men of the same ages.

A possible explanation for the better achievement of older married men is that the settled life of marriage, with a decrease in outside social activities requiring time and energy, may favorably affect achievement. Married students may also have more clearly defined educational goals than they might have had as single students, and hence greater motivation to achieve.

For some years people believed that the tendency to marry while in college was a temporary wartime phenomenon. College administrators took temporary measures to house the married students. On some campuses today, married students are still living in the old "temporary" structures, which are substandard housing after many years of use. Most universities have built modern housing units for married students. Such housing areas provide nursery and grammar schools for the children of students.

Getting married while in college has continued, but with the current trend toward delayed marriage, the percentage of married undergraduates will doubtless decrease. In the United States, in 1960, 28 percent of women in the age group of 20 to 24 were single, but by 1975, 40 percent of this age group were single. This tendency for people to delay marriage until older was probably brought about by the economic recession, the fact that more women attend college, and newer attitudes about marrying young. A large percentage of graduate students will be married since they are in an older age group.

## SUCCESS OF COLLEGE MARRIAGES

Through the years several studies have asked married students the question, "Knowing what you now know, would you marry before finishing college?" Three-fourths of the couples have said they would marry while in college if they had it to do over again.[1, 2, 3] Those who said they would not or who were not certain whether they would, gave reasons such as difficulties in earning a living as married students, in finding housing, and in doing satisfactory college work. Although these are the reasons most often given, other findings suggest that the real reasons may have been deeper. Many of those who doubted the wisdom of their college marriages expressed dissatisfaction with their marriages for other reasons. If they had waited until after college to marry, they might not have married each other at all.

It is difficult to get accurate information on the success of student marriages. However, what evidence is available seems to indicate that the majority of married students make a better than average success of their marriages. For both to be students, being involved in studies and in campus life during the early months of their marriage may give them some advantages over couples who marry later when each is in a different work world, or when one is in a job or profession and the other a homemaker.

## SOME CONSIDERATIONS IN COLLEGE MARRIAGES

In one of our studies of college marriages, the students listed some advantages they valued in college marriages, most of them being related to the emotional security that marriage may provide. Many of the men felt that being married as a student gave their lives greater stability, made them more purposeful, and made it easier for them to settle down to work. This feeling of stability and purposefulness might be expected to be reflected in higher grade averages for married students.

Many factors important in contributing to success in marriage are about the same whether people marry in college or after college. But additional problems arise in college marriages that are not necessarily present in other marriages.

**Willingness to give up life of a single student.** Most young people enjoy the social side of college life. In the process of mingling in groups and enjoying college social life, they may find one person whom they want to marry, but they still may not be ready to sacrifice their other activities for marriage. These students are not ready to settle down to marriage even if they are in love. The person who is not ready to give up single

[1] Judson T. Landis, "On the Campus," *Survey Midmonthly* 84:1 (January 1948), 17–19.

[2] Harold T. Christensen and Robert E. Philbrick, "Family Size as a Factor in the Marital Adjustment of College Students," *American Sociological Review* 17:3 (June 1952), 306–12.

[3] Ross Eshleman and Chester L. Hunt, "Social Class Influences on Family Adjustment Patterns of Married College Students," *Journal of Marriage and the Family* 29:3 (August 1967), 485–91.

habits is not ready for marriage, whether he or she is in or out of college.

**Readiness for parenthood.**   Probably most couples who marry in college plan to postpone having children. It would seem, then, in view of today's contraceptive knowledge, that there need be no thought about the possibility of an unplanned pregnancy's interrupting educational plans. But, for reasons not completely clear, unplanned pregnancies continue to occur among married students, as well as among other groups in the population. A wide variation exists in attitudes toward and knowledge about reliable contraceptive measures. Some student couples whose plans for staying in school depend on postponing parenthood until after graduation have inadequate knowledge and insufficient understanding of conception control; they believe methods to be reliable that are not.

Whatever the explanation for the continuing unplanned pregnancies even among people who do want to plan their families, students who marry must consider the possibility that marriage may mean parenthood. They should assess their readiness to cope with what parenthood would mean to them at this time.

To become parents, planned or unplanned, at any time, but especially while still in school, involves an entirely new level of responsibility and potential strain. Being parents is not an easily handled extracurricular activity. The subject of contraception will be discussed further in a later chapter.

**Willingness of both to work and cooperate.**   When both husband and wife are attending classes and perhaps working part-time, or when one is in school and the other working, they find it necessary to organize their activities with great efficiency. If, in addition, there is a child to care for, couples need to be supermen and superwomen in order to meet all their responsibilities adequately. The success of college marriages means that many young couples are adequate for these requirements. But a man or boy who expects to be waited on, who considers it unmasculine to do dishes, scrub floors, or diaper babies, is likely to be a problem husband in a college marriage. And a girl who wants to be free from hard work and struggle, and who cannot be happy if she has to miss some areas of college life, should not marry while she is still in college. For even if there is plenty of money and there are no babies, working at marriage while both are students requires unselfish cooperation and some sacrifice of personal preferences.

**Present income and parental support.**   During the fifties and sixties a great many married students were able to earn their living by holding part-time jobs, without having to depend on their parents. In the 1970s jobs are far more scarce and inflation has increased the cost of food, rent, and tuition. Most students now must look to parents or other sources for financial help if they are to remain in school.

Students who are considering marriage often reason that since their parents support them during college when they are single, why should they not continue to support them if they marry while in school? If they can afford it, they would like to continue the financial backing so their children may finish their education. But they recognize that certain problems may arise if they continue to support their married children even though the children are still students. Few parents can look upon their children as independent married adults as long as they are contributing a major part of the children's support. The situation is more complicated because money contributed is for the use of the child-in-law as well as their own child. In-law friction may easily arise. In our study of 3189 students in 18 schools, more than 80 percent of both men and women said they thought the girl who married as a student should continue in school, but only a third of the men and a fourth of the women thought the parents ought to continue to support a married daughter. However, half the men and a third of the women thought their parents *would* continue support through school if they married. Possibly these attitudes have not changed today, but the practical facts are that inflation and the high costs of an education make it more difficult for parents to help significantly with their children's support.

Some young people are willing to accept the parental support, but they are not willing to accept any "interference" that may come with it. If there is to be parental subsidy, parents and children need to be objective about the situation. Otherwise misunderstandings may bring disillusionment and disappointment to parents and unhappiness to children. Some married students who try to face problems realistically feel that they must earn their own way after they marry. Whether parents will support their married children in school is likely to be determined in part by their approval or disapproval of the marriage as well as by their financial position. Parents who approve their daughter's marriage to the man she chooses may reason that it remains their responsibility to pay for her education; that a young husband who is a student is doing enough if he can help to support his wife and should not be expected also to pay for her education.

A review of research findings on the subject of parental financial support for married children points to the conclusion that such aid is becoming more general in all social classes in our society, whether or not children are students. One study that examined and compared parental assistance among blue-collar workers and white-collar workers found that parental help is most extensive during the first few years of the children's marriage.[4] White-collar families give more help for a longer period of time, probably not only because they may have more financial resources but also because of their children's longer educational requirements and

[4] Bert N. Adams, "Structural Factors Affecting Parental Aid to Married Children," *Journal of Marriage and the Family* 26:3 (August 1964), 327–31.

delayed readiness to earn incomes. The help given by middle-class parents is usually financial; the help given by working-class parents is more likely to take other forms, such as child care. In both classes of families the wives' parents tend to do more for the young married couple than do the husbands' parents. After an analysis of research studies, Sussman and Burchinal concluded that changes may be occurring in the family system toward a weakening of the financial autonomy of the nuclear family unit.[5] Evidence suggests some blurring of the distinct lines formerly drawn between "yours" and "ours" after children marry.

With or without parental financial help the majority of student couples agree that, if they marry in college, both must do all they can to help with their own support. If only the husband is a student, the wife usually works; if both are students, both hold part-time jobs if possible. Many students solve the problem by waiting to marry until at least one of them is within a year of graduation, since financial arrangements are far easier to make for one year than for three or four.

The precedent has been set, and young people will continue to marry while in college. The more general acceptance of the fact that married women will continue to work outside the home, widespread confidence in contraception, and a gradual change in attitudes of parents toward supporting sons or daughters after marriage—these factors will help to establish the custom of college marriages.

Nevertheless, those who are considering such marriages are realistic if they recognize that they face certain alternatives that do not usually confront couples who wait to marry until after their education is complete. If they want to live independent of outside financial help, they will have to work harder than will couples who marry later. If, on the other hand, they marry expecting help from parents or others, they will, during their college years, be in something of an interim stage—no longer dependent children, but not yet independent adults. They also need to face the fact that *both* should be willing to work at household tasks and to care for children that may come.

## FOR MARRIED STUDENTS THE FUTURE IS NOW

Sometimes married students sacrifice too much of the present for what they think of as the future. They may put too much of their effort into the life they hope to have after their education is finished and they can begin to make their own living. They think of their present arrangement —in which one of them works to support them both, or in which both work in order to remain in school—as an interim. Some such couples work so hard that they have little time or energy to enjoy life together or to

---

[5] Marvin B. Sussman and Lee Burchinal, "Parental Aid to Married Children: Implications for Family Functioning," *Marriage and Family Living* 24:4 (November 1962), 320–32.

appreciate fully the positive values in their present life as a married couple. The first years of marriage are very important in establishing patterns of response and habits of mutual enjoyment in a relationship. Too great a sacrifice can be made in order to keep on schedule toward a planned future. Some couples who decide to marry while in college and undertake the additional responsibilities that come with marriage may need to be willing to take longer to finish their education. If both must work, they might choose to think in terms of five years rather than four for getting the college degree, and in terms of spreading the graduate work over more years. Such a plan may involve less strain and allow more time for living and building satisfying relationships without any sacrifice of permanent goals.

People contemplating a college marriage, like those contemplating any marriage, must have perspective on life as a whole and a realistic conception of what is a successful marriage. If they are willing to begin at once to work at building together the kind of cooperation and mutual support that is necessary for a good marriage, they can cope with whatever special problems are involved in marriage while in college.

## MARRYING A DIVORCED PERSON

With the present divorce rates, approximately one-fourth of all marriages involve one member who has been married before. An analysis of re-marriage in the United States reveals that the divorced have a tendency to marry others who have been divorced.[6] However, many people marrying for the first time marry divorced people. Are there special problems in marriages of this type? How may a previous divorce affect a second marriage?

> A young woman went to a marriage counselor for what she considered to be a routine premarital consultation. She told the counselor happily about her wedding plans and asked for any advice he might offer to help her make a good beginning in marriage. Incidentally, she mentioned that her mother had not yet been told of her plans because it was something of a problem to know how to break the news that her fiancé had only recently been divorced. There had never been a divorce in her family and she felt that her mother might be prejudiced and doubtful about her marrying a divorced person. The girl said to the counselor, "I feel that my future husband's having been divorced is not important as far as our happiness is concerned. All that is in the past. It was not his fault, and it would be ridiculous to attach any importance to whether or not a person has been married before."

This view is not unusual. Nevertheless, marriage to a divorced person does include special factors that differentiate such marriages from mar-

[6] *Socio-economic Characteristics of Persons Who Married Between January 1947 and June 1954: United States,* U.S. Department of Health, Education and Welfare, Vital Statistics—Special Reports 45:12 (9 September 1957), 286.

riages that are the first for both partners. These marriages differ in the following ways.

**Attitudes toward second marriages.** Public custom is to smile with approval upon "first" marriages. The wedding is acknowledged, approved, supported, and celebrated with an enthusiasm that is not always given when one partner has been married and divorced. The difference may be slight, but even if there is no active disapproval, many of the couple's friends may assume an attitude of watchful waiting to see how it turns out. This is in contrast to the attitude of optimistic acceptance that is usually given to the first wedding for both.

A study done some years ago showed clear differences between attitudes toward a first and a second marriage [7] (Table 9-1). The greatest difference was when both had been previously married. For example, if neither had been married before, 81 percent were given showers by friends; if both had been married before, only 32 percent were given showers. If the wife had been married before, the pattern of activities connected with the wedding was similar to that when both had been married before. However, if only the husband had been married before, the wedding activities approached those in which neither had been married. This difference in the way friends and family respond to first and second weddings continues today. Regardless of the general acceptance of divorce, friends and families seem to give unrestrained support and celebration only to the first wedding.

In our study of marriage among 581 former college students, there were 39 couples in which one or both had had a previous marriage.

TABLE 9-1    Varying pattern of wedding activities according to previous marital status of spouses *

|  | Both first marriage | Wife first, husband before | Husband first, wife before | Both married before |
|---|---|---|---|---|
| Engaged | 89.0% | 74.0% | 69.0% | 54.0% |
| Engagement ring | 84.0 | 64.0 | 60.0 | 43.0 |
| Shower | 81.0 | 57.0 | 27.0 | 32.0 |
| Formal wedding | 70.0 | 29.0 | 25.0 | 6.0 |
| Church wedding | 81.0 | 45.0 | 23.0 | 25.0 |
| Bride's family paid for wedding | 46.0 | 23.0 | 15.0 | 3.0 |
| Reception | 88.0 | 79.0 | 52.0 | 45.0 |
| Wedding trip | 95.0 | 79.0 | 76.0 | 62.0 |

* Hollingshead, "Marital Status and Wedding Behavior."

[7] August B. Hollingshead "Marital Status and Wedding Behavior," *Marriage and Family Living* 14:4 (November 1952), 308–11.

Table 9-2 summarizes some differences between the approaches to marriage by the couples in first and in second marriages. A comparison of courtship behavior of the two groups shows that those without previous marriages and divorces had a courtship pattern that has been found to be predictive of success in marriage. Their pattern was significantly different from the approach to marriage by the group with previous marriage and divorce in their backgrounds. Of the divorced and remarried group, a larger percentage had no formal engagement. If there had been an engagement, it had been of shorter duration. Their marriage had had less parental approval and they had shown that they themselves had had less confidence that their marriage would work.

Almost half of divorced people remarry very soon, within a year after their divorce. Some who divorce do so to marry another with whom they have become involved before they ended their first marriage. The question arises for many as to whether the remarrying is a rebound reaction or whether the remarriage is a form of adjustment to the trauma of the marriage failure. The person marrying someone recently divorced should be aware that the divorced person may be marrying quickly for the wrong reasons.

**Families have doubts.** Family doubts or outright opposition, which must be reckoned with in the success or failure of any marriage, are more likely to exist when one partner has been divorced. The family of the one with no previous marital record is likely to view the marriage with

**TABLE 9-2**  The approach to marriage, as reported by 581 couples, 542 couples married for the first time and 39 couples in which one or both had been married before

| Approach to marriage | First marriages (N–542) | Second marriages* (N–39) |
|---|---|---|
| Had informal engagement | 88% | 62% |
| Length of engagement— | | |
| 0–2 months | 12 | 33 |
| 1 or more years | 21 | 8 |
| Parental approval of marriage | | |
| Both approved | 90 | 77 |
| Confident marriage would be happy | | |
| Very confident | 58 | 51 |
| Premarital intercourse with someone other than spouse— | | |
| Men—none | 58 | 33 |
| Women—none | 83 | 50 |
| Premarital intercourse with spouse | 35 | 75 |

* It was a second marriage for 29 men and 16 women.

mingled hope and fear for the future, whether or not the fears are justified by the circumstances of the previous marriage.

The family of the divorced partner cannot help but make comparisons between the new spouse and the former one. Is the new choice better or worse? Views will vary, depending on family attitudes toward the circumstances of the first marriage and divorce. Consequently, the first marriage and divorce are facts of life that will enter into in-law relationships and associations with friends, even when the married pair sincerely believe that "all that is past."

**If there are children.** In addition to factors related to family and social attitudes, many second marriages involve children from the previous marriage. Marriage to a divorced person with children makes it necessary for the second mate to adjust to emotionally difficult circumstances. Some people find it very difficult to accept situations that arise if husband or wife has visitation rights with children in custody of the former mate. To know that the spouse sees the former mate when visiting the children may arouse feelings that make trouble in a second marriage.

If the previously married mate has financial responsibilities for the children, another kind of adjustment is necessary. Financial pressure may be severe if the husband must pay alimony or child support. Few men can earn enough money to support two families adequately. Frequently it becomes necessary for a second wife to work to help support her family because of financial pressures arising from obligations her husband has to a first family.

The person who has not been married before needs to be thoughtfully aware of these situations and many more that inevitably exist in marriages involving children by a previous marriage.

**How much did the divorced person learn from marriage failure?** A significant point to be considered by the young person who contemplates marrying a divorced person is the attitude of the previously married one. If he or she feels sure that there was no personal blame in the marriage failure that occurred, there is good reason to question whether this person is a good partner for a second marriage. For marriage failure, like marriage success, is usually achieved by two working at it together. We have often wondered at the naiveté of young people who say, "I know he'll make a wonderful husband (or she'll make a wonderful wife). He (or she) had a rough time in the first marriage, but it was not his (or her) fault." The divorced person who has learned from experience and is able to recognize what personal mistakes contributed to the first marriage failure is far more likely to make a success of a second marriage. Many people do learn by bitter experience, not how to control the second mate better, but how to understand their own weaknesses and strengths, how to choose more wisely a second time, and how to work more effectively at building a successful marriage.

Among the people who make a success of a second marriage are those who have grown to greater maturity by the time they marry again or who have been able to learn from their mistakes, whether the mistakes were in the choice of a mate or in meeting problems. In the very unhappy group of those who fail a second time may be found those who could not accept their share of the responsibility for the first failure, but blamed the mate for all problems. When they make a later marriage they will expect the next mate to make up for all their early troubles; they will set impossible standards for the mate and none for themselves. A young person considering marriage with a person previously married and divorced should ask above all, "What has the person learned that might have helped in the first marriage, and that would help make a better marriage for us?" A previous marriage is a fact of life to be lived with.

## MARRIAGES INVOLVING SEPARATION

There are two types of separation which may occur in marriage. One may take place for a short period in early marriage. It may be necessary to attend different colleges or to accept jobs in separate communities or for one to accept a job elsewhere to support the other while the spouse completes professional training. The second type may be on a regularly recurring basis throughout marriage. Such a separation is associated with the jobs held by certain people: those who make the military, especially the navy, a career; airline pilots and personnel who are frequently away from home for several days at a time; salespersons who are required to travel as a part of their job; and those in government who live away from home perhaps because it seems best to keep an established residence for the family. We will discuss some of the implications for both types of separation and adjustment in marriage.

Many couples who are in love or engaged and who face temporary separation because of some unavoidable circumstance naturally feel impelled to win some measure of security by marrying quickly in order to ensure their future together, even though for the present they must be apart.

Some good relationships cannot survive a separation of more than brief duration. In other cases, a separation may help one or both to become more objective about a relationship that would have had little chance of being permanently satisfactory if it had survived; thus, the separation serves to break up a potentially disastrous relationship. Clearly, it is better in such cases if the separation occurs before rather than after the wedding.

People who are thinking of getting married and know that they will have to be separated for periods of time face unusual problems. There are many women who could not tolerate the loneliness of being stationed at a military base while their husbands were on duty away from home for months at a time. The couple planning marriage with the prospects of long separations should consider realistically how sexual needs will be met. Are they liberated enough that they can accept how each spouse may need to find sexual satisfaction while they are separated? Do they agree on what their behavior will be? Are they in agreement that both or possibly just one of them can be faithful during separations, recognizing that temptations and sexual needs will be strong?

**Postponing adjustments.**   In cases where separation must occur soon after marriage, the adjustments that must inevitably be made in learning to live with each other are postponed. Time passes; a couple may be married months or more without having had the opportunity or the necessity to make adjustments that are usually made soon after the wedding. Usually when a married couple are together during the first year of marriage they go almost everywhere together. They try to please each other in every way possible. In the process they tend to grow closer together in their habits and their ways of reacting to situations. They may never again have quite so strong an urge to work at giving their marriage a good start. With couples who undergo early separation the situation is different. After their separation has ended and they come together to begin life as a married couple, they learn that the interim has not been a blank; both have continued to develop independently.

**Loneliness and the married feeling.**   Couples who have had to be separated soon after marrying sometimes say that they have never got to "feeling married." Therefore, while they are apart they are tempted to date others just as if they were in fact unmarried. The temptations may be increased by the loneliness arising from the separation. Many people cannot endure the strain of long-continued loneliness. They may have a need to associate with and possibly to date others. Yet if they do this, the two will inevitably be farther apart when they are reunited.

A reasonably long acquaintance is especially important before marriages that are to be followed by separation. Couples need time to get to know each other well and to be sure of their love for each other before they marry, so that when the natural doubts arise later during separation they will have the confidence to cope with the loneliness. Even when a marriage could be a potentially good one, if the acquaintance before marriage is short, there is not enough basis of understanding and confidence to tide the couple over the periods of loneliness and uncertainty that inevitably occur during separation.

**Age is a factor.**   The age of the young people is significant in these situations. All the handicaps that ordinarily exert pressure on marriages of the very young will be intensified by separation. The person who may have some reluctance to "settle down" and give up the pleasures of youthful freedom from responsibility will find the strain of being married and separated from the mate even more difficult.

**Alternatives, if marriage would involve separation.** Some couples want to marry before separation because they are afraid they will lose each other if they do not. Perhaps they really will lose each other if they postpone marriage. But would their love survive if they were married? The fact of a wedding ceremony will not necessarily insure the survival of an emotional attachment. If their love for each other and their habits of companionship are not well established, it might be safer for them to part as friends or as an engaged rather than as a married couple. Sometimes questionable behavior during a separation can be accepted and forgiven by an engaged couple, while it would be grounds for divorce if they were married. If they can survive an engagement apart, they have a better chance to make a success of marriage, once they are together. If they cannot survive such an engagement, less damage will have been done than if they had married and their separation had resulted in a broken marriage. Experiences of two couples show the alternatives:

> Bob and I became engaged at Christmas time, and in February he left for an on-the-job training period. We couldn't bear the thought of losing each other and we almost decided to marry then. It would have meant being apart for six months as a married couple instead of as an engaged couple, because he wouldn't be free to marry until August if we waited. I felt absolutely sure of our love for each other, and yet I kept wondering why I was afraid I would lose him if we waited to marry until after my graduation and his first few months were completed. I wondered if perhaps I really trusted him less than I thought. We had a hard time deciding, but at last he left and I stayed to finish the year and graduate in June. I have been so happy that we made this decision. We write to each other every day, and he phones me as often as he can. I miss him terribly, so much so that sometimes when he phones me I just can't think what I want to say and the conversation is not very satisfactory. But just the same I think that through our letters we have come to understand each other even better, and above all we now feel secure about our future relationship. The separation has not raised doubts in our minds but has made us able to decide that our wedding is worth waiting for. In the years after we are married I'll never wonder whether I would have lost him if we'd waited. I *know* we can be faithful to each other.

Another young woman said:

> I made the same decision you did. I wanted to graduate before we married so I let Tom go without me. We planned to be married a few months later. But we hadn't been apart two months before he was dating other girls. I was terribly upset at first, then I began to realize that another boy whom I sometimes studied with was more my type. I began going out with him, and now Tom and I have decided it would have been a mistake if we had married. It just didn't last when we were apart.

**Parenthood and separation.** Some couples go ahead and have a child, reasoning that while the wife is waiting out a necessary separation is a good time for a pregnancy and the baby's infancy. With other couples, an unplanned conception may occur early in the marriage preceding the separation. If a child is born when the parents are separated for much of the time, a special adjustment for all three—father, mother, and child —will be necessary later. At best, far greater effort must be made if all are not to be cheated of the privilege of growing to understand one another during the child's infancy. A husband's career that keeps him away from home much of the time causes him to become a "weekend father" who must fit into a family that has been organized without his presence. By necessity, the mother must make the day-to-day decisions for the children, and the father becomes an outsider who may or may not fit easily into the family circle.

**Reunion after a long separation.** Although every effort has been made to keep in touch with each other, most couples are not prepared for some of the readjustments that may come after they have been separated for some time. During the absence each may tend to build up an idealized picture of the other and of their relationship. During separation they do grow apart in some ways; instead of thinking together as one, they have been thinking as two independent individuals. Each may have some new ways or new ideas that may seem out of character to the other. They may have forgotten each other's annoying habits and mannerisms. When they are united, they must again face the realities of being just ordinary human beings with the usual faults and idiosyncrasies. For some it will take time to get back to their old basis of living as husband and wife. For those who had a hasty marriage following a short acquaintance, it may mean starting almost from the beginning of courtship and—for the first time—really getting to know each other.

Many people have had the experience of meeting a friend after a long absence. The two are happy to meet, they greet each other with enthusiasm, and then stand with nothing to say; an unexpected distance has developed with time and change. Married people sometimes have an experience similar to this when they get together after long separation.

For those with a firmly based relationship, the strangeness can be temporary and quite easily overcome. Most factors involved in relationships for married couples who are necessarily separated need not be crucial or damaging if the problems are understood and approached constructively. Knowing what some of the problems are likely to be and facing these situations together may prevent some unhappy occurrences.

The person who values the close type of relationship involving all family members would see danger signals in making a marriage where separation would be involved.

MARRIAGE UNDER SPECIAL CIRCUMSTANCES

Many young people will continue to go into military service or into groups such as the Peace Corps unmarried and without any serious attachment to someone back home. Some of them will reach the point of readiness to marry during the time that they are away from their accustomed associations. They are likely to find a person who seems to be a desirable mate among whatever group they are with at that time.

**Some points to consider.** Certainly, successful and happy marriages are made between couples who meet in situations far from home and different from their accustomed environments. The man who has given some thought to what he hopes for in his future marriage and who is aware of the relevance of background factors to marriage success can, if he becomes ready to marry, find a wife while away from home. But to avoid a hasty or unwise marriage, any young person should recognize some special considerations before becoming involved in serious courtship while far from his or her usual associations.

For one thing, the young man in military service is likely to feel more lonely at times than ever before, and so feel more urgently a need for companionship with women. Because of his own special needs, it may be particularly hard to be objective about the traits of the young women available.

The young woman who is working in a city away from home, or who is in the Peace Corps, in school abroad, or in any other situation similar to those in military service, will be confronted with like decisions. Generally, in the United States and in other countries, a wife is likely to enter the social class to which her husband and his family belong. Therefore, if she marries a man of a different social level or a different race or nationality, it is into his world that she may expect to move. It is less likely that he will move into hers. Can she make the adjustments that will be required? Will his people be able to accept her? Will he seem a different person to her—or she to him—when they see each other against the background to which each is accustomed?

## IN SUMMARY

The choice of whether to marry under any of the special circumstances discussed in this chapter confronts many college students today. Each person so confronted must consider the factors involved and the available alternatives. Many people can make a success of marriage even under the most difficult circumstances. Whether or not circumstances are difficult is less important than whether people are able to view the situation realistically and evaluate accurately their ability to cope with eventualities before making a lifetime decision.

## REVIEW QUESTIONS

1 What changes encouraged an increase in marriages among college students? Is marriage while in college increasing or decreasing?

2 What opinions do students express about their attitudes and their parents' attitudes concerning marrying while in college?

3 Give some of the advantages and disadvantages of college marriages.

4 Why would some couples hesitate to marry in college if they had it to do over again? What seems to underlie their doubts?

5 What special problems should couples consider if they plan to marry while in college?

6 How much does it cost a college couple to live today?

7 Should parents continue to support a son who marries while still a student? Should the parents of a girl continue her support after marriage? What opinion did students express on these questions?

8 What are college administrators now doing to provide for the needs of married students?

9 In what respects do second marriages differ from first marriages?

10 What did Hollingshead find in his study of ritual and ceremony accompanying first and second marriages?

11 What attitudes characterize those divorced persons most likely to make a success of second marriages? What attitudes characterize those likely to fail if they marry again?

12 What are some factors involved in separation during the early years of marriage?

13 Should a couple marry if there is danger that the separation ahead might result in their not marrying each other? Discuss.

14 What are some of the problems in marriages in which the husband's job takes him away from home weeks or months at a time?

15 Why is reunion after separation sometimes difficult?

16 What is meant by the term "marriage readiness"? Why may this apply to people in military service, the Peace Corps, or working away from home?

17 What are some specific points for one to consider before marrying while away from one's usual environment?

## PROJECTS AND ACTIVITIES

1 Collect figures on the cost of living from several married students and report to the class.

2 *Panel Discussion.* The married students in the class discuss the financial aspects of being married while in college.

3 *Role Playing.* Alice and Bill are juniors at the university. They have been supported by both sets of parents since marrying a year ago. Bill has planned to go on to graduate school. Alice has found that she is pregnant. *Scene.*

Alice is reading a letter from her parents in which they say that, since their agreement was to support Alice through college, they feel that if she must drop out of school on account of the baby, Bill should take over the responsibility for support.

# PREMARITAL SEXUAL RELATIONS

# 10

The past fifteen years have brought a change in the attitudes of people in our society on many social issues. All segments of society and all age groups are questioning and reexamining values, norms, and assumptions long accepted as valid. The Vietnam War, the worldwide population explosion, new discoveries in every area of scientific research, and a new awareness of inequalities and injustices inherent in our definitions of racial and sexual differences—all these things have given impetus to change. Basic questions are being raised about taboos, social standards, and mores regulating sexual behavior. Laws passed approximately a hundred years ago regulated every aspect of sexual behavior. Now they are being challenged, and many of them are being replaced by more appropriate ones based on changed definitions of normal and abnormal, moral and immoral.

In a time of rapid change it is not possible to predict accurately just what the ultimate value system will be. Predictions have been made regarding an end to all wars, families being limited to one child, a married priesthood, free abortions for all women desiring them, liberal drug-use laws, an end to all laws regarding sexual behavior of consenting adults, and the general acceptance of coitus from puberty on as social interaction.

A study of the history of this century, as well as of times past, raises serious doubts about at least some of those predictions. Lewis M. Terman studied the sexual behavior of people coming to adulthood between 1910 and 1930. He concluded that sexual standards had been changing in the 1920s so rapidly that by the 1950s all women would have coitus with the future spouse before marriage.[1] But all the research from the thirties to the sixties showed that actually there was little or no change in premarital

[1] Lewis M. Terman, *Psychological Factors in Marital Happiness* (New York: McGraw-Hill Book Company, Inc., 1938), p. 323.

sexual behavior during that period of time. Norms of behavior tend to move like a pendulum. Historically, after a time of freedom from restraints, people tend to perceive some unacceptable behavior accompanying the personal or moral freedom they have had and to move back toward greater restraint in behavior. Our discussion here is not so much concerned with making predictions for the future as with examining evidence available today that can be useful for college students as they think out their own policies and make their choices.

Research evidence suggests that a change in attitudes is occurring toward the value placed upon the virginity of women before marriage. That this change would now occur seems logical in view of some new developments. The present surge toward equality between men and women negates or raises serious questions about the double standard in sexual behavior. The development of the oral contraceptive, the ready legal availability of contraceptives, and the legalization of abortion all may certainly be expected to have some impact upon attitudes of girls and women toward coitus, both marital and premarital.

Some writers in the press picture all young people as having made a transition from old-fashioned morality to a new custom of having sexual intercourse with casual dates and acquaintances promiscuously. But such assumptions are not supported by research. A more accurate assessment is offered by researchers who describe the attitudinal and behavioral trend as in the direction of premarital permissiveness when there is affection plus commitment to a permanent relationship.

## CONFORMITY OR NONCONFORMITY TO MORAL CODES

Studies by Ehrmann at the University of Florida in the early fifties [2] and our study of 3000 students in 11 colleges and universities in 1952–1955 showed a high percentage (from 88 to 91 percent) of university women reporting that they had refrained from premarital sexual relations. Most past studies did not attempt to discover differences in conduct during different stages of dating and courtship. What evidence we have shows that virginity still remains high among people who have had no serious emotional commitments, and decreases as couples approach marriage.

Martin Luther and others of his time tended to emphasize the "I will marry you" as the important commitment, rather than the "I do," and thus, historically, sexual intercourse tended to be permissible after the engagement. In general, this point of view was not in the past accepted by the majority of people in our country. We have no way of knowing what actual behavior was during engagement in early America. In the colonial period, couples had less opportunity for sexual intercourse than they do now; yet even in those days every community had its subjects for gossip, and "shotgun" weddings seem to have been common enough to

[2] Winston W. Ehrmann, *Premarital Dating Behavior* (New York: Holt, Rinehart & Winston, Inc., 1959), p. 34.

PREMARITAL SEXUAL RELATIONS

have had a recognizable place in social custom. Some years ago, Burgess and Wallin, in their study of 1000 engaged couples, found that 46 percent of their sample had had sexual relations by the time of the wedding.[3]

Current research does not show a developing pattern of sexual promiscuity among college people today. Rather, the studies reveal a pattern of increasing physical intimacy among couples in serious relationships or as couples approach marriage, and sexual intercourse may be a part of this intimacy.

We have summarized patterns of premarital behavior among college people as reported by 3189 students in 18 colleges in 1967. Of the women and men who had never had a serious love relationship, well over 90 percent of the women and over 60 percent of the men were virgins. When premarital sexual behavior was analyzed by current dating status of the 2184 women, it was found that 15 percent of those not now dating had at some time had premarital sexual relations; the percentages for those now casually dating were 20 percent and for the engaged 44 percent. There were 1677 men and women who had had a serious love relationship that had been broken. The pattern of behavior at each stage of courtship among these is shown in Table 10-1.

When the pattern of sexual behavior among women was analyzed for the 18 different colleges, the pattern was found to be the same for all schools in that as commitment to marriage increased the percentage engaging in more intimate physical behavior increased. The percentage engaging in each type of behavior tended to be about the same in all courtship stages in the schools in all parts of the United States, with two exceptions: one state university and one church-affiliated school showed significantly fewer people engaging in coitus at each stage of courtship.

More than half the serious affairs reported upon had started when

**TABLE 10-1** Patterns of sexual behavior at each stage in relationships later broken, as reported by 1677 students in 18 colleges

| Stage of the relationship | Percentages reporting sexual relations | |
| --- | --- | --- |
| | Men | Women |
| During casual dating (524 men, 1153 women) | 4.0% | 1.0% |
| During steady dating (524 men, 1131 women) | 29.0 | 12.0 |
| During understanding engagement (240 men, 570 women) | 52.0 | 27.0 |
| During formal engagement (52 men, 93 women) | 48.0 | 45.0 |

[3] Ernest W. Burgess and Paul Wallin, *Engagement and Marriage* (Philadelphia: J. B. Lippincott Company, 1953), p. 331.

the people were 17 years old or younger. They seem to have been typical of the love relationships that begin between high school student couples and end either before high school graduation or after the couples separate to go to different colleges. Half the relationships had lasted from seven months to two years, and a fourth more had lasted two years or longer.

Some of the evidence suggests that permissiveness with serious commitment may tend to lead toward behavior bordering on promiscuity. Our studies show that a larger percentage of the women who had had two or more "understanding" engagements had had premarital sexual relationships than the women who had progressed through a single serious love relationship to formal engagement. The young woman who has defined sexual relations as within her moral code in one serious relationship has made this definition for herself and tends to follow the pattern in a second or third serious relationship.

A study of a national sample of 4611 women of all social levels and races, made by Kantner and Zelnick in 1972, found that 14 percent had had coitus by age 14 and 46 percent by age 19. The percentage varied greatly by social class and by race. This study did not measure degree of intimacy by the dating stages leading up to marriage. Since nonwhites and lower social classes marry at a much younger age, the study probably tells us more about the sexual behavior of these groups. The predominant pattern for women in these groups was to have had coitus with only the person whom they planned to marry.[4]

A Gallup Poll of a representative sample of people in 1973 found that 48 percent of adults believe that premarital sexual intercourse is wrong. Attitudes differed according to age and marital status of the respondents. A larger percentage of younger people and the unmarried approved of having coitus before marriage.

## CHANGING ATTITUDES ON PREMARITAL SEXUAL BEHAVIOR

In successive studies from 1952 to 1971 in many universities and colleges, we have used the identical rating scale used by Cornell University in 1940. Changes in attitudes expressed by students on approved standards are revealed in Table 10-2. In the 1940s and 1950s the majority of men and women approved the standard of no coitus for either sex before marriage. In our sample, a major change began in the 1960s, and by 1971 the majority expressed the belief that coitus should be permissible for both sexes before marriage. By far the greatest change in expressed attitudes was on the part of women in 1971 compared with women prior to that time. Fifty-nine percent of the women and 70 percent of the men expressed acceptance of premarital coitus as permissible for both sexes; 16 percent more men and 19 percent more women approved of coitus during engagement.

[4] John F. Kantner and Melvin Zelnick, "Sexual Experience of Young Unmarried Women in the U.S.," *Family Planning Perspective* 4 (October 1972), 9–18.

TABLE 10-2

Percentages of students in four different time periods checking each of four statements representing attitudes on premarital sexual standards

| Approved standard | Cornell 1940 | 11 Colleges 1952 | 18 Colleges 1967 | 2 Colleges 1971 |
|---|---|---|---|---|
| | | Men | | |
| | (N–73) | (N–1,056) | (N–1,005) | (N–63) |
| Sexual relations: | | | | |
| For both | 15% | 20% | 47% | 70% |
| None for either | 49 | 52 | 24 | 13 |
| For men only | 23 | 12 | 8 | 1 |
| For engaged persons only | 11 | 16 | 22 | 16 |
| | | Women | | |
| | (N–100) | (N–1,944) | (N–2,184) | (N–135) |
| Sexual relations: | | | | |
| For both | 6% | 5% | 21% | 59% |
| None for either | 76 | 65 | 39 | 15 |
| For men only | 11 | 23 | 17 | 7 |
| For engaged persons only | 6 | 7 | 23 | 19 |

Christensen and Gregg, studying student attitudes on acceptable premarital sexual behavior in 1958 and 1968, found the same change in attitudes that we have indicated above, with attitudes of women changing more rapidly than those of men.[5] Louis Harris and Associates polled a national sample of college students in 1970 and found that 72 percent approved of premarital coitus during formal engagement. This is about the same percentage as expressed approval in our study in 1971, if all categories of "approval" are combined. In our study, 7 percent of women still expressed belief in a double standard. Only 1 percent of the men thought there should be a double standard. Nearly equal percentages— 13 percent of men and 15 percent of women—thought there should be no sexual intercourse for either before marriage. These attitudes show a strong shift from attitudes of students in 1952, when 52 percent of the men and 65 percent of the women felt the sexual standard should be virginity for both before marriage.

Some researchers who found the attitudes of college students on acceptable sexual standards changing in the late 1960s concluded that, although expressed attitudes were changing, there had been no change in actual premarital sexual behavior over several generations.[6] All of our re-

[5] Harold T. Christensen and Christiana F. Gregg, "Changing Sex Norms in America and Scandinavia," *Journal of Marriage and the Family* 32:4 (November 1970), 616–27.

[6] John H. Gagnon and William Simon, "Prospects for Change in American Sexual Patterns," *Medical Aspects of Sexuality* (4 January 1970), 100–17.

search with young people in the late 1960s and the early 1970s indicates that in the past decade sexual behavior has been changing, along with attitudes. Others studying students in the late 1960s and the 1970s have also observed this trend.[7] A larger percentage of young people, especially women, now have had coitus with someone other than the one they will marry, since people may have several serious relationships before marriage.

## MOTIVATIONS FOR VIRGINITY

Studies of different student generations, past and present, show that those who choose to remain virgins today give about the same positive reasons as students gave in the past: family training, religion, and the idealism associated with the desire to wait until after the wedding. Negative motivations—such as fear of pregnancy or of social ostracism and fear that lack of virginity might hinder chances for marriage—have less weight today (see Table 10-3).

**TABLE 10-3**   Reasons for having refrained from premarital sexual relations, according to students in three different periods of time

|  | Cornell 1940 | 11 Colleges 1952 | 18 Colleges 1967 |
|---|---|---|---|
| **Reason for chastity** | | **Women** | |
| I want to wait until married | — | 81% | 75% |
| Family training | 71% | 66 | 59 |
| Religious beliefs | 21 | 32 | 44 |
| Fear of pregnancy | 68 | 27 | 35 |
| Fear that sexual relations will stand in the way of marriage | 42 | 21 | 18 |
| Fear of social ostracism | 22 | 17 | 10 |
|  | | **Men** | |
| I want to wait until married | — | 50% | 44% |
| Family training | — | 41 | 37 |
| Religious beliefs | — | 33 | 39 |
| Causing pregnancy | — | 27 | 32 |
| Fear that sexual relations will stand in the way of marriage | — | 19 | 12 |
| Fear of social ostracism | — | 12 | 5 |

[7] Robert R. Bell and Jay B. Chaskes, "Premarital Sexual Experience Among Coeds, 1958 and 1968," *Journal of Marriage and the Family* 32:1 (February 1970), 81–84; Christensen and Gregg, "Changing Sex Norms in America and Scandinavia"; Eleanore B. Luckey and Gilbert D. Nass, "A Comparison of Sexual Attitudes and

The positive motivation for the idealism concerning sexual intercourse and marriage has its source in family attitudes and teachings, in religion, and in a desire to have a lasting and happy marriage. Ira Reiss, in reporting on his study of attitudes concerning sexual permissiveness, noted that people from families where parents are happily married and religiously oriented express less permissive attitudes toward premarital sexual freedom than people from families with opposite characteristics.[8]

## PREMARITAL SEXUAL EXPERIENCE AND SOME SOCIAL VARIABLES

In the past sociologists have studied people who do and who do not have premarital coitus and have attempted to relate their findings to how these people succeed in marriage. Typical of this type of study is ours of three groups: 1163 married people, 155 people having marriage counseling, and 164 divorced people. Our study found that 38 percent of the married, 58 percent of the divorced group, and 73 percent of those having marriage counseling had had premarital coitus. The difference among the groups is clearly significant. The same study found that 5 percent of the married were pregnant before marriage, 11 percent of the divorced, and 23 percent of the marriage counseling group. We cannot assume a direct causal relationship between the premarital experience and the poor marital adjustment, because many complicating factors are related to premarital experience as well as to marital adjustment. For example, the same study found the unhappily married and the divorced to have had short acquaintances before marriage, to have had more parental opposition to their marriages, and to have had more doubts ahead of time about whether their marriages would be a success. All of these variables are associated with failure in marriage. The following case illustrates the interlocking of different variables that affect success or failure in marriage:

> A couple dating steadily during their senior year in high school engaged in sexual intercourse. Just after graduation, when they were both 17, the girl learned that she was pregnant. When they told their parents that they intended to be married, both families objected. The boy's family felt that the girl was from an undesirable family, a family of less social standing and education. The girl's family had had high hopes for the future of their daughter, since she had made a brilliant scholastic record in high school. She had talked of becoming a doctor, and her family was anxious to help her toward her goal. Both families agreed to the wedding only when they were told of the pregnancy.

Behavior in an International Sample," *Journal of Marriage and the Family* 31:2 (May 1969), 364–70; Vance Packard, *The Sexual Wilderness: The Contemporary Upheaval in Male–Female Relationships* (New York: David McKay Company, Inc., 1968); Ira E. Robinson, Karl King, Jack O. Balswick, "The Premarital Sexual Revolution Among College Females," *The Family Coordinator* 21:2 (April 1972) 189–94.

[8] Ira L. Reiss, "Premarital Sexual Norms," *Journal of Marriage and the Family* 27:3 (August 1965), 314–23.

After five years of marriage, this couple was extremely unhappy. The wife held a deep resentment because she had not been able to go to college or prepare for the career she had hoped for. She also rejected her baby, and the baby developed into an unhappy problem child. She was unable to respond sexually to her husband throughout almost all the marriage, although she had enjoyed coitus before marriage. An offhand diagnosis might seem to be that the premarital coitus and resulting forced marriage were the whole cause of the trouble, since the wife rejected everything associated with the premarital experience. But analysis of the factors involved in the case brought to light other circumstances that made diagnosis far less simple. Although the wife's mother seemed conscientious and eager to help her daughters, this daughter, at 22, stated that for as long as she could remember she had felt a bitter antagonism toward her mother. She was intensely attached to her father and said she had always resented being a girl and wished she were a man. Moreover, all through the young couple's marriage, a violent antagonism persisted between the two parental families, both of whom blamed the child-in-law for all the marital difficulties as well as for the original sexual activity that had caused the marriage.

The young couple was also plagued with financial difficulties, for the husband had trouble holding a job. His family sympathized with him in his job difficulties, always making excuses for his failures and blaming circumstances or other people. They were willing to help him with gifts of money, and they resented his wife's feeling that he ought to be able to support her and the baby without financial help from his parents.

Our study of 3189 college and university students in 1967 attempted to find whether there were personal and family variables that differentiated the students who had engaged in premarital coitus; and whether these variables might also be related to success in marriage. The study found that those who considered themselves indifferent or antagonistic to religion and those who said they had no religious faith had much larger percentages who reported being nonvirgins.[9] Those who classified themselves as devout or very devout religiously reported the highest percentage of virgins. Being devout rather than nondevout or reporting no faith have also been found to be associated with low divorce and with happiness in marriage. Our study found that students were more likely to report they were virgins if they also reported their parents' marriages were happy rather than unhappy, their parents were not divorced, or they felt close to their parents rather than distant.[10]

There are doubtless many values, attitudes, and beliefs that children absorb from their families, so that children from families with conventional beliefs are more likely to have conventional beliefs that in turn are

[9] Judson T. Landis, "Variables Associated with Virginity and Non-Virginity Among 3189 College and University Students" (Paper read before the family section, Annual Meeting of the Pacific Sociological Society, Los Angeles, 18 April 1970).

[10] Landis, "Religiousness, Family Relationships, and Family Values in Protestant, Catholic, and Jewish Families," *Marriage and Family Living* 22:4 (November 1960), 342–47.

associated with successful marriage. It is a cluster of behavioral patterns developed in the home, rather than any one factor, that relates to attitudes of the individual toward premarital coitus.

Kantner and Zelnick found in their study of a national sample of 4611 women of all races that premarital coitus was highest among those who had had only a grade school education and decreased among those with more education, being the lowest among those with a college education.[11]

Henze and Hudson found, in comparing college student couples who had and who had not lived together, that those who were living together were less religious, identified with a liberal life style, and were more likely to use drugs.[12]

Vener and Stewart studied the sexual behavior as well as the attitudes and behavior of high school students in 1970 and again in 1973, both studies in the same school.[13] They found that having coitus at an early age was not an isolated factor in the students' lives. In comparing the students who had had coitus with those who had not, they found those having had coitus were more likely to have the following characteristics: to have committed delinquent acts such as shoplifting, car theft, vandalism, assault, and reckless driving; to have used both soft and hard drugs; and to have rejected traditional institutions as measured by their attitudes toward the police, religion, and the schools.

Jurich and Jurich studied students in eight different colleges and found a close association between their being religious and their acceptance of traditional standards such as premarital chastity.[14]

## GUILT FEELINGS AND COURTSHIP BEHAVIOR

We have research findings from 270 students who had had serious love relationships involving coitus; they evaluated their feelings about having had coitus during the relationships (see Table 10-4). More than half the men and almost a third of the women did not feel that their behavior had been wrong. As would be expected, a much larger percentage (70 percent) of the women than of the men had doubts or felt guilty. Women, more than men, are brought up to believe that they must uphold a standard of premarital chastity. Women who have had coitus in past

[11] Kantner and Zelnick, "Sexual Experience of Young Unmarried Women."

[12] Lura F. Henze and John W. Hudson, "Personal and Family Characteristics of Cohabiting and Noncohabiting College Students," *Journal of Marriage and the Family* 36:4 (November 1974), 722–26.

[13] Arthur M. Vener and Cyrus S. Stewart, "Adolescent Sexual Behavior in Middle America Revisited: 1970–1973," *Journal of Marriage and the Family* 36:4 (November 1974), 728–35.

[14] Anthony J. Jurich and Julie A. Jurich, "The Effects of Cognitive Moral Development Upon the Selection of Premarital Sexual Standards," *Journal of Marriage and the Family* 36:4 (November 1974), 736–41.

relationships now broken may have more feelings of guilt than women still in love or engaged to the man with whom they have had coitus. Those from broken affairs are now nonvirgins and face some implications for the future. These women may be troubled if they feel they must tell the man they may some day marry, or if they feel they have let their family down by not living up to expectations, or have failed to live up to their self-expectations. We compared the reactions of presently engaged couples who were having coitus with those who had broken engagements. There is a contrast in what the engaged and those with broken engagements reported. See Table 10-4 for the differences between the groups. The engaged group were still planning marriage and their evaluation of coitus is seen in that perspective. Among these engaged couples who do not marry there may be many who will, if studied after this engagement is broken, report guilt feelings about going as far as they have gone in lovemaking.

Christensen and Gregg found more expressed guilt or remorse among midwestern college students having had coitus than among a group of Danish students.[15] This would be expected because of the historical acceptance of coitus during engagement in Denmark. With changing attitudes toward premarital coitus in our country, guilt feelings in the future will tend to decrease. Christensen and Gregg found, in repeating in 1968 a study first made in 1958, that college students reported fewer feelings of guilt and remorse in 1968. The Christensen studies were made in a western university, a midwestern university, and a Danish university; the restudy found the decrease in guilt feelings in all three universities.

**TABLE 10-4** Percentages of 270 students who had had sexual relations during engagement reporting their personal feelings after the engagement was broken, compared with 122 couples currently engaged *

| Feelings about having premarital sexual relations | How did (does) it affect you personally | | | |
| --- | --- | --- | --- | --- |
| | Broken engagements | | Currently engaged | |
| | Men N–117 | Women N–153 | Men N–122 | Women N–122 |
| I felt it was all right | 56% | 29% | 80% | 75% |
| It did (does) not affect me one way or another | 8 | 1 | 2 | — |
| I had (have) some doubts | 19 | 25 | 10 | 14 |
| I felt (feel) guilty | 13 | 25 | 4 | 8 |
| I felt (feel) extremely guilty | 4 | 20 | 4 | 3 |

* The 270 formerly engaged were among the 3189 students in the 18 colleges studied in 1967, and the 122 currently engaged were couples at the University of California, Berkeley, and Chico State College studied in 1967.

[15] Christensen and Gregg, "Changing Sex Norms in America and Scandinavia," p. 626.

Bell and Chaskes did a similar study of students in 1958 and again in 1968 and found the same trend toward less expressed guilt or regret among those studied in 1968.[16]

A better perspective on feelings of guilt about having had coitus in a serious relationship is obtained when we consider that young people in our studies who did not have coitus but engaged in other forms of intimacy also expressed some degree of guilt. This is especially true of girls. Because of the values (or the assumed values) of parents, the church, and friends, many girls feel guilty when they first engage in intimate forms of kissing, necking, and petting. When relationships are broken, they express regrets or guilt feelings about how far they went in lovemaking even though they stopped short of coitus. A girl with conservative values may experience more guilt about petting than a "liberated" girl experiences about having had coitus. The teachings one has had in the family cannot be overlooked in understanding how people react to the stages of lovemaking during courtship.

## EFFECTS OF PREMARITAL COITUS ON THE RELATIONSHIP

Some years ago Burgess and Wallin, and later Kirkendall, studied couples to determine what if any effects premarital coitus had on their relationships.[17] Kirkendall's studies were in the form of self-evaluations by the men in the cases. In recent years we have repeated Burgess and Wallin's early studies with college students.

Table 10-5 summarizes the responses in our study of 270 formerly engaged students and 122 currently engaged couples. The predominant pattern reported by the formerly engaged as well as the presently engaged is that having sexual intercourse tended to bring them closer together emotionally. Two-thirds of the people who had been engaged and over 90 percent of the presently engaged reported coitus had affected their relationship positively. A fourth of those who had broken their engagements reported that coitus had been disruptive to their relationship.

This type of study may or may not be helpful in evaluating premarital sexual intercourse and its effect. It tells us that whatever couples do in mutual agreement tends to intensify a relationship. In expressing physical intimacy from the level of hand holding, kissing, necking, petting, to coitus, a couple takes steps in the direction of greater and greater closeness in a relationship. At any stage something may intervene to stop further steps in intimacy. Parental opposition to the dating, conflicts over various differences, or one person's insisting upon going further than the

16 Bell and Chaskes, "Premarital Experiences Among Coeds," pp. 81–84.
17 Ernest W. Burgess and Paul Wallin, *Engagement and Marriage* (Philadelphia; J. B. Lippincott Company, 1942); Lester A. Kirkendall, *Premarital Intercourse and Interpersonal Relationships* (New York: The Julian Press, Inc., 1961).

TABLE 10-5

Percentages of 270 formerly engaged students who had had intercourse during engagement and 122 currently engaged couples reporting the effects of intercourse on the relationship

| | Effect on relationship in broken engagements | | Currently engaged | |
|---|---|---|---|---|
| Effect on relationship | Men N–117 | Women N–153 | Men N–72 | Women N–72 |
| Brought us closer together | 50% | 46% | 79% | 88% |
| Brought us somewhat closer together | 22 | 19 | 14 | 9 |
| Did not affect relationship one way or another | 9 | 7 | 1 | 1 |
| Tended to be disruptive | 11 | 15 | 6 | 2 |
| Very disruptive | 7 | 13 | — | 1 |

other wishes in physical intimacy may be intervening factors. Our studies show that at whatever stage couples agree to decide to draw the line in intimacy, it tends to bring them closer together. Those who decide to stop at the light petting stage report that that drew them closer together. Their ability to agree on the subject of intimacy seems to be the key to their relationship. The following excerpt from the report of a female university student in 1972 illustrates some of the points discussed here:

I was never told anything about sex at home. I only found out what the physical act of procreation was in seventh grade, told to me by a girl friend. My first reaction to this knowledge was surprise and a vague feeling of embarrassment, perhaps because I felt I was the only one in the class who did not know until then. My knowledge was very sketchy until tenth-grade biology. I still am learning the subtleties involved. I don't recall my mother specifically instructing me to remain chaste, but I do remember her telling me that light petting was acceptable. I also remember her telling me while I was attending junior college that she did not know whether premarital intercourse was wrong or not. I always felt that intercourse outside of marriage was morally wrong, although I do not really know why. I remember in my freshman year in college how shocked I was to hear that two of my best friends were no longer virgins. I had assumed that my friends would not have sexual intercourse. On the other hand, I believed in the double standard that males could do what they pleased but females could not. I soon developed the philosophy that no one has the right to judge another's actions. I was fairly consistant in my own behavior until I met my fiancé. I felt that hugging and kissing were acceptable for casual dates, and very light petting with a steady boyfriend. After going with my fiancé about one and a half years, we began more extreme lovemaking. However, I was having serious doubts as to whether or not it was right. These doubts may have occurred because even though he proposed, I was not sure that I would marry him. And heavy petting somehow seemed immoral with someone to whom I was not totally committed. In the last six months, however, my attitude toward marrying my fiancé has improved so that my behavior has been fairly consistent with my moral attitudes. We have been doing some heavy petting but I have not been feeling guilty. I am happy with this outcome because we are both virgins, and both of us hadn't done more than light petting before we met each other. We have not had intercourse, although my fiancé would like to. He has respected my wishes. Even though intercourse would not be such a big step, I would like to mark my marriage with the start of intercourse. In another way I am glad that we have progressed so far. For example, if we had only necked just before marriage, I think our honeymoon would have been disastrous, both of us being rather shy and naive.

## PREMARITAL COITUS AND BREAKING RELATIONSHIPS

Burgess and Wallin's study of 1000 engaged couples done some years ago has some implications for our discussion here. They found that a larger percentage of those having premarital sexual intercourse broke their engagements and did not go on into marriage.[18] Different explanations could be given for this finding. One could be that if a relationship tends to be exploitative, usually on the part of the man, the woman may become aware of an exploitative pattern in their association. This could be especially true if she has been overpersuaded and has guilt feelings. Another factor may be that in some cases coitus is started early in the relationship before there has been time to explore other facets of personality. Once there has been more complete exploration of personalities and more thorough acquaintance, one or both may see that they should not marry. In such cases, if they had not had coitus or if they had found coitus unsatisfactory, the relationship would probably have ended sooner and with less trauma.

Conversely, premarital coitus may lead some people to fail to break a relationship and to marry when the relationship would better be broken. A man may find it difficult to break off a relationship with a woman if he knows he is the only man with whom she has had sexual intercourse, or if she becomes pregnant.

If the man has been brought up to feel his responsibility in such a situation, the couple will probably marry in spite of all evidence of potential failure. A male student's report illustrates this:

Our courtship, if it can be called such, developed along the lines of an exploitative pattern. At the time I was running around with a gang of boys who, as a group, thought it smart to have sexual intercourse if possible while still remaining free of any involvements. After meeting my wife, however, I withdrew from this group to a great extent. We soon began having sexual intercourse and became quite emotionally involved. This was her first experience, and she was undoubtedly more emotionally involved than I. She worried a lot about becoming pregnant, and very soon she did become pregnant. By this time I was in love and wanted to marry her. We planned to elope and be married at once, but she found herself unable to tell

[18] Burgess and Wallin, *Engagement and Marriage.*

her mother of the pregnancy, and her mother insisted that we should be married either at a church or in her home. This meant some delay. We began our married life in a small apartment and were fairly happy for the first couple of months. Finally her family began to ask questions, and the truth came out. The family took her pregnancy very hard at first and my wife quarreled with them and became very unhappy.

She insisted that she was glad we were married. But other things in her actions and things she said made me feel that she felt that I had married her only because I was forced to and that she felt she had been trapped without knowing for sure that she wanted to marry me. Our child is now two years old. At present we seem to have little in common except our child. I have come to agree with her that we probably would never have married each other if it had not been for the pregnancy.

## PREMARITAL BEHAVIOR AND PREGNANCY

Despite advances in contraceptive knowledge, the rate of illegitimate births among unmarried women ages 15–44 increased steadily between 1940 and 1973. There is no accurate information on the percentage of unplanned pregnancies in marriage, but what information is available indicates the rate is high. Ryder and Westoff conducted a study of a national sample of 6752 women and found that new birth control devices had cut the contraceptive failure rate in half during the past ten years. Despite this, they found that 14 percent of the women had an unwanted pregnancy, and 26 percent more had become pregnant sooner than planned. There were approximately one million abortions performed in 1975. An estimated 75 percent were performed on unmarried women and 25 percent on married women. These statistics would certainly indicate that conception control as practiced today remains far from perfect.

**Lack of caution.** The conditions under which premarital coitus takes place and individual lack of caution both contribute to premarital pregnancy. In our study of single college students in 1967, we found that of 704 women who had had coitus, 15 percent had depended upon the "safe period" as a means of contraception; a fourth of the group had made no provision whatever for preventing conception. Fewer than a fifth of them were taking the oral contraceptives to avoid pregnancy. In 1971 we repeated the study with 116 single men and women students who were or had been in relationships involving coitus, and found that 37 percent of the women involved had used the pill. Although more were using the pill in 1971, 15 percent of those having sexual intercourse still depended upon the so-called safe period, and 15 percent had taken no preventive measures at all. In 1967, of 72 engaged couples who reported that they were having coitus, about a fourth were using the oral contraceptive and about half were depending on a variety of other methods of varying degrees of reliability. A reckless or naive approach to premarital sexual experience, even when people are engaged and hope to plan their lives, is revealed by the reports that half of those who were having coitus said they "were petting and it just happened." Ten percent more reported, "We planned it but we had made no plans for contraceptives." Less than a third reported making specific plans and being prepared with contraceptives. The picture, as it emerges from this research, is that having coitus in love relationships, before marriage as well as in marriage, is not a rationally planned activity; it just "happens" in the average case. After an accidental pregnancy early in marriage, couples become more rational about lovemaking and establish some consistent course of action to control conception and plan their families. For many women, before marriage, such rational planning for conception control goes against their sense of values and their feelings about lovemaking and sexual intercourse. Some of their comments to us make this explicit: "It wouldn't seem right," "It would seem so calculated," "I wouldn't *plan* to have premarital sex." But these same girls were having premarital sexual intercourse without "planning."

A study of 642 women who were seeking abortion at Stanford University Hospital found that these women did not understand contraceptive methods and were careless in their use of contraceptives. They were young women, more that 70 percent under the age of 25, a group that one might think would be well informed. Table 10-6 summarizes the most common reasons they gave to explain their unwanted pregnancy. It should be noted that a third were depending on the safe period, and one-third more reported using a contraceptive that did not work.[19]

It is safe to predict that for some years to come much premarital coitus will continue to be unplanned and unprepared for and so will involve the possibility of a premarital pregnancy.

**Alternatives when pregnancy occurs.** A premarital pregnancy is an eventuality that can hardly be faced realistically ahead of time. When the situation is purely hypothetical, a couple may believe that they could handle the problem fairly well if it should arise. When it is no longer hypothetical and a woman finds or suspects that she is pregnant, serious decisions must be made and no happy solution is possible. One possible solution is marriage, if the man and woman are suitable marriage partners. Sometimes, however, marriage for couples caught in these circumstances may not be the answer. The woman may consider abortion, but she lives with her own definitions and feelings about abortion and these may make it a traumatic choice for her. The other alternative is to try to make plans that will enable her to go safely through the pregnancy and give birth to the baby. The solution means that parents or others must be trusted and able to give the needed help. Under only the best possible circumstances may parents or friends be able to minimize the trauma for the mother. More unmarried mothers today than for some decades past decide to keep and rear a child. But to make that choice,

[19] *Western Journal of Medicine*, 122:1 (January 1975).

TABLE 10-6

Women seeking abortions. Percentage of respondents in the study group who checked each Contraceptive and Sexual Attitude Questionnaire item, indicating it played a role in the occurrence of their unwanted pregnancy. (N = 642)

| Item number | Questionnaire item | Percent of respondents checking item |
|---|---|---|
| 1 | I thought it was during the safe period | 35 |
| 2 | I took precautions but the contraceptive method didn't work | 33 |
| 3 | I was afraid of the side effects of certain contraceptives | 29 |
| 4 | I thought it couldn't happen to me | 27 |
| 5 | I put the possibility of pregnancy out of my mind | 21 |
| 6 | I didn't thing pregnancy was likely because I had intercourse so infrequently | 14 |
| 7 | I didn't think I would get pregnant because I have often had intercourse without precautions and have never gotten pregnant before | 14 |
| 8 | I realized that if I did get pregnant I could probably get an abortion | 13 |
| 9 | I decided to take a chance and count on good luck | 12 |
| 10 | I had planned not to have any more intercourse for a while | 11 |
| 11 | I just never got around to getting contraception | 10 |
| 12 | I got carried away before I could think about contraception | 9 |
| 13 | I halfway wanted to get pregnant | 8 |
| 14 | He was supposed to withdraw but he didn't | 8 |
| 15 | I was embarrassed or afraid to see a doctor about contraception | 8 |
| 16 | I didn't like deliberately planning for the possibility of intercourse | 8 |
| 17 | I loved him and nothing else mattered | 8 |
| 18 | I knew I might get pregnant but that uncertainty didn't concern me very much | 6 |
| 19 | I was in the process of beginning a new contraceptive method | 6 |
| 20 | I didn't think I was fertile | 6 |
| 21 | I was afraid someone would find out if I tried to get a contraceptive | 6 |
| 22 | I assumed that he would take some kind of precautions | 5 |
| 23 | I felt that having intercourse on that occasion was worth the chance of pregnancy | 5 |
| 24 | My judgment was affected by alcohol | 5 |
| 25 | I wanted to prove my love by taking a chance | 4 |
| 26 | I was embarrased or afraid to talk to him about contraception | 3 |
| 27 | I sort of liked putting myself in a risky situation | 3 |
| 28 | I felt a contraceptive would interfere with the natural expression of love | 3 |

a woman must be among the extremely liberated group, for the norm in our society is still that it is better for babies to be born to a father and a mother who are married to each other. The unmarried mother bringing up her child alone will find that there are many severe problems of adjustment for the child and for herself. If the baby is not kept, but given for adoption, the mother may hope that the entire experience is in the past. But if she later marries happily and has other children, her love for them may bring her a new awareness of the one that was given away. As time passes and she watches her children grow up, the thought of the first-born whom she was not able to know can become more painful. People are likely to be totally unconscious of this aspect of unmarried parenthood during the time when a premarital pregnancy looms chiefly as an immediate problem to be solved. Future mental conflict may operate also in the case of the unwed father, and for many of the same reasons.

## VENEREAL DISEASE AND CURRENT SEXUAL NORMS

So far in this chapter we have discussed different aspects of premarital sexual intercourse as it applies in meaningful relationships between couples in their approach to marriage. It is not our purpose here to explore deviations in society or personality factors among the sexually promiscuous.

However, in the 1970s, among people who do not consider themselves promiscuous but whose premarital sexual standards allow intercourse without anticipation of marriage, an increasing number are becoming victims of venereal disease. Because of realistic treatment and control programs at all governmental levels, venereal disease decreased to such a low point by the 1950s that it could have been eliminated entirely if the programs had been continued. It was assumed that the battle was won and the public became complacent. By 1960 the diseases were increasing, and by the early 1970s syphilis and gonorrhea reached epidemic proportions. Whereas there were only 5000 cases of syphilis reported in 1958, almost 92,000 cases were reported in 1976; 225,000 cases of gonorrhea were reported in 1958, but over two million cases were reported in 1976.

The increase in venereal disease has been explained in several ways: increased sexual promiscuity, viruses becoming immune to drugs that have been effective in the past, ignorance about venereal disease, cutting off of funds to eradicate venereal diseases through public health services, and, finally, a change in the contraceptives most generally used.

In the past, educational programs emphasized the seriousness of venereal infections and the necessity to use prophylactic devices as partial protection. With the widespread acceptance of contraceptive pills and intrauterine devices for contraception, along with an increase in coitus between people in temporary relationships, protection against venereal infection greatly diminished. Research has now found that women using the oral contraceptive contract venereal infections more readily than others do because the hormones in the pill increase alkalinity and moisture in the genital tract thereby making conditions more favorable for growth of infection.

State laws have been relaxed in recent years to curb the rapid spread of venereal disease among the very young. With the passage of the Twenty-first Amendment giving 18-year-olds the right to vote, many other rights have also been granted. All states now allow people 18 and over to get medical treatment for venereal disease without parental consent. In all states but Wisconsin teenagers under 18 as well can get treatment for venereal disease without parental consent.

In attempts to control the venereal disease epidemic, realistic educational programs are proposed for schools and colleges and more adequate funds for treatment facilities. Research continues for better methods of detecting gonorrhea in women and for more effective cures since penicillin is rapidly becoming ineffective as a cure. People who believe in individual sexual freedom owe it to themselves and to others to be responsible in cooperating toward the control of venereal disease.

Both gonorrhea and syphilis are very serious and crippling diseases, although this is usually not realized since the diseases can be cured. The success of cure and avoidance of permanent damage are based upon early detection and treatment. Gonorrhea is usually detected in the male but is often impossible to detect in the female until after permanent damage has been done. Syphilis may go undetected in its early stages and, if not treated, has permanent disastrous effects on the individual's circulatory and nervous systems.

## SEXUAL FREEDOM AND RESPONSIBILITY

It is true that greater individual choice about many matters, including sexual behavior, exists in our society today. People making personal decisions about sexual behavior sometimes overlook the fact that every increase in freedom brings an equal increase in responsibility. The broadened responsibility is not assigned; it is automatically another face of freedom.

Freedom to choose one's course of action in sexual behavior means also the necessity to consider possible emotional and social effects upon another person and that person's life as well as upon one's own life. The responsible individual will recognize that a relationship may have different meanings and different levels of commitment for the two involved. Such differences mean a possibility of emotional trauma for one or both. Beyond the responsibility to one's partner and oneself are, of course, one's broader obligations to society. Among these are individual responsibility to build the kinds of relationships that contribute to the mental, physical, and emotional health of individuals and to successful and happy families.

## RESPONSIBILITY TO CHILDREN AND TO SOCIETY

Those who choose the way of sexual freedom should never forget their obligations if conception occurs. Children need to be loved and cared for by two people who are ready for parenthood. Children have a right to loving care, food, shelter, and medical attention. Failing families, families in which these needs are not provided, produce emotionally unhealthy children. Mental illness, emotional problems, dependency, and delinquency are all evidence of failing families. Failing families put a burden upon the taxpayers for tax-supported programs that take care of families who cannot meet their own responsibilities.

In 1974 there were eight million children and three million parents or guardians supported by the Aid to Families with Dependent Children program. Most of the children were born either to unmarried mothers or to young parents whose marriages failed. The cost of the total program to the taxpayers in that year was more than 12 billion dollars.

Those who assume the right of sexual freedom should be mature enough to think of the rights of the other individuals involved, the implication for their own lives, the effect on their children's lives, and the economic cost to taxpayers.

## REVIEW QUESTIONS

1   What prediction did Terman make regarding sexual behavior, based on his studies in the 1920s? What accounts for the failure of his predictions to become reality?

2   What developments may be conducive to a change in attitudes of women toward premarital virginity?

3   Do present research studies show a pattern of sexual promiscuity among young people?

4   What appears to characterize the pattern of sexual behavior among college students as shown by research studies?

5   What family background factors tend to be characteristic of people who are less permissive in premarital sexual attitudes and behavior?

6   Discuss the implications of premarital behavior and some related factors for marital success.

7   What are some of the social characteristics and behavioral patterns between those having and not having premarital coitus? How do they differ?

8   What are some of the situations that influence how much guilt people feel about having premarital coitus?

9   How can the continuing high rate of premarital pregnancies be explained in view of available contraceptives?

10   What factors have contributed to a new venereal disease epidemic?

11   What is meant by the statement that "Responsibility is but another face of freedom"?

12   What are some of the direct and indirect costs of sexual freedom to society?

## REPORT

Report on the programs in your state or community designed to reduce the incidence of venereal disease.

# MIXED MARRIAGES

# 11

Studies of marital success and failure have established that, in general, marriages have a better chance for success when couples are from a similar background. The more their two families are alike in beliefs, attitudes, values, educational level, and many other characteristics, the greater are the chances for their marriage to succeed. The success of marriages of people of widely different backgrounds depends on the individuals involved, but the chance for success is greater if those who marry across lines of difference are aware at the outset that they will have to work harder for a good marriage than they would have to do if they married someone with a similar background. All couples have some problems after they marry; in a mixed marriage the number of problems is increased and some problems that might normally exist are intensified. Any marriage involving extreme differences may be called a mixed marriage, although the term is usually applied to those in which there is a difference in race or religion, and sometimes nationality, since these differences show the problems of mixture most clearly.

## SOURCES OF PROBLEMS IN MIXED MARRIAGES

Some problems in mixed marriages arise from the nature of the family itself. Families value their own ideas, traditions, and life styles and they hope to perpetuate these patterns in the lives of their children. The children's departure from family values is threatening to the parental family. As children grow up and absorb attitudes or beliefs from outside sources that do not coincide with the teaching or thinking of the family, the parents may interpret the new attitudes or behavior as a rejection of family norms.

During the dating years, conflicting points of view may come into focus for the first time if a son or a daughter dates one whose background shows marked contrasts to that of the parental family. If dating is prolonged with such a person and it appears that a serious relationship might develop, parents are likely to be disturbed. The greater the difference in background factors, such as social class, religious faith, race, or cultural characteristics, the greater the parental opposition. Opposition to the dating across such lines is usually shared by both parental families; it is not one-sided. The orthodox Jew (usually the boy) who considers marrying outside his faith and culture knows that orthodox rabbis would refuse to marry him and that his family may reject and disinherit him if he makes such a marriage.

It is difficult for black families and white families to accept interracial dating of their children, even in cases in which the couple might have many background factors in common. For example, such a couple might be college graduates, members of the same church, perhaps both their fathers successful business or professional men, but the racial difference would still loom large to their families.

The feelings and attitudes on the part of the parental families about a mixed marriage are a continuing part of the adjustment of any such marriage. A nonmixed marriage is more likely to have the wholehearted support of parents, friends, community, and church. All expect the marriage to succeed. In a mixed marriage, especially one involving extreme differences, the two who marry are essentially on their own. Their marriage must be launched and survive mainly on the basis of the relationship they are able to build. They do not have the social and family support given to other marriages.

Families, with the aid of certain social factors, are relatively successful in maintaining their values and traditions through their children's marriages. Glick found in a study of religious homogamy in 35,000 households in the United States that Protestants, Catholics, and Jews tend to marry within their own faith to a much larger degree than would be expected by chance. Protestants make up 66 percent of the population, and on a chance basis 53 percent would marry within the Protestant faith; but in practice, 91 percent make homogamous Protestant marriages. Catholics make up 26 percent of the population, and the expected homogamous marriages would be 16 percent; in practice, 78 percent marry within the faith. Jews make up 3 percent of the population with an expected homogamy of 2 percent; in practice, 93 percent make homogamous marriages.[1]

[1] Hugh Carter and Paul Glick, *Marriage and Divorce: A Social and Economic Study* (Cambridge, Mass.: Harvard University Press, 1970).

It now appears that many of the forces that helped families maintain homogamy in the past are breaking down and that these changes may have far-reaching effects on dating and marriage. Many people now hold the view that the family of mankind is of greatest importance and that the individual family might be better served if homogamy were less emphasized. The strong push toward integration in housing, schools, churches, and job opportunities influences dating across lines of difference.

Family opposition to mixed marriages will not disappear overnight, or perhaps ever. However, if differences decrease between groups in our society, as they are doing in some areas of life (such as religion), the implications of intermarriage will tend to have less significance. A major example of change is to be seen in the stated positions on mixed marriage by various religious groups over a period of time.

## PROTESTANT–CATHOLIC MARRIAGES

For centuries, Protestants and Catholics have stood in opposition to interfaith marriages because each felt that the beliefs of the other approached the heretical. Each faith wanted to insure that the children born within it would grow in the "right" faith, and each taught its adherents that they should marry within the faith. When Catholics decided to marry outside their faith, the Catholic Church made specific requirements in the form of a prenuptial agreement to be signed by both the Protestant and the Catholic desiring to marry. In signing the agreement, they promised that any children born would be baptized and educated in the Catholic faith, that birth control would not be practiced, that the Protestant would permit the Catholic to continue to practice his or her religion without hindrance, and that no ceremony other than that of the Catholic Church would be performed.

Protestant denominations did not require Catholics to sign such an agreement, and many Protestant leaders felt that the Catholic prenuptial agreement was objectionable and unfair. As a result of this feeling, Protestant denominations in the 1950s passed resolutions affirming the position of their denominations regarding mixed marriages with Catholics.[2]

The resolution passed by the Lutheran Church–Missouri Synod, quoted below, is interesting because its wording reveals how emotionally loaded for some groups the subject of mixed religious marriages has been:

> Whereas the Roman law pertaining to marriage between Lutherans and Roman Catholics requires instruction from a priest and/or the signing of a Roman prenuptial

[2] Such resolutions were passed by the American Baptist Convention, the Southern Baptist Convention, the International Convention of the Disciples of Christ, the Lutheran Church–Missouri Synod, and the United Presbyterian Church of the U.S.A.

contract and—Whereas, said contract involves a sinful promise or oath; violates the Christian conscience; condemns unborn children to the soul-destroying religion of the Anti-Christ; and is diametrically opposed to the eternal truths of God; and— Therefore, be it Resolved that we plead with our pastors and congregations to deal with this matter in their respective congregations in a firm, evangelical manner, and Resolved, that we ask The Family Life Committee to provide our people with pertinent information as soon as possible.[3]

The statement of policy issued by the United Presbyterian Church was somewhat less strong:

. . . the General Assembly counsels Presbyterians to refrain from marriage with Roman Catholics as long as the demands and rulings of that Church remain unchanged. . . . The Roman Catholic attitude with reference to mixed marriage makes it impossible for a wholesome family religious life to exist and continually requires the Protestant to surrender or compromise his personal convictions. What is even more serious, it involves the signing away of the spiritual birthright of unborn children by denying them the possibility of any religious training in the home other than that prescribed by the Roman Catholic Church. It is far better that the parties concerned should not marry than that these tragic results should follow.

Statements from other Protestant denominations all expressed similar views with varying degrees of intensity.

## ECUMENICAL DEVELOPMENTS

Beginning in the late 1950s and continuing into the 1970s, religious leaders of all faiths have been reevaluating what the function of religion should be in society. Conferences of laymen and church leaders have been held on state, national, and international levels to consider the views and responsibilities of churches. The blunt statements of Protestant denominations quoted above have now been tempered by greater insight and understanding. A significant change in interfaith marriage policy has taken place in the Catholic Church. In 1966 the Ecumenical Council of the Catholic Church recommended far-reaching changes in Catholic policy on many matters, including interfaith marriages.

As recommended by that council and amended by Pope Paul VI, the prenuptial agreement now provides for only one thing: that the Catholic party promise in the presence of a priest that all children born to the marriage shall be baptized and educated solely in the Catholic religion. This promise may or may not be in writing, depending upon the individual priest. The non-Catholic is no longer asked to make such a promise, although he or she is informed of the promise made by the Catholic partner. Even though the non-Catholic, in conscience, will not agree to

---

[3] Resolution adopted in convention by the Lutheran Church–Missouri Synod, Houston, Texas, June 1953.

have the children brought up in the Catholic faith, the bishop may grant a dispensation for the marriage.

The new regulations make it possible for the bishop, in granting a dispensation for a mixed marriage, to alter the traditional Catholic "form of marriage" in that a couple may now obtain permission to be married in a non-Catholic church or in a synagogue by a non-Catholic clergyman or rabbi or in a secular setting by a justice of the peace. All such marriages are now recognized by the Catholic Church as valid.

The only requirements for a mixed marriage involving a Catholic now are:

1  The couple must obtain permission, called a "dispensation," from the bishop.
2  After the dispensation is granted, there must be some form of public ceremony.

With the widespread use of contraceptives among Catholics, it was thought that the liberalized position of the prenuptial agreement would be followed by a liberalized view of the use of contraceptives. However, after much study, Pope Paul VI issued an encyclical in 1968 condemning the use of contraceptives by Catholics. Studies by Father Andrew Greeley of national samples of Catholics found that in 1961, before the encyclical had been issued, 45 percent of Catholics approved of the use of contraceptives; by 1974, 83 percent of Catholics reported they approved of the use of contraceptives.[4] These findings would indicate that there is little difference between Catholics and other faiths in their approval of birth control.

## ATTITUDES OF YOUNG PEOPLE ON MIXED MARRIAGES

Changes in student attitudes parallel changes among other groups in society. Over the past 20 years our studies of student attitudes have involved more than 6000 students in all parts of the country.[5] Students in 1967 and 1971 expressed far more willingness to marry across religious lines than students in 1952. In 1967, 75 percent and, in 1971, 91 percent said that, other things being equal, they would marry into a different faith, whereas in 1952 only 55 percent expressed that view. However, among those willing to marry across religious lines, we have found no increase in willingness to adopt the faith of the spouse. In 1952 and 1967, only 23 percent of the men and, in 1971, only 21 percent said they would adopt

---

[4] Andrew Greeley, William C. McCready, and Kathleen McCourt, *Catholic Schools in a Declining Church* (New York: Sheed and Ward, Inc., 1976).

[5] For a detailed summary of the 1952 study of student attitudes on mixed marriages, see Judson T. Landis, "Religiousness, Family Relationships, and Family Values in Protestant, Catholic and Jewish Families," *Marriage and Family Living* 22:4 (November 1960), 345.

the faith of the spouse if they made a mixed marriage. Of the women, about 33 percent in 1952 and 1967, and 26 percent in 1971, reported that they would change faiths, a decrease from the percentage in 1952.

This unwillingness to adopt the spouse's faith, and at the same time a greater willingness to intermarry, may reflect an awareness that lines dividing different religions are becoming less rigid and, therefore, for the spouses to have different religions might be less disruptive to the marriage than in the past. It may also represent an increased tendency today to accept people as they are, as individuals, and to expect one's friends or spouse to give to oneself the same kind of acceptance, including one's religion. Complete acceptance of another does not mean trying to change that person. Possibly these attitudes expressed by students in 1971 imply a definition of marriage as a relationship in which neither one must give up deeply held beliefs or values in order to merge identity with another person.

All our studies show that willingness to marry outside the faith is closely related to family religiousness; the devout are less willing to make a mixed marriage than are those indifferent to religion. Among the different faith groups, Catholics are most willing to marry outside the faith and Jews least willing. Both Catholics and Jews express less willingness than Protestants to change to the faith of the spouse if they intermarry.[6]

Our discussion up to this point is not meant to imply that because of the various kinds of changes we have been considering, it no longer matters whether one marries across lines of difference. In reality, mixed marriages have some built-in, special adjustments to make. Regardless of intellectualized minimizing of differences, deeply held values are a part of one's personality, and so are one's cultural background and even some aspects of one's nationality and racial background. In a relationship such as marriage, it matters deeply to individuals to be able to share all possible facets of life. If there is too much difference, inevitably they will experience some strains.

## FAILURE RATE IN RELIGIOUSLY MIXED AND NONMIXED MARRIAGES

Sociologists have made a number of studies to determine the divorce rate of Catholic–Protestant marriages.[7] Findings based on information

[6] Ibid., pp. 241–47.

[7] Loren E. Chancellor and Thomas P. Monahan, "Religious Preference and Interreligious Mixtures in Marriages and Divorces in Iowa," *The American Journal of Sociology* 61:3 (November 1955), 233–39; Thomas P. Monahan and William M. Kephart, "Divorces and Desertion by Religious and Mixed-religious groups," *American Journal of Sociology* 59:5 (March 1954), 454–65; Lee G. Burchinal and Loren E. Chancellor, "Survival Rates Among Religiously Homogamous and Interreligious Marriages," Agricultural and Home Economics Experiment Station, Iowa State University, Research Bulletin 512 (December 1962), p. 758.

gained from students' reports of their parents' marital status and religious affiliation all show a higher divorce rate among the parents who had married across religious lines than among the nonmixed parental marriages.

One of these studies was our analysis of data from 4108 mixed and nonmixed marriages among the parents of college students.[8] Special attention was given to conflict situations resulting from the religious differences; types of solutions attempted for the conflicts; the adjustments reached by the parents on the religious training of the children; and the eventual religious choice of the children. Using separation and divorce as an index of failure, the study showed that mixed marriages in which both husband and wife held to their separate religious faiths have always had a much higher rate of failure than other marriages. Where both parents were Catholic, the divorce rate was lowest, only 4.4 percent of the marriages ending in divorce; if both were Protestant, 6.0 percent ended in divorce. Of the marriages in which neither parent claimed any religious faith, 17.9 percent ended in divorce. The highest divorce rate of all existed in marriages in which the husband was Catholic and the wife Protestant. Of this group, 20.6 percent were divorced (see Figure 11–1).

Two earlier studies made in Washington and Maryland showed approximately the same results.[9] A factor explaining the lower divorce rate in Catholic mother and Protestant father unions is the hesitancy of the

[8] Judson T. Landis, "Marriages of Mixed and Non-Mixed Religious Faith," *American Sociological Review* 14:3 (June 1949), 401–7.

[9] H. Ashley Weeks, "Differential Divorce Rates by Occupation," *Social Forces* 21:3 (March 1943), 336.

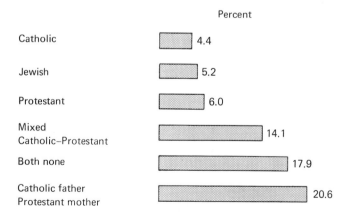

Percent

| | |
|---|---|
| Catholic | 4.4 |
| Jewish | 5.2 |
| Protestant | 6.0 |
| Mixed Catholic–Protestant | 14.1 |
| Both none | 17.9 |
| Catholic father Protestant mother | 20.6 |

FIG. 11–1 Religious affiliation and percentage of marriages broken by divorce or separation (4108 marriages). From Judson T. Landis, "Marriages of Mixed and Nonmixed Religious Faith," *American Sociological Review* 14:3 (June 1949), 401–7.

Catholic woman to seek divorce.[10] There may be as much difficulty in the Catholic mother and Protestant father unions as in any other combination, but they are less likely to end in divorce because the wife does not believe in divorce; she is more likely to stay in the marriage even if it is unhappy. On the other hand, if a Catholic father and Protestant mother union is unsatisfactory, the Protestant wife will not be as hesitant to ask for a divorce.

Another study that provided information concerning divorce rates of parents' marriages was made in a number of the major cities of the United States in the 1950s, gathering data from more than 40,000 families.[11] This research showed the divorce rate to be approximately three times higher in Catholic–Protestant marriages than in marriages between two of the same faith.

## WHY THE HIGH DIVORCE RATE IN CATHOLIC–PROTESTANT MARRIAGES?

Heiss found that "in general, the intermarried as compared with the intramarried are characterized by: (a) nonreligious parents, (b) greater dissatisfactions with parents when young, (c) greater family strife, (d) less early family integration, (e) greater emancipation from parents at the time of marriage." [12]

One study found that a larger percentage of mixed marriages were forced by pregnancy than was true of a comparable sample of in-faith marriages.[13] Rebellion against the family and its social values may motivate some people toward a mixed marriage. Such rebellion may not be exclusively against the family but also may be against society in general for discriminating against certain groups. Some people make mixed marriages because they have failed to find satisfying heterosexual relationships within their own group. Some may enter mixed marriages because they hope to achieve increased status, real or imagined. None of these motives can be helpful as a positive force toward good marital adjustment. They are all oriented to factors outside of and possibly irrelevant to the interaction of the two who will live their lives as a married couple.

One researcher who asked spouses in interfaith marriages to relate the most common causes of friction in their marriages reported the following conflicts, in order of frequency:

[10] Howard M. Bell, *Youth Tell Their Story* (Washington, D.C.: American Council on Education, 1938), p. 21.

[11] Carle C. Zimmerman and Lucius F. Cervantes, *Successful American Families* (New York: Pageant Press, Inc., 1960), pp. 153–54.

[12] Jerold S. Heiss, "Premarital Characteristics of the Religiously Intermarried in an Urban Area," *American Sociological Review* 25:1 (February 1960), 47–55.

[13] William P. Pratt, "A Study of Marriages Involving Premarital Pregnancy" (Ph.D. diss., Ann Arbor: University of Michigan,).

1   Conflict over what religion the children would follow

2   Conflict over church attendance

3   Conflict over interference by in-laws in religious matters

4   Conflict over size of family and/or spacing of children

Most of the couples reported having experienced one or more of the problems listed.[14]

**Religious faith of children in Protestant–Catholic marriages.** Since the Catholic has promised that he or she will bring up the children in the Catholic faith, and the non-Catholic is aware of the promise, the question of the religious training of the children would seem to be settled at marriage. But it is difficult for young unmarried people to project ahead and to know how they will feel when they have their children. After they are married and the children arrive, many people find that some things begin to matter to them more than they had anticipated. At this time, or later when the children are old enough to begin religious instruction, the question will come up for rethinking and some agreement will have to be reached. Our study of mixed marriages among the parents of college students gives some indication of what the eventual decision was about the religious upbringing of the children in these marriages.[15] There were 305 marriages of mixed Catholic–Protestant backgrounds; however, in 113 marriages one spouse had dropped his or her faith and had accepted the faith of the spouse. There were, then, 192 marriages that were mixed in that each spouse maintained his or her original faith. In these 192 marriages, half of the 392 children had been reared in the Protestant faith. The remainder had been reared in the Catholic faith (45.0) or had no faith (5.0). The most common tendency seems to be that the children follow the faith of the mother. Approximately 65 percent of the boys and 75 percent of the girls followed the faith of the mother.

**Parental policy on religious training in Protestant–Catholic marriages.** The students in our study of mixed marriages who were the products of Protestant–Catholic marriages were asked to describe the policy of their parents on religious instruction. A ranking from most common to least common practice revealed the following:

1   Mother took all the responsibility for the religious training (36 percent).

2   Our parents told us about both faiths but let us decide for ourselves when we were old enough (27 percent).

3   The responsibility for religious instruction was equally divided between our parents (20 percent).

[14] Alfred J. Prince, "A Study of 194 Cross-Religion Marriages," *Family Life Coordinator* 11:1 (January 1962), 3–6.

[15] Landis, "Marriages of Mixed and Non-mixed Religious Faith."

**4** We took turns going to both the church of my father and the church of my mother (7 percent).

**5** Father took all responsibility for the religious training (4 percent).

**6** Some of us went with my father to his church and some went with my mother to her church (3 percent).

In these findings, the dominance of the mother in the religious training of the children is observable.

There is some evidence that the Catholic father makes a stronger effort to defend his faith than the Protestant father does, in that the Catholic father has more to do with the religious training of the children. Croog and Teele, studying boys born to mixed Catholic–Protestant marriages, found that only 27 percent had followed the faith of the Protestant father, whereas 53 percent had followed the faith of the Catholic father.[16] The Catholic father's insistence upon having a place in the religious instruction of the children may be one factor explaining the high divorce rate when Catholic men marry Protestant women. In marriages of this combination, the divorce rate was 20.6; it was only 6.7 percent when Protestant men had married Catholic women. Half of the nominally Protestant men who had married Catholic women were not church members, and they were willing to let the wife rear the children in the Catholic faith without much conflict.

**Change to faith of spouse.** In our study, one Protestant–Catholic couple in three attempted a solution whereby one of the spouses accepted the faith of the other, usually before marriage. The shifts from Catholic to Protestant and from Protestant to Catholic were equally divided. Prince found that of those in his study who converted, twice as many wives as husbands changed to the faith of the spouse. He also found that most conversions to the faith of the partner took place before the end of the first year of marriage.[17] What evidence we have indicates that in the past mixed marriages had a better chance of success if the two could accept the same faith. In our study, among the cases in which one spouse changed to the faith of the other, the divorce rate was lower than in cases in which each held to his or her own faith.

## JEWISH–GENTILE MARRIAGES

The ecumenical movement has not had the same impact upon Jewish attitudes about mixed marriages as upon Protestant attitudes. Jews for many years have practiced ecumenicism in working with other faiths in all types of community activities, but Jewish leaders—orthodox, reform,

---

[16] Sydney H. Croog and James E. Teele, "Religious Identity and Church Attendance of Sons of Religious Inter-Marriages," *American Sociological Review* 32:1 (February 1967), 97.

[17] Prince, "A Study of 194 Cross-Religion Marriages."

and conservative—have not changed their position regarding interfaith marriages. They feel that the only way that Jews will survive as Jews is to resist interfaith marriages, since the Jewish people make up only 3 percent of the total population of the United States.

On the basis of a Gallup Poll in 1965 and again in 1971, it was found among Jews that 83 percent in 1965 but only 41 percent in 1971 were opposed to marriage with non-Jews. However, the great change in attitude was on the part of younger people rather than the leaders.

Jews recognize two types of Jewish–Gentile marriages: intermarriage and mixed marriage. Intermarriage is marriage between a converted Gentile and a Jew. Orthodox, conservative, and reform rabbis will perform marriages of converted Gentiles and Jews; however, this type of marriage is discouraged, since Jews do not feel that Gentiles converted to Judaism are faithful Jews. When the Gentile does not accept Judaism, the marriage is termed a mixed marriage.

Orthodox rabbis still hold to the ancient Jewish tradition in their opposition to mixed marriages and will not perform mixed marriage ceremonies. Reform rabbis are opposed to officiating at a mixed marriage, yet it has been estimated that as many as 35 percent of reform rabbis do perform mixed marriage ceremonies.[18]

Early studies of Jewish–Gentile marriages in New Haven between 1870 and 1950 found a very low interfaith marriage rate, approximately 5 percent.[19] Studies in New York, Cincinnati, and Stamford also found the low interfaith marriage rate.[20] Studies in recent years all indicate an increasing mixed marriage rate among Jews, and it is probably as high as 15 to 20 percent today. In interfaith marriages, the Jewish man is far more likely to marry outside the faith than is the Jewish woman. Whether Jews marry outside the faith is related not only to the degree of religiousness but also to the proportion of Jews in the population in a given area.

As with Catholics, Protestants, or denominational groups such as the Mennonites, who strongly prefer that their children marry within the group, Jews tend to have a higher proportion of marriages across religious lines if they live in an area where they are a distinct minority. Young people tend to marry within their own group if suitable mates are available, but when their own numbers are small, they must marry outside the group if they are to marry at all. Among Jews, marrying outside the faith is also associated with being born in the United States, having more than a high school education, having a high professional status, and being "conservative" or "reform" rather than "orthodox." [21]

It is estimated that half of the six million Jews in the United States

[18] Albert I. Gordon, *Intermarriage* (Boston: Beacon Press, 1964), p. 187.

[19] Ruby Jo Reeves Kennedy, "Single or Triple Melting Pot? Intermarriage Trends in New Haven, 1870–1950," *American Journal of Sociology* 57:1 (July 1952), 56.

[20] Milton L. Barron, "The Incidence of Jewish Intermarriage in Europe and America," *American Sociological Review* 11:1 (February 1946), 11–12.

[21] Gordon, *Intermarriage*, pp. 204–5.

live in New York City and the surrounding area. The potential for finding a Jewish mate is great, then, in New York City compared to Iowa, Nebraska, or even Washington, D.C. The interfaith marriage rate in Washington, D.C., was found to be 17 percent, 53 percent in Iowa.

## DIVORCE RATES IN JEWISH–GENTILE MARRIAGES

Zimmerman and Cervantes, in their study of 42,258 marriages in five large cities, found that when Jews had married outside their faith the divorce rate was higher than in marriages between Catholics and Protestants. Their findings showed, as have the other studies, that it was usually the Jewish man who married out of the faith rather than the Jewish woman, and in these marriages the divorce rate had varied from 25 percent in Boston to a high of 62 percent in Omaha.[22]

**Conflict in Jewish–Gentile marriages.** Most of the differences we have discussed in relation to Protestant–Catholic marriages exist in Jewish–Gentile marriages as well. In addition, cultural differences make adjustment more difficult in Jewish–Gentile marriages than in Protestant–Catholic marriages. Discrimination has forced Jews to emphasize family and group solidarity even more than other groups do. The Jewish family is a closely knit in-group into which it is often difficult for an outsider to fit. Family resistance to accepting the member from the out-group may be shown by both the Gentile and the Jewish families.

[22] Zimmerman and Cervantes, *Successful American Families*, p. 154.

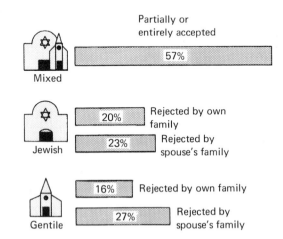

FIG. 11–2 Family acceptance and rejection in Jewish-Gentile marriages. Young people in love may bridge the gap in a mixed marriage, but it is more difficult for their families to merge their different backgrounds. Data from J. S. Slotkin, "Adjustment in Jewish-Gentile Intermarriages," *Social Forces* 21 (December 1942).

The views of Jewish families are logical since records show that those who marry outside the faith do tend to be lost to the faith and, in many cases, to the culture as well. The Greater Washington Study of 2400 intermarried Jewish families found that two-thirds of the families were bringing up the children as non-Jews. This study found that the children were more likely to follow the faith of the mother. Forty-four percent of the Jews in the Washington study identified themselves with some religion other than Judaism, and 29 percent identified with no religion at all.[23]

A case illustrates some of the kinds of considerations facing a couple contemplating a Jewish–Gentile marriage:

> Ann, a college girl in a midwestern school, fell in love with Art, a Jewish boy from New York. They decided to marry, but Ann's parents objected. Ann could not understand this. She was not acquainted with prejudice against Jews. In her small town there was only one Jewish family, and they were highly respected. In her college no distinctions were made between Jewish and Gentile students. Ann and Art planned that after marriage they would live in the East near his family. An older friend from whom Ann sought advice suggested that Ann go to New York City for a semester and take work toward her degree, meanwhile using the opportunity to become acquainted with Art's family. The plan was agreed upon, and Ann spent a semester in the eastern school. Art's family treated her with kindness and tried to make her feel that they would accept her as a member of the family, but at times she was uncomfortably aware that they were not happy about Art's decision to marry her. She felt that she could accept Art's religion and she liked his family, but she found it difficult to adjust to family customs that were quite different from those of her own family. She also concluded that she did not love him enough to endure with him the discrimination that she found in some places where she went with him. She realized, too, that she would be halfhearted in her acceptance of his life and that she might not be willing to have her children brought up in his faith and subjected to the discrimination she had observed. She decided not to go ahead with the interfaith marriage.

This girl's analysis of her attitudes and feelings concerning her own and her fiancé's different backgrounds enabled her to recognize that she was not capable of overcoming the difficulties that would be involved in the intended marriage. It is true that she might have been just as unable to cope with a marriage involving any difference at all. Perhaps she could only be happy married to a "local" boy in her own church and neighborhood. Some young people in a similar situation may find that, to them, the difficulties would not be insurmountable. Such persons may well decide, after cautious analysis of themselves and of the circumstances, to proceed with an interfaith marriage. However, they should be fully aware that it is easy to underestimate the importance of cultural and religious differences when one is emotionally involved during the courtship period and that it is hard to be realistic about the future. One tends to put future problems out of mind and avoid facing them before marriage.

[23] Gordon, *Intermarriage*, p. 206.

## MIXED MARRIAGES BETWEEN RELIGIOUS AND NON-RELIGIOUS PEOPLE

The individual who has a religious orientation to life may find that it is the same as a mixed marriage if he or she marries someone who is not religiously oriented. The contrasts in beliefs between the religiously oriented and nonreligiously oriented may be as great as the contrasts between Jews and Gentiles or Catholics and Protestants. Our study of mixed and nonmixed religious marriages, with a total of 125 couples in which the wife was a church member and the husband was of no religious faith, revealed that 16 percent had ended in divorce. When the wife was Protestant, the divorce rate was almost as high (19 percent) as when the Protestant wife married a Catholic. The high divorce rate in this combination of spouses may result in part from a clash of sacred and secular values. Available information seems to indicate that young people should compare and contrast their religious values and philosophies, as well as the differences in their specific religious faiths.

## INTERNATIONAL MARRIAGES

Many mixed marriages involve more than one type of mixture. With increased differences between the backgrounds of a couple, more adjustability and greater effort is required of each member of the pair if they are to build a good marriage.

The complicated set of differences that may be involved in a marriage can be recognized in this case:

At the time the case came to our attention, the couple had been married for 14 years. They lived on the plains of western Oklahoma in a fairly comfortable four-room farmhouse set in the midst of acres of wheatland. There was no tree on their land, nor were there any trees in sight in any direction from their house. The husband was a hard-working man of crude appearance. He owned his land, but he was not well off.

The wife was of French parentage. She had met and married her husband while he was stationed in France during his military service. She had never been happy in the marriage, and she was never able to adjust to the circumstances of their lives. Her reasons for her unhappiness were, "He told me he had a big American ranch, and I pictured beautiful trees and hills like my own France. So I left my family and came with him. This is what he brought me to. At home we had lots of fun and music, and I gave music lessons to the children of the village. But here it is always quiet—he never talks and he never laughs. When I've wanted a piano he says we can't afford it. In my family we could get along without a tractor but not without a piano. My family were so happy for me when I had a chance to marry him, so when I was disappointed, I couldn't write and tell them. It seemed better to stay and try to make the best of it, but I don't know if I did right. He doesn't think I am a good farmer's wife.

The husband also was unhappy in the marriage. It was impossible for him to understand how his wife could look look upon the vast wheat fields of his native state as less desirable than the small crowded village from which she had come.

All of her feelings about their home baffled and irritated him. He saw her as simply unwilling to accept the good life that he provided for her. But the two were in agreement in trying to stay together. The husband felt responsible for his wife's support, and she was unwilling publicly to admit defeat.

It will be seen that this marriage involved several kinds of differences. The most obvious was the nationality difference. They had to learn to understand each other's language. But more crucial in the marriage may have been the differences in their conceptions of what made life enjoyable. The fact that, because of their different backgrounds, they spoke a different language in many important areas of living was the real problem.

Many international marriages involve a difference in religion, as well as in customs and manner of living. That two people are from different countries—with nationality differences alone—may be of little importance to their happiness if they happen to be of the same religion and of approximately the same economic level and if the things they value in life are similar.

**International marriages may require special adaptability.** As means of travel and transportation become ever more advanced, more young people will consider marrying others from distant parts of the world. This is especially true on university campuses to which outstanding young people from all over the world come to study. Any woman who contemplates marriage with a man from a different part of the world should try to get a realistic picture of family life in the country from which he comes. She should also study herself and take time to know whether she is willing to work at adjusting to the life into which her marriage will take her. For, although ways are changing in countries all over the world and women are achieving an improved status in many countries, changes remain uneven or slow, and the American woman who marries into a culture significantly different from her own must be willing to do much of the adjusting. She cannot count on bringing swift changes in the ways of that world into which she will move.

An American woman married a man from East Pakistan and fled his country later with the complaints, "His mother sat on the floor to sew! They expected me to stay behind a wall with the other women! They always had tea instead of coffee, and I couldn't bear their food!" This girl probably would have had trouble even if she had married a man from her own home town. She would have found habits in her mother-in-law that were different from her own mother's habits; she would have encountered customs in her husband's family that she was not used to. Her attitudes were probably too rigid to enable her to accept, and adjust to, the differences that can be expected in any marriage; naturally, she had no chance at all for success when she married into a culture extremely different from her own.

Some international marriages also include a difference in race. Such marriages were relatively rare in the United States a generation ago. But the World Wars, the Korean war, the war in Vietnam, and the continued stationing of American men in many parts of the world have meant an increase in interracial marriages. Moreover, the various governmental educational programs that bring young men and women from all over the world to American universities in increasing numbers have resulted in more American marriages which have contrasting racial, religious, and national backgrounds. Interracial marriages are viewed with alarm in many parts of the United States, especially by parents.

**Black–white marriages.** Many of our states have had laws prohibiting interracial marriage, especially between a black and a white. In 1967 the United States Supreme Court handed down a ruling that, in effect, declared all such laws unconstitutional. (See Chapter 13 for a summary of laws dealing with interracial marriages.) However, social attitudes change slowly. As recently as 1965 a Gallup Poll found that 48 percent of adult Americans approved of laws making interracial marriage a crime. A follow-up Gallup Poll in 1972 found that 58 percent of blacks and 25 percent of whites approved of marriage between blacks and whites. A much larger percentage of college-educated people approved of black–white marriages than did the less educated. Heer and Bernard suggest that black–white marriages take place between people who live in areas in which integration is far enough advanced so that young people of both races go to school together, and perhaps live in the same neighborhoods. Evidence shows that those likely to marry each other come from similar socioeconomic and educational backgrounds.[24, 25] Even so, their marriages may be disapproved by people of both races in their communities. In 1972 the black students on the campus of a major state university successfully prevented the administration from appointing a black man as the new director of student affairs because his wife was white.

In black–white marriages the male is more often black and the marriages more often involve prior divorce for both; the female is more often foreign-born or of foreign parentage and both are older than the average age at marriage. Today less than 1 percent of all marriages in the United States are interracial.

Little reliable data is available on the success of interracial marriages because of the relatively small numbers that take place. Probably the best data we have come from the California divorce statistics, which in 1966 began requiring divorcing people to list their race. These data show that interracial marriages are terminated much sooner than *intra*racial mar-

[24] David M. Heer, "Negro–White Marriages in the United States," *Journal of Marriage and the Family* 28:3 (August 1966), 262–72.

[25] J. Bernard, "Note on Educational Homogamy in Negro–White and White–Negro Marriages, 1960," *Journal of Marriage and the Family* 28:3 (August 1966), 274.

riages, and that black–white marriages are terminated sooner than all other types of mixed racial marriages.[26] Heer found in analyzing data of the census from 1960 to 1970 that black–white marriages have a high divorce rate.[27]

**Some problems of interracial marriages.** Some specific problems other than prejudice against such marriages must be faced in interracial marriages. The children of mixed racial marriages are sometimes subjected to discrimination by both the races. People who can endure criticism or prejudice when it is directed against themselves may suffer intensely when such attitudes strike at their children. For this reason some of the most difficult problems in mixed racial marriages as in marriages of mixed religion arise in relation to the children. Parents may possibly change their religion when they see that their differences are the cause of insecurity or confusion for their children, but, of course, they cannot change their race. The fact that there is no sound biological basis for the opposition to interracial marriages becomes merely an academic point; as long as prejudice against such marriages still exists, social attitudes are likely to create special difficulties for interracial marriages.

Couples of mixed race may have difficulty finding satisfactory housing in many parts of the United States, in spite of laws designed to protect them. They may also be deprived of congenial companionship among other married couples in their community unless they can find and associate with other "mixed" couples. Young people who make mixed marriages while in a university community, where attitudes are more inclined toward acceptance of such marriages than in other communities, may encounter new problems when they settle elsewhere. Whether the problems are distressing or traumatic to a couple will depend on their own values and on the quality of the relationship they have been able to achieve in their marriage. In some cases, if the mixed marriage was made hastily and without realizing the type of problems that will inevitably arise, one or both may tend to react by blaming the other or the other's family for troubles, so that when the pressure of opposing backgrounds becomes severe the marriage may not survive.

It is important to recognize that interracial marriages, and international marriages involving religious and cultural differences, inevitably require more of the individual than is required in the usual type of marriage between people of similar backgrounds.

This part of our discussion of mixed marriages may seem to be pessimistic, but rather, it is realistic from the viewpoint of individuals most concerned about having a happy marriage. Certainly, some marriages

[26] *Divorce in California* (Sacramento: Department of Public Health, Bureau of Vital Statistics, October 1967), p. 29.

[27] David M. Heer, "The Prevalence of Black–White Marriages in the United States, 1960 and 1970," *Journal of Marriage and the Family* 36:2 (May 1974), 246–57.

involving several different kinds of mixtures with the potential for the whole range of mixed-marriage problems turn out to be successful and happy.

When such is the case, the success is due to qualities of flexibility within the two individuals themselves. They have the ability to face their problems, to do what they can about them, and to accept circumstances or situations many other people might consider unendurable.

## DIFFERENCES THAT DO NOT CONSTITUTE A MIXED MARRIAGE

**Intelligence and education.**  Differences in intelligence, under some circumstances, may involve hazards to happiness for one or both spouses. Terman's research examined this kind of difference more intensively than succeeding studies attempted to do, and found that when the husbands were far superior to the wives in intelligence, the husbands rated their happiness low although the wives rated happiness high.[28] If the intelligence ratings were reversed, the husband being inferior to the wife, the wife's happiness score was low. Couples with the highest happiness rating for both husband and wife were those in which the husband and the wife were about equal in intelligence (Fig. 11–3).

Several studies have been made in an attempt to discover whether educational differences of the spouses affect adjustment in marriage. The majority of these studies show that the same amount of education is slightly favorable to good adjustment in marriage.[29] Possibly, if someone from a family of highly educated people who place great value on education married into a family with little or no formal education, the marriage

[28] Lewis M. Terman, *Psychological Factors in Marital Happiness* (New York: McGraw-Hill Book Company, Inc., 1938), p. 193.

[29] Kirkpatrick, Hamilton, Landis, Terman.

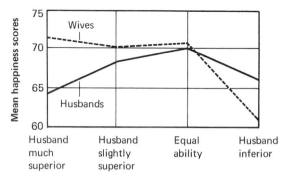

Relative mental ability

FIG. 11–3  Mean happiness according to rated mental ability of spouses. From Lewis M. Terman, *Psychological Factors in Marital Happiness* (New York: McGraw-Hill Book Company, Inc., 1938).

would involve elements of a mixed marriage, since educational differences may represent significant differences in family background in such other matters as viewpoints, values, and goals in life.

Studies of graduates of several colleges and universities found that approximately 40 percent of the women married men from the same institutions. Further, a series of studies have found that people tend to marry others with about the same intelligence as measured by IQ tests. Homogamy definitely operates in mate selection on the basis of education and intelligence.

**Physical differences.**   Physical differences such as a difference in height are noted here because they tend to loom large in the minds of some people, sometimes larger than other differences that are not so visible but that have serious implications for marital success.

It is not the physical difference, but rather the attitude held toward the difference, that may cause problems in a marriage. A tall woman who feels embarrassed and conspicuous when dating a man shorter than herself would adjust more happily in a marriage with a man her own height or taller. A man who feels inferior and conscious of his shortness when with taller girls might better marry a girl no taller than himself, unless he can change his attitude. If he is uncomfortable about their difference in height, his attitude may cause his wife to feel disparaged and uncomfortable about her own tallness. People who feel there is something wrong with their physical appearance as a couple may have the effect upon each other of destroying self-confidence rather than of building up each other's self-esteem. In such cases, although the height difference in itself is of no significance, feelings about it may have an adverse effect upon the relationship.

**Age differences.**   Various studies have attempted to determine whether age differences between spouses affect the happiness of marriages. The findings of Burgess and Cottrell are representative. They found no consistent relationship between ages of the spouses and their mutual happiness, although the combinations with the largest percentage of good adjustments were those in which the wife was older than the husband. After analyzing these data, Burgess and Cottrell state, "When we summarize the findings regarding age differences, the popular romantic notion that, for marital happiness, the husband should be somewhat older than the wife, is not substantiated for the group studied." [30]

If a woman marries a man ten years older than herself, it may mean that she has been conditioned to respect older men, or has idolized her own father, or only that she is more mature than others of her chronological age. Similarly, the man who marries an older woman may do so because he needs to be mothered and because she wants to mother

[30] Burgess and Cottrell, *Predicting Success or Failure in Marriage*, pp. 161–64.

someone, or they may both simply be self-confident people indifferent to age differences. The marriage will be above average in happiness if it meets the needs of both.

Only when age differences are extreme, such as a variation of 20 years or more, might age differences constitute a mixed marriage, and not necessarily so even in such cases. But if, because of great disparity in age, the two belong to two different generations with contrasting values, recreational and cultural interests, and viewpoints, their differences may be as great as if they had married into different cultures. Such a marriage could involve many of the problems occurring in mixed marriages of other types.

People do tend to marry those within their own age group. One survey of American families found that when husbands were between 14 and 24 years of age, 93 percent of their wives were of that age. Among older people, not so large a percentage were within the same age group, but the majority of wives and husbands were within the same age group at all ages.[31]

## SUMMARY

A mixed marriage may result from a combination of factors, all of which make for extreme difference. The greater the number of contrasts, the more hurdles will have to be surmounted to achieve happiness in the marriage.

Consideration of all types of mixed marriages forces the conclusion that, whether the difference is in race, religion, nationality, or certain other characteristics and circumstances in the individual's make-up or background, a marriage that involves differences serious enough to make it a "mixed" marriage will require special effort to make it a success. Further, it seems that the differences in mixed marriages do not necessarily decrease with the passing of time after marriage. They tend to become magnified in the minds of the couple and their families. To achieve happiness in such marriages, individuals must be mentally and emotionally mature and must possess more than average understanding and tolerance.

When considering any marriage, one needs to evaluate honestly his or her own marriageability and the degree of determination to work at making a good marriage, no matter what circumstances may arise. This is more true of those making a mixed marriage than of the usual couple.

## REVIEW QUESTIONS

1  Define mixed marriage. How do the adjustment problems of mixed marriages differ from adjustment problems in other marriages?

[31] Metropolitan Life Insurance Company, "The American Family Today," *Statistical Bulletin* 41 (1960), 7.

**2** What are the two items a Catholic promises in the prenuptial agreement?

**3** How do you account for the fact that the intermarriage rate of Jews in Iowa is much higher than in New York?

**4** What are the attitudes of Catholic and Protestant young people toward marrying outside their faith, as revealed by studies of students since 1952? Toward changing to the faith of the spouse?

**5** What percentage of Catholics marry outside their faith?

**6** What are some of the factors explaining the higher divorce rates in mixed marriages?

**7** What has research revealed about the faiths of children reared in Catholic–Protestant marriages? How is this explained if agreement has been made before marriage that the children will be reared in the Catholic faith?

**8** What seems to be the most common parental policy on religious instruction?

**9** Give some of the reasons for the higher divorce rate in Catholic father–Protestant mother marriages.

**10** What is the position of the three large Jewish groups toward mixed marriage? Toward intermarriage?

**12** Cite factors that make for conflict in Jewish–Gentile marriages.

**13** Do differences in intelligence or education between spouses make for unhappiness in marriage? High divorce rate?

**14** What do research studies show in regard to differences in age of spouses and happiness in marriage?

**15** Discuss some unsound motivations for intermarriage.

## PROJECTS AND ACTIVITIES

**1** Have a rabbi, a priest, and a minister present their views on mixed marriages to the class.

**2** In order to break down religious, nationality, and racial prejudice, there should be a biological fusing of different groups; or we might say that for the good of society one should make a mixed marriage. Is it possible to harmonize this point of view with what has been said about mixed marriages in this chapter?

# ENGAGEMENT

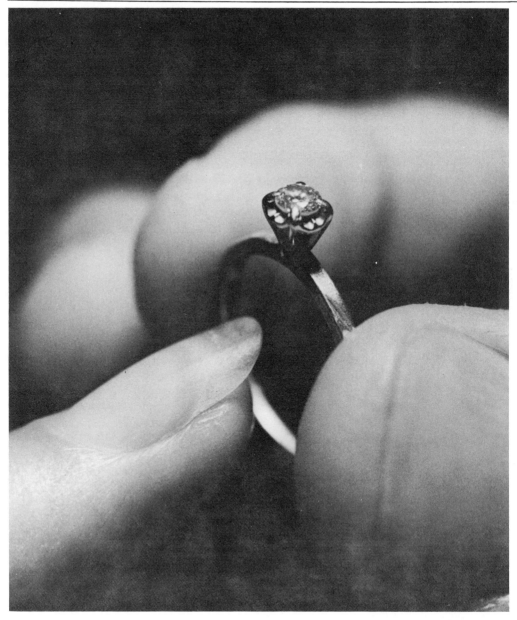

# 12

In the past a promise to marry constituted a legal contract. If a man broke an engagement against the will of the woman she could sue him for damages. In 1976 a judge ruled against a Washington woman who was suing her ex-fiancé for damages amounting to over a half-million dollars because he had broken the engagement. The woman reported that she had sold her home and furnishings, and that the couple had bought a new home. The judge ruled that, in this modern age, engagement is not viewed as legally binding and dismissed her case.

Formerly, it was not unusual for the parents of a girl to approach the man she was dating if he had not proposed within reasonable time and ask whether he had "serious intentions." Parents believed that it was not fair for a girl to have her time taken up with the attentions of a suitor who did not intend to marry her, and that a man should not be too slow in making up his mind. Because of social changes and the far greater freedom of young people in courtship choices and behavior, parental action of this type is not likely to occur today. Parents may worry over the fact that a daughter is wasting her best years on a man who does not intend to marry her, or who is not a suitable marriage prospect, but they take no direct action. A concern of parents today is for a daughter who may be living with a man of whom they do not approve. They may believe the man to be already married, and may realize that he has no intention of ever marrying their daughter. The parents see their daughter as not permitting herself to have normal dating experiences which could lead to a desirable marriage.

## AVERAGE TIME—FIRST DATE TO ENGAGEMENT

The majority of people among the college population do not rush into engagements. We asked more than 500 single and married students who had been engaged to state how much time had elapsed between the first date and the engagement. A summary is presented in Table 12-1. Nearly one-half had dated for a year or more before becoming engaged, 53 percent were engaged within the first year of dating, and 27 percent were engaged within less than five months.

In a recent study of 122 engagements, those couples who were formally engaged told how much time had elapsed during each stage of their courtship.[1] The couples reported an average of five months of casual dating with each other, eight months of dating steadily, and eight months during which they had had an "understanding"; they had been formally engaged an average of six months, and the average time until the wedding was seven and one-half months. The average time from first date to marriage would be approximately three years.

The 122 engaged couples described the progress of the development of their love from the first dates to engagement. With most of these couples, love developed gradually as they became well acquainted. (See Table 12-2.)

TABLE 12-1    Average length of time elapsed in 546 courtships from the first date to engagement

| Length of time | Number | Percentage |
|---|---|---|
| 1–2 weeks | 11 | 2.0 |
| 3–4 weeks | 15 | 3.0 |
| 1–2 months | 50 | 9.0 |
| 3–4 months | 70 | 13.0 |
| 5–8 months | 105 | 19.0 |
| 9–11 months | 39 | 7.0 |
| 1–2 years | 142 | 26.0 |
| 3 years up | 114 | 21.0 |
| Total | 546 | 100.0 |

TABLE 12-2    Description of the progress of love up to engagement, as given by 122 engaged couples

| Progress of love | Men (N–122) | Women (N–122) |
|---|---|---|
| We both fell in love at first sight | 4.0% | 4.0% |
| I fell in love at first sight | 1.0 | 3.0 |
| Fiancé(e) in love at first sight | 0.0 | 1.0 |
| One fell in love first, the other later | 33.0 | 30.0 |
| It was a gradual falling in love for both | 62.0 | 62.0 |

[1] Judson T. Landis, research among students at University of California, Berkeley, and Chico State College, see footnote 6, p. 44.

ENGAGEMENT

## IMPORTANCE OF BECOMING WELL ACQUAINTED

It is important that people become thoroughly acquainted before engagement or marriage. The stability of a marriage depends on qualities within the marriage itself, and outside institutional forces that exert pressures to keep marriages intact are less powerful. Marriages last if comradeship, cooperation, emotional security, and affectional satisfaction are present. If some of these elements are not present, there is a good chance that the marriage will fail. Our studies of three groups—those successfully married, couples having counseling, and those divorced—showed that among the happily married group were more who had had long acquaintances and more who had taken time for an engagement stage of courtship before marrying (see Table 4-2).

## BECOMING ENGAGED AND ENGAGEMENT RITUALS

Our study of engagements showed that there had been a proposal of marriage by the man in about 75 percent of the cases. In these cases most of the women (82 percent) said that the proposal was not a surprise, and 93 percent accepted at once. If there has been good communication and a satisfying relationship between a couple for some time, as was true of these couples, the marriage proposal and acceptance are not a sudden development. About one-fourth of the couples said that there was never any formal proposal and acceptance, but that "we just understood that we were engaged."

As for the places in which couples become engaged, if there were such a specific occasion, one-fourth of this group became engaged while in automobiles, and about one-half while at the home or college residence of one of them.

Half of the men in this group of engaged couples went through the formality of asking the woman's parents for permission to marry her. However, the custom is not the same as in former generations, when the man was expected to go alone to the girl's father and ask him for his daughter's "hand in marriage." In two-thirds of the cases in which parental permission was asked, both members of the engaged pair went together to ask for parental approval, and they consulted both parents together, not just the father. In many cases the asking procedure is more nearly just a ritual of informing the parents of plans, not in asking for permission that could be refused or given.

Table 12-3 summarizes other rituals observed by the engaged couples. Notice that a larger percentage of the women than of the men reported having certain rituals.

In our 1967 study, the 581 couples who had highly successful marriages reported that in their approach to marriage they had gone through all the stages that are still the custom on college campuses. Specifically,

TABLE 12-3

Percentages of 122 engaged men and 122 engaged women reporting specific rituals during engagement

| Rituals | Men (N–122) | Women (N–122) |
|---|---|---|
| Using pet names | 66.0% | 74.0% |
| Using a special language | 53.0 | 65.0 |
| Considering a certain song "our" song | 49.0 | 54.0 |
| Sharing special jokes | 64.0 | 70.0 |
| Going to certain places | 73.0 | 74.0 |
| Observing significant dates | 77.0 | 74.0 |

94 percent had dated each other steadily and 88 percent had had a formal engagement. In contrast are findings from another group of people in the same study, 155 who were all clients in a marriage counseling center associated with a court of conciliation. Among these people in troubled marriages, only 37 percent had had a formal engagement stage in their courtship, and 71 percent had dated each other only "casually." This is not to imply that having had or not having had an engagement stage during courtship was the crucial factor in the marriage problems of the second group. Among people who marry hastily after only a brief period of friendship there may be more individuals who are impulsive and incautious in decision making in other matters as well. The group reporting no engagement also includes a higher percentage of previously married people. Whatever the explanation, the engagement stage in courtship has been skipped more frequently by couples whose marriages have serious problems than by happily married couples.

## RINGS AS SYMBOLS

The ancient Egyptians used a ring as the symbol of a pledge. This custom has come down to us and is widely followed in present-day dating and engagements. Various kinds of rings are given in each of the stages of courtship from casual dating to formal engagement and marriage. The ring recognizes a friendship or relationship, but when given during less serious dating stages it has no precisely defined meaning. In our studies, the students who had had serious love relationships reported on what symbol had been given at each stage of their affair. More than a third of the girls had worn a ring during steady relationships and the understanding engagement. Pins, such as fraternity or sorority pins, are not used by many couples today. Over 80 percent of those who were formally engaged had marked this stage with a ring. Kinds of rings given differ in different stages of courtship. At the time of formal engagement the girl usually receives a ring of either intrinsic or special symbolic value.

## SIGNIFICANCE OF ENGAGEMENT

When a couple becomes engaged, they usually believe that the matter is settled for all time. However, as they come to know each other better during this period, they sometimes decide to break their engagement. Thus engagements today differ from those in earlier days, when the promise to marry was considered a legal contract that would eventuate in marriage. In those days the engagement was a period specifically for planning and preparing for the wedding. In practice, it has now also become a period of more intimate acquaintance, during which both partners may more accurately evaluate marriage desirability. We recognize that many promises to marry should never have been made and that it is better to break an engagement than to go into an unsuitable marriage that may later be dissolved. However, many people find it very difficult to break an engagement that has been announced. If family and friends accept the match as settled, one who begins to have doubts is inclined to struggle with the doubts and to believe that the uncertainty is due to prewedding jitters. Painful emotional experiences and some unworkable marriages could be avoided if more caution preceded engagement.

## BROKEN ENGAGEMENTS

Earlier studies of engagement disclosed that a large percentage did not end in marriage.[2] These studies were made after wars, and the disruption of lives during wartime conditions leads to a high incidence of broken engagements.

Evidence available more recently seems to show that for years the incidence of broken engagements has not changed greatly. Of the 581 married couples in our 1967 study, 20 percent of the men and 33 percent of the women said they had broken one or more engagements before the engagement that led to their marriage. These people had been in the engagement period during the 1950s. Our study of broken love relationships among people who were students in 1967 showed that one-fourth of both men and women had broken one or more engagements. Some of these students, predictably, will have other broken engagements before they marry.

Earlier studies of broken engagements did not analyze the data with respect to whether the relationships had been broken after a formal engagement or after an "understanding" that may have been defined as more of a commitment by one member of a couple than by the other. In our 1967 study, those reporting distinguished between "understanding" engagements and formal engagements; the findings showed that 78 percent of the broken relationships had been understanding engagements

2 Ernest W. Burgess and Paul Wallin, *Engagement and Marriage* (Philadelphia: J. B. Lippincott Co., 1953), p. 273.

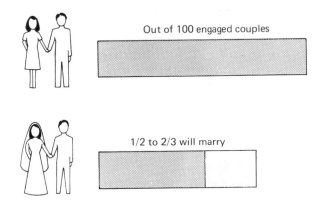

Out of 100 engaged couples

1/2 to 2/3 will marry

FIG. 12–1  Many engagements do not end in marriage.

and only 22 percent had been formal engagements. Apparently, the understanding stage of a courtship tends to weed out relationships that would not result in satisfactory marriages; those who go ahead into a formal engagement have a more serious commitment and are less likely to break the relationship.

## WHY ENGAGEMENTS ARE BROKEN

Whether a relationship is broken during serious courtship or following a formal engagement, the reasons for the break probably have the same pattern. A couple's association during serious courtship provides opportunities for greater realism about the possibility of a successful marriage between them.

Table 12-4 summarizes the reasons given by 810 students who had broken one or more engagements. The causes of broken engagements given by the students can be grouped as follows:

TABLE 12-4    Percentages of 810 students in 18 colleges giving specific reasons for broken engagements

| Cause of breakup | Men (N–240) | Women (N–570) |
|---|---|---|
| Parents | 11.0% | 12.0% |
| Mutual loss of interest | 8.0 | 8.0 |
| Partner lost interest | 13.0 | 10.0 |
| I lost interest | 18.0 | 22.0 |
| Separation | 19.0 | 19.0 |
| Contrasts in background | 11.0 | 14.0 |
| Incompatibility | 10.0 | 15.0 |
| I was not ready for marriage | 18.0 | 25.0 |
| Partner was not ready for marriage | 7.0 | 18.0 |

1 One or both lost interest

2 One or both not ready for marriage

3 Separation

4 Incompatibility

5 Contrasts in family background

6 Influence of family and friends

7 Other factors, such as fear of marriage

**Loss of interest.**   More than a third of the men and women said that the reason the engagement was broken was that one or both lost interest. A higher percentage of women said that they had lost interest, and a smaller percentage admitted that it was the man who lost interest. Are women quicker to perceive that a planned marriage would be unworkable and so "lose interest"? Or are women less willing to admit that the man lost interest and broke the engagement?

Engagements after a short acquaintance are often based on some superficial attraction that may wear off as the couple becomes better acquainted. Love-at-first-sight engagements are frequently of this type, since they may have no basis in common bonds. Therefore, they may not survive the more careful scrutiny of the engagement period. The element of adventure or new experience, which may have represented romance when the couple became engaged, may wear off during the engagement period and leave little to hold some couples together.

**Separation and maturing.**   When engaged student couples separate to attend different colleges, the engagement has little chance of withstanding the years of separation. Both are constantly in the company of other young people, and they are likely to become interested in dating someone among the new acquaintances and to drift apart.

An important cause of broken engagements is the rapid emotional maturing of people of courtship age. The young person who becomes engaged while in high school but who does not plan to be married before finishing college will change and mature greatly during the four years. His conception of a desirable mate will be so modified that the high school sweetheart may later fail to measure up. People find that the mate they choose at 22 or 24 may bear little resemblance to the one they would have chosen at 18 or 20. Many of the broken engagements were made at an early age, when the individuals were immature; these engagements could not stand the test of more mature judgment. In addition to increased maturity, interests and values may also be changed by college experience. Among the most common reasons given by students in 1967 was that one or both were not yet ready for marriage. With more than half of the 810 students who had broken engagements, the relationship had begun when they were under 18 years old. Many of the loves had started when the young people were in the early years of high school.

As they grew older they realized that they had become seriously attached at too young an age and that they were not ready for marriage.

**Incompatibility.** During the engagement period, with more time spent exclusively together, the couple may learn more about what values and basic interests they actually have in common. Sometimes they discover more divergence between them than they had recognized when their relationship was more casual. Also, habitual ways of behaving toward family members and others are likely to become apparent if the association is given time.

The serious dating stage of a romance may accomplish many of the purposes of engagement. A steady couple may associate together in almost all ways as if they were engaged, and if they are alert to danger signals and it seems best not to go on to marriage, they can break off their relationship early enough so that both may be spared the unhappy emotional effects that would accompany a broken engagement.

**Cultural contrasts.** Many "mixed" engagements do not survive the contrasts in backgrounds. Engagements are often entered into before the young people have had any opportunity to know each other's families. If it is a mixed engagement of nationality or race, the couple may have thought the difference was of little importance while they were dating; but as they approach marriage and become better acquainted with the future in-laws, each may find it difficult to accept the cultural background of the other. Resistance to the engagement on the part of the family or families may also contribute toward breaking a "mixed" engagement.

**Friends and family.** During engagement, friends and families have an opportunity to get acquainted with the prospective husband or wife. Most young people find it difficult to go ahead with a marriage if their intended is looked upon unfavorably by friends and family. When a young woman recognizes that her fiancé is not liked by her family, it not only hurts her pride but may also cause her to look at him more candidly. Our study of the divorced people and of the couples having marriage counseling showed a clear relationship between parental approval of a marriage and success or failure in the marriage (see Table 4-2). Our findings also indicate that the way the wife's family feels about the forthcoming marriage is a more significant indicator than the way the husband's family feels.

Other studies of divorced people support the conclusion that the degree of approval of friends and family is rather closely related to how marriages succeed.[3] Goode points out that one factor in the greater success

[3] William J. Goode, *After Divorce* (New York: The Free Press, 1956), pp. 81–85; Harvey J. Locke, *Predicting Adjustment in Marriage* (New York: Holt, Rinehart & Winston, Inc., 1951), p. 119.

ENGAGEMENT

of approved marriages might be that friends and family who approve will make an effort to help when crises arise. If there has been disapproval, active support for maintaining the marriage might be lacking since the family felt pessimistic about the outcome from the beginning.

**Other factors.** During the financial planning that usually must be done by an engaged pair, the economic values are more likely to be revealed, so that each comes to know how the other thinks. A clash in economic values may cause the couple to recognize other basic value differences that they did not become aware of until they began financial planning.

Sometimes an overdependence upon parents on the part of one or the other does not show up until a couple are thoroughly acquainted during engagement. For a young man or woman to be too dependent upon parents, or strongly dominated by parents in choices and decisions, may mean the person is not yet ready for engagement or marriage and still needs some years for growing up. Extreme rebellion is one face of dependency. The person who makes a choice because of parents' opposition is no more independent than the one who decides because they favor the choice. He or she is still basing actions and choices upon parents and their views rather than considering all evidence and making an independent judgment.

There are many reasons, then, why couples break their engagements, and most of them are sound. Engagement provides the couple with an opportunity to hesitate on the verge of marriage and to make sure the marriage has a chance for success. However, too many broken engagements in the experience of one person may mean that the individual is reckless or superficial in relationships with others, making commitments impulsively or for exploitative or selfish motives without having a serious intention to marry.

## RECOVERING FROM EMOTIONAL INVOLVEMENT WHEN ENGAGEMENT IS BROKEN

When an emotional commitment has been made, whether the engagement is formal or an understanding, breaking an engagement usually involves some trauma for one or both. Responses of 810 formerly engaged people who reported on how long it takes people to get over the emotional shock of a broken engagement are summarized in Table 12-5.

For some people there can be a feeling of relief when an engagement is finally ended. As we have pointed out, the broken engagement is more likely to take place in "understanding" engagements when people are not as deeply involved as in the formal engagement. If both have come to see danger signals in their relationship or have found themselves growing apart, they may mutually agree that the relationship should end. The very

TABLE 12-5

Length of time to get over emotional involvement of the engagement, as reported by 810 formerly engaged students

| Length of time | Men (N–240) | Women (N–570) |
|---|---|---|
| by final date | 7.0% | 12.0% |
| 1–2 weeks | 16.0 | 10.0 |
| 3–4 weeks | 13.0 | 10.0 |
| 1–2 months | 18.0 | 17.0 |
| 3–5 months | 22.0 | 21.0 |
| 6–12 months | 13.0 | 22.0 |
| 1 year and over | 11.0 | 8.0 |

quick recovery of some people suggests that in many cases the engagement does end when both have reached a point of readiness for the break. The final break is no shock or surprise to either one. If the break is one-sided and one remains eager to marry, the shock is far greater. Or if there had been a formal engagement and both were seriously committed to the planned marriage, breaking the engagement may be traumatic.

When one is in the midst of the emotional turmoil that may occur at the time of a broken engagement, the experience seems unique. The tendency is to feel that no one else has ever endured the same ordeal. It is helpful in such circumstances if one can realize that, not only have others suffered similarly, but the experience tends to follow a rather specific pattern.

A number of years ago Kirkpatrick and Caplow made some interesting studies of the patterns of emotional trends in the courtship experience of college students.[4] Their findings remain enlightening. The students cooperating checked graphs representing their feelings during the readjustment period after broken love affairs had ended.

More than half said Graph B among the four graphs in Figure 12-2 represented their readjustment feelings. That is, their feelings approached indifference to the former loved person and no serious trauma remained. Fifteen percent indicated that there was a temporary flare-up of affection for the loved one, which soon decreased and became indifference (Graph A). Another 15 percent went through a period of recurring upsurges in affection for the former loved person before tapering off to a state of indifference (Graph D). In 11 percent of the cases, what had been love

[4] Clifford Kirkpatrick and Theodore Caplow, "Emotional Trends in the Courtship Experience of College Students as Expressed by Graphs with Some Observations on Methodological Implications," *American Sociological Review* 10:5 (October 1945), 619–26.

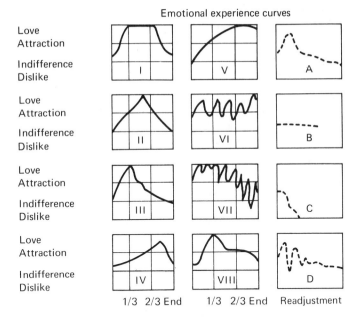

FIG. 12–2 Emotional trends in the courtship of college students as expressed by graphs. Of 400 university students who had had 900 love affairs, the largest percentage thought Graph 1 most nearly represented their feelings toward the loved one during the love experience.

turned into dislike (Graph C). In approximately 90 percent of the terminated love affairs reported, a normal state of adjustment, indifference to the former person loved, was achieved.

In our study among students, we included a section adapted from Kirkpatrick and Caplow's study of adjustment reactions to broken love affairs among students.[5] Table 12-6 summarizes the responses of 1894 of the students who had broken off serious love affairs. It is interesting that the adjustment reactions are quite universal and that men and women resort to the same ones with about the same frequency, except that a larger percentage of women "preserve keepsakes" and remember unpleasant associations. Most of the adjustments are normal and acceptable reactions, although some tend to be neurotic or would have to be classed as neurotic if they were extreme or long continued. The girl who constantly daydreams about the former lover, refuses to date others, and imagines that he is unhappy with his new girl friend or wife, is developing an unhealthy mental state and may need counseling to reorient her life.

The findings on how long it takes to get over broken engagements

[5] Kirkpatrick and Caplow, *American Journal of Sociology* 51 (September 1945), 114–25. Reprinted in Judson T. Landis and Mary G. Landis, eds., *Readings in Marriage and the Family* (Englewood Cliffs, N.J.: Prentice-Hall, Inc., 1952), pp. 79–90.

TABLE 12-6

Percentages of 1894 students from 18 colleges in 1967 giving adjustment reactions when most serious love affair ended

| Reaction | Men (N–624) | Women (N–1270) |
|---|---|---|
| Remembered pleasant association | 70.0% | 75.0% |
| Got dates with others | 62.0 | 68.0 |
| Daydreamed about partner | 40.0 | 37.0 |
| Preserved keepsakes | 21.0 | 41.0 |
| Avoided meeting him (her) | 30.0 | 33.0 |
| Read over old letters | 23.0 | 31.0 |
| Attempted to meet him (her) | 25.0 | 21.0 |
| Remembered unpleasant association | 21.0 | 32.0 |
| Frequented places of common association | 22.0 | 20.0 |
| Liked or disliked people because of resemblance | 12.0 | 14.0 |
| Daydreamed | 11.0 | 12.0 |
| Avoided places of common association | 17.0 | 19.0 |
| Resolved to get even | 5.0 | 5.0 |
| Thought of suicide | 5.0 | 5.0 |

point up a common relationship in love affairs: the one-sided involvement. One member of the couple may feel very much in love and wish to continue a relationship, while the other prefers to end the affair. When the affair ends, one is relieved, the other hurt.

The emotional upset for the one hurt may be compared with a case of some of the childhood diseases, in that such cases follow a definite course. Mothers of children who are ill and feverish sometimes become frantic with worry during the time when the illness is at its worst stage, just before recovery begins. At this point the family doctor will attempt to comfort the mother and the patient by telling them that it is a "typical" case, that there are no complications, and that if the patient is kept comfortable and given reasonable care, nature will bring about recovery. When several children in succession in a family have to be nursed through such illnesses, the mother learns to ease each child through by giving good care and by encouraging the patient to recognize that the disease is taking its course and will soon be over. Friends and family of the person suffering from a broken love affair have much the same role. They can do little except to try to live peaceably with the emotionally upset individual, meanwhile hoping there will be no "complications," such as a sudden marriage on the rebound or an unhappy clinging to grief.

It is hard, however, to convince the victim of a broken love affair that this one is a "typical" case. A part of the process of attaining maturity is learning by experience that recovery, in the sense of regaining emotional balance, is possible from even the most devastating loss or bereavement.

The person who can work at absorbing tasks as soon as possible after emotional loss can hasten such recovery. The students who reported broken love affairs said that "getting dates with others" was one of their most common adjustments to a broken affair. That is a good adjustment if the dates are an attempt to enjoy life by mingling with others and to widen a circle of associations rather than an attempt to get even with the former partner.

## WHEN ENGAGEMENT MUST BE BROKEN

To end an engagement when one of the pair has concluded that the marriage cannot work out is sometimes difficult. Some engagements are broken in immature ways, with a careless disregard for the feelings of the partner, or even with a deliberate attempt to hurt. It is humiliating to both men and women to be unexpectedly rejected and to have to face friends and family after the fiancé(e) has broken the engagement. But sometimes, even if the one who breaks the engagement shows all possible consideration for the feelings of the other, the one most hurt by the break may regress to an immature level of behavior in an attempt to hold the unwilling partner. Threats of violence to oneself are common. Sometimes threats are made to "tell" things that might be damaging to the partner, and pathological individuals may even resort to threats against the life or person of the partner. These are ways of reacting to situations in which individuals feel extremely frustrated. Children may react to a blocking of their wishes by running away or by telling their parents of intention to run away. In childish ways they are attempting to bring sorrow to the parents by harming themselves. Immature adults who threaten suicide when a love affair is ended against their will do so because they wish to force the loved one to worry about them and to feel responsible for such behavior. They hope their actions will cause the loved one to decide he or she loves them too much to risk allowing them to harm themselves. Sometimes jilted lovers drink to drown their sorrow, hoping to force a reconciliation and a happy marriage.

If one partner threatens violence when the engagement is broken, the one wishing to break the engagement should look upon the threats objectively. In the first place, there is little chance that they will be carried out. Children who start to run away from home to hurt their parents seldom run more than a block. Making threats is an indication of immaturity and instability; such threats are convincing proof of the desirability of breaking the engagement. If fiction pictured life situations rather than romantic fantasy, it would tell what happened later in the married life of the couple who weakened and married because one reacted to disappointment by turning to liquor. Instead of living happily ever after, they would be spending the rest of their lives trying to pacify a spouse who resorted to sulking, temper tantrums, or drunkenness whenever things failed to go according to his or her wishes. Immature patterns of behavior do not change with marriage any more than selfishness is cured by marriage.

The quick marriage to someone else may be another form of reaction. Marriages on the rebound have little chance for success, for the new choice may be made not on the realities of the new relationship, but on the basis of resentment toward the former love. Courtships in which one or both partners have not had time to get over previous love affairs should not end in engagement or marriage until ample time has elapsed, so that both may evaluate their chances for happiness as carefully as if it were the first love affair. They need to be sure that they have had time to let their wounded affections heal and that no spite or "rebound" is involved. Quick marriage after a broken affair usually indicates that the person is seeking an escape and that emotions may still be involved with the former loved one.

When an engagement must be broken, it is better if both can recognize that a one-sided affectional attachment would result in unhappiness in marriage. Impossible as it may seem at the time, the rejected one will find that there are others who have as many and perhaps more of the desirable traits of the ex-partner.

## LENGTH OF ENGAGEMENT

How long should engagements be to result in the best adjustment in marriage? Some people can get thoroughly acquainted during a relatively short period of engagement, whereas others may be engaged for years without having settled many of the questions that should be faced during the engagement. Some couples defeat the purposes of the engagement period by concentrating so exclusively on wedding plans that they make little progress toward really knowing each other.

In the past, when engagements were for the purpose of planning and preparing for the wedding, short engagements were considered desirable. Since engaged couples had greater freedom, it was thought that long engagements would lead to premarital sexual intercourse. Therefore, short engagements were recommended so that couples could be ushered quickly and safely into marriage. Actually, many factors help to determine premarital sexual behavior other than how long a couple dates or is engaged. In our study of two groups of engaged couples, we found that there was little relationship between length of engagement and whether or not they had coitus.

Sexual behavior during engagement is determined less by how long and how much couples date each other than by their acceptance or rejection of virginity as a value and by certain other factors. Research studies show the following factors to be among those related to premarital sexual behavior: the social class a couple represent, their parents' marital stability, their religiousness, and how they assess the happiness of their parents' marriage. All evidence shows that the values held, far more than length of acquaintance, determine premarital sexual behavior.

Research studies show that longer engagements are among the factors predictive of happiness in marriage. It might be expected that short acquaintances would be followed by long engagements, but the opposite seems to be true. Those who are acquainted the longest before engagement tend to have the longest engagements.[6] The type of person who will take a longer time to build a relationship before considering marriage may also take time to approach marriage after the engagement. This willingness to proceed carefully is part of the explanation for the greater success of marriages following longer engagements.

Another factor in the success of marriages following longer engagements is, of course, the weeding out of the poorer marital risks. Many of the people who were not engaged or who were engaged for a short time would not have married had they had a longer engagement.

Certainly, time alone is not the crucial factor. But the time factor may be an indicator of other elements in the engagement. Research findings show that most people usually need more than a few weeks or months to achieve certain growth tasks that are important functions of the engagement period. Time is needed for two people to learn to understand accurately each other's attitudes and viewpoints, since communication is not accomplished only by conversation. For example, a couple may have wide differences in attitudes on such matters as having children. In a short engagement, the subject of having children may be touched on, if at all, in a romantic, idealized way. The one who hopes to have children and who especially values family life with children may assume that the other feels the same. But sometimes, as time passes, he or she may discover that the attitudes of the other were not accurately perceived. In a longer engagement such attitudes are more likely to be determined. The couple may then be able to talk over their feelings honestly. They may reach a compromise in their attitudes and so be able to marry with an understanding that will help them avoid shock or disillusionment later, even though they do not feel exactly the same on such an important matter. Or, as time passes during engagement, discernment of their differences in this or any other area of life may cause them to conclude that they are too far apart to marry happily. In a short engagement, the wedding day will arrive before there has been time enough to think constructively or objectively about mutual or antagonistic values.

Of course, a couple could be engaged for a long time and merely

[6] Goode, *After Divorce*, p. 81.

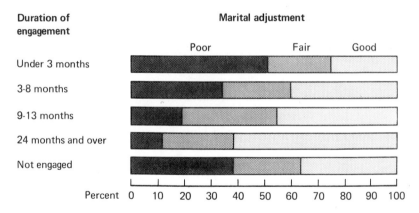

**Duration of engagement**

**Marital adjustment**

Poor      Fair      Good

Under 3 months

3-8 months

9-13 months

24 months and over

Not engaged

Percent 0   10   20   30   40   50   60   70   80   90   100

FIG. 12–3 Duration of engagement and marital adjustment. Long engagements often weed out couples who would not make a success of marriage. From Ernest W. Burgess and Leonard S. Cottrell, *Predicting Success or Failure in Marriage* (Englewood Cliffs, N.J.: Prentice-Hall, Inc., 1939).

mark time; when they marry, their tasks of adjustment will be much the same as those who have had very short engagements. For example: Mrs. B. went to a counselor after six months of marriage, disappointed and disillusioned. She explained that their engagement had lasted for almost two years and remarked, "I always thought that after a long engagement a marriage couldn't fail. But we hadn't been married more than a few weeks before I saw all kinds of traits in him that I never had even thought of. He seems to be a completely different person from the man to whom I was engaged."

A review of the experience of this couple revealed that, although the engagement had lasted for almost two years, the couple had actually been together for no more than a total of a month, if all the days they had spent in each other's company were added together. Moreover, most of the times that they had been together had been special occasions when it was easy for each to show a side of the personality attractive to the other. Their true selves had little chance to show, and their association remained on the level of dating, with no serious exploration of the attitudes, values, or traits that would be important in their marriage.

## RECOGNIZING DANGER SIGNALS

Interviews with many engaged couples have revealed that for some couples danger signals become evident only after they have been engaged for a period of time. Elements in their interaction with each other and their two families that should warn of possible unhappiness and maladjustment in marriage often go unrecognized at first.

John and Barbara met as students at a West Coast school, began dating in April, and were engaged in October. Just before Christmas, John discussed his engagement with a counselor. He said, "I often have a feeling that we might be talking at cross-purposes when we discuss plans for the future. Usually she expresses agreement with my ideas about the kind of life I'd like us to have; then after I leave her, I feel uncertain. It seems that whenever we talk about something that means a lot to me, I end up with the feeling that none of my ideas or thoughts look very good when brought out into the open. Since we've been planning to marry I seem to have been discarding as impractical or rather silly a great many of the hopes I've always had for the future. I realize it's important to be practical, but I've always felt that there are some things that can't be judged or decided on the basis of strictly a dollars-and-cents value. Perhaps I'm just worrying over nothing or only having a small case of prewedding jitters."

John visited Barbara's home for the Christmas holidays and met her family. Barbara had told him that they were a happy family. During his visit in her home he noticed that her mother was extremely dominating; the 28-year-old brother, who was unmarried and living at home, and the father took orders constantly from the mother, but not without showing antagonism. Barbara's two older sisters, aged 26 and 30, came for Christmas and he learned for the first time that they were both divorced. The whole family had the habit of making jokes at each other's expense, or of openly disparaging each other with no pretense of humor. John came from a family who were mutually supportive, and he found himself very uncomfortable in the atmosphere of his fiancée's home.

He had known that Barbara had moody spells, but he was now bothered by a similarity between some of her moods and the behavior he observed in her unhappy brother and sisters.

He noticed also that the family valued everything in terms of money. They frankly appraised the cost of Christmas gifts they received, and he realized that the gift he had spent so much careful thought in choosing for Barbara embarrassed her before her family because it was less expensive than some of those exchanged by other members of the family. He began to remember his vague feelings of disappointment on past occasions when he had given her small gifts that were inexpensive or contrived, but that he thought had special significance.

If John had not visited Barbara's family, he probably would not have recognized the danger signals indicating that a very great difference existed between him and Barbara in their conceptions of happiness, life goals, and values.

If elements exist in the personalities of two people or in their relationship that would make the success of their marriage extremely difficult or impossible, such danger signals are obvious. A special task of the engagement period is to become able to recognize such warnings.

## REASONS FOR FAILURE TO RECOGNIZE DANGER SIGNALS

Some couples even during long engagements fail to recognize danger signals because they have decided to marry and have resistance to accepting and facing facts that might prevent them from marrying. Such couples may fill their pre-engagement and engagement time with focusing on matters outside their relationship, and so forestall exploring or assessing their own interaction and potential chance for success in marriage. For example, if there is family opposition to their marriage, a couple may spend most of their time and attention fighting the opposition—the families, friends, minister, priest, or rabbi—and never seriously consider whether they should marry each other regardless of opposition. They will not let themselves consider the danger signals for fear those who disapprove of their marriage may be right. After they are married they may discover that most of what they had in common was their battle against the opposition; they had little basis for a good marriage.

Some couples concentrate on a special event, such as plans they are making for after they are married, and their concentration on the future may cause them to lose sight of the present need to explore the interaction between them and to see whether they should or should not marry each other. To illustrate:

> Two students met in the spring of their senior year in college. They discovered that they shared an interest in travel. Both had saved and planned to take a trip to Europe after graduation. Their romance developed rapidly and they became engaged. During the next few weeks they were absorbed in planning for their wedding and for a European trip, now to be their honeymoon. They returned in the fall full of enthusiasm about their trip, but they began to discover at once that they had almost nothing else in common. By Christmas time they were in trouble. The wife wanted to feel settled in her home town and was anxious to buy a home. The husband was teaching there but he considered it a dull place and had no intention of remaining for more than a year or two. He objected to the idea of buying a home at any time in the foreseeable future, preferring to remain free of any permanent obligations that might tie him down. They could not agree on having children, and each was bored with the people the other chose as friends. In fact, they were in conflict about almost all the permanent goals and the basic values by which each lived. Within a year after their marriage they had separated.

Some other couples waste their engagement time by concentrating their attention on planning the wedding. The wedding itself becomes so important to them that they lose sight of the purpose of the engagement. They may even unconsciously keep their minds on "plans" to avoid facing danger signals.

The custom in some communities of choosing tableware patterns and registering such patterns with stores from which wedding gifts may be purchased, of planning elaborate weddings, or of writing and memorizing personal wedding ceremonies, and many other customs related to engage-ments and weddings serve to help couples block facing and evaluating danger signals that are present in their relationship.

Engaged couples should have in mind the clear distinction between the wedding and the marriage. The wedding is a step, an occasion marking a new beginning; the marriage is a lifetime of living together. In the long view, the kind of wedding the couple may have is unimportant in comparison with the kind of marriage theirs is to be. Engagement is the time to consider what the marriage can be.

The following discussion of engagement as a bridge to marriage points out matters that can serve as guides for recognizing danger signals. Vague feelings of uneasiness or disappointment in communication and understanding may be significant.

## ENGAGEMENT AS A BRIDGE TO SUCCESSFUL MARRIAGE

**Establishing the habit of talking things over.**   The habit of talking things over so that the two can understand each other's views and feelings is essential for a successful marriage. This habit could become established, if people are aware of its importance, during the engagement. Some people communicate more easily than others; they are able to express themselves in ways that are understood and they can draw out expressions of feelings and attitudes from others. Other people have difficulty revealing themselves even to those close to them. Some couples may avoid even talking about subjects or ideas about which they suspect that they do not agree. It is worthwhile for the engaged couple to talk over as many as possible of their differences that will be important during marriage.

**Money matters.**   For example, handling money is often a focal point of friction within marriage. An engaged couple needs to discuss frankly their attitudes about money. What does each one consider worth sacrificing and saving for? Do they agree? How important does each feel it is to have *enough* money, and what is "enough"? In their two-parent families how was money handled? Do each think his or her family had the "right" views about money? Was there friction over money in the parent families? If so, can the engaged couple determine how the friction might have been avoided or resolved? What ideas have they about how they could handle such problems that might arise in their marriage?

There is value for engaged couples who look at such potential problem areas of life before they are married. At this time, the questions may be merely interesting topics for discussion, yet by discussing them frankly, viewpoints can be understood and progress made toward mutually acceptable viewpoints. If such things are not discussed, or if they are only briefly considered and then avoided because the two cannot talk about them freely without creating tension, real difficulties may arise after marriage. After marriage, the use of money is no longer merely an interesting subject for discussion. It is a matter of great importance. The better they understand ahead of time each other's attitudes and habits relative to earning and spending money, the easier this area of their married life will be. It can come as a serious shock to a newly married person to conclude that the mate is "extravagant" or "financially irresponsible" or "materialistic" or "wasteful"—if each has not understood or accepted the other's attitudes on financial matters before marrying.

**Having children.** Engaged couples also need to discuss their feelings about having children and their conceptions of themselves as future parents. To many people, in spite of an awareness of worldwide population problems, having a child or children is an essential part of a happy marriage. Some people believe that they should not have children but should adopt if they wish to have the experience of parenthood. However, feelings about adoption are very complicated, and the two may have conflicting responses to the idea if they explore their attitudes honestly.

**Life goals and values.** Couples need to compare their standards on goals and values. The woman whose greatest wish is to live in her home town among people she has always known may not find happiness married to a man who would gladly move from place to place if that seemed necessary to his occupation. And he, in turn, might feel hindered if it became necessary for them to live permanently in one place in order to keep his wife happy. However, such a difference need not be a real problem if it is considered before marriage.

Feelings and beliefs about religion need to be shared and understood. The person who values an active religious life may be disappointed if married to one uninterested in religion.

Differing attitudes on the value of an education may create problems, unless both have completed their education before marriage or have understood what amount of education was desired or planned by each. It is hard for a young couple to weather student life as a married couple if either one feels that the required sacrifices are unwarranted.

**The parent families and roles.** Engaged couples also need to take a candid look at their two parent families in the matter of the roles played by the parents. Is the father the traditionally dominant head of the house in one family, while in the other the mother dominates? Are both families similar in being father-dominated, mother-dominated, or equalitarian in roles? The kinds of masculine–feminine roles in the parent families will be a factor in the new marriage. It need not be a disrupting factor. Just discussing such a subject and exploring different attitudes about roles that each might be capable of taking in marriage will increase the likelihood that the couple can be comfortable in whatever role pattern they eventually create in their own marriage.

It is important that both try to be honest in assessing their own attitudes about roles and in revealing their views to the partner. Views may change with time and circumstances. Studies of college students on role changes in recent years have found great confusion of attitudes on the subject. The women's liberation movement, the lower birth rate, the desire of women to have a career along with being a wife and mother, and the scarcity of jobs have all contributed to a need to assess what roles husbands and wives should play in marriage. Studies show that, in general, college people are accepting new roles for women but they are not in agreement on what the roles should be. Men still tend to be traditional in refusing to accept women in certain roles. The man who feels that he can support the family and that his wife should not work at an outside job may change his mind later under financial pressure or if such a role is disagreeable to the wife. But such changes do not necessarily occur. An educated woman who hopes to have a job or career in addition to her home and family should know exactly what the attitudes of her future husband are. Will he feel threatened if he is not the family head in a traditional sense? Should she follow him and live where he has a job or should they live where she has a job? How will he feel if she makes more money than he does? In a tight job market he might not be able to find a job. Could he adjust to staying home and caring for the home and children?

The engagement should serve to reveal attitudes and emotions about masculine–feminine roles to both members of a couple. An honest assessment of their attitudes may enable them to make adjustments before they marry. If the divergence between them is too great, they should recognize their differences as a major danger signal.

**Personal marriage contracts.**   Some couples who discuss the problems of roles and other differences decide to make personal contracts defining their roles and duties in marriage. A study of these contracts shows that they may be illegal, that they tend to emphasize the negative aspects of the relationship, that they tend to deal with trivial differences, and that couples cannot anticipate the serious differences they will have after marriage. Further, the contracts are inflexible and do not make provisions for changes that must be coped with after marriage. Probably the greatest benefit of the contract is that it forces open discussion of differences before marriage. Such a discussion should bring some of the couple's conflicting views into the open and should help to establish a basis for rational considerations.[7]

[7] J. Gibson Wells, "A Critical Look at Personal Marriage Contracts," *The Family Coordinator* 25:1 (January 1976), 33–37.

How the question of coitus during engagement is handled by a couple often predicts the level of their success in marriage. If one partner is persistent in wanting to engage in coitus during engagement in spite of the reluctance of the other, especially if the reluctance is based on conscientious beliefs or on a desire to reserve sexual intercourse for marriage, a difference in values and in basic attitudes is apparent. Such persistence may indicate that an exploitative pattern exists in the relationship. The persistent one is concerned chiefly with his or her own wishes and has little regard for the feelings, beliefs, or needs of the other. Such self-centered attitudes are conducive to unhappiness in marriage. Arguments or conflicting views about coitus during engagement must be recognized as a danger signal.

Coitus during engagement may divert the couple's attention from other facets of their relationship that need exploring; it may also disrupt a potentially good permanent relationship. Evidence suggests that premarital coitus should not be regarded as a test, or as a sure prediction, of what the sexual adjustment in marriage will be. In our study of engagements, among the couples who were having coitus, 5 percent of the women reported having orgasm "always," 37 percent "usually," in contrast to 24 percent of married women who reported "always" and 50 percent "usually." Of the engaged women having orgasm in coitus "sometimes, seldom, or never," there were 58 percent, compared to 25 percent of the married women.[8] These young women and their partners might easily conclude that they are mismatched, or the man might believe that his fiancée is not capable of adequate sexual response. The explanation must lie elsewhere, for it is extremely improbable that such a high percentage of young women in love would have such a low response level if they were married. Of this group of women, 25 percent reported that they had doubts about whether their having coitus with the fiancé was right, or that they felt guilty about it; about half of them were not using any effective method of contraception. Considering those findings, their inability to have orgasms seems normal for their situation, and could not be considered predictive of what their response might be if they were married, free of guilt feelings, and using reliable contraceptives.

It seems that coitus during engagement might cause a couple to have needless doubts about the possibility of a future satisfactory sexual adjustment in marriage. Before we leave the subject of coitus during engagement, a relevant finding from the study of broken love relationships

[8] For studies of sexual responses in married women, see Alexander L. Clark and Paul Wallin, "Women's Sexual Responsiveness and Marriage," *American Journal of Sociology* 71:2 (September 1965), 187–96; see also O. Bruce Thomason, "Differential Non-Sexual and Sexual Behavior in the Marital Adjustment of Penn State Alumni" (Ph.D. diss., Pennsylvania State College, 1951).

should be noted. Of the students who reported that they had engaged in coitus in a former engagement now broken, 50 percent said they had never taken reliable contraceptive precautions. The finding suggests a lack of effective communication between those couples and a naive or irresponsible approach to premarital coitus.

## LIVING TOGETHER BEFORE MARRIAGE AS TEST OF COMPATIBILITY

Today many couples who are considering marriage decide to live together during the latter period of courtship. Rather than seeing engagement as the final step before marriage, these couples consider engagement, living together, and then, if everything goes well, marriage, as the proper sequence of events. They are interested in all areas of their relationship but especially in the sexual aspect, because great emphasis has been put on the fact that a bad sexual adjustment is a cause of failure in marriage. Research does show that if both husband and wife are about equal in sexual drive it makes for a better sexual adjustment. The greater the difference in sexual needs, the greater the difficulty in adjusting satisfactorily.

Couples who choose to have coitus before marriage as a test of their sexual compatibility might consider the following:

1  The lack of complete privacy, the fear of being discovered, the fear of pregnancy, and family training and religious teachings are inhibiting factors, especially in a woman's response to sex.

2  The inability of the woman to enjoy the relationship through orgasm is the rule rather than the exception. It takes time and favorable circumstances for many women to learn to enjoy sex.

3  Reliable contraceptives are important in exploring coitus before marriage.

4  In early sexual attempts, often the man is so excited that he has little control and cannot prolong sexual play in order to bring satisfaction to the woman.

5  Women who do develop early in their sexual drive and who do not have strong inhibitions will usually respond sexually before marriage and in marriage.

6  Women who have developed strong sexual drives may wish to reconsider whether they should marry a man who has infrequent desire for sexual intercourse. The sexual drive of the man will probably never be stronger than it is in his teens or early twenties. An expectation that he will become more interested in sexual intercourse with age is unrealistic. The woman's sexual drive may continue to be strong or grow stronger as she reaches her thirties and forties.

7  The man who concentrates on satisfying his own sexual needs without regard to the needs of the woman may carry this pattern into marriage. It could stem from selfishness, or ignorance of sexuality.

8  Being equal in sexual drive should not be considered the only key to happiness in marriage. The total relationship is the important thing.

It is almost impossible to know what the ultimate sexual adjustment will be with any couple. Living together before marriage may help in seeing danger signals, but often the meaning of these danger signals will not be recognized until the couple has lived together for many months. The understanding of one's own sexuality and sexual needs develops slowly; the understanding of the sexual needs of another develops even more slowly.

In talking with couples who have lived together before marriage, we have found that many are surprised that they still have doubts about their relationship. They thought living together would definitely determine for them the extent of their compatibility. But after some months their doubts remained and they discovered some new points of difference.

From conferences with such couples and others who have married after such a trial arrangement, we have concluded that there is no magic short cut for couples in determining what their future adjustment will be. During the period of living together they have had to go through many of the usual adjustments that newly married people have had to work their way through, but in this arrangement they have not had the security of marriage to motivate them.

## CONFESSING THE PAST

At some time during an engagement one may feel that he or she must tell the other all about incidents in the past, some of which are regretted. What rule should be followed when the urge comes to tell all? Four questions might be considered.

1  *Why* do I feel I must tell of this experience or incident?
2  Will our marriage be happier if I tell?
3  Will my fiancé(e) be happier if I tell?
4  If I must tell, is my fiancé(e) the best person to whom I should tell it?

If people analyze their motives carefully, they may find that they have one of two motives for wanting to confess. They may simply want the pleasure of reliving or exhibiting the past, without realizing that an element of self-aggrandizement is involved in the confession. On the other hand, the urge to discuss past incidents or experiences may arise from inner pressures or guilt feelings, which might be less burdensome if they were shared with another. Neither of these motives is sufficient reason for telling regrettable past actions or past experiences to the fiancé(e). Confessions made for no other reason than those mentioned may cause unhappiness for the loved one, and may raise doubts and questions that will have an adverse effect on the happiness of the marriage. The very telling of relatively insignificant past events may exaggerate their importance. If there is a strong urge to relieve guilt feelings, confession might better be made to someone other than the loved one. A minister, priest, or marriage counselor who will listen and can give wise counsel would be a better choice.

However, it is necessary to tell certain things to one's future spouse. Things ought to be told that, if known, might lead to a better relationship in the marriage, or those that, if found out later, might make trouble in marriage. If either member of the couple has had venereal disease, has had an illegitimate child, has been married before, or has a prison record, the mate should know about it before marriage. These matters could seriously affect the marriage, and their effect might be far more damaging if they were unknown to the spouse until after the wedding. The person who marries someone who has had a venereal disease has a right to evidence that a permanent cure has been effected. Previous parenthood, a former marriage, or a prison record are things that may not remain unknown. Therefore, the future wife or husband should be told of such past experiences.

Table 12-7 summarizes our study of what events or circumstances people had in their backgrounds and how much of this information they told the person to whom they were engaged. It shows that both men and women tend to tell about most of the items on the list if they had occurred. The men tend to reveal more information about the past than do the

**TABLE 12-7**  Percentage of 122 engaged men and 122 engaged women reporting past experiences or facts in family background and the percentage who told fiancé(e) about these facts *

| Experiences or facts | Men | | Women | |
|---|---|---|---|---|
| | In background | Told fiancée | In background | Told fiancé |
| Dating history with others | 97.0% | 93.0% | 98.0% | 94.0% |
| Necking experience with others | 83.0 | 93.0 | 80.0 | 68.0 |
| Petting experience with others | 74.0 | 82.0 | 57.0 | 64.0 |
| Premarital sexual relations | 47.0 | 91.0 | 23.0 | 86.0 |
| Personality faults | 32.0 | 92.0 | 43.0 | 94.0 |
| Serious problems in the family | 27.0 | 94.0 | 30.0 | 92.0 |
| Previous engagement | 11.0 | 100.0 | 10.0 | 100.0 |
| Crime in the family | 7.0 | 78.0 | 3.0 | 75.0 |
| Personal crimes | 5.0 | 100.0 | 1.0 | 0.0 |
| Insanity in the family | 3.0 | 75.0 | 7.0 | 88.0 |
| Having had venereal disease | 3.0 | 75.0 | 1.0 | 0.0 |
| Having been married before | 2.5 | 67.0 | 1.0 | 100.0 |
| Suspected bad heredity | 2.0 | 100.0 | 3.0 | 25.0 |
| Having had a nervous breakdown | 2.0 | 50.0 | 2.5 | 67.0 |
| Child out of wedlock | 2.0 | 50.0 | 2.5 | 67.0 |

* Landis, findings from a study of 122 engagements at the University of California, Berkeley, and Chico State College in 1967.

women. The engaged people reported that almost all of the telling had been done during steady dating or during the "understanding" stage before formal engagement. In about 50 percent of the telling it was one's confessing about the past that prompted the other also to confess. These couples evaluated the effects of having confessed the past. Approximately 5 percent regretted having told about the past and felt that it would have been better if neither one of them had made such confessions. Whether a marriage turns out to be happy or unhappy will probably have something to do with the long-term evaluation of having told the mate about the past. In unhappy marriages, confessions of past actions could become one of the points of friction in family disputes in later years.

## THE PREMARITAL EXAMINATION

It is advisable to have a premarital examination from a competent physician. All but five states now require an examination for venereal disease before a marriage license can be obtained. A premarital examination should provide the following:

1   A complete physical examination
2   A pelvic examination for the female
3   Attention to diseases or defects that might be hereditary
4   An opportunity to secure reliable contraceptive information
5   A blood test
6   A chance to ask questions about sexual functioning

If there is a Planned Parenthood clinic in the area, it is a good place to go for the premarital examination. The doctors who work with Planned Parenthood have a special interest in the questions confronting people approaching marriage. Such clinics are usually better qualified to discuss the different aspects of sex in marriage than is the average medical doctor. Planned Parenthood centers prefer that couples come to the center well ahead of the wedding date. The premarital examination should be completed before the last hurried days preceding the wedding, and if a contraceptive pill is to be used, its use must begin approximately one month before it will be effective. The view of some Planned Parenthood clinics is that a woman planning to use an oral contraceptive should begin its use two or three months before her wedding, to allow time to get past disturbing physical symptoms that may occur with the first use of the pill.

## PARENTAL APPROVAL AND PLANNING THE WEDDING

Marriages that are planned and made known have a better chance than those that are kept secret. Sometimes, when parents are opposed to the marriage, the young people see elopement as their only choice. When parental opposition is the reason for a secret marriage or an elopement, the marriage is less likely to turn out happily than if an elopement is for reasons of economy or for some other reason of convenience. If strong parental opposition exists, the couple should seriously consider whether the reasons for the opposition are valid. If they decide to marry in spite of opposition, they should make every effort to secure the cooperation of the families before the marriage. Often the parents will consent when they see that the young people are determined to marry. However, if the opposition continues, the marriage is handicapped. Family ties of affection are not easily broken. There is likely to be an emotional antagonism toward the parents and there may be unhappiness for the couple who marry despite opposition.

Traditionally, the bride plans and pays for the wedding and the groom plans and pays for the honeymoon. Many couples write their own wedding ceremony and are married with rituals that have personal meaning for them. If a minister is to officiate at the wedding, he or she is experienced and may be helpful in planning. Whether the wedding is to be large and elaborate or small and simple will depend upon the wishes of the pair and upon their situation. From the viewpoint of marital success, the important thing is that the wedding marks a change in status. Since it is uniting two families to form a new kinship group, there are advantages in having both families present at the wedding.

## THE HONEYMOON

The function of the honeymoon is to give the couple a chance to settle into their new status as a married couple, unhindered by the presence of interested friends and relatives. Young people are sometimes disappointed because they approach the honeymoon unaware of its broad, general function, believing that it will be chiefly a time of perfect sexual fulfillment. Sexual fulfillment may not be complete during the honeymoon, for most couples need time and experience to achieve the understanding and perception of each other necessary for a mutually satisfactory sexual relationship. The honeymoon is an important beginning of their companionship as a married pair as well as of their sex life. They may need weeks or months of living together before their sex life becomes as mutually satisfying as they may have thought it would automatically become on their honeymoon. The most important accomplishment of a honeymoon is to establish a pattern of understanding cooperation and unselfish consideration for each other in all their relationships.

In setting the wedding date, girls usually try to plan so that they will not be menstruating during the honeymoon. Such planning is an attempt to have conditions as ideal as possible for the beginning of sex life after marriage. But many girls find that the added strain of the last few days or weeks preceding the wedding may cause menstruation to be delayed until the relaxation that may come with the honeymoon.

If the honeymoon is to serve its function, a few points must be considered when it is planned:

1 Whether the time alone, away from friends and relatives, is to be only a day or two or much longer, the plans should provide for privacy and anonymity. Most newly married couples want only to be an inconspicuous married couple. Anonymity may be found in a hotel in the city or a cottage in the country, on a lake or ocean cruise, or hiking in the mountains. The important consideration is that if possible the couple should go where no one knows them.

2 The honeymoon should provide freedom from fatigue and nervous tension. Strenuous travel schedules should be avoided. If a couple tries to cover a predetermined amount of territory and to make sure that they miss nothing of educational or cultural value, they may find themselves working so hard at having a wedding trip that the purpose of the honeymoon is defeated.

3 The kind of plans made should depend upon what activities both can enjoy. If they like to see and do the things that are offered by a large city, they may choose to spend their honeymoon in that way. If they are both enthusiastic campers or if they enjoy hiking or fishing, they may plan a honeymoon of that type. The point is that the honeymoon is a time for them to enjoy each other in an environment that allows them to be themselves and to relax in each other's company.

4 The cost of the honeymoon should be kept well within what they can afford so that they will be as free as possible from financial pressure or worry.

If a couple has made good use of their engagement period, it will have served its basic purposes, and a good foundation for marriage will have been built. In such cases the honeymoon is not likely to offer shocks or unanticipated discoveries. Before the wedding, the two will have come to know each other so well and will have built so much understanding between them that the honeymoon can be a relaxed and happy beginning to their married living.

## OUTLINE FOR SELF-STUDY:
## TO ASSESS A RELATIONSHIP

If you are engaged or about to be engaged, think through the following questions and attempt to evaluate your relationship and its potential for success if you marry. (If you are not seriously dating now, apply these points to a dating relationship or love affair you have had in the past. Can you see why the relationship did not survive?)

### I QUARRELING IN YOUR RELATIONSHIP

Do you quarrel? How often? How intense are the quarrels? Is your quarreling becoming less frequent or more frequent? Have quarrels resulted in blocking off certain touchy issues that are no longer discussed? Have you taken positions in a quarrel that you find yourself defending in later quarrels? Have some of the quarrels made for a better understanding and more accepting attitudes between you?

## II YOUR ATTITUDES TOWARD YOUR ENGAGEMENT

Have you ever broken or considered breaking this engagement? How many times? Are you ever bothered by doubts about whether you should go on with your plans? Are you proud and happy about your engagement, confident and secure in your feelings about the future? What attitudes toward your engagement are you aware of among your friends and family? Are you proud of your fiancé(e) around your friends and family? Do you feel uncomfortably apologetic or feel that you must make excuses for things he or she says or does?

## III YOUR RESPECT FOR EACH OTHER

Do you respect this person and all that he or she represents? In judgment? Ideals? Goals in life? Moral standards? Habits? Vocational choice? Religion? Does your basic respect for all that he or she is enable you to act in ways that make your fiancé(e) feel supported and built up? In turn, does he or she respect you and make you feel valued and appreciated for all that you are? Do you respect his or her friends and family? Do you feel that they accept you and think well of you? If you do not, can you weigh honestly the basis of the nonacceptance and determine whether serious differences exist between you?

## IV DECISION MAKING IN YOUR RELATIONSHIP

Think about the pattern of decision making between you. How do you arrive at decisions? Does one tend to have the major voice in decisions, or do you talk things over and decide together? Do you usually feel satisfied about the wisdom of decisions you have made together, afterwards, when you are alone? If the present pattern of decision making continues in your marriage, will you both be happy and satisfied with it?

## V YOUR CONFIDENCE IN EACH OTHER'S ABILITY TO COPE WITH LIFE

Do you ever feel that you are the victim when he or she has a bad day? Do either of you take out unpleasant feelings or aggressions on your friends or family, or do you resort to escapes such as moodiness, brooding, temper spells, reckless driving, or excessive drinking? If your fiancé(e) acts in any of these ways, how do you react now? Can you live comfortably with this pattern? Will you feel the same about it later if the two of you marry and have children to bring up?

## VI CONSIDER YOUR TOTAL RELATIONSHIP

A love affair may be based on one or two satisfying elements, such as a strong mutual interest in music, sports, or religion, or on a compelling physical attraction. A broader basis is necessary for success in marriage. How many satisfying areas of mutuality do you have? Are there things you cannot talk to each other about because of lack of mutual interest, antagonistic viewpoints, or because doubts cause you to block off discussing them?

Does the relationship bring out the best in you? How do you feel after you have been together? Elated? Confident? Ambitious? Uncertain? Moody? Depressed?

Have you tried to get each other to change in many ways?

Are you more comfortable with each other than with anyone else? Can you be yourself happily in this relationship without strain?

As you look at all aspects of your association with each other—your feelings about each other and about your engagement, your habitual ways of treating each other, your agreement or disagreement on important matters, your ability to talk over and share together all that matters to each of you—can you conclude that your engagement or relationship is a dependable bridge to successful marriage?

## REVIEW QUESTIONS

1  What relationship is there between length of acquaintance and happiness in marriage?

2  What is the purpose of the engagement period today? How does this differ from the past?

3  How permanent are engagements?

4  What are common reasons for breaking engagements?

5  What are some of the most common trends in courtship, as represented by graphs?

6  Does the research on broken engagements give encouragement to those suffering with broken hearts? Discuss. Apply this same principle to other emotional crises.

7  What are some common reactions to the frustration that comes with breaking an engagement?

8  What should the attitude of the wounded partner be when an engagement is broken?

9  Why do long engagements predict success in marriage?

10  What did the case of John and Barbara (page 195) reveal about recognizing danger signals?

11  Give some of the reasons why couples fail to recognize danger signals.

12  Cite some subjects that should be discussed during the engagement period.

13  What are some of the weaknesses of personal marriage contracts as a way of settling differences before marriage? Do marriage contracts have any value?

14  Will living together before marriage be a fair test of the equality of a couple's sexual drive? Why?

15  Will living together give couples definite answers as to whether they should marry? Why?

16  Give reasons for or against confessing the past.

17  What questions should be considered before confessing one's past?

18  Give the chief reasons for a premarital examination.

19  Are elopements as happy as conventional marriages? Why?

20  What points should be considered in planning the wedding and the honeymoon?

## PROJECTS AND ACTIVITIES

1  Let each student consult two other students who have broken an engagement to find out just why the engagements were broken. Summarize the class findings.

2  Study several movies to see what pattern of behavior is depicted when the hero or heroine is frustrated in love.

# LEGAL CONTROL OF MARRIAGE

# 13

The state has a stake in every marriage. It exercises control over the making and keeping of marriage contracts through legal requirements and restrictions. The state's basic interest is in the children who may result from marriage, but it is also concerned with the rights and responsibilities of the individuals who marry. Both men and women are guaranteed privileges and assume obligations when they make a marriage contract. The children of legal marriages are legitimate and have clearly defined inheritance rights. The law attempts to guarantee the children a stable environment for growth. Thus the state regulates who may marry and exercises control over the dissolution of marriage.

Marriage laws, like other laws, are designed to protect the interests of both the individual and society. The individual yields a measure of personal freedom for the good of society and is compensated by guarantees of personal security and social stability.

## MARRIAGE LAWS ARE SLOW TO CHANGE

There is much debate and discussion concerning the changes that are coming about in the traditional "nuclear" family which has existed for generations. The nuclear family consists of the husband, wife, and children as an exclusive relationship for a lifetime. To replace the traditional family, there is talk of group marriage, open marriage, communal marriage, contract marriage with renewable terms and provisions, and marriages that have all the usual elements except for a legal ceremony and registration. Some couples who are living together have drawn up special contracts spelling out duties, obligations, personal freedoms, rights to alimony, and many other items.

Laws regulating traditional marriage are slow to change. Whether couples live together with or without marriage, if special contracts have been drawn up they have little validity before the courts if the agreements differ from the established state marriage laws. A wife may waive her right to alimony in the contract with her husband and yet be awarded alimony in case of divorce because that is the official state law.

Some laws regulating marriage are out of date. Existing laws assume that people are marrying for the first time, that women and children are subservient, that the man is the breadwinner, and that the rights of all family members must be protected by the state. More than one-fourth of marriages today are among people who have been married more than one time following divorce or widowhood.

## PROBLEM OF REGULATION

Almost everyone agrees that laws governing marriage are necessary. There is much disagreement, however, as to the kind and extent of regulation that will achieve the desired ends. Although there is general agreement that it is not desirable for the biologically unfit to perpetuate themselves through children, opinions differ concerning who the biologically unfit are and how to control their relationships. Some believe they should be prevented from marrying; others maintain that preventing their marrying will not prevent their reproducing, and that it is better to legalize their union in order to give their children legitimacy. Still others advocate permitting the biologically unfit to marry if they first submit to a sterilization operation.

It is agreed that young people should not marry before reaching a mature stage of development, yet there is no agreement on when people are mature enough to marry. One state permits boys 15 years old to marry if they have parental consent; other states set the age at 18. One state sets no minimum age for marriage if the children have the consent of their parents and a judge. Girls may be legally married in some states at 14; in others they are not legally old enough until they reach 16 or 18. Where the age for legal marriage is low, the belief is that a high age requirement would promote sexual promiscuity. In the states where the age requirement is high, the reasoning is that, even though more promiscuity may result among those below the legal age for marriage, a higher age requirement makes for more stable marriages and so is better for the individual and for society.

Usually states accept marriages as valid even though they do not conform to legal requirements, provided no one takes action to have such marriages annulled. Those who administer marriage laws differ about permitting individuals' choices to take precedence over established regulations. The problem is to exercise enough regulation to achieve desired ends, but not so much that people will flout the laws and form illegal unions.

Marriage laws are in the hands of the separate states, and in attempts to solve the problem of effective control for the good of society a great variety of laws have been enacted. The result has been confusion. There are 50 different sets of marriage and divorce regulations, since the states have acted independently of one another. In addition to statutory laws, there is the common law. The common law is a body of unwritten and legal precedents which have developed throughout history. If no statutory law exists, the common law steps in to protect rights of family members, or in some cases the state law may be set aside in favor of the common law.

It has been observed that, by traveling 15 miles to enter three different states, a man would be considered a married man in one state, a single man in another, and a bigamist in the third. The courts have given contradictory decisions on the legality of divorces granted in one state to citizens of another state. However, in 1948 the Supreme Court ruled that the Massachusetts courts erred when they declared divorces invalid that were obtained in Florida and Nevada, and that each state must give full faith and credit to the official acts of other states. Lawmakers are showing an increasing awareness of the complications arising because of the diverse laws, and attempts are being made to bring about greater uniformity.

We shall look at some of the more common regulations concerning marriage. In some cases the laws of Michigan will be quoted, not because they are "model laws," but because they include most of the regulations found in other states, and because the reader will gain a better understanding of the nature of some of the marriage regulations if specific laws are quoted.

## MARRIAGE IS A CIVIL CONTRACT

Laws specify that marriage is a civil contract between two individuals. The marriage contract differs from ordinary contracts in that: (1) it cannot be rescinded or its fundamental terms changed by agreement between the two parties; (2) it results in a *status;* (3) it merges the legal identity of the parties; and (4) the tests of capacity differ from those applied to ordinary contracts (in other words, those who may not bind themselves by ordinary contracts may make a valid marriage). The marriage contract is not valid unless the two have the ability to consummate the marriage. Although a marriage can be contracted easily, it cannot be dissolved by mutual agreement as other civil contracts can be terminated. Society is profoundly interested in the family as an institution and, once the marriage contract is made, society tries to see that the contract is not readily dissolved. To get out of the contract, the individuals must go through court procedure.

The important point that makes a marriage contract valid is the consent of the two parties to the agreement. What really marries the couple is their mutual and willing expression of "I do" when they accept each other as husband and wife. The law prescribes a wedding license and someone to officiate, but although both these requirements are met, if one partner has been forced into the marriage by the other, no marriage has taken place, since willing consent was not given to the contract by one party. Coercion or unwillingness on the part of one partner makes the contract void. On the other hand, common-law marriage can take place without either the officiant or the license, if the couple willingly agree to live as husband and wife and do so.

The following is an example of a specific law covering the marriage contract:

> Michigan 12691. Marriage, as far as its validity in law is concerned, is a civil contract to which the consent of parties capable in law of contracting, is essential.
>
> Contract: Chastity is not a requisite to validity of a marriage and while marriage is, in a very important sense, a contract, it is also a relation governed by rules of public policy, which apply to no mere private agreements. Intention is the essential ingredient, as in every other contract, and, when one of the parties, instead of assenting to the contract, positively dissents from it, there can be no legal or valid marriage, although a ceremony is gone through by the officiating minister or magistrate. A contract of marriage cannot be presumed when such presumption would do violence to facts in the case. This section does not make a ceremony essential to validity, and a common-law marriage, when shown, binds the parties.

## EUGENIC REGULATIONS

All states have regulations governing the marriage of those who are mentally ill or mentally retarded. People who are not of sound mind cannot make a legal contract of any type, and therefore are incapable of contracting a marriage. Emphasis on this matter is changing, however, and the more generally accepted present-day reason for preventing these marriages is the assumption that the mentally defective might have defective children. Three states—Nebraska, South Dakota, and New Hampshire—have amended their laws so that feeble-minded persons may marry if they have had a sterilization operation. Medical research continues to discover previously unsuspected causes of mental defects and disease, with the result that some handicaps formerly assumed to be inheritable are now known to be relatively "accidental." Therefore, the more valid reasons for restricting the marriage and reproduction of mentally defective people are social; that is, regardless of the cause of their handicaps, people who are mentally defective cannot give the nurture that children require.

If they marry and reproduce, their children are more likely to become public charges than are the children of normal parents. Laws preventing the marriage of mental defectives have accomplished little. In the rare cases where such laws are enforced, the mental defectives are likely to have illegitimate children.

Although all states have some mental requirements for marriage, little is done to enforce such laws. The couple may be required to swear that they are of sound mind, but how many people will state that they are of unsound mind when applying for a marriage license?

In 1935 Connecticut passed a new type of venereal disease law, often referred to as the eugenic marriage law. Since then, 46 states have passed laws that require both men and women to have a physical examination for venereal disease shortly before marriage. The examination is valid for a period of from 7 to 40 days, the time limit varying in different states. If the marriage does not take place within that period, the examination must be repeated. In the majority of states the test is for syphilis only, but in the others it includes all venereal diseases. The costs of making physical examinations and laboratory tests are borne either by the individual or by the public health department. If the tests are not free, some states set the maximum fee a doctor may charge. Today almost all states accept out-of-state laboratory tests for people who are going to another state to be married. (Table 13-1 summarizes the marriage laws in the various states.)

**TABLE 13-1**

Marriage information by state, 1975. *Sources:* Legal information, *Information Please Almanac* questionnaires to states; Marriage statistics, National Center for Health Statistics, Department of Health, Education, and Welfare.

| State | Legal minimum marriage age | | | | Blood test required | Waiting period[1] | |
| | With parental consent[3] | | Without parental consent | | | Before license | After license |
| | M | F | M | F | | | |
| --- | --- | --- | --- | --- | --- | --- | --- |
| Alabama | 17 | 14 | 21 | 18 | yes | none | none |
| Alaska | 16 | 16 | 18 | 18 | yes | 3 da. | none |
| Arizona | 18 | 18 | 18 | 18 | yes | none | none |
| Arkansas | 18 | 16 | 18 | 18 | yes | 3 da. | none |
| California | 18 | 16 | 18 | 18 | yes | none | none |
| Colorado | 16[21] | 16[21] | 18 | 18 | yes[18] | none | none |
| Connecticut | 16 | 16 | 18 | 18 | yes | 4 da. | none |
| Delaware | 18 | 16 | 18 | 18 | yes[11] | none | 24 hr.[5] |
| D. C. | 18 | 16 | 21 | 18 | yes | 5 da.[6] | none |
| Florida | 18 | 16 | 21 | 21 | yes | 3 da. | none |
| Georgia | 18 | 16 | 18 | 18 | yes | 3 da.[7] | none |
| Hawaii | 17 | 17 | 18 | 18 | yes | none | none |

TABLE 13-1 (Continued)

| State | Legal minimum marriage age | | | | Blood test required | Waiting period [1] | |
| | With parental consent [3] | | Without parental consent | | | Before license | After license |
| | M | F | M | F | | | |
|---|---|---|---|---|---|---|---|
| Idaho | 18 | 16 | 21 | 18 | yes | 3 da. | none |
| Illinois | 18 | 16 | 21 | 18 | yes | none | none |
| Indiana | 17 | 17[12,17] | 21 | 18 | yes | 3 da. | none |
| Iowa | 18 | 16 | 18 | 18 | yes | 3 da. | none |
| Kansas | 18 | 16 | 21 | 18 | yes | 3 da. | none |
| Kentucky | 18 | 16[19] | 18 | 18 | yes | 3 da. | none |
| Louisiana | 18 | 16 | 18 | 16 | yes | none | 72 hr. |
| Maine | 16 | 16 | 18 | 18 | yes | 5 da. | none |
| Maryland | 18 | 16 | 21 | 18 | no | 48 hr. | none |
| Massachusetts | 14–17[12] | 12–15[12] | 18 | 18 | yes | 3 da. | none |
| Michigan | 18 | 16[8] | 18 | 18 | yes | 3 da. | none |
| Minnesota | 18 | 16 | 21 | 18 | no | 5 da. | none |
| Mississippi | 17 | 15 | 21 | 21 | yes | 3 da. | none |
| Missouri | 15[12] | 15[12] | 18 | 18 | yes | 3 da. | none |
| Montana | 18 | 18 | 18 | 18 | yes | 5 da. | none |
| Nebraska | 18 | 16 | 19 | 19 | yes | 2 da. | none |
| Nevada | 18 | 16 | 18 | 18 | no | none | none |
| New Hampshire | 14[12,15] | 13[12,15] | 18 | 18 | yes[11] | 5 da. | none |
| New Jersey | 18 | 16 | 18 | 18 | yes | 72 hr. | none |
| New Mexico | 16 | 16 | 18 | 18 | yes | none | none |
| New York | 16 | 14[9] | 21 | 18 | yes | none | (10) |
| North Carolina | 16 | 16 | 18 | 18 | yes | none | none |
| North Dakota | 18 | 15 | 18 | 18 | yes | none | none |
| Ohio | 18 | 16 | 21 | 21 | yes | 5 da. | none |
| Oklahoma | 18[17] | 15[17] | 21 | 18 | yes | none[14] | none |
| Oregon | 18 | 15 | 21 | 18 | yes | 7 da. | none |
| Pennsylvania | 16 | 16 | 18 | 18 | yes | 3 da. | none |
| Rhode Island | 18 | 16 | 18 | 18 | yes | none | none |
| South Carolina | 16 | 14 | 18 | 18 | no | 24 hr. | none |
| South Dakota | 16 | 16 | 18 | 18 | yes | none | none |
| Tennessee | 16 | 16 | 18 | 18 | yes | none[14] | none |
| Texas | 16[13] | 16[13] | 18 | 18 | yes | none | none |
| Utah | 16 | 14 | 21 | 18 | yes | none | none |
| Vermont | 18 | 16 | 18 | 18 | yes | none | 5 da.[16] |
| Virginia | 16 | 16 | 18 | 18 | yes | none | none |
| Washington | 17 | 17 | 18 | 18 | no | 3 da. | none |
| West Virginia | 18 | 16 | 18 | 18 | yes | 3 da. | none |
| Wisconsin | 18 | 16 | 18 | 18 | yes | 5 da. | none |
| Wyoming | 18[20] | 16[20] | 18[20] | 18[20] | yes | none | none |

[1] In some states, waiting period may be waived or reduced by court order. [2] By place of occurrence. [3] In most states, persons younger than the age shown may be married by court permission. [4] Provisional figures; data represent marriages reported, marriage intentions filed, or marriage licenses issued. [5] 96 hours if nonresidents. [6] Day of appli-

There are few other physical prohibitions to marriage, although it might be desirable to have more. A few states have regulations against marriage of people with infectious tuberculosis, epilepsy, alcoholism, or any communicable disease.

## AGE FOR MARRIAGE

States usually set minimum age requirements for marriage: one age that is legal if the parents give their consent, and another at which young people may marry without parental consent. The most common legal age for marriage with the consent of the parent or guardian is 18 for boys and 16 for girls. Thirty states have adopted this standard.

The most common minimum age for marriage without the consent of the parents or guardian has been 21 for boys and 18 for girls. Approximately three-fifths of the states have set these ages. The next most common age has been 21 for both men and women. One state, New Hampshire, allows boys of 14 and girls of 13 to marry if they have permission from their parents and from a judge.

With the passage of the Twenty-sixth Amendment to the Constitution all of these age requirements will be reconsidered. If 18- to 21-year-old people can vote and make other legal contracts, can they also make contracts to marry without parental consent? The new Texas Family Code allows a couple to become husband and wife by simply filing a declaration of informal marriage with a county clerk. The state attorney general has ruled that teenagers in Texas can declare themselves informally married without parental consent as long as the boy is at least 16 and the girl 14 years old.

In the United States, as in other countries, it is less the law than the attitudes of people toward child marriages that determine whether children will marry. The largest percentages of child marriages are in the southern section of the United States, although some other states have laws differing little from those of the southern states (see Figure 13-1).

---

cation and day of pickup are included in 5-day waiting period. [7] If applicants are under 21 but over 19 and female is not pregnant. [8] Consent of one parent or guardian necessary for female only. [9] Females 14 to 16 years old must also have consent of judge of Family Court. [10] Marriage may not be solemnized within 10 days from date on which specimen was taken for serological test, and not until 24 hours after issuance of marriage license. Waiting period may be waived by court order. [11] Blood test may be waived by court order. [12] Need court order. [13] Parent must appear in person or provide doctor's affidavit of his or her illness. [14] 3 days if either party is under legal age. [15] If pregnant. [16] After date on which marriage application has been filed with town clerk, excluding date of filing. [17] Males under 18 and females under 15 only if female is pregnant. [18] Blood test for rubella and RH type not required of females over 45 years or found by physician to be incapable of bearing children. [19] No parental consent if female is pregnant. [20] If under 18 or 16 need court order. [21] Males and females under age of 16 may obtain a license with judicial approval.

**State rankings of all marriages involving
teenage brides and grooms by age**

Brides

Grooms

Percent

50 40 30 20 10 0 0 10 20 30 40 50

| Rank | State | Brides % | Grooms % | State | Rank |
|------|-------|----------|----------|-------|------|
| 1 | Kentucky | 47.4 | 24.7 | Kentucky | 1 |
| 2 | Alabama | 46.5 | 22.5 | North Carolina | 2 |
| 3 | North Carolina | 45.4 | 22.5 | South Carolina | 3 |
| 4 | South Carolina | 44.7 | 20.3 | Missouri | 4 |
| 5 | Arkansas | 44.2 | 20.0 | Alabama | 5 |
| 6 | West Virginia | 42.3 | 19.6 | Utah | 6 |
| 7 | Utah | 42.0 | 19.5 | Arkansas | 7 |
| 8 | Mississippi | 40.6 | 18.6 | Tennessee | 8 |
| 9 | Louisiana | 40.1 | 18.3 | Mississippi | 9 |
| 10 | Missouri | 39.4 | 18.1 | Indiana | 10 |
| 11 | Kansas | 39.0 | 17.8 | Texas | 11 |
| 12 | Tennessee | 38.9 | 17.8 | West Virginia | 12 |
| 13 | Indiana | 38.6 | 17.7 | Louisiana | 13 |
| 14 | Iowa | 38.3 | 17.3 | Michigan | 14 |
| 15 | Texas | 38.2 | 17.1 | Iowa | 15 |
| 16 | Montana | 37.2 | 16.5 | Kansas | 16 |
| 17 | Oregon | 37.2 | 15.3 | Oregon | 17 |
| 18 | Maine | 36.6 | 15.1 | Georgia | 18 |
| 19 | Maryland | 35.5 | 14.7 | Ohio | 19 |
| 20 | Vermont | 35.2 | 14.5 | South Dakota | 20 |
| 21 | Michigan | 35.1 | 14.1 | Delaware | 21 |
| 22 | North Dakota | 35.0 | 14.0 | Maine | 22 |
| 23 | South Dakota | 34.0 | 14.0 | Nebraska | 23 |
| 24 | Georgia | 33.8 | 13.7 | Idaho | 24 |
| 25 | Nebraska | 32.9 | 13.7 | Virginia | 25 |
| 26 | California | 32.8 | 13.6 | California | 26 |
| 27 | Wyoming | 32.5 | 13.2 | Wyoming | 27 |
| 28 | Virginia | 32.4 | 13.1 | Montana | 28 |
| 29 | Idaho | 32.3 | 13.0 | Vermont | 29 |
| 30 | Ohio | 31.4 | 12.9 | Maryland | 30 |
| 31 | Alaska | 31.1 | 12.1 | Pennsylvania | 31 |
| 32 | Delaware | 31.1 | 11.3 | Minnesota | 32 |
| 33 | Wisconsin | 30.5 | 11.3 | North Dakota | 33 |
| 34 | Minnesota | 29.9 | 11.1 | Illinois | 34 |
| 35 | Florida | 29.3 | 11.0 | Florida | 35 |
| 36 | Illinois | 28.4 | 11.0 | Wisconsin | 36 |
| 37 | New Hampshire | 28.3 | 9.2 | Massachusetts | 37 |
| 38 | Pennsylvania | 27.3 | 9.1 | Rhode Island | 38 |
| 39 | Hawaii | 24.2 | 9.0 | Alaska | 39 |
| 40 | Massachusetts | 24.1 | 9.0 | New Hampshire | 40 |
| 41 | Rhode Island | 23.5 | 8.1 | Hawaii | 41 |
| 42 | New Jersey | 22.9 | 8.1 | New Jersey | 42 |
| 43 | New York | 22.7 | 7.7 | New York | 43 |
| 44 | Connecticut | 20.6 | 7.4 | Connecticut | 44 |
| 45 | District of Columbia | 19.2 | 6.3 | District of Columbia | 45 |

Under 18 Years    18-19 Years    Under 20 Years

FIG. 13–1   As reported by 44 states and the District of Columbia, 1969.

An important reason for discouraging early marriage is that very young people are not likely to be able to cope with the responsibility of parenthood. Boys who marry early may not be in a position to support families. In addition, very youthful marriages are less stable.

It must be remembered that many child marriages are forced because of pregnancy. In most states judges have the right to waive the minimum ages for marriage if the girl is pregnant. In such marriages there may be disparity in age; usually the man is a number of years older than the girl. A man of 70 once married a girl of 13. The girl believed herself to be in love with the man, and her parents willingly gave their consent to the marriage. That the law does not attempt to judge the results of marriage contracts is shown by the Michigan law, which states: "Marriage is a contract which the legislature may not dissolve, though contracted for convenience with unhappy results."

Although states prohibit marriages below certain ages, a marriage of people below that age usually stands as valid if it has been consummated. If an interested person takes the case before a court, offers proof that one or both are below the legal age, and asks annulment, the court may annul the marriage. Otherwise it stands.

## MARRIAGE BETWEEN RELATIVES

All states prohibit marriages between close blood relatives. Brothers and sisters, fathers and daughters, mothers and sons, grandfathers and granddaughters, grandmothers and grandsons, aunts and nephews, and uncles and nieces may not marry in any state, with one exception. Rhode Island suspends its own marriage law in order to accommodate itself to the Jewish law, which permits the marriage of an uncle and a niece, but not of an aunt and a nephew. The next most common prohibitions against marriages of consanguinity are that first cousins and brothers and sisters of half blood may not marry. Both prohibitions are found in 29 states. Only six states prohibit the marriage of second cousins.[1] Although many states do not permit first cousins to marry within their borders, a number of them do recognize the marriages of first cousins who go to another state to marry and then return to their home state to live. This policy seems inconsistent, but it is commonly followed by states in order to prevent confusion and to guarantee the legitimacy of children born of such marriages.

The strongest objection to marriages of close blood relatives arises from the incest taboo. However, there are biological reasons for opposing a consanguineous marriage, since relatives are more likely to carry the same hereditary defects in their germ plasm. If marriage takes place

[1] Indiana, Minnesota, Nevada, Ohio, Washington, and Wisconsin.

between closely related people, defects are more likely to show up in the children, who can inherit the same traits from both sides of the family. In animal breeding it is common to "line breed" to build up a particular stock, that is, to mate mothers and sons and fathers and daughters. The principle.is that superior stock produces superior stock. In stock breeding the defective strains have been eliminated so that mating of blood relatives does not present the risk that it does in human mating, where it is impossible to eliminate the undesirable strain. If first cousins were of the best hereditary stock, from a biological point of view, first-cousin marriage would be desirable.

The incest taboo is carried to an unreasonable and illogical extreme in the laws prohibiting marriage because of affinity. There is no biological reason why in-laws or step-relatives should not marry. In Michigan, the law goes so far as to say a man may not marry his stepmother or his wife's grandmother, and goes on to include every possible relative-in-law or step-relative among those an individual may not legally marry. Surely there is no more valid basis for objection to a man's marrying his former wife's grandmother, if he wishes to do so, than to his marrying any other grandmother. Only seven other states have all the prohibitions found in the Michigan law.[2] Twenty-six states have no regulations at all on marriages of affinity. The most common regulations are those prohibiting the marriages of stepparents to stepchildren (23 states), parents-in-law to sons- and daughters-in-law (20 states), and a man or a woman to granddaughter- or grandson-in-law (18 states).[3] All these prohibitions, when considered objectively, seem to have no reasonable basis. They are simply based on misunderstanding of blood relationship and on the general aversion to incest.

## INTERRACIAL MARRIAGE REGULATIONS

At one time 40 of the states had laws prohibiting interracial marriages. Sixteen states still had such laws in 1967 when the United States Supreme Court ruled unanimously that all laws prohibiting marriage between whites and nonwhites are unconstitutional. In the northern states a trend toward repealing such laws had developed fairly rapidly after the courts ruled on a California case in 1948.

California's law against interracial marriages was declared unconstitutional when a woman of Mexican descent and a black man who were refused a marriage license appealed to the courts for a ruling. The court declared the law unconstitutional for several reasons, among them the

[2] Kentucky, Maine, Maryland, Massachusetts, Rhode Island, South Carolina, and Vermont.

[3] Chester G. Vernier, *American Family Laws* (Stanford, Calif.: Stanford University Press, 1931), Vol. I, pp. 183–84.

following: (1) a marriage contract is a fundamental right of free men; (2) marriage is the right of individuals and not of special groups; (3) legislative control of marriage must be based on proved peril to the parties involved or to the state; (4) the law discriminates because of race or color; and (5) the law is not meeting a definite need. Since both parties applying for the license were Catholic, they declared that their religious freedom was hampered by the law because they could receive all the sacraments except that of marriage.

There was no great increase in interracial marriages in California after the law was declared unconstitutional. By 1959 there were 1455 interracial marriages, or 1.4 percent of all marriages. The most common combinations were black men to white women, white men to Japanese women, and white men to Chinese women. Looked at in percentages of total marriages for their group, whites and blacks tend to marry within their own racial groups more than is true of any of the other races in California. Half of American Indians, men and women, had married outside their race, 20 percent of Japanese women and 11 percent of Japanese men married outside their race, and 18 percent of both Chinese men and women married outside their race.[4] Racial origin is no longer required on applications for marriage licenses in California, and such information has not been collected in other states where there is a potential for many mixed racial marriages of blacks, Orientals, Indians, and whites.

Monahan has analyzed all data on interracial marriages as recorded in states that belong to the United States Divorce Registration area, before and after the Supreme Court decision in 1967.[5] Although many states such as California have outlawed the registration of marriages by race, Monahan was able to get the data from 36 states that have records from 1963 to 1970. Although the data are inadequate, Monahan came to the following conclusions after studying the records: In black-white marriages, 70 percent or more involve a black man and a white woman; in marriages of other races with whites, the male is more often white. Between 1963 and 1970 the rate of intermarriage of blacks with other races has doubled from 1.4 percent to 2.6 percent (intermarriage rates vary greatly by regions and by states). In the 23 Northern and Western states, black interracial marriages have exceeded 7 percent; in states having a very small black population, such as Maine, Vermont, New Hampshire, South Dakota, Montana, and Hawaii, black mixed racial marriages approach or exceed 50 percent of all black marriages. The bulk of interracial marriages of blacks in the South has taken place since 1967.

[4] California Public Health Statistical Report, Vital Statistics for Calendar Year 1959, Part V.

[5] Thomas P. Monahan, "An Overview of Statistics on Interracial Marriage in the United States, with Data on its Extent from 1963–1970," *Journal of Marriage and the Family* 38:2 (May 1976), 223–31.

The overall incidence of interracial marriage is small but is rising, particularly the marriages of blacks and whites. Less than three-fourths of one percent of marriages in any one year are interracial.

Biologically there is no reason why the races should not intermarry, but the pressure of social attitudes has been a factor affecting these marriages. If no stigma were attached to interracial marriage, no race problem would exist, since the acceptance of biological fusion represents complete acceptance of a minority group. In parts of the United States, such stigma is still attached to such marriages.

## MARRIAGE LICENSE

All states have adopted the system of requiring a license in order to keep records of marriages. Although their laws require licenses, many states recognize marriages without a license. As we have pointed out earlier, it is not the license that marries the couple, and nearly a third of the states recognize common-law marriage, which takes place without a marriage license. Quakers and some other religious groups are exempted from getting marriage licenses because of their religious beliefs. Georgia, Maryland, and Ohio permit the substitution of the published banns for a license.[6] No marriage license is required of Texas couples who file a "Declaration and Registration of Informal Marriage" according to the new Family Code.

A license grants a couple legal permission to be married. However, those qualified to officiate at a marriage may refuse to marry a couple even though a license to wed has been secured. Some ministers are in the habit of questioning couples about their previous marital status and the circumstances of any previous divorce. If a minister concludes that a contemplated marriage has no chance for success, or that for moral reasons the church should not sanction the marriage, he may refuse to perform the ceremony, since the license is permissive and not mandatory.

Here is a typical law regarding the marriage license:

Michigan 12705. It is necessary for all parties intending to be married to obtain a marriage license from the county clerk of the county in which either the man or the woman resides. If both parties are non-residents of the state, it shall be necessary to obtain such a license from the county clerk of the county in which the marriage is to be performed.

## WAITING PERIOD

Two policies are usually followed if a waiting period is required between the time of the application for a license to wed and the marriage. Most

[6] Vernier, *American Family Laws*, p. 60.

states follow the policy of not delivering the license for some time after the application is made, three days being the most common period of waiting. Or the license may be issued at once but not become valid for a certain number of days. All states except Nevada either require a waiting period or have a venereal disease law, which serves much the same purpose of delaying hasty marriages. In many states, a judge may waive the waiting-period requirement under certain conditions. If the girl is pregnant, if both members of the couple are old enough and have considered their decision, or if other circumstances seem to make the waiting period unnecessary, they may apply to a judge who may have the power to waive the waiting period.

The waiting-period requirement, like the physical examination for venereal disease, is relatively recent. Maine is the only state that has always required a waiting period or the publishing of banns. The custom of publishing advance notice through the posting of, or the reading of, the banns started early in the Middle Ages and has continued among Catholics to the present. Publishing of the banns was made mandatory by the Fourth Lateran Council in 1215. It is now recognized that this old church custom was important in preventing hasty marriages.

Laws that require a waiting period should reduce the number of ill-advised marriages, and available evidence indicates that they do tend to serve this purpose. Records show that many couples who apply for marriage licenses do not return at the end of the waiting period to get the licenses. A study comparing nonreturnees for marriage licenses in Milwaukee County, Wisconsin, with couples who did return for their licenses and marry found that the nonreturnee pairs tended to have characteristics of marriages more likely to fail.[7] More of the intended marriages of the nonreturnees would have been hasty marriages, as indicated by lack of wedding plans; more were forced by pregnancy; more were being undertaken in spite of legal obstacles to the marriage; more of the nonreturnees had had previous marriages; and more were of low occupational status.

No information is available as to how many who do not return for their licenses do proceed to marry by traveling to some other state where the license requirements are more lenient. The effectiveness of any one state's laws can be hindered because of the lack of uniformity in requirements among different states.

Premarital requirements still vary widely among states. In the late fifties and early sixties, six states introduced new premarital requirements, namely, Arizona, Iowa, New Mexico, South Carolina, Indiana, and Mississippi. The new laws dealt with such matters as blood tests, proof of age,

[7] Gordon Shipman and H. Yuan Tien, "Non-Marriage and the Waiting Period," *Journal of Marriage and the Family* 27:2 (May 1965), 277–80.

FIG. 13-2 Known for its easy divorce laws, Nevada also extends a helping hand to couples who wish to be quickly wed. For about $35.00, a minister, witnesses, lighted candles, and flowers can be purchased as a "package wedding."

parental consent, and a waiting period between applying for and receiving the license. A comparison of the combined marriage totals in these six states for the last full year before the law changed with the totals for the first full year following the new laws showed that marriages declined by 47 percent. For individual states, the decline was from 23 percent in Iowa and South Carolina to 667 percent in Mississippi.[8] The precise explana-

[8] Alexander Plateris, "The Impact of the Amendment of Marriage Laws in Mississippi," *Journal of Marriage and the Family* 28:2 (May 1966), 206–12.

tion for this great decrease in marriages is not clear. A certain percentage probably represents the actual prevention of ill-advised marriages. The requirements may have caused another percentage of applicants to postpone their intended marriages until they could meet the requirements for age proof, parental consent, or blood tests. Undoubtedly, others went to adjoining states with different requirements, when that was possible, and married. An analysis of divorce statistics for 1966 in California showed that many couples bypassed the California laws by crossing the state line to be married in Nevada, where requirements are lenient. The duration of those marriages was shorter than of the marriages that had met California requirements and had taken place in the state. The analysis showed also that only 18 percent of the couples marrying for the first time had gone to Nevada to marry, whereas 45 percent who had had a previous marriage had crossed state lines to be married.[9] Detailed studies of the apparent effects of laws dealing with premarital requirements continue to provide information that should accelerate the trend toward uniform requirements in all states.

## WHO IS QUALIFIED TO PERFORM MARRIAGE CEREMONIES?

In all states except two, marriage ceremonies may be performed by either civil or religious authorities. In Maryland and West Virginia, the ceremony must be performed by religious authorities. People usually prefer to be married by the clergy; three-fourths of all ceremonies are performed by a minister, priest, or rabbi. Of all the civil authorities qualified to officiate at weddings, the justice of the peace most often officiates.

In some states, the legality of the marriage is doubtful if the officiant is not properly qualified. However, in other states, the legality of the marriage is not affected by the status of the officiant. Some couples, either through sentiment or because of confusion concerning the nature of a legal wedding ceremony, have two weddings. If they have been married in a civil ceremony, they may later have the religious wedding. The important thing is that the couple is acting in good faith.

The Michigan law states:

12701. No marriage solemnized before any person professing to be a Justice of the Peace or a minister of the gospel shall be deemed void. *Provided* the marriage be consummated with a full belief on the part of the persons so married that they have been lawfully joined in marriage.

In 41 states, Friends or Quakers and members of other denominations having special methods of solemnizing marriages are exempted from the

[9] *Divorce in California* (Sacramento: Department of Public Health, Bureau of Vital Statistics, October 1967), pp. 64–65.

law that requires an officiant. Members of these sects are permitted to solemnize their marriages according to the method prescribed by their religion. In the Quaker marriage ceremony, the man and woman marry each other without the aid of an officiant. The marriage is a civil ceremony in which the groom states, "I, John Jones, take thee, Mary Smith, to be my wedded wife," etc. The bride repeats, "I, Mary Smith, take thee, John Jones, to be my wedded husband," etc. After the pledges have been made, leaders or chosen people sign the wedding certificate, and the couple are as legally married as if they had been married by a minister or some other official.

## VALIDITY OF MARRIAGE

On this point the Michigan law says:

> 12696. The general rule of law is that a marriage valid where it is celebrated is valid everywhere; and the converse to this is equally general, that a marriage void where it is celebrated is void everywhere. Whatever the form of the ceremony, if the parties agreed personally to take each other for husband and wife and from that time lived together professedly in that relation, presentation of these facts would be sufficient to show marriage as binding upon the parties, which would subject them and others to legal penalties for disregard of those obligations.

In general, the spirit of the above law exists in other states. That is, if a marriage is void where it is celebrated, it is usually void everywhere. Exceptions occur in a few states that make marriages void if the parties married in order to evade a state law. These states are Illinois, Louisiana, Massachusetts, Vermont, and Wisconsin. Twelve other states have laws prohibiting out-of-state marriages to evade the state law, but in most of these states such marriages would still be considered legal.

As the various state laws now stand, it is easier for each state to recognize the marriage laws existing in other states.

## COMMON-LAW MARRIAGE

Common-law marriages are still valid in 14 states. Ten more states recognize the validity of common-law marriages if entered into prior to the enactment of any new laws outlawing common-law marriages in the state. States outlawing common-law marriages recognize their validity if they were valid in another state where contracted. Common-law marriages are marriages in which a man and a woman mutually agree that they will live together as husband and wife. No license or marriage officiant is employed, nor is any specific ceremony necessary. If the validity of the marriage is questioned, the couple must show that they are living as husband and wife. If either is already married, or if other legal reasons make a regular marriage impossible, the couple cannot marry by common law. In the states where common-law marriages are valid, they are as binding as other marriages. In these states, a common-law marriage must be dissolved through divorce, according to the divorce laws governing all other marriages, before either party may remarry.

Common-law marriages were frequent in Europe during the Middle Ages but were abolished by the Catholic Church in the Council of Trent in 1563. England abolished common-law marriages in 1753. Common-law marriages were suited to the frontier life of early America, since it was often impossible to get a minister when people were ready to marry. In many frontier communities, people who died were buried with little ceremony, and a funeral was held weeks or months later when the circuit rider came around. In the same way, couples pledged themselves as husband and wife and began housekeeping, sometimes having a wedding later when the circuit rider appeared. Others dispensed with the wedding, and their pledges and their living together as husband and wife were accepted as a marriage.

## A NEW TYPE OF COMMON-LAW MARRIAGE

Today couples who are rebelling against the traditional marriage ceremony and who decide to live together in an unmarried relationship do not always recognize the implications of such a relationship. Although the state in which they live may have abolished common-law marriage, the courts may judge the relationship as a marriage if the relationship had the characteristics of a legally married couple. One attorney has advised unmarried couples who live together to follow certain rules: (a) keep separate bank, credit, and income tax accounts; (b) identify yourself as single; (c) use your own name; (d) avoid having children; and (e) before sharing in a financial or business venture, consult an attorney and have an agreement drawn up.

If informal unmarried relationships become numerous, there will be many cases in which courts will have to decide the rights of the individuals when the relationship ends. Cases in California and Washington (two states that have abolished common-law marriages) may indicate a trend. Paul and Janet, an unmarried couple in California, lived together for eight years. During that time they had four children, bought property, and filed joint income tax returns. When Paul petitioned to dissolve the relationship, the courts were called in to decide Janet's rights to property. The court ruled that the property was "family property," and Janet was awarded her share.

In a Washington case, an unmarried couple had reared children, born to them, and had acquired and managed a cattle ranch. When the man died, the courts decided the survivor had community property rights similar to those of a legal wife.

Those couples living together without a traditional marriage live in a condition of uncertainty because their rights to food stamps, social security, alimony, child support, child custody, mortgage and bank loans, inheritance and survivor's benefits, and income tax benefits are not clearly defined. The laws define the rights of those who live within the framework of traditional marriage, but the courts have to decide by common law the rights of those living outside traditional marriage. Change will come about slowly toward accepting unmarried relationships as binding and toward uniform interpretation of the rights of those involved.

## VOID AND VOIDABLE MARRIAGES

Certain marriages are considered void from the beginning, and certain others are voidable. In a void marriage it is not necessary to have the marriage annulled or to take any legal recourse. Although there was mutual consent, a license to wed, and a qualified officiant, no marriage took place since a legal reason such as consanguinity, feeble-mindedness, or an already existing marriage prevented it.

Some prohibited marriages stand as valid unless reason is shown why the marriage should be declared void. These are voidable marriages and are dissolved through annulment rather than through divorce. Annulment differs from divorce in the following ways:

1   It proceeds on the assumption that no valid marriage ever existed between the parties.
2   Property is to be returned to each.
3   Usually neither is entitled to further rights of support.
4   Children are considered illegitimate unless they are protected by some other law.

In some states, the difference between annulments and divorce is not clear. There are states that make no distinction between the two, so the only ending for an illegal marriage is divorce. The most common grounds recognized for annulling marriages are age, insanity or lack of understanding, force or fraud, bigamy, and impotence.

The most common reason given for having marriages annulled is fraud. The French war bride of a veteran who claimed to be the owner of a big plantation in Georgia had the marriage annulled on the grounds of fraud when she found that actually he lived with his parents in a three-room shack on a 20-acre farm. Almost half of all annulments are for misrepresentations of this type. Fraud may not be the real reason for some of these annulments. Couples must give reasons that are acceptable to the court if they are to get out of a bad marriage, and since fraud is an acceptable reason, that may be the one most frequently offered.

The second most common reason for annulments is bigamy. About 35 percent are for this reason. Although bigamous marriages are usually void from the beginning, it is usual to have them annulled through court action. No doubt then remains about the marital status of the individuals, once court action has been taken, whereas confusion might arise if no legal action had been taken, especially in states where the law is confusing.

In most states, those who marry under age are legally married unless action is taken to have the marriages annulled. A few years ago a Tennessee girl of 9 married a man 22 years old. At that time Tennessee had no statute on age for marriage, and the common law prevailed. In common law, marriages of children under seven years of age were void. Since both members of the Tennessee couple and their parents were satisfied with the marriage, nothing could be done to dissolve it. The marriage stood as legal, since the common law provided that marriages of children over seven were voidable but not void. In some states, this marriage would not have stood, and probably the man would have had charges brought against him.

In addition, annulment can be secured because of mental incapacity and physical incapacity or impotence. Impotence is not to be confused with sterility, which is inability to reproduce. Impotence is the inability of either the male or the female to have sexual intercourse, but it usually refers to the male. It is recognized in many states as cause for annulment of marriage. The majority of states also recognize mental incapacity as grounds for annulment.

Some causes for annulment, such as insanity or impotence, cannot be used if the marriage has been allowed to stand unchallenged for a certain period of time. Approximately a third of annulments come within the first year of marriage. Annulments account for only a small percentage of marriage dissolutions, for no more than 2 percent in most states.

New York and California are the only states in which it is not unusual to seek annulment rather than divorce when a marriage is to be broken. In California 12 percent and in New York 40 percent of marriages terminated were ended through annulment. Until 1967, when New York liberalized its divorce laws, residents tended to seek annulments if they did not go out of the state for divorces, because New York laws recognized adultery as the sole ground for divorce. With the liberalized law, annulments may become less common in New York, but not necessarily so, since the precedent has been established there for ending marriages through annulment. Immediately after the liberalized law in California in 1970, the annulment rate decreased 32 percent, but the rate remains high. An analysis of annulments in California shows that people securing annulments tend to be at the extremes in age: either young, as indicated by the fact that many are students, or past middle age, as many of the annulments are granted to people in their sixties. The couples tend to have had more than one marriage, to have gone outside the state to be married, and to have married across lines of race or religion.[10]

### Catholic annulment

Annulment may become a more common method for dissolving Catholic marriages. In recent years the divorce rate among Catholics has approached the rate among non-Catholics. Several leaders of the Catholic Church in the United States are seeking to make annulment easier as a way out of bad marriages while still holding to the sacramental nature of marriage and the concept of the indissolubility of a valid marriage. The argument being emphasized in annulment is that "deficient personalities" cannot meet and live up to the requirements of a marriage. Among Catholics, marriages of long standing can be annulled using the new personality-deficiency approach. Church courts are being expanded and streamlined in the United States to hasten annulments. In 1968 there were only 650 annulled Catholic marriages; this had increased to 10,000 by 1975. Catholics who have their marriages annulled are free to remarry and retain their standing in the Church. The Catholic annulment procedure differs from the civil annulment. The Catholic couple must first get a divorce through the civil court like any other couple. They then apply to the church court to have that court declare that there never had been a valid marriage.

## LEGITIMACY OF CHILDREN OF ANNULLED MARRIAGES

If a marriage is proved illegal and the couple had children during the period when they thought they were married, are their children legitimate or illegitimate? Again there is confusion. Several of the states have passed no regulation on this point and still follow the common law which held that such children were illegitimate.[11] The usual policy of the states that have legislated on this point is similar to the following law, which declares that children of void or annulled marriages are legitimate.

> Michigan 12750. Upon the dissolution of a marriage on account of non-age, insanity, or idiocy of either party, the issue of the marriage shall be deemed to be in all respects the legitimate issue of the parent who, at the time of the marriage, was capable of contracting.

[10] *Divorce in California,* pp. 72–76.

[11] Maryland, Mississippi, North Carolina, Pennsylvania, Tennessee, and Washington.

In some states, the children of certain types of illegal marriages are considered illegitimate. Children of incestuous and bigamous unions are more likely to be considered illegitimate than the children of other prohibited unions.

## LEGAL STATUS OF ILLEGITIMATE CHILDREN

Although many states have made efforts to legitimize children born of void and annulled marriages, progress has been slow toward an enlightened viewpoint concerning children born out of wedlock. Traditionally, sexual intercourse outside of marriage has been frowned on, and if the sexually delinquent became diseased or if pregnancy resulted, society has had little sympathy. This attitude applied not only to the parents but to the children as well. The status of illegitimate children was such that it was hard for them to live normal lives. It was public knowledge that they were illegitimate because birth certificates carried the information, and under the law these children could not inherit property from either parent.

Some progress can be seen in present-day thinking on the problem of illegitimate children. It is now considered that children should not be discriminated against because of their origin. In 1973, 13 out of every 100 babies born in the United States were from illegitimate unions. The present illegitimacy rate varies greatly by race, being eight times higher among nonwhites.[12]

To register babies born out of wedlock as illegitimate is still the practice in 34 states and the District of Columbia. In these states, whenever the birth certificate must be shown, the illegitimate birth becomes known to others. Birth records are public records kept at the county seat

[12] *Vital Statistics of the United States 1967*, Vol. 1, Natality, Tables 1–26, 1967.

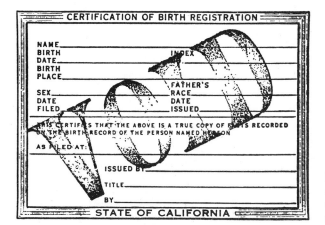

FIG. 13–3 Copy of a short form birth certificate as provided in some states.

and, as such, are open to public inspection. Some states have revised their laws so that birth certificates showing illegitimacy are recorded only at the state capitol. Even this method, however, is small protection, for the illegitimacy still shows up on the birth certificate, which must occasionally be shown.[13]

Some states have changed their laws so that all citizens receive a short form of their birth certificate which lists only essential facts: name, sex, and place and date of birth.

Two states, Arizona and North Dakota, legitimize *all* children and give them equal rights. The Arizona law states:

> Every child is the legitimate child of its natural parents and is entitled to support and education as if born in lawful wedlock, except the right to dwelling or a residence with the family of its father, if such father be married. It shall inherit from its natural parents and from their kindred heirs, lineal and collateral, in the same manner as children born in lawful wedlock. This section shall apply to cases where the natural father of any such child is married to one other than the mother of said child, as well as where he is single.

Arizona and North Dakota are realistic in recognizing the rights of all children regardless of their origin. In 44 states, the "natural" child does not have the right to inherit from the father.[14] In all but one state, Louisiana, the illegitimate child may inherit from the mother. The most common limitation on inheritance is that, although the illegitimate child may inherit from the mother, such a child cannot inherit from the mother's lineal or collateral kindred. The Michigan law represents this point of view. It states, "Every child is heir of his mother, but it [illegitimate child] is not allowed to claim, as representing his mother, any part of the estate of any of her kindred, either lineal or collateral."

Although 48 states have laws that may require a father to support his illegitimate child, it is often difficult to prove paternity.[15] Unless the mother of the child initiates action to prove the paternity of the child, the father need take no responsibility for the child's support. One study found that within one year after divorce, 58 percent of fathers were making support payments as ordered by the court, and that after four

[13] Arizona, Arkansas, California, Colorado, Connecticut, Idaho, Maryland, Massachusetts, Nebraska, New Hampshire, New Mexico, New York, Oklahoma, and Vermont had eliminated the question of legitimacy from the birth certificate by 1955. *Vital Statistics of the United States 1955*, vol. I (Washington, D.C.: Bureau of Census, 1955), 23.

[14] In Arizona, North Dakota, Iowa, and Wisconsin, the illegitimate child may inherit from the father, and bills have been introduced in several other states which, if passed, will grant children full inheritance rights from both parents regardless of the marital status of the natural parents.

[15] Texas and Virginia have no legislation applying to the father of an illegitimate child.

years, only 33 percent were making support payments for their children.[16]

The Scandinavian countries have the most advanced legislation on illegitimacy. In general, the state takes the responsibility for the protection of the child in that it establishes paternity, provides equal rights to inheritance, protects the child through the father's continued support until maturity, and gives the mother regular social security benefits in addition to special benefits, since she is unmarried. The parents are not forced to marry, but the child is guaranteed rights and protection equal to those of children whose parents are married. Of the children under the supervision of child-welfare guardians in Sweden, in one year paternity was established in 85 percent of the cases, largely through the father's own admission of his responsibility.[17]

In the United States, when the mother takes the initiative and establishes paternity, and the court orders the father to support the child, little real guarantee of permanent support for the child is made. If the father falls behind in payments or ceases altogether to contribute to the child's support, it is up to the mother to take legal action. In many cases, however, the mother is unable or unwilling to take such action and the child is the victim.

If children born out of wedlock are to have an equal chance with others to become desirable citizens, it would seem that the following policies should be universal:

1   Legitimize all children and give them equal rights regardless of the circumstances of their birth.

2   Provide birth certificates that do not call for paternity information.

3   Give the state responsibility for establishing paternity.

4   Give the state responsibility for enforcing parental support of all children.

5   Provide adequate financial support for all children in need.

6   Provide more adequate maternity care for unwed mothers.

7   Create general acceptance of the fact that there are no "illegitimate" children, and that for the good of society all children must be freed from any stigma attached to their birth.

One registrar of births, in a state that still records "legitimate" or "illegitimate" on each birth certificate, when asked why the state did not change its policy on registering births, responded: "It just is not legal to do what some states are doing in not registering the paternity of children. Their action would not stand up in court at all, and there is danger that

---

[16] Citizens' Advisory Council on the Status of Women Memorandum: The Equal Rights Amendment and Alimony and Child Support Laws (Washington, D.C., January 1972).

[17] Social Sweden (Stockholm, Social Welfare Board, 1952), pp. 214–19.

the practice will result in many legal tangles." This person was sincere, but was focusing attention entirely on an outmoded legal viewpoint rather than on our society's obligation to more than four hundred thousand children born out of wedlock each year. Evidence indicates that this legalistic way of thinking is giving way to a more socially desirable point of view. Laws need to be adjusted in the light of their effect on the welfare of young citizens.

An analysis of existing marriage laws points to the conclusion that a great many state laws need revision. Marriage education in colleges and high schools throughout the country should lead to a better understanding of the broad social purposes underlying legal regulation of marriage and, in turn, to revision of marriage and divorce laws so that they may contribute more effectively to the stability of family life.

## REVIEW QUESTIONS

1   What is meant by saying the state has a stake in every marriage?

2   In what ways do state laws regulating marriage seem to be out of date?

3   What special problems does the state face when it attempts to regulate marriage?

4   How does a marriage contract differ from other civil contracts?

5   What one thing is essential to make a marriage binding?

6   Give some of the most common eugenic regulations of marriage.

7   Why is it difficult to enforce some of the eugenic regulations?

8   What is the most common legal age for marriage without the parents' consent? With consent?

9   Folkways and mores rather than the law determine the age at marriage. Explain.

10   Give some of the common regulations of marriages of consanguinity. Of affinity.

11   Why is there a great variation among states on marriages of affinity?

12   What were the reasons given by the Supreme Court for outlawing state laws against interracial marriages?

13   Summarize the conclusions about the incidence of, and the characteristics of, black–white marriages since they have become legal.

14   Is it possible to marry without a marriage license?

15   Cite evidence to show that requiring a waiting period between making application for a license to marry and the marriage is a good regulation.

16   Define common-law marriage. What are some of the problems couples living together without formalizing their marriage may face when they end the relationship: a) if they have bought property? b) if one wants to separate or divorce? c)if one dies? d) if they separate and remarry without seeking a divorce?

17   Distinguish between void and voidable marriages. Give an example of each.

18 How does annulment differ from divorce?

19 Give the most common grounds for annulment.

20 What is the legal status of children of void marriages?

21 What changes are taking place to protect children born out of wedlock?

22 Give some additional recommendations for action to protect the children of unwed parents.

## PROJECTS AND ACTIVITIES

1 *Special report.* Have one member of the class consult a statute book from your state and report on some marriage laws in your state.

2 *Special report.* Gather all the available information on your state's policy on children born out of wedlock.

3 Have one member of the class get copies of all the legal forms required for marriage and the registration of births in your state. Post these on your bulletin board.

# ACHIEVING ADJUSTMENT IN MARRIAGE

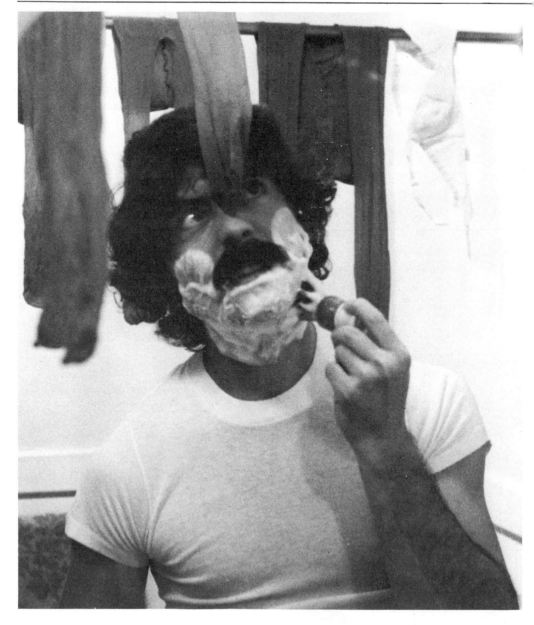

# 14

Before marriage, people in love have a tendency to emphasize the similarities in their ways of thinking rather than the differences. It is easy for a couple to idealize each other and to impute attitudes that may not exist. After they are launched upon life as a married couple, personality traits and value systems will become more apparent. Gradually, the two may recognize that they are not in such close agreement on everything as they had thought during the engagement.

In our studies of three different groups—married couples, couples having marriage counseling, and divorced people—those responding assessed their agreement in different areas of husband–wife relationships. The 122 engaged couples also rated their agreement on the same scale in the same areas of living. Figure 14-1 summarizes the assessment of their agreement in four areas. Marked differences appear between the extent of agreement reported by the engaged and the other groups.

In the more difficult areas of marriage adjustment—sex, money, in-laws, child-rearing—to be discussed in later chapters, the engaged couples in this study were even less aware of any differences. Does this mean that previously nonexisting differences in feelings, preferences, or behavior arise after the wedding, or simply that the married people recognize that agreement is not so complete as it may have seemed during engagement?

Recognition of areas of disagreement unacknowledged during engagement becomes normal after marriage, and some degree of it occurs quite universally. If the two people are from similar family backgrounds, their values may be much the same. If it is a "mixed" marriage, there may be practically no agreement. Married couples become conscious of differences in several well-defined areas in which they have to build a co-operative relationship. As one studies large numbers of marriages that

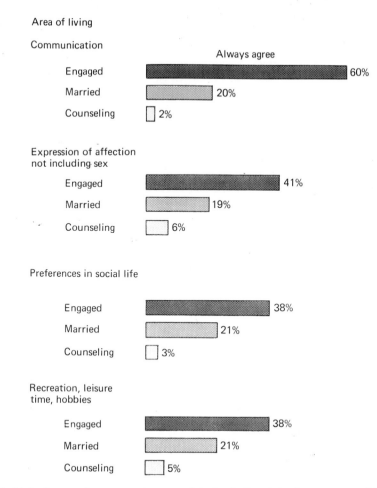

Area of living

Communication

Always agree

Engaged [60%]

Married [20%]

Counseling [2%]

Expression of affection
not including sex

Engaged [41%]

Married [19%]

Counseling [6%]

Preferences in social life

Engaged [38%]

Married [21%]

Counseling [3%]

Recreation, leisure
time, hobbies

Engaged [38%]

Married [21%]

Counseling [5%]

FIG. 14–1 Degree of agreement in areas of husband-wife relationships as reported by 122 engaged couples, 581 married couples, and 155 people seeking marriage counseling.

have lasted happily for years, the evidence becomes more and more convincing that successful marriages do not just happen. A conscious recognition of the need to work at building a successful marriage has proved to be the important factor in the success of many marriages, and the failure to recognize this necessity has resulted in failure in many others.

## ADJUSTABILITY REQUIRED IN ALL RELATIONSHIPS

In most situations involving human relationships, elements of conflict are present. Marriage is no different from other relationships in this respect.

Whenever two or more people attempt to live harmoniously together, adjustments must be made. People in college dormitories, in sorority or fraternity houses, in communes, or in any type of housing situation in

ACHIEVING ADJUSTMENT IN MARRIAGE

which several roommates or housemates live together learn that living with others under any circumstances requires cooperation, self-discipline, and a willingness to share and to compromise. One person who is selfish and demanding or thoughtless and inconsiderate of the rights of others can create constant friction and unpleasantness.

Learning to get along with roommates or housemates is in some ways a good preparation for married life. One learns to be tolerant of the wishes and peculiarities of others and develops the ability to use tact and to avoid friction-provoking issues. Married life requires the same finesse. However, in marriage, people are inclined to take their differences more seriously and to project themselves into controversial issues because they feel they belong to each other; they cannot go their separate ways and avoid differences so easily as can roommates. In addition, the marriage relationship involves sex, which plays an important part in determining levels and types of interaction. The sexual part of their interaction may serve as a strong bond that holds husband and wife together and aids them in working out points of difference, or it may serve as a focal point of friction so that they react more emotionally in all other areas requiring adjustability.

## PATTERNS OF MARITAL ADJUSTMENT

Most people in the early years of marriage may believe that the joys and satisfactions and the frustrations and disappointments they experience in their married living are unique to themselves. They do not realize that their experiences tend to fit a pattern being repeated in the lives of thousands of their contemporaries. Many married people would probably become less disturbed by the frustrations and disillusionments that may occur at some stage of marriage if they knew how common this is in marriage. The need is to recognize that certain developmental tasks confront all married couples.

These developmental tasks differ at each of the four or five stages of the married life cycle: (1) in early marriage; (2) after children come; (3) in middle life after the children leave home; (4) after retirement time comes; (5) when crises occur, such as death, serious illness, or financial disaster. Some of the tasks that confront newly married couples are accomplished easily and smoothly, such achievements contributing to the couple's sense of unity and to their awareness that they are establishing a firm foundation for permanent happiness and success as a married couple. Others may be more difficult for some couples. Nevertheless, *all* couples must build their marriages on the basis of satisfactory working arrangements in certain basic areas of living. The specific areas in which adjustability and cooperation are necessary are: sexual relations; money matters; religion; social activities and recreation; in-law relationships; associating with friends individually or as a couple; and, after children come, their training and discipline.

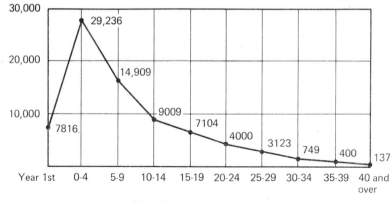

Number of
separations

FIG. 14–2  Time from the wedding to separation in marriages that failed (69,292 first marriages among couples filing for divorce, separate maintenance, or annulment in California in 1966). From *Divorce in California* (Sacramento: Department of Public Health, Bureau of Vital Statistics, October 1967), Table 16, p. 128.

It is safe to assume that in all marriages differences of opinion and potential conflict situations will arise in one or more of the areas requiring agreement or cooperation. The quality of a couple's overall relationship will be influenced by the methods used in meeting these situations. How potential conflict situations are resolved and how soon they are resolved are fundamental to the happiness of the marriage partners. That the first year of marriage is a crucial time for making adjustments is emphasized by the fact that marriages that fail tend to do so in the first year. A marriage fails psychologically and the couple separate sometime before they divorce; records show that more divorces are granted for couples in the third year after the wedding than in any other year. Figure 14-2 summarizes data on the time interval between marriage and separation in marriages that failed.

Ways of solving conflicts in marriage tend to fall within three different patterns. Some couples are able to develop a relationship in which both *compromise* to a certain extent and find a middle ground of agreement satisfactory to both. Few couples agree from the beginning in all areas of living. Through compromise, they may reach an adjustment after a few years that gives them a feeling of confidence and security in their marriage. In the most satisfactory adjustments, neither one feels that there has had to be too great a personal sacrifice in compromising.

In another type of adjustment, two people find that they hold quite seriously opposing viewpoints or that they have antagonistic characteristics, but they accept the fact of their differences and *accommodate*

ACHIEVING ADJUSTMENT IN MARRIAGE

themselves to the situation in any one of several ways. They may not be able to reach a compromise that is entirely satisfactory to them both, but their accommodation involves little or no outwardly expressed aggression or antagonism. They resolve their differences on certain matters by striking an equilibrium in which each tolerates the behavior of the other with little or no protest. Both may recognize that they have not reached a satisfactory agreement, but their state of accommodation will be such that their differences place relatively little strain upon the marriage. During the process of accommodation, the couple may discuss issues and attempt to reach mutuality of views. Sociologists speak of cooperation or collective effort for common ends as a form of accommodation. And certainly such cooperation is an important part of the picture in this type of adjustment in marriage. Differences in viewpoint and reactions to undesirable characteristics may be "tabled" in the interests of shared goals and values. The undesirable conditions will continue to exist but will not be allowed to hinder cooperation toward mutually desired ends. This form of accommodation is seen among couples who differ seriously on such points as religion or social activities, but who present a united front for the benefit of their children, or among couples whose financial security depends on there being an absence of conflict and on cooperation between them, such as in a business venture or a work situation. Such couples often table their serious differences, or at least control their actions so that no outward conflict shows, and concentrate on the cooperative effort that is necessary for their economic advancement and security.

A third form of adjustment in marriage is a *state of hostility*. Constant quarreling and bickering go on about the points on which the two differ, or tension is produced by antagonisms that may be expressed in words and made evident by behavior. The two cannot cope in any satisfactory way with their differences. They reach an impasse or a relationship that is either static and inflexible, characterized by hostility, or that moves toward a breakup of the marriage.

This state of hostility may be illustrated by a couple who differ on recreational interests. The husband does not like to dance but is an enthusiastic golfer. The wife continues to try to force her husband to take her to parties. When he refuses, she retaliates by hiding his golf clubs, going home to mother, or going out without him. Or she may appear to have given up her own interests but continue to hold resentful feelings. This resentment may find expression in a refusal to participate in other activities that the husband enjoys, or refusal to cooperate in sexual intercourse. The husband may retaliate by spending more and more time on recreational interests with others. In this way a couple may settle into a permanent state of antagonism and conflict.

Another couple with different habit patterns in their methods of facing problems might have the same differences but adjust to the situation in a more desirable way through the process of accommodation. They might compromise and each become able to participate in at least some of the recreational interests of the other, whether or not with pleasure. Or they might accommodate themselves to the situation by accepting their difference, each going his or her own way as far as possible, but with little or no hostility over their inability to enjoy the same things.

## IMPORTANCE OF ADJUSTMENTS MADE EARLY IN MARRIAGE

The process of achieving some level of pair adjustment is in the forefront during the early months or years of every marriage. In successful marriages, adjustments that are relatively satisfactory are made during this early period. Nevertheless, adjustability will be called for throughout the married life of each couple. As they go into new stages of life, they will encounter new conditions that require them to be flexible and to have an open mind toward differences in viewpoint. No matter how satisfying a closeness two people achieve, they remain two individuals, and each will have his or her own way of reacting to new experiences. When children are born, when children mature and leave home, when grandparents must move in to live with the family, when their financial situation changes for the better or the worse, and when illness or death comes into their lives, new levels of adjustment will have to be achieved. Relationships do not remain static in the face of changing circumstances and conditions.

However, couples who are able to make satisfactory adjustments in most areas of married living in the early years of their marriage are more likely to be able to cope with later requirements that life makes upon them. If a good understanding and mature affection exist between them, they will better adjust more readily later, perhaps scarcely recognizing some of the new developments as potential sources of conflict. But if within some segments of their lives chronic conflict exists before new problems arise, a couple may find that new developments will put an intolerable strain on their relationship.

## THE TIME FACTOR IN ADJUSTMENT

It takes time to accomplish a satisfactory working arrangement in areas where there is disagreement, and the couple should not become discouraged early. In our study of 581 couples, 25 percent said they had at sometime in the adjustment process discussed divorcing, and 18 percent had seriously considered it.

Research has revealed that certain areas of living seem to require more time for adjustment than do others for most couples. Just as there seems to be a pattern in the kinds of adjustments people reach in their marriages, so also the time factor in their progress toward working arrangements falls into a pattern. A comparison of findings on adjustment in marriage today with findings from our study of 409 couples 30 years ago shows that the problems couples face in marriage have changed little with changing times.[1]

The 409 couples in that study had been married an average of 20 years, some of them for as long as 40 years, and they represented successful marriages; no divorced couples were included. In that study and in the 1967 study, husbands and wives responded independently of each other concerning the adjustment processes in their marriage. Therefore, it was possible to see how well couples agreed about their ways of achieving working arrangements in the different areas of living.

Among the 409 long-married couples in our earlier study, most agreed on the length of time that had been required to arrive at whatever adjustment they had made. But about one couple in ten disagreed. In some cases one spouse would report that the couple had been in agreement from the beginning of the marriage, whereas the other spouse might say that satisfactory adjustments in certain areas had taken years or had never been made.

Each spouse stated whether he or she felt they had agreed satisfactorily from the beginning of the marriage, whether months or years had passed before satisfactory adjustment was achieved, or whether they had never worked out their differences in an area. All checked specifically their success or failure, and the time required to adjust in each of these areas: spending the family income, relationships with in-laws, sexual relations, religious life, choosing and associating with friends, and social activities and recreation. Figure 14-3 summarizes the results of that study.

Notice that more time was required for reaching a plateau of adjustment in sexual relations and in spending the family income than in any other areas. Approximately half of the couples agreed that their sexual adjustment had been satisfactory from the beginning. The remainder (47 percent) either disagreed on how long it had taken, agreed that months or years had passed before they achieved a good adjustment in sex, or agreed that they had never arrived at a satisfactory relationship.

On spending the family income, the picture is about the same. Social activities and recreational interests and in-law relationships were equal in time required for adjustment after marriage. Approximately two out of three of the couples had agreed satisfactorily from the beginning; the remaining third had either required time to adjust or had never arrived at a good working relationship. Three out of four of the couples in these marriages had been in accord from the beginning in religious life and in associating with friends. These two areas presented the least difficulty. The husbands, considered as a group, gave the six areas the same rating on length of time required for adjustment as did the wives as a group.

---

[1] Judson T. Landis, "Length of Time Required to Achieve Adjustment in Marriage," *American Sociological Review* 11:6 (December 1946), 666–77.

|  | Spouses agreed | Disagreed | 1-12 Months | 1-20 Years | Never |
|---|---|---|---|---|---|
| Sexual relations | 52.7% | 12.3% | 12.5% | 10.0% | 12.5% |
| Spending family income | 56.2% | 11.4% | 9.0% | 13.1% | 10.3% |
| Social activities | 67.1% | 9.5% | 4.3% | 5.3% | 13.8% |
| In-law relationships | 68.6% | 10.9% | 3.9% | 7.0% | 9.6% |
| Religious activities | 74.0% | 7.6% | 1.6% | 6.8% | 10.0% |
| Mutual friends | 76.4% | 7.8% | 4.6% | 3.3% | 7.9% |

☐ Spouses agreed they had worked out satisfactory adjustment from beginning

▓ Spouses disagreed as to whether they had worked out satisfactory adjustment from beginning

▨ 1-12 months

▨ 1-20 years

☐ Never made satisfactory adjustment

FIG. 14–3 Percentage of 818 spouses reporting various periods of time required after marriage to achieve adjustment in six areas. People who had been successfully married for an average of 20 years had experienced greater difficulty in adjusting in certain areas. From Judson T. Landis, "Length of Time Required to Achieve Adjustment in Marriage," *American Sociological Review* 11:6 (December 1946).

And those who had been married under 10 years agreed with those who had been married 30 years or more.

More of those married from 30 to 40 years had achieved a satisfactory adjustment in all areas except one—sex. It may be that in these older marriages a better sexual adjustment had once existed, but at the time of responding to the questionnaire the couples had reached a period in life requiring a change in their sexual adjustment.

At the time of that research we had no dependable clue to why these long-married people reported a less satisfactory adjustment in sex than in other areas. When we began the 1967 study with the 581 college-educated couples, we hypothesized that this new generation of successful marriages would show sex to be less of an adjustment problem. This hypothesis was based on the notion that, before such contraceptives as the ovulation-inhibiting pills were available, and before attitudes had changed so much toward acceptance of equality and mutuality in sexual experience, factors handicapping sexual adjustment operated more strongly than now. But the findings show that sexual adjustment remains a major problem area in many marriages today. Fear of pregnancy was apparently not so crucial a factor in sexual adjustment in the marriages in the earlier studies. The subject of sexual adjustment will be considered more extensively in the following chapter.

## LEVELS OF ADJUSTMENT IN MARRIAGE

After the couples in our early study recorded how long it had taken them to reach established levels of adjustment in the various areas of living, they stated whether the working relationship they had reached in each area was satisfactory to both, satisfactory to one, or unsatisfactory. The unsatisfactory adjustments might more accurately be called conditions of stalemate or failure to adjust.

The fewest had arrived at a mutually satisfactory adjustment in sexual relations; the most had arrived at a mutually satisfactory adjustment in associating with friends. The adjustments in the various areas were either states of accommodation or of conflict in from one-third to one-fifth of the marriages. In sexual relations, more than one-third of the couples had either made a compromise adjustment or continued in conflict. The couples had arrived at mutually satisfactory adjustments in from about two-thirds to four-fifths of their relationships in the seven areas (see Figure 14-4).

Our study of the marriages of college-educated people found few major differences in the nature of marital problems as reported by this later generation of people and those reporting more than 20 years earlier. In first order in the later study were listed sex, finances, "communication," in-laws, and child rearing. Hence, the problems rated as looming large in marriage in the past generation seem to remain the first-rated problems in marriage, although today's couples listed some additional areas, such as difficulties relating to communication, differences over household tasks, problems related to the husband's work—his constant absence from

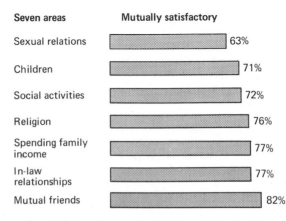

FIG. 14-4 Percentage of 409 couples agreeing that they had arrived at mutually satisfactory adjustments in seven areas.

home or the necessity to move about because of his work—and difficulties arising from differences over "time"—the use of time and contrasts in habits of punctuality or tardiness.

It is doubtful that inability to communicate with each other is a new development in marriage in this generation. Married couples may now be more aware of lack of communication when it exists, and less willing to accept it without a struggle, because of the more general recognition by college-educated people today of the importance of communication in all relationships. The emphasis on lack of communication as a problem may also mean that, after some decades of marriage-education courses in schools and universities and widespread discussion of the subject of marital adjustment in the public press, couples may tend to anticipate certain kinds of response and interaction in marriage that may not have been expected by people in earlier times. Today the emotional-companionship aspects of marriage have greater weight than have some functions formerly considered more basic.

As to problems related to the husband's work, some general social and economic changes have occurred that tend to focus attention on this point. Increasing urbanization of the country means more commuting husbands and more suburban families in which the wife may resent the burden of carrying family responsibilities with little help from a commuting husband. More wives also hold jobs today, so that difficulties may easily arise over division of household tasks and family responsibilities.

Couples in our earlier studies were adjusting in marriage during years of economic depression when wives did not hold outside jobs and could not afford to concern themselves with such matters as the husband's necessary absence from home because of his job or the necessity to change residence because of the husband's work. Problems over time allocation and differences over habits of punctuality naturally arise among couples who both work, or who live by the frequently intense, regimented social or professional schedules of middle-class couples today. With people for whom life moved at a slower, less complicated pace, "time" problems might be expected to assume less magnitude.

Yet these "new" problems listed by the present generation of married people are not the ones they ranked highest. Their reports agreed with those of the earlier couples in giving highest ranking to problems in the areas of sex, finances, in-laws, and child rearing.

## BECOMING AWARE OF DIFFERENCES

Some differences couples have early in marriage are not a surprise to them; others come as a shock. In the study of 581 couples, those who were having disagreements reported on when they had first become aware of their differences, whether before marriage or in what year of marriage. The findings showed that couples are likely to recognize differences in religion before marriage, especially if it is a mixed religious marriage. They are likely also to be somewhat, but not entirely, aware ahead of time of possible problems within in-law relationships. That is, they may recognize whether they are congenial with each other's families or whether there are antagonisms or irritations that might be troublesome.

Differences over punctuality or tardiness and differences in recreational interests tend to be recognized during courtship. However, the more serious differences that may have a disruptive effect on the marriage —differences over sex, and disagreement in the area of finances—do not usually show up until after people are married (see Figure 14-5). The problems arising from differing viewpoints about child rearing naturally arise even later.

Differences over sex, the use of money, showing affection, lack of communication, and preferences in social life tend to show up in the first year. Many couples become aware of unanticipated differences with in-laws for the first time after the birth of a child, and during the second or third year or later couples must face their differences over how to train and discipline children.

Early in marriage, couples continue to cope with the differences they may have recognized before marriage, if those differences have not been resolved, and they also come to recognize for the first time other potential problems. Some disagreements they may have had before marriage take

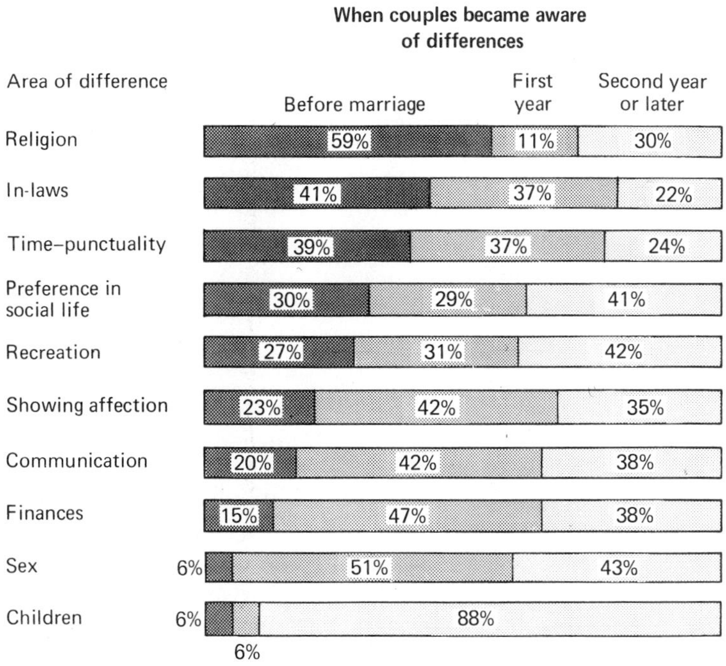

FIG. 14–5 Areas of difference and the stage in the relationship when they became aware of their differences (581 couples reporting).

on a different meaning after marriage, so that what might have seemed a solution in the engagement period is no longer adequate.

In some areas couples may have little or no agreement, and yet the disparity in their views or attitudes may not be disruptive to their overall relationship. For example, in politics one may be a Republican and the other a Democrat, and they may at times debate the subject without ever being able to persuade or change each other's views. Yet politics may remain more or less a side issue with them, without ever becoming emotionally disturbing to their relationship. Only when contrasting political views represent a wide contrast in values to live by and in moral and ethical convictions could the difference be expected to disrupt a marriage.

The group of 581 couples we studied, were well above average in marital happiness and success. They actually reported a minimum of serious differences in their marriages. It must be concluded that they had made better than average mate-choices. They also found relatively satisfactory ways of coping with the differences that did exist in their marriages. Most had encountered some problems, and their assessment of the comparative significance of the various areas of difference is a significant contribution to our understanding. For example, although not many of the couples had differences about the husband's work, those who did, found it quite disruptive to their relationship. The areas of disagreement which they reported most frequently were sex, dissatisfaction with communication, and differences over the use of time or lack of punctuality. In the marriages in which these differences existed, they were more disruptive to the marriages than other differences.

## BECOMING AWARE OF DIFFERENCES AND MARITAL HAPPINESS

In our study of married couples, married couples having counseling, and divorced people, we compared the three groups to see whether those who were happily married had discovered more of their differences *before* marriage than did those who were unhappily married. The divorced reported having had the least awareness of differences before marrying, the unhappily married were next, and the happily married reported having been aware before marriage of most of whatever differences existed. The unhappily married and the divorced reported discovering their differences usually during the first months or years of marriage. These findings might be expected since, as noted in other chapters, happily married people on an average have longer periods of acquaintance before marrying than have couples who fail in marriage.

## TIME REQUIRED TO ADJUST AND HAPPINESS IN MARRIAGE

The study of the 409 long-married couples showed a close relationship between agreement or early adjustment to differences and happiness in the marriages. More than a half of the couples rated their marriages as very happy if agreement had existed from the beginning or if they had been able to get together on differences immediately, whereas only a fifth rated their marriages as very happy if they had been unable to adjust at the beginning.

Some couples rated their marriages as very happy, even if there had been one area in which they had never been able to agree. But if there had been failure to get together fairly well in two areas, 77 percent were average or unhappy, and all those who reported unsatisfactory adjustments in three or more areas rated their marriages as average or unhappy. Of the 409 couples, only 11 reported failure to adjust in as many as three areas. It seems safe to conjecture that the explanation is that people who could not resolve their differences in as many as three areas would probably not remain married, and no divorced or separated couples were included in that study. In successful marriages, if a measure of success is performance of the marriage, husbands and wives have managed to work out their differences in at least four of these major areas of living. In marriages that can be called happy as well as successful, the man and woman are likely to have achieved good working arrangements in all seven areas.

## QUARRELING

In almost all marriages, even those with no basic differences, some quarrels are likely while the two people are in the process of developing the many facets of their relationship as a pair. Some of the quarrels, though painful, may serve to bring into the open differences that can be resolved, once they are faced. But couples discover that quarrels may damage their relationship, driving them apart and leaving hurts that are slow to heal.

Research studies of engaged couples have shown that those who do not have arguments and quarrels are less likely to break their engagements. The quarreling pattern during engagement is predictive of unhappiness in marriage. Similarly, it may be said that a quarreling pattern in marriage is destructive in its overall effect upon marital happiness. This is true even though some of the quarrels, especially in the early months of marriage, may serve to bring resolvable differences into the open. If conflict during the early adjustment stages in a marriage impels people toward a realistic assessment of the values worth struggling to preserve in their marriage, and *if they can go on to make the necessary accommodations,* only then can the conflict serve a constructive function.

Many quarrels serve no purpose other than as an outlet for accumulated tensions in one or both partners. It is sometimes argued that marital quarrels are necessary and useful as tension relievers. Most people recognize that it is not practical to express negative emotional reactions freely in their relationships outside the family. They exercise self-restraint in their dealings with friends, acquaintances, or business associates because

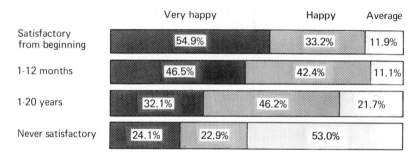

| | Very happy | Happy | Average |
|---|---|---|---|
| Satisfactory from beginning | 54.9% | 33.2% | 11.9% |
| 1-12 months | 46.5% | 42.4% | 11.1% |
| 1-20 years | 32.1% | 46.2% | 21.7% |
| Never satisfactory | 24.1% | 22.9% | 53.0% |

FIG. 14–6  Time needed to adjust in six areas of marriage and happiness in marriage, as reported by 409 couples. The sooner couples merge their interests and find satisfactory working arrangements, the more likely they are to find happiness in marriage.

they know that if they did not they would soon have few friends and no job. But they may use the family as a shock absorber, and home as the place where they relax self-restraint and give vent to the frustrations and tensions that accumulate in other areas. If we could consider solely the need of the individual for tension release, we might say that providing a place for such release is a function of the family or, more specifically, of marriage. We could then agree that a spouse should accept explosive outbursts of the mate as attempts to help make a constructive adjustment to life outside the home. Husbands and wives then could feel that in serving as sparring partners who knew when to retreat and when to meet violence with violence, they would be enabling each other to maintain emotional balance. Unfortunately, that is not the effect that quarreling usually has, and people do not react so rationally to a quarreling situation.

The experience of Sally and Bill, a young married couple, reveals how the negative effects of quarreling in the average marriage tend to nullify any positive effects.

Bill's work requires him to be in constant contact with other men, many of whom are working under pressure in highly specialized jobs. Bill's immediate superior is a perfectionist about his work and has little understanding of human nature. While on the job, Bill works at maintaining harmonious relationships with his co-workers and his superior; this requires serious effort, and sometimes strains his self-control severely. After an especially hard day, Bill comes home to find that Sally has invited the Browns in for waffles and a game of bridge. Bill doesn't like waffles. In his family, waffles were not considered a suitable substitute for a good dinner after a day's work. Moreover, the Browns are a couple he finds hard to tolerate. They have been friends of Sally's since childhood and she can see nothing wrong with them. But to Bill they are just a shallow pair who are not even good card players. Their conversation frequently is concerned with occurrences far back in the past before Bill met Sally, and these reminiscences irk Bill.

So the stage is set; conditions are perfect for a quarrel. Bill explodes. He gives vent to all the resentments that have been accumulating all day long. He goes further and expresses himself freely concerning the Browns and some of Sally's other friends, past and present. While he is getting things off his chest, he tells what he thinks of any family who would let a daughter grow up thinking that *waffles* were a suitable meal for a hungry man. And since he is on the subject of cooking, he throws in for good measure a few references to the good cooking he was used to before he left his mother's house and married Sally.

According to some theories, Sally, after responding with some uncomplimentary references to Bill's family background, his friends, and his general behavior, would cry; they would kiss and make up, and their love would be on a better basis than before because of the progress toward understanding growing out of the quarrel. But is that the way it really works? Has enough constructive good been accomplished to compensate for the damage that has been done? One thing has been accomplished that may be considered a step in their adjustment. Sally has decided she will not ask the Browns in any more, because it just is not worth it if it so upsets Bill. She also secretly resolves that if she is going to have to give up her friendship with the Browns, she is justified in insisting that Bill drop certain friends of his for whom she has no affection. She will take that up later.

The quarrel has served as a tension reliever for Bill. But he does not feel any better for it. He is ashamed of the things he said about Sally's family, and he realizes that the comparisons he made between his mother's cooking and Sally's will only widen the rift that is already developing between Sally and her mother-in-law. And worst of all, four-year-old Johnny was wakened by the quarrel and came downstairs crying just after Sally began to cry. When Johnny saw Sally crying, he could hardly be comforted. After they got him back to bed, Sally remarked with bitterness that Johnny was getting to be a naughty and unhappy child. She said, "Every time he hears us quarrel he is worse for days."

As might be suspected, Sally and Bill were developing a quarreling pattern. Their quarrels were becoming more rather than less frequent. Each quarrel added a few more barbs that rankled. Each left a few smoldering resentments that might break out on another occasion. Although some of their quarrels settled issues, inasmuch as one decided to change an attitude or both decided to compromise, most of the verbal battles settled nothing at all. They simply added scars. Both Sally and Bill grew more adept at responding with remarks that touched sore points. In the quarrel described above, Sally might easily respond to Bill's disparagement of her family by suggesting that a possible reason for the recent failure of Bill's father in a business venture was his inability to get along with co-workers. This reference would be especially puncturing to Bill's self-confidence and would serve to produce still more tension for him on other occasions when he found the going hard in his relationships at the office. Thus a vicious circle: more tension, more quarrels, more emotional scars, and Bill and Sally driven apart in understanding and affection.

In the average marriage, few quarrels can be considered constructive. The possible benefits—release of pent-up emotional tension for one or both and bringing differences into the open in order to resolve them—may in many cases be accomplished by more constructive means. Significantly, many marital quarrels do not stem from any real differences that need to be resolved or from any underlying dissatisfaction with the mate. They do not eliminate differences. Disputes between married people are no different from those between friends outside marriage. Few friendships can survive constant or frequent quarrels. Friends learn to curb the impulse to say bitter words in the interest of preserving the friendship. In the same way, happily married couples learn to withhold the bitter criticism or the cutting retort in order to avoid unpleasantness and to enjoy a happier companionship.

## DISCUSSING DIFFERENCES

In our study of 581 couples, two-thirds of the husbands and wives reported that they avoided any discussion of their differences as one method of coping. Some couples learn early in marriage that there may be no solution to a specific difference and that discussion of it only brings unhappiness. About 10 percent of those in this study reported seldom or never resolving differences with their spouses by discussion.

The question of discussing differences that become apparent is complicated. Theoretically, a difference cannot be resolved unless it is openly faced and discussed. But to imply that all differences should be discussed assumes that all differences that may exist between two people married to each other *can* be satisfactorily resolved, an assumption not necessarily true. It depends on the kind of difference. If there is a wide chasm between their feelings about basic values in life or a conflict between fundamental attitudes that they hold because of their own backgrounds and lifetime experiences, discussion may be futile or even destructive in its effects.

People who are happily married are far more likely to report that their differences are usually solved by discussion. But those who are happily married have few serious differences; they can operate on a level of discussion that does not become emotional. Those who rate their marriages as average or unhappy are far more likely to report that discussion sometimes, seldom, or never resolves differences (see Figure 14-7). These same people also report that they keep their differences to themselves or that they become emotional if they do try to face their differences. They tend to feel that their choice is between constant conflict or adjusting as well as they can and achieving some sort of accommodation. Their accommodation may continue to include some negative feelings about the spouse and about the marriage.

Probably almost all couples find during the exploratory early years of marriage that in some areas there can be no discussion. In happy marriages based on wise mate-choice, there are more areas of only slight disagree-

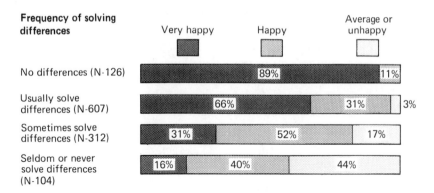

FIG. 14–7 Frequency of solving differences through discussion as given by 581 couples (of those who had differences) and self-ratings of marital happiness. Discussion of differences is more likely to result in a solution to the differences in happy marriages than in unhappy marriages.

ment and fewer of serious disagreement; therefore discussion can lead to a meeting of minds. In the early years of marriage, people tend to sort out differences; they gradually learn that it is better for the relationship if they avoid discussing certain matters. On some issues one or both can change their attitude in order to reach a better understanding.

A couple who are creatively building a good relationship for a lifetime can look with some objectivity at situations that seem to provoke antagonisms between them. They can ascertain which are serious and which are only the predictable frictions of two people living together, frictions they can minimize or ignore.

Many couples recognize that it is better not to discuss problems or to try to talk about "touchy" subjects when they are physically tired, certainly never when they are hungry.

One couple, both of whom were working at jobs outside the home, reported that in the early months of their marriage they found themselves involved in frequent arguments. Upon analyzing the situation, they realized that these arguments invariably occurred late in the afternoon when both were just home from work and were preparing dinner together. They therefore made it a rule to have dinner earlier and to refrain from any but the most casual conversation until after they had eaten and had relaxed. They realized that both had been reacting in a childish manner because of fatigue and hunger. Actually there were no differences between them worth arguing over. It is safe to say that a great many marital quarrels would never occur if people could analyze the immediate reasons that provoke the irritation and recognize that a feeling of mild antagonism or opposition might become much more intense if emotionally expressed. We are inclined, when faced with opposition, to express things more strongly than we feel them, with the result that our feelings become more intense in order to back up our words. Happily married people know that giving frequent expression to their affection for each other seems to build up and to increase their love. Love thrives on expression and response. So it is with anger, irritation, and criticism. The free and frequent expression of such feelings increases their strength and magnifies the importance of situations which might better have been passed over and forgotten.

## KINDS OF RESPONSES TO PRESSURE IN MARRIAGE

The value of making the effort to cope with minor irritations and frustrations as well as major differences by peaceful rather than explosive means is shown clearly by an analysis of findings from our study of college-educated people. The couples reported on ways in which they behaved when they encountered differences. After a series of experiments in which groups of married people made lists of the ways in which they behaved when they had differences and described the feelings they had after such behavior, a checklist was prepared and checked by the 581 couples in this study (see Table 14-1).

**TABLE 14-1**  Ways of reacting to differences and feelings resulting from their behavior, as reported by 581 husbands and 581 wives

| Ways in which couples reacted to their differences | Percentages reporting the kinds of behavior listed | | Feelings usually resulting (understand each other better, feel good about spouse, feel more secure, feel relieved of tension) | |
|---|---|---|---|---|
| Behavior resulting in positive feelings | Husbands | Wives | Husbands | Wives |
| 1  We discuss differences peacefully | 82% | 88% | 94% | 96% |
| 2  After discussion we compromise | 74 | 82 | 94, | 95 |
| 3  After discussion spouse generally has his (her) way | 74 | 77 | 64 | 56 |
| 4  After discussion I generally have my way | 73 | 75 | 74 | 67 |
| 5  I do something nice for spouse | 72 | 74 | 94 | 93 |
| 6  I cool off for a time | 89 | 73 | 72 | 66 |
| 7  I confide in someone other than spouse | 21 | 44 | 66 | 62 |

TABLE 14-1 (Continued)

| Ways in which couples reacted to their differences | Percentages reporting the kinds of behavior listed | | Feelings usually resulting (have more tension, feel guilty, angry, unloved, discouraged) | |
|---|---|---|---|---|
| Behavior resulting in negative feelings | Husbands | Wives | Husbands | Wives |
| 1 We start peaceful discussion but we get emotional | 69% | 77% | 72% | 72% |
| 2 I keep differences to myself | 70 | 71 | 87 | 91 |
| 3 We argue and quarrel | 69 | 72 | 80 | 79 |
| 4 Spouse brings up problem but I get emotional | 63 | 73 | 80 | 86 |
| 5 We avoid any discussion of our differences | 64 | 67 | 64 | 77 |
| 6 I bring up problem but spouse gets emotional | 67 | 57 | 84 | 88 |
| 7 We do not talk to each other | 55 | 56 | 91 | 95 |
| 8 I leave the room | 46 | 53 | 77 | 84 |
| 9 Spouse leaves the room | 45 | 47 | 91 | 95 |
| 10 I take frustration out on others | 44 | 46 | 88 | 95 |
| 11 Spouse refuses to have sex relations | 48 | 24 | 92 | 93 |
| 12 I refuse to have sex relations | 29 | 40 | 90 | 97 |
| 13 I slam doors | 25 | 30 | 69 | 69 |
| 14 Spouse slams doors | 27 | 25 | 89 | 91 |
| 15 I drink when we have differences | 18 | 9 | 56 | 66 |
| 16 Spouse drinks when we have differences | 11 | 12 | 72 | 81 |
| 17 Spouse strikes or slaps me | 8 | 8 | 82 | 89 |
| 18 I strike or slap spouse | 8 | 6 | 83 | 77 |
| 19 I cry | 8 | 76 | 60 | 55 |
| 20 Spouse cries | 62 | 7 | 87 | 78 |
| 21 I get physically ill | 7 | 16 | 91 | 96 |
| 22 Spouse gets physically ill | 14 | 8 | 92 | 98 |

The list of kinds of behavior under pressure that cause negative feelings is much longer than the list of actions having a positive effect. This is probably to be expected, since only persons especially creative in relationships might be capable of reacting to differences in ways that produce positive rather than negative feelings. The more usual response to provocations would be an immediate emotional reaction without pausing to consider what long-term effects it might have on a relationship. Nevertheless, a considerable number of people reported that they meet their differences in such ways as peaceful discussion and compromise, by one or the other's giving in to the mate, by just "cooling off" for a time, or by doing something nice for the spouse—that is to say, by making a specific effort to act positively instead of negatively. All these ways of coping resulted in more positive feelings about the mate and about the marriage. Such negative feelings as an increase in tension, guilt, or anger, or discouragement about the marriage resulted when people argued or quarreled, engaged in emotionally loaded talk, or resorted to such things as slamming doors, withdrawing from association with each other, or, in some cases, physical attacks.

It must be remembered that this group of people were considerably above average in marital happiness. Their serious differences were relatively few compared to other groups of marriages that have been studied, and on the whole they coped unusually well with what differences they did have.

When two people live together as intimately as do a husband and wife, even though no major differences exist between them, many little things can cause irritation. Mannerisms or habits that might pass unnoticed in friends or casual acquaintances may assume importance and provoke annoyance when practiced by one's wife or husband. Carelessness with cigarette ashes, table manners, eating habits, turning down the page corner to mark the place in a book, leaving a ring in the bathtub, or being slow to come to the table when meals are ready may become so irritating to the spouse that emotional explosions occur. These trivial things which often cause friction in marriage have been called "tremendous trifles." [2]

We quote below a wife's description of some differences that could be treated as serious problems or as trifles, depending upon the two people and their temperaments and adjustability.

> It was difficult to get used to sleeping in a small double bed. We are both tall and I had always slept alone and I needed more blankets than he did. We were embarrassed to have our friends discover that we had bought twin beds a few months after we married. When we could afford it, we purchased a king-sized bed and a dual-control electric blanket and moved back together again to sleep. Whoever crossed the line could either freeze or roast, but for the first time we could both be comfortable in the same bed. Now the children use the twin beds.
>
> We discovered quite a few other things that could be a nuisance, but we managed to adjust. We discovered that he is a morning person and I am a night person. He likes the house to be cool and I like it warm. He wants to eat right away in the morning and I'm not hungry until later. All these differences in our temperaments and physiology took time to recognize and to adapt to. We both wanted to have personal freedom but also to give in enough to make the other one comfortable.

[2] Ray B. Barber, *Marriage and the Family* (New York: McGraw-Hill Book Company, 1953), pp. 221–23.

Why such matters become so tremendous for some couples is not easy for the outsider to understand, but they harass many marriages. The happy couples are those who can preserve a sense of proportion about the relative importance of events, but that is not always easy. A sense of humor helps. A great many things cannot be explained, interpreted, or corrected, but will diminish in importance if a couple can laugh over them together. A small boy, when taken to task by his mother for an annoying habit said, "I don't know *why* I do it. Let's just laugh it off." That is often the best solution to annoyances in marriage. Certainly, it is a much surer road to peace and happiness than for either spouse to try to change the ways of the other. Moreover, as a tension reliever, a hearty laugh is at least as effective as an angry explosion, and far more pleasant to live with.

If at times too much tension has been built up either over irritations at home or because of pressures in outside relationships, it is possible to find tension relievers other than having conflict with the spouse. Some people have discovered that taking a walk or ride will help them to regain perspective. One businessman, who found his security threatened by a change in ownership of the organization for which he worked, preserved his emotional balance by using his spare time to grub out trees that he did not want in the garden area. He learned that an hour or two of working with the spade and an ax helped his emotional balance and enabled him to live peaceably with his wife and family. Some husbands and wives go to a movie or a concert, read an absorbing book, or take a drive in the country when they feel under emotional pressure. Any activity that enables people to get far enough away from problems to look at them objectively is an aid to the perspective which is vital to marital happiness.

Resorting to such tension-relieving activities is not just an "escape." It is constructive, because often, when the individual has turned to other interests in order to relieve feelings, he or she realizes that there was no point important enough in itself to quarrel over; the difficulty was personal and could be corrected only by a change in one's own attitude.

## PERIODS OF STRESS OR CRISIS IN MARITAL ADJUSTMENT

Most marriages will encounter problems that, at the time, are more serious than the ordinary situations requiring adjustability in husband–wife relationships. The special encounters with serious differences may amount to crises in relationships. In some marriages, the crisis or stress may be sudden and unexpected; in others, unrecognized differences may build up emotional tension over a period of time and culminate in a crisis. Almost inevitably the effect of such a crisis is to force a couple toward a more realistic assessment of their relationship. They may have been evading a difference in a particular area for some time, but a crisis period makes evasion no longer possible.

In our study of three groups of marriages (Table 14-2), all completed identical questionnaires reporting on crises experienced in their marriages, the year or years of the marriage in which the crises had occurred, what their response had been at the time, and what they felt the long-term effects had been. Crises among all three groups had been more often in the areas of sex, finances, in-laws, child rearing, and communication.

The areas of crisis were nearly the same in all three groups, although not arranged in the same order of frequency, and they were assessed as more severe among the marriage counseling and the divorced groups. One-third of the happily married and four-fifths of the unhappily married saw their crises as serious or very serious. In all three groups, the most serious stress situations tended to occur in the first five years of marriage. Table 14-2 summarizes the ways in which these people reacted to crisis. The happily married, more than the other groups, could discuss the problem peacefully, and a much smaller percentage reacted by being physically or mentally ill, talking to others about the problem, or considering divorce. The women seem to have been more perceptive than the men about whatever problems existed and more inclined to take some specific action in response to problems.

## CRISES AND LATER MARITAL ADJUSTMENT

The three research groups attempted to evaluate the effects of crisis periods upon their later marriage adjustment. Their responses (Table

TABLE 14-2

Ways of reacting to crisis in marriage, as reported by 581 married couples, 155 unhappily married people having counseling, and 164 divorced people

| Ways of reacting to crisis | Married (N–1027) | Counseling (N–155) | Divorced (N–164) |
|---|---|---|---|
| Peacefully discussed the problem with spouse | 69.0% | 35.0% | 45.0% |
| Tried to understand spouse's point of view | 65.0 | 58.0 | 50.0 |
| Tried to change | 55.0 | 52.0 | 50.0 |
| Tried to change spouse | 42.0 | 50.0 | 49.0 |
| After discussion and/or reading, came to an understanding | 31.0 | 8.0 | 9.0 |
| Talked to someone other than spouse about problem | 24.0 | 60.0 | 56.0 |
| Blamed spouse for everything | 18.0 | 25.0 | 20.0 |
| Blamed myself for everything | 15.0 | 25.0 | 21.0 |
| Considered separation or divorce | 14.0 | 44.0 | 49.0 |
| Got sick physically and/or emotionally | 12.0 | 36.0 | 37.0 |
| Sought professional help alone or with spouse | 10.0 | 29.0 | 66.0 |
| Looked for affection from other sex away from home | 6.0 | 6.0 | 9.0 |
| Started action for divorce | .5 | 12.0 | 25.0 |

ACHIEVING ADJUSTMENT IN MARRIAGE

14-3) show rather clearly the effects of stress periods followed by re-
conciliations upon relationships in marriage. There are various positive
and negative effects, but almost always couples are forced to face reality
in their relationships.

An important phase of the adjustment process for couples in the early
months or years of marriage is their being forced to realize what marriage
itself requires and to recognize they have less complete agreement in
many areas than they had thought. For some couples, this reassessment
results in a higher level of understanding and greater satisfaction. For
others, it results in compromises and adjustments on a less satisfactory
level than they had hoped for; they are somewhat disillusioned, but still
their marriage survives. For still others, the early stress periods mark the
beginning of a series of crises, resulting in progressive deterioration in
their relationship toward extreme unhappiness and probable divorce.

A study of the findings indicates that marriages that profited from

**TABLE 14-3** Percentages of 581 married couples, 155 people having marriage counseling, and 164 divorced people reporting on how crises affected their marriages

| Effects on marital adjustment | Married (N–1027) | Counseling (N–155) | Divorced (N–164) |
|---|---|---|---|
| **Made us face reality** | | | |
| Made us face the problem | 54.0% | 15.0% | 13.0% |
| Made me more realistic in my expectations of marriage | 49.0 | 31.0 | 25.0 |
| Made us assess what we did have in common | 41.0 | 34.0 | 33.0 |
| Made us realize we could never agree on this particular matter | 18.0 | 37.0 | 59.0 |
| Now I can see that the stress period was unnecessary | 13.0 | 6.0 | 3.0 |
| Differences in values and interests became glaringly apparent for the first time | 11.0 | 48.0 | 54.0 |
| **Brought positive feelings between us** | | | |
| Helped us understand each other | 42.0 | 6.0 | 4.0 |
| Increased our ability to communicate | 38.0 | 7.0 | 2.0 |
| Brought us closer together | 33.0 | 5.0 | 1.0 |
| Made our marriage happier | 16.0 | 3.0 | .5 |
| **Resulted in feelings of alienation** | | | |
| Undermined both of our egos, self-confidence, self-esteem | 15.0 | 50.0 | 64.0 |
| Tended to break down our ability to communicate | 13.0 | 64.0 | 70.0 |
| Made permanent "scars" in our relationship | 11.0 | 66.0 | 72.0 |
| Drove us farther apart | 8.0 | 75.0 | 80.0 |
| Tended to solidify patterns of destructive behavior toward each other | 5.0 | 34.0 | 37.0 |

crisis situations were those based upon relatively wise mate-choices in the beginning; they actually had few potentially disastrous differences. These couples could become realistic about marriage and its responsibilities and could rise to the challenges. Among the ones whose crises had been largely destructive were some who probably should not have married each other at all. Unwise mate-choice had united people too far apart in important matters to overcome their disparities. Many such couples survived a series of crises before they divorced. In the group whose crises were chiefly destructive may also be more who lacked some of the important traits of marriageability; their responses to stress are of a kind that contribute to alienation.

## STRESS AND MARITAL ADJUSTMENT—A SUMMARY

In recent years some writers have argued for the use of aggressive behavior in solving conflict situations. Bach and Wyden, in their book *The Intimate Enemy,* state that "couples who fight together are couples who stay together—provided they know how to fight."[3] Do the actions implied in "letting it out," "hanging loose," "therapeutic aggression," "physical combat" with fists or "combat pillows" have the effect of lessening tension in relationships, as some advocates believe? Straus studied college-student families and found no basis to support theories of "agression." He found that the more often couples resorted to verbal aggression the more likely they were to resort to physical aggression. Those who resorted to aggressive behavior found that it increased their tension. Straus's respondents reported that couples who faced their problems in an intellectual way were better able to solve them.[4]

Straus's research supports the conclusion of our studies which have been presented on the previous pages. Habitual quarreling, aggressive behavior, and physical combat eventually result in the deterioration of a marriage. If differences are to be resolved, they are best resolved through rational discussion.

## HUSBAND OR WIFE DOMINANCE AND FAMILY SUCCESS

The traditional view of husband–wife roles in our culture has been that the husband is the dominant partner. However, analysis of data from research studies of dominance indicates that the most successful family life is found in families having an equalitarian type of husband–wife relationship, when success is viewed in terms of closeness of children to parents, low divorce rate, children holding high self-conceptions, and other such factors.

[3] George R. Bach and Peter Wyden, *The Intimate Enemy: How to Fight Fair in Love and Marriage* (New York: William Morrow & Co., Inc., 1969).

[4] Murray A. Straus, "Leveling, Civility, and Violence in the Family," *Journal of Marriage and the Family* 36:1 (February 1974), 13–27.

Findings of our research among university students (summarized in Figure 14-8) show a close relationship between the way in which the students perceived the pattern of dominance in their families and the way they assessed their parents' marital happiness. Those who saw their parents as having a 50–50 division of control also assessed their parents' marriages as happy. The relationships viewed as most unsatisfactory were in families in which the mother was definitely the dominant member, but homes strongly dominated by either the mother or the father are assessed by the children as among the least satisfactory. Our research showed also that children tend to feel closer to the less dominant parent, whether it is the father or the mother.[5] That inequality in dominance is not a desirable type of marital pattern is shown by reports of married couples about themselves. In our research, married couples assessed their own happiness and also reported on their dominant pattern as they saw it. The findings agreed with results of research among students reporting on parents' marriages (see Figure 14–9).

There can be many reasons, not understood by outside observers or even by the children of a couple, why one member of a couple seems to dominate. In some families the mother may take most of the responsibilities usually assumed to be the prerogatives of the family head and make most of the decisions, chiefly because the father does not accept such responsibility; such a dominance of the mother arises out of necessity. Even though the situation has not been considered ideal according to norms in our society, such a family still functions more effectively than it could if both parents abdicated responsibility for decision making. After studying the pattern of dominance in 731 Detroit families, Blood and Wolfe concluded, "The circumstances which lead to the wife's dominance involve corresponding inadequacies and incompetencies on the husband's

[5] Judson T. Landis, "A Re-examination of the Role of the Father as an Index of Family Integration," *Marriage and Family Living* 24:2 (May 1962), 127.

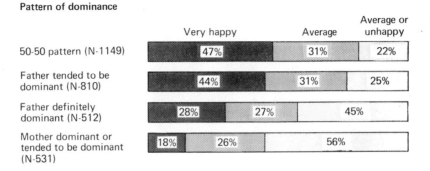

FIG. 14–8 Interaction pattern in the home and parental marital happiness, as reported by 3189 students.

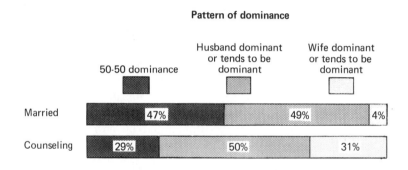

FIG. 14-9 The pattern of dominance, as reported by 581 married couples and 155 unhappily married people having marriage counseling.

part. An inadequate husband is by definition unable to make a satisfactory marriage partner. So the dominant wife is not exultant over her 'victory,' but exercises power regretfully by default of her 'no good' or incapacitated husband." [6]

In other families, either the wife or the husband may dominate primarily because of a personal drive and need to control others. Because of traditional role definitions in our society, the tendency is to view the dominant wife with more doubtful or critical attitudes than are directed at the dominant husband, regardless of the underlying reasons for dominance in a specific case. A husband may exercise most control in decision making from necessity, just as some wives must do. Or his control may arise from immaturity and an excessive need to claim all possible prerogatives of his sex. Whatever the underlying reasons, male dominance is usually given the benefit of the doubt; the dominant husband is defined as masculine, i.e., "strong," even if in a specific case the dominance may be evidence of weakness. Certainly, in some marriages, outsiders or even the couples' own children would name as the dominant one the member of the pair who is really the weaker, the stronger one having learned to cater to the emotional needs of the weaker one by acquiescing in the behavior defined as dominant. In such marriages it is difficult, if not impossible, for any outsider to determine the source or extent of the real power in decision making. In other words, apparent dominance is not necessarily the same as decision making or control in a family's affairs.

Further, the reaction of the other member of a pair to the mate's dominance may not correspond to the reactions of observers. The one who seems to be dominated may be unaware of any lack of independence. He or she may welcome the dominance because it meets personality needs. On the other hand, one member may have resentful feelings that seem to outside observers out of all proportion to any clear dominance by the spouse.

[6] Robert O. Blood, Jr., and Donald M. Wolfe, *Husbands and Wives* (New York: The Free Press, 1960), p. 45.

ACHIEVING ADJUSTMENT IN MARRIAGE

Some people are self-disciplined and mature enough to welcome constructive criticism from the spouse. Such individuals will evaluate criticism objectively and make successful efforts to correct undesirable personality traits in themselves. For most people contemplating marriage, however, it is safer and less likely to lead to disappointment if both members proceed on the assumption that the partner will do little changing. It is better to face the questions, "Do I love her (or him) enough to accept this as trivial?" "Can I refrain from making him (or her) uncomfortable by agitating for change?" If the chosen mate has traits that loom large and seem very annoying before marriage, there is no reason to believe they will be less irritating after the wedding. Happy marriages are those made between people whose faults are tolerable to each other. Wives have frequently said of someone else's husband, "How can his wife endure that way of his! I couldn't stand it if my husband behaved that way." Yet she herself may have a husband with faults that seem far worse to the other woman. So it is best to look, not for a faultless mate, but for one who can be loved for his or her traits when viewed as a whole, and whose faults are not especially irritating to the other.

During the courtship period, it is natural for a measure of uncertainty to exist. Both partners may need frequent assurances and demonstrations of love. One or the other may occasionally indulge in attempts to keep the other guessing by pretending indifference or by showing attentions to other members of the opposite sex with the intention of arousing jealousy in the loved one. An excessive desire to test and to prove the love of the partner is an indication of lack of inner security and lack of confidence, which may cause the immature demands for reassurance to be carried over into marriage and cause unhappiness.

Granted that a certain minimum of affectional testing may occur during courtship, it is not desirable to carry this pattern into marriage. One of the joys of a good marriage is the calm of emotional security that comes with the knowledge of being wholeheartedly loved. In a happy marriage, both partners express and demonstrate their love so that neither one has occasion for doubt. Attempts to test love by pretending indifference or by trying to arouse jealousy are threats to the success of the marriage. Being able to "take each other for granted" and to trust each other without limit is one of the reasons why people make the commitment that marriage is; it also is a benefit offered by few other relationships in life.

## FINALLY—

Since the success of a marriage depends greatly on what goes into the marriage, the most important prerequisite for a happy marriage is to choose one's mate wisely. However, even when the choice is less than perfect, people can learn to become good husbands and wives through thoughtful, cooperative effort. There is hope even for those who have not made a wise choice, if they comprehend the different facets of life in which they must work together, and if they work to establish satisfactory and happy levels of adjustment in their relationships.

> People who share a cell in the Bastille or are thrown together on an uninhabited island will find some possible ground of compromise if they do not immediately fall to fisticuffs. They will learn each other's ways and humours so as to know where they must go warily and where they may lean their whole weight. The discretion of the first years becomes the settled habit of the last; and so, with wisdom and patience, two lives may grow indissolubly into one.[7]

## REVIEW QUESTIONS

1 Contrast the interaction of courtship adjustment with the interaction of marriage adjustment.

2 What does the study of engaged and married couples reveal about agreement in relationships?

3 How does marriage adjustment in a "mixed marriage" differ from marriage adjustment in a conventional marriage?

4 In what ways is adjusting to a marriage partner comparable to living with a roommate?

5 In what years are marriages most likely to fail as measured by separation and divorce?

6 What are the three chief forms of resolving conflict in marriage adjustment? Illustrate each with cases of marriages you have observed.

7 Name seven potential conflict areas in marriage interaction that may call for adjustment.

8 Which areas seem to require the longest time for adjustment? In which areas are there fewest mutually satisfactory adjustments after some years of marriage?

9 Is a quarrel in marriage ever strictly constructive and not destructive?

10 How much have the major problem areas in marriage changed in a period of 20 or 25 years?

11 What are some of the "new" problem areas in today's marriages? Explain why such problems are noted by couples today.

12 What does the study of 581 couples show in regard to when couples become aware of their differences in areas of living? Relationship of happiness and the time when couples become aware of their differences?

13 Discuss some of the effects of quarreling in marriage adjustment.

14 Are happily married couples always able to resolve their differences through discussion? Why?

15 What does the study of 581 couples show about their ways of reacting to their differences and their position and negative feelings for each other? (See Table 14-1.)

[7] Robert Louis Stevenson, "Essay on Marriage," *Virginibus Puerisque.*

ACHIEVING ADJUSTMENT IN MARRIAGE

16 What are "tremendous trifles" in marriage?

17 Contrast the ways in which happily married, divorced, and counseling couples react to crises in marriage. What seemed to be the long-time effects of the crises for the three groups of couples? Which couples profited most from the crises?

18 What does research show about using aggressive behavior as a way of solving conflicts?

19 What do studies of dominance in marriage show about happiness in marriage?

20 Discuss the statement that the dominating partner may actually be the weaker rather than the stronger person in the marriage.

21 Explain how there may be a distinction between dominance and real decision-making power.

## PROJECTS AND ACTIVITIES

1 Give a case of a family difference that started as a discussion but ended in a family fight.

2 Make a list of "tremendous trifles" that have caused trouble in some family you know well.

3 *Role playing.* (a) John comes from a home run by a neat and orderly mother who always had his clothes pressed and ready for him. He has been married to Joan for six months and has become annoyed at her housekeeping and her failure to be responsible for having his clothes ready for him. Scene: John is hurrying to get to work and finds that he has no clean socks. Joan comes into the room at this moment.

(b) John and Joan have been married six years and have children 1, 3, and 5 years old. The baby has been sick and Joan has had a hard day. When John comes home from work, dinner is not ready, although Joan knows that this is the evening when John has an early bowling date.

# SEXUAL ADJUSTMENT IN MARRIAGE

# 15

A mutually satisfactory sexual relationship is a basic factor contributing to happiness in marriage. People contemplating marriage may assume that sexual gratification is the all-important factor upon which success or failure depends. However, since marriage is made up of a complicated set of interdependent elements, sexual satisfaction is affected positively or negatively by factors in other areas of living. It, in turn, contributes negatively or positively to the overall marital adjustment. The sexual relationship cannot be considered an independent factor.

## THE SEXUAL RELATIONSHIP AND ADJUSTMENT IN OTHER AREAS OF LIFE

Other kinds of conflict may cause the failure of marriages in which the sexual phase seems satisfactory to both partners. Inability to agree on the use of money, for example, with frequent quarrels over finances, may cause a couple to part in spite of sexual compatibility. Friction about in-laws may create such animosity between husband and wife that they will part regardless of the bond provided by their sexual adjustment.

Moreover, if conflict exists in some areas of a marriage, it is likely to be reflected in the sexual adjustment of the couple. Since sexual inter-course is the most intimately cooperative activity of marriage, some partners may have coitus less frequently if antagonism exists between them. If they are at odds over other matters, one or the other may reject the spouse's sexual approaches, with the result that other conflicts become exaggerated.

Conversely, marriages in which the sexual adjustment is poor may endure because of the strength of other bonds. Sharing of interests in children, friends or relatives, religion, recreation or work, and in many phases of daily living all contribute to a good marriage. Since all facets of a marriage are closely interrelated, it is often impossible to determine whether a poor sexual adjustment is a cause or a result of dissatisfactions in other aspects of the life of a couple.

Sexual relationships, more often than other phases of marital interaction, seem to be the focal point of tensions because constantly recurring biological urges force couples to reckon with this part of life and because sexual compatibility requires cooperation. Two people who differ on religion may agree to disagree and may live together happily. A couple may have widely divergent ideas concerning the use of money, yet if they have enough money so that their differences do not cause financial hardship, they can tolerate their differences and live in peace. But in the area of sexual relationships the issue must be faced, for the sexual urge is comparable to hunger. It seeks periodic satisfaction of needs, and these periodic needs make more specific requirements of the other person than do other physical needs. Hunger can be satisfied with no great difficulty if the partner responsible for cooking dinner is too tired or too busy or even if one just neglects to get a meal. A hungry spouse can raid the refrigerator. A man may say, "She can't cook, but I love her and we don't go hungry." But with sexual intercourse it is different. There is no acceptable detour by which needs can be met habitually if the mate is too busy, too tired, absent, or uninterested.

If, for any reason, a low level of cooperation exists in a marriage, the sexual adjustment can become an emotional problem. An added reason why differences become so emotional is found in the expectations with which people marry. Because people are likely to be specifically aware of their sexual needs before they marry, they tend to expect that marriage will inevitably provide satisfaction of those needs. That expectation is one of the impelling motivations toward marriage. Therefore, in marriage, if one feels any deprivation because needs are inadequately or irregularly met, the tendency is to react not only with the emotion resulting from the pressure of unsatisfied sexual needs but also with frustration arising from the feeling that the mate *ought* to make possible the avoidance of such pressures. Thus an explosive potential is a built-in element of sexual adjustment in marriage.

Studies among happily married couples all agree that couples who have achieved the highest degree of mutuality in their sexual relations are among the most happily married. Burgess and Wallin, in their study of 1000 engaged couples, followed up with research concerning the sexual adjustment of these couples after they had been married about five years. They found a high association between the couples' sexual adjustment and their overall marital adjustment.[1] Dentler and Pineo studied these same couples after 15 years of marriage and found that the high relationship between sexual adjustment and general marital satisfaction tended

[1] Ernest W. Burgess and Paul Wallin, *Engagement and Marriage* (Philadelphia: J. B. Lippincott Co., 1953), pp. 687–93.

SEXUAL ADJUSTMENT IN MARRIAGE

to remain constant.[2] Our studies also show a far higher degree of agreement in sexual relations among happily married couples. Figure 15–1 summarizes our findings.

A study of the sexual behavior of 2262 wives found that those wives who reported their marriages as unhappy in contrast to those who reported their marriages as happy, were the ones who were much more likely to have had extramarital intercourse.[3] This might be expected since people who are unhappily married are frequently considering divorce, and extramarital affairs often take place during the predivorce months.

The personality traits each partner takes into marriage will have much to do with the degree of sexual mutuality achieved. People who are perceptive of the reactions of others and considerate of others' needs are the ones who seek to share gratification rather than to achieve only self-gratification. Those who are selfish, impatient, unaware of the needs of others, and unwilling to learn from others will have far less to contribute toward the achievement of a rewarding sexual relationship in marriage. These personality factors are of greater relevance in sexual adjustment than is simple biological adequacy.

## MUTUALITY IN SEXUAL INTERCOURSE

In earlier days, the public attitude was that sexual intercourse in marriage was to be enjoyed by men and tolerated by women, although this attitude may not have prevailed in individual marriages. Traditionally, it was not recognized that husbands had any obligation toward attempting to achieve mutuality in the sexual act. And many women accepted a passive role, in the belief that coitus was one of their marital duties not intended to involve much personal pleasure. Evidence of too much pleasure

[2] Robert A. Dentler and Peter Pineo, "Sexual Adjustment, Marital Adjustment and Personal Growth of Husbands: A Panel Analysis," *Marriage and Family Living* 22:1 (February 1960), 45–48.

[3] Robert R. Bell, Stanley Turner, and Lawrence Rosen, "A Multivariate Analysis of Female Extramarital Coitus," *Journal of Marriage and the Family* 37:2 (May 1975), 375–83.

**Agreement on sexual relations**

**Happiness in marriage**

| | Always or almost always agree | Occasionally disagree | Frequently, usually, or always disagree |
|---|---|---|---|
| Happy or very happy | 25% | 54% | 21% |
| Average, unhappy, or very unhappy | 6% 23% | 71% | |

FIG. 15–1 Degree of agreement on sexual relations and happiness in marriage, as reported by 581 couples.

in sexual intercourse was even to be avoided by self-respecting wives, since it might be taken as an indication of unladylike tendencies. In the past, many marriages considered to be happy operated on that basis.

Wives who wholeheartedly accepted a passive role and who married with no other expectation may have escaped some of the conflicts that some women experience today. People now generally believe that coitus in marriage should be mutually gratifying; some, indeed, attach too great an importance to the woman's ability to enjoy sexual intercourse during the early days of marriage. Disillusionment may result at this point for newly married couples. For here a cultural lag exists. Our generation has discarded the belief that woman is entirely the passive, man entirely the active sexual partner, and theoretically we believe in mutual sharing of sexual pleasure. But some adverse conditioning of girls in the realm of sexual understanding remains, and the general preparation for marriage, which would make mutual sharing a more easily attainable goal, has not kept pace with young peoples' attitudes and expectations.

The crucial period is the first few months or years of a marriage. If too much disillusionment and frustration develops, undesirable patterns may become so set that it will take much effort by one or both partners to remedy the defects in the adjustment pattern. However, some couples whose early sexual experiences have been a disappointment do achieve mutually satisfactory sexual adjustments even after as long as ten to twenty years of married life. Much conflict in the early years of marriage could be avoided if people were well prepared with knowledge of the differences in the sexes, emotionally and physically.

## CAUSES OF POOR SEXUAL ADJUSTMENT

Research shows three broad classifications under which the complaints about poor sexual adjustment in marriage fall: (1) problems due primarily to a lack of biological and psychological knowledge; (2) problems due to social conditioning; and (3) problems due to biological or organic factors. Very few cases fall within the last classification.

Most difficulties in sexual adjustment are due to causes based on social conditioning or on lack of knowledge. Even today, when nearly all taboos against public discussion of sex have disappeared, many men and women marry with a vast amount of misinformation concerning sexual functioning. In fact, the presentation of sex by the media to which most people are exposed distorts the facts to such an extent that many people may be more misled or misinformed than formerly when rigid taboos existed. In addition to mistaken ideas about biological and psychological functioning, the wife or husband, sometimes both, may bring to marriage attitudes that handicap establishing a good sexual relationship. Some children, perhaps girls more often than boys, are still being conditioned to look upon sex with shame, aversion, or fear. When a man and woman have sexual difficulties in their marriage, it is sometimes hard to determine whether lack of knowledge or social conditioning is the cause. Despite adverse conditioning, many couples could respond and cooperate in building good sexual relationships if both were well enough informed to understand their own and their mate's reactions.

## TIME AND PSYCHIC UNITY AS FACTORS IN SEXUAL ADJUSTMENT

Many people marry believing that, since sex is based on biological drives, one need only follow one's biological inclinations to have a good sexual adjustment. This attitude may lead to early disillusionment. In a loving marriage, sexual pleasure is a part of the reciprocal gift of the relationship, since coitus requires a giving and receiving type of cooperation. The desire for sexual intercourse is not necessarily simultaneous for two people. Since one partner's thoughts and inclinations may be elsewhere at the time that the other can think only of sexual urges, some "ceremony" attending sexual approaches is, if not a practical necessity, at least an effective help toward mutual meeting of needs. The psychic and emotional factors in sex within marriage are equally as important as the biological impulses. Results of research among married people indicate that, because of the psychic and emotional factors, many couples do not immediately achieve a sexual relationship that is in all ways satisfactory. They need time and understanding, and some patience.

Our study of the length of time required after marriage for 409 couples to achieve satisfactory sexual adjustment revealed that one-eighth needed weeks or months, but reached an adjustment they considered satisfactory within a year. One-tenth of them required an average of six years to work out this part of their marriage, for some as long as twenty years (see Figure 15–2).

In the average marriage, a measure of uncertainty, awkwardness, and even tension in coitus may occur at first. Since the newly married couple expect to live together for many years, it is surely worthwhile to proceed slowly and to build a permanently satisfying sexual relationship. For after

**Length of time required**

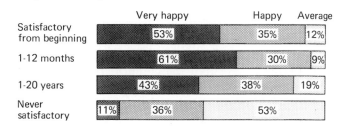

FIG. 15–2  Length of time required to adjust in sexual relations and happiness in marriage, as reported by 409 couples.

this is established, the sex life of the couple will contribute greatly to their feelings of mutual contentment and well-being. Happily married couples report that their sexual adjustment becomes an increasingly satisfactory bond as years pass.

In a study that included the sexual aspects of the honeymoon, nearly half of 177 wives characterized the first coital experience as "unsatisfying" or "very unsatisfying," yet only 17 percent evaluated the total sexual experience of the first two weeks of marriage as unsatisfactory.[4] This suggests that for many of the couples happy relationships were being created in all the different areas of life during the honeymoon, so that even though a completely satisfactory sexual relationship was not established so early, the honeymoon was a successful beginning of married life for these couples. Since sexual adjustments improve with the growth of communication in marriages, all available evidence indicates that a good sexual adjustment is usually established gradually, and does not occur automatically on the honeymoon.

Evidence shows that many couples cannot know before marriage what their sexual adjustment will be even if they have premarital coitus. Of the 581 couples who reported on their differences over sex, only 6 percent had been aware of their differences before marriage, 51 percent during the first year of marriage, and 43 percent during the second year or later (see Figure 14-5). It comes as a shock to many couples to find, after they are married, that they have conflicts over sex. We compared reports of the 122 engaged couples on their agreement or disagreement with reports of 581 married couples, 155 people having marriage counseling, and 164 divorced people. The findings show overly optimistic views among the engaged group. Half of the engaged couples were having coitus; the couples who were refraining probably assessed agreement in terms of values that they believed they had agreed upon concerning premarital and marital sex. The high degree of agreement reported by the engaged couples who were having coitus, contrasted with reports from the married couples, shows that the engaged group assessed their mutuality unrealistically, for sexual compatibility between a couple is not decreased by marriage (see Figure 15-3).

A basic factor in the success of any marriage is the ability of each partner to give support to the ego of the other, to build up rather than to deflate. In the sexual phase of marriage, a man's ego is perhaps more deeply involved than a woman's because of social conditioning in our culture.

People who have had premarital experience with several others may believe they are prepared for marriage, but they may have learned little that will help in working out a satisfactory sexual relationship within their marriage. Our study of 581 married couples found that the men

---

[4] Eugene J. Kanin and David H. Howard, "Postmarital Consequences of Premarital Sex Adjustment," *American Sociological Review* 23:5 (October 1958), 561.

SEXUAL ADJUSTMENT IN MARRIAGE

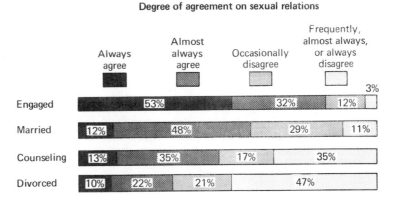

**Degree of agreement on sexual relations**

|  | Always agree | Almost always agree | Occasionally disagree | Frequently, almost always, or always disagree |
|---|---|---|---|---|
| Engaged | 53% | 32% | 12% | 3% |
| Married | 12% | 48% | 29% | 11% |
| Counseling | 13% | 35% | 17% | 35% |
| Divorced | 10% | 22% | 21% | 47% |

FIG. 15–3 Degree of agreement on sexual relations, as reported by 122 engaged couples, 581 married couples, 155 people having marriage counseling, and 164 divorced people.

who had been promiscuous—in that they reported having had coitus with as many as nine women before meeting the one they married—were twice as likely after ten years of marriage to report sex to be a serious problem in their marriages as were men who had not been promiscuous.

This finding is open to a variety of interpretations, but one conclusion can be drawn: Premarital experience with many or several people is definitely not an adequate preparation for marital success. Men and women who at marriage have open minds and are willing to learn and to work at reaching a good understanding are more likely to achieve success.

## CULTURAL CONDITIONING OF SEXUAL RESPONSE

The way the subject of sex is handled in our culture complicates sexual adjustment in marriage. In some families, when young children first begin to ask questions about sex, parents may be unwilling or unable to answer. When a child engages in any type of sexual play or experimentation, parents are likely to be worried or shocked and to show it, or to reprimand the child. It is very difficult for some parents to recognize and appreciate in a positive way that sexuality is a part of every human being at every age. They are disturbed or made uncomfortable by any kind of expression of sexuality in their children. Consequently, the child may form negative or confused attitudes about sex.

Girls are likely to be impressed more than boys with sexual taboos, since greater social stigma is still attached to the girl who deviates from socially acceptable behavior. Many parents solve the practical problem of protecting a daughter by trying to impress her with the dangers which may result from sexual activity. Such policies may create emotional attitudes that later handicap her sexual adjustment.

Conditioned responses built up over a period of years preceding marriage will not change suddenly after marriage. Reluctance to discuss sex makes it difficult for some couples to cooperate when cooperation is most essential. An understanding of the reasons underlying their attitudes can help to overcome the effects of early conditioning.

Ignorance concerning the facts of physical structure and functioning handicaps some young women. This is responsible for some of the tensions associated with the first experiences in sexual intercourse after marriage. The premarital conditioning of the husband has usually been different from that of the wife. Boys are likely to grow up thinking of coitus as pleasurable, with little reason to be aware of any unpleasant or painful concomitants of sexual functioning. If boys are punished for their early experimentations, it is seldom with the zeal that is applied when girls are the offenders. Some parents tend to view boys' infractions of rules in sexual behavior as evidence of potential virility, and to be lenient in dealing with such behavior.

If both partners in marriage understand and make allowances for differences in experience and conditioning, they can better cooperate toward a satisfactory sexual adjustment.

## DIFFERENCES IN SEXUAL RESPONSE

Many people are baffled because they cannot understand the reactions of their spouses. A puzzled young husband stated that his wife's "sex drive varies with the success of daily affairs." This pattern of responsiveness also characterizes some men in marriage, so that some wives have the same complaint. However, many men find that they can enjoy coitus regardless of how other phases of the marriage are going. A man may be at odds with his wife and critical of nearly everything she does, yet desire coitus. The wife may resent this attitude. Some wives complain that husbands show affection only when they are interested in coitus. The woman's viewpoint is likely to be that sexual intercourse is the ultimate expression of love that includes the whole personality, so that if personality clashes or antagonisms develop over things in their daily association, she is likely to be less interested in coitus. Her husband's ability to desire it in spite of other personal factors is evidence to her that his interest in her is only physical and for his own gratification.

A husband can be equally resentful of his wife's attitude. He may feel she withholds response from him as a method of revenge or retribution. It may be difficult for one to realize that at times the mate's *ability* to respond sexually may depend upon a general response to the spouse's personality. When a couple can accept the fact that this difference is not a peculiarity of their own marriage but, rather, a difference common to many marriages, they can view it in a different light. It is often a help to young married couples facing problems to realize that they are not alone. The problems that trouble them have been encountered to a greater or lesser degree in almost all the marriages about them. The happy marriages with which they are acquainted have been achieved, not because these conditions did not exist, but because the couples have accepted them realistically and have worked their way through them successfully.

The experience of the couple in the following case, as reported by the wife, illustrates some of the points in our discussion:

> Until I was in high school I did not have much accurate information on sex. I read everything I could get my hands on and somehow developed a fairly wholesome attitude toward sex. All during my teens I looked forward to being married and to the sexual aspect of marriage. It seemed to me something enjoyable and much to be desired.
>
> During our courtship we developed complete freedom of discussion about sex. Both of us felt a need for sex, yet our convictions told us that premarital sexual relations were against what we believed to be right and contrary to what we really wanted in our relationship. We talked over the problem openly but never did find a satisfactory solution outside of marriage. Because we both felt such a desire for sex, we thought marriage would be the cure-all, and we went into marriage thinking all problems would be solved. We had probably not taken into account the fact that in marriage we would be faced with many events that would interfere with our being able to have sexual intercourse.
>
> In the months after marriage we found ourselves in the abnormal position of working long hours in the night shift of a cannery. I was so physically fatigued that at times I could not engage in sex at all, which left my husband frustrated. Because I was tired I was often irritable, and this interfered with my response. Even now, while we are both busy at school and outside work, we often face this same problem, but both of us have grown immensely in understanding. My husband finds sex satisfying at any time, providing he knows I enjoy it too. He is very understanding and makes sexual intercourse for me something very enjoyable in our marriage. We are learning to accept differences in sex drive and how to anticipate the feelings of the other. We are learning that sex is a reflection of and a contribution to our happiness. The emotional type of affection so prominent in our courtship is being enriched into a mature relationship.

## STRENGTH OF SEX DRIVE

Various views are held concerning inherent biological differences between the sex drives of men and women. One difference seems to be that the ability to experience mature sexual orgasm occurs later in girls than in boys. In our study of students in 18 schools, of 2184 women reporting on age at first orgasm response, 64 percent had never experienced it or were not sure they had. Of those who were certain they had experienced orgasm, 9 percent reported the first experience to have been at age 15 or younger, in contrast to 90 percent of the men who reported first orgasm response to have been at age 15 or younger. Of the women who had experienced it, 63 percent said the first experience had been between the ages of 16 and 19, and 31 percent at ages over 20. We repeated the study in 1971 and found that 18 percent (of 132 women) reported orgasm at age 15 or younger, 46 percent between ages 16 and 19, and 36 percent at ages 20 and over. Of the total group of women in 1971, a larger percentage had experienced orgasm at some time than was true of the women reporting in 1967 (51 percent compared to 36 percent).

In our study of married couples, the most common sexual problem reported was that one mate tended to be more interested in frequent coitus than the other. In earlier research studies, it was husbands who complained of lack of interest or inadequate sexual response of the wife; the newer findings show that in a growing percentage of marriages having sexual problems, wives make that complaint about husbands, although more often the complaint still comes from husbands.

In a study of 641 couples who had been married an average of four years, Thomason asked spouses to report on their mutual willingness to have coitus. In approximately 60 percent of the cases, the husbands and wives both said "as often as each wished." In about 30 percent of the cases, both the husband and the wife reported that the husband wished to have coitus more often than did the wife.[5]

Apparent disparities between sexual desire and sexual response in mature men and women have traditionally been explained by the simple assumption that women have less sexual drive and sexual response than have men. Another explanation must be considered. In our culture today, even though the concept is accepted that either marriage partner may initiate sexual intercourse according to need or desire, it is the man who usually initiates it. He does so when he is ready and able; his state of mind and body is such that there is seldom any doubt about his ability to complete the sex act at the time he initiates it. His wife's best time for response, the time when she would initiate lovemaking if it were left to her, may not coincide with his at all. In cases in which the wife habitually initiates lovemaking when she feels the inclination, she probably finds more occasions when her husband is too sleepy or too involved in other complications in his life to be interested in sex. In fact, more wives today than formerly do have these specific complaints. Probably an increasing proportion of marriages are no longer traditional regarding which one initiates lovemaking or which has the greater sex drive.

When the husband is customarily the initiator, a man who, for example, habitually is most aware of his need for coitus upon waking in the morning may be married to a wife whose metabolism is such that she awakes slowly and is never likely to be sexually responsive early in the day. Or a man who is very tired at night but habitually awakes in the middle of the night after a few hours sleep, conscious of sexual desire, may be married to a wife who finds it difficult to fall asleep at night but who, once asleep, cannot respond sexually if awakened. Even if neither

[5] Bruce Thomason, "Marital Sexual Behavior and Total Marital Adjustment: A Research Report," in *Sexual Behavior in American Society,* ed. Jerome Himelhoch and Sylvia Fleis Fava (New York: W. W. Norton & Company, Inc., 1955), p. 159.

husband nor wife is much interested in sex when overworked or exhausted from loss of sleep, and both can respond when rested and relaxed, one may believe the other lacks sex drive. People of equal sex drive may differ in the timing of their greatest responsiveness, just as people who are equally robust in general health may differ in times of day or night when they are most alert and capable of productive achievement in any kind of activity.

So far there has been little research into marriages in which the wife customarily initiates coitus; all conclusions about responsiveness and drive are based on marriages following the traditional pattern of the husband as initiator. Our further discussion of sex drive and response in this chapter is based on research revealing patterns of marital interaction as they tend to occur, whether they arise from biological differences or from cultural and social factors.

Some wives at marriage are sexually "unawakened" and they need time to achieve full response and satisfaction in coitus. In our study of college students in 18 colleges, 13 percent of the married women students said they had never experienced orgasm, although they had been married an average of three years. Table 15-1 summarizes this study and compares our findings with those of similar studies in the past by Terman and Thomason.[6] The pattern of orgasm response had changed very little.

In 1971 we repeated the study of the married women in our classes and found the pattern of orgasm response to be the same as shown in the previous studies. In approximately half the cases in all studies, the wives experienced orgasm within the first month of marriage, and one-fourth more within the first year of marriage. The remaining fourth took one or more years, or had never experienced orgasm. Findings of our study show that a larger percentage of those who at marriage had been nonvirgins (55 percent) than of the virgins (33 percent) experienced

TABLE 15-1

Percentages of wives in three studies stating various lengths of time before orgasm was experienced in marriage

| Length of time<br>year study made | Terman<br>(N–792)<br>Married: 11 years<br>1935 | Thomason<br>(N–641)<br>4 years<br>1950 | Landis<br>(N–215)<br>3 years<br>1967 |
|---|---|---|---|
| Honeymoon to 4 weeks | 51.0% | 50.0% | 58.0% |
| One month to 1 year | 25.7 | 23.0 | 22.0 |
| One year or more | 16.0 | 12.0 | 7.0 |
| Never | 7.1 | 7.0 | 13.0 |
| No reply | — | 9.0 | — |

[6] Lewis M. Terman, *Psychological Factors in Marital Happiness* (New York: McGraw-Hill Book Company, 1938), p. 306; Thomason, "Marital Sexual Behavior."

orgasm on the honeymoon, but by the end of the first year of marriage, 80 percent of both groups had experienced it. Sixteen percent of those who had been virgins and 9 percent of the premaritally experienced had never or were not sure they had ever experienced orgasm. These studies emphasize that a wide range exists in the sexual response of wives in the early months of marriage and that time is needed for growth in this area. When marriage partners seem unequally matched in sex drive in the early years, both will need to compromise, but they need not conclude that they are permanently handicapped, for time may show that the difference is not great. It should be noted that a difference in sexual response early in marriage is by no means a universal problem, although it does cause trouble in a percentage of marriages.

In considering this topic, there is sometimes a concentration on techniques by which a husband or wife may arouse increased response in the mate. The emphasis tends to be on the physical element, ignoring the fact that desire and responsiveness depend also on psychological and emotional elements. Expression of affection, assurances of love and appreciation, and a high level of communication between husband and wife are necessary elements.

## SEXUAL RESPONSE AND THE MENSTRUAL CYCLE

Some husbands are unaware that the mood of the wife changes with the time of her menstrual cycle. Her ability to be aroused and her reaction to coitus may differ at various times of the month. Although variations occur in individuals, studies show that with most women the periods of time just before or just after menstruation are times of greatest sexual interest. Terman found that one-half of the women in his study recognized greater desire just before or just after menstruation, about twice as many after as before.[7] In another study, 181 single college girls kept a record of the day-to-day changes in their physical and emotional feelings throughout one or more monthly cycles.[8] One item they recorded was any change in awareness of sexual desire. This study showed that, if any noticeable upswing in desire occurred, it was just before or just after menstruation, with slightly more reporting upswings before than after.

Undoubtedly it is helpful for husbands and wives to have some understanding of how fluctuating hormone levels characterizing each stage of the female monthly cycle affect moods and emotions. In 1942 Benedek and Rubenstein published the first study in the relationship between monthly cycle phase and emotional state.[9] They found that during the

[7] Terman, *Psychological Factors in Marital Happiness*, p. 351.

[8] Judson T. Landis, "Physical and Mental-Emotional Changes Accompanying the Menstrual Cycle in Women," *Proceedings of the Pacific Sociological Society* 25:2 (June 1957), 159–62.

[9] Therese Benedek and B. B. Rubenstein, "The Sexual Cycle in Women: The Relation Between Ovarian Function and Psychodynamic Process," *Psychonomic Medicine Monographs* 3:1 and 3:2 (1942), viii–307.

first half of the monthly cycle women felt more alert and happy; just before menstruation they felt more tense, anxious, and aggressive. In 1963 Coppen and Kessel studied 465 women and found that they were far more depressed and irritable before menstruation than at midcycle.[10] This was true of neurotic, psychotic, and normal women. Other researchers have found the premenstrual phase associated with feelings of helplessness, anxiety, hostility, and yearning for love.[11]

These typical and "normal" changes in a woman's emotional state during a month can certainly have an important impact on marital sex life as well as on other aspects of the couple's relationship.

## DIFFERENCES IN TIMING AND ORGASM RESPONSE

Although there is reason to believe that male–female biological differences in sex drives are no greater in variation than the variation between individuals within each sex, still a difference between the manner and duration of reaction in men and women does exist. Men tend to be more easily aroused and more quickly satisfied, women slower to arouse and capable of longer response.

It is desirable for both to receive emotional release through orgasm in sexual intercourse. However, research shows that in some marriages the wife seldom or never experiences what is known as full climactic response, yet she receives pleasure and satisfaction from coitus. There are many levels of sexual enjoyment; orgasm is only one. The love play leading to coitus may be satisfying without orgasm. It is not necessary, nor is it possible, for all responses to conform to a typical physical climax. Nevertheless, if the wife expects and desires orgasm and is frequently disappointed, the sexual side of the marriage will be adversely affected.

It is important for couples to know that, in general, men's sexual desire and response are more specific and localized than are women's. The average woman reaches a climax more slowly and her reaction is more diffuse; the emotional reaction is of longer duration and subsides more slowly.

There are couples in which each is capable of only one orgasm, and experiencing it together might be most enjoyable for them. On the other hand, some wives can experience orgasm in sex play before coitus and then a final orgasm simultaneously with the husband. Since most husbands lose erection with orgasm, the wife must be considered first. Here the average husband has more responsibility than the wife, because his responses are likely to be faster than hers. By exercising a measure of control and by studying his wife's reactions, the husband can help them progress toward the goal of mutually satisfactory sexual experiences.

[10] Alec Coppen and Neil Kessel, "Menstruation and Personality," *British Journal of Psychiatry* (1963), 711–21.

[11] Judith M. Bardwick, "Her Body, The Battleground," *Psychology Today* 5:9 (February 1972), 50–54, 76–82.

Thus the highest level of emotional and affectional, as well as physical, union may be achieved.

Successful coitus should result not only in physical release or satisfaction for the husband and the wife but in a general sense of well-being for both, in a feeling of security resulting from the psychic and physical union. Sex manuals often emphasize the importance of simultaneous orgasm. Rather, emphasis should be upon mutuality in satisfaction, which may or may not include simultaneous orgasm. In many marriages, simultaneous orgasm is impossible because of individual differences. The wife with a capacity for multiple orgasm may be left unsatisfied or frustrated by sexual relationships in which the partners make a simultaneous initial orgasm their goal.

## OTHER FACTORS

Quite commonly, the achievement of a successful sexual relationship depends in part on other factors such as fatigue of one or both partners. The circumstances under which coitus is attempted must also be suitable. There must be privacy, a confidence that there will be no interruption, and pleasant surroundings. If either feels that haste is necessary because of other obligations or impending interruptions, a mutually gratifying experience will be less likely.

One couple was having conflict in sex in their marriage. After three months of marriage they both felt disillusioned. The wife was finding coitus repugnant; the husband said bitterly that he felt he had married a frigid woman. An analysis of the facts revealed that their problem was due at least in part to the circumstances under which they were living. Because their parents had wanted them to wait until after graduation to marry, they were keeping their marriage a secret from their friends and families. Any time they spent together was necessarily clandestine and in surroundings different from those desirable for consummation of marriage by bride and groom. Whenever they were together as husband and wife, they felt the pressure to be careful that their relationship not be discovered. These things weighed more heavily on the wife than on the husband, although she had not recognized the connection between them and her inability to respond sexually. After consulting a counselor and thinking through their situation, the couple announced their marriage and began living together openly thus removing the inhibiting psychic factors. The wife's ability to respond sexually improved, and they reached a much better adjustment in sexual relations.

## FREQUENCY OF COITUS

Some people who marry are hampered by preconceived ideas about just how frequently coitus should occur. There can be no set rule about what is "right," or even customary. Frequency is entirely an individual

SEXUAL ADJUSTMENT IN MARRIAGE

matter, to be determined by mutual desires, the success of a couple's over-all relationship, the type of life they lead, and other factors. Great differences exist in frequencies found to be satisfactory in different marriages. In our study of 330 couples, approximately one-half reported a frequency of two or three times per week, and this did not differ significantly among the age groups, which were from 20 to 25 up to 38 through 45. Nor did the reported frequencies differ significantly between the educational levels represented: those with less than a high school education, high school graduates, and those who had attended or graduated from college. A larger percentage of couples who were not over 31 years old and of those who had no more than a high school education reported a weekly frequency of four times or more than was true of the older and more highly educated couples. The study emphasized the wide range of frequency of intercourse in marriage: 14 percent reported coitus less often than once a week, 19 percent nearly or about once a week, 51 percent two or three times a week, and 16 percent four or more times a week.[12]

It is not unusual for people to behave unreasonably when their sexual desires are blocked. To the mate, this behavior may seem an immature and undisciplined response. In some cases neither husband nor wife will recognize the source of the behavior. It is impossible to estimate the proportion of marital difficulties arising because of explosive behavior on the part of husbands whose sexual desires are blocked. Cases of wives who are sexually frustrated may be somewhat less frequent in our culture, but such frustration is equally demoralizing to a marriage. If both husband and wife recognize that their needs may differ, and if both are willing to compromise, they can eliminate much unpleasantness and build a sex life that is quite satisfactory for both, even though they must cope with their individual differences. Kephart has suggested that in our culture one male–female difference is that a wife may have no specific periodic desire to seek coitus such as her husband has, yet she may be capable of intense response even though she has not sought sexual intercourse.[13] If this is true, development of good communication between man and wife can contribute greatly toward mutuality in sex life. Sexual adjustments that are perfect at all times are probably relatively rare. The tempo of modern living—success and failure in work, sickness of the spouse or the children, worry and anxiety—all affect the desire and capacity for sexual enjoyment in both men and women. For these reasons it must be recognized that a successful sexual adjustment is one that provides a satisfying experience for both partners most of the time, but probably not all of the time. The emotional and psychological factors associated with sexual intercourse, and the integration of coitus within the framework of

[12] Judson T. Landis and Thomas Poffenberger, "Marital and Sexual Adjustment of 330 Couples Who Chose Vasectomy as a Form of Birth Control," *Journal of Marriage and the Family* 27:1 (February 1965), 57–58.

[13] William M. Kephart, *The Family, Society, and the Individual* (Boston: Houghton Mifflin Company, 1972), p. 443.

a total relationship that is satisfying to both, are the tests of a good sexual adjustment.

## LACK OF STANDARDIZATION IN TEACHINGS AND ATTITUDES ABOUT SEX

When any two young people marry, they are almost certain to bring two different and often contrasting sets of attitudes toward sex to their marriage. Adequate institutional provision for teaching sexual behavior and practices has not been provided for young people.

Research on sexual behavior in marriage indicates that no single pattern in marriage is generally accepted as normal and proper. Rather, a wide range of practices may be looked upon as normal and right, or as improper and wrong, according to the individual's background. This variation in what is considered right, proper, and normal in coitus can make for misunderstanding, even repulsion and disgust, between two young people who come from families or economic groups with contrasting attitudes toward sex in marriage. What one spouse accepts as normal the other may feel is abnormal or perverted.

Two young people who find differences in their attitudes toward sex in marriage will sometimes have difficulty in harmonizing their attitudes. One may be sure his or her standards are best because they are based on religion or morality or "what is right." The other may be equally sure that desirable practices can be based only on what is "normal" biologically. An added difficulty arises because few couples will be able to recognize rationally even that their fundamental attitudes do differ or to see to what extent the differences exist. They will simply marry, expecting much from sexual relations, and if all is not perfect at once or soon, the husband may decide he has a frigid wife, or the wife may decide she has married a selfish and insensitive husband. Or either one may decide that the other is oversexed or overaggressive sexually. The couple may not have analyzed the real problem: a fundamental difference in attitudes toward normal sexual expression in marriage. People who understand that such differences exist in our culture should be able to cope with problems arising from differences between them.

## OUTSIDE HELP FOR PROBLEMS

People who have difficulties in their personal adjustments in marriage often hesitate to seek outside help. They will readily seek medical help in case of illness, and many will discuss their physical ailments freely with friends and neighbors. But when it comes to working out husband–wife relationships, many couples feel they must maintain a pretense of perfect harmony and never openly admit to any problems of adjustment. Attitudes of society have supported this viewpoint. Couples have been expected to conceal their hostilities and to work out their problems alone. They could perhaps go to their priest or minister or rabbi with a confession of failure, or go to a lawyer for advice concerning a divorce, but not much help was available in finding a constructive solution. Little progress was made toward the understanding and cure of mental illness so long as families hid their mentally ill members and tried to keep secret the illness they felt was a disgrace. An open recognition of any problem is necessary before progress can be made toward a solution.

Much frustration, unhappiness, and ultimate divorce could be avoided if couples would acknowledge their common marital difficulties and realize that it is not an admission of defeat to seek help from an outside source. Yet there is a shortage of people qualified by training, experience, and personality to help troubled married couples. Some ministers and doctors have studied to become qualified to handle the special problems of marital adjustment, since they realize there are not enough other qualified counselors. But many more specially trained marriage counselors are needed. It is seldom wise to seek help from neighbors, friends, or relatives, for these people would be inclined to be prejudiced in favor of one spouse or the other, and unable to view the situation objectively.

A trained counselor is in a position to look impartially at the total marriage situation.[14] The counselor may let the couple talk it out, suggest certain readings, or make suggestions according to what he or she observes as an outsider. In many marriage situations, it could be very helpful to the relationship for each spouse to have a chance to talk about personal problems with an unprejudiced outsider. As two people live together, they will find solutions to many marital problems without the aid of a counselor. Some excellent help is available in books and articles.

A number of books treat the physiology and psychology of sex. Public libraries are becoming increasingly aware of their obligation to provide such books to meet the needs of people. However, since in many communities these books are still unobtainable from libraries, those interested may need to buy them. It is desirable for couples to own helpful books that may be reread when questions arise after marriage. Much of the material dealing with the subject of sex will have greater meaning some time after marriage. Readers are inclined to skip over important points that may be beyond their present understanding.

## SEX IN MARRIAGE AS A POSITIVE VALUE

A satisfying sexual relationship is one of the positive elements contributing to the well-being of each partner and of the married pair. The couple who find satisfaction together in sex are more likely to be successful and happy in their relationship in other areas of living and to have a home in which children will find happiness. They will also be better able to

[14] The American Association of Marriage and Family Counselors can supply the names of counselors in one's area and general guidelines for seeking their help. Address: AAMFC, 6211 W. Northwest Highway, Suite 2900, Dallas, Texas 75225.

condition their children to look upon sex as an element to be valued in personality and in relationships. Just as we appreciate good food, comfortable shelter, and the security of a workable philosophy of life or a religious faith, so we recognize sexual fulfillment as a powerful and constructive force influencing the happiness of individuals. It can be the most complete form of love expression, contributing to the mental, emotional, and physical balance necessary for a happy and successful marriage.

## HELPS TOWARD A GOOD SEXUAL ADJUSTMENT IN MARRIAGE

1   Try to become informed accurately before the wedding about the facts of sexual relations in marriage. Read together a good sex manual during engagement, and go to a qualified person for premarital counseling.

2   Learn to talk over sexual reactions in marriage in order to be perceptive of the feelings of the spouse. Sex is an area of living in which each one receives greater satisfaction if one is able to bring satisfaction to the other.

3   When differences are discovered and frustrations arise (as is true in all marriages at times), try to accept such differences without resorting to accusations or blame. The task is to recognize that there are differences in response and to work to understand and cope with these differences.

4   Keep a perspective on the whole relationship. A sexual adjustment is good if the two find satisfaction in most, but not necessarily all, of their attempts. In marriages with excellent sexual adjustments, times of frustration and failure for one or both may occasionally occur.

5   Try to develop a sense of humor, which helps ease failures or embarrassments in sexual matters.

6   Remember that good sexual adjustments usually take time. Early experiences are merely the beginning, not the ultimate test of what a sexual relationship in marriage is to be.

## REVIEW QUESTIONS

1   How important is a good sexual adjustment in marriage?

2   In what ways may failure to adjust in spending the family income affect the sexual adjustment?

3   What special factors, which do not operate in making other marital adjustments, serve to focus attention on working out sexual adjustments?

4   Contrast the attitudes of two generations ago toward sexual expression in marriage with the attitudes of today.

5   Name the three broad classifications that include most of the causes of poor sexual adjustment in marriage.

6   Discuss the time element in sexual adjustment. What do studies of the honeymoon reveal about sexuality?

7   What does the study of engaged couples having coitus reveal?

8 How does conditioning before marriage affect the sexual functioning of men and women?

9 How does day-to-day living affect sexual adjustment?

10 Studies of men and women seem to show a difference in the strength of the sexual drive. Why might this difference be due to cultural factors?

11 Why may there appear to be a marked difference in the strength of the sexual drive of the husband and wife in the early months of marriage?

12 How does the menstrual cycle affect sexual adjustment?

13 Timing is essential in a successful sexual adjustment. Discuss.

14 What should be the guide in determining frequency of coitus?

15 If a couple finds they are having difficulty in arriving at a mutually satisfactory sexual adjustment, where may they get help?

## PROJECT

As a special project, two or three students can query all agencies in your community that might be doing marriage counseling to learn what facilities are available to the public. Report to the class.

# IN-LAWS AND MARRIAGE ADJUSTMENT

# 16

When some people marry, they are vaguely aware that they are getting, along with a spouse, a new family: a mother-in-law, a father-in-law, brothers- and sisters-in-law, even aunts-, uncles-, and grandparents-in-law. Others marry feeling secure in the belief that marriage is for only the two of them and are quite unconscious of the in-laws. Those who do realize that one marries a family as well as a mate have a variety of attitudes. Some who have been conditioned by years of exposure to mother-in-law jokes marry with a fatalistic attitude that in-law trouble is a part of marriage. Some others look forward with pleasure to associating with a large family group. A person who has had no sister or brother may hope to have the lack filled by a brother-in-law or sister-in-law. Whatever the attitudes of those marrying, in-laws and in-law relationships will need to be considered. How important a factor in their adjustment, how disturbing or how satisfactory and rewarding their in-law relationships become, will depend on special factors in themselves and in their families.

## VARIETY OF PATTERNS OF IN-LAW INTERACTION

Great differences exist in the pattern of in-law relationships among families in the United States. There are couples whose marriage does in fact cause a happy uniting of two families, with the in-law situation representing the expanding and extension of already satisfying and congenial family associations. When this occurs, the parent families may become friends if they are not already. The parents-in-law share interests other than the children, children-in-law, and grandchildren they acquire in common. The married couple can build a good relationship of their own independently, and also enjoy associating with both in-law families free from disturbing factors such as embarrassing disparities or competitiveness between their families.

At the opposite extreme are couples whose in-law relationships are so unsatisfactory that they function as a focal point of marital dissatisfaction. In such families, the in-laws may have nothing whatever to do with each other; or any contacts they do have may be characterized by competitiveness or by misunderstanding and antagonism. In these cases, each of the married partners views his or her in-laws negatively, is disparaging toward them, feels threatened by them or resentful toward them.

Probably the experience of the vast majority of married couples falls somewhere between the two extremes. There are probably as few ideal in-law relationships as there are "perfect" marriages, in the sense that no troublesome or disturbing problems ever arise. Those couples whose in-law relationships are totally unsatisfactory are likely to be among the group whose marriages include other elements so disruptive that their marriages fail. Many married couples, along with their parents, do accomplish a satisfactory in-law relationship.

## NEW RELATIONSHIPS:
## A GROWTH TASK OF THE EARLY YEARS OF MARRIAGE

The special kind of growth required at this stage of life is difficult for many people, and logically so. The young person at marriage undertakes three distinct, yet interlocking, though somewhat contradictory achievements in reorganizing basic personal relationships in life: (1) He or she must build a new pair relationship with the mate. (2) He or she must at the same time grow into a new kind of relationship with his or her parents, a partial withdrawing from accustomed closeness in favor of the new closeness with the spouse. (3) He or she must establish a new relationship with the in-law family, a relationship having some of the elements that have long existed with his or her own parental family.

There is a tendency at marriage to focus exclusively on building the new pair relationship and to be unaware of the necessity also to alter relationships with one's own family, as well as to build new relationships with the family into which one has married. Or one may be conscious of the importance of trying to establish workable relationships with the new family, but quite unconscious that readjustment must be made in the pattern of interaction with one's own family. For many people it is difficult to achieve these different growth requirements with equal ease. Moreover, a different aspect of the same kind of growth is required of the parents, as well as of the newly married pair. It is not surprising, therefore, that any one of those involved, or perhaps all of them, may experience some measure of failure or inability to cope with the new challenges, with the result that "in-law problems" arise.

To speak of in-law problems is simply to recognize that the capacity for growing into new relationships varies greatly among people. Naturally, such problems are much more characteristic of the early years of marriage than of the later years.

## IN-LAW RELATIONSHIPS AS A PROBLEM AREA IN MARITAL ADJUSTMENT

From the 1940s to the present, a number of researchers have used various approaches in attempting to assess in-law relationships as a factor in marital happiness or failure, and to determine the nature of problems that arise in families as they work out their relationships. Each major study has contributed insights on some aspects of the subject and has supported and reinforced the findings of other research studies. Some clear patterns emerge, and the significance of in-law relationships as a factor in marriage apparently remains similar in successive generations in our society.[1]

In our early study of the length of time required to achieve adjustment in marriage, couples married for an average of 20 years were asked what had been their most serious problem in achieving happiness in marriage. The women mentioned in-law relationships second, the men mentioned in-laws third among six chief areas of daily living. These people had been married long enough to have faced most of the issues that arise in married life. Since none of this group was divorced and 83 percent classified their marriages as happy or very happy, they would tend to understate rather than overstate the seriousness of in-law friction as it would exist in a representative cross section of marriages that included a large proportion of newly married.

The same questions were also answered by a group of 544 Michigan State University student couples who were still in the first few years of marriage. These couples provided more detailed information on many facets of the subject, and their responses provide greater insight into the whole range of in-law relationships. These couples gave in-law relationships first place in their list of difficult areas. A comparison of findings from the two groups shows that in-law disagreements affect the early

[1] See Judson T. Landis, "Length of Time Required to Achieve Adjustment in Marriage," *American Sociological Review* 11:6 (December 1946), 666–77; Landis, "On the Campus," *Survey Midmonthly* 84:1 (January 1948), 19; John L. Thomas, "Marital Failure and Duration," *Social Order* 3:1 (January 1953), 26; Theodore B. Johannis, Jr., "The Marital Adjustment of a Sample of Married College Students," *The Coordinator* 4:4 (June 1956), 24–31; Evelyn Millis Duvall, *In-Laws: Pro and Con* (New York: Association Press, 1954); Paul Wallin, "Sex Differences in Attitudes to In-Laws—A Test of a Theory," *The American Journal of Sociology* 59:5 (March 1954), 466–69; Mirra Komarovsky, "Continuities in Family Research," *The American Journal of Sociology* 62:1 (July 1956), 42–47; Thomas, *The American Catholic Family* (Englewood Cliffs, N.J.: Prentice-Hall, Inc., 1956), p. 235; Robert O. Blood, Jr., and Donald M. Wolfe, *Husbands and Wives* (New York: The Free Press, 1960), p. 247; Robert M. Gray and Ted C. Smith, "Effect of Employment on Sex Differences in Attitudes Toward the Parental Family," *Marriage and Family Living* 22:1 (February 1960), 36–38.

years of marriage more than the middle and later years, although some couples settle into a permanent state of friction with their in-laws. Some of the younger couples experiencing difficulty in early marriage probably did, in the course of time, resolve their differences and reach a good understanding with the in-laws; if they had been queried on their relationships years later, they would probably have reported their relationships with in-laws to be much better. The long-married group included fewer with in-law difficulties, because those who were not able to solve the problems had in some cases ended the marriage by divorce; for others, the situation had resolved itself through the increased maturity of all involved or because time removed the parents-in-law as a factor. When John L. Thomas examined 7000 Catholic marriage failures that had gone through the Catholic Separation Courts, he found that only 7 percent of *all* the failures were attributed to in-law problems, but in the marriages that failed *during the first year*, in-law problems were named as the most common cause.[2]

That the younger married couples report in-law problems more often is understandable, since to make the transition from being an unmarried member of one's own family to becoming a member of an enlarged family circle with the wedding is one of the major developmental tasks of early marriage. To integrate oneself happily into the family of the spouse, a family whose ways and attitudes may not correspond to the long-accepted ways of one's own family, requires special tact and perceptive understanding, and to do this at the same time when it is necessary also to achieve a new level of independence from the parental family is an added complication. People who can be challenged to create good relationships with their new in-laws can be rewarded by added happiness in their marriage.

## SPECIFIC PATTERNS OF IN-LAW FRICTION

The pattern revealed by all research studies seems to be that the wife more often thinks that in-laws are a problem, and her feelings are most often directed toward the husband's mother.[3] Among the 544 student couples, those who reported that they felt in-law relationships were a source of friction in their marriages specified which in-law relationship they saw as the center of the trouble. Table 16-1 summarizes their responses.

The findings suggest that in-law friction has a feminine pattern, since mothers-in-law, sisters-in-law, and wives are involved more frequently than are fathers-in-law, brothers-in-law, or husbands. The brother-in-law seldom receives any blame for contributing to tense in-law relationships.

[2] Thomas, "Marital Failure and Duration."
[3] See Thomas, *The American Catholic Family;* Duvall, *In-Laws.*

IN-LAWS AND MARRIAGE ADJUSTMENT

TABLE 16-1

Percentages of 116 husbands and 160 wives reporting various in-law relationships that were causing friction in marriages *

| | Husband | Wife | Both |
|---|---|---|---|
| Mother-in-law | 42.0% | 50.0% | 46.7% |
| Father-in-law | 15.0 | 11.0 | 12.3 |
| Brother-in-law | 3.0 | 6.0 | 5.0 |
| Sister-in-law | 16.0 | 13.0 | 13.8 |
| Two or more of the above | 24.0 | 20.0 | 22.2 |

* Judson T. Landis, study of 544 student couples.

Sociologists have advanced various theories to explain why in-law problems fall into a feminine pattern and have attempted to test some of the theories through research. However, the studies reveal that girls are more attached to their families, without providing support for the theory that this attachment becomes a factor in marital friction over in-laws. Studies seem to show that if a husband and wife are equally attached to their respective families, the wife is more likely to feel threatened by the husband's parental attachment than is the husband by the wife's.[4]

## IN-LAW ADJUSTMENTS AND HAPPINESS IN MARRIAGE

Our study of the 544 student couples in the first years of marriage revealed a close relationship between happiness in marriage and getting along with the in-laws. Of those couples who had an excellent in-law adjustment, 67 percent said their marriages were very happy, but of those in which the in-law relationships were fair or poor, only 18 percent classified their marriages as very happy. In another study, we compared the responses of three groups—the married, the counseling group, and the divorced—with the engaged on agreement with in-laws or prospective in-laws. The results show that the happily married have better relationships than the couples having counseling and the divorced, but the engaged couples believe that they have more agreement than do the happily married couples (Figure 16-1). About half the engaged couples were aware that they were not in complete agreement about their two families. In view of all previous research, it is predictable that more of them will discover differences about in-laws after they are married.

Ability to create and maintain pleasant and peaceful relationships with in-laws seems to be characteristic of the type of person who can accomplish the many other growth tasks necessary for achieving happiness in marriage.

[4] See Gray and Smith, "Effect of Employment on Sex Differences."

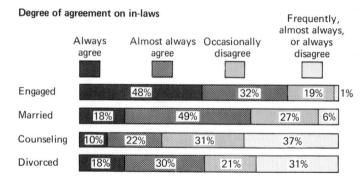

FIG. 16–1  Degree of agreement on in-law relationships, as reported by 122 engaged couples, 581 married couples, 155 people having marriage counseling, and 164 divorced people.

## AN ANALYSIS OF THE CONFLICT SITUATION

If we would understand the in-law conflict situation, we must reflect further on the family life pattern. For the first 20 years of the person's life the mother is deeply involved with the children. As young children, they look to her for most of their needs; to them she represents security. She influences their decisions as they grow older. The average father is likely to be more occupied with making the family's living and less closely associated with the children. He has more interests outside the home, whereas even the working mother is likely to center more of her interests in the home and the children. This pattern may develop in the children a greater dependence on the mother. Even in the most successful families, most people have not been completely weaned psychologically when they marry; a pattern built up over a period of 20 years will not disappear with the wedding ceremony. After the wedding, many mothers will continue to give helpful suggestions to the son and, in turn, the son will continue to consult with the mother if that has been his habit. This same pattern will be found in the wife's family. Here the problem begins in many marriages. Each spouse, while continuing accustomed relationships with his or her own family, may feel resentful of the close relationship between the other spouse and his or her family. The offering of parental counsel may seem to the son- or daughter-in-law to be parental interference, and the fact that the spouse seeks parental advice may be interpreted as an indication that he or she has more respect for and confidence in the parents than in the mate.

A natural situation exists, with good intentions on the part of all concerned, yet unless the patterns of a lifetime are altered fairly rapidly, and unless all the individuals try to advance into a new level of maturity, trouble may arise.

The two statements below reveal the beginnings of growth in the attitudes of two young people toward their parents. The first, from a young husband:

**Length of time required**

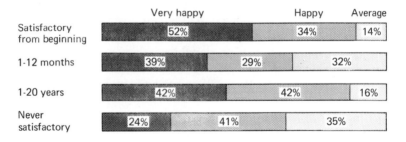

FIG. 16–2 Percentages of 409 husbands and 409 wives reporting various periods of time required for adjustment in in-law relations and happiness in marriage.

My mother welcomed us with open arms after our honeymoon and was just full of ideas on how to help us. She would load us down with food of every imaginable sort, slip me five dollars for fuel for our car, which she also had given us. The payoff came when, after I mentioned merely conversationally (I thought), that our mattress had a broken spring, she wrote and said she was bringing us a new one. Margaret hit the ceiling and said Mother would never let us be independent if this kept up. She was certainly right, yet I could not help but realize that I, myself, had unconsciously spurred my mother on. I knew that I depended entirely too much on my mother, and I realized that I had to change in order to have a satisfactory marriage. My mother was the victim, for, as I would never have done before, I called her and told her as nicely as I knew how that we could not possibly accept the mattress. She protested, saying that she enjoyed doing what little she could to help us. But help was not the issue; my maturity was the issue. If I accepted the mattress, there would be similar things I would be accepting. For some time my mother was deeply hurt, and I was deeply hurt over the whole situation.

But eventually my mother came to realize that perhaps she had interfered somewhat, even though she had tried to help us. I now look back and view the situation as constructive, a trivial situation to an observer perhaps, but a major step toward our independence and my maturity.

## And from a young wife:

I have had an adjustment to make—that of psychologically leaving my family's home. Before I was married, I was very close to my family, especially my mother. When I got married, however, I found that if things did go wrong for a day or so, I owed it to myself and to Jerry not to go home with the problem. If Jerry and I had an argument and I took my side of it to my mother and father, they would be inclined to take my side, and would find it hard to forgive Jerry easily, as I could do after we had solved the problem and made up. As time goes on I have come to understand that I no longer need to depend so much on the love and security that my parents gave me, for I have my husband and *our* home. (But it's still nice to know my parents are there.)

When misunderstandings have developed, both the children and the parents are inclined to lose their objectivity. To the parents, the son-in-law or daughter-in-law may seem to be ungracious and unappreciative, and the son-in-law or daughter-in-law may view parental interest or help as interference. Some comments made by young people about their parents-in-law are illuminating here:

"They try to run our home."
"They treat us as children."
"They give us too much advice."
"—try to help too much."
"—try to influence our lives."
"—hover over us."

These comments are more likely to be made by the son- or daughter-in-law about the spouse's parents than about one's own. This same young person may be continuing to seek counsel from his or her own parents with no thought that the spouse might interpret the situation as parental "interference." Personal conferences with some of the young people who made such comments about their parents-in-law revealed that frequently they were shocked when they realized that the spouse had exactly the same criticism, but directed at the in-law parents.

It seems that during the early years of marriage many couples find it hard, if not impossible, to discuss with each other their feelings concerning the in-laws. Each fears that he or she will appear to be motivated by personal jealousy or pettiness. The fact that an element of jealousy actually is present does not make objective discussion any easier. We list some further comments made by daughters-in-law, which indicate that an element of jealousy or at least a competitive attitude toward the parents-in-law does exist:

"His mother insists on first place with my husband."
"They still think he belongs to them."
"They don't accept my status as daughter-in-law."
"They try to steal my place as his wife and the mother of his child."

It will be readily seen that the young wife would find it difficult to discuss these complaints lucidly and convincingly with her husband. She would find this inability to talk it over wth her husband disconcerting. In such a situation, a wife may seek to relieve her emotional turmoil by talking with her own parents or friends who may be sympathetic about what she feels to be a problem, rather than discussing it with her husband.

The comments quoted above are from daughters-in-law, but many sons-in-law also find it hard to accept and tolerate close affectional bonds between the wife and her family.

## PARENTS AS A FACTOR IN IN-LAW RELATIONSHIPS

Some parents, as well as the children, show immaturity in their in-law relationships. Some mothers cling to their children, refuse to let them grow up, and continue to make decisions for them long after the children should be thinking for themselves. This type of mother has not matured to the point of being able to accept life as it is. She resists the natural course of events, which is that children must grow up and adjust away from their parents if they are to marry and have families of their own, allowing their own families to become more dear to them than their parents. The mother who fails to accept this viewpoint and who tries to hold the first allegiance of her children will probably have trouble with her children-in-law.

**Regression in parents and children.** One aspect of mother-in-law trouble centers in regressive tendencies that may show up in people when they are faced with problems. As one looks back, life may seem to have been easier and simpler than it is at present. In early marriage, the inevitable problems to be solved surprise and baffle some people who believed that marriage would end all problems; their urge is to return to their home emotionally and sometimes physically. This tendency toward regression appears in sons and daughters after marriage and also in parents who encourage their married children to come to them with their troubles.

Many mothers experience a crisis in their lives when children marry and leave home. This may be especially true of mothers who have not worked outside the home and who have centered all their time and energy in their home and children. Their lives have been full of homemaking and child rearing, and when the last child has gone the mother may feel the emptiness deeply. So the married daughter who returns home with problems may find her mother waiting with welcoming arms. Both mother and daughter have regressed, and the young husband understandably feels anger toward his mother-in-law, whom he blames for complicating his life.

Fathers are not so likely to try to regulate the lives of their children, since they are usually less close to the children emotionally. The father has his job and is as absorbed in that after the children marry as he has always been. He may even feel relieved privately when the last daughter is married, if he has been supporting her during the teen years. But the mother's loss of the children through marriage and her subsequent loneliness must be taken into consideration when we attempt to understand in-law problems.

Some newly married couples are able to understand the special problems their mothers may have at this stage of life. But as the report by the husband below shows, such problems tend to be more complex than merely the fact of a lonely mother. The traits of everyone involved contribute to complicating the adjustments.

Ann and I believe that my mother needs to feel accepted and temporarily given more attention until she gets over the shock of my father's recent death. We are trying to make her feel as secure as we can without endangering our own relationship. At first this was difficult because when she visited us she tended to assert too much authority over Ann in the kitchen. Ann herself felt insecure about her cooking, and the fact that my mother had so much advice to give only made Ann feel inadequate. She was decent enough not to let my mother know her feelings and lately she has been more confident and can adjust more to my mother's need to help and give advice.

We have to make a similar adjustment for Ann's mother. She has very limited outside interests and is oversolicitous toward us.

Another complication is that both our parents usually come to visit us at the same time. This means double trouble because the two mothers are somewhat jealous of each other. At the same time, they are oversensitive to each other's feelings. I don't believe that either mother would knowingly hurt the other, but I do believe that each has a strong ego drive to compete for our attention. One mother will tell how she makes something; then the other will tell how she makes it. Each seems convinced that her way is the best. We try to head off these encounters, but sometimes we cannot.

Another complication for which I am to blame is my own prejudice in favor of my family. I recognize that a certain amount of this is quite normal, but I tend to go overboard at times. I think that my family is better than Ann's. At times I have found myself building my family up to Ann, to the detriment of her own. I do not believe that this family prejudice was ever as strong in me as it has been during the past month, and I'm not sure why I've developed it, except that I may be unconsciously siding with my mother when she and Ann's mother compete. Now that I have seen it in myself, I am trying to cope with it.

A better relationship with our in-laws has developed by our not seeing them as often. We try to limit visits to twice a month.

**Distance may be an asset.** The American ideal has been that when young people marry they live alone. In practice, some young people do live with or near the parents when they marry. In this case, their process of growing up and becoming psychologically weaned from the parents may be delayed. Continuation of the parental-dominance and child-dependence patterns of the spouse near whose parents they are living is often intolerable for the other who has married into this family.

When parents are close by and a part of a couple's daily life, a complicating factor is the tendency for the young couple to fail to take full responsibility for their own actions. If things go wrong in the household, if their children are spoiled and tempers are short, there is a scapegoat handy to blame. It is easy to think that things would be otherwise if only in-laws were not present to complicate life. There is often a tendency for one of the pair to discuss problems with someone in his or her own family rather than trying to work them out with the mate.

As long as our American family system continues in its present form, newly married couples who can live some distance away from *both* their families probably have an advantage in establishing a good adjustment in their own marriage.

**Contrasting backgrounds as a factor.** In marriages in which the two young people come from contrasting backgrounds, such as different nationalities, religions, economic classes, or social classes, all the usual factors that make for family misunderstandings are present in addition to the contrast in backgrounds. These contrasts contribute to unsatisfactory in-law relationships. This kind of difficulty was discussed in Chapter 11, "Mixed Marriages."

Again, friction may develop because parents are critical of changes they see occurring in young people after marriage. Some people resist change of any kind. If parents are of this type, and if they are not wholehearted in accepting the son- or daughter-in-law, it is easy for them to feel critical of any changes in behavior or attitude evident in their own son or daughter after he or she marries. They may attribute the changes to the influence of the in-law spouse rather than recognizing that growth and change are inevitable for the person who attains a mature independence. Parents in such a situation who cannot resist offering reproof or advice are likely to provoke resentment in the son- or daughter-in-law. Their attitudes will be sensed, adding force to resentment against the advice.

## AGE AT MARRIAGE AND IN-LAW DIFFICULTIES

In our studies, men who married under the age of 20 took longer to achieve a good understanding with the in-laws than those who married later, and women who married at ages under 20 were having more difficulty with in-laws than were the young husbands. The husbands and wives who married at 24 or over had the best adjustment with the in-laws. Blood and Wolfe also have found that the younger the bride, the more frequently couples report disagreements with their in-laws.[5] Parents probably interfere more when they feel their children are not mature enough to marry, and married couples who are young and immature may be especially sensitive to parental interference. Moreover, people

[5] Blood and Wolfe, *Husbands and Wives*, p. 248.

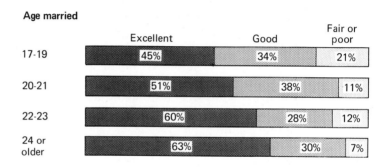

**Age married**

|  | Excellent | Good | Fair or poor |
|---|---|---|---|
| 17-19 | 45% | 34% | 21% |
| 20-21 | 51% | 38% | 11% |
| 22-23 | 60% | 28% | 12% |
| 24 or older | 63% | 30% | 7% |

FIG. 16–3  Age of 544 wives at marriage and in-law adjustment.

who marry at younger ages are likely to be less well established economically and so more dependent on help from parents or others. Approximately one-fifth of couples live with their parents if the husband is under 20. Younger couples are usually not as free to be independent as are older couples, and yet they may be especially resentful in situations arising from their dependence upon parents or other family members.

## BEHAVIOR ARISING FROM IN-LAW DISHARMONY

So far we have given attention to conflicts between parents-in-law and sons- and daughters-in-law in an attempt to clarify somewhat the background factors of such difficulties. The whole interactional pattern is complicated, for just as the young people fail to understand their parents-in-law, so they are puzzled and frustrated by the reactions of their spouses to the in-law situation. In our research, previously quoted, some comments from young husbands were:

"She takes her mother's advice no matter how bad it is."
"She tells her mother too much about our personal affairs."
"She is too much at their beck and call."

Some comments from both husbands and wives were that the spouse:

"Is tied to their apron strings."
"—wants to live near own folks."
"—is too worried about them."
"—gets homesick."
"—agrees with them (though they're ignorant) just to pacify them."

When the partners find it hard to understand these attitudes in each other, they tend to resort to certain irritating types of behavior. The husband or wife may behave in an unpleasant manner to the in-laws; behave unpleasantly to the spouse in the presence of the in-laws; or attempt to thwart the mate in in-law relationships by refusing to have anything to do with the in-laws. Such comments as, "He (or she) makes the in-laws feel unwanted," "won't talk to them," "argues with them," give an idea of some overt expressions of feeling toward the in-laws.

Few sons- or daughters-in-law engage in this behavior as a conscious effort to offend the in-laws. The offenses are usually no more deliberate than the interference by the parents is a deliberate attempt to make trouble. The offending actions may mean only that the spouse is ill at ease and feels insecure in the presence of the in-laws. More rarely, it may be a response to a mutual dislike existing between a spouse and the in-laws.

In many cases the wife or husband feels critical of the spouse's behavior toward the mate in the presence of the in-laws. Both husbands and wives are likely to be especially sensitive to the impression that the mate is making on the in-laws. Since they hope to give the impression that unity and solidarity exist in the marriage, any direct or implied criticism from one directed about or toward the other in the presence of the in-laws is very disturbing.

Again, the comments of certain individuals are enlightening:

"He embarrasses me in front of them."
"—ignores me when we are with them."
"—doesn't show any affection when the in-laws are around."
"—criticizes me in front of the in-laws."
"—doesn't take my side if I differ with the in-laws."

All of these comments indicate that the son- or daughter-in-law feels the need of "backing" from the mate in the presence of the in-laws. He or she wants it demonstrated that there is love and respect from the mate. Many things a husband does may provoke no irritation at all when he is alone with his wife, but the same words or actions in the presence of the in-laws will cause the wife to feel she has lost face and has been repudiated before those whom she especially desires to impress. Husbands react similarly to the face-losing situations.

## MAINTAINING PERSPECTIVE ON IN-LAW RELATIONSHIPS

It is of the greatest importance for young people entering marriage to have a realistic understanding of the in-law interactional pattern. It helps to realize that most parents are just as interested in the success of the marriage as are the couple, and that the son- and daughter-in-law have as many attitudes provocative of conflict as have the parents. If the in-law son or daughter can analyze with some objectivity the emotions motivating their own behavior, they will find it easier to maintain perspective on in-law relationships.

If the young wife finds that it is painful to admit that her husband is the special man she chose to marry, at least partly because his mother did some things right in rearing him, she might reexamine her own attitudes. She will probably find that she is reacting to her own feelings of insecurity in her overreaction to her mother-in-law. Some mothers-in-law, in the interest of peace, make an effort to keep out of the way of sons-in-law or daughters-in-law who are too easily threatened.

## SUCCESSFUL IN-LAW RELATIONSHIPS

As we stated early in the chapter, the ability to get along well with the in-laws is one of a number of characteristics found in those who have the capacity for meeting adjustment requirements constructively. The couples in our in-law study who supplied information on difficulties in this area listed their solutions. The most successful in their relationships were those who willingly compromised for the sake of harmony, or who made friends with the in-laws and actively liked them. Their comments were of this type:

"I fit in with their ways of doing things."

"I made up my mind to get along."

"I treat them as my own family."

"I respect their views."

"We visit them often but not for very long."

"I am helpful whenever possible."

"I try to be agreeable and friendly to them."

"I ignore things that irritate."

"I realize they have developed their ways over a long period of time so I don't try to change them."

"I try to be sensible about it and not condemn them for faults, because I have faults too."

All these comments indicate a positive frame of mind that will avoid or resolve in-law friction.

A few couples reported that they had met problems by simply not trying to get along with the in-laws. Most of those who had chosen that solution had managed to live far away from the in-laws and to see them infrequently. Comments made by the couples in the study of older-generation marriages revealed that many of the couples in the older generation had met their problems by this substitute solution. That is, they avoided any open conflict with in-laws by having nothing to do with them. Sometimes that is necessary even though it is not a very happy solution. There are advantages for families that can happily expand to include a wide kinship circle. The small nuclear family of parents and children alone is deprived of enrichment that can come through association with loving grandparents, aunts, and uncles. People who can approach in-law relationships with an appreciation of the positive aspects of the enlarged kinship circle are giving themselves and their future children special benefits.

Young people who are still immature may have a better chance to grow up if they are away from family during the first adjustment period of marriage. The too-interested parents may also find interests other than the lives of their children if the children are not living nearby during the first months after they marry. So, although putting distance between the married couple and the in-laws may not be the most constructive or desirable solution, it sometimes serves to facilitate other adjustments during the early years of marriage. By thus postponing conflict, young people may attain a more satisfactory marital adjustment and in time may become able to live near the in-laws and enjoy a pleasant relationship with them. The better solution, of course, is for all those involved to strive to understand the nature of this part of marriage and to achieve the maturity necessary for growing into new relationships as early as possible.

## DO IN-LAWS BREAK UP MARRIAGES?

Of themselves, poor in-law relationships probably do not actually cause the break-up of many marriages, although divorced people may blame the in-laws for the marriage failure. The same personality traits that create or contribute to in-law problems also contribute to other kinds of difficulties within a marriage. Even if the in-laws are in fact difficult and have a tendency to make trouble, they are unlikely to break up the marriage of a young couple who are working out their adjustments together, who can freely and objectively discuss their families, and who are secure in each other's affections. Many of the comments from young people who complain that they have in-law trouble reveal that some of the trouble lies within the complaining individuals themselves. Some people would have "in-law trouble" regardless of whom they married or what kind of people the in-laws were, and if their marriages fail they will insist that the cause was in the in-laws, not in themselves.

## IN-LAW RELATIONSHIPS DURING THE LATER YEARS OF MARRIAGE

Most of our discussion thus far has been of in-law relationships in the early years of marriage, for it is then that friction is mostly likely to occur. In-law problems of later marriage are different. After a few years have passed, the many adjustments which faced the newly married couples have been worked out, and the new family has become a solid unit. Each

FIG. 16–4 "We just now finished dinner, Mother. Oh, meat and biscuits and gravy. Dessert and coffee. No, I didn't have a vegetable. Yes, I know I should. Now don't worry. What? Oh, she baked a cake. Ha-ha-ha! You're a scream, Mother! . . ." From *The Saturday Evening Post*, Hank Ketcham.

partner is more sure of his or her place in the affections of the spouse and does not need so much reassurance around the in-laws. Most people will have achieved by this time a measure of the necessary adjustment. Some comments by the long-married group suggest the nature of the situations more common in the later years:

"My husband's father lives with us. He has many irritating habits and attitudes that trouble my husband more than they do me."
"My husband's mother tried to be in full charge of all of us until her health failed and she became a helpless invalid."

And from a husband:

"My father was compelled to live with us after my mother died and he was irritable and childish, making it hard for my wife."

Today, when it is becoming possible for the majority of old people to be relatively independent because of social security benefits, Medicare, and similar programs in our society, the nature of in-law problems among long-married couples may be changing. Since most elderly parents prefer not to live with their children unless necessary, cases in which family problems center around an aged parent should be fewer and less typical.

## OUTLINE FOR SELF-STUDY: IN-LAW RELATIONSHIPS

The key to successful in-law relationships is in developing a mature understanding of the complicated relationships that result when two families are connected by a marriage. You are probably an in-law now, whether or not you are married. If you are not, you will be some day. Consider the answers to the following questions:

1 Have you ever been critical of any in-law (brother-, sister-, mother-, or father-in-law) in your immediate family? Try to decide whether your evaluation of that person is objective or subjective.

2 Consider the following situation: The son works for his father and some day will inherit the business. After college he wanted to go into a profession but the father insisted that he come home and go into the family business. After two years of marriage his wife feels smothered by the attention of the in-laws. Her mother-in-law drops in frequently and makes suggestions on such matters as how to decorate the home, how to care for the baby, what to feed her husband. Her husband's younger brothers and sisters stop in every day on the way home from school. The couple is doing well financially but the daughter-in-law feels overwhelmed by her husband's large family.

Can you put yourself in the place of the wife in this case and understand her feelings? Can you imagine yourself the husband and think of his reactions to his wife's attitude? What advice would you give to each? Why would you so advise them? Can you determine how much of your reaction to the case arises from your own experiences or your attitudes toward your own in-laws?

3 If you are married (or planning to be), what kind of an in-law are you?

a. Try to assess your level of maturity in your relationships with your in-laws. Can you recognize and accept in yourself immature attitudes toward the in-laws and at the same time keep from letting your feelings control your actions or words?

b. Did you consider the preferences and wishes of both families in planning your wedding? Do you habitually look for the best in your in-laws? Do you tend to tell your family and friends about the good things you see in your in-laws? Do you consider your in-laws among your real friends? Do you feel that your in-laws understand and appreciate you?

c. Have you and your spouse grown together enough so that you can speak of *our* families rather than *my* family and *your* family? Do the two of you make your decisions before you consult your families? Have you become able to communicate freely with your families but at the same time stand as an independent unit living your own lives and making your own decisions?

d. As you look ahead, would you say that you are developing a pattern that will make for a happy family in the larger sense? That is, good relationships between the grandchildren and the grandparents, cousins and cousins, and so forth?

e. If you feel that you have "in-law problems," would an outsider agree that you have a real grievance or would he or she conclude that the things bothering you are insignificant, or imagined, or spring from your own traits?

## REVIEW QUESTIONS

1 Why are people often unaware that, in reality, marriage unites two entire families?

2 How important are in-laws in marriage adjustment?

3 In what relationships are in-law frictions most common?

4 How is happiness in marriage associated with the length of time required to create good relationships and an ultimate adjustment with the in-laws?

5 "In-law friction in the early years of marriage is a normal outgrowth of parent–child relationships." Explain.

6 "They give us too much advice." Analyze this tendency in parents-in-law.

7 Why do couples find it difficult to discuss their in-law differences?

8 Give several reasons why the age from 45 to 60 is a crisis period for the average mother.

9 Why is in-law friction more likely if the children live with or near the parents-in-law?

10 Discuss in-law problems in "mixed" marriages.

11 Why should in-law friction be more pronounced among those who marry young?

12 What three common forms of interaction between the husband and wife develop from frustrations in in-law relationships? Illustrate each.

13 It has been said that most in-law friction is due to two women trying to be first in the affections of one man. What is the basis for this belief?

14 How do in-law problems among middle-aged couples differ from those of the early years of marriage?

15 Discuss some advantages families have if they can maintain close, friendly relationships with grandparents (parents-in-law), aunts, uncles, and cousins.


## PROJECTS AND ACTIVITIES

1 Make an objective analysis of the in-law relationships in your immediate family. If the in-law relationships are harmonious, why are they this way? If there is difficulty, who do you believe is at fault? Write a paragraph describing an in-law relationship pattern.

2 *Role playing.* a. Jack and Marilyn have been married two years and have been getting along very well. They live away from both families. Jack's mother came to visit them six weeks ago and at present shows no indication of wanting to go home. Marilyn had understood that the visit would be for two weeks. Marilyn has felt "left out" in many of the discussions between Jack and his mother, and she finds herself resenting her mother-in-law.

Scene: Jack's mother has gone to a movie for the evening, and Marilyn has decided to have a frank talk with Jack. Before she has a chance to say anything, Jack mentions that his mother has been so much help with the children and housework that he thinks it would be a good idea if she stayed indefinitely.

b.  Two young couples are seated playing bridge for the evening.

Scene: Couple #1 mention that they have in-law problems. In the conversation that follows, couple #2 bring out positive feelings about in-laws while couple #1 continue to find fault with their in-laws.

# RELIGIOUS ATTITUDES
# AND MARRIAGE

## CHAPTER 17

Most people, by the time they reach a marriageable age, have a pattern either of religious or nonreligious orientation, which will have become a part of their personality structure. It may not be easily changed. Couples approaching marriage need to consider whether they are together in their religious attitudes. Their agreement or disagreement and the extent of their religious or nonreligious orientation will affect the happiness and success of their marriage.

## RELIGIOUS AFFILIATION AND MARITAL SUCCESS

Research shows that generally, in the first half of the twentieth century in our culture, the presence of a religious faith has been associated with more favorable chances for marital success.

When the measure is marital permanence or marital breakup, studies covering approximately 25,000 marriages have shown that there were three times as many marital failures among people with no religious affiliation as among those religiously affiliated. In marriages between persons of different religions, religion may be a disruptive factor, yet the failure rate of marriages of mixed religions has been generally lower than that of marriages where there is no religion.

In research done in the thirties, Lewis Terman found that those whose religious training had been extremely strict or rigid tended to be similar to the group with no religious training insofar as marital happiness was concerned, although they had a somewhat higher happiness rating than did the no-religion group.[1] In another study 20 years later relating religious upbringing to marital adjustments, Peterson classified religious

[1] Lewis M. Terman, *Psychological Factors in Marital Happiness* (New York: McGraw-Hill Book Company, 1939), p. 164.

backgrounds according to five types, ranging from those that rigidly control the individual along puritanical lines and are emotionally oriented to the agnostic or nonreligious group.[2] He found the most low-adjustment scores among those individuals who had the very rigid type of religious background, and the most high-adjustment scores among those who were in the middle group classified as religiously liberal.

## RELIGIOUSNESS AND RELATIONSHIPS WITHIN THE FAMILY

In recent decades a trend has been observable in the United States toward secularization and away from a formerly more widespread religious orientation. Findings from our study of 3189 students in 18 schools in 1967, compared with findings from 3000 students in 11 colleges in 1952, do not significantly reflect this trend. It appears that religious differences, when they exist in families, continue to be disruptive. On the other hand, families united in their religious beliefs and emphasis, whatever these beliefs are, are among the happier families.

Analysis of the reports by university students concerning the religiousness of their parental families as they perceived it, and their assessment of various aspects of the relationships within their families, emphasizes the relationship that exists between religion and successful family life.[3]

The responses were analyzed separately for Catholics, Protestants, Jews, and those of no faith, and by the reported devoutness of each group. In general, findings from all four groups show a high association between family religiousness and successful family living. The parental divorce rate had been four times higher in nonreligious families than in devout families. Further, the students from devout homes, in contrast to those from nonreligious homes, reported being closer to their parents and having a higher conception of self as measured by such factors as their appraisals of their own personality, their feeling of ease in making friends with the other sex, and their confidence that they would be able to have a successful marriage.

Of the four groups (Catholic, Protestant, Jewish, no faith), those from the group having no faith reported the largest percentage of divorced parents and the largest percentage of parents unhappily married.

Several studies have been made in the 1970s of religiousness and the behavior and attitudes of young people. All studies found that young people from religious homes hold attitudes and have engaged in behavior

[2] James A. Peterson, "The Impact of Objective and Subjective Religious Factors on Adjustment and Maladjustment in Marriage" (Ph.D. diss., University of Southern California, 1951); quoted in Peterson, *Education for Marriage* (New York: Charles Scribner's Sons, 1956), p. 328.

[3] See Judson T. Landis, "Religiousness, Family Relationships, and Family Values in Protestant, Catholic, and Jewish Families," *Marriage and Family Living* 22:4 (November 1960), 341–47, for a report of the 1952 study.

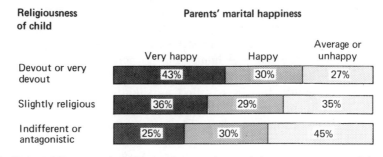

| Religiousness of child | Parents' marital happiness | | |
|---|---|---|---|
| | Very happy | Happy | Average or unhappy |
| Devout or very devout | 43% | 30% | 27% |
| Slightly religious | 36% | 29% | 35% |
| Indifferent or antagonistic | 25% | 30% | 45% |

FIG. 17–1 Religiousness of children and parental marital happiness, as reported by 3189 students from 18 colleges, 1967.

which would support the stable traditional family.[4] They were less likely to have had premarital sexual intercourse, to have used drugs, to have lived with a member of the other sex, to have committed delinquent acts, or engaged in other manifestations of rebellion and rejection of society.

That a religious orientation seems to be a benefit in family living might be explained in various ways. For example, most churches emphasize the value of religious participation by family groups, and today the forces that separate the members of the family and direct their interests into widely divergent channels are more numerous than are the opportunities for partipation in any activity as a family unit. Hence, for children to participate with their parents in the activities of a church often aids in building family solidarity. Going to church together on Sunday morning, if it is the habitual practice of a family, may acquire special significance for both children and parents. It is an occasion when they are together as a family, wearing what one child happily called "our Sunday morning faces." The occasion is different from most of their other associations, which for many families tend to fall into a pattern of merely crossing paths as each hurries about the business of his own separate life and activities. A family orientation to religion seems to add to children's feelings of identification with their parents and so to contribute to their sense of security.

## STUDENT VIEWS ON FAMILY RELIGIOUS EMPHASIS

We asked 625 university students in family sociology classes to report on their attitudes toward the religious emphasis in their childhood homes,

[4] Arthur M. Vener and Cyrus S. Stewart, "Adolescent Sexual Behavior in Middle America Revisited: 1970–1973," *Journal of Marriage and the Family* 36:4 (November 1974), 728–35. Anthony P. Jurich and Julie A. Jurich, "The Effects of Cognitive Moral Development upon the Selection of Premarital Sexual Standards," *Journal of Marriage and the Family* 36:4 (November 1974), 736–41. Lura F. Henze and John W. Hudson, "Personal and Family Characteristics of Cohabiting and Noncohabiting College Students," *Journal of Marriage and the Family* 36:4 (November 1974), 722–26.

and to say whether they intended to follow approximately the same policy when they were married and had children of their own. Only 2 percent of the students thought there had been too much emphasis on religion in the parental home, and 35 percent said they thought there had not been enough. Most critical among the students were those from parental homes that were rated as slightly religious or indifferent to religion; these expressed the view that they intended to have a different policy with their children. There was little difference in the response patterns of men and women in the study. Slightly more women than men thought there had been too little emphasis on religion in the parental home, and more intended to have a different policy with their own children.

When the students were asked what religious policies they intended to have for their own children, all faith groups listed, in first order, family church attendance and Sunday school; second, bedtime prayers; and third, grace at meals. The findings of this study do not provide an explanation for why a third of these university students said they would like to have had more emphasis on religion in their parental homes. Whether these people as children had felt different from other middle-class children among their associates who were from church-going families, whether they envied the family interaction among their church-attending friends, or whether they felt that there were some specific things lacking in their own families, we can only conjecture.

## NATURE OF RELIGION AS IT RELATES TO FAMILY LIVING

To assess further the contribution of religion to marriage and family life, let us consider some aspects of the nature of religion. Philosophers and theologians offer a variety of definitions of religion from which we may choose. William James said, "Religion means the feelings, acts, and experiences of individual men, so far as they apprehend themselves to stand in relation to whatever they may consider the Divine."[5] John Dewey: "Whatever introduces a genuine perspective is religious."[6] William Ernest Hocking: "Religion is the habitual reference of life to divine powers."[7] And John Herman Randall: "Religions differ widely but, like art, religions all do the same things for men. They are all man's quest for the divine and his attempt to order life in its light."[8] Randall said further, "All religions embrace a code for the guidance of living and a set of ideals toward which human life should be directed."

[5] William James, *The Varieties of Religious Experience* (New York: Longsmans, Green & Co., Inc., 1902), p. 31.

[6] John Dewey, *A Common Faith* (New Haven: Yale University Press, 1934), p. 24.

[7] William Ernest Hocking, *Types of Philosophy* (New York: Charles Scribner's Sons, 1929), p. 26.

[8] John Herman Randall, *Preface to Philosophy* (New York: The Macmillan Company, 1946), Part IV, "The Meaning of Religion."

Summarizing the meaning of these statements, we see that they all emphasize the orientation of the individual to realities outside physical existence. Such orientation can aid people toward developing and maintaining a perspective on life and its problems. Life thus has the possibility of becoming more than the present moment or the immediate problem. Whatever helps individuals to maintain a sense of proportion about factors in their lives and in the world about them should increase personal adequacy in a relationship such as marriage.

## RELIGION AND ADULT NEEDS

Few adults are self-sufficient or entirely secure emotionally. It is inevitable that crises arise in life that shake confidence in material things and in the social environment. Change is constant. Political changes, changes in customs and behavior patterns, changes in our manner of life as a result of technological developments, changes in our closest associations brought about by the death or absence of friends and loved ones—all these things upset individual security and we look for something of permanent and unchanging validity to hold to. For many people a religious faith provides the security that enables them to maintain emotional balance in the face of life's fluctuations. The security sought in religion is not dependent on material things but, rather, upon an inner security that must be based on values that, for the individual, have an unchanging validity.

It is true that some unhappy, poorly adjusted, and intolerant people are religious. Extremes in religion are sometimes attempts to escape from realistic acceptance of the responsibility for living and adjusting among others. There is a difference between a functioning religious faith and bigotry, which may be dedicated to the acceptance of certain dogma and intolerant of all other beliefs. The person with a positive religious faith that impels him or her to behave toward others according to standards based on respect and acceptance of them as individuals of equal worth is more likely to be capable of satisfactory relationships with others, and hence is a better choice as a marriage partner.

## CURRENT EXPRESSIONS OF A NEED FOR RELIGION

Since the 1960s many people, especially young people, have been turning to religion or to semireligious groups to help them find meaning and understanding in their lives. Young people have turned to Jesus communes, to Transcendental Meditation, and to many forms of Oriental philosophy, especially Indian philosophy. In many of these groups emphasis is placed upon self-understanding and meditation as a way to find meaning in life. Some of the people joining these groups were among the "lost generation" who have tried communal sex, soft and hard drugs, drifting with no thought of permanent jobs, and in general, those who had rejected society. Their attention is now directed toward finding meaning and security in life through some form of religion.

It is impossible to evaluate the long-term effects of these new forms of religious or semireligious movements upon the individual and his functioning as a spouse or a parent. Possibly the present feeling of need for this type of experience will soon diminish, and there will be no long-time effects on family life.

## RELIGIOUS PHILOSOPHY AND FAMILY LIVING

Certain essentials of a religious philosophy are especially relevant to marriage and family living in our culture. Central in Judeo-Christian teachings is the individual; the emphasis is on respect for the essential rights of each personality. Ideally, a religious faith impels one toward unselfishness and sympathy for the needs of others, rather than concern only for one's own personal needs and satisfactions.

Our discussion of what a religious faith may mean in terms of an individual's interaction in marriage and family living concerns itself with the ideal, and in daily living the ideal may not be achieved. In a certain proportion of families, the religious orientation and the implementation of the religious philosophy in the life of the family do include many elements of the ideal.

The person who has a faith that "works" in his or her own life may make a better marriage partner. He or she will strive to understand the viewpoint of the other person. Ideally, the religious person will show a willingness to compromise for harmony and to respect the personality of the partner, refraining from ridicule or the belittling attitudes that are so devastating to the happiness of a wife or husband. Such a person will build up rather than destroy the self-respect and self-confidence of the partner. If religion gives an inner security, it can be a source of strength in times of crises that come to every family. The religious person may be better able to maintain a perspective on life and its values, so

FIG. 17–2 Place of marriage, as reported by 581 married couples, 155 people having marriage counseling, and 164 divorced people.

that when trouble comes he or she will be better able to withstand the pressure.

Another characteristic that gives religion relevance to family life is that it demands *self-discipline*. Religious people do many things because they believe they should; they refrain from doing other things because they believe they should not do them. They also act or refrain from acting in certain ways out of consideration for the feelings and attitudes of others. The attitude that says, "If the taking of meat offends my brother, I will take no meat," [9] is one that will serve to limit conflict in the daily contacts in life.

Self-discipline is a valuable asset for those who would work out happy relationships in marriage. No matter how interesting an unpredictable and undependable person may be as a temporary companion, that type of person is usually difficult to live with as a permanent partner in all the affairs of life. Innumerable occasions arise in family living when the course of life and love is smoother and happier for all if each member can be depended on to behave as a disciplined individual—to follow the course of action that is for the best interests of all, even when it requires a sacrifice of personal preference.

## RELIGION AND HAPPINESS

Elsewhere we have stated that some people who are unhappy in their marriages would not be happy in any event, married or single. To be able to give happiness to others, one must have the elements of a happy existence within oneself. Religion should contribute to personal happiness because religious people have a basis for confidence in their own destiny, and believe in the permanence of certain universal principles. They cannot be blindly optimistic for they are aware of the evil and ugliness in society as well as the goodness and beauty to be found in life. But they can give others the benefit of the doubt, assuming that others' motives and intentions are as generous as their own. This religious attitude contributes to the happiness of people who are not tormented by suspicions and distrustful doubts concerning their associates. It also contributes to the happiness of others by helping them to feel valued as individuals.

## RELIGION AND PARENTHOOD

People who have the inner security of a religious faith have less need to strike out at others in the world about them, or to be overly critical, aggressive, or bitter. As parents, they should be better able to consider the individuality of each child, not just selfishly as it relates to themselves or the family, but in terms of the ultimate possibilities that are within

[9] I Corinthians 8:13.

the child. They can seek to understand and to help the child develop in his or her own way toward the highest potentialities. Such parents will not take the position of demanding instant obedience on the basis of an arbitrary parental authority that bolsters their own egos, but will adopt policies designed to help children develop self-control and a positive philosophy of life for themselves. Ideally, religious parents will not try to force their beliefs on their children, but rather will live so that their children will be inclined to give consideration to the important values by which to live.

## IN SUMMARY

Young people contemplating marriage will do well to take stock of their religious attitudes and those of their future mate, remembering that no person is without a "religion" of some kind in the sense of devotion to a value or a set of values. Most irreligious people are committed to some set of values. Does this commitment enable them to overcome or cope with inner fears and anxieties? Does it direct them toward an understanding of others and a tolerance for the things that matter to them? Does it enable them to face life with equanimity? Or are they seeking security in possessions, in dominance over others or in individual freedom that denies freedom to others?

Those who desire a good marriage will want to start with every possible advantage in favor of the success of the marriage. Religious attitudes are often a key to the general personality pattern of an individual. This explains in part the greater success of marriages between those who have a positive religious belief.

## REVIEW QUESTIONS

1  What do research studies reveal concerning religion and marital adjustment?

2  Summarize the research findings concerning family religiousness and students' self-concepts.

3  How can religious participation serve as a family bond making for family unity? Disunity?

4  What specific contribution to individual adjustment may result from religion as defined early in this chapter?

5  In what ways does a religious faith fulfill basic needs of adults in the modern world?

6  What are some current expressions of the need for religion?

7  List five ways in which religion should contribute to marital adjustment if one follows Judeo-Christian teachings.

8  In what ways should religious faith contribute to the general happiness of the individual?

9  May the person with a religious philosophy be expected to have other characteristics that make for successful marriage adjustment? Discuss.

## PROJECTS AND ACTIVITIES

1   Have representatives from the Protestant, Catholic, Jewish, and any other faith represented in your community talk to your class on the subject of religion and marriage.

2   *Panel Discussion.* What religion means to me.

3   Give a book report on one of the current best-selling books with a religious theme. Analyze the book, and tell why the religious theme has a strong appeal.

# FINANCES AND ADJUSTMENT IN MARRIAGE

## CHAPTER 18

Almost all married couples find it necessary to compromise in order to achieve a good working relationship in the area of finances. Family discord is frequently attributable to a failure to agree on money matters. It will be remembered that the study of the length of time required to adjust in marriage revealed that it had taken the longer married couples more time to work out problems centering around spending the family income than problems in any other area except sexual relations. Approximately one couple in five had never satisfactorily agreed about finances, although the couples had been married an average of 20 years. Our study of the three groups of couples—the marriage counseling group, the divorced, and the married couples—showed that all three groups listed finances either in first or second place as a cause of their problems in marriage. Responses of the engaged couples in our study showed that most of them were unaware of potential differences over the use of money. Figure 18-1 summarizes the responses of all four groups on their agreement or disagreement in the area of finances.

**Degree of agreement on family finances**

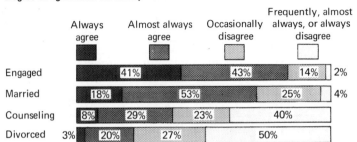

FIG. 18–1 Degree of agreement on family finances, as reported by 122 engaged couples, 581 married couples, 155 people having marriage counseling, and 164 divorced people.

Why should spending the income be a problem in marriage? Here it is necessary to look at the values that each partner brings into the marriage. Our society emphasizes money and material possessions, but there is no unanimity on value-standards. Many people reject the materialistic values long accepted in our society, but they have their own variety of wants that represent but another facet of the emphasis placed upon possessions. The necessity for making choices in using money is the key to some difficulties husbands and wives experience in the early years of marriage. Members of a couple have come from families in which standards differ, and when they marry they may have reached different levels in their own individual formulation of value-standards.

We observed a young couple shopping together in a supermarket. The wife was putting items in the shopping cart and the husband was following her, taking things out of the basket and placing them back on the shelves. He seemed to be acting automatically, unaware of the implications of what he was doing. Out-of-season foods, and some things that he apparently considered "unnecessary" to their living, were being put back on the shelves. If we had been able to follow the young couple around long enough to observe developments when the wife realized that her shopping was being censored, the situation would no doubt have provided a good example of how differences in economic values and attitudes can become an emotionally explosive issue.

But contrasts in values may go far deeper than is evidenced by choices made in a supermarket. For example, a husband may be from a family in which the available money was spent for good clothes, new cars, or for entertaining. With this background, his values may center around making a good impression on neighbors and friends. His wife might come from a family whose chief values were getting an education, or saving for the future, or owning a home. During the courtship period the wife may have been impressed by the husband's willingness to spend for her pleasure or benefit. However, after marriage this same free spending by her husband may be a source of friction. If the wife becomes conscious of the limitations of their income, she will probably feel that they should be saving money for a home and for other things that are important according to her set of values. To her, the expenditures they enjoyed during the courtship period can now be foregone in order to have money for things she considers of more permanent value. The husband, who has been accustomed to thinking of money as a means of providing pleasure and enjoyment, may not be in sympathy with what he looks on as a sacrifice of the present for the future. He may find it hard to understand the wife's seeming change of attitude after the marriage. It would take some time for such a couple to get together on use of the income.

During the courtship period a man may be proud of his fiancée because she is always attractively dressed. He is pleased when his friends admire her appearance. After the wedding he may still wish to be proud of his wife's appearance, but may find that their income is insufficient to permit her to have the kind of clothes she has been accustomed to buying. The wife may feel that she could easily cut down on the food bill to enlarge the portion of the budget allocated for clothes. However, if the husband happens to be from a family that believed in "setting a good table," he will not take kindly to the idea of saving on food to spend on clothes. The wife will find it hard to understand why he has changed so much since marriage. The necessity to harmonize their views and still cope with practical financial urgencies may produce strain in the marriage. Patterns of spending and value systems developed over a period of years will be slow to change. To each, his or her own pattern seems "right." In some marriages, the partners will never reach complete agreement on the use of money.

**Contrasts in ways of controlling money.** In some families, the father takes all responsibility for spending the money; in some, the mother. Other families divide the responsibility about equally. Thus, contrasting family economic systems can be observed. The young man who comes from a family in which the father has taken all responsibility may be inclined after marriage to think he should control family finances. The fact that his mother always asked his father for money when she needed it seemed perfectly natural to him. If this young man should marry a girl from a family in which the money had been controlled by the mother or controlled democratically by both parents, there is a good chance that misunderstandings will arise. This wife would resent having to ask her husband for money and to account to him for expenditures. The husband might be unaware of her viewpoint and at a loss to understand why his wife should react emotionally to a financial arrangement that seemed reasonable to him.

When couples differ greatly on how the money should be used or controlled, the feeling of frustrated irritation each may have at times affects their behavior in a variety of ways. The husband or wife may become overly critical of the mate's actions in unrelated matters. Either one may find it easier to be generally critical than to discuss the focal subject of family economics. A husband may engage in behavior his wife does not approve, such as going out in the evening or drinking too much. Or he may just become moody and hard to live with, behaving in general like a worried and irritable person. It is not always the husband who worries about finances. Among marriages having serious problems over finances, many cases occur in which careful planning and good money management by the wife are upset by the husband's impulsive spending. Another kind of problem fairly common in our motor-oriented society is that some husbands have an overwhelming weakness for cars, and the financial situation of young families can be kept precarious for years because of unwise expenditures for cars. The wife may worry about the situation but be unable to control it.

## GROWING TOGETHER ON ECONOMIC VALUES

Young married people are inclined to feel that it is conceding defeat to admit that they differ widely on economic values or anything else. In the early years of marriage, many try to keep believing they agree on everything. In so doing, they make no progress toward harmonizing their ideas. It is far better for the couple to recognize at marriage that they will surely differ on some matters but that they can discuss and work out differences as they arise.

The time to talk things over is at the time any difference in viewpoint becomes evident, *before* the situation reaches an explosive point. Some traditionally oriented men still marry believing that it is a sign of weakness for a man to need his wife's help on money matters. Yet relatively few wives may willingly allow the husband to manage and make all decisions about money matters. Most couples find they must talk matters over and share responsibility for decisions, neither one having arbitrary control over financial decisions.

## BUDGETING OR FINANCIAL PLANNING

Even in times of economic prosperity, most couples have to do some careful planning if their money is to be stretched as far as it must be to meet all their needs. A budget is not primarily a plan to save money; it is a plan to distribute the income so that the family may have what they consider most essential. The term *budget* has unfortunate connotations for some people. Many have tried to follow some ideal plan that did not fit their situation. A budget should not be a hard-and-fast list of

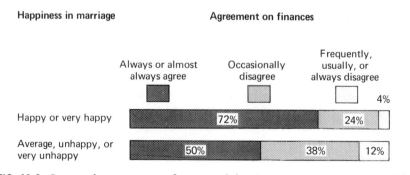

FIG. 18–2 Degree of agreement on finances and happiness in marriage as reported by 581 couples.

predetermined expenditures, an ironclad arrangement allowing for no flexibility in the use of income. It should be a spending plan based on an estimate of the family's income and expenditures for a realistic list of items. Whatever the married couple may call it, they will need to plan their spending so that they get the most value from their money.

One of the chief values in keeping a budget in the early years of marriage is that it causes a couple to study their spending and encourages them to talk over and plan together about money matters. It is a good idea for an engaged couple to work out a financial plan before they marry. They should discuss their attitudes on spending money and discover some of their points of agreement and difference at a time when they can discuss their differences more objectively than might be possible after they are married and are faced with financial pressures. It should help also to be more realistic about how they can afford to live after marriage, lessening a tendency to blame each other if they later have financial problems. However, most couples will not be realistic about money before marriage. If they attempt to discuss the matter and it appears that they differ, they will abandon the subject because of a conscious or unconscious wish to believe that they agree on everything. With some couples, one partner may suspect that they are far apart in their views on the use and handling of money but may deliberately avoid discussion of the subject before marriage because of a determination to marry anyway, and a belief that "everything will be all right once we are married."

Marital tension is sometimes increased through attempts to follow a financial plan that is too rigid. If they cannot make the budget work, a couple may begin to blame each other for the failure. If one believes in a plan that includes keeping a record of every cent spent, and the other is not good at remembering where and for what the money went, constant irritation may center around finances.

Some people who object to keeping records use the system of putting money that is to be used for different purposes in different envelopes. The theory is that when a fund is exhausted the expenditures stop. It is not necessary to point out the complications that may arise with that system also.

Nothing is to be accomplished by one partner's trying to use a carefully worked out financial plan as a means to force the other into line in the spending of money. If this attitude exists, something more fundamental is wrong in the relationship of the couple, and budget keeping will not correct the difficulty. It will simply serve as a focus for their friction.

## WHO SHOULD HAVE MAJOR RESPONSIBILITY?

Ideally, the responsibility for managing family finances should be shared equally. But from a practical viewpoint, one or the other can regularly be responsible for paying bills, keeping the checkbook balanced, seeing that payments for insurance and taxes are made when due, and other such tasks. Which one takes these responsibilities should depend upon circumstances, such as whether both work outside the home or whether one is more interested, is more experienced, or has more financial ability.

Many men appreciate having their wives take major responsibility here. One wife said:

> We had constant arguments over money in the early years of our marriage. I was often irritated because my husband would say there wasn't enough money for things I felt we needed. I believed that he was not in sympathy with what I felt to be 'needs,' and that if he had wanted the things there would be enough money for them. Finally, we decided to try a different system. He turned over his salary to me with the understanding that I would handle it. My problem was to make it stretch to cover our fixed obligations and the other things I wanted. I no longer felt critical of him, for often I found there really wasn't enough money for what I felt were 'needs' and I revised my ideas about where the money should go. I enjoy planning and trying to make the money stretch. My husband likes this arrangement.

Of course, such an arrangement is based on mutual confidence and cooperation. A husband who spends money carelessly or on impulse can upset his wife's financial management just as she can upset family finances by failing to cooperate if he is handling the money. Common sense about money is not a sex-related trait.

Many couples manage to share the responsibility quite equally. They have a joint checking account and both try to use good judgment in spending. This system is sometimes hard to carry out smoothly in the first years of marriage. After people have lived together for some time and have reached agreement on financial planning and spending, they can have gained confidence in each other's judgment and handle the money together more easily.

There are some men who feel they must handle the money in order to preserve their dominance in the family. A young man from a patriarchal family may feel that to turn over the money management to his wife is to abdicate his place as head of the house. If a husband attempts to use the allowance system as a means of control, it may indicate that other adjustment failures are present in the marriage. In such marriages, the husband may feel that, although his wife dominates in many areas of family living, he can occasionally make the final decision about money. However, if one's position in the family is maintained by using power through money control, the affectional interaction in the family is probably unsatisfactory.

There are many approaches to managing the family income. In some homes, the children are given a part in deciding how the income shall be used. However, financial worries are hard enough for adults, and little is to be accomplished by having children feel much of the burden of financial responsibilities. As children grow older, they can be encouraged to take more part in money management in the family.

The fundamental thing is to try to understand each other's viewpoints and attitudes and to achieve as much agreement as possible. If a couple find that one system does not work satisfactorily for them both, they can try another. Success is more probable if people can throw aside preconceived ideas and be adjustable. Money should be used to help smooth the path, not to provoke family battles.

## STAGES IN THE FAMILY'S FINANCIAL LIFE CYCLE

The financial situation of families tends to vary at different stages of life, and the differences fall into fairly characteristic patterns. People who have an understanding of this overall view, and the ways in which financial needs change as families advance through life, can handle their finances more satisfactorily at each stage.

**Stage I.** The first stage begins with marriage, when the couple are about 22 to 25 years old. This is the financial honeymoon period. In many cases both members of the pair are working, and there may have been some parental subsidy or financial gift at the time of the wedding, as well as other wedding gifts that amount to an initial subsidy. Thus launched, and with two incomes, the average couple feel little financial strain at first. They are inclined, under our present credit system, to be overly optimistic in the things they buy, basing their monthly ability to pay on their two incomes.

**Stage II.** The second stage comes very quickly for many couples. The first child is born, and the wife may stop work or cut down on the hours or days she works. Perhaps a second child may follow within two years. Expenses suddenly more than double during the very time when the income is reduced. This stage, about ten years, when the partners are 25 to 35, is a period of financial strain approaching crisis for many couples. The husband's earning power is probably slowly increasing, but does not even approach the increase in expenses. Medical bills, baby sitters, food, clothing, the continuing need for home furnishings not yet accumulated—all together can equal more than one income is able to cover. This is the stage in which the couple's ability to make their money go far enough is tested.

**Stage III.** During the years 35 to 45 the burden is still heavy but may begin to ease. At this stage the children are in school, and the mother may begin to work at least part time to add to the family income. The college-educated father's earnings have increased by this time, and teen-age children may even be earning enough to cover some of their own expenses.

**Stage IV.** The years from 45 on, for the educated couple, are financially the easiest. The husband's income is probably at its peak, and necessary family expenses have decreased. In many cases the wife is holding a full-time job. The children either may be away from home and earning their own living or may be in college. The parents may now be able to help with college educations or to buy things they had not been able to afford during the earlier stages. At this time they can concentrate more on making financial investments that will ensure their continued security.

For college students reading this text, the stages of financial life other than the first and possibly the second are likely to seem too far in the future to have immediate significance. But a look at the whole of life in its successive stages helps to clarify the specific objectives of the present stage in which one finds oneself.

## SIGNIFICANCE AND TASKS OF STAGES I AND II

It becomes clear that the college or early years of marriage are not the time for investing for old age. They are, rather, the time for learning to handle money wisely, establishing habits of financial responsibility, learning to cooperate in financial matters, and determining what the two are willing to sacrifice and what are the necessities for which they must provide. Newly married couples who have this perspective will try to control their expenditures during the time when they have two incomes, realizing that the situation is likely to be temporary. Rather than getting too deeply involved with time payments for furniture and other things, they can try to build up a little reserve against the time when they may have only one income and be confronted with unexpected expenses.

Clearly, Stage II—the child-bearing stage of life—is the one that places the heaviest financial strain on the average couple. And this stage may come fairly soon after marriage, often within one or two years. If sound spending habits have already been established it will be of great help now. The remainder of our discussion in this and the following chapter will deal with considerations for couples in the first two stages of married living.

## CASH OR CREDIT?

Some couples decide at marriage that they will buy only what they can afford, paying the entire price at the time of purchase. They save until they have the cash to buy one item of furniture at a time, usually planning to live in a furnished apartment or house until they accumulate enough furniture to buy or rent unfurnished housing. Other couples decide that since the credit system in the United States makes buying so easy, there is no reason to wait to own things until they can save enough cash. They may find that they can rent an apartment or house for less money if it is unfurnished, and decide to use the difference to help with time payments on things they want.

Early in marriage, every advantage is on the side of using caution in buying on credit. It is very easy for a couple, even with a good income, to get so deeply into debt that they will have a long, hard struggle to get out of debt.

To quote a wife, married six years and the mother of two children:

> We can have *anything* we want. Our credit is still good. But lately I've wished there wasn't such a thing as an add-on charge account. We've kept buying and adding on and getting farther and farther behind until our payments each month are almost as much as John's whole paycheck. I wake up in the night worrying about what we'll do if one of us gets sick or some sudden expense comes up. John thinks I should go back to work even though it does mean leaving the children with a sitter, and I suppose that's what I'll do. But I know what will happen. We'll keep on buying things—there's plenty that we still need—and all I earn will just go the same way. Things won't get any easier.

An analysis of bankruptcy records in the United States in 1971 by the Family Economics Bureau of the Northwestern Life Insurance Company showed that 90 percent of bankruptcies were by families, not businesses. They found that, typically, the head of the bankrupt family in 1971 was 30 years old, honest and hardworking, with a blue-collar job and a larger than average family. The most common cause for the financial failure was found to be poor money management, usually with overbuying on credit. Other causes of failure were unexpected layoffs, elimination of overtime pay, and unexpected medical bills. An earlier analysis of bankruptcy records in 1966 showed that in a certain proportion of families, a few years after going into bankruptcy—which meant wiping the debt slate clean and starting over—the same families were again in a state of financial crisis although the family head's income had been continuously equal to that of the average working-class family in the same area. Clearly, for these families it was not inability to work or earn money that caused the crisis, but rather failure to manage their income well enough to allow for predictable expenses.[1]

## INSTALLMENT BUYING

The carrying charges one pays for the convenience of buying on credit must be recognized by the buyer as interest. Since the buyer is not usually posting security, except that one does not own the goods until the last payment is made, the carrying charges in terms of interest may be anywhere from 0 to 500 percent. This extra "hidden cost" involved in credit

[1] Robert O. Herman, "Families in Bankruptcy," *Journal of Marriage and the Family* 28:3 (August 1966), 324–30.

buying can add up to a considerable amount of money. Its total can be large enough to make the difference between a fairly comfortable solvency and real financial hardship for the family. A great variety of installment plans are offered to the consumer, and, until the passage of the Truth-in-Lending law in 1968 requiring sellers to state on the sales contract the actual amount of interest being charged, few consumers had any idea what interest rates they were paying on installment purchases. Now buyers can know whether they are agreeing to pay 6 percent, 20 percent, or more. They can consider whether it might be better to borrow elsewhere at lower interest cost.

Before buying on time, the intelligent buyer will also read carefully the terms of the contract. What if he or she cannot make the payments? What does it say about repossession? What about fines for failure to pay? Does the dealer turn the time payment contract over to some other agency? Can a claim be made on goods other than those purchased? Does the purchaser get a rebate on the carrying charge if the total cost is paid before it is due? The buyer should know the answers to these and other questions before signing a time payment contract. Many couples who would not put a second mortgage on their home to borrow the purchase price of an item from a bank or other reputable lending agency will readily buy on terms that are far more expensive.

## USING CHARGE ACCOUNTS

There is little doubt that the best buying policy for the average family for a while after marriage is to buy for cash. This helps them to become realistic about exactly how far money will go and can help prevent overbuying while satisfactory consumer habits are established.

Nevertheless, in the second stage, after there are children and both may be heavily involved with responsibilities, there are some advantages to be found in the wise use of charge accounts. One advantage of charging goods is convenience. If articles have been charged and the buyer finds after getting them home that they are not suitable, it is simple and easy to return them and be given credit. With a charge account, the busy person can phone for information about the articles needed and do much of the routine buying without going to the store. Another advantage is that a complete record of expenditures comes with a bill at the end of the month. Payment is made in a lump sum and record keeping is facilitated.

Of course, the conveniences offered by charge accounts are reflected in the prices paid for goods. The store that charges and delivers and then accepts returned goods that do not suit the customer must be paid for these services. Enough general markup has to be made to allow for the goods that are sometimes returned after being carelessly handled. Sales organizations that accept charges based on credit cards must pay a percentage to the credit card organizations; they therefore add such costs to prices.

One woman said:

> I use the services offered by the stores where we have charge accounts. I never take the time to go to the stores when my shopping can just as well be done by phone or mail. I realize that I pay more for the goods, but we can afford to pay that cost easier than we could afford a second car for shopping or a baby sitter for the children so I could go to shop. The time and energy I save are worth a lot. And, too, my sales resistance is not as good as it should be, and when I buy by telephone or mail, I buy only definite needs. So we think it all balances out.

Another young wife said:

> We don't keep any charge accounts and we have no credit cards because if I can charge, I buy everything I see that I want as I walk through a store, then we have an awful time paying the bills.

If either the husband or the wife cannot resist overbuying when the purchases are to be charged, it is better not to have charge accounts or credit cards.

In making the decision whether to use some charge accounts, a couple or a family must consider their own situation. Can they afford to pay for the services offered by charge accounts? Do they need these services? What about the sales resistance of the family? Have they learned to consider before buying, or is it impossible for them to pass up items that make a momentary appeal? The little boy who said, "I saw a honey of a squirt gun. If I still want it next week I am going to buy it," had already learned that a good way to stretch money is not to buy until one is sure that one really wants or needs the thing that looks so desirable at the moment. All these things enter into whether the family should buy only for cash.

## JUDGING GOODS

When it comes to the actual buying of goods, the family buyer can learn much. In buying foods, it is necessary to read labels carefully and decide for oneself which brands and sizes are best to buy. Not all nationally advertised brands are necessarily the best buys. It is sometimes confusing to find in the same store several different brands of the same canned vegetable with wide variations in price. Many people think that buying one of the higher-priced cans will mean getting better quality. But other factors than quality have a part in determining price, so that paying higher prices does not insure getting the best. If the shopper is in doubt, it is a good plan to buy one of each price level, take them home, and compare them to know the difference. Buyers who do this often make interesting discoveries. Sometimes the lowest-priced can of food, or the medium-priced one, will prove to be of the best all-round quality. Sometimes the smaller carton will actually contain a larger quantity, for despite efforts by the states and the federal government, there has been little effective legal control of deceptive packaging. Unfortunately, the grades, standards, and sizes stamped on food packages are not very enlightening to the buyer. The best solution is to make it a habit to read labels, note weights, observe whether foods are wet-pack or dry-pack, sweetened or unsweetened, and then choose as intelligently as possible, continuing to make tests.

Many of the same considerations apply to buying clothing and household items. A high price does not guarantee quality. Nor is the cheap item necessarily a bargain. Sometimes it is a waste of money to buy the cheapest; it would be better to pay more and have a more durable item. But that is not always so. One must learn to distinguish the good from the shoddy rather than to judge the value of an article by its price. The intelligent buyer will try to judge wisely and make tests. It is wise also to study the published consumer information available from reliable and unbiased sources.

## HELP FOR CONSUMERS

The task of the family shopper who must make the family income go as far as possible has become increasingly complicated. In 1961 a Senate investigating committee was authorized to "examine, investigate, and make a complete study of the nature and extent of trade practices affecting consumers." The testimony at these Senate committee hearings brought out many facts about the problems of the average family shopper. The quantity and variety of merchandise available to shoppers today seem unlimited; techniques of displaying and advertising consumer goods have become highly developed. But many of the advances in marketing techniques are more confusing than helpful to the consumer. There is far too little standardization in packaging. As never before, the shopper should take time to read the fine print. A primary concern is about packaging confusion in the food industry, because expenditures for food have so much importance in the budgets of low-income families.

Since 1962 the federal government has had a Consumers Advisory Council to examine government policy and programs related to consumer needs and help promote the flow of consumer information. Some governors have created in their states the position of Consumer Counsel; they have appointed to these positions persons whose duty it is to make available to consumers helpful information about products for sale and help protect consumers' interests. New regulations regarding automobile safety, meat inspection, tighter control of new drugs, and truth in food packaging were passed in 1967 to protect consumers. One benefit has been to bring about more alertness on the part of the buyers, who are now more aware of the need to look for actual weights on food packages rather than to judge by size of the package, to recognize that such terms as "jumbo size" do not necessarily mean any larger quantity than if no such words appeared, and to read labels carefully instead of assuming that the contents of a package conform to an attractive picture on the label.

For a number of years certain unofficial agencies and organizations have been working to help consumers become better informed. Such an organization is the Consumers Union, which buys on the open market samples of food, clothing, appliances, cars, and most of the other things a family uses, and subjects them to rigid laboratory use tests.[2] CU then publishes ratings and comparative buying information designed to increase the buyer's chances of getting his money's worth. The organization publishes a monthly magazine called *Consumer Reports*, which discusses developments and considerations of special interest to shoppers as well as rating articles and explaining the basis on which the ratings were made. Such publications can be a valuable type of consumer education, whether or not the individual buyer follows the specific buying recommendations.

Since the 1960s Ralph Nader and his group of investigators have been studying many consumer products and presenting their findings to the public. Such crusading in the interests of consumers provokes controversy in our economically oriented society. Nevertheless, the activities of groups like "Nader's Raiders" stimulate buyers to study values, to be aware of pitfalls in buying, and to develop some measure of healthy skepticism regarding advertised products.

## CARE OF GOODS

Proper care of clothing and furniture is an important means of making the money go further. Careful laundering of clothing, dry cleaning, and mending when needed will lengthen the life and add to the good appearance of clothing. Intelligent care should also be taken of various types of woods and materials. Good furniture can become increasingly beautiful with the right care, or it can deteriorate until the family is ashamed of it and wants to replace it. Excellent pamphlets on the care of furniture and clothing are available at little or no cost from the federal government.

## WHEN TO SHOP

Grocery stores usually offer the best prices as well as the best selection of articles on a special day and on the weekend. Most of the grocery buying may well be done once a week when advantage can be taken of better buying opportunities.

2 Consumers Union of U.S., Inc., 256 Washington St., Mount Vernon, N.Y. 10550.

Off-season buying also pays dividends. Winter clothes can be bought more reasonably during the January sales when merchants are anxious to clear their stocks. There are some goods that one would not wish to buy in off seasons because of style changes, but a great many things, particularly children's clothing, can be purchased at these times if foresight is used.

Some goods can be bought *in season* to advantage. This is true of most farm products. Family meals may be planned to take advantage of seasonal buying, when such foods as oranges, grapefruit, lettuce, cabbage, and asparagus are abundant on the market and when the prices are lowest. Canned fruits are often featured in sales during the canning season in late summer and fall. Hence this is the time to buy a supply of canned goods.

## SOME METHODS FOR MAKING THE MONEY STRETCH

1  Take proper care of clothing, household tools, and equipment.

2  Wear suitable clothes for the type of work being done.

3  Learn to use a screwdriver, hammer, saw, pipe wrench, and paintbrush. Although cartoonists enjoy showing the household goods submerged because the man of the house has attempted to fix the plumbing, people with some mechanical aptitude can make worthwhile savings if they learn to make the minor repairs that are regularly required around a house.

4  Work at developing the family's own resources in the matter of recreation. A good time need not be gauged by how much it costs.

5  Families who enjoy such activities as vegetable gardening and canning or freezing foods from their garden or from the markets at certain seasons may save money by these activities.

## WHAT ABOUT BORROWING?

Whatever the attitude of the family toward borrowing money, it is sometimes necessary. Unexpected expenses may arise, such as illness or accident, before there has been an opportunity to accumulate savings. Some who are accumulating savings toward a home or some other major expenditure prefer to borrow to meet unexpected expenses rather than to dip into accumulated savings.

Several sources of credit are open to people who want to borrow. The interest rates charged vary greatly from one agency to another, according to the risks involved in the lending. Some agencies specialize in lending money to high-risk classes of people and therefore charge high rates of interest. The problem for the individual consumer is to find the agency that will lend him money at the lowest rate. It is important to shop carefully before buying credit. Because of a lack of information, many people with a good credit rating pay unnecessarily high interest rates by borrowing money from agencies that specialize in lending to people who have a poor credit rating.

Usually it is cheaper to borrow on property than on a promise to pay. Tangible evidence of ability to repay is worth more to the lender than the borrower's promise. For this reason, agencies that ask the borrower to give collateral can lend money cheaper than those that simply require the borrower's signature. Many people will resist mortgaging the home, car, or furniture to secure a loan, and so will pay unreasonably high rates of interest. Loans that are justifiable and that are not beyond the borrower's ability to repay should be secured as cheaply as possible, even if it does require mortgaging property. If there is danger that the loan cannot be repaid and that the property might be lost, the borrowing should not be done in the first place. Life insurance policies can also be used as collateral. The insured may borrow from the insurance company, or he may deposit his policy with a bank as security for a loan.

## SMALL-LOAN COMPANIES

One of the most highly advertised forms of credit is that offered by small-loan companies. These companies operate under laws enacted to eliminate illegal lenders, but not all states have such laws. In 1916, after a number of years of research on lending practices, the Russell Sage Foundation drafted a Uniform Small Loan Law as a model. The Foundation has constantly revised its original recommendations for the benefit of states who wish to enact fair and up-to-date small-loan laws.

The Uniform Small Loan Law states that those lenders who choose to be licensed under the law may make charges higher than those that are otherwise considered legal, on condition that the lender will submit to rigid regulation and supervision. The recommended law permits the charging of 3½ percent per month on the unpaid balance. Some state laws do not permit an interest rate as high as this; some other states have no small-loan laws to control rates.

Small-loan companies specialize in lending money to borrowers who have little or no security. They may require a chattel mortgage and may take wage assignments as security. But usually all they have as security is the borrower's promise to pay. The rates of interest are extremely high because of the risk involved. Too many people who could borrow from banks, insurance companies, or credit unions borrow from small-loan companies at a rate of interest that they cannot afford to pay.

However, the small-loan companies still serve a useful purpose. People without security could only borrow money through illegal lenders or loan sharks if it were not for these companies. In states with small-loan laws, consumers should make comparisons of the legal lenders, because a legal rate may still be an exorbitant rate.

## CREDIT UNIONS

Credit unions are permitted, by the Federal Credit Union Act, to charge interest at the rate of 1 percent per month on the unpaid balance. Although this rate is higher than those who borrow would pay if they could furnish security and borrow from a bank, it is still a considerably lower rate of interest than they might have to pay through installment buying or to a small-loan company. Credit unions are formed by groups of people who have money to lend, or who wish to borrow relatively small amounts without security.

## COMMERCIAL BANKS

Some commercial banks have set up personal loan departments and, although their interest rates are higher than those charged when the borrower has assets, the rates are usually considerably lower than those of a small-loan company. Table 18-1 tells you at a glance the average rates of interest charged by different types of lending agencies over a period of years. Rates that are federally controlled vary with financial conditions in the country.

TABLE 18-1    Rates per year on consumers' credit

| Financing agency or type of loan | Common charge | Range of charges |
|---|---|---|
| A. Cash lenders | % | % |
| Insurance polices | 6 | 5–6 |
| Credit unions | 12 | 6–12 |
| Industrial banks | 15 | 12–24 |
| Remedial loan societies—other loans | 18 | 15–30 |
| —pledge loans | 24 | 9–36 |
| Commercial bank—personal loans | 12 | 8–36 |
| Consumer finance companies— | | |
| under small-loan laws | 30 | 16–42 |
| Pawnshops | 36 | 24–120 |
| Illegal lenders | 260 | 42–1200 |
| B. Retail installment financing in five states having rate legislation—12-month contract | | |
| New cars | 12 | 8–24 |
| Used cars under two years old | 24 | 9–31 |
| Used cars over two years old | 30 | 9–43 |
| Other commodities | 24 | 9–34 |
| C. Retail installment financing in states without rate legislation—12-month contract | | |
| New cars | 12 | 9–120 |
| Used cars | 40 | 9–275 |

The married couple must necessarily pay for housing either through renting or purchasing property. Some people who are quite well informed on other phases of financial management are naive when it comes to making decisions about what is reasonable or practical to do about housing.

Economists have figured out some practical rules that can be helpful. A rule of thumb that works for the average family is this: Whether renting or buying, the family cannot afford to commit themselves for a monthly housing expense that is more than one week's take-home pay. And "housing expense" means the total: the entire rent if renting, and if buying, the total of all payments, taxes, insurance and other costs one has as a buyer that one does not have as a renter.

Thus, if the family has a take-home salary of $800 a month, the couple could probably afford to pay rent of $200—no more. Or they might safely buy a house on which the monthly payments, without taxes, insurance, or upkeep were about $140.

The purchase of a house is a type of "installment buying" that is in a separate classification from the other installment purchases already discussed. A house, unlike furniture, electrical appliances, or other perishable items that can be bought on credit, will keep a certain value or may increase in value as time passes. For the past 35 years the economic situation has been very favorable in the long run to the home buyer. A house that cost from $6000 to $8000 in 1940 would, in many parts of the country, sell for $40,000 or more in 1977.

It is true that the home buyer who pays down 20 percent of the purchase price of a house and contracts to pay off the mortgage on the remainder over a period of 30 or 35 years will be paying in interest over the entire payment period an amount equal to the price of the house. This interest payment may seem a formidable expense, but buyers must recognize that despite the portion of payments that go for interest, they will still spend no more for housing over the entire payment period than they would pay in rent if they did not buy. And if they buy, the "rent money" is buying and paying for an equity (ownership) that can have permanent value as an investment.

Another practical rule is designed to help home buyers determine what price range they can afford when buying a house. The average family can safely buy a home costing two and a half times the annual income of the family. For example, if their income is $14,000 annually, the family could safely pay between $30,000 and $40,000 for a house.

Some newly married couples who are both working are overly optimistic about their financial situation and assume financial obligations that they cannot possibly meet if it becomes necessary for one of them to stop earning. When future financial commitments are made, therefore, whether for a house, furniture, or other things, the safest policy is to count on only the income that is permanent and likely to increase rather than decrease.

Some couples will buy their home even if they know that they may not choose to stay permanently in the same area. They will plan to sell the equity they have acquired in the property when they decide to move. When housing costs remain stable or continue to inflate, this policy enables people to "get ahead" somewhat sooner financially. Nevertheless, home ownership does involve responsibilities from which the renter is free. All houses require repairs and upkeep; home owners must be willing to give time and attention to such matters and must also have the money to pay for maintenance services which they cannot themselves maintain.

If the decision is to buy rather than to rent, here are some points to consider:

1  Is it better to buy a new house or an older one? Old houses are usually cheaper, have more space inside and outside, are landscaped, and are likely to be in settled neighborhoods with established schools and shopping services. New houses have the latest conveniences in kitchen appliances, heating, and plumbing and may need fewer repairs, but usually are less spacious, and may be less well built than are some older ones. They also may involve extra expense for curtains or carpeting, items which often come as part of the price of an older house. The cost of these things must be added to the original price.

2  Will this house suit the present size and living habits of the family?

3  Is it a house that will sell readily if the family should have to move later? Does it fit in with the other houses in the neighborhood? A house that is noticeably better or worse than others in the neighborhood is harder and less profitable to sell.

4  Is the house structurally sound? Check the roof, the plastering, the floors, the plumbing, and the understucture to see that the house is well built and in good repair. Old houses are often better constructed than some of those being built today. If in doubt about construction, have the house inspected by a city housing inspector to see that it meets necessary code requirements.

5  Does the electrical wiring meet present-day standards? Many older houses will need rewiring in order to carry the load of the appliances used today by the average family.

6  What about the heating system? Some old houses will need heating system repairs, and in some new houses the system may be inadequate for heating the entire house.

7  In many parts of the country, it is important to check for termites and other wood-destroying organisms. An expert will usually do the inspecting for a set fee, and the offer to buy can be contingent upon correction of any existing damage at the seller's expense. Some state and local laws require termite inspection when property is sold.

8  Is there room for an expanding family? Could another room be added as the family grows? Are there adequate closets? Is the room arrangement convenient?

**9**  Is the price right and are the conditions of sale reasonable? How much would a bank lend to help finance the house? The amount the bank will lend is a clue to whether the price is right. Are the payments low enough so that unforeseen expenses could still be met? Is the interest rate on the mortgage in line with current interest rates?

**10**  Is it necessary to pay the price asked? Most old houses and some new houses have two prices, the asking price and the price at which the house will sell. The asking price is usually from one thousand to several thousand dollars above the expected selling price. The actual price to be paid will depend on how many houses are on the market at the time, and whether the buyer has had experience in buying a house. Those buying a house for the first time are often uninformed about the pricing system in real estate dealings.

**11**  Is the title to the property clear? Any offer to buy should be contingent upon guarantee of a clear title. A qualified real estate firm will usually protect the interests of both the buyer and the seller, but the buyer should make sure this is done.

## OUTLINE FOR SELF-STUDY: ECONOMIC VALUES

To examine your own attitudes about money and its handling, think through the following outline. If you are engaged or married, it is suggested that the two of you go through the outline together and assess your agreement and your ability to cooperate in matters involving money.

### I  YOUR VALUES AND SPENDING HABITS

**1**  If an outsider were to judge by the way your parents spend their money, what would be the conclusion about your family's values? Would this same pattern of value exist among your grandparents? Aunts and uncles?

**2**  In general, does your family's way with money seem right and satisfactory to you, or do you disagree with some of their values or their financial habits?

**3**  As you think of how you spent your allowance or money you have earned, what things do you seem to value most? When you are short of money, what things do you sacrifice first?

**4**  Do you usually think it over before making a major purchase or do you "buy at sight"?

**5**  Compare your spending habits with the spending habits of your three best friends, or your fiancé or spouse. Does the comparison show a difference in basic values? If so, how much could you change if change seems desirable?

**6**  Do you prefer to buy on credit an item you want and do you enjoy it while you pay for it, or do you enjoy more the things that you wait to have until you can pay cash for them?

**7**  Do you have a tendency to go without things that you need or want, even if you might be able to afford them?

**8**  How many times have you bought things that you did not need, or that you did not use after you had bought them? How did you feel about the purchase?

**9**  When you have paid a high price for a possession, do you feel better about the item than you would if you got it as a bargain? Or do you get more pleasure out of your "bargains"?

**10**  If you had to borrow $3000, would you prefer to borrow it from a bank, a loan company, or a relative? How would you feel about paying the same interest rate to each of the three sources?

**11**  Some people are "compulsive spenders." That is, they cannot resist spending whatever money they have available at any given time, since the act of spending gives them pleasure. At the opposite extreme are people who hate to part with money even for necessities. It is keeping and accumulating money that gives them pleasure. In between are those who see money simply as a useful commodity; they spend or save according to a rational plan based on needs. Try to classify yourself in relation to these three types.

**II**  ASSUME THAT YOU ARE MARRIED AND YOUR TAKE-HOME PAY IS $800 PER MONTH. MAKE OUT A BUDGET FOR TWO. INCLUDE SPECIFIC AMOUNTS FOR ALL OF THE FOLLOWING THAT YOU CONSIDER NECESSARY IN A FAMILY BUDGET. IF YOUR MONEY WILL NOT COVER EVERYTHING, ON WHICH ITEMS COULD YOU SPEND LESS?

| | | |
|---|---|---|
| 1 | Rent and utilities (heat, electricity and gas, telephone, water) | $_____ |
| 2 | Groceries | _____ |
| 3 | Clothing | _____ |
| 4 | Furnishings for the home | _____ |
| 5 | Insurance: life, car, illness, home | _____ |
| 6 | Recreation | _____ |
| 7 | Gifts to charity, friends, relatives | _____ |
| 8 | Taxes | _____ |
| 9 | Transportation | _____ |
| 10 | Auto expenses: gasoline, payments, repairs | _____ |
| 11 | Savings and investments | _____ |
| 12 | Miscellaneous expenses: cleaning and laundry, haircuts, dues, subscriptions | _____ |
| 13 | Medical and dental care (not covered by insurance) | _____ |
| 14 | Others, specify _____ | _____ |
| | Total | _____ |

## REVIEW QUESTIONS

**1**  What are the basic factors making for misunderstanding between husband and wife over the use of money? Give three illustrations.

**2**  Why do attitudes toward the spending habits of the spouse sometimes seem to change after marriage?

3   What is the real purpose of a budget?

4   What are three common family patterns of controlling the family purse?

5   Give some arguments in favor of the wife's having the major responsibility for handling family finances.

6   List and distinguish between the different stages in the family's financial life cycle.

7   What are some financial errors easily made by couples in the first stage?

8   Why is Stage II difficult for many families?

9   What are the chief advantages and disadvantages of buying on a cash basis? Of using charge accounts?

10   What agencies have been organized for the specific purpose of protecting the consumer?

11   What are the questions a couple should consider before they borrow money?

12   How do you explain the fact that people will shop around for groceries but not for credit?

13   What questions should a buyer ask before buying goods on an installment contract?

14   Where does one usually pay a higher interest rate, at a bank or on an installment contract?

15   What are small-loan companies? How are they controlled?

16   Why are small-loan companies permitted by state laws to charge such high interest rates?

17   What are the small-loan regulations in your state?

18   Where can one usually borrow money at the lowest rate of interest?

19   What are the chief causes of family bankruptcies?

## PROJECTS AND ACTIVITIES

1   *Role playing.* John is a generous spender. Scenes:

a.   During their engagement, John has just presented Mary with an expensive ring upon which he has made a down payment. He hopes to have it paid for by the time they marry.

b.   After five years of marriage, two children, and many unpaid debts, John brings Mary an expensive dress as a gift.

2   *Special reports.* (a) Give a general, overall report on the method and work of Consumers Union. (b) From a recent issue of *Consumer Reports* give the findings and ratings on some consumer goods.

3   Report on the progress in your state in providing a program or laws designed to protect the consumer.

4   Have a student "shop" with all the lending agencies in town to see where one can borrow money and at what interest rates. Report findings to the class.

5   Mr. A. wants to buy a new television set but does not have the cash. He decides to borrow the money. He consults all lending agencies in his community in shopping for the credit. Play the role of Mr. A. and ask all the questions he should ask each lender.

# BUYING LIFE INSURANCE

The family's program of spending for insurance is an important phase of family finance. A wisely planned insurance program can guarantee security for the dependent members of the family in case of misfortune. However, unwise expenditures for insurance can complicate the financial problems of families and leave them without protection at a time when they most need it. The average couple beginning their married life believe that they should have some insurance but they find it difficult to determine the best of the many types of insurance policies for which they should obligate themselves. They may be inclined to buy insurance from the first salesman who approaches them and to buy whatever policy the agent recommends.

The insurance needs of a family vary with each stage of life. Insurance needs in Stages I and II, as these financial life cycle stages were outlined in the preceding chapter, are considerably different from the insurance needs of the family in the later stages of life. There are several basic classifications into which the various types of insurance policies logically fall, and certain of the classifications of insurance are far more appropriate for the first two stages of life than for the later years.

Young married couples who have small children or who will soon start a family are not ordinarily in a position to look upon insurance as an investment for the future. They must plan in terms of buying the largest amount of immediate protection for their security at the lowest cost in dollars. The time when they can better afford to think of insurance as an investment is in the later stages of life. However, as we will discuss later, insurance should never be thought of as a way to "invest" money, at any stage of life. It should be thought of as a "service" you pay for to protect the family in case of a loss.

## INSURANCE AS PROTECTION, NOT INVESTMENT

The protective function of insurance is simply to provide an income for the dependents who would be left without support if the wage earner should die or become disabled.

For some reason, it is hard for people to look at life insurance as they look at home or car insurance. The average family insures the house for a period of three to five years. If no fire or other disaster occurs, they are thankful, and they do not waste time on regrets that they had no cash return to show for the insurance. They bought protection, which meant that they could leave the house with the confidence that if catastrophe struck they would have the means to secure another home. It is with the same attitude that they insure the car against fire, theft, or collision. They consider the money well spent for *protection* and do not regret that they have had no occasion to collect on the insurance. It is this principle on which life insurance bought on the wage earner of the young family should also be judged.

A reason for the tendency to think of life insurance as an investment as much as protection is that there was a time in the history of our country when the value of the dollar was relatively stable. People could buy a $5000 endowment insurance policy and have confidence that they would be paid $5000 of the same value 30 years in the future. They received their money back with approximately 3½ percent interest when the endowment matured. However, during the past 35 years the value of the dollar has decreased greatly. The man who took out a $5000 35-year endowment policy in 1942 to mature at his retirement in 1977 would be paid the $5000, but that amount would be worth only about $700 in terms of the purchasing power of the dollar in 1977. People who put their investments in such tangible property as real estate or stocks have seen their investments snowball in value, whereas those who placed their investment dollars in insurance have seen their investments become almost worthless in terms of today's dollars. The family who bought a $5000 home in 1942 would find its value had increased to $30,000 or more by 1977. Most economic authorities today believe that the inflationary trend of the past 35 years will not be reversed. If inflation continues or is not reversed, young wage earners today should spend their insurance money to buy immediate protection for their dependents in case of the death of the wage earners, and keep the investment part of their financial planning separate.

## ORDINARY INSURANCE

Most readers of this book will be interested in what is called ordinary insurance. Ordinary insurance includes four basic kinds of policies: (1) term, (2) whole or straight life, (3) limited payment life, and (4) endowment. The classification is used to distinguish these policies from industrial and group insurance.

**Term insurance.** Two basic types of term insurance are sold today—
"level term" and "decreasing term." Level term insurance is written for
a certain specified length of time—one, five, or ten years—and the
premiums are figured on the probability of the individual's dying during
that period. At the end of the period the insurance can be renewed for
additional terms up to the age of 65 or 70 without medical examination.
If the insurance is renewed, the premium is slightly higher, since the
insured is older and the chance of dying is greater than during the
previous period. Decreasing term insurance is usually written for a period
of 20, 30, or 40 years; the premiums remain the same for the entire period,
but the amount of protection decreases gradually until there is no protection at the end of the period. The young person should not buy a policy
that decreases too rapidly since he or she will need maximum protection
up to approximately age 45. Term insurance does not contain any saving
principle; it is bought for precisely the reason that car insurance is
bought—protection.

Term insurance is the most practical buy for the young family. Next
to group insurance, the insured gets the most protection for money spent,
since he or she is paying solely for protection and paying only at the
rate of his or her present death risk. This type of insurance makes it
possible for the young person with a limited income to provide very well
for dependents in case of his or her death. Those who have debts can
carry enough insurance to cover the debts, with a minimum outlay in

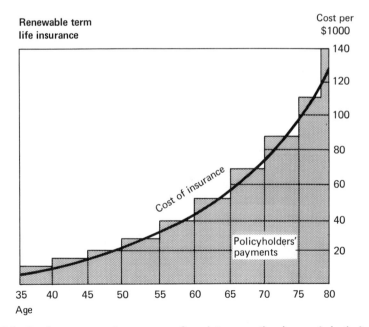

FIG. 19–1  Premiums on term insurance are figured to cover the chance of death for the
present age of the insured. Each renewal calls for higher premiums.

premiums. Under present economic conditions, the young family head, rather than starting a permanent insurance program featuring savings, might well take out term insurance for the first 20 years of marriage and wait to see what happens to the value of the dollar. Then he or she can convert to other policies if the currency has stabilized.

The term policy gives maximum protection at minimum cost during the years when the family is most dependent and would suffer most if the wage earner died. As children leave home and there is no longer need for so much protection, some of the term policies can be dropped. Only the protection needed at any one stage of life should be paid for.

In the last 20 years the proportion of term insurance sold has jumped from 33 to 61 percent of total insurance sold. One insurance authority who has studied life insurance from the buyer's point of view has concluded: "In most instances term insurance should be used to provide not only for temporary needs, but also for those more permanent requirements, a part of which may continue to exist during the policyholder's productive years. The flexibility of renewable term insurance and its low premium outlay fully warrant its predominant use under today's economic conditions in all well-planned life insurance programs." [1]

**Whole or straight life policies.** The whole life policyholder pays a fixed premium each year as long as he or she lives, and the insurance company agrees to pay the face value of the policy upon death. The policy has been set up to distribute the cost of the protection through the lifetime of the insured, eliminating the necessity for progressively higher premiums as the insured grows older. For a young man, the premiums are higher than would be necessary to cover the cost of protection at his age; for an older man, they are lower. Although the face value of the policy is not payable until death—unless the insured lives to be 96, when all whole life policies endow—the insured may at any time withdraw the cash or loan value of the policy. Whole life policies have a cash or loan value chiefly because the younger people in the insured group pay higher premiums than are required by the mortality risk at their age.

This policy distributes the cost over the lifetime of the individual and is a permanent plan of insurance for the dependents of the insured. A disadvantage of whole life insurance is that for young people with several dependents it provides less protection for the money. The same amount of money spent on term insurance would provide more than twice as much protection. Another disadvantage is that the savings aspect of the policy is unsound in today's economy; the policy may well be of far less value in 25 years than the money that has been put into it.

[1] *Life Insurance and Annuities from the Buyer's Point of View* (Great Barrington, Mass.: The American Institute for Economic Research, 1966), p. 14.

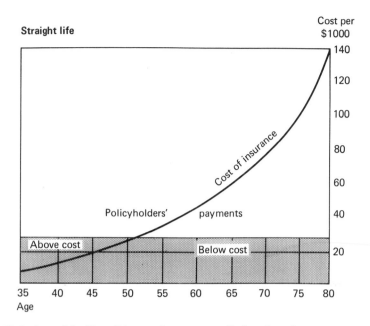

Straight life

Cost per $1000

Cost of insurance

Policyholders' payments

Above cost

Below cost

Age: 35  40  45  50  55  60  65  70  75  80

Cost per $1000: 140  120  100  80  60  40  20

FIG. 19–2  In straight life policies premium costs are distributed so that a young man pays more than is necessary for protection. As he grows older, however, he will pay less than is necessary for protection.

**Limited payment policies.**  All limited payment policies are modifications of the whole life plan. The total cost of the insurance is paid in 10, 20, or 30 years instead of throughout the lifetime of the insured. This type of policy is suitable for those few people who have high earnings for a few years early in life but whose earning power is likely to decrease rather than to increase. Such people as professional athletes or entertainers with peak incomes only in certain years may buy fast-paying-up policies during their period of especially high income. Limited payment policies are not advisable for the college-educated professional person whose income reaches its peak in middle age or beyond. For the average family, the great disadvantage of this kind of insurance is that during the years when the dependency load is greatest, the insured is paying large premiums and yet is providing little protection for the dependents. Term or whole life policies would give the family more protection when they need it most.

**Endowment insurance.**  Many people buy endowment insurance because they feel that it is one policy on which the insured can collect. The endowment policy emphasizes savings rather than protection. Endowment policies usually run for periods of from 10 to 30 years, with the

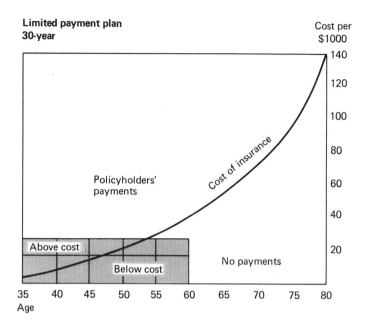

**Limited payment plan 30-year**

Cost per $1000

Policyholders' payments

Cost of insurance

Above cost

Below cost

No payments

Age

35  40  45  50  55  60  65  70  75  80

140
120
100
80
60
40
20

FIG. 19–3 With limited payment policies, premiums are figured so that one pays the total costs of insurance during the most productive years.

provision that if the insured dies during the period, the beneficiaries will receive the face value of the policy. If the insured outlives the contract, the face value will be paid to the insured. What the company actually does is to take out a decreasing term policy to cover the life of the insured in case of death. The rest of the money is invested. If the insured does not die, the term policy is canceled and the insured is paid the face value of the policy.[2] Endowment insurance is "temporary" insurance that emphasizes savings. At the end of the term, the individual has no insurance, since the policy is canceled and the insurance company keeps the profit it has made on the insured person's money.

We should emphasize that endowment insurance is largely for the person who wishes to use insurance as an investment. All other types of insurance will provide more protection for a comparable amount of money. The young man or woman 22 years old, for an annual premium of $100, could have $19,500 in protection in a 5-year renewable and convertible term policy, but only $2200 in protection with a 20-year endowment policy (see Table 19-1).

[2] Some companies write participating endowment policies in which the insured gets the $1000 face value of the policy plus additional earnings.

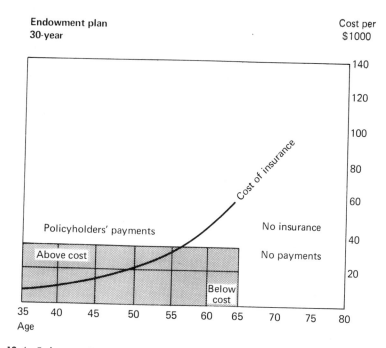

Endowment plan
30-year

Cost per
$1000

Policyholders' payments

Above cost

No insurance

No payments

Below cost

Cost of insurance

Age

FIG. 19–4  Endowment insurance calls for high premiums for a limited period.

## SHOULD INSURANCE ALSO BE "SAVINGS"?

The person who thinks of buying such insurance as whole or straight life and endowment policies as a means of investment or of accumulating savings might better consider another plan for his investments. One might better take out a decreasing term policy for protection and, instead of having the company invest the money, personally invest the difference between what the term policy and what the policies featuring investments would cost. If a person knows how to invest wisely, the long-term return is likely to be far greater than it would have been had he or she permitted the insurance company to do the investing. The insurance company makes investments that keep up with inflation, but their profitable investment gain is not passed on to the policyholders. The difference between the cost of a straight life policy and renewable decreasing term, if invested each year at 6 percent, would give equal protection through the years, and the insured person, at age 65, would have built up a far larger retirement fund than the whole or straight life policy would provide.

Those selling insurance feel that the insurance company is better qualified to invest money than is the individual. They recognize that insurance is not a profitable investment for the buyer, especially in times of inflation. Companies are now considering what they can do to take care of problems of inflation and deflation for the insured. Some consideration has been given to paying annuities or benefits in terms of the value of the dollar at the time due. This is the only way the insurance buyer could get real protection for the future.

Insurance agents also argue that, if people are not forced to save, many of them will not do so, and that therefore the compulsive nature of the endowment insurance contract is a benefit. They support their position by pointing out that in the great majority of cases life insurance is the only savings middle- and low-income families have been able to accumulate. There is some validity to their arguments, since some families do need a "crutch" to help them save. However, many different ways are now available. Automatic payroll deductions, monthly investment plans, automatic transfer of a fixed sum from checking to savings account, and monthly investment in mutual funds are only a few of the many ways that help people save.

The insurance agents' argument that insurance results in forced savings is not necessarily sound because, when financial reverses come, the majority of people with low incomes are forced to drop their insurance. The lapse rate on ordinary policies in commercial companies was approximately one-third of the new policies written in 1936. A more recent study examined records of policies purchased in 1949. The study followed the records for nine years and found that 12 percent of the purchasers had let their policies lapse within two years; by the ninth year, 23 percent had cashed in their policies. This was during a boom period in the economy.

The "forced savings" argument is not sound because, when policies are cashed in within the first three years, everything is lost—no "cash value" accumulates in that time. The premiums for this period go largely to the agent selling the policy and for administrative costs in setting up a new policy. If the money had been invested in another form of "forced savings" such as government bonds, there would be no loss for the person who had to withdraw savings. The facts about the lapse rate of insurance policies among families with moderate or low incomes emphasize the necessity that the family should make the most economical and practical choice when buying insurance. The probability, then, of having to drop insurance under the pressure of financial difficulties is decreased.

## GROUP INSURANCE

Group insurance covers more people today than any other type of insurance written. It is insurance written upon groups of people having a common employer such as a university or college or a unit of government. People in the military service, federal employees, and members of unions and other such groups are usually eligible for group insurance. The insurance is term insurance on a year-to-year basis, written without physical examination, and the costs are usually shared by the employer and the employee. Group insurance is a very good buy for the many people eligible for it. The premiums are low, since it is term insurance and because the "handling costs" are low. Handling costs can be kept low because the company employing the insured worker pays the premiums in a lump sum, one policy is written to cover the entire group, physical examinations are eliminated, and commissions paid for selling the insurance are low.

The maximum amount of insurance the employees can carry is set, and when they leave such employment they must convert to some other policy. They can usually do this, within a specified time limit, without a physical examination. Most people will want to take advantage of group insurance if it is available to them; it is a good supplement to any regular insurance program.

## BUYING INSURANCE ON CHILDREN

Parents who wish to provide for their children's college education often consider taking out an endowment policy on each child to mature when the child is ready for college. Some insurance companies specialize in this type of insurance for parents of young children. Authorities on family insurance are agreed that any insurance to provide for the education of a child *should be placed on the one who will be responsible for paying for the education of the child and not on the child to be educated.* If one parent should die before the child reached college age, the other might find it impossible to keep up the insurance payments on the child, and there would be little guarantee of a college education. The best endowment for the child's education would be term insurance on the wage earner's life together with a program of systematic saving, so that whether one parent lives or dies, funds will be provided for the education

TABLE 19-1          What $100 a year will buy in insurance protection (approximate amounts)

|  | Amount of Ins. $100 a year will buy |
|---|---|
| Term (5-year renewable & convertible) | $19,500 |
| Term (10-year convertible, nonrenewable) | 19,300 |
| Straight Life | 7,000 |
| Life-Paid-Up-at-65 | 6,250 |
| Modified Life (5 years) | 6,000 |
| Family Income (20 years) | 5,600 |
| Endowment at 65 | 5,400 |
| 20-Payment Life | 4,100 |
| Retirement Income at 65 | 3,960 |
| 20-Year Endowment | 2,200 |

of the child. Many families are not aware of this sound principle in buying insurance.

## COSTS OF INSURANCE

It is almost impossible for the consumer to compare costs of insurance. The claim is made that competition between companies keeps the cost of insurance about the same in all of them. The Temporary National Economic Committee's study of insurance companies, however, showed that the net cost for the same protection varied in different companies from $36.20 to $133.94. The American Institute for Economic Research found that two companies had very different administrative expenses; for one the cost was $4.63, and for the other $9.52 per $1000 of insurance.[3] The cost of insurance varies according to the size and age of the company and its ability to invest funds, to administer the company efficiently, and to keep mortality expenses down through wise selection of insurees.

The insurance consumer is often confused when he tries to compare costs. He or she learns that in a mutual company one will pay a high premium but receive a dividend each year, whereas in a joint-stock company one will pay a low premium and receive no dividend. In the mutual company, the insured pays more than necessary and the company simply returns the overpayment in the form of a dividend. The insured should not be misled by dividends; what one really should know is the net cost in different companies. A careful analysis was made of the net costs in many different companies operating in the United States to determine how much costs vary from company to company for the same policy.[4] All factors were taken into consideration in computing the net costs in the different companies. For the ordinary life policy, the 20-year net cost at age 35 for $1000 protection varied from $110 in the least expensive company to $208 in the most expensive company. Table 19-2 summarizes the approximate costs of various ordinary insurance policies per $1000 of insurance.

## DETERMINING NEEDS

Because of differing needs, it is impossible to lay down universal rules on how much insurance each person should buy. In determining individual specific needs, one should take into consideration (1) age, (2) debts, (3) dependents, (4) present earnings, (5) possible future earnings, and, if married, (6) earning ability of the spouse. People in their teens or early twenties without debts or dependents need not be much concerned about taking out insurance.

As obligations become greater and as dependents increase, the in-

---

[3] *Life Insurance and Annuities from the Buyer's Point of View,* p. 39.
[4] Ibid., p. 49.

BUYING LIFE INSURANCE

TABLE 19-2    What various policies cost

| Type of policy | Age at which policy is issued | | | | | |
| --- | --- | --- | --- | --- | --- | --- |
| | 20 | 21 | 22 | 23 | 24 | 25 |
| Five-Year Term | $ 5.65 | $ 5.70 | $ 5.80 | $ 5.90 | $ 6.00 | $ 6.10 |
| (Renewable and convertible) | | | | | | |
| Ten-Year Term | 6.80 | 6.90 | 7.00 | 7.10 | 7.20 | 7.30 |
| (Renewable and convertible) | | | | | | |
| Straight Life | 14.15 | 14.50 | 14.85 | 15.25 | 15.65 | 16.10 |
| Life-Paid-Up at 65 | 16.20 | 16.60 | 17.10 | 17.60 | 18.15 | 18.70 |
| 20-Payment Life | 25.85 | 26.30 | 26.75 | 27.25 | 27.75 | 28.30 |
| Retirement income at 65 (male) | 25.50 | 26.30 | 27.15 | 28.05 | 29.05 | 30.15 |
| 20-Year Endowment | 46.95 | 47.00 | 47.05 | 47.10 | 47.15 | 47.20 |

surance program should be suitably adjusted, as discussed in the section on term insurance. If the wife has special training that would make it possible for her to support herself and the children if her husband should die, less protection may be necessary than in cases where it would be a hardship for the wife to provide for herself and the dependents.

As a couple become established, they can consider permanent investments. If they have taken out five- or ten-year renewable and convertible term insurance policies in their twenties, they may, in their early forties, wish to convert some of these policies to permanent insurance such as whole life policies. If their dependency load is no longer heavy, they may wish to drop some of the term insurance at this time since it has served its purpose. The need then will be for savings or for an annuity for support in old age, rather than for protection for dependents.

Figure 19-5 shows the consumption unit responsibility of the male head in the average American family from age 20 to 62. This is a concrete way of picturing the succeeding stages in the family's financial life cycle. An "adult consumption unit" is the amount spent a year for food, clothing, shelter, medical care, recreation, and other items by an average adult male. At age 20, the average American family head is supporting slightly more than one unit. This responsibility gradually increases until age 39, when a maximum of 3.75 units are being supported. After age 39, the family responsibility gradually decreases as the children take over their own support. Some companies are now writing family policies that combine a straight life policy with a term policy. The term part of the policy is gradually decreased and finally dropped when the family is grown; the straight life part continues for life. The combination of straight life policy and decreasing term policy is sound. But many companies are promoting a "family-style" policy that covers all family members. These policies usually protect the husband with a straight life or endowment policy and the wife and children with term policies that are decreased and dropped or become convertible as the children get older. Such a "family-style" policy violates sound insurance principles by placing almost

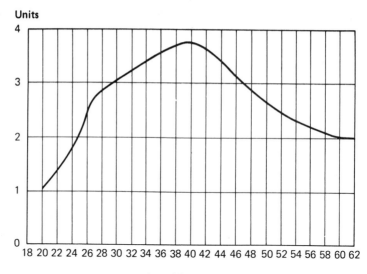

**Units**

**Age of family head**

FIG. 19–5 Consumption units in the average American family according to age of male family head. Insurance purchased would provide maximum protection when the wage earner has the greatest consumption unit responsibility.

half the protection on the wife and children rather than on the wage earner. It is well to remember when considering any insurance plan that *the average family needs no insurance on children and little, if any, on the wife; all available insurance money should be spent on the one who is the permanent support of the family.*

## WHERE TO BUY INSURANCE

After people have carefully considered their present needs and future prospects, they are ready to consider where best to buy insurance. Buyers should choose an agent with whom they wish to deal after selecting the company from which they wish to buy insurance, rather than following the too common practice of buying at random from the first or the most personable agent who approaches. It must be remembered that our discussion is for the majority of people who have limited incomes or who want to have the most for their money. People with ample funds may spend conspicuously and wastefully for insurance as for other items, without serious results.

The next step is to consider where the most protection can be bought at lowest cost. If the individuals are eligible to take out insurance with some special group, it will be to their advantage to do so. In addition to group insurance available for workers in business or industrial organizations, there are provisions for other special groups. Examples are the

Teachers Insurance and Annuity Association of America,[5] which was endowed by the Carnegie Corporation to make it possible to sell insurance to teachers without profit, with the overhead being paid by the endowment, and the Presbyterian Ministers' Fund, which offers insurance to all Protestant ministers, their spouses, and students of the ministry. The cost of life insurance written for any special group is usually low. A person living in Massachusetts, Connecticut, or New York may go to any bank and buy Savings Bank Life Insurance at a very low rate because the profit motive has been removed by eliminating salespeople and the overhead of an insurance company.

**The life insurance agent.** People who are not eligible to buy insurance through any group plan should seek an agent of a life insurance company. When talking with agents, it is well to remember several things. In the first place, the agency method of selling insurance emphasizes chiefly one thing—selling. In the companies with the best standards, agents are carefully selected on the basis of personality and are then trained to become masters in the art of salesmanship. The agent's business is to sell insurance, not to be an expert adviser on general family finances. Naturally, a successful agent can be expected to push the types of policies that sell best and return the highest commission.

The American College of Life Underwriters was organized to ensure that qualified people enter the insurance field. Those who successfully pass the examinations given by this organization are recognized by the designation C.L.U. (Chartered Life Underwriter). Approximately 2 percent of life insurance agents are C.L.U. people.

Some insurance companies have a good training program for agents before they are permitted to sell insurance. Other companies encourage their agents to take in-service courses to qualify them for their work.

An agent may be sincere in recommending a certain policy, but it is up to the buyers to determine wisely for themselves what policy will meet their personal needs. They should not feel that they must buy from the first agent with whom they discuss the matter, any more than they must buy the first house a real estate agent shows them or the first car an auto salesman demonstrates. Intelligent buyers will shop for insurance just as they shop for anything else that involves a commitment to long-term financial expenditures. Careful buyers will not buy a policy until they have asked the agent to submit the plan in writing so that it can be studied. Then they will be able to compare the policies of the several companies under consideration and can avoid haste in buying. One should certainly never buy any policy that he or she does not clearly

[5] For information write, Teachers Insurance and Annuity Association of America, 730 Third Avenue, New York, N.Y. 10017.

understand. Before buying any policy one should also check on the rating of the company.

## CONFUSION ARISING FROM POLICY LABELS

In recent years insurance companies have coined many new labels for policies. Advertisements list the Family Income Policy, Modified Life, the Benefactor Policy, the Family Protection Policy, the Newlywed Policy, the Extra Protection Policy, and many others. These labels may confuse some consumers of insurance, making it more difficult to know what is the most suitable insurance. Actually, there are still only four basic types of ordinary insurance policies: term, straight or whole life, limited payment life, and endowment. Every other type of policy is a variation or combination of these.

## PREFERRED RISK

In buying insurance, it is well for buyers to determine if they are in a "preferred risk" group. Many of the readers of this text are in a preferred risk group because they have or will have a college education, they are in good health, and they will enter a profession. Many life insurance companies now issue straight life policies for a special "minimum face amount" and "preferred risk." The minimum policy may range from $5000 up to $25,000. The policy costs less because of the lower-risk group insured, because the agent gets a low commission, and because it is cheaper to write the larger policies.

Some companies now recognize the fact that women are a lower risk group than men and offer policies for women at reduced premiums based on their longer life expectancy. Companies also offer lower rates to non-smokers than to cigarette smokers because of the nonsmoker's greater life expectancy.

## BUYING INSURANCE WHILE A COLLEGE STUDENT

College students are a special risk group; their mortality rates are so low that insurance companies can afford to insure them at lower costs than they can the general population. However, college students as a group have less need for insurance than any other segment of the population. Because old-line insurance companies recognize this, they do not push special sales of insurance on college campuses. They are critical of the few insurance companies that see college students as a tempting market for sales and that do assign especially trained agents to sell insurance on campuses.

Many students, approached for the first time by sellers of insurance, buy policies that are unsuitable, that serve no useful purpose, and that are an unnecessary added expense. The following points should be considered by students who are beginning to think of their future insurance needs and plans:

**1**  No item, whatever its price, is a "bargain" if it can serve no purpose for the buyer. The fact that insurance companies can offer low rates to students is irrelevant because, unless the students have debts or dependents, they do not need insurance.

**2**  Any insurance policy should be designed to meet the specific buyer's needs, and an individual college junior's or senior's insurance needs have nothing to do with whether ten members of the class of 1976 of dear old Alma Mater (whose pictures the agent may show) bought the insurance. Any such sales approach should be suspect. The seller may appear to be a wonderful person and a pleasant companion who may wine and dine the prospective buyer, but that is no reason to buy insurance. The seller who is offering something the buyer needs and ought to be able to pay for is not obliged to resort to such selling tactics.

**3**  Students with no dependents should not commit themselves for unnecessary future expenditures. That the offer is made to let the student "buy now and pay later" has no relevance. No saving is accomplished by buying at a younger age; there is actually only a very slight increase in the premium rate between ages 20 and 25 (see Table 2); the person who takes out straight life insurance at 20 and pays until age 65 will pay the same total amount as the one who takes out the same policy at 25 and pays until age 65. There is no reason to buy insurance before it is needed and before it is known what the dependency load or real insurance needs will be.

The "buy now–pay later" plan is no more desirable for newly married students than for the single student. If the newly married couple cannot pay the cost now, they will be even less able to next year or the following year, after a baby has been born to them. For newly married students who are self-supporting, the only logical insurance needed is a minimum of term insurance, which can be increased later as needed.

**4**  The student years are not the time to consider any kind of endowment policy or policy involving "investment." At this stage of life, young people are actually making a major investment by spending money for education that will increase their permanent earning power. For a number of years after graduation, most people need maximum protection for their dependents and, during these years, their earning power is not as great as it will be later. Investment responsibilities can be met as earning power increases.

**5**  The college years are not the time for either men or women to buy any kind of *permanent* insurance. For most college students or graduates still in their 20s, insurance plans should be flexible so they can be adjusted to meet changing life situations. The college girl who is told by an insurance seller, as some have reported being told, that she will find it easier to "get a man" if she has her own insurance should realize that obligating herself or a hypothetical husband to keeping up insurance she does not need could hinder rather than help her prospects!

It might seem that today's students would be well enough informed so that they could not be persuaded to buy unneeded insurance policies.

However, 40 percent of all insurance sold by one life insurance company is now sold to students. A study of a national sample of young people between the ages of 14 and 22 in 1971 found that almost half had life insurance on themselves.

Some insurance companies see students as an available market and have stepped up efforts within the past few years in college communities. Some companies that formerly approached only seniors now are promoting sales to all academic class levels. In some university communities, personable young men who were formerly campus leaders are recruited as salesmen. They may live near campus, become a permanent part of campus groups, and, in a sense, assume the role of "financial adviser" to students. Various kinds of pressure tactics are used by some unscrupulous salesmen to persuade students to buy. Since the passage of the Twenty-sixth Amendment, students report having been reminded by a salesman that they are now adults since they are past 18, and so should not consult their parents or other experienced advisers about a possible purchase such as life insurance. In some cases, students who protest that they cannot afford such insurance at this point are encouraged to sign notes for future payments. Such notes are now legally binding on anyone over 18 years old, and some students who later regret having signed up under pressure are sued for collection of the notes.[6]

## PAYING PREMIUMS

The buyer will have a choice of payment premiums quarterly, semi-annually, or annually. The privilege of paying quarterly or semi-annually will add to the cost of the policy. On a $10,000 whole life policy, the extra charge per year will be between $10 and $20 if the buyer pays quarterly.

If one cannot make payments annually, it may be more economical to take out policies for smaller amounts and have them dated so that they come due at different times of the year. If one has $10,000 insurance protection, it might be an advantage to have two $5000 policies, one due each six months. This also has another advantage if the policy is term insurance. One policy can be dropped when it has served its usefulness. Some of the special policies are issued in minimum amounts of $5000, $10,000, or $20,000, and usually cost less than policies issued in smaller amounts.

## BENEFICIARIES

Some people contemplating marriage have insurance policies in force that were purchased for them when they were children. These policies

[6] For a consideration of insurance selling to students, see "Life Insurance on Campus: Caveat Emptor," *Consumer Reports* 37:1 (January 1972), 50–51. *Consumer Reports* is planning a longer report on all aspects of life insurance in a forthcoming issue.

are likely to be industrial endowment policies taken out to provide for their college education. The parents are usually the beneficiaries named on the policy. If the person marries and the policy is still in force, the question arises: Should the spouse be named as beneficiary, and when should this change be made? Since the parents have paid for the policy, the individual may feel that it would not be right to make the spouse the beneficiary.

If the son or daughter is still in debt to the parents for a college education or for other reasons, it might be well to continue the parents as beneficiaries until the debt is paid; that is, if it is a debt for which the parents expect payment. If there is no recognized debt, then old or new policies taken out for either person should be changed to make the spouse the beneficiary. Since marriage is a joint venture—a partnership in material things as well as in love—the beneficiaries should be changed at the time of marriage. There is no point in waiting months or years to take care of this important detail. Sometimes couples hestitate to change the beneficiary because they still feel obligated to their parents. A part of mature development after marriage is recognizing that one's first obligation is to the spouse and not to parents. For spouses to change beneficiaries shows confidence and trust in the new relationship.

## IN SUMMARY

If there is a limited income, it is important that all insurance be placed on the one who supports the family. Usually this is the husband. He could support himself and the children if the wife died, but if he died the wife might find it difficult to rear the children without his support. It must be remembered that we are speaking of the average American family with limited money for insurance; the money must buy the greatest possible amount of protection for dependent members of the family. Families with unlimited means may wish to insure all or none of the family members, since their provisions for security are different.

## REVIEW QUESTIONS

1  Why is a discussion of life insurance pertinent in a book on successful marriage?

2  How are the insurance needs of a family different in Stages I and II (see Chapter 18) from their needs in the later stages of life?

3  What is the chief purpose of life insurance? Why are some people confused as to its primary purpose?

4  What are the four basic types of policies sold under the heading of ordinary insurance? Which of these is the most commonly sold in face values of policies?

5  What is the chief function of term insurance? Are all term policies convertible? Renewable?

**6** What advantages does a straight life policy have over a term policy?

**7** Do all straight life policies have a cash or a loan value? Explain.

**8** What is the principle of the limited payment policy? Under what circumstances would it be unwise to take out a limited payment policy?

**9** Why do many people choose an endowment policy? What financial plan might offer more benefits than an endowment policy?

**10** Why is group insurance a good buy?

**11** Is it wise for families with limited incomes to take out endowment policies on their children for the education of the children? Explain.

**12** Do insurance policies that offer the same protection cost the same in different companies? Explain why or why not.

**13** How can the consumer of insurance determine the true net cost of an insurance policy?

**14** What factors should be taken into consideration in determining one's insurance needs?

**15** What is meant by "consumption unit responsibility"?

**16** How should one go about buying insurance? Is the life insurance agent objective in recommending the right policy for the client?

**17** What is meant by the term "preferred risk"?

**18** What points should students consider before buying life insurance?

**19** Give some of the arguments which insurance agents use in selling insurance to students.

**20** What are some advantages of having two $5000 policies rather than a single $10,000 policy?

## PROBLEMS TO SOLVE

**1** John and Mary Smith are 25 years old. John has completed law school and is beginning his practice. He is in debt several thousand dollars for his college education and, in addition, must meet the expenses of getting started in his practice. John and Mary have one son, James, who is a year old, and they expect another baby in six months. John has no insurance but is interested in buying some. What would you recommend that he buy?

**2** John and Mary Smith are now 40 years old. John is well established in his law practice and all debts have been paid. They have four children, ages 16, 15, 13, and 10. John followed your earlier advice and bought the policies recommended. Would you recommend any changes in his policies at this time? If so, what changes would you suggest?

**3** An insurance agent has approached you about a policy and has made it sound so good that you feel you must buy it. You have never heard of the insurance company, but the agent assures you that it is a good one. What should your procedure be?

**4** For some 20 years the value of the dollar has been slowly decreasing as we have been in a period of inflation. Under these conditions what type of investments offer the most protection for a family? Endowment insurance? Stocks? Bonds? Annuities? Straight life insurance? Buying a home? Real estate? Defend your answer. Which would provide the greatest protection if money were to increase in value, or if we were to have deflation?

**5** *Role playing.* Two scenes between a life insurance agent and a client: (a) Show how life insurance *should not* be bought or sold. (b) Show how life insurance *should* be bought or sold.

# DIVORCE

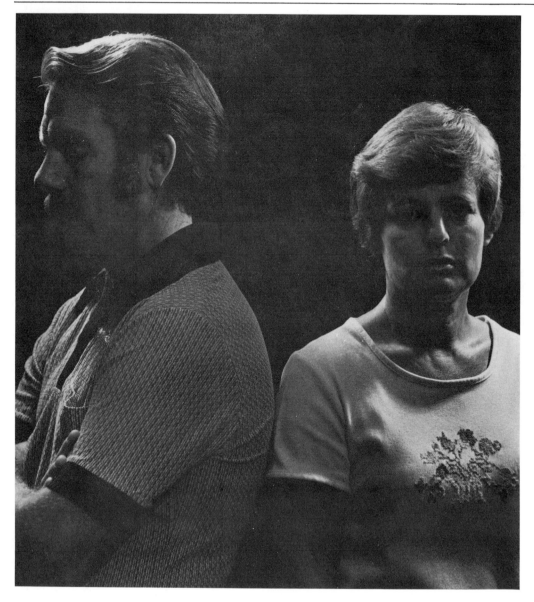

Throughout this book we assume that for most people it is possible to build a good marriage. Our view is that one of the chief positive elements in the process of adjustment in marriage is that both individuals move away from functioning as two separate, independent personalities toward a *pair* identification. In a successful marriage, people become able to think in terms of the marriage and their mutual identity as a married couple as much as of themselves as individuals.

This chapter departs from that approach to deal with the one marriage out of three that ends in divorce. In an unsuccessful marriage either the pair identity does not develop or may develop only partially. The marriage still may not have the elements for survival. The partners must then go through the process of withdrawing emotionally and returning to the premarital state of individual identity. This process is far more painful than are the early problems of adjustment in marriage. Adjustments made in successful marriages are based on a sense of hopeful building. Personal compromises or sacrifices are rewarded by deeper understanding and involvement in the meaningful relationship. In failing marriages the necessity to withdraw from the pair identification involves disillusionment and disappointment. It means going back to a situation already willingly relinquished. The adult who has known a close relationship with another finds it painful to return to the kind of aloneness that characterizes the premarital years.

When two people marry, the assumption is that the contract is for a lifetime; the words "until death" have been a part of wedding vows for generations. Some couples today, in an attempt to be realistic about marriage, believe that the contract should be for as long as love lasts, or for a stated term of years, renewable by mutual consent if the marriage continues to be a successful relationship. Whatever reservations may be verbalized, most people who marry are making a commitment to each other that they hope and believe will be permanent. The act of contracting a marriage with all the emotional, social, financial, and other legally recognized obligations involved has profound significance for couples at the time of their wedding. Nevertheless, many of the couples who marry will find so many unresolvable differences between them that they will later go through the painful process of divorcing.

## EXTENT OF MARITAL BREAKUP

Discussions of marriage failure usually cite that for some years the national divorce rate has been approximately one divorce for every three marriages. In some states the rate is one divorce for every two marriages. The crude divorce rate in a state is misleading, however, since it simply counts the number of marriages in a given year compared to the number of divorces in that same year. It does not consider factors such as a mobile population and effects of raised or lowered birth rates that result in increases or decreases in numbers of individuals in the age groups most divorce-prone.

The current increase in the number as well as rate of divorces is explained in part by the population explosion after World War II. The young people born then are marrying now, and the bulk of marriage failures come in the early years of marriage. Figure 20-1 gives the divorce rate per 1000 for each age group in the U.S. population. The rate for teen-aged wives was 30.6 per 1000, the highest of all age-specific rates. An increase in marriage failure is predictable when an increasing number of the total population is in the divorce-prone age group. Factors such as new attitudes toward divorce as an acceptable alternative in problem marriages also affect the rate.

Dissolving unhappy marriages through divorce was rare in the early part of this century. In 1900 there were approximately ten divorces for every hundred marriages. The rising divorce rate has been viewed as evidence of a breakdown of the family. It may only mean, however, that today a higher proportion of people will end intolerable family situations rather than endure them. There is no reason to believe that in the past any higher proportion of marriages were happier than at present. Nor did low divorce rates necessarily mean that marriages were happier, but rather that the process of terminating a marriage was more difficult legally and socially. Figure 20-2 summarizes the trend since 1920. A high in the number of divorces (610,000) and in the ratio of divorces to marriages (33 divorces to 100 marriages) was reached after World War II in 1946.

After World War II the divorce rate decreased until 1963, when it began to rise again. It now stands at an all-time high—approximately one million divorces in 1976. The divorce rate has been increasing more rapidly in the northeastern and southern sections of the country be-

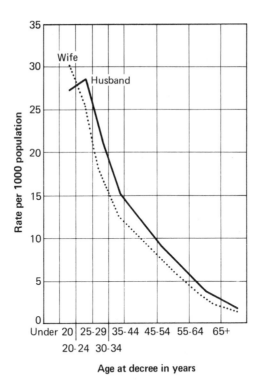

FIG. 20–1 Divorce rates by age at decree, United States, 1965. *Divorce Statistics Analysis, United States, 1964 and 1965,* Washington, D.C.: Vital and Health Statistics, U.S. Department of Health, Education, and Welfare, Series 21, No. 17 (October 1969).

cause in states within those areas it had previously been very difficult to get divorces. Because of the recent liberalized divorce laws in these states, the divorce rate has risen rapidly compared to states that have always had liberal divorce laws.

## LAWS REGULATING MARRIAGE AND DIVORCE

The trend is away from laws rigidly restricting divorce toward more recognition of realities in human relationships. New laws acknowledge the concept that to be a constructive rather than destructive force in society, a marriage must be based upon a meaningful relationship between the partners, and that the good of society is not served by forcing unhappy couples to remain legally married. Concerned groups continue to study the subject with a view to proposing legal reforms that protect both the individual and society. One aspect of the problem is how to prevent marriages that have little or no chance for success.

Historically there were few limitations upon getting married, but divorce laws were extremely restrictive. The laws and public opinion

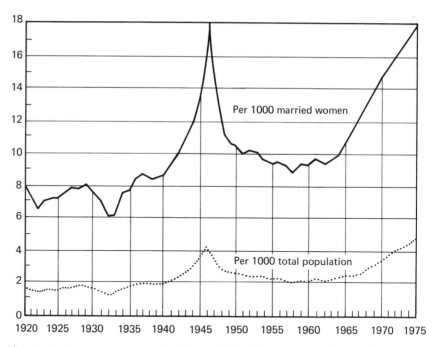

FIG. 20–2 Divorce rates in the United States, 1920–1975. *Increases in Divorce, United States, 1967*, Washington, D.C.: Vital and Health Statistics, U.S. Department of Health, Education and Welfare, Series 21, No. 20 (December 1970; corrected to 1975).

took the position that a marriage once contracted must be permanent. Laws are now being adopted which ask the question, "Is this a non-workable marriage?" If it is, then new laws aid in ending such a marriage, and making it possible for the couple to make a new start.

**The adversary concept in divorce laws.** Divorce laws were, and still are in most states, based on a concept of guilt or innocence. The assumption is that, if a divorce is sought, one is the innocent victim who has a right to have wrongs redressed, the other is the offender to be punished through a divorce and divorce settlement. This type of "adversary" proceeding in divorcing has been followed for generations and has been slow to change.

Under adversary proceedings one member files for the divorce, more often the wife than the husband. She must list the "grounds" for the divorce. These differ in states but include such offenses as adultery, mental or physical cruelty, fraud, impotence, and others. The one who sues must make accusations against the mate in court and must produce witnesses to support the accusations. The judge renders the final decision on the basis of testimony given in the case. If the judge grants the divorce, guilt is established, the worldly goods are divided, the amount of alimony is set, custody of the children is decided, and the amount of child support is determined.

Under the adversary concept in divorce laws, for a couple to agree that their marriage is hopeless and seek a divorce is called *collusion,* and if collusion is proved the divorce cannot be granted. Nevertheless, to avoid some bitterness, many couples do agree privately to divorce, even though one member may be unwilling; they agree as to who shall file for the divorce and what grounds will be used. Then the nonfiling member simply does not appear or present any defense, and usually the divorce is granted. However, many couples whose marriage is breaking up cannot agree on anything about the divorce any more than on other matters. One then may choose to contest the divorce. Divorces that are contested are a minority of those sought, fortunately, for in contested divorce actions the damage to individuals and to children involved is likely to be severe. A Michigan lawyer said, "Some of the contested divorce dockets in major cities are so overcrowded that delays in hearing these cases and rendering final judgment vary from two to five years. The marital existence of the parties and their children is held pendulously—in a state of purgatory. All normal functions cease between the parties until judgment day which may or may not end in a divorce." [1]

## CHANGES IN DIVORCE LAWS AND PROCEDURES

Some progress is being made toward changing divorce laws and the no-fault divorce is replacing these adversary proceedings. In 1969, California, followed by Iowa in 1970 and Florida, Michigan, and Oregon in 1971, made the first major reform in divorce laws in over a hundred years. These states have abandoned the idea of adversary proceedings and accepted the concept of "no-fault" divorce. Under the new laws, a married person may file a court petition for dissolution of his or her marriage without having to make accusations against the mate.

States adopting the new code use the term "dissolution of marriage" rather than divorce. The Iowa code defines the term "dissolution of marriage" as synonymous with the term "divorce." In California, if the court finds there are "irreconcilable differences" and there are no chances for reconciliation, the marriage is dissolved and the decree becomes final in six months. Property is divided and support for minors arranged as formerly. In Iowa and Michigan, dissolution is granted if "there has been a breakdown of the marriage relationship to the extent that the legal objects of matrimony have been destroyed and there remains no reasonable likelihood that the marriage can be preserved." In Florida, Colorado, and Oregon, a marriage is dissolved if the court finds the relationship is "irretrievably broken."

[1] Norman N. Robbins, "Will Arbitration Ease the Crowded Divorce Docket?" *The Family Coordinator* 19:4 (October 1970), 374.

In 1970 the revised Texas Family Code added a new ground for divorce, called "insupportability," defined as "discord or a conflict of personalities that destroys the legitimate ends of the marriage relationship and prevents reasonable expectations of reconciliation."

Now that some states have abolished adversary proceedings in terminating marriages, other states are following the trend. Between 1971 and 1974, 23 states had adopted some form of no-fault divorce. However, many of the states do not yet have true no-fault divorces as defined by the states mentioned above. Most of the states have simply added no-fault as an additional ground for divorce, which means that the adversary concept still prevails in divorce cases. State legislatures are considering changing procedures to the no-fault concept.

## The conciliation court

If the divorce judge has any question about whether a marriage has failed, the judge may recommend that the couple go to a marriage counselor for advice before making a final court decision. The concept of requiring counseling before divorce developed in the 1930s in Los Angeles, where the first "conciliation court" was established. State law now provides for such counseling centers throughout California. Several large cities throughout the nation have established "conciliation courts." The courts are staffed with qualified marriage and family counselors. Attorneys and judges may refer couples for counseling to help the couple determine whether there is basis for saving the marriage or whether it is one that should be dissolved. The weakness of the counseling procedure is that often couples who do need long-term counseling do not obtain it because of overcrowded schedules. Another weakness is that couples seek counseling when it is too late. Usually the marriage is beyond reconciliation by the time couples see their attorney or petition the court for divorce.

**Effect of legal changes on marital breakup.** It is sometimes argued that to make divorce laws more lenient will result in a flood of divorces. Only scant statistical evidence is yet available on this point. What evidence we have is from California, the first state to have the new laws. The dissolution law in California went into effect in January 1970, and in that year dissolutions (divorces) increased 46 percent over divorces in the year 1969. But some other factors contributed to the increase. For example, in the same year the waiting period for a divorce or dissolution to become final was reduced from one year to six months. Until this time, many Californians who wished to remarry went to Nevada to divorce because in Nevada a final divorce could be secured in six weeks. There was a 35 percent decline in Nevada divorces the year after California shortened its time necessary to obtain a divorce. Moreover, in California, for years, many couples have secured annulments instead of divorces, partly because the annulments were immediately final. With the new dissolution law, annulments decreased 32 percent in 1970 as compared to 1969.

In California, the divorce rate declined the second year after the no-fault law was passed, but since that time the divorce rate in that state has continued to increase as it has in all other states. Until 1968 New York had one ground for divorce, adultery. In New York that year, there were only 4000 divorces, but when five additional grounds for divorce were added in 1968, the divorce rate increased rapidly. In 1974 there were over 55,000 divorces granted in the state of New York. As noted previously, the divorce rate is increasing most rapidly in those northeastern and southern states in which divorce laws have been most restrictive and are now being liberalized. In the past, couples who wished to divorce went to states like Nevada with easy divorce laws; with the recent liberalized divorce laws, they now divorce in their home state. It is possible now for poorer people to get a divorce. In the past only the middle and upper classes could afford to take up residence in a state that granted easy divorces. Although divorce is still expensive it is now more within the reach of the poor.

When we consider the many circumstances that contribute to marriage failure it seems apparent that there is little hope of eliminating failure, short of abolishing marriage itself, an untenable proposal. People need, now as they have in the past, the kind of committed relationship found only in marriage. Rather than staying locked in destructive marriages, the goal should be to improve the mate-selection process and to advance the extent and quality of premarital education so that fewer of the predictably disastrous marriages would occur.

## DIVORCE AS A SOCIETAL ADJUSTMENT

Sometimes a backward look can provide perspective on present developments. Just after World War II, when divorce rates skyrocketed, some people concluded that the family was doomed. Viewed in perspective, it appears that the number of divorces at that time was inevitable and probably a healthier development for society and individuals than if many thousands of the couples who married hastily during the war had not divorced. In a way divorce serves as a safety valve which protects the institution of marriage. From 1940 to 1945 the courtship and mate selection process had broken down. Thousands of couples married for the wrong reasons. Men married to evade the draft; couples married in panic after brief acquaintance because the man was to be shipped out; people married under the stress of emotional turmoil fearing that the man would never live to return from war. Many people who would in other circumstances have looked cautiously ahead and hesitated to marry each other plunged into marriage with the feeling that there might be no future for them, that the present hour or moment was all that they could count on. Thousands of the couples who married with these motives had very little basis for creating a permanently satisfactory relationship in marriage. Later, when the men returned from military service and the couples confronted the realities of living together under ordinary day-to-day conditions, many of them divorced. Society is probably better off today than if the war-induced marriages had all been permanent. True, the breakup of so many marriages meant severe trauma for individuals. However, the divorces were a social adjustment, not an indication that marriage as an institution was failing.

## MOVING TOWARD DIVORCE

Chapter 14 explored the subject of the universal adjustment requirements in marriage, especially in the early years. The average married couple goes through a process of reassessing themselves and their relationship after the wedding. Many arrive at better patterns of interaction after they have survived some crisis periods. For others, the stress periods become a series of crises; the relationship deteriorates progressively and divorce becomes a consideration.

In the majority of marriages that fail, the beginning of disillusionment comes early. The process of moving toward divorce is a gradual adjustment process having some similarities to the process by which marriage adjustment moves toward success rather than failure.

In the successful marriage, the two encounter situations that force them to become more realistic about what marriage is and about their own and the mate's personality and values. In the marriage that will fail, the same thing occurs, but in these marriages each step toward a realistic assessment of each other or of their interaction represents a deeper disillusionment. They fail to discover counteracting or compensating factors to balance the disillusionments. Thus, instead of making a deeper commitment to each other, they create situations resulting in more frustration, tension, and stress.

This stage of early disillusionment is a time of severe inner turmoil for an individual, producing different reactions depending upon the personality and the maturity or immaturity of the individual. However one may react outwardly, pain and suffering characterize the process of confronting a discrepancy between the realities in a deteriorating relationship and the hopes and dreams that carried one into the marriage. The pain is proportionate to the depth of the emotional commitment made at marriage, and with most people that commitment involves the whole personality. Therefore, most people strongly resist, at first, defining their problems in terms that might imply failure.

A wife of three months cried as she told a close friend of having almost daily quarrels with her husband. The friend suggested finding a marriage counselor, but the wife said, "Oh no, it's nothing *serious*. We love each other. That's why we married." She clung to the concept of "love" for some months in an attempt to avoid facing what she feared might be true of her relationship with her husband. For a while she tried to focus upon things in her situation that had functioned in her decision to marry him. She talked about her husband's appearance, saying to her friend, "I'm so proud of him. He's such a handsome man. I love to be seen with him." After a few months she began to want to have a baby, and talked idealistically of her feelings about her future children. She and her husband both relied more and more upon what might be termed the superficial appearances or aspects of marriage in their efforts to escape facing their incompatibilities. They bought a small home and furnished it as extravagantly as they could; they dressed well and entertained their friends frequently. They approached, in appearance and activity, the "typical" young married couple as presented in advertisements. There was almost a total absence of communication between them on any matter of deep concern. In a relationship without substance, it became increasingly difficult for them to create any pattern of interaction that could meet mutual and individual needs acceptably. Yet their commitment to the marriage was such that they used all possible rationalizations to block or postpone a necessity to redefine their relationship.

**The alienation process.**    In many cases alienation is gradual. At first, the quarreling may be a couple's refusal to believe that they really have disparities that cannot be remedied. Each wants to believe that the other can change, that they can change provocative circumstances, or even that one can change oneself enough to eliminate troubling differences. And each tries to make or force changes. But as time passes, if repeated times of stress do not result in better understanding and a resolving or diminishing of differences, one or both may begin inwardly to draw back into an assessment of the marriage that is more characteristic of the single person considering a possible marriage before he or she is unalterably committed to it.

Sometimes the process of alienation may be short, if the mate choice is recognized to have been unfortunate and serious points of difference emerge soon after the wedding. In other cases the process may extend over many years before the marriage eventually breaks. In these marriages, since both resist the thought of failure, they may go ahead and have children and then use the requirements of child rearing, earning a living, homemaking, and social life or community participation to drain off energy that might otherwise have gone into conflict or hostility toward each other. Some of such couples over a period of years do become able to tolerate whatever level of relationship they have, but such a basis is precarious. When the time comes that the income is established and the children are older and some responsibilities decrease, their basic incompatibilities or the emptiness of their relationship may again emerge. Whether they will ever divorce depends somewhat upon factors in their background.

Not all marriages that are terminated are necessarily the most unhappy marriages. Many very unhappy marriages continue for a lifetime. The couple in an unhappy marriage who are devout in religion are more likely to stay married than couples indifferent to religion. A woman with little education or with no vocation by which she could earn her living is more likely to remain in an unhappy marriage than is a woman with a job or a profession.

The person with divorced parents or who has a number of divorced relatives and acquaintances is more likely to end an unhappy marriage than is one from a family with no history of divorce. To one accustomed to divorce in the family, the idea of divorcing quite readily comes to mind in times of crisis. One from a family with no history of divorce, who may have thought of divorce as a disaster for others, may struggle for years in an unhappy marriage before becoming able to think of divorce as a possible alternative.

In a study of 667 intact, unhappy marriages and 203 unhappy divorced marriages, we found that those who divorced were more likely to be indifferent religiously, to have married young, to be of the professional class, the wife to be employed outside the home, and to have more education.[2] In another study quoted in Chapter 6, we found a high relationship between a divorce and the number of divorces that had occurred among grandparents, parents, aunts, and uncles.[3]

A study of health and marital experience in an urban population found that people who remained in an unhappy marriage were less healthy; that is, they reported more physical disability, chronic illness, neurosis, and depression than did those either divorced or happily married of the same race, sex, and age.[4] Whether that finding means that mental and physical ill health occurred prior to the deterioration of the marriage and contributed to it or were consequences of an unhappy marriage is uncertain.

## DECIDING TO DIVORCE

Once divorce as a possible solution comes into an individual's thinking, a multitude of complications and considerations must be faced. Few people can go through this stage without suffering from doubts and ambivalent feelings. They tend to move toward divorce and then to hesitate and entertain hope that perhaps it need not be. In every close relationship contradictory feelings tend to exist. In a deteriorating mar-

[2] Judson T. Landis, "Social Correlates of Divorce or Nondivorce Among the Unhappily Married," *Marriage and Family Living* 25:2 (May 1963), 178–80.

[3] Landis, "The Pattern of Divorce in Three Generations," *Social Forces* 34:3 (March 1956), 213–16.

[4] Karen S. Renne, "Health and Marital Experience in an Urban Population," *Journal of Marriage and Family* 33:2 (May 1971), 338.

riage one's feeling for the mate may swing between love and hate, resentment against present and past wrongs and a longing for the meaningful relationship that once was believed to exist or was hoped for.

Even in marriages that fail some important needs are met. The troubled person considering divorce constantly attempts to sort out the elements that have given meaning to the marriage and weigh them against those that are intolerable. Some people move through this process blindly, wavering between feelings of despair and hope; others can cope with it fairly rationally. People who have counseling at this stage are often encouraged to try to assess their situation by making specific lists that represent the good and the bad or the satisfactory and intolerable elements in the marriage. Through such an assessment, one may become more aware of some satisfactions in the marriage that would be experienced as extreme losses if the marriage breaks. It may also help the person to face the truth about the extent of the areas of hopeless failure.

At this stage many people resort to behavior that for them is out of character. People who were formerly even-tempered may become irritable and unreasonable and begin to have difficulty with colleagues on the job and in other relationships. Sometimes men struggling with the ego deflation which may result from a sense of failure in a relationship, may become aggressive and domineering and cause problems for their co-workers or for the organization in which they work. Many people begin to have health problems formerly unknown to them.

Some people will begin to have an affair. The affair may be an attempt to prove to oneself that the failure is the partner's, not his or her own. Or it may be a blind search for solace in a time of emotional turmoil. It may be motivated by feelings of revenge for wrongs. Or it may be a testing, perhaps unconsciously, to see whether, *if* the marriage should break, it would be possible to find another relationship to fill the void. An affair may even be a vague effort to cause the partner to make the decision about breaking the marriage rather than to have to make it oneself. In our society it appears that men more than women think they need to have another relationship before they can make a rational decision to get out of a failed marriage. Women seem to be more able to move toward divorce on the basis of terminating an intolerable situation and they may have no wish to become immediately involved in a substitute relationship.

The trauma of this stage of approaching divorce may cause many people to become involved in extramarital affairs. They seem unable to go through the breakup process without someone to whom they can turn. In many such cases, once the marriage is ended the new affair breaks up. If immediately after the divorce is final the individual marries the new "love," the new marriage does not have a high predictability of success.

During the process of deciding whether or not to divorce, the person faces other difficult considerations. What will parents and family think? How will friends react? Will friends take sides and leave one isolated?

Will it be possible to have again a meaningful relationship with someone? A woman said despairingly, "I know this isn't much of a marriage. But it's the only one I have. Can I face being *alone* for the rest of my life?" Apparently her husband had the same uncertainties, for this couple wavered for three years, separated, and tried reconciliation several times before they were finally divorced.

Practical questions have to be faced. What about the cost of a divorce? How and where will one live? If a woman has not continued to work during her marriage, how can she earn a living after divorce? Will education or job training be necessary? Can the man earn enough to help support two households or meet his obligation to the children? Studies on alimony payments and child support reveal that the majority of men do not continue support for long. Facing these practical problems may cause individuals to hesitate for a long time even though the marriage is unhappy.

## THE DIVORCE DECISION WHEN THERE ARE CHILDREN

So far our discussion has not considered children, but has focused upon the problems only of the married couple. Today 60 percent of divorcing couples have children. More than one million children under 18 are living in homes of divorced parents. When there are children, every aspect of the problem is far more complicated. Feelings of failure and guilt that one has as he or she struggles toward a decision are intensified when it becomes apparent that the children are reacting to the tensions of their parents. Parents see a child becoming unhappy and insecure or worried and tense because of the parents' problems. They are aware of the belief that parents should stay married for the sake of the children. Likewise, parents are aware of the child's feelings about the possibility of divorce. Children are likely to fear and dread their parents' divorcing as much as they might fear their deaths. For the parents to break up is an ultimate threat to the security of children. So parents must face how divorce will affect their children. Will it damage their development more than the unhappy situation is damaging them? And, even if one believes the children would actually be better off free of living with two unhappy parents, one may still wonder, "Will the children blame me? Will they hold it against me that we divorced? What if they decide to live with the other parent?"

One attorney who has practiced family law for 27 years kept a record of the most prevalent concerns asked by clients who were divorcing or had been divorced. These are listed below. The comments reveal that the vast majority are expressed concerns about the children.[5]

[5] Norman N. Robbins, "End of Divorce—Beginning of Legal Problems," *The Family Coordinator* 23:2 (April 1974), 185–88.

May I change my child's name in school when I remarry?

How do I change custody?

May I take my child out of the state?

May my children stay with my parents?

My child is dirty and poorly dressed when I call for him.

My former wife never has my child ready on time for visitation.

Can I make provision for my child's custody by will?

May I prevent my ex-husband from taking my child with him on dates?

How can I make certain that my support payments are regular?

My husband left the state, how do I collect my alimony and support payments?

My former husband always brings the children home late from visitation or they eat hot dogs and are sick.

My child doesn't want to visit his [or her] dad (or mother).

I want to change my child's religion, may I?

My child needs a serious operation, can I get my ex-husband to pay?

My child has a special aptitude in art, can I get my ex-husband to pay?

My child is 22 months old, can my ex-husband (or wife) take him [or her] out of my home?

I don't want my ex-wife (or husband) in my house while she (or he) visits with the child.

May I bring my dates home, will it jeopardize my custody?

If I marry out of my race or religion, will I lose custody?

If I marry out of my race or religion, will I lose visitation?

How old does a babysitter have to be?

My children's grades are poor and they are always dirty, can I get custody?

My second husband took indecent liberties with my child, will I lose custody?

How much can I chastise my child?

How can I get more visitation rights?

How can I decrease visitation rights?

How can I get more support or alimony?

How can I decrease support or alimony?

How can I get my former husband to provide for my son's college education?

How do I protect my children in case of my death:

A. Will my husband get custody?

B. If my husband is unfit, does he get custody?

Some research findings can be helpful for parents concerned about divorce as it affects children, although much more research is needed. We studied the maturation and dating of children from parents with happy marriages, unhappy intact marriages, and unhappy broken marriages. We found that, on the majority of items, children from unhappy intact marriages made a poorer showing than children from divorced marriages.[6] Nye did a similar analysis and came to a like conclusion. He found that children of divorced marriages fell into a more favorable

[6] Landis, "A Comparison of Children from Divorced and Nondivorced Unhappy Marriages," *The Family Life Coordinator* 9:3 (July 1962), 61–65.

category than did the children from unhappy nondivorced marriages in 26 of 29 categories.[7]

Merely to observe, however, that children in unhappy homes are handicapped does not mean that for the parents to divorce will inevitably improve the children's situation. What happens to children's development if the parents divorce will depend upon a number of factors, some of which are: how the breakup process is handled; which parent has custody afterward and how that parent is able to meet the responsibilities of parenthood; whether or not the parents remarry; and their success or failure in second marriages.

The parent with custody of the children (usually the mother) has sudden new responsibilities to carry alone. Such a woman said, "You are suddenly totally responsible for yourself, the children, the finances, the car, the house. If the gutters are clogged, you've got to climb the ladder and clean them. If the baby has a fever at three in the morning, you've got to call the doctor and find an open drugstore and worry all by yourself. You must make all the decisions. There's no one to lean on or to share with; no one to comfort you—and no one to blame when things go wrong."

If a mother must work to earn a living, there are baby-sitter problems, worries over whether the children are being taken care of properly, necessary efforts made for trying to keep up with difficult schedules of living and working. The absent father suffers another aspect of these problems. He may feel deeply his isolation from his children, may have the same worries about whether they are being taken care of well enough, and yet be unable to have a hand in their circumstances. He may feel that his only share in his children's lives is financial. A recently divorced father said, "I miss them most at breakfast time. I have coffee and a doughnut alone and think of the children at breakfast together and so full of life and good spirits, and I feel a terrible loss."

Another phase of the adjustment comes when one realizes that a divorce is never "final" when children are involved. Some contact between the formerly married parents will continue for many years. Child-support payments and visits the children have with the nonresident parent have a continuing potential for stress for both parents. Two years after her divorce a mother said, "After I managed to get through with the whole painful process of the divorce, I thought I would be free. But now I realize that I'll *never* be free. As long as Jim and I both live he's a complication in my life because of the children."

The divorced parent has also to make a decision, and live with it consistently, about how much to tell the children about reasons for the divorce, and what attitude to take toward the other parent. There may be a temptation for one to disparage the other parent and destroy the

---

[7] F. Ivan Nye, "Child Adjustment in Broken and Unhappy Unbroken Homes," *Marriage and Family Living* 19:4 (November 1957), 356.

respect or affection the children have for their nonresident parent. Many mothers in this situation try to preserve the children's love for the father by refraining from any criticism of him and presenting him in as good a light as possible. However, the children may experience emotional turmoil if they idealize the absent father and seem to blame the mother for his absence.

It may become especially hard for the mother and often for both parents if the children play one parent against the other in the remarks which they make when visiting with the other parent. The "power of the children" as go-betweens can be effective in their control of the parents in many ways. Children can use their power to get material things, to upset their parents as a conscious or unconscious way of getting even for what the parents have done to their security, or as a way to upset the parent when the child is having a bad day.

## TRAUMA OF CHILDREN IN DIVORCE

The trauma of marriage failure is not necessarily limited to the divorcing pair. How much their children may be adversely affected depends upon many factors in the family situation. If the divorce occurs very early in the children's lives—even in some cases before birth—there is no reason why their experience should be any different from that of children reared by a single parent. If the mother remarries and the second marriage is a good marriage, the children cannot be considered, in effect, children of divorce.

In an unhappy marriage in which an inadequate father deserts when the children are small and the mother takes all responsibility for rearing the children, the children may have little trauma unless the mother is bitter and resentful. They may be better off than if such a father had stayed in the unhappy marriage. The mother's capacity for being a good mother determines whether the children suffer any ill effects of the separation or the divorce.

To learn something of how children go through divorce with their parents, we had the cooperation of 295 university students who were from divorced homes.[8] Our first finding was that approximately a third of these people had been too young to realize or remember the family situation at the time of the divorce. The only thing on which they could report was their reactions (when they were older) to being from a home that was different from their friends' homes. Having to explain the absence of their father, envying those who had a father, and having to admit that their parents were divorced were some of the situations causing embarrassment.

There were 183 people who had been five or older at the time of the

---

[8] Landis, "The Trauma of Children When Parents Divorce," *Marriage and Family Living* 22:1 (February 1960), 7–13.

divorce, old enough to recall the circumstances and their own reactions. These formed the group for detailed analysis in the study. The analysis found that the children who had been in the youngest age group, aged five to eight, were less affected by the situation leading up to the divorce and in adjustment to divorce than were the older children. In general, the five- to eight-year group tended to feel secure, happy, and less aware of predivorce conflict than did the older children. At the time of the divorce fewer felt upset by the divorce; they reported less threat to their security; they did not feel "used" by their parents against each other during and after the divorce; and they seemed to suffer less trauma in facing friends. Older children reported having felt greater trauma on most of these items.

In analyzing the data we found that, contrary to our expectation, many of the children reported believing their homes to be very happy and their family closely united before they realized their parents were going to divorce. It might seem that openly expressed hostility and unhappiness would be evident in all homes before a divorce, but this is not the way the children always see it. Our analyses showed that trauma experienced by children is related to how they viewed the home before the divorce.

We divided the respondents into three groups: those who saw the home as happy in terms of their feeling of security, unity, lack of conflict; those who saw the home as very unhappy with no family unity, much open conflict, and the children's feelings of insecurity; and a third group made up of those between the two extreme groups in their views of the home.

The results of the study show that children who saw their homes as happy suffered the most severe trauma at the time they learned there was to be a divorce. Those who knew the home was unhappy had suffered for years before the actual divorce. Table 20-1 summarizes the reactions of the children when they were first informed of the impending divorce. Over 50 percent of the children from the unhappy families thought the divorce was best for all concerned, while only 20 percent of those from homes they viewed as happy had this feeling. Over 40 percent of those from the happy group could not believe divorce could happen to their families; only 16 percent of those in the unhappy group felt that way. Table 20-1 summarizes other reactions that point up the trauma experienced by those who saw their homes as satisfactory before learning of a possible divorce.

Once a divorce had become a fact, the children who saw their homes as unhappy reported greater feelings of security and greater personal happiness, while those who had seen the home as happy and secure before the divorce reported greater loss of security and less personal happiness after the divorce.

In a way, children who find themselves in a very unhappy home anticipate divorce even though they still suffer when it happens. Children

TABLE 20-1

The immediate reaction reported by 183 children of divorced parents when learning their parents would probably separate or divorce

| Reaction | ⅓ Happiest N–61 | ⅓ Unhappiest N–61 | Total * N–183 |
|---|---|---|---|
| Thought it was best for all concerned | 19.7% | 54.1% | 34.4% |
| Couldn't believe that it had happened to us | 42.6 | 16.4 | 33.3 |
| Fought against it and tried to prevent it | 13.1 | 11.5 | 14.2 |
| I was happy | 1.6 | 14.8 | 6.0 |
| I was unhappy and upset | 52.5 | 57.4 | 51.9 |
| I was worried and anxious about my future | 14.8 | 27.9 | 20.2 |
| Hated father | 4.9 | 19.7 | 8.7 |
| Hated mother | 1.6 | 8.2 | 3.3 |
| Did not understand | 18.0 | 8.2 | 12.0 |
| Indifferent | 6.6 | 3.3 | 4.9 |
| Miscellaneous reactions | 19.7 | 11.5 | 15.3 |

* Total represents two-thirds shown, plus one-third of sample not shown.
   Landis, "The Trauma of Children When Parents Divorce," *Marriage and Family Living* 22:1 (February 1960), 7–13.

who see their homes as satisfactory are not prepared for divorce, and at the time feel a greater threat to their security. This does not mean that the children who see their parents' marriages as happy are damaged any more severely than are the others. A sudden tragedy in the family is hard for children but it may still not be as damaging in the long run as chronic conflict. Moreover, children who experience security, unity, and happiness seem to be fortified by this background so that they may have more strength and ability to adjust to the divorce situation.

The findings suggest that some parents who divorce are more capable than others of handling their unhappy marriages and eventual divorces and thus avoiding severe damage to the children. While married, they do not have open conflicts before their children, and when the divorce does take place they know how to ease the trauma for their children. They do not "use" their children against each other during and after the divorce. Table 20-2 summarizes ways in which some parents "use" children before, during, and after divorce. Children who saw their homes as unhappy before divorce also reported being "used" by their parents more than was reported by children who saw their homes as happy. Over 60 percent of the children from homes viewed as happy reported they were never "used," in contrast to only 25 percent of those from unhappy homes.

One other index of adjustment to divorce for children was in how they felt divorce affected their relationships with friends and associates. Table 20-3 summarizes the responses of the happy and unhappy groups and the entire group of 295 studied. Here the adjustments seem to be about the same for all groups. Notice that over 40 percent reported that the divorce had no effect upon their relationships with friends and asso-

TABLE 20-2

Percentage distribution of specific ways in which 295 children of divorced parents reported they were "used" by one parent against the other before, during, or after divorce

| Way in which parent "used" child | ⅓ Happiest N–61 | ⅓ Unhappiest N–61 | Total * N–295 |
|---|---|---|---|
| One tried to get information from me about the other | 21.3% | 41.0% | 21.0% |
| Asked to testify against one parent in court | 4.9 | 21.3 | 7.8 |
| Asked to back up one parent or other in family quarrels | 1.6 | 31.1 | 9.8 |
| Not permitted to talk to one parent | — | 3.3 | 1.0 |
| Not permitted to see one parent | 3.3 | 8.2 | 4.1 |
| One told untrue things about the other | 18.0 | 42.6 | 17.6 |
| One gave messages to me to give to the other | 9.8 | 11.5 | 7.1 |
| I was used as a go-between in quarrels | — | 13.1 | 3.7 |
| One or both played on my sympathy | 14.8 | 52.5 | 25.8 |
| Neither ever used me | 60.7 | 24.6 | 44.4 |
| Miscellaneous responses and too young to remember | 4.9 | 9.8 | 20.0 |

* Total represents two-thirds shown, one-third not shown, plus 112 respondents who were too young to remember family before divorce but old enough to remember post-divorce years.

Landis, "The Trauma of Children When Parents Divorce," *Marriage and Family Living* 22:1 (February 1960), 7–13.

ciates, and that almost three-fourths of all groups reported they did not need to resort to "face-saving" techniques.

## ADJUSTMENT OF CHILDREN TO THE STEPFATHER

A group of sociologists studied the adjustments of children to a stepfather. Their research supports our findings in that the remarriage of the mother after divorce and the presence of a stepfather does not mean that the children are affected adversely.[9] How the children are affected depends upon many conditions which existed before the divorce, and on

[9] Kenneth L. Wilson, Louis A. Zurcher, Diana Claire McAdams, and Russell L. Curtis, "Stepfathers and Stepchildren: An Exploratory Analysis From Two National Surveys," *Journal of Marriage and the Family* 37:3 (August 1975), 526–35.

TABLE 20-3

Percentage distribution of adjustments reported with friends and associates by 295 children of divorced parents

| Description of adjustment | ⅓ Happiest N–61 | ⅓ Unhappiest N–61 | Total * N–295 |
|---|---|---|---|
| *Did you feel that your parents' marital status had any effect upon your social acceptability with friends and associates?* | | | |
| I felt different from other children | 23.0% | 29.5% | 22.7% |
| I felt inferior to other children | 13.1 | 23.0 | 16.3 |
| Embarrassed to face friends | 11.5 | 11.5 | 10.2 |
| Was ashamed that parents were divorced | 29.5 | 23.0 | 21.4 |
| It was a blow to my pride | 8.2 | 8.2 | 6.8 |
| Had no effect at all upon me | 49.2 | 41.0 | 42.4 |
| We moved and new friends did not know | 3.3 | 19.7 | 10.2 |
| Envious of those with happy homes | 1.6 | 4.9 | 5.4 |
| My friends were from divorced homes, so accepted | 6.6 | 6.6 | 3.4 |
| Did not tell friends or talk about it | 1.6 | — | 2.0 |
| Miscellaneous responses | 4.9 | 1.6 | 13.6 |
| *Did you feel the need of "face-saving" techniques when discussing or having to give information on the marital status of your parents?* | | | |
| Sometimes lied about where one parent was | 11.5 | 8.2 | 9.5 |
| Said one parent was dead | 4.9 | 8.2 | 3.7 |
| Said one parent was on a trip, at sea, or would be with us later | 4.9 | 1.6 | 4.4 |
| Talked as though parents were not divorced | 19.7 | 16.4 | 15.3 |
| Associated largely with other children who were from separated or divorced homes | 3.3 | 3.3 | 3.7 |
| Did not mention divorce except to those who came from broken homes | 3.3 | 4.9 | 6.8 |
| Never felt need to "save face"—just told the truth | 72.1 | 75.4 | 70.5 |
| Avoided subject, but truthful if asked | 16.4 | 11.5 | 14.9 |
| Never had to give information | — | 1.6 | 1.4 |
| Miscellaneous responses | — | — | .7 |

* Total represents two-thirds shown, plus one-third not shown, plus 112 respondents who were too young to remember family before divorce but old enough to remember postdivorce years.

Landis, "The Trauma of Children When Parents Divorce," *Marriage and Family Living* 22:1 (February 1960), 7–13.

their adjustment to the divorce and to the parent's second marriage. The adjustment of the child to the new family may be positive, negative, or mixed.

## THE PERMANENTLY DIVORCED

Divorce seems to remove some people from the marriage market who will remain in the divorce category. Divorces caused by alcoholism, drug addiction, impotence, homosexuality, and some severe personality disorders tend to account for a certain proportion of the permanently divorced. Census data show that divorced men and women have higher death rates at all ages than do the single or the married. This is to be expected for deaths caused by suicide and alcoholism, but it also applies to many diseases. However, the permanently divorced are a small minority. Most divorced people do remarry and so are removed from the statistical category of the divorced. The next chapter will discuss remarriage.

## REVIEW QUESTIONS

1 Summarize the trend in the divorce rate from 1920 to the present.

2 What are some explanations for fluctuations in the divorce rate?

3 What is meant by the term "divorce-prone age group"?

4 Explain some differences between adversary divorce proceedings and no-fault dissolution of marriage.

5 What is the purpose of the conciliation court? How does it work?

6 Discuss the statement, "Liberalizing the divorce laws results in a rapid increase in divorce." Think of the changes in the laws in California and New York in discussing the statement.

7 Explain the statement that the sudden increase in the divorce rate immediately after World War II may have been somewhat healthy for society.

8 Compare or contrast the early adjustment phase of marriage in successful and in failing marriages.

9 Describe the process of alienation as outlined in this chapter.

10 What are some of the factors associated with whether unhappily married couples divorce or decide to stay married?

11 What are some special types of ambivalent tendencies and feelings experienced by persons deciding about divorce?

12 What are some motivations that may lead an individual in a failing marriage to have an affair with an outsider?

13 What percentages of divorcing couples have children?

14 What are some of the concerns parents have about their children when they are considering divorce?

15 Which children seem to show the better adjustment, those from unhappy nondivorced homes or those from divorced homes?

16 What are some of the predivorce situations in a home that are associated with the amount of trauma experienced by children?

17 Give some of the reactions children expressed when they learned their parents were going to divorce.

18 How does divorce affect the security of children?

19 What situations seem to determine how the security of children is affected when parents divorce?

20 In what ways do parents "use" their children during and after divorce?

**21** Give some of the ways in which children of divorced parents react in associating with friends.

**1** Ask a representative of Parents Without Partners to speak to the class. Ask especially about problems of divorced parents and programs organized by Parents Without Partners and other agencies to aid divorced or single parents.

**2** Interview (or invite to the class) a lawyer or a judge who is qualified in the area of divorce laws.

**3** Make a special report to the class on the status of divorce laws in your state. Is there a marriage dissolution or no-fault divorce law? If not, are efforts being made to revise the present law?

**4** Report on what provision is made in your community for marriage and family counseling.

# REMARRIAGE

## CHAPTER 21

Throughout this book we have been discussing first marriages and the problems of adjustment in first marriages. We have also focused upon those who marry young—in their teens or twenties—since 77 percent of men and 86 percent of women marry before age 30. This chapter focuses on marriages which are for one or both a remarriage. The high divorce rate coupled with the increase in life expectancy has resulted in more people marrying a second or third time. In past generations many marriages were broken by death at young ages—through loss of women in childbirth and through diseases that took the lives of young people. Today widowhood tends to come late in life. In 1976 there were 22 million people 65 years of age and older, many of whom are widowed and desire to remarry.

In this chapter we discuss the remarriage of the divorced and widowed, and some of the adjustments in these marriages. Divorced people have a higher remarriage rate than the widowed, mainly because they are younger and have greater opportunity. The marriage rates for both men and women who have been divorced are higher than for single people of the same sex and age group. Women who divorce under the age of 25 have the highest remarriage rate of all. Of women who divorce under the age of 40, 90 percent eventually remarry. Divorced men are more likely to remarry than are divorced women. Divorced people tend to enter a second marriage soon. Data from 15 states show that 50 percent of people remarry within shortly more than one year after divorce.[1] The quick remarriage is explained in part because some

---

[1] "Remarriage Statistics," summarized in *Journal of Marriage and the Family* 36:2 (May 1974), 302. Reprinted from *Remarriages United States,* Vital and Health Statistics, Series 21, No. 25, Publication No. (HRA) 74–1903.

who divorce have found a new mate before the divorce is final. In fact some may be in no hurry to divorce until they have found a new mate.

Second marriages differ from first in that the age disparity of the spouses is greater. The divorced man of 30 marries a woman 5 years younger; the divorced man of 35 marries a woman 5 to 10 years younger. This disparity limits opportunities for divorced, single, or widowed women to marry men of their own age group. They must marry older men if they remarry. Divorced women as well as men with children in their custody are further handicapped in marrying a second spouse.

## SUCCESS IN REMARRIAGE

Paul Glick of the U.S. Census Bureau has been studying marriage and divorce trends for the past 35 years. He estimates that less than half of the people in second marriages remain married, in contrast to first marriages in which two-thirds of the people remain married. If approximately half of the divorced people make successful second marriages, and by so doing have eliminated bad marriages, then we might look optimistically upon divorce and remarriage. The individuals involved and society in general would doubtless profit by this change. In the past students of the family may have focused upon the atypical group of people who divorce and remarry repeatedly, people who can find mates but who cannot create and maintain a successful relationship. The tendency to focus on the failures rather than the successes of those who do succeed in second marriages has been due to the general attitude of society toward divorce. An objective appraisal of divorce and remarriage would indicate that for many it is the right solution.

The group whose second marriages last are likely to be average people who are capable of making a success of marriage if they remarry under different circumstances and after they have become more mature and realistic about marriage. The first marriages were likely to have been contracted at very young ages or after short acquaintance, may have been forced by pregnancy, or may have involved extreme differences in background and personality. Many of these people are able to learn from their mistakes and to approach a second marriage more cautiously. They may have learned something of the necessity to adjust and compromise in a relationship and they may have fewer unrealistic expectations of the mate.

The statement is often made that second marriages are actually happier than first marriages. If people in second marriages are asked how the second marriage compares with the first, the respondents tend to report that the second is better; at least half will report the second to be happier and more successful. But it should be noted that, for these people, first marriages had had a 100 percent failure rate. Naturally they report the second as better, even though some of these marriages may also end in divorce. Probably these same people, if queried during the early months or years of a third marriage, would report that it was better than the two preceding, both of which had failed.

All studies of marriage and divorce show that a larger percentage of first marriages are successful than of second or succeeding marriages. A number of states now keep records on number of times married for all couples who make application for a marriage license. Monahan made detailed analyses of the data from Iowa for the years 1945–1947, 1948–1950, and 1953–1955. He found that second and successive marriages are not so enduring as first marriages. Figure 21-1 summarizes this research for the years 1953–1955.[2] We do not have a similar study of first and second marriages for a recent year, but the pattern shown is probably the same although the divorce rate in each category is much higher today. It will be observed that first marriages have a low divorce rate (16.6 percent) compared to marriages between two people who have both been divorced once (34 percent). Of the marriages between partners who have been divorced two or more times, about eight out of ten ended in divorce (79.4 percent).

Monahan's analyses also showed that, with each successive marriage, previously divorced people tend to divorce more quickly if they divorce. The median duration of marriage before the first divorce was 6.5 years; if both had been divorced once, it was 3.5 years; and if both had been

[2] Thomas P. Monahan, "The Changing Nature and Instability of Remarriages," *Eugenic Quarterly* 5 (June 1958), 73–85.

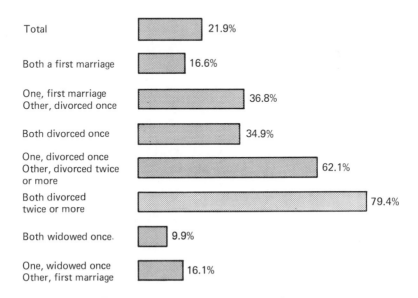

FIG. 21–1  Ratio of divorces per 100 marriages of selected type of marital background (divorced-widowed combinations excluded), Iowa, 1953–1955. Thomas P. Monahan, "The Changing Nature and Instability of Remarriage," *Eugenic Quarterly* 5 (June 1958).

divorced twice, the duration of the marriage before the next divorce was only 1.7 years.[3]

## PROBLEMS OF ADJUSTING TO DIVORCE

How people adjust to divorce is dependent upon many factors in their lives associated with their marriage, as well as upon their personality development from childhood to adulthood.

Society has made provisions for helping people through most personal crises; in a time of crisis there are standards of accepted behavior. If there is death in a family or serious sickness, friends and neighbors know what to do and are ready to help the family or the individual. But when a marriage ends, there is no supportive ritual to ease the individuals through the crisis.

Studies of divorced women showed that "divorce trauma" was greater: if they were religious, if the husband had suggested the divorce, if the suggestion came unexpectedly, if they still cared for the husband, if they personally disapproved of divorce, and if family and friends disapproved of divorce.[4, 5] Another study found that both men and women who were actively associating with family and friends or participating in organizations experienced less trauma than did those not actively engaged.[6]

The personality that the divorced person has developed before the divorce has much to do with the adjustment. The habitual methods the person has used in facing problems are most important because there are many problems to face after a marriage fails. The immediate solution of some problems, such as division of property, alimony, and child support, may have been spelled out in the divorce settlement, but there are many other problems to face in adjustment.

1 Often there is an immediate financial problem. If the woman has not been employed, what kind of employment could she find? Is she qualified for any type of work or must she take additional training? Most divorced women do enter the job market because alimony and child support do not provide adequate support. The man's obligation to share his income with the former wife and children often means he cannot remarry unless his new wife will help finance the marriage.

2 There is the question of where to live. Should they continue living in the same community where they will be in contact with mutual friends and asso-

---

[3] Monahan, "The Duration of Marriage to Divorce: Second Marriages and Migratory Types," *Marriage and Family Living* 21:2 (May 1959), 136–38.

[4] Morris Rosenberg, *Society and the Adolescent Self-Image* (Princeton, N.J.: Princeton University Press, 1965).

[5] William J. Goode, *Women in Divorce* (New York: The Free Press, 1956).

[6] Helen June Raschke, "Social and Psychological Factors in Voluntary Post-Marital Dissolution Adjustment" (Ph.D. diss., University of Minnesota, 1974).

ciates, or should one or both move to a different community? Should one keep the apartment or home, or should each make a clean break and start over? Should the wife move back to her home community so that the children can be with the grandparents and other family members?

3   There is a question about what living arrangements are best for the children. Almost 90 percent of children continue to live with the mother. Which is better for children—regular visiting rights for the father or a permanent break with him? The divorce settlement will have spelled out the specific rights of custody, support, and visiting rights, but the terms of the settlement do not necessarily result in a smooth relationship. Fathers often fail to make payments for support, to adhere to scheduled times to see their children, or to try to build harmonious relationships. Often there is a pulling and hauling and, in general, a discordant relationship between parents in the early adjustment after divorce.

4   The social life of divorced people must be reorganized. Usually it cannot continue with the same friends. Married people usually have couples as their best friends. The divorced person is single and must adjust to the world of the singles if he or she is to remarry.

5   Divorced people must make their own decisions and abide by them. In marriage, no matter how bad, usually the husband and wife have worked together in making day-to-day decisions about their lives. Possibly each blamed the other if the decisions were bad, but it was two people together trying to solve problems. With divorce, each spouse must make decisions, and there is no other one to blame if wrong decisions are made.

6   Divorced people often continue to struggle with the fact of failure in an important venture in their lives. Although divorce is widely accepted today, it still represents failure. Adjusting to any failure in life takes time and effort and may damage one's self-confidence.

7   Some divorced people may go through periods of questioning whether they did the right thing, and a small percentage of divorced couples remarry each other. Confusing questions may arise for divorced people, such as: "I blamed him (or her) for the failure but possibly I was at fault." "Just what did we do wrong in our marriage?" "If I had it to do over again, what would I do differently?"

## DIVORCE MAY OFFER NEW HOPE

Although divorce may exchange new problems for old, it can also have many positive aspects which offer new hope for the individuals involved. Throughout this book we have placed emphasis upon building a successful marriage relationship through wise choice of mate based upon long courtship, maturity, and learning to live successfully with another in marriage. At the same time, we recognize that the courtship process fails in many cases; people marry who should not have married. For such marriages, the most constructive outcome is divorce. In general, society profits from happy rather than from unhappy marriages. There can be advantages in ending an unhappy marriage.

1 The individual may regain a degree of emotional health not experienced in years. Many people are emotionally destroyed by the conflict and the indecision that they experience when going through the psychological failure of a relationship. They may be unhappy, depressed, and difficult to live with because they cannot adjust to a bad relationship.

2 The person may experience a general improvement in physical health. It may be easier to work and to sleep. With the cessation of worry and indecision, there may be fewer physical signs of ill health, such as headaches or stomachaches, and there may be a noticeable increase in energy.

3 It is often true that divorce itself is not difficult; it is the indecision leading up to divorce that is disturbing. With the act of divorce, the person may feel relieved that it is finally over. Often, in looking back, people cannot understand why they waited so long to make the decision to divorce when they can now see that the marriage had been destructive for some years.

4 Divorce gives people a chance to remedy a mistake. Couples who marry very young, who marry because of pregnancy, or who were too immature may end a bad marriage. It is not too late for them to continue their education, make plans for a different future, and become mature before making a second marriage.

5 Often, relationships with family and friends become strained in a bad marriage. Once the marriage is broken, the person may be happy and rebuild relationships with friends and family.

6 If there are children, their emotional security may improve after the divorce, especially if the predivorce years were characterized by much open hostility and conflict.

7 The individual may remarry and substitute a happy marriage for an unhappy one. Although divorced people who remarry have a higher divorce rate than people married only once, almost half do find happiness in a second marriage.

## COURTSHIP AND THE DIVORCED

Many researchers have studied the progress of courtship among those who marry for the first time, but little attention has been given to courtship leading toward second marriages. The depiction of love and romance in novels, poetry, and the media usually results in warm feelings about those in love. Everyone loves a lover, or those in love. Although this warm acceptance may be more characteristic of first marriages, it also applies to second marriages. Friends and family may be concerned that the divorced one will not find a new mate. They expectantly watch the developments in a possible romance. They may also initiate dates for the divorced person.

Divorced people are in a vulnerable position in new courtships. One of the considerations of people in an unhappy marriage is that perhaps the unhappy marriage is better than no marriage. They have thoughts that they may not be able to marry again, so they question if they should give up the unhappy certainty for an uncertain future. After the divorce is final and they start dating, they may not be cautious in marrying again. The fact that the majority do marry relatively soon would indicate a lack of caution, and that they may have married on the rebound. It also indicates the vulnerability of those who divorce. They may have less insight into danger signals than have couples in first marriages. They have usually gone through a traumatic experience, often an ego-deflating experience of feeling rejected by the spouse, and/or of losing confidence in their own judgment in having chosen that spouse.

With the resumption of dating, divorced people tend to move quickly from first dates to marriage. It may be that both individuals are lonesome and have missed having a close loving relationship. It is easy for such a couple to rush into marriage without taking enough time to study their total relationship. Since both have been married before and may be feeling the need for coitus, a larger percentage of divorced people than single people start having sexual intercourse during courtship.

In Chapter 9 we pointed out that the courtship activities leading up to remarriage differ from those in first marriages in that people marrying for a second time are less likely to become engaged, or to have bridal showers, church weddings, or wedding trips.

We do not wish to convey the impression that there is little or no romance in second marriages. The divorced, like those entering first marriages, may enjoy detailing every step in their courtship. As much emphasis may be placed on when and how they met, their first impressions of each other, their favorite songs and eating places, their common interests, and the physical attractiveness of one to the other as in first marriages. They may want a large church wedding, reception, and all the frills that often go with a first wedding. We knew one couple who had been having sexual intercourse for months but decided they would not have coitus for six weeks prior to the wedding so they would have "something to look forward to on our honeymoon," as related by the woman. They came for counseling because he could not live up to the agreement and had broken down her door, resulting in her having called the police.

## Problems of dating

The problem of finding dates with people who are interested in marriage is probably as difficult for the divorced as for those who have never married. They are usually older and may not have the opportunity to meet eligible people at work or at social events. One national organization, Parents Without Partners, serves as a common interest group for divorced or widowed people with children. Some churches have special interest groups for older unmarried people.

For divorced women who date, there are common complaints. Some believe that most of the men they date want sex but not marriage. They believe that men tend to want sexual intercourse almost immediately, and the men tend to think divorced women would feel the same. Divorced women who have gone through an unhappy experience in their marriage are likely to be looking for an understanding relationship, not only sexual relations.

Another problem often mentioned is that too many married men assume divorced women are starved for sex and try to take advantage of them. There are also married men who hold out the promise of breaking up their marriage to marry divorced women.

Further, divorced women mention that they do not feel they are trusted around former couple friends. They feel the wives are afraid divorced women will get romantically involved with their husbands.

## PROBLEMS OF ADJUSTMENT IN SECOND MARRIAGES

It is difficult to discuss the problems of adjustment in remarriage because there are multiple combinations of partners on the basis of prior marriage experience. In Chapter 9 we discussed some of the special problems that arise when a single person marries a divorced person. But this is only one type of remarriage. Some of the others are: divorced married to divorced; divorced married to divorced with no children, or one with children, or both with children; divorced of about the same age marrying, or divorced marrying with great differences in ages; and divorced people marrying at different life stages.

We shall comment briefly on the possible problems of adjustment in some of these types of remarriages.

Divorced people tend to marry those who have been divorced. Fig. 21-2 summarizes the number of times husbands and wives have been married at the time of the current marriage. It is noted that the predominant pattern is that people marrying for the first time marry others marrying for the first time, and that divorced people tend to marry divorced people. Those divorced two or three or more times tend to marry those divorced two or three or more times.

The tendency of those divorced to marry other divorced people follows the general pattern of mate selection in our country. People of similar backgrounds, interests, and life experiences meet and find a basis for companionship. In the case of the divorced marrying the divorced, one of the reasons they are attracted to each other is that they have the common experience of divorce in their backgrounds. The fact that both are divorced often means that two people are marrying who have personality defects which contributed to the first marriage failure. If both are unmarriageable in some respects, then this fact contributes to their chances for failure in a second marriage.

### The multiple divorced

In Fig. 21-1 it is noted that more than two-thirds of remarriages fail if one or both have had two or more previous marriages fail. The failure of the multiple divorced to adjust in marriage is doubtless explained by their having many personality traits which make them permanently unsuitable for marriage. Possibly more of this group could make stable marriages if they had psychiatric help and marriage counseling over a period of years.

### The young divorced

The problems of adjusting in marriage of people divorced in their twenties are probably not greatly different from those marrying for the first time, if no children are involved. In 1975, 41 percent of men and 52 percent of women divorced before they were age 30. Divorces that take place in the early twenties are among marriages of short duration and thus the individuals have not built up habit patterns as have people who divorce when they are in their thirties or forties. Some research indicates that divorces among the very young are not as traumatic as among those who divorce after several years of marriage.

### The middle-aged divorced

People who divorce after being married several years have more problems of adjustment in a remarriage. There are many reasons for this. Habit patterns developed through living with another for several years

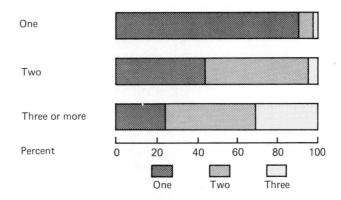

FIG. 21–2 People marrying for the first time tend to marry others marrying for the first time. Divorced people tend to marry divorced people. *Socioeconomic Characteristics of Persons Who Married Between January 1947 and June 1954: United States.* U.S. Department of Health, Education and Welfare, Vital Statistics—Special Reports, 45:12 (9 September 1957), 286.

cannot be altered easily. Although the divorcing couples conflict in various areas of living, there are usually some areas in which they agree. It is inevitable that one will make comparisons of the current spouse with the former. If these comparisons are verbalized, this results in trouble.

The previous spouse is a part of the new marriage in many ways. If the new couple continues to live in the apartment or home of one member, and if furnishings or possessions of the previous spouse are in evidence, there is the continuing reminder of the former spouse. If one or both have children by the previous marriage, constant attention is necessary in order to live harmoniously with each other's children and to be fair in disciplining and loving them. There are also necessary contacts with the previous spouse over visiting rights and other matters dealing with the children.

When divorced women marry divorced men who are older, a problem often arises over whether they should have more children. His children may be in their teens or older, and she may have young children or none. If the younger woman wants to start a family she may meet great resistance on the part of her spouse since he may have no desire to share the responsibility of babies again. If the husband had a vasectomy after having a first family, there could be the problem of an operation to see if fertility might be restored.

Adjustment in the area of making and allocating the money is difficult in remarriage, especially if the husband has made a large commitment to support his first wife and children. The new wife may have to work to help support the new marriage. This she may willingly agree to do before marriage, but after marriage she often finds it increasingly difficult to sacrifice buying things she needs so that the previous wife and children can benefit. If after remarriage the couple decide to have children, an increased financial strain is felt, and the wife may become more unhappy about the support to the husband's first family.

When people in middle age or older remarry, the economic problems often center around how each will spend or dispose of the money and property they bring to the marriage. If the children are grown, the couple may make a special contract or agreement on how each is to dispose of personal property at time of death. Regarding inheritance, each may feel greater financial responsibility to children and grandchildren than to the new spouse. Further, some people who remarry at later ages remarry with uncertainty, thinking, "If the marriage does not work out, we will avoid financial tangles when we separate."

### Single women marrying divorced men

The reader may refer to our discussion of this type of marriage in Chapter 9, page 125.

## DIVORCED PEOPLE LIVING TOGETHER BEFORE REMARRIAGE

Since almost half of divorced people who have failed in one marriage fail in a second marriage, and almost two-thirds who have been married more than once fail in subsequent marriages, a strong case could be made for divorced people living together before they formalize a new marriage contract. As we have pointed out earlier in this discussion, divorced people are often vulnerable when remarrying, especially if they remarry quickly. Their remarriage may be their way of adjusting to a crisis in their lives; it may be to prove that they are desirable to another; it may be because of loneliness, inability to make friends, inability to make day-to-day decisions about the children and money; because of sexual urges; or because they need adult companionship. A trial relationship during the postdivorce adjustment period might be preferable by far to another formalized marriage and another divorce. A sufficient waiting period would also give divorced people time to seek marriage counseling before remarriage. Unwise decisions are often made during a crisis in life. Once the crisis has been resolved, the individual is more likely to be able to make a wise decision for the future. This especially applies to those going through postdivorce adjustment.

## PROBLEMS OF ADJUSTING TO WIDOWHOOD

The widowed, like the divorced, go through a period of trauma, but this is looked upon entirely differently than is the trauma of divorce. Many customs and rituals have been established to help the widowed during their period of crisis. Sympathy is expressed by people who know the widowed. Many people offer a helping hand to sustain them through the crisis; this is done especially for women.

Some of the problems of adjustment for the widowed are the same as those for the divorced, such as: finances; where to live; loneliness; making decisions alone; planning for the future, and whether to think of remarriage. The age at which widowhood takes place alters the solutions to these various problems. Remarriage is seen as the best solution for many widowed people.

## REMARRIAGE OF THE WIDOWED

In 1976 there were 22 million people 65 years of age and older in the United States, and the number will increase for some years. On an average, women live approximately eight years longer than men, the result being a much larger number of widows than widowers in the population. In 1970 there were about ten million widows but only two million widowers in the total population aged 14 years or older. The great surplus of widows are in the older age groups. Because of the favorable sex ratio, widowers are much more likely to remarry and to remarry sooner than are widows. Women widowed at young ages (under 40 years) are more likely to remarry than are women who have never married. Of those widowed before age 25, 90 percent remarry. The older the women are when widowed, the greater the odds are that they will not remarry.

Those widowed tend to marry other widowed people. Widowed women especially marry widowed men rather than marrying the single or the divorced. This results because the widowed are more likely to know other widowed people, and their widowhood is a point of congeniality and a similar life experience which may draw them to each other. The number of people 65 and over who are marrying has increased in recent years, but the number of people in that age group has also increased. Consequently, we do not know whether there has been an increase in the percentage of people marrying in the 65-and-over age group.

## SUCCESS IN REMARRIAGES AMONG THE WIDOWED

Available data suggest that the divorce rate among the remarried widowed is lower than in any other group, even lower than among those in a first marriage. One study found that two-thirds of widowed remarriages were rated as "very happy" or "happy." [7] Another study found that nearly three-fourths of widowed remarriages studied were successful.[8]

The success of remarriages among the widowed may be explained by the fact that the widowed who had happy first marriages are more likely to remarry. In addition, their previous happy marriage indicates that they were marriageable. They knew how to choose wisely the first time and learned how to adjust in a first marriage. This pattern tends to be repeated in a second marriage.

## COURTSHIP OF THE WIDOWED

The courtship of the widowed is greatly influenced by the age of people when widowed, whether it is when young, middle-aged, or older.

### Courtship when young

Courtship and marriage after widowhood in early life have the complete approval of friends and family. It is expected that there will be a remarriage. If the widow or widower has children, there is additional

[7] Jessie Bernard, *Remarriage: A Study of Marriage* (New York: The Dryden Press, 1956).

[8] Walter McKain, *Retirement Marriage* (Agricultural Experiment Station Monograph 3, Storrs, Conn.: University of Connecticut, 1969).

sympathy expressed by friends and family, and the hope that the widowed will be able to remarry and thus have another parent to help with the children. Friends cooperate in arranging social events for the widowed with unattached members of the other sex as a way of promoting romance. There may also be an unconscious motivation on the part of friends and family. They may feel a degree of responsibility for looking out after the widowed and the children. After there is a remarriage, friends are relieved of this responsibility.

Widowers seem to have an advantage over widows in dating, courtship, and remarriage at all ages. The widower in his twenties or thirties can choose from the single, widowed, or divorced women his age or much younger. The widow is usually limited to meeting a potential husband in the small group of single or widowed men older than she is. She finds that most of those she can date are either single older men who for some reason are not interested in marriage, or are married men. The largest source of prospective mates is among men who have been divorced.

Widowed as well as divorced women frequently say that the men they date seem to think of them as easily accessible sex partners. The widow who has had a happy first marriage often finds it difficult to find someone suitable among the single and divorced men she meets. She is faced with the decision whether to marry a man who does not meet her expectations or whether to remain single. Men sometimes feel ill at ease in dating a widow because they feel the widow idealizes her former mate and they cannot measure up to her expectations. Men feel more at ease with the divorcee because she does not idealize the former spouse.

## Courtship in later life

People who are widowed in middle age or older tend to date those of long-standing acquaintance. Lifelong friends and neighbors are in the near age group when widowhood may take place. Relatives are also a possibility. It is not unusual for a man to marry a sister-in-law or for a woman to marry a brother-in-law. Possibly one of the reasons for the high success rate of marriages among the widowed is that they have usually known each other many years.

Courtship among older people serves the same functions as it does among younger people, although there are some differences. Older people are more conscious of the attitudes of friends, family, and the community toward their new relationship. One study found that "the courtship pattern of older men and women tends to be more circumspect, their judgments more carefully weighed, and their decisions more responsive to outside influences." [9] Older people feel they must inhibit their desires to express affection openly for fear others will think them foolish or "in their second childhood." The dating of older people tends to be in

[9] McKain, *Retirement Marriage*, p. 21.

associating with others and in attending social events, rather than in being alone together.

The biggest problem for widowed women is that it is difficult to find eligible men to date. At age 50 and over there are three or four widowed women for every widowed man.

Another problem that both men and women have in considering remarriage when they are older is the attitudes of their children. Society generally has recognized that older people as well as young people have a strong need for love and companionship. Yet, when it comes to their own parents wanting to remarry, children seem to be less understanding. The children may also be less objective about the courtship and possible remarriage because of what it may do to their inheritance. Before marriage, older people often recognize the concerns of their children about inheritance and make special contracts, or revise their wills so that the children of each parent will be protected.

## ADJUSTMENT PROBLEMS OF THE WIDOWED IN REMARRIAGE

### Adjustment in early life

The problems of adjustment to remarriage among those who are widowed when young are very similar to the problems of those who are divorced at young ages. The special problems they face grow out of the interaction which develops between two people with marital experiences prior to the new marriage. To illustrate: Consider the differences in the adjustment required between two people widowed in their early twenties with no children, in contrast to a single woman marrying a widower with teenage children; or between two widowed parents, each with young children, who marry, in contrast to widowed parents, each with teenage children, who marry.

The problems faced in these various combinations of marriages are similar to those of the divorced who marry with like combinations. One element that is different in remarriage of the widowed in contrast to the divorced is that often one or both of the widowed have had a happy first marriage. The experiences of the happy first marriage are a constant reminder to each spouse of the expectation of the other. Each must try to measure up to the spouse of the *real* or *imagined* good marriage the other had had. In the case of adjustment of the divorced, often the previous marriages had been unhappy and the present spouses are not being measured by any previous good relationship or standard. The widowed are also more likely to work through their problems of adjusting in marriage, while the divorced, since they have failed in one marriage, may be more likely to see divorce as the solution to problems of adjustment. The adjustment of the widowed is easier than that of the divorced in that the widowed husband is not paying alimony or child support to his first wife and family.

The widowed who remarry in later life have many problems of adjustment associated with having been married for many years to one spouse. The habit patterns of a lifetime are ingrained in both individuals, and these habits are slow or impossible to change. They are very much a part of the new marriage with which people have to live. Attitudes about politics, religion, eating habits, recreation, sexual behavior, and use of money have been well established in each spouse. Some of the problems of adjusting in these remarriages are discussed below.

1   People for whom social security payments are the main source of income may face a serious problem of how to support themselves if they marry. They might have met in a retirement community and found it possible to live on their social security individually, but since the social security payments are lower for a married couple than for two single people, they might have difficulty if married. For this reason, some people on social security do not formalize their new living arrangement with a marriage.

2   If the couple have sufficient funds for retirement, problems often arise associated with their living arrangements after marriage. The more likely arrangement is that they will live in the home or apartment belonging to one or the other. There are often problems in this situation for the one who gives up his or her living arrangement and moves in with the other. The one moving in may feel that it is not home, even though many things are brought from his or her previous home. There are constant reminders of the former spouse in how the home is furnished. There may be reticence on the part of the new mate to change anything in the home. It takes time to develop a feeling of belonging. The spouse who continues living in his or her home faces fewer problems of adjustment because he or she feels at home with the surroundings as they have always been. This spouse may like things as they have been and can see no need for change. If there are sufficient funds, possibly the solution to the many problems involving the place in which to live would be for the two to acquire a new home together.

3   Couples of all ages have to adjust to each other's annoying habits, to ways of thinking, and to methods of doing things. Probably, older people have acquired certain manners and have become more rigid in behavior patterns which were tolerated by the first spouse. These same behavior patterns or habits may become real annoyances in a new relationship. Each spouse may have to make a great effort to modify behavior patterns and to adjust to the other's habits if the two are to enjoy their companionship.

4   There may be fewer problems in the in-law area of living because the parents of the couple may have died and in-law relationships are now with the children and grandchildren. There are exceptions to this, of course. The couple may have to take in or support one of the aged parents. It becomes a problem associated with the duty of caring for an aged one, which often is not pleasant. Sometimes the remarried parents have to continue support for their own children who have not been able to get established economically. In such cases one may resent seeing their money going to support the other spouse's children.

5 Little research has been done on the sexual adjustment in marriages of older people. They are more likely to put greater emphasis on companionship in remarriage, but the majority who marry in their sixties are still interested in sexual intercourse. The sexual drive continues until late in life for most people if they have good health. The urge for satisfaction is not as strong; the need is not as frequent, but satisfaction is more difficult to obtain. Couples may marry and one or both may be no longer interested in coitus. Couples who are older may have an advantage in working out a mutually satisfactory sexual adjustment since they may be able to discuss freely their needs and desires.

6 One situation older people face which is more in the forefront of their thinking is the inevitability that one or both may soon become sick or disabled. The realization of the shortness of life is ever present. No matter how happy the remarriage, they know they cannot look forward to many years together.

## REVIEW QUESTIONS

1 Why has there been an increase in remarriages in the past few years?

2 How does the remarriage rate of the divorced compare with the marriage rate of the single? The widowed?

3 How successful are remarriages of the divorced? What factors seem to be associated with the success of remarriages? What did Monahan find through his research on remarriage?

4 Give several of the problems divorced people commonly experience after divorce. What situations are associated with the degree of trauma after divorce?

5 Give several positive aspects of ending a bad marriage.

6 Why are the divorced sometimes vulnerable when they renew dating and courtship?

7 How does dating and courtship prior to remarriage differ from that of first marriages?

8 Name some of the problems divorced women frequently mention about their dating.

9 Are divorced people more likely to marry divorced or never-married people? Why would you expect this to be true?

10 How do the problems of adjusting in remarriage differ among those who divorce and remarry when young in contrast to those who marry when in middle age?

11 Review the special problems when a young single woman marries an older divorced man (Chapter 9).

12 Why might a strong argument be made for divorced people to have marriage counseling before they remarry? Or a trial period of living together?

13 How does adjustment to widowhood differ from adjustment to divorce?

14 How does the remarriage rate differ among widows and widowers? Why?

15 How successful are remarriages among the widowed?

16 Describe the dating and courtship of those widowed early in life. Do men or women seem to have greater advantages? Why?

17 What problems do people widowed in middle age or older have in remarrying? Are men or women more likely to remarry? Why?

18 What are several of the special problems older widowed people have in adjusting to remarriage usually not found in young remarriages?

# REPRODUCTION

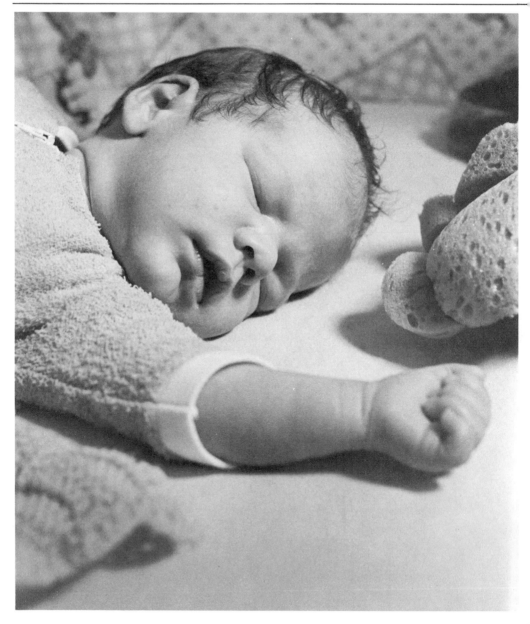

# 22

This chapter will present as clearly as possible in a brief space some essential facts of the reproductive process that should be understood by individuals before marriage.

## THE FEMALE REPRODUCTIVE SYSTEM

The female reproductive system consists of external and internal organs. The external are (1) two labia majora, (2) two labia minora, and (3) the clitoris. Collectively these are called the vulva. The labia majora are folds of tissue that form the outer rim or boundary of the vulva. The labia minora are inside, or between, the labia majora and are thinner, elongated folds of mucous membrane. The clitoris is a small organ situated at the point where the upper edges of the labia minora join. It is exclusively an organ of sensation.

The internal organs are (1) the vagina, (2) the uterus, (3) two Fallopian tubes, and (4) two ovaries. The vagina is an elastic passageway between the uterus and the vulva, opening into a small space called the vestibule, between the labia minora. The vagina serves as the female organ of copulation, and is the birth canal. It is also the passageway for the menstrual flow. The vaginal opening is partially closed by a membrane called the hymen. Superstitions exist concerning the hymen, not only among primitive people but also in the United States. Chief among these erroneous beliefs is that the hymen is an infallible index to a woman's virginity. Actually, its presence, absence, or structure is unreliable as a means for the layman to determine either virginity or nonvirginity. Natural variations in size, structure, and thickness of the hymen are great—from membranes that are of such slight development that they are hardly discernible, or so loose and dilatable that they survive intercouse and even the birth of a child, to others that are very thick and strong, with only a tiny opening into the vagina.

The uterus is a pear-shaped, muscular organ normally about three inches long and two inches wide. It serves as the home of the fetus during the period of gestation. Its muscular walls increase in thickness and size during pregnancy and serve as the chief force in expelling the child during the birth process. The uterus opens into the vagina through the cervix, a muscular ring at the lower end of the uterus.

The ovaries are the gonads or sex glands of the female. They have two chief functions. They produce the reproductive cells called ova or eggs, and they manufacture the hormones (estrogen and progesterone) responsible for the development of female characteristics and for the processes that result in menstruation. The Fallopian tubes conduct the egg cells from the ovaries to the uterus. The meeting of an egg cell with the sperm, and its subsequent fertilization, usually takes place in the larger part of the Fallopian tube. Each tube is about four inches long; its smaller end opens into the uterus, and its larger end lies closely around the surface of the ovary but not directly connected to it. The end that is in contact with the ovary is made up of numerous fingerlike projections, which are for the purpose of intercepting the egg, when released from the ovary and starting it on its way through the Fallopian tubes to the uterus.

## THE MALE REPRODUCTIVE SYSTEM

The male reproductive system consists of the following organs or structures: (1) two testicles or testes, (2) two epididymides, (3) two vasa deferentia (the testicles, epididymides, and part of the vasa deferentia are contained in the scrotum), (4) two seminal vesicles, (5) the prostate gland, and (6) the penis.

The testes are the gonads, or sex glands, of the male. Each testicle is about the size of a walnut and they are suspended in the scrotum, a pouch or sac hanging between the thighs just behind the penis. The temperature of the testicles is usually somewhat lower than that of the rest of the body. It is probably because they need a temperature lower than the body temperature in order to function that they lie outside the body rather than inside, as do the female gonads (ovaries). The testicles have two chief functions. They secrete the male sex hormone (testosterone), which has much to do with the development of such male characteristics as body build, deep voice, and distribution of body hair. They also produce the reproductive cells, called spermatozoa or sperm cells. The manufacture of sperm cells begins at puberty and continues for many years. The number of spermatozoa produced decreases with age; in a few men their production ceases after middle age. However, cases are on record of men as old as 90 who have fathered offspring.

Convoluted along one side of each testicle within the scrotum is the epididymis, a loosely coiled tube into which the sperm cells are emptied for storage. The epididymis is connected to a tube called the vas deferens, which serves to suspend the testicle from the body and also to carry the sperm cells up out of the scrotum toward the seminal vesicle and the prostate gland. After the vas deferens leaves the scrotum, it extends up over the outside of the pubic bone and enters the abdominal wall through a very small opening in the muscles. It is this small opening or muscular ring that sometimes becomes enlarged or ruptured, allowing a portion of the abdominal lining or of the intestine to protrude through the opening, in the condition called "inguinal hernia."

After entering the abdominal cavity, the vas deferens joins the seminal vesicle and then passes through the tissue of the prostate gland to enter the urethra. There is uncertainty about where the sperm are stored for immediate ejaculation. It appears that they are stored in the ampulla, which is between the vas deferens and the seminal vesicle. The seminal vesicles secrete a fluid that, combined with the fluid secreted by the prostate gland and sperm, forms the semen, and is the material ejaculated in sexual intercourse. During intercourse the seminal vesicles and the prostate gland contract and force their contents out through the urethra. When the glands become full, they sometimes empty themselves in what are known as "seminal emissions" or "nocturnal emissions," that is, emissions of seminal fluid during sleep. Nocturnal emissions are very common and usually quite regular during adolescence or for males who do not have an outlet through sexual intercourse or masturbation. They are a natural result of glandular activity and are in no way harmful. The penis, through which the urethra makes its way to the exterior, is the male copulatory organ, corresponding to the vagina in the female. It is composed of special tissue, in reality a spongy network of blood vessels which, during sexual excitement, become engorged and congested, causing the penis to enlarge, harden, and become erect in position. This condition enables the penis to enter and deposit semen within the vagina.

## CONCEPTION

Approximately once each month, from puberty until the menopause, ovulation takes place in the female reproductive system, although individual differences exist in the frequency of ovulation and in the number of ova released with each ovulation. During ovulation the egg is released from the ovary and starts its course to the uterus. It is swept into the Fallopian tube by the fingerlike projections that lie closely about the ovary. If sperm are present, the egg usually meets them somewhere in its course through the tube and is fertilized there.

During sexual intercourse, millions of spermatozoa are deposited in the vagina near the entrance to the uterus. The sperm cells are extremely motile and begin moving rapidly in all directions, some of them entering the uterus and traveling on into the tubes. If an egg is encountered, the sperm cell unites with the egg cell and conception has occurred. The fertilized egg continues through the Fallopian or uterine tube to the uterus, where it implants itself, and development of the embryo proceeds. If sperm do not appear while the egg is progressing toward the uterus and fertilization does not take place, the egg soon dies and, together with other elements that were involved in its production, is later cast off during the menstruation process.

## MENSTRUATION

Throughout the ages, menstruation in women has been the subject of much speculation and superstitious belief on the part of both laymen and medical men. Only within the last hundred years has any reliable scientific information been available, and research continues to add answers to some of the baffling questions that have existed about this function. In general, however, it may be said that menstruation is the result of failure of conception to occur. During the time that the egg is maturing and ready to be released from the ovary, elaborate preparations are being made within the uterus to receive a fertilized egg. The exact manner of these preparations and the factors that initiate them are complicated and very interesting. For our purposes, it is sufficient to say that within the ovary are produced hormones (estrogen and progesterone) that are carried through the blood stream to the uterus, where they cause certain changes to take place. A steadily increasing growth of the mucous membrane lining of the uterus (endometrium) occurs, and also a gradually increasing supply of blood in the endometrium. Another change takes place in the endometrium that is specifically designed to provide anchorage for the fertilized egg (zygote) if it arrives to ensure that it will not be cast off before it is firmly implanted. All these preparations are completed in each monthly cycle in time to receive the egg. If no sexual intercourse takes place, or if sperm have been deposited but have failed to reach and fertilize the egg, the egg disintegrates and fails to arrive in the uterus as expected. Since all the preparations for the egg are useless, the uterine surface, which has enlarged and become full of blood, is cast off and makes its way out of the body in what we call menstruation.

It has been said that no woman is the same in moods and behavior every day of her approximately 28-day cycle because she is influenced by the effect of glandular secretion. On the other hand, men tend to show more evenness in behavior and feelings because their glands tend to function the same day after day with no alternating or balancing of sex hormones. In the woman there must be a balancing of estrogen and progesterone as she goes through the monthly cycle. An alternation in balance is necessary to produce the stages of the cycle, such as the buildup of the uterine wall in preparation for ovulation and fertilization, or for the deterioration of the uterine wall and subsequent menstruation. It is thought that an imbalance in the estrogen-progesterone level brings on the many and varied feelings women have leading up to menstruation. There may also be weight gain because of the tendency of the body tissues to retain water at this time. The physical and emotional changes commonly experienced preceding menstruation have been called the "premenstrual syndrome."

To get a better understanding of some of the physical and mental–emotional changes accompanying the menstrual cycle, 400 women in family sociology classes were asked to cooperate in keeping daily records of their changes in feelings for from one to three months.[1] When the study was completed, we had fairly complete records on 334 cycles as reported by 181 women whose cycles had ranged from 20 to 42 days. A summary of the study is given in Tables 22-1 and 22-2. The first quarter would begin with the first day of menstruation; the fourth quarter would be the one leading up to the next menstruation. It will be noticed from the tables that certain physical and mental–emotional symptoms were reported with far greater frequency during the first and fourth quarters of the cycle.

The most common physical symptoms were decreased energy, skin eruptions, tenderness of the breasts, and headaches. The most commonly reported mental–emotional states were depression, tendency to worry,

TABLE 22-1

Daily physical changes during 334 menstrual cycles, as reported by 181 women, summarized by quarters of the cycle

| Physical symptoms | First quarter (N–334) | Second quarter (N–334) | Third quarter (N–334) | Fourth quarter (N–334) |
|---|---|---|---|---|
| Decreased energy (easily fatigued) | 63.5% | 25.4% | 27.8% | 44.0% |
| Skin eruptions | 52.7 | 26.9 | 29.0 | 57.8 |
| Headache | 40.1 | 20.4 | 18.9 | 32.6 |
| Increased appetite | 29.6 | 21.9 | 23.1 | 30.2 |
| Decreased appetite | 44.9 | 17.4 | 16.8 | 21.0 |
| Chills | 22.5 | 3.6 | 4.8 | 16.5 |
| Cramps | 56.6 | 3.3 | 3.9 | 22.5 |
| Nausea | 24.0 | 4.5 | 6.0 | 9.9 |
| Poor coordination | 19.2 | 9.6 | 5.4 | ,14.7 |
| Swelling or tenderness in breasts | 30.2 | 3.6 | 10.2 | 44.0 |
| Weight gain | 24.3 | 6.9 | 12.0 | 21.3 |

[1] Judson T. Landis, "Physical and Mental–Emotional Changes Accompanying the Menstrual Cycle," *Research Studies of the State College of Washington, Proceedings of the Pacific Sociological Society* 25:2 (June 1957), 155–62.

TABLE 22-2

Daily mental–emotional changes during 334 menstrual cycles, as reported by 181 women, summarized by quarters of the cycle

| Mental–emotional state | First quarter (N–334) | Second quarter (N–334) | Third quarter (N–334) | Fourth quarter (N–334) |
|---|---|---|---|---|
| Depressed | 47.9% | 29.0% | 31.7% | 48.2% |
| Tendency to worry | 34.4 | 25.4 | 24.9 | 35.9 |
| Tendency to cry easily | 41.3 | 21.0 | 26.9 | 42.8 |
| Inability to concentrate | 48.8 | 25.4 | 26.3 | 38.6 |
| Inability to make decisions | 20.4 | 12.6 | 11.7 | 19.2 |
| Forgetfulness (absent-mindedness) | 23.1 | 11.7 | 16.2 | 16.8 |
| Disorganized at work | 32.9 | 15.6 | 17.1 | 21.0 |
| Irritable (touchy, argumentative, quarrelsome) | 35.9 | 16.8 | 22.2 | 36.8 |
| Uncooperative toward others | 18.3 | 9.6 | 14.1 | 18.0 |
| Tendency to nag | 13.8 | 8.4 | 8.7 | 20.1 |
| Critical of others | 24.6 | 14.4 | 19.2 | 28.1 |
| Feeling of being unloved or unappreciated | 17.7 | 9.9 | 12.9 | 26.3 |
| Affectionate toward others | 47.9 | 40.7 | 36.8 | 36.5 |
| Increased sexual desire | 44.3 | 29.9 | 29.0 | 38.0 |
| Decreased sexual desire | 24.9 | 10.5 | 11.7 | 18.3 |

tendency to cry, inability to concentrate, irritability, affection toward others, and increased sexual desire.

Several other studies have attempted to find the mental–physical–emotional characteristics of premenstrual tension.[2,3,4,5] These studies have found similar characteristics as did our study. In addition, one study found that wives' negative behavior also caused some husbands to report more physical–emotional problems during the period of the wives' premenstrual cycle. Some evidence indicates that women are more likely to have accidents, attempt suicide, commit assaults or crimes, or to require hospitalization for emotional troubles during the premenstrual days. With menstruation over, there often follows a feeling of physical, emotional, and mental well-being. Some women can feel a sharp pain when the ovum is released from the ovary 12–14 days after the beginning of menstruation, the time at which conception is most likely to take place.

The evidence shows that certain changes in emotions and in physical functioning do commonly accompany stages in the menstrual cycle.[6] But

[2] Katharina Dalton, *The Premenstrual Syndrome* (Springfield, Ill.: Charles C Thomas, Publisher, 1964).

[3] Dalton, *The Menstrual Cycle* (New York: Pantheon Books, Paperback Library, 1972).

[4] J. H. Morton, *American Journal of Obstetrics and Gynecology* 65 (1953), 1182.

[5] Julia A. Sherman, *On the Psychology of Women: A Survey of Empirical Studies* (Springfield, Ill.: Charles C Thomas, Publisher, 1973).

[6] See discussion of swings in mood associated with the menstrual cycle, in Chapter 15, Sexual Adjustment in Marriage, pp. 278–79.

menstruation is not an illness and usually is not accompanied by serious pain, although about half the women in our sample reported having cramps during menstruation. Most girls look on menstruation as a normal function related to femininity. Possibly some of the symptoms experienced are a reflection of their attitude toward and what they have learned about menstruation. They may have been conditioned to feel different at certain times of the month and so they may play the role of feeling different and give undue attention to the "premenstrual syndrome," whether real or imagined. If menstrual periods are regularly accompanied by severe pain, medical help should be obtained, for such pain is evidence of abnormal functioning.

## The "safe period"

The rhythm method or safe period, sometimes depended on as a means of controlling conception, is based on the principle that conception can take place only at the time when the egg is in the Fallopian tubes. If intercourse is limited to other periods of the month, conception will not occur. This theory is sound, but since so many factors remain unknown at the present time, the theory is not reliable in controlling conception.

Research biologists are agreed that conception can take place only when the egg is present, but they do not know exactly when the egg will be expelled from the ovary. In general, this takes place during the middle of a regular 28-day menstrual cycle. However, not all cycles are regular, and ovulation is believed to take place about 14 days before the onset of the next menstruation. This of course means that ovulation is not in the middle of the cycle in a 21-day or a 40-day cycle, or in any other that regularly or occasionally varies from the 28-day cycle. For some years, women who hoped to control conception through the rhythm method were taught to use a temperature chart to establish the time of ovulation. A sudden rise in body temperature of about three-fifths of a degree in midmonth was thought to indicate ovulation. However, it is now known that the temperature rise indicates the hormonal changes that take place *near* the time of ovulation but does not accurately indicate the exact time. Research at Sloane Hospital for Women found that the interval between ovulation and temperature rise may vary by as much as four days.[7] In some cases evidence seems to show that ovulation may occur at times other than about two weeks preceding the next menstruation. We know that more than one egg can mature at one time, since this occurs when fraternal twins are conceived. It is also possible then that eggs may be released at different times in the cycle. Moreover, it is now known that some women do not ovulate during every cycle. Progress in medical research has led to a new recognition of individual differences in

[7] C. L. Buxton and E. T. Engle, "Time of Ovulation," *American Journal of Obstetrics and Gynecology* 60:3 (September 1950), 539–51.

functioning. There is far less tendency than formerly to believe that, even when general patterns of biological functioning have been determined, any one individual can be expected to function according to a regular pattern.

Authorities do not yet know the length of time the egg may live if it is not fertilized or the length of time the sperm cells will survive in the uterine cavity. One researcher believes that the spermatozoa retains its capacity to fertilize the egg cells no longer than 24 hours, and that the egg is capable of fertilization no longer than 12 hours.[8] Others disagree. All the uncertainties and unpredictable factors mean that the "safe period" is not reliable as a method of controlling conception.

## TESTS FOR PREGNANCY

Although it is usually impossible for a doctor to determine pregnancy with certainty during the first two months after conception, tests have been devised that are almost 100 percent accurate if administered properly. The best known of these tests, the Friedman and the Aschheim-Zondek, work on the same principle. After conception takes place, a new hormone is secreted and excreted in the urine. If the urine is injected into a virgin female animal, it will cause the genital tract to mature and ovulation to take place within from one to four days. The Friedman test uses rabbits, the Aschheim-Zondek uses mice or rats, and a more recent test uses frogs. One advantage of the frog test is that the induced ovulation takes place in from six to eighteen hours. Consequently, this test will show the existence of pregnancy almost at once.

Another pregnancy test, which does not use animals, is the cervical color test. In pregnancy, the cervix deepens in color and by the fortieth day a test matching cervical color with prepared color slides is usually strongly positive.[9]

Usually, only those women whose commitments make it necessary for them to know at once go to the trouble and expense of having a test for pregnancy. Most women wait until other evidence indicates whether or not they are pregnant.

## PRESUMPTIVE SIGNS OF PREGNANCY

Signs that are not based on biological tests or the doctor's diagnosis after an examination are said to be presumptive. In the early months of pregnancy, the following are presumptive signs: (1) skipping menstrual period, (2) nausea or "morning sickness," (3) increased frequency of urination, and (4) increasing tenderness of the breasts. None of these

[8] Edmond J. Farris, *Human Fertility and Problems of the Male* (White Plains, New York: The Author's Press, Inc., 1950), p. 145.

[9] Farris, *Human Ovulation and Fertility* (Philadelphia: J. B. Lippincott Co., 1956), pp. 133–36.

REPRODUCTION

by itself is conclusive, since each may be due to some other cause. A combination of these signs, however, could be considered evidence that pregnancy may exist. However, pregnancy may exist without some of these signs appearing at all. In some cases of pregnancy, menstruation may continue for one or two periods. Conversely, failure to menstruate cannot be taken as an absolute sign of pregnancy because it may instead be the result of nervous tension or worry, or even climatic changes. Also, many women have no nausea during pregnancy. Although more than half of all pregnant women report nausea or morning sickness, some women have had nausea when they thought they were pregnant but actually were not; on discovery that they were not pregnant, the nausea disappeared. Nevertheless, in our study of 212 couples who had gone through their first pregnancy, we found many cases in which the wife reported to have had nausea before she suspected that she was pregnant.[10] Wives who have been using contraceptives or who for some other reason believe it is impossible for them to become pregnant have sometimes experienced nausea as an early symptom. This suggests that the nausea of early pregnancy has a basis in metabolic changes or in changes in the glandular balances that may occur with conception.

## POSITIVE SIGNS OF PREGNANCY

By the third month the doctor's examination will usually be accurate in determining whether pregnancy exists. By this time there will be an enlargement and softening of the cervix. The fetal heartbeat can be heard during the fourth or fifth month, at which time the mother can "feel life," or the movement of the fetus. Shortly after this time, changes in the mother's figure will become evident.

## BOY OR GIRL?

Since parenthood begins before the child is born, couples are curious about the child's sex some months before birth. Superstition and "folk" beliefs about guessing the child's sex are common. Some of these say that a boy is carried high, will kick the mother's right side, will cause the mother to prefer sour foods, will cause more nausea, or will be more active, and that a girl will cause the opposite effects. All of these beliefs are without foundation.

Researchers continue to seek ways to discover the sex of the child before birth. But, so far, they have not found means that can be used in average pregnancies to satisfy the curiosity of parents. A procedure called "amniocentesis," in which a small sample of the amniotic fluid is taken for analysis, is used in certain pregnancies when, for special

[10] Shirley Poffenberger, Thomas Poffenberger, and Judson T. Landis, "Intent Toward Conception and the Pregnancy Experience," *American Sociological Review* 17:5 (October 1952), 616–20.

reasons, it is necessary to obtain sloughed-off cells from the growing baby and study them. It has been found that, through these procedures, it is also possible to discover the sex of the child, but because amniocentesis requires hospitalization, involves some risk, and is very costly, it would never be attempted simply to discover the sex of the unborn baby without some crucial reason for needing such information. Thus, for the present, parents wait until their child is born to know whether they have a son or a daughter.

The sex of the baby is determined at the time the sperm unites with the egg, and nothing can be done to change the sex after that. All eggs are alike, but there are two types of sperm cells, those with an X chromosome and those without the X chromosome; sperm cells without the X chromosome are designated as "Y." If the egg is fertilized by a sperm having an X chromosome, the baby is a girl; if fertilized by a sperm having a Y chromosome, the baby is a boy. Scheinfeld worked out a simple chart that describes the process by which sex is determined (see Figure 22-1).[11] Since it seems to be chance whether an X or Y sperm will fertilize an egg, it might be expected that an equal number of boys and girls would be born. However, the sex ratio at birth is 105.5 boys to 100 girls, and at conception it has been estimated to be between 120 and 150 boys to 100 girls. Several theories have been advanced to explain why more Y sperm cells than X reach their mark. Some of these theories are that the Y sperm cells are able to move faster or that the acidity of the female genital tract is more often fatal to X sperm.

## MULTIPLE BIRTHS

Identical twins result when a fertile egg divides into two embryos. (Siamese twins develop if the egg does not completely divide.) Identical twins, then, are developed from a single egg and a single sperm and usually grow with one placenta. It is often difficult to know whether twins are identical or fraternal, but a series of tests have been developed that can make the distinction. Twins that are not identical grow when two eggs are fertilized simultaneously. Individuals produced by this type of multiple birth are no more alike than are other brothers and sisters who are produced by single births. Fraternal twins may be of different sexes, whereas identical twins are always of the same sex, since they are the result of an egg fertilized by a single sperm, either X or Y.

Other multiple births, such as triplets, quadruplets, and quintuplets, may be identical, fraternal, or a combination of the two. The Dionne quintuplets, girls born in Canada in 1934 who all survived to adulthood, are thought to have been the result of one fertilized egg that divided and

[11] Amram Scheinfeld, *Women and Men* (New York: Harcourt Brace Jovanovich, Inc., 1943), p. 12.

REPRODUCTION

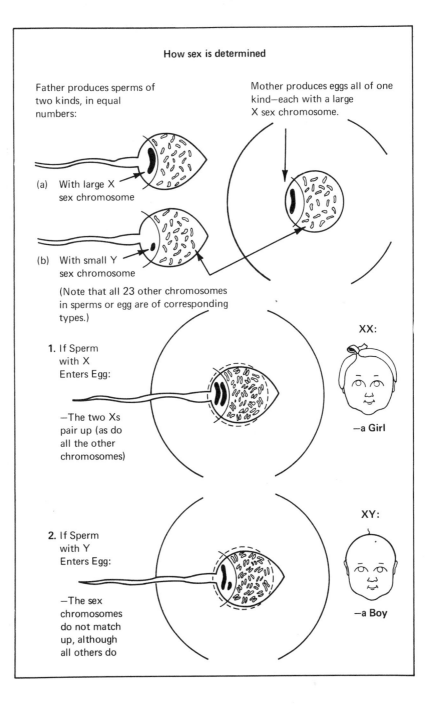

FIG. 22–1  Amram Scheinfeld, *Women and Men* (New York: Harcourt Brace Jovanovich, Inc., 1943).

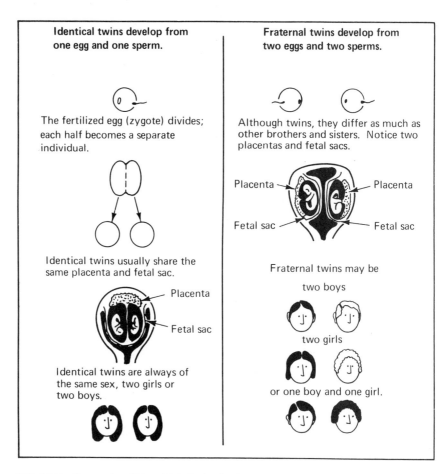

**Identical twins develop from one egg and one sperm.**

The fertilized egg (zygote) divides; each half becomes a separate individual.

Identical twins usually share the same placenta and fetal sac.

Placenta

Fetal sac

Identical twins are always of the same sex, two girls or two boys.

**Fraternal twins develop from two eggs and two sperms.**

Although twins, they differ as much as other brothers and sisters. Notice two placentas and fetal sacs.

Placenta

Placenta

Fetal sac

Fetal sac

Fraternal twins may be

two boys

two girls

or one boy and one girl.

FIG. 22–2 The way in which multiple births develop.

produced five individuals. Division into two would have produced identical twins.

For many years it had been observed that multiple births seemed to run in families, and that if a woman had one multiple birth she was more likely than other women to have a second multiple birth. The mystery of multiple births is better understood today because of research on infertility.

The fertility hormone which causes the ovaries to release the ovum is secreted by the pituitary gland. The hormone can be extracted from the urine of women who are past the child bearing age. When given to non-fertile women, it causes the ovaries to release ova, often one ovum from each ovary, producing twins. Sometimes several ova are released at one time, resulting in several babies. Evidently, multiple births in families in the past were due to an excess of this hormone being released by the pituitary gland. The time may come when the dosage of the fertility hormone can be controlled so that it will cause the ovaries to release one, two, or more ova. Couples would then be able to decide how many babies they wanted at one time.

The incidence of multiple births increases until the mother is 39 years old and decreases slightly thereafter. The ratio of multiple births is higher among nonwhites than among whites.

## PREGNANCY

**Choosing a doctor.** As soon as pregnancy is suspected, the couple should find a doctor. During the first days and weeks after conception, if any recognized complication arises, medical advice is imperative. The task of choosing a doctor is relatively simple for those who have lived in the same community or city for many years. They may already have a family doctor who will either continue with care or will suggest an obstetrician. The problem is more complicated for couples who are newly located and without a family doctor. To such couples, the choice of a doctor may present a puzzling problem. It is essential that they find one whom they believe competent to handle any complications that might arise. Otherwise, worries and doubts may disturb their peace of mind unnecessarily during the pregnancy. In many communities, the couple may inquire at a hospital and secure a list of the doctors or obstetrical clinics in the area. Most hospitals will not make specific recommendations. The couple may consult the latest edition of the *Directory of Medical Specialists* in any public library. It lists specialists in obstetrics and gynecology who have been certified by the American Board of Obstetrics and Gynecology.

In many communities, prospective parents may choose an obstetrician who practices with a group of two or three other doctors. Two or more obstetricians, along with a pediatrician or a doctor in general practice, share offices and cooperate in their practice. The prospective mother can choose the doctor she prefers, but may at some time during the pregnancy have consultations with the cooperating doctors also, so that in case of any emergency, any one of the doctors could be ready to help. This kind of arrangement can allay doubts or feelings of insecurity she may have about the care that will be available to her at the time of the birth.

Some prospective parents are too timid in their preliminary consultation with a doctor. A qualified doctor knows the importance of rapport between the obstetrician, and the patients and will be willing to talk with the couple frankly. The doctor will take time to get acquainted with them. At this time, the doctor will designate what the fees are, what hospitals are available, and will answer other questions the couple may wish to ask. After making a choice and having had a consultation, the couple should follow the doctor's advice during the pregnancy and birth of the child.

Early in the pregnancy the doctor will give the expectant mother a thorough physical examination to determine her general health. The doctor will be interested in her health background, including the obstetrical history of her mother and sisters, and will check blood pressure and make tests for venereal disease. Throughout the pregnancy the doctor will keep a close check on all conditions and developments in order to be able to anticipate any complication that may arise at the time of the birth and so be prepared to cope with it. All these things are an important part of the services of the obstetrician.

## PHYSICAL AND PSYCHOLOGICAL DEVELOPMENTS

Pregnancy is accompanied by a number of physical changes, some of which are readily apparent. The one of which both husband and wife are usually most conscious is the wife's gaining weight and her change in figure. With the physical changes, there are also emotional and psychological effects, which sometimes cause difficulty in the couple's adjustment. If the child is desired by both and the pregnancy occurs after being planned, difficulties may be somewhat less likely to arise, for both enter the experience with a feeling of sharing and mutual responsibility. They know that, although it is the wife's part to go through the physical processes of pregnancy and birth, the whole undertaking is as vitally important to the husband as to her. Such couples often find the months preceding the birth of their child among the happiest in their lives. Even so, it sometimes comes as a shock to them to find that the wife may possibly lose all sexual desire early in the pregnancy. This often occurs. Occasionally, a woman may have more sexual desire during pregnancy, but many women have reported that, although they feel excellent physically and feel affectionate toward their husbands, they seem incapable of their usual sexual response when pregnant.

If the couple did not desire a child and if conception occurred without their having planned for it, they sometimes experience more emotional upset and more problems of adjustment (see Figure 22-3), although it is possible that some of these difficulties may arise regardless of whether the child was desired. Some wives consider pregnancy an illness and demand all the privileges of a semi-invalid. Other wives may resent the loss of their figures and react emotionally, blaming the husbands for the inconveniences of pregnancy. Some couples have their first difficulties in sexual adjustment at this time.

In the previously quoted study of 212 pregnancies, information was secured on changes in sexual desire of husbands and wives during the first pregnancy.[12] Half the wives and three out of four of the husbands said they saw no change in sexual desire during the first trimester, but

[12] Judson T. Landis, Thomas Poffenberger, and Shirley Poffenberger, "The Effects of First Pregnancy Upon the Sexual Adjustment of 212 Couples," *American Sociological Review* 15:6 (December 1950), 767–72.

REPRODUCTION

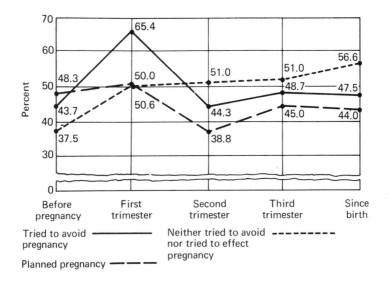

FIG. 22–3 Percentages of 212 wives experiencing emotional upset (frequently or sometimes) during five periods of marriage, classified by intent toward first pregnancy.

that the desire of both decreased rapidly through the next two trimesters. More than one-fourth of the wives noticed a marked decrease in sexual desire with the onset of pregnancy, and less than one in five noticed an increase in sexual desire with pregnancy. We do not know why this change in sexual desire takes place, but, since the pattern of the husband is similar to that of the wife, it appears that there is a strong psychological basis for it. However, some couples, unable to appreciate that the wife's sudden loss of interest in sex is only a temporary condition, may lose perspective and decide that the marriage is in trouble. The husband may show his frustration by becoming critical of his wife and irritable. His wife is in no mood to take such behavior. She feels that he should be more considerate than usual rather than less so during her pregnancy. Thus, sometimes tensions and unhappiness result that could be avoided if both had a better understanding of pregnancy and could maintain a better perspective of the situation.

The wife is usually healthy and can live normally and happily during these months. Our study of pregnancy showed that more than half the wives noticed no change in their health, one-third said their health was better, and only one in ten said her health was poorer during pregnancy. Nausea is a common discomfort, especially during the first three months. More than half the wives in our pregnancy study reported having had nausea in the first trimester, but only 15 percent reported it during the last three months of pregnancy (see Figure 22-5).[13] Most of those who had nausea considered it a discomfort rather than "ill-health." Rosengren

[13] Poffenberger, Poffenberger, and Landis, "Intent Toward Conception."

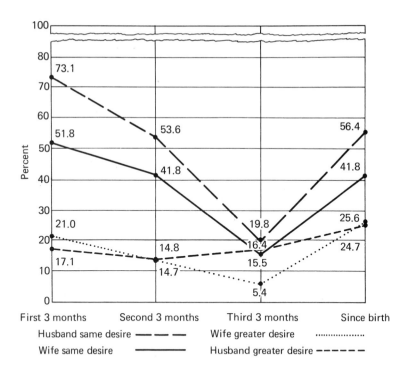

FIG. 22–4 Percentages of 212 husbands and wives rating sexual desire in three periods of pregnancy and since birth, as compared with desire before pregnancy.

found in a study of pregnant women that their assuming a "sick" role was related to whether they were unhappy and insecure in other aspects of their marriages and in their general outlook on life.[14]

In many of the adjustments during pregnancy, it is logical that the husband should be the one most willing to compromise and sacrifice his personal desires. Our research among young couples indicated that husbands did identify closely with their wives; the wives found their husbands more helpful, thoughtful, and affectionate than ever before. However, if the husbands noticed any change in the dispositions of their wives, it was that some wives were harder to live with during pregnancy.

A woman is not likely to feel very kindly toward her husband if he shows embarrassment or unwillingness to be seen with her when her pregnancy is apparent, or if he makes any remarks that are critical rather than complimentary about the clothes she wears when pregnant.

Fortunately, nature seems to offer compensation; many women have an unusual feeling of well-being during pregnancy—their complexions are better and, in general, their appearance, with the exception of their figures, improves. One study found that the majority of husbands rated

[14] William R. Rosengren, "Social Sources of Pregnancy Illness or Normality," *Social Forces* 39:3 (1961), 260–67.

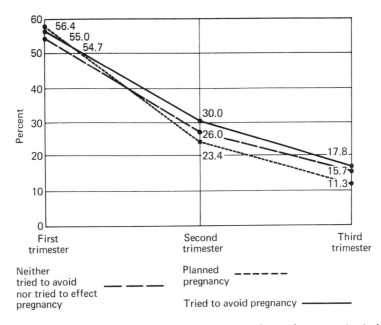

FIG. 22–5 Percentages of 212 wives experiencing nausea (frequently or sometimes) during trimesters of pregnancy, classified by intent toward first pregnancy.

their wives as attractive or more than usually attractive to them physically during pregnancy.

Within about six weeks after the birth of the baby, sexual desire returns to about the same level as before conception and normal sexual relations can usually be reestablished. Of course, a baby in the house means extra work and loss of sleep, factors likely to have an effect on the sex life of new parents.

## PRENATAL INFLUENCES

There is some tendency for prospective mothers to worry about the possibility that their child might be abnormal in some way. Such worries are probably more common during first pregnancies than during succeeding ones, for it seems logical that a woman who has given birth to one or two healthy, normal children would have more confidence and fewer fears of the unknown. In our study of first pregnancies among 212 wives in Michigan some years ago, slightly more than two out of five reported having had such worries during the first pregnancy.[15]

Medical scientists agree that accurate knowledge is still incomplete concerning many factors affecting the growth and development of the unborn. It is known that use of some drugs, exposure to excess radiation, or the mothers having certain virus diseases can affect the unborn

[15] Poffenberger, Poffenberger, and Landis, "Intent Toward Conception."

child's development. Evidence shows that most of these factors, to be damaging in effect, must be operative at a precise point in fetal development. It has been determined within the past few years that cigarette smoking by the pregnant mother retards fetal growth in size and weight. Research at the Columbia–Presbyterian Medical Center in New York City found that nicotine passes quickly from the mother through the placenta to the fetus; its effect is greatest during the later months of pregnancy and contributes to low birth weight and premature birth.

Doctors now are not so rigid as before in their advice to mothers about keeping their weight low during pregnancy. It is recognized that a reasonable gain of about 25 pounds or, in some cases, more probably leads to a better birth weight in the child, and that prenatal mortality tends to increase as birth weight decreases.

In past generations, because there was no known explanation for abnormalities, folklore and old wives' tales offered explanations that were widely accepted. Mothers could only fear the worst or hope for the best, but could have no realistic understanding of the subject. As research continues to accumulate more accurate knowledge about prenatal development and about potentially damaging factors, more is known about precautions that can be taken.

Since evidence became conclusive in the 1940s that German measles contracted by the mother during the first weeks of pregnancy could have damaging effects on the baby, pregnant women have become generally aware of the necessity to avoid exposure to this disease. In 1967 the U.S. Public Health Service announced the development of a new, rather simple blood test for German measles (rubella) antibodies. By means of this test, a woman can know ahead of time whether she is susceptible to that disease. If her blood shows antibodies, she has already had a mild case, perhaps without even noticing it, and she need not worry about contracting it during her pregnancy and risking damage to her child. For people not immune to rubella, a vaccine is effective as prevention. However, the vaccine cannot be used if a woman is already pregnant, or even during months when she might possibly become pregnant, for the vaccine can have the same prenatal effects as would a case of the disease. As a preventative of birth defects, the rubella vaccine can only be effective if used in the general population of children or of girls before they reach the age for potential pregnancy.

Since the 1940s new knowledge has been gained of the dangers of some extreme vitamin deficiencies and of certain drugs. When it was first recognized that some drugs prescribed for pregnant women could cause severe damage or deformity in the developing fetus, it was believed that the effects could occur only if the drugs were used during the early weeks of pregnancy. It is now known that some kinds of damage can result from drugs used at later stages of fetal development, and that much remains unknown about possible effects of many drugs, even those most commonly used.

In recent years there has been concern about the use of drugs such as tranquilizers and marijuana. It is as yet not completely known how these drugs affect the developing fetus. Cases have been found in which babies born to alcoholic mothers show symptoms of alcohol addiction at birth, and after birth have the withdrawal symptoms of an alcoholic. Evidence also indicates that the baby of an alcoholic mother may have brain damage, or may have deformities of the heart and nervous system. The evidence is strong enough to suggest that alcoholic mothers should consider having their pregnancies aborted.

Expectant mothers today are usually warned to avoid *all* drugs or medication except in cases of extreme necessity. Moreover, doctors are more alert to the dangers of deficiencies in expectant mothers of the basic vitamins such as the B complex.

## THE Rh BLOOD FACTORS

During the early part of pregnancy, when the doctor tests for venereal disease a test for the Rh factor in the blood of the mother may also be made. This factor was first discovered in the blood of Rhesus monkeys. Like many other discoveries, its importance in childbearing has been exaggerated in the minds of many people. At first, it was even proposed that tests for this factor should be required before marriage and that people with incompatible blood should not marry. Now the Rh blood factors are better understood and can be coped with in childbearing.

About 85 percent of white persons have the Rh factor in their blood and are called "Rh positive"; 15 percent do not have the factor and are called "Rh negative." The Rh negative mother who conceives by an Rh positive father will sometimes give birth to an Rh positive child. When this happens, if any minute amount of the baby's blood gets into the mother's circulation—an occurrence that is extremely rare no matter what the blood types are—the mother's blood stream builds up antibodies against the incompatible blood elements. The presence of these antibodies in the mother's blood will not usually affect first or second pregnancies; it may cause jaundice and anemia in later babies. It is estimated that among couples with an Rh positive father and an Rh negative mother, only one in 300 pregnancies is actually affected by the wrong combination. Where periodic tests during pregnancy show that the mother's blood is building up the antibodies to the point of danger, doctors now prepare for the emergency and at birth the baby is given transfusions, which gradually replace the blood with which the child was born.

There are some obstetrical specialists who, when trouble is suspected in cases of parental blood incompatibility, take samples of the amniotic fluid at intervals to learn whether antibodies are present in the baby's waste products in the fluid. If the tests show increasing presence of the antibodies, the doctors may induce birth as early as possible or perform an early Caesarian section. Thus most babies from the small percentage that would be affected by the incompatibility of their parents' blood can be saved.

Prospective parents do much needless worrying if they know they have the "wrong combination" of blood. For example, a mother of four healthy children, all born before tests for the Rh factor were being made, who learned during her fifth pregnancy that she was Rh negative and her husband Rh positive, worried all through her pregnancy. Although this child also was healthy and unaffected, she was afraid to attempt another pregnancy. Probably she would have been afraid to have any children after the first one had she known about the Rh factor at that time.

Statistically, prospective mothers have every right to be optimistic today about the normality of the unborn child. Hospital and medical records show that the great majority of babies are normal and free of even the most minor defects. If all defects, serious and minor, are considered, an individual mother's chances of having a normal baby are several hundred to one.

## FETAL DEVELOPMENT

After fertilization, the egg immediately begins the process of division and growth, and continues through the tube where it met the sperm. It is believed that about three days are required for the fertilized egg to reach the uterus. Once there, it appears to rest for several more days. During this time, however, a process is taking place by which a part of the ovum is preparing to continue its development into a new individual, and another layer of cells is preparing for its special function of securing nourishment for the fetus during the months of its growth in the uterus. This second layer of cells forms the placenta, which becomes a flat, broad structure attached to the side of the uterus. It has numerous villi that penetrate the uterine lining and through osmotic action secure nutritive substances from the mother's blood. Waste products of the developing fetus are also given off by the same process, to be carried away by the mother's blood. All nutritive substances and waste products pass through a membrane by absorption. The placenta is connected to the umbilicus of the fetus by a cord containing the blood vessels that carry the nourishment and waste products back and forth. After the placenta has formed and established itself, membranes develop from the margin of the placenta and surround the fetus. This membranous sac fills with a watery fluid in which the fetus lives until almost time for birth. This fluid is called the "amniotic fluid" and serves to protect the fetus from outside shocks, as well as to keep the temperature constant. This sac of fluid breaks sometime during the birth process. Whether it breaks early or late will not affect the ease or difficulty of the birth.

The length of time required from conception to birth is between 266 and 270 days, or roughly nine calendar months.[16] Doctors usually figure that the birth is due 280 days from the beginning of the last menstruation. However, since conception in a 28-day cycle takes place approximately 12 days after the onset of the last menstruation, 268 days may be a more accurate figure. It is also known that individual differences exist in length of the gestation period, just as such differences exist in processes such as ovulation. A study in which the date of conception could be definitely known, either because the women had conceived by artificial insemination or because coitus had taken place only once during the month, found that age may have something to do with length of gestation. In the age group 20 to 23, gestation had averaged 272 days; in the age group 36 to 39, it had averaged 263 days.[17]

During gestation the embryo develops in size and complexity. By the end of the fourth week, the embryo is about a quarter inch long and is composed of a body and small buds that will later be the arms, legs, eyes, ears, and nose. By the end of the sixteenth week, the fetus is approximately five inches long and quite well developed; the sex organs, which until this time have appeared much the same for both sexes, have now differentiated. During the first two months the new individual is called an embryo; after that and until birth it is called a fetus. From this time on, the fetus grows in length and in weight, most of the weight increase coming during the later weeks of the prenatal period. The weight is approximately doubled in the last four weeks before birth. Studies of prenatal and infant development within recent years have changed medical attitudes toward birth weight. It is now recognized that the increase in weight before birth is an important contributing factor in the healthy growth and development of the infant during the months after birth.

## BIRTH

After approximately 38 weeks of growth, the fetus is ready to be born. A specific hormone functions at this time to initiate the birth process. Once the process has begun, it proceeds through three definite stages that result in releasing the child from the mother's body.

The first stage of labor is the longest and, for many mothers, the most tiresome. This stage may last anywhere between 2 and 20 hours, or more. The cervix at the uterus opening is composed of a circular band of involuntary muscles, which serve to hold the unborn child safely within the uterus until the time for birth. The uterus itself is composed of longitudinal muscles, also involuntary, which have become strong and tough in order to hold the baby during pregnancy, and which

[16] H. L. Stewart, "Duration of Pregnancy and Postmaturity," *Journal of the American Medical Association* 148 (March 1952), 1079–93.

[17] Farris, *Human Ovulation and Fertility,* p. 119.

contract during labor to dilate the cervix so that the baby can leave the uterus, and to push the baby through the cervical opening when dilation has been completed.

These processes of the first stage of labor are all accomplished by the action of involuntary muscles. The first awareness a mother has that the birth is near is usually sensations of muscle twitching or contracting that may be very much the same as the cramping sensations she may have had during menstruation. Many women have such cramping or contracting sensations at intervals for several days, or even longer, before they can be sure that the baby is about to be born. Actually, these intermittent cramps often accomplish the preliminaries of the first stage of labor for some women; by the time they become aware that the first stage of labor is definitely under way, a considerable amount of dilation of the cervix is already accomplished.

Most women agree that the sensations in this first stage are not so much pain as discomfort. Nevertheless, when a woman is in the hospital and the contractions are regular and rhythmic, if the first stage is slow and drawn out, she is likely to have feelings of discouragement or distress, to feel at times that she is involved in a tedious and tiring process that is endless.

There is nothing a mother can do at this stage to help expedite the birth. The involuntary muscles perform their function far better if she can be relaxed in mind and body. Undoubtedly, the process is slowed if the mother is tense or frightened, as she is likely to be if she does not understand what is happening. If she does understand, through adequate preparation, and if she knows that there is no set time limit within which this stage of the process can be expected to be accomplished, she is much more likely to be able to relax and conserve her strength for the next stage, in which she can help.

The second stage begins when dilation is complete; the cervix has opened and the baby is ready to be expelled from the uterus and pass through the birth canal (vagina) to be born. This stage is usually fairly short, from a few minutes to an hour or so. When this stage begins, the mother is taken to the delivery room of the hospital for the actual birth. Now she can help the process along, and the help she gives is real labor. Through controlled breathing, by alternately taking and holding deep breaths, she can bear down and help push the baby through the birth canal.

The third stage is the expelling from the uterus of the placenta, after the child is born. When the entire birth process is over, the tissues of the mother begin to return to their former state. The uterus begins a series of contractions and gradually returns to approximately its original size and shape. These changes returning to a prepregnancy condition usually take about six weeks.

There are many conflicting views among medical people and others concerning the pain accompanying childbirth. Some mothers say that the process was exhausting but that the sensations they had could not, in their view, be called intense "pain." Other mothers say that, in their experience, "labor pains" are unquestionably intensely painful. One doctor said of the second stage of labor, "It is certainly work, just as playing a game of football or running a race is work. How much of it is 'pain' is a matter of viewpoint or definition, and that differs with different women." Certainly, the facial expressions of many athletes in action could be interpreted as expressions of pain, but few of them would call their sensations pain. Undoubtedly, pain thresholds vary greatly with different individuals, and individuals have different concepts or definitions of pain. Most authorities agree that fear or tension increases pain in any circumstance, and childbirth may involve special tensions arising from a fear of the unknown or fears that have been built up by misinformation and lack of knowledge.

Studies by anthropologists of pregnancy and childbirth among primitive people show striking differences in the ease or difficulty of giving birth. The findings suggest that cultural conditioning and a society's attitudes toward childbirth are effective influences upon the process. Niles Newton studied two different Indian cultures in Central America and in Bolivia. One group, the Cuna, surround pregnancy and birth with great secrecy and many taboos. Girls are kept in ignorance as long as possible, and births occur in isolated secrecy. The other group, the Siriono, are very free and open in all ways about pregnancy and birth, births even taking place in a central hut with many people of both sexes present throughout. Of her observations Dr. Newton comments, "In the Cuna culture where frightening ritual accompanies labor, girls tend to have extreme and sometimes lengthy labor with periods of unconsciousness. In contrast, the relaxed, casual Siriono have startlingly quick labors, quicker by far than the labor of a typical woman in a Western industrial culture." [18]

Progress is being made toward a better understanding by laymen and doctors of the facts about the birth process in our culture. Clearer distinctions are now drawn between the mother's part and the doctor's part in "delivering" the baby. More doctors and laymen are recognizing that if nature takes its course the mother is more than merely present and heavily anesthetized while the doctor engineers the birth. In the usual normal birth, the important functions of the doctor are to stand ready to help in case of emergency, to see that anesthetics are provided if the mother needs or wants them, and to give reassurance and emotional support to the mother while the birth proceeds.

Various views are held concerning the use of anesthetics for mothers in childbirth. Doctors today tend to be more cautious in their use than they were some years ago, when many kinds of anesthetics were used extensively and some babies suffered harmful effects. Especially during

[18] Niles Newton, "Childbirth and Culture," *Psychology Today* 4:6 (November 1970), 375.

FIG. 22–6  Before labor: thick pelvic floor, cervix closed, uterus relaxed.

the first stage of labor, most doctors agree that quiet and as much rest as possible are most important. During the second stage, when the child is actually born, most doctors use some kind of anesthetic, unless the

FIG. 22–7  Labor: uterus contracting, cervix dilating, bag of water below head.

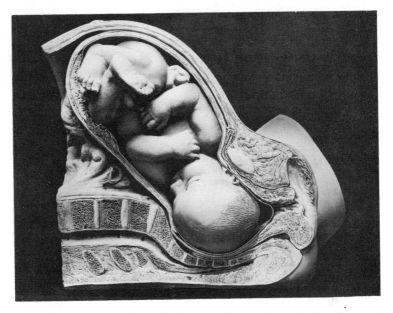

FIG. 22–8 Full dilation: head deep in birth canal, pull of uterine contractions draws cervix up.

mother prefers not to have it. Many mothers, because they want to be fully conscious and to know when the baby is born, prefer to have little if any anesthetic. This viewpoint among mothers is increasing because

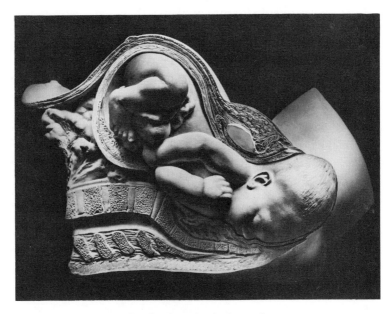

FIG. 22–9 Head turns upward, pelvic floor slips back over face.

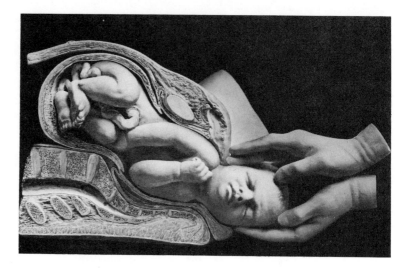

FIG. 22–10  Birth of the shoulders, turning to fit passage.

of the work of doctors who advocate "natural childbirth." These doctors believe that if mothers are thoroughly informed about what actually takes place in the birth process, if they are familiar with how the birth of the baby is to be handled—including some knowledge of hospital conditions and routines—and if they have confidence that the doctor will be standing by, ready for any emergency, they will go into the birth process free of tension and able to give birth naturally to the child with a minimum need or desire for anesthetics.

The policy of doctors who are exponents of natural childbirth is based on the view that it is the mother herself who needs to be prepared to give birth and who can best determine how painful is her experience and at what point she may want an anesthetic. These doctors do not promote the idea that there is any virtue in pain or that giving birth should be a test of endurance. They believe, rather, that a woman who is in good condition for the effort and fairly free of fears and tensions can give birth more quickly and with less physical or emotional trauma if the process is interfered with as little as possible. They hold that unnecessary or excess anesthesia may constitute interference.

These views are supported by research studies carried out at certain medical schools. A study was made of 1000 consecutive deliveries in the Yale University Service of the Grace-New Haven Community Hospital. All the mothers took part in the Training for Childbirth Program, which gave both physical and psychological preparation. Doctors organizing the program explained, "The educational aspects of our program consist of four talks given to prospective parents, and four exercise classes given by a nurse. . . . Following the fourth class, which is given in the third trimester of pregnancy, the women visit the obstetrical division of the hospital, meet members of the personnel, see the labor and delivery rooms, and learn how the delivery tables and anesthesia apparatus operate. The patient in labor is in a room by herself; during this period she may have her husband with her if she wishes. The patient is kept informed of her progress and during active labor is not left alone. Attention is focused upon her needs and what she is trying to accomplish. Any therapy or instruction is in the hands of a nurse or a physician. Activity and busyness on the part of those attending her are kept to a minimum." [19] That policy is typical of the best natural childbirth procedures.

Of the 1000 consecutive births reported in the Yale study, the average length of total labor, whether the birth was of a first baby or not, was 10.3 hours; only eight babies out of 1000 died.

Helen Heardman studied the duration of labor among 1000 women who were having their first baby; 500 of the mothers had gone through the "natural childbirth" training program and a control group of 500 had no special training. The average length of labor was approximately six hours shorter for the 500 who had gone through the training program, and there was a far larger percentage of normal deliveries in this group.[20]

Many doctors consider it routine to conduct classes or to have an assistant conduct classes for expectant mothers. Training similar to that described in the Yale program is usually given. One company has prepared a series of films showing normal labor and childbirth which are used at the conclusion of the training programs.

The education of young people should emphasize the normality of the birth process and of the launching of a new individual into life, rather than possible pain or risk.

Giving birth to a child today is not dangerous for the mother, as was true at one time. In the United States today, approximately one mother in 8000 dies in childbirth. The discovery and development of new drugs to prevent infection have done the most to reduce the dangers that once existed in childbirth. More progress is still needed to make good medical care available to nonwhite mothers and mothers from the lower socioeconomic classes. Childbirth risks are more than twice as great among this group. Almost all white mothers are attended by a physician and have their babies in hospitals. The most favorable age for giving birth to children is between 20 and 24 years, although if there is adequate medical care the risk is not great at any age.

[19] Herbert Thoms and Robert H. Wyatt, "One Thousand Consecutive Deliveries Under a Training for Childbirth Program," *American Journal of Obstetrics and Gynecology* 61:1 (January 1951), 205–9.
[20] Herbert Thoms, *Training for Childbirth* (New York: McGraw-Hill Book Company, 1950), p. 76.

## DECIDING ABOUT CIRCUMCISION

Before the baby is born the doctor will want to know whether the parents want the baby circumcised if the baby is a boy. The vast majority of boys born in the United States today are circumcised soon after birth, although it is not the general custom in any other country except Israel. Among Jews, the custom was prescribed in the Old Testament as a religious ritual. Genesis 17:11 quotes God as saying to Abraham, "And ye shall circumcise the flesh of your foreskin; and it shall be a token of the covenant betwixt me and you," and in 17:14, "And the uncircumcised man child whose flesh of his foreskin is not circumcised, that soul shall be cut off from his people; he hath broken the covenant."

Circumcision in the United States has religious significance only in the Jewish faith, and it was not commonly performed until recent years among non-Jews. People are now questioning the practice of routine circumcision. Those who favor circumcision argue that it is easier to keep the glans of the penis clean if the foreskin is removed, and that there might be a positive relationship between having a foreskin and getting cancer of the penis. Those who think the foreskin should not be removed believe that cleanliness can easily be achieved for most men, and that there is no added danger of cancer. They also believe that removal of the foreskin causes nerves in the glans without the protective cover to become less sensitive, and that sexual pleasure is reduced. Some consider circumcision an unnecessary disfigurement. Prospective parents should probably study the arguments pro and con before making a decision on circumcision.

## ROOMING-IN

Certain things can be done from the very moment of birth to give children a good emotional start. The earliest experiences an individual has with the mother are believed to affect later human relationships and to influence the total personality. Many hospitals now follow a plan designed to give children a better emotional start in life than they were given in the past. This is called the rooming-in plan, under which the babies are not kept in a central nursery but remain in the rooms with their mothers. Mothers are encouraged to do as much as they want to in caring for their newborn babies. Mothers acquire confidence in caring for their babies while in the hospital under direction of a nurse, and they learn from one another, since several may be in one unit of rooms. Breast-feeding is encouraged. More mothers seem to be able to nurse their babies when the babies are with them, and when the mother and baby are able to work out their own schedule, than when the baby is fed only at stated intervals according to hospital schedules.

New mothers may be more enthusiastic about rooming-in than mothers with several children. The latter may look forward to a vacation when they go to the hospital. Many hospitals have an arrangement of rooms that permits the mother to have her baby with her and still turn the baby over to the care of nurses when she wants to be free to rest. But even mothers of several children are likely to prefer to have their babies with them, because they want to know that their babies are comfortable at all times. Under the system in which babies are all kept in a central nursery, mothers often can hear babies crying and each one may worry over whether it is her baby that needs attention.

Hospitals and doctors using the rooming-in plan believe that a close relationship between mother and baby is important during the first days and weeks of the baby's life, and that it will produce better mental and emotional health for both mothers and babies.

## REVIEW QUESTIONS

1  Explain the basis of menstruation.

2  What are some of the physical states more commonly experienced during the first and fourth quarters of the menstrual cycle?

3  What are some of the mental–emotional states more commonly experienced during the first and fourth quarters of the menstrual cycle?

4  What are some of the unknowns that make the "safe period" or rhythm method unreliable for conception control?

5  What are some of the tests used for pregnancy?

6  What is the principle of the pregnancy tests?

7  Is it possible to determine the sex of an unborn child?

8  How is sex determined? Why are more boys than girls conceived?

9  What does new research reveal about the probable cause of multiple births?

10  Are multiple births more common among nonwhite or white mothers?

11  Where can one find help in choosing an obstetrician?

12  What are some of the common problems facing a couple during pregnancy?

13  Is the unborn affected by the mother's use of alcohol? drugs? cigarettes?

14  Explain the Rh blood factor.

15  Trace the development from fertilization to birth of the baby.

16  What are the three stages in the birth process? At which stage is the mother encouraged to help in giving birth to her child?

17  Explain the theory of "natural childbirth" as you understand it.

18  How are expectant mothers prepared for "natural" childbirth?

19  What is the origin of the custom of circumcising boys? Give the arguments for and against circumcision.

## PROJECT

1  Ask an obstetrician who believes in "natural childbirth" to speak to your class on pregnancy and childbirth.

2  Make a special report on the effect upon prenatal development of drugs used by the mother during pregnancy.

# FAMILY PLANNING

Although one of the functions of marriage is to perpetuate the race by producing and nurturing offspring, some married couples choose not to have children. Throughout history, couples who married expected to have children; if no children came, the marriage could be dissolved. Such marriages can still be dissolved in some countries; and in two states in the United States, inability to have children is a legal reason for divorce.[1]

## DESIRABLE FAMILY SIZE

Through the years we have queried college students concerning the number of children they considered desirable in the ideal family. The number given gradually increased until 1957. From that time there was no significant change until the late 1960s. The average number of children considered ideal by young people in 1936 was 2.3; in 1947, 3.0; in 1957, 3.4; in 1967, 3.5; and in 1971, 2.5. In 1976 a Gallup Poll showed that college-educated people considered 2.0 the ideal number of children. It is possible that the contrast in economic conditions between the depression of the 1930s and the prosperity of the 1950s and 1960s caused young people to think differently about the desirable number of children. War and threat of war may also have brought about a shifting of values toward greater emphasis on family living and the presence of children as contributing to happiness in the 1950s and early 1960s.

The rapid shift in attitudes about family size between 1967 and 1971 was spurred by several factors. One was recognition of ecological problems arising from overpopulation. Suddenly, the idea that several children were necessary for family happiness was rejected in favor of lowering

[1] Pennsylvania and Tennessee.

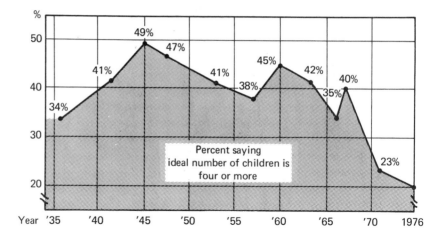

FIG. 23–1 Percentages of Americans stating that four or more children is the ideal family size, 1935 to 1976 (Gallup Poll). Men expressed a desire for smaller families than women, Protestants smaller than Catholics, college-educated smaller than high school or grade school graduates, and people under 30 years old smaller than those over that age.

the birth rate as necessary for survival. Another factor was probably related to the emerging independence of women and the surge toward sexual equality. More men and women now hold that a variety of roles other than motherhood are potentially satisfying and rewarding for women.

The Gallup Poll has surveyed a representative sample of the total population since 1935 on ideal family size. Figure 23-1 summarizes the percentages of Americans who said four or more children was the ideal size in each survey year.

## THE BIRTH RATE, PUBLIC ATTITUDES, AND SOCIOECONOMIC FACTORS

As public attitudes change on the desirable number of children, a change also occurs in actual family size. Around the beginning of this century the belief grew that people should have only the number of children they could care for and educate adequately. Contraception began to be accepted more widely and the birth rate gradually fell from 1900 to the 1930s. In the 1930s it was feared that the population of the United States would not reproduce itself; concern arose because the better educated and more privileged people had the lowest birth rate. With World War II attitudes again changed. People who had had small families had another child if they could or they tried to adopt children. Adoptable babies were very scarce and a "black market" in adoption developed. The birth rate rose sharply after World War II and for 20 years families were larger, until the sudden drop in the birth rate during the 1960s. Figure 23-2 summarizes birth rate trends since 1920.

Birth rates vary also in relation to certain socioeconomic factors. Rates have been proportionately higher among low-income groups than among high-income groups in both the city and the country. College-educated people have had fewer than their proportionate share of children. However, the current decline in the birth rate is even more rapid among the poor and the less well educated, especially among the black poor, than among groups of higher income and better education.

The number of children born varies among people of different religious faiths. Studies show that Catholics are most prolific, Protestants next, and Jews least. Mixed marriages of Catholics and Protestants have fewer children than do Protestant or Catholic marriages. But within all three religious groups, as in the population in general, those with higher incomes and more education and those in urban areas have proportionately fewer children than do the others of their faith.

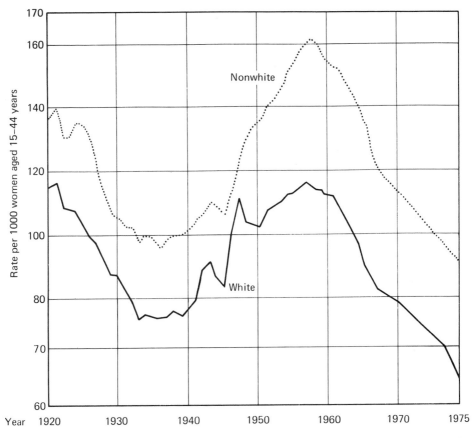

FIG. 23–2 Live births per 1000 women aged 15–44 for the United States 1920 to 1975 by color.

Although people have been interested in contraception for centuries, serious research is relatively recent. Papyrus rolls of as early as 1850 B.C. contain formulas for inducing abortion, and by the fourth century B.C. measures had been found for preventing conception. However, for centuries little progress was made toward developing contraceptive methods that were effective and acceptable.

The world population explosion of the 1950s and 1960s forced open discussion of contraception and general recognition of the need for more effective methods of limiting births. The overpopulation throughout the world has become a problem because better nutrition and medical care allow more babies born in underdeveloped countries to survive, grow up, and reproduce. It has become evident that saving a larger percentage of the babies born will result in a population too large for the world's space and food supply, hence the worldwide concern with curbing the birth rate.

Although attention was first focused on the underdeveloped countries and their rising population, the rapid growth in population in the United States now causes concern. In the decade of the 1960s, a frank and open approach was made to the problem of birth control by scientists, religious leaders, and legislators.

## RELIGIOUS GROUPS AND CONTRACEPTION

The sexual and reproductive behavior of people has long been considered a part of moral behavior and so has been under the watchful eye of the religious. The morality of contraception was debated by religious leaders for years and, as use of contraceptives increased and the birth rate declined in the 1920s and 1930s, all faiths made official pronouncements on the moral issues involved. The chief Protestant denominations and the reform and conservative Jews took positions favoring the practice of birth control. The National Council of the Churches of Christ in America, representing 25 of the largest Protestant denominations, issued a favorable statement of policy in 1938.

In 1934 the Rabbinical Assembly of American Jews (the conservative group) passed a resolution on birth control that concluded: "We urge the passage of legislation by the Congress of the United States and the state legislatures to permit the dissemination of contraceptive information by responsible medical agencies. We maintain that proper education in contraception and birth control will not destroy but rather enhance the spiritual values inherent in the family and will make for the advancement of human happiness and welfare."

The official position of the Catholic Church was given by Pope Pius XI in 1930 when he stated that birth control is "unnatural and intrinsically evil and therefore not to be justified for any reason, however grave." Any contraceptive other than refraining from intercourse during the fertile period was defined for Catholics as "unnatural."

Contraception no longer created problems as a moral issue for Protestants and Jews in the 1960s. Some faith groups made even more liberal pronouncements than they had made in the 1930s. As early as 1959, reform Jews passed a resolution urging the elimination of all restrictions and prohibitions against the dissemination of birth control information and the rendering of birth control assistance by qualified physicians, clinics, and hospitals. Protestant denominations took similar stands. It is only the hierarchy of the Catholic Church that has not yet been able to resolve the moral issue of birth control. The position taken by Pope Pius XI still stands as the official position. Committees appointed by the Pope as well as other committees of law and church leaders have continued to recommend that the position of the Catholic Church be changed. Many Catholics, often upon the advice of their priest, consider the question of using contraceptives to be an individual decision, rather than being bound by the teachings of the church. Our study of college and university students of the Catholic as well as Protestant and Jewish faiths showed wide acceptance as far back as 1967 of the view that contraceptives should be made available to all (see Table 23-1).

## LEGAL ASPECTS OF CONTRACEPTIVES

In the past, laws concerning contraceptives were made to limit their use, sale, and distribution. The Comstock Act, passed in 1873, prohibited the sending of contraceptive information through the mails. As late as 1965, the United States Supreme Court declared unconstitutional a Connecticut law which forbade any person to use contraceptives.

With the population explosion there has been a rapid change in laws to allow and facilitate the distribution of contraceptives. Abortion, illegal in all states a few years ago, has now been legalized and accepted as a means of controlling the birth rate. One of the most extreme changes in attitudes and laws on contraceptives is in the area of making contracep-

**TABLE 23-1**    Views of 3189 Catholic, Protestant, and Jewish students from 18 colleges in 1967 on whether birth control information should be available to married mothers, to ,unmarried mothers, to all others

| Religious faith | Should be available to following groups | | |
| | Married mothers | Unmarried mothers | All people |
| --- | --- | --- | --- |
| Catholic (N–663) | 96.0% | 86.0% | 87.0% |
| Protestant (N–1990) | 98.0 | 91.0 | 91.0 |
| Jewish (N–119) | 99.0 | 97.0 | 97.0 |

tives available to teenagers. As of 1976, in 25 states teenagers could obtain contraceptives without parental consent through the Planned Parenthood centers, from doctors, and through public health agencies. This change was brought about partly because of the rapid rise in illegitimate births among those under 15 years of age and those in the 15 to 19 age group. The increase of sexual intercourse among teenagers resulting in unplanned pregnancies not only contributes to the population explosion but also places a much greater burden upon taxpayers to support those unqualified for parenthood. Availability of contraceptives may reduce the number of unplanned pregnancies among the teenage population. We say *may* decrease the unplanned pregnancies, because teenagers are often uninformed and careless in the area of contraceptives. The birth rate will continue high in this age group unless a widespread program of education is initiated, or these pregnancies are terminated by abortion.

## NEW METHODS OF CONTRACEPTION

During the past fifteen years, and especially during the past ten years, researchers have made great progress toward improved methods of conception control. It is recognized that, to be perfect, a method has to do many things: it has to be effective, simple to use, and inexpensive; in addition, it has to be free of unpleasant or harmful side effects. Its use must be independent of coitus and have no effect upon sexual desire or enjoyment; it must be long-lasting and yet reversible if pregnancy is desired; and it must protect against the spread of venereal disease.

No method of contraception yet meets all those standards. As of this writing, there are three or possibly four methods that, with further research, may approach the desirable standard: (1) hormonal inhibitors, (2) intra-uterine devices, (3) reversible surgical sterilization, and, possibly, (4) an infertility vaccine.

## HORMONAL INHIBITORS

Intensive research continues with orally administered synthetic hormones that suppress ovulation. The possibility of using pills for contraception was first discovered as a result of research aimed at regularizing the menstrual cycle to make the determination of the "safe period" more reliable. It was found that when synthetic female hormones were taken according to an exact schedule, the effect was the prevention of ovulation; thus no conception could occur as long as use of the hormones continued according to schedule. The researchers also found that, after use of the hormones was discontinued, fertility was increased. Recognition of the implications of the use of hormones for treatment of infertility and for conception control spurred efforts in this area of research.

The most commonly used oral contraceptives suppress the action of the pituitary gland, which stimulates the ovaries to ovulate each month. If the hormones are taken from the fifth day after the first day of menstruation for 20 days, the ovaries do not release an egg and the woman is sterile for that month. If used with no deviation from the schedule, the hormone pill seems to be nearly 100 percent effective as a contraceptive. However, because use of the hormones interferes with the endocrine system, the Pure Food and Drug Administration authorities were cautious about approving it for public use.

Knowledge of the long-term effects of birth control pills cannot be certain until after many more years of use and research. In addition to possible concerns about breast and uterine cancer, the Pure Food and Drug Administration has found that women who suffer from migraine headaches may be more subject to strokes when using the pill, that it may affect blood clotting and be a causative factor in strokes, that it may be a causative factor in visual disorder, and that it may inhibit bone growth if taken before people reach their physical growth. Women who have the trait for sickle cell anemia are warned against taking the pill since it may increase the chance of their developing blood disorders. Ten percent of all black people have the sickle cell trait but most of those carrying the trait are not aware that they carry it. It is now known that women who are aware that they carry the trait and women in whom sickle cell anemia has already been diagnosed should never take the pill.

Medical records are continuously checked in efforts to determine with certainty all conditions related to use of the hormone pills. After studying and reviewing all research on this contraceptive, covering approximately ten years of use, the Pure Food and Drug Administration felt that the evidence was strong enough that women should be given more warning against possible dangers than had been required earlier. In 1970 the Administration directed that all manufacturers include the following warning with each box of the pills:

> The oral contraceptives are powerful, effective drugs. Do not take these drugs without your doctor's continued supervision. As with all effective drugs they may cause side effects in some cases and should not be taken at all by some. Rare instances of abnormal blood clotting are the most important known complications of oral contraceptives. These points were discussed with you when you chose this method of contraception. While you are taking these drugs, you should have periodic examinations at intervals set by your doctor. Tell your doctor if you notice any of the following: 1. Severe headache; 2. Blurred vision; 3. Pain in the legs; 4. Pain in the chest or unexplained cough; 5. Irregular or missed period.

Since 1970 the Pure Food and Drug Administration has continued to make known to doctors and the public new findings on the harmful effects of the pill. The earlier findings of harmful effects have been substantiated by continuing research. In addition, the pill seems to be associated with an increased incidence of heart attacks among women over 30, and certain liver tumors.

A report of Planned Parenthood in 1976 warned women over 40 about the dangers of the pill, and indicated that it would not prescribe the pill to women in this age group unless they signed a consent to relieve the organization of any responsibility, since their research showed women of this age group to be more prone toward heart attack, stroke, pulmonary embolism, hypertension, thrombophlebitis, and gall bladder disease.

Research continues on hormonal inhibitors: morning-after-coitus pills, lowering the dosage in pills, once-a-month pills, once-in-six-months pills, intrauterine devices containing hormonal inhibitors, as well as pills for men. All of these are in the experimental stages, and some have been found to be dangerous. There is evidence that the "sequential pill" may cause cancer of the uterus. The morning-after-coitus pill is of such danger that it is recommended for use only in emergency cases, such as after rape.

Although long-term effects are still under study, short-term effects are easily observed and documented. A certain proportion of women have unpleasant side effects for from one to three months after they begin using the oral contraceptives. Since the contraceptive, in effect, produces a simulated pregnancy, many of the same symptoms appear which normally occur early in pregnancy. Some women experience nausea and digestive upsets, weight gain, emotional depression, reduced sexual desire, or skin problems. With some women these side effects are severe enough so that they discontinue use of the pill rather than persevere through several months to learn whether the symptoms will disappear after a time. However, just as with real pregnancy, some women feel better physically and emotionally than usual and have no unpleasant symptoms at all.

During the past 15 years, millions of women have adopted the pill as a form of birth control because it is effective if used correctly; it is independent of the sex act; for many women, it has no apparent side effects; and it is relatively inexpensive. All the dangers of using the pill are not yet known. But as Planned Parenthood points out, for women under the age of 40, one is more likely to be killed in a car accident than to die from use of the pill.

The use of the pill has contributed to the current epidemic of venereal disease. Evidence seems to suggest that women using the pill contract venereal disease more readily when exposed to it than do others, because the pill reduces acidity in the genital tract and so creates a more favorable environment for growth of venereal infection. The venereal disease epidemic today is attributed in part to the fact that the pill is now more widely used than are condoms, which did provide some protection against venereal disease.

Renewed attention is now being given to a method of birth control that received widespread attention in the 1930s. Dr. Ernst Grafenberg developed an intrauterine ring that was inserted in the uterus. It was found to be effective in preventing conception, but many side effects were reported and the method fell into disrepute in the United States. With the development of plastics and the discovery that, when introduced into the body by certain surgical procedures, the plastics were nontoxic, attention again turned to intrauterine techniques for preventing conception. Stainless steel had been developed and it too had been found to be nontoxic to the body. Today there are stainless steel, copper, and plastic devices that, when inserted in the uterus by a doctor, prevent conception as long as they remain in place.

It is not known why the "foreign" object in the uterus prevents conception.[2] The current theories are: (1) The foreign body in some way prevents the spermatozoa from passing through the uterus into the Fallopian tubes; (2) it causes excessive contraction of the uterine muscle walls and thus blocks the processes that normally would provide a receptive surface for the egg; (3) it causes excessive Fallopian peristalsis so that the egg, even if fertilized, reaches the uterus in far less than the normal 72 hours required for this two-and-one-half-inch journey and so is too immature to implant itself in the still unprepared endometrium.

The intrauterine devices have many of the elements of a perfect contraceptive; they are inexpensive and permanent, and for many women they produce no side effects. Because of their low cost, simplicity, and permanence, this is the most common type of birth control being used in India at the present time. However, the IUDs have the weakness that they may be expelled without the woman's being aware of it. The most common complaints about the IUDs are that they may cause some women to have severe cramps, to get a bacterial infection, or to have heavy menses. In addition, about 3 out of 100 women become pregnant in spite of the presence of the IUD. If pregnancy occurs, the IUD cannot then be removed without causing an abortion. Dr. Tietze, coordinator of all Planned Parenthood research projects, studied 22,000 women using IUDs and found that 30 to 40 percent either expelled or, for various reasons, removed the devices.[3]

Research continues on the use of intrauterine devices. New ones are being constructed that do not expel as easily as some of the earlier types. The IUDs are becoming more widely used as more women are reluctant to use the hormone pill and desire another form of contraception. Even though improvements are made in the IUD, many women will still object to having a foreign object placed permanently in their bodies.

[2] Adapted from Christopher Tietze, "Spirals, Loops and Rings Tested as Contraceptives," *Medical World News* (8 November 1963).

[3] Ibid.

Continued research shows that there is some cause for worry in the use of the IUD. A study by gynecologists at the University of Washington in 1975 concluded that approximately 60,000 of the four million IUD users develop dangerous and painful infections each year as a result. A string attached to the IUD which makes it possible to see whether the IUD has been expelled may serve as a pathway for bacteria to enter the uterus and cause infection. One device, the Dalkon shield, which was sold for many years, had to be withdrawn from the market in 1976 because it induced infection. To protect the public from harmful medical devices Congress passed legislation in 1976 bringing all such devices, including the IUD, under the control of the Pure Food and Drug Administration.

## VASECTOMY AND SALPINGECTOMY

In the past, sterilization operations have not generally been thought of as a means of birth control, although they have been used to keep the unfit from reproducing, and have been used extensively for women who would be in serious danger if they had a pregnancy. The current interest in population control is causing sterilization, especially vasectomy, to be considered as a means of birth control. In the male, vasectomy involves tying and cutting the vas deferens; in the female, salpingectomy involves tying and cutting the Fallopian tubes. The vasectomy operation is very simple, inexpensive, and usually done in a doctor's office using only a local anesthetic. The salpingectomy is much more expensive, since it must be done in a hospital, and it entails an incision in the abdominal wall to reach the Fallopian tubes. The vasectomy operation takes from ten to fifteen minutes, and doctors may charge from 75 to 500 dollars. The man need not be hospitalized or lose time from work. Except for one factor, the vasectomy would seem to be an excellent form of birth control, since it is less expensive and more effective, is not related to coitus, does not interfere with pleasure or decrease sexual desire, and does not threaten physical health in any way. That the operation is neither quickly nor surely reversible, however, is still a major handicap. Objections to the operation, such as fear of loss of sexual potency, fear that the operation might cause pain, and other possible psychological problems, could be overcome through a better understanding of the operation. Vasectomy is not illegal in any state, but there are doctors who consider it illegal and will not perform it. To overcome fears of illegality, more states may need to pass laws similar to one passed in Kansas, which specifically states that vasectomy is legal for birth control purposes.

Sterilization operations are often confused with castration, which is the removal of the testicles and which does affect sexual functioning in the male. Tying or cutting the tubes in either the male or the female simply prevents the release of sperm or eggs into the genital tract and does not affect sexual functioning. All the hormones controlling sexual functioning and insuring maleness or femaleness continue to be secreted and to enter the blood stream as before.

In our study of 330 men who had had a vasectomy as a means of contraception, 60 percent felt that their marital adjustment had improved, largely because of improved sexual adjustment. Reasons for improved sexual adjustment were removal of the wife's fear of pregnancy and a lessening of tension over use of unsatisfactory contraceptives, Almost three-fourths reported that sexual enjoyment was greater for both husband and wife after the operation; this was supported by their reporting an increased frequency of coitus after the operation, especially among those under age 25.[4]

Husbands and wives do not decide to have the vasectomy without some concern. The men reported that, before the operation, they had feared it might be painful or that their sex drive might be affected, or they had worried because they might later change their minds and want more children and not be able to have the operation reversed. The men reported that their wives had been concerned ahead of time about the effectiveness of the operation, whether it would affect masculinity, and whether the vasectomy might encourage sexual promiscuity by the husband.

In a study of 887 doctors in two countries, we found that 60 percent approved of vasectomy as a form of birth control.[5] The most frequent reason given by the doctors against the operation was that the man might later change his mind. Of the 45 doctors who had tried reversal operations on men (230 cases of attempted reversal), 53 percent of the operations had resulted in viable sperm, and at the time of the study 23 percent had resulted in pregnancies.

Male or female sterilization is gaining rapid acceptance as a form of birth control for those who have completed their families. It is estimated that no more than 100,000 sterilization operations were done in 1960, while there were more than 1,300,000 in 1975, and one-half of these were vasectomies. Men have become more educated about the nature of the operation and no longer fear losing their potency. Also, there is now greater hope that the vasectomy can be reversed. One doctor has found that with the use of a high-powered microscope it was possible to rejoin the tubes and restore fertility in almost 100 percent of the operations. Researchers are working on valves that can be inserted in the vasa to cause sterility for only as long as desired, and on other procedures for making reversal easier. Until reversal can be guaranteed, sperm banks

[4] Judson T. Landis and Thomas Poffenberger, "The Marital and Sexual Adjustment of 330 Couples Who Chose Vasectomy as a Form of Birth Control," *Journal of Marriage and the Family* 27:1 (February 1965), 57–58; also Landis and Poffenberger, "Hesitations and Worries of 330 Couples Choosing Vasectomy for Birth Control," *Family Life Coordinator* 15:4 (October 1966), 143–47.

[5] Landis, "Attitudes of Individual California Physicians and Policies of State Medical Societies on Vasectomy for Birth Control," *Journal of Marriage and the Family* 28:3 (August 1966), 277–83.

have been established in some cities so that a husband may store sperm before the operation as a precaution in case he should later wish to father another child. At that time, his wife could receive his sperm through artificial insemination.

Research also continues in search of more acceptable methods of female sterilization. Some techniques have been developed that are relatively simple and that require only a few hours in a hospital. One of these—laparoscopic tubal sterilization—is done by cutting and tying the Fallopian tubes through a very small incision made in the abdomen. The operation does not require more than a temporary stay in the hospital and in most cases is much cheaper than the major surgery required in the past. The operation is still much more expensive than is a vasectomy for the male, and is not reversible.

The first vasectomy clinic in the United States was opened at the Margaret Sanger Research Bureau in 1969. Today vasectomy clinics are in operation in most large communities. The U.S. Office of Economic Opportunity now permits its funds to be used for voluntary sterilization of men and women in low-income families. Colorado and Tennessee now provide free sterilization operations for the indigent. The Supreme Court has held that it is unconstitutional for a hospital to refuse its facilities for a voluntary contraceptive sterilization operation.

It is too early to know, but it is possible that sterilization will become the chief means of birth control for couples after they have had the desired number of children, or before they are ready for children if a reversing process is perfected or if sperm banks become generally acceptable and available.

## GETTING RELIABLE INFORMATION

Today married couples who wish to limit the size of their families or to space the births of their children will not find it difficult to secure reliable information. The one agency that keeps up on all developments in conception control and has the information available is the Planned Parenthood League of America.

The League has affiliated clinics throughout the United States to provide this information to couples approaching marriage. In some communities without Planned Parenthood offices, there are public health services and public or private hospitals with family planning clinics that provide the information. Many doctors are becoming better informed, although clinical training in contraception is still not a part of medical training in many medical schools.

## LIBERALIZING ABORTION LAWS

For years the desirability of liberalizing abortion laws was debated by doctors, church leaders, social workers, sociologists, parents, and others in the United States. Japan, Sweden, Poland, Mexico, and other countries had experimented with liberalized abortion laws for some years. A change in public attitudes toward abortion took place in the late 1960s. The following points were widely considered and debated in relation to proposals for liberalized abortion laws in the United States:

1   It was estimated that there were almost one million illegal abortions being performed in the United States each year.

2   The death rate and serious complications resulting from illegal abortions were known to be high.

3   Unwanted pregnancies contributed to the population explosion, especially among the lower classes.

4   The burden of supporting unwanted and illegitimate children through government assistance was great.

5   It was suggested that it was not in the best interests of society for women to be forced to bear unplanned and unwanted babies.

6   And, finally, there was the belief, often voiced by the women's liberation movement, that a woman has the right to control the uses of her body.

Bills were introduced in state legislatures to liberalize abortion laws, but it was not until 1967 that the first such law was finally passed (in Colorado). By 1972, 16 other states had passed such laws. Most of the state laws follow the American Law Institute's Model Penal Code. The measure allows abortion up to the sixteenth week of pregnancy if a board of doctors agrees that the pregnancy endangers the physical or emotional health of the woman, if there is suspicion of fetal abnormality, or if pregnancy is the result of rape or incest. Some states went far beyond the suggested model law, permitting abortion up to the twentieth week upon demand by any pregnant woman, and permitting abortions for women from out of state with no required waiting period. New York has no residency requirement.

The long legal struggle over the right to abortion was finally ended in 1973 when the United States Supreme Court decided that it was the right of a woman (guaranteed by the 14th Amendment on personal liberty) to decide whether or not to terminate her pregnancy. The court decision gave women the legal right to abortion during the first three months of pregnancy, with considerable latitude during the last six months. However, since the Supreme Court decision in 1973, some states enacted laws to make abortion virtually impossible and many hospitals refused the use of their facilities for abortions. In a new decision in 1976, the Supreme Court declared unconstitutional a new abortion law in Missouri which stated a woman had to get her husband's consent before she could have an abortion. The court also struck down the provision in the Missouri law that a person under 18 had to have parental consent for an abortion. State laws in 25 states permit teenagers to obtain abortions without parental consent.

It has been estimated that there were as many as one million illegal abortions in the United States up to the time of the Supreme Court decision. In 1975 alone, there were approximately one million legal abortions to three million live births.

Although the legality of abortion has been established by the courts, for many the moral and religious concerns remain. Anti-abortion groups have organized to get a constitutional amendment passed which would make abortions illegal unless the life of the pregnant woman is in danger. A Gallup Poll in 1976 found that 45 percent of Americans favored the amendment and 49 percent opposed the proposed amendment. Although the "pro-life" movement was initiated by Catholic groups, the Gallup Poll indicates that many people are still questioning the morality of abortion.

A Field Poll in 1976 of attitudes on abortion in California found much wider acceptance of abortion since 1969, but approval depended upon circumstances. Three-fourths of the various groups, including Catholics, reported they approved of abortion if the baby might be born with a serious deformity. On the other hand, fewer than 50 percent disapproved of abortion for any reason. Other studies show that there is greater disapproval as the pregnancy gets closer to term.

Abortions performed in hospitals today are quite safe. The resulting emotional and psychological effects depend upon how the woman views the right to life, which in turn is dependent upon her upbringing and development up to the time of the considered abortion.

## HAVING CHILDREN AND MARRIAGE STABILITY

Married couples encounter less strain in their relationships if they postpone parenthood until they have had time to work out some of their problems of adjustment in marriage. There are always some new and different problems of adjustment during pregnancy and child rearing. Further, since marriage failure comes early, children have greater protection against being brought up by unhappy or divorced parents if parenthood is postponed until the couple has tested their own potential for building a good marriage. Christensen, by means of record linkage research, studied 1531 marriage licenses in Indiana.[6] He noted the date the couples married and then linked this date with the date of birth of the first child and examined also the divorce rate among the couples. The results of his study are summarized in Figure 23-3. It will be observed that the divorce rate was highest in those marriages in which pregnancy had occurred before marriage. This would be expected because many of these were forced marriages and might not have taken

[6] Harold T. Christensen and Hanna H. Meissner, "Studies in Child Spacing: III—Premarital Pregnancy as a Factor in Divorce," *American Sociological Review* 18:6 (December 1953), 641–44.

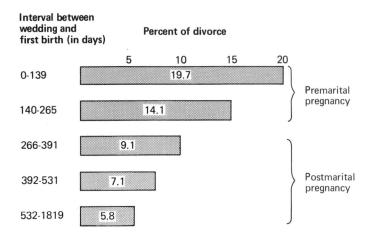

Interval between
wedding and
first birth (in days)

Percent of divorce

FIG. 23–3 Divorce percentages distributed according to the spacing of the first birth from marriage (sample of 1531 cases from Tippecanoe County, Indiana).

place had it not been for the pregnancy. The most pertinent part of the research for our discussion here is that the divorce rate was higher among those couples whose first conception occurred soon after marriage than among those couples who waited months or years before having children. Our research on adjustment to pregnancy [7] and similar research by Christensen [8] found a very high percentage of unplanned pregnancies among couples who conceived early in marriage. Christensen found low marital adjustment scores among these same couples.

## WHY HAVE CHILDREN?

Many couples have children simply because nature takes its course. They marry with the expectation that they will have children. They give little thought to whether they actively wish to have children, but they welcome the children when they come. Some others desire children because of a wish to have a stake in the future. They may feel a conscious desire to keep a grasp on youth and life through the lives of their children, or they may feel an undefined urge toward self-perpetuation. People may desire children also because they believe that children are necessary to a complete and happy home life. Studies of college students show that most of them hope to have a child or children eventually. Whatever the reason back of the desire for children, having children

[7] Shirley Poffenberger, Thomas Poffenberger, and Judson T. Landis, "Intent Toward Conception and the Pregnancy Experience," *American Sociological Review* 17:5 (October 1952), 616–20.

[8] Christensen and Philbrick, "Family Size as a Factor in the Marital Adjustment of College Students," *American Sociological Review* 17:3 (June 1952), 306–12.

does give married people not only a stake in the future but an interest in the present. Matters that we may shrug away as of no concern to us suddenly take on importance after we become parents.

Several attempts have been made to determine the relationship between happiness in marriage and the size of the family. Terman, Hamilton, and Bernard found no significant differences between the happiness scores of childless and parental husbands and wives. In our study of 409 couples, those without children tended toward the extremes in their adjustments, being either very happy or very unhappy, while those with children approached an average in happiness.

Several difficulties are involved in trying to determine the effects of children on the happiness of a marriage. Of importance is the duration of the marriages studied. Studies of people who are in the early months or the first year of marriage may show a high percentage of happy marriages, most of which will be childless but in these marriages of short duration the childlessness is not significant. In marriages of short duration, the partners are likely to rate the marriage as very happy simply because they are still in the honeymoon stage. Even if they suspect their marriage is less happy than they had anticipated, they are not so likely to admit it as are couples who have been married longer. For the latter, their desire to have or not have children may be more important than the actual presence or absence of children. If the coming of undesired children forces a couple to give up the type of life they had planned, or if unwanted children come to a couple who are already unhappy in marriage, having children may increase the adjustment problems. Burgess and Cottrell found that couples who had no children but desired them, and couples who had one or more children because they desired them, were the happiest in marriage.[9] It seems that a couple's

[9] Ernest W. Burgess and Leonard S. Cottrell, *Predicting Success or Failure in Marriage* (Englewood Cliffs, N.J.: Prentice-Hall, Inc., 1939), p. 260.

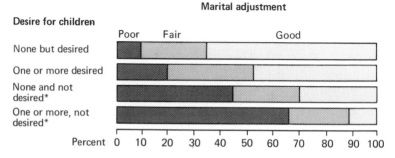

FIG. 23–4 Desire for children and marital adjustment. Children may serve as a bond to hold husband and wife together, or the coming of unwanted children may serve as an added handicap to marital adjustment.

agreement in desiring children indicates good marital adjustment. Consequently, whether or not they are successful in having children, they are among the happier couples. Burgess found that those who had no children because they did not want them, and those who had children in spite of not intending to have them, were among the less happy.[10] Reed, in a careful study of 1444 Indianapolis couples, found "an increase in marital adjustment with increasing success in controlling fertility according to the desires of the couples."[11]

## REVIEW QUESTIONS

**1** What size family have college students considered the ideal during the past 40 years? What are some of the factors that have caused people to change their concept of the ideal size during these years?

**2** How have birth rates differed by residence? Income? Religion? Education? Occupation?

**3** What are the official pronouncements of different religious faiths on the use of contraceptives?

**4** How have laws changed on regulating the sale of contraceptives in recent years?

**5** What are the new methods of contraception being given most attention today?

**6** What are the chief concerns about the use of hormone pills?

**7** What are some of the adverse effects of using IUDs?

**8** Give the arguments for and against vasectomy and salpingectomy for birth control.

**9** Summarize the trend of changes in laws governing abortion.

**10** The legality of abortion has been settled, but the morality of abortion has not. Discuss.

**11** Name some of the reasons people desire to have children.

**12** Discuss the effects of children on happiness in marriage.

## PROJECTS AND ACTIVITIES

**1** Make a tally of what the students in your class consider the ideal number of children in a family. How does it compare with the figures given in the text?

**2** Diagram your family tree for as many generations as you can. List the number of children born to each couple for each generation. Do you find a gradual decrease in the number of children in each generation?

[10] Ibid., p. 260.

[11] Robert B. Reed, *Social and Psychological Factors Affecting Fertility*, Part VII (New York: Milbank Memorial Fund, 1948), p. 423.

# CHILDLESS MARRIAGES
# AND ADOPTION

In 1974, 13 percent of all married women past the childbearing age had borne no children. It is almost impossible to discover what proportion of the childlessness that shows up in census reports is due to biological causes and what proportion is due to contraception. Some authorities have concluded that from one-half to two-thirds of childless marriages are involuntarily sterile. Many more couples are relatively infertile and therefore unlikely to have more than one or two children. The problem of sterility is faced by almost 150,000 newly married couples each year. Many young people who marry are concerned only with planning not to have children until they are ready to have them. Some people are shocked and disappointed to find, if they later want children, that because of low fertility or infertility they are not able to have them.

Throughout history, folk beliefs assumed that the cause of a sterile marriage is always to be found in the wife. Even within this generation, when no children are born to a married couple who desire them, the wife often is the first to seek medical advice. Some couples refuse to entertain doubts about the ability of the husband to father offspring. However, more accurate information about the reproductive processes based on research shows that in the majority of cases of sterile or relatively infertile marriages, both the husband and the wife show some evidence of infertility; the cause is not wholly in one or the other partner. When causes can be definitely discovered, it has been found that at least a third of the causative factors are in the husband. Of 486 couples unable to have children who sought help at the Wistar Institute, almost half the wives became pregnant when they resorted to artificial insemination by a donor other than the husband.[1]

[1] Douglas P. Murphy, "Donor Insemination—A Study of 511 Prospective Donors," *Fertility and Sterility* 15:5 (September–October 1964), 528–33.

There are a number of specific causes of sterility. The female genital tract is normally acid, but it may be too acid for the sperm to survive, especially if the sperm are not vigorous. Extra secretions from the cervix may prevent the sperm from entering. Some failure in glandular functioning may hinder implantation of the egg after it has been fertilized, so that the fertilized egg does not remain to grow in the uterus. Since the sex cells are very susceptible to the effects of X-rays and radium, either partner may become temporarily sterile after exposure to radiation. The sex cells of a particular couple may be incompatible and destroy each other, a condition called genetic incompatibility. The general health, mental or physical, of one or both may make it impossible or unlikely that conception will occur. Age is also a factor, younger women being far more likely to conceive than older women. Some cases of failure to conceive are due to the failure of the couple to have intercourse during the time of the month when the egg is available for fertilization. Recent research indicates that normally fertile women will produce a normal egg cell in slightly over eight out of ten menstrual cycles, whereas women of subfertility ovulate normally in less than half of the menstrual cycles. Some wives in this second group who were tested regularly in every cycle for more than a year ovulated only three or four times in that period of time.[2] In many men, spermatozoa are not produced in sufficient quantity or of vigorous enough quality, and the result is lowered fertility. Fallopian tubes may be closed by infection, injury, or disease, so that the sperm cannot meet the egg to fertilize it.

The current epidemic of gonorrhea will probably result in more women being sterile, since untreated gonorrhea often scars and seals the Fallopian tubes so that conception can never take place. A woman may contact the disease and be unaware that she has it. Smears must be taken by a doctor to determine the presence of gonorrhea in women, and the method is not completely reliable. Once the Fallopian tubes in the female become sealed, there is no remedy for the sterility.

Since any one of these factors, or a combination of several of them, may play a part, fertility may be seen to be relative. A couple may be infertile temporarily, or they may have a low fertility so that they would be unlikely ever to have many children but still might have one or two, or they may be permanently sterile.

## PROGRESS IN OVERCOMING STERILITY

Progress is being made in understanding the causes of infertility and in correcting or overcoming the causes to make it possible for infertile

[2] Edmond J. Farris, *Human Fertility and Problems of the Male* (White Plains, N.Y.: The Author's Press, Inc., 1950), p. 191.

couples who want children to have them. As recently as ten years ago, only a fourth to a third of the infertile couples seeking help from specialists might hope to conceive. Today with new knowledge and new treatments available, nearly two-thirds of such couples are likely to be able to have children. The greatest aids in effecting pregnancy are through (1) a better understanding of the time of ovulation and (2) hormone or chemical treatment to stimulate ovulation.

**Determining the time of ovulation.**   Many women are fertile for only a few hours in a month, and the newer methods of ascertaining time of ovulation are especially valuable in effecting conception with these women. The Wistar Institute of Anatomy and Biology developed a rat hyperemia test by which urine from the subject is injected into young female rats on each of the days when ovulation is most likely to take place; the ovaries of the rats show reactions indicating exactly when ovulation is occurring. After two months of testing, the exact day of ovulation can be determined for an individual and conception can be attempted in the third month. To test this prediction of ovulation, couples cooperating with the Institute attempted conception only once during the month, or artificial insemination was attempted but once. The rat hyperemia test was found to be accurate.

A temperature reading as an attempt to determine the time of ovulation has been used by people who could not effect pregnancy, as well as by those who desired to postpone conception by relying on the "safe period." However, a rise in temperature may not indicate ovulation. With one experimental group of women, Dr. Farris of the Wistar Institute found in predicting ovulation by the rat test that almost half conceived before there was any change in their temperature reading, 15 percent when the temperature was at its lowest point, and the remainder during a rise in temperature. Farris concluded that, although the temperature reading has helped some people to achieve pregnancy, it also contributes to infertility if it is depended upon as an indication of ovulation.

For some time it has been thought that, in a regular cycle of 28 days, ovulation would be most likely to take place on the fourteenth day. However, the researchers at the Wistar Institute have found that it is more likely to take place on the twelfth day. Figure 24-2 has been worked out to show when 364 conceptions actually took place among couples who came to the Wistar Institute for help. Clearly, there is great variation in the time of the fertile period in women having the same length cycle. The most fertile period in women with a 20-day cycle is from the sixth to the thirteenth day after the onset of menstruation, and the most fertile period for women on a 40-day cycle is from the fifteenth to the twenty-third day after the onset of menstruation. In general, the Wistar Institute research places the most likely day of ovulation as the middle day of

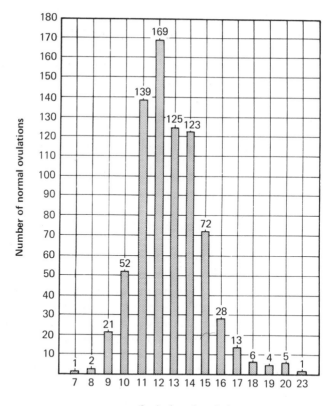

FIG. 24–1 The day of ovulation, as determined by the rat test. The day of the menstrual cycle in which 761 ovulations occurred in 232 women prior to conception. Ovulation took place between days 7 and 23, with cycle day 12 being the most common. Edmond J. Farris, *Human Ovulation and Fertility* (Philadelphia: J.B. Lippincott Company, 1956).

the menstrual cycle minus two days, with fertility extending from approximately two days before that time until about five days afterward, or about eight days.[3]

**Stimulating ovulation.** The use of hormones (the pill) has resulted in two discoveries, both aids in overcoming infertility. Doctors Rock and Pincus, who first experimented with the steroid hormones, had in mind regularizing the menstrual cycle more nearly to the 28-day cycle to aid couples who wished to use the "safe period" as a means of birth control. In the course of their research, they also discovered that, after women stopped using the pill, they were more likely to ovulate than they had

[3] Murphy, "Donor Insemination."

CHILDLESS MARRIAGES AND ADOPTION

FIG. 24–2 The fertile and infertile periods. Day on which 364 conceptions took place, in relation to the length of the menstrual cycle. (Study based on 100 donor inseminations, 30 husband artificial inseminations, and 234 cases in which only one coitus occurred during cycle.) Rat hyperemia test used to determine time of ovulation.

| Average length of cycle | Number of conceptions | 6 | 7 | 8 | 9 | 10 | 11 | 12 | 13 | 14 | 15 | 16 | 17 | 18 | 19 | 20 | 21 | 22 | 23 |
|---|---|---|---|---|---|---|---|---|---|---|---|---|---|---|---|---|---|---|---|
| 20 | 1 | | | | | | 1 | | | | | | | | | | | | |
| 21 | 0 | ←—————Fertile————→ | | | | | | | | | ←——————————Infertile—————————→ | | | | | | | | |
| 22 | 0 | | | | | | | | | | | | | | | | | | |
| 23 | 6 | | | 1 | | | 1 | 3 | 1 | | | | | | | | | | |
| 24 | 11 | | | | | 7 | 4 | | | | | | | | | | | | |
| 25 | 22 | | | | 4 | 9 | 6 | | | 2 | 1 | | | | | | | | |
| 26 | 43 | | | | 3 | | 19 | 7 | 9 | 3 | 1 | | 1 | | | | | | |
| 27 | 73 | | | 2 | 5 | | 22 | 17 | 10 | 8 | 7 | | 2 | | | | | | |
| 28 | 68 | | | | 1 | | 12 | 28 | 17 | 7 | 2 | 1 | | | | | | | |
| 29 | 46 | | | 1 | 1 | | 3 | 17 | 14 | 5 | 5 | | | | | | | | |
| 30 | 32 | | | | | | 2 | 7 | 12 | 5 | 3 | 1 | 1 | 1 | | | | | |
| 31 | 24 | | | | | | 3 | 3 | 5 | 4 | 4 | 4 | | 1 | | | | | |
| 32 | 10 | | | | | | | 2 | 1 | 4 | 2 | | | | 1 | | | | |
| 33 | 7 | | | | | | | | 1 | 4 | 1 | 1 | | | | | | | |
| 34 | 7 | | | | | | | | 2 | 3 | 2 | | | | | | | | |
| 35 | 6 | | | | | | | | 2 | 1 | | 1 | | | | 1 | | | 1 |
| 36 | 0 | | | | | | | | | | | | | | | | | | |
| 37 | 1 | | | | | | | | | | | 1 | | | | | | | |
| 38 | 4 | ←——————Infertile——————→ | | | | | | | | 2 | 1 | | | 1 | | | | |
| 39 | 1 | | | | | | | | | | | | | 1 | | | | | |
| 40 | 0 | | | | | | | | | | | | | | | | | | |
| 49 | 1 | | | | | | | | | | | | | | | | | 1 | |
| 62 | 1 | | | | | | | | | | | | | | 1 | | | | |
| 364 Totals | | 1 | 7 | 26 | 73 | 82 | 70 | 40 | 35 | 14 | 7 | 3 | 2 | 2 | 0 | 1 | 1 | | |

Pattern of highest incidence of ovulation calculated by formula

Ave. length 3 con. cycles / –2 = Optimum day of ovulation — Formula

been before its use. Thus the use of the pill not only helped those wishing to avoid pregnancy, it also became an aid to those wanting to become pregnant. It helped achieve pregnancy by pinpointing the expected time of ovulation and by stimulating the ovaries to expel ova each month when that might not ordinarily have occurred.

More recent research has found that failure to ovulate may be traced to a lack of the pituitary hormones, which stimulate the ovaries to release eggs. The pituitary hormone lacking in infertile women is now given to stimulate ovulation. A problem is that in some cases many eggs are released and multiple births result. In some cases women who had been unable to have children have given birth after using the new ovulation stimulants to as many as six or seven infants from one pregnancy. With continued research, fertility specialists believe that the dosage can be regulated so that it will not cause multiple births.

All such findings should make it possible for many couples who desire to have families to have children before they pass the childbearing age. Many fertility clinics have now been established to help infertile couples conceive. Planned Parenthood League offices also provide information or suggest sources of information for couples who want but have failed to have children, as well as for those who do not want to have them.

**Artificial insemination.** Some couples who have been unable to have a child attempt conception through artificial insemination with the husband as donor. If this fails, they may then resort to artificial insemination and trust their doctor's judgment in the choice of donor. Staff members of the Wistar Institute report that many couples choose donor insemination when every other procedure to bring about pregnancy has failed. In a follow-up study of 38 couples who had had children by means of artificial insemination, the following reasons were given for their decision: (1) the wife's urgent desire to experience pregnancy, (2) dissatisfaction with adoption agencies, (3) benefits it is thought the child will derive from maternal heredity even though paternal heredity will not be from the "father," (4) the belief that they will have a closer relationship with the infant than would be possible in adoption, and (5) the desire to conceal infertility.[4] It appears that young people tend to reject the idea of artificial insemination by donor other than the husband. On this subject the responses of 3189 students in 18 colleges showed that 65 percent of the Catholics, 76 percent of the Protestants, and 80 percent of the Jews said that if they could not achieve pregnancy, they would be favorable to artificial insemination with the husband as donor; but only 10 percent of the Catholics, 17 percent of the Protestants, and 19 percent of the Jews said they would accept unknown donor insemination.

The legal status of artificial insemination by donor is not clear. A Chicago judge held that artificial insemination is adultery when the donor is a third party. However, the New York Supreme Court held that a child conceived by artificial insemination is legitimate. Since artificial insemination is becoming more common, the legal aspects will doubtless be cleared up through new court decisions and new laws.

## ADOPTION OF CHILDREN

Not only childless couples, but many couples who fail to have more than one or two children before the childbearing age is past, wish to adopt a child or children. Some other couples, aware of world problems arising

---

[4] Edmond J. Farris and M. Garrison, "Emotional Impact of Successful Donor Insemination," *Obstetrics and Gynecology* 3 (1954), 19–20; or Farris, *Human Ovulation and Fertility*, p. 146.

from overpopulation, decide that they should not give birth to any children or at least to not more than one or two. They may not want to miss the experience of living with and rearing children in a family, so they decide to adopt.

Attitudes about adoption have changed greatly. In early American history, all needy children, those who were orphaned or those of illegitimate birth, were kept in institutions, at first "almshouses" and later orphanages. Here they received the minimum essentials of physical care until they were old enough to be released to make their own way in the world. In those days, adoption of a child was looked upon as an act of philanthropy, and it was assumed that few adopted children could be expected to have the capacity to bring credit to their adoptive parents. In 1909 President Theodore Roosevelt called the first White House conference to consider the problems of child welfare. Out of that conference and succeeding ones grew a new understanding of the needs of children, with new programs for providing for them.

New policies were developed to give aid to mothers of dependent children so they could keep and rear them. States established strict legislative control of adoptive procedures. Social agencies and legal authorities assumed the responsibility for making sure that all adoptions took place under the supervision of legally constituted agencies. Public policy continues to oppose and attempts to prevent the making of informal adoptive arrangements by unwed mothers and their doctors or lawyers.

At the same time that the policies of public agencies reduced the number of children for adoption, many of the old superstitions and prejudices about inferiority of adopted children were discarded. Adopting children became accepted and approved among people of all social levels, especially among the middle and upper-middle classes. These policies meant that for many years it was very difficult for couples to adopt children. Prospective parents were on long waiting lists, the ratio of adoptive parents to available adoptable children being as much as twenty to one. One factor that helped to maintain that ratio was prospective parents' preference for an infant rather than an older child, and the policy of social agencies of making every effort to keep children with their natural mother before arranging to release them for adoption.

Social agencies dealing with adoption generally assume that the best place for children is in their own home, if that is possible. Whether this assumption is sound enough to provide the basis of generally applied policy has not been established. Findings of some studies of child development suggest that the natural mother is not necessarily the person best qualified to meet the physical and emotional needs of the child. Nevertheless, children are not available to adoptive parents until all possible attempts to help the children's own parents keep them have failed. When natural parents cannot keep their children, the children are placed in foster homes under the supervision of social agencies for as long as there is any hope that they might eventually be returned to their own parents. When no other arrangement is possible, a child becomes available for adoption.

Attitudes about adoption and policies for dealing with adoptions continue to change, and the changes help alter the ratio between potential adoptive parents and children. For example, more people are now interested in adopting children who are no longer infants and children who would formerly have been considered unsuitable for adoption. Some couples deliberately seek to adopt handicapped children who require special physical or emotional nurture. Agencies have also changed their outlook concerning adoptive parents. They are now less restrictive in such requirements as age and home ownership. There is less emphasis than formerly upon perfect "matching" of parents and children in such matters as physical type and ethnic origin.

Because of these changes in policy and in attitudes, and also because of factors such as a high birth rate following World War II and the Korean War, there was a time in the 1960s when a fairly equal balance of adoptive parents and available children existed. People could decide to adopt a child and carry out their plan with little delay.

This situation has changed. The birth rate has been falling rapidly for the past ten years so that today there are not enough babies to satisfy the number of people who wish to adopt. Those desiring white infants may have to wait years to get a baby through approved adoption agencies or, if they adopt through a doctor or an attorney, may have to pay thousands of dollars. At the same time the birth rate has been falling, the desire to adopt has increased. Couples with no children or couples who have had only one or two children often want to have more children. If teenagers use contraceptives effectively, or if they resort to abortion more frequently, the chief supply of babies for adoption will diminish, and those who wish to adopt will find it almost impossible. Cases have been reported of couples having been charged by some lawyers as much as $10,000 to adopt a baby, in addition to all expenses of the natural mother during her pregnancy and delivery.

## POINTS TO BE FACED BEFORE ADOPTING

Before a couple seeks to adopt a child, there are questions they should face that go much deeper than "Do we want a child?" and "Will we be able to find a child available to us for adopting?"

**Why do we wish to adopt a child?** Are we hoping that a child will be a possible source of ego satisfaction to ourselves? Will we seek to make the child a reflection of ourselves—projecting onto him or her our ambitions and interests?

Sometimes investigators for welfare agencies and couples themselves assume that being educated and of the professional class, and having adequate financial means, are sufficient qualifications to adopt children. But very unhappy situations may arise for both children and parents if such couples are determined to fit adopted children into a certain mold according to their standards. One of the most essential qualifications of adoptive parents should be their ability to allow the adopted children to be themselves and to develop according to their own capacities, free of pressure designed to fit them into some predetermined mold. Many children brought up by their own parents become warped and unhappy because of the pressures of parents determined to fulfill their ambitions through the lives of their children. The danger may be even greater with adopted children.

**Are we thinking of the needs and rights of the children we might adopt or are we looking to them to provide companionship or fulfill other needs for a child or children we already have?** Couples thinking primarily of the needs of a child already in the home are likely to overlook some of the needs of the adopted one. Each child must be understood and loved for herself or himself, whether or not the needs of another child are helped or whether or not new problems are created. Quite often, bringing another child into the home does create new problems, or at least the situation brings into the open problems that were already there. People who have the capacity to be wise parents will be able to help all children work through problems that arise, but this can be done only if they adopt a child for himself or herself and study personality and needs, without unrealistic expectations about what a certain child can do for the home or for another child. The following case illustrates the kind of situation that may develop:

> Mr. and Mrs. A. were professional people in their late 30s in comfortable financial circumstances. They desired a companion for their five-year-old daughter, so they adopted a four-year-old boy. From the beginning, the children did not get along well together. Since the parents felt that their daughter needed to learn to play with others, they went ahead with the final adoption.
>
> Whenever the children quarreled, the parents were inclined to see the side of the little girl; having had her from birth, they understood her and made allowances for her faults. They made an effort to apply justice in their dealings with the two children, but the love they felt for the girl was lacking in their attitude toward the boy; consequently, he was often punished for his naughtiness, whereas the little girl could get by without her misdeeds being noticed. When issues between the children had to be decided, it was much easier for the parents to see the viewpoint of the little girl than of the boy, so rulings were seldom in his favor.
>
> The little boy was extremely desirous of affection and often showed an aggressive attitude toward his foster sister. He was always punished for this, for he was bigger and stronger than she was, and the parents feared he would hurt her.

They pointed out that the little girl never resorted to such behavior. As time passed, the boy became accustomed to being always the loser and always in the wrong. He withdrew to himself and avoided as much as possible playing with his adopted sister or with other children. When he did play with other children he was sly in his dealings, taking what he wanted by stealth rather than ever facing an open issue. As he grew older, his adoptive parents bewailed the fact that he was untruthful, underhanded, lacking in self-confidence, and lacking in affection for others. At school he was overaggressive with those younger than he, but was constantly the victim of those his own age, being frequently chased or teased by the other boys.

It was impossible for the parents to see that their own treatment surely had contributed to developing the undesirable traits. They had adopted him thinking only of the needs of their daughter and giving little thought to his needs; they had not loved him for himself but constantly compared him with the other child. Their conception of justice was to judge both children by the same rules, all of which had been made to fit the needs of the girl.

The boy became a very unhappy child and a serious disappointment to the parents. The girl developed traits of smug self-righteousness. Her assumption that the scales of justice would always be weighted in her favor created later problems for her.

**Are we capable of carrying through undertakings once begun, or are we likely to make alibis for our mistakes and refuse to accept the responsibility if the child's emotional growth is unsatisfactory?** Sometimes adoptive parents, with problems like those in the case above, resist accepting responsibility for the directions in which the child develops. There is a temptation to blame undesirable traits on something in the child's hereditary background rather than to work with patient perseverance and love to help the child develop in the best possible way. The couple who would adopt must first settle in their own minds that they are undertaking exactly the same degree of responsibility for an adopted child that they would have if they gave birth to the child.

**Are we capable of making a success of our marriage with or without a child, or are we expecting an adopted child to improve our marriage?** Marriage counselors not infrequently hear from couples having trouble in marriage. "We are trying to find a child to adopt. We feel that if only we had a child it would bring us closer together."

No couple should adopt a child unless they have already been able to build a satisfactory relationship between themselves. If they cannot cope with their two-way relationship, adding a third person would certainly complicate their situation and intensify their pressures. Successful parenthood requires more cooperation and self-sacrifice than does marriage without children. Children need protection against being placed with adoptive parents whose search for a child is an attempt to escape from their own problems and frustrations in life, or from their inability to cope with the requirements of marriage. Sometimes the very desperation with which a couple seeks to adopt a child is evidence of a neurotic adjustment to life.

**Are we too old to adopt?**  That is likely to be a difficult question for people to face. Sometimes people put off having children until late in the childbearing years and then decide that they wish to have children by adoption; or they wait for years, hoping to have a child of their own, and at last, when they are approaching middle age, seek to adopt. Some simple mathematics will help find the answer to this question. How old will the parents be when the child is an adolescent? When he or she is 15 or 16 and behaves like any normal adolescent—noisy, exuberant or depressed, sometimes irresponsible, often unreasonable, delighting in crowds, confusion, and activity—will the parents be too old "to take it"? Over-age parents are likely to resist and feel impelled to thwart the normal behavior of youth; in such cases the accompanying pressures may cause rebellion on the part of the young person, and result in sorrow and grief for the parents.

Another aspect of the age question is this: If the parents are middle-aged when they adopt, their life expectancy is less than that of average parents. Unless they adopt an older child, their child might be orphaned at a younger age than if adopted by young parents. It may not be fair, then, for people who are beyond their middle thirties to adopt. Some adoption agencies seek to protect children by refusing to allow placement with over-age parents, but many couples resent the age limitation and persist in trying to adopt children through sources that impose no age limitations.

When the decision has been made to adopt a child, a couple should become acquainted with and follow legal regulations in the state in which they live and in which the adoption occurs. If this is not done, future developments may bring sorrow to the adoptive parents and the child. All of those involved need to be protected by careful legal procedures in order to ensure that the adoption cannot be later challenged and the child removed from the adoptive parents. Occasionally, court cases arise in which a natural mother seeks to regain custody of a child whom she gave for adoption several years previously. Some judges tend to attach major importance to the claims or the wishes of the natural mother, and in some cases foster parents have been ordered to relinquish a child after they have had the child since its birth. Such a situation is likely to be traumatic for the child as well as for the adoptive parents, and could be avoided if people were careful to follow legal adoptive procedures and thus secure as far as possible the status of the child.

Once a couple is ready to undertake adoptive parenthood, they should be able to approach it with as much confidence in the child's potential as they would have if the child were born to them. Few of us check carefully into the hereditary background of our mates before we marry; in almost every combination of parents there is the possibility that undesirable traits may appear in the offspring. With adopted children, parents at least have the protection of a thorough physical and mental examination of the child before adoption. They can have the advantage of knowing ahead of time what special physical and mental handicaps the child may need help in overcoming. Most states require a trial period before the adoption becomes final. If valid objections are discovered during the trial period or if parents are doubtful and uncertain about whether they can be adequate parents to the child, they should not proceed with the adoption.

Once children are legally adopted they are members of the adopting family as much as if they had been born to the adoptive parents. They are entitled to all the rights and subject to all the obligations that would have come with natural birth into the family. People who would make any reservations in the matter of name or inheritance should not adopt children.

## DILEMMA OF ADOPTIVE PARENTS

H. D. Kirk theorized, as a basis for his studies of adoption, that in our society the biological foundations of parenthood are widely assumed to be a necessary condition for the most satisfactory parental role performance, and that a consciousness of such attitudes affects the feelings of nonchildbearing couples about themselves and about their functioning as adoptive parents.[5]

He illustrated adoptive parents' reactions to what he called their dilemma by analyzing the following kinds of incongruities confronting them. They are supposed to tell the children about their origin; they were not born to the parents. But they must at the same time maintain the pretense that they are a regular, normal, average family like all other families—that the children and they are not "different" just because they happen to be adopted. Kirk cited a number of different mechanisms by which adoptive parents try to cope with this situation: they emphasize physical resemblances between themselves and the child; if they adopt more than one child, they space ages of the children and adoptions to fit the pattern of biological families; in telling the children about their

[5] H. D. Kirk, "A Dilemma of Adoptive Parenthood: Incongruous Role Obligations," *Marriage and Family Living* 21:4 (November 1959), 316–26.

origin, they try to ignore the existence of the natural parents, or if they recognize it they depersonalize the natural parents by such means as referring to them as "the lady who brought you into the world" or "the woman you were born to"; they make use of what Kirk calls the "chosen baby myth" which attempts to quiet anxieties of both parents and children by assuring the children that they were especially chosen and reassuring themselves that they were all "meant to be together," or that God had a hand in bringing them together in a special way.

Malinowski has pointed out that myths serve a function, especially where there is sociological strain, and Kirk believes that the "myths" used in adoptive situations are evidence of such strain.[6] He says that the mechanisms are attempts to deny or reject the differences between the adoptive and the biological family situation. It seems logical to accept the view that certain emotional conflicts are inherent in the adoptive relationship in our society. Because of this, adoptive parents need to be better prepared for their task than natural parents. A trend in the 1960s and 1970s toward crossing racial and nationality barriers in adopting may have a healthy effect toward resolving this "dilemma," as described by Kirk. It would seem that when married couples choose to adopt children who are very different from themselves or who are handicapped physically or emotionally, surely they must be able to view the children as individuals with their own special needs, as they might not be able to do if they had chosen them on the basis of their similarity to themselves or to children born to them.

Certainly many adoptive parents do as well with adopted children as they would have done with any children born to them. Nevertheless, adoptive parents are required in some ways to be superior in knowledge and preparation for parenthood, since it is always a challenging job and, clearly, there *are* more potential problems in being successful parents of adopted children.

### Honesty with child about adoption

It can be readily understood why some parents might try to avoid telling children that they are adopted. But such a policy has resulted in shock and sorrow for children when they later learned the truth. In spite of their own feelings about it, most adoptive parents recognize that it is better for the children to know that they are adopted while they are very young, so that they live with and accept the fact that they were not born physically to their parents, before it has much specific meaning for them.

In cases in which parents adopt children of another race or nation-

[6] B. Malinowski, *Magic, Science and Religion* (New York: Doubleday & Company, Inc., 1954), p. 126.

ality, so that differences in physical appearance are clearly apparent, the question of whether or not to tell is less likely to arise. The fact that they were not born to these parents will be evident to the children as soon as they are old enough to observe that most children resemble their parents in traits such as skin color or hair type. Parents who adopt children of another race or culture probably have resolved this matter in their own minds or they would not have adopted these children.

For parents who have followed the earlier custom of adopting children as much like themselves as possible, a challenging, often very difficult task is to handle the facts of origin in a way that will help the children make the best possible emotional development, not only when they are young but also later when they are in the teens and are deeply aware of all the implications of their birth and adoption.

It has been common practice for adopted children to be told stories about being "chosen" children, with great emphasis and detail given to how carefully their parents searched for them and chose them. But it is doubtful whether the story of being chosen and adopted should be used as a bedtime story any more than parents would use the story of physical birth as a bedtime story to children born to them. There are good reasons for this statement.

**Telling about adoption can be overdone.**  First, some parents in their zeal to impress children with the fact that they were wanted and chosen overdo their emphasis on the adoption, and in the end the children may be as troubled as if they had not been told of their adoption. In either case, they succeed in impressing the children more than is necessary with the painful fact that they are *different* from other children, and this can be confusing.

> A little boy of three, whose parents had conscientiously told and retold the story of his being a chosen child, seemed to delight in hearing the story. At bedtime, he would cuddle into his bed and say, "Now, tell me about when you got me." But his mother became aware that he was very intense about the story and sometimes would be slow to go to sleep afterward, then would sleep restlessly and cry out in his sleep. This mother said, "All the books told us to be sure to let him know he was a chosen child. But no one warned us not to make too big a thing of it. We had to learn the hard way how complicated the thoughts and feelings of a little child are, and to try not to overdo what we thought was being truthful with him about his origin."

So parents of young children need to be realistic about this. They should be open about the adoption, but they should be careful not to give any more emphasis or attention to the subject while the children are young than they would normally give to the facts of natural birth— a subject it is safe to say most parents do not pursue and dwell on unduly with their children. Any specific questions children ask should be honestly and accurately answered, just as parents try to answer questions they ask about all other subjects. Far more important than how they acquired the children is that they love them now for themselves. Their love for them is the one truth that can help to compensate for the fact that as a family they are different from most of the families around them.

To overdo the "chosen" aspect of adoption is not really being accurate or honest, no matter how sincere the intentions. This overdoing grows out of the parents' need to resolve their own anxieties in the matter. The truth is that the majority of adoptive parents probably would have chosen to have their children born to them had it not been for factors beyond their control. What has that truth to do with the adjustment of the children? Perhaps not very much while the children are young, but far more as they grow up.

## ADOLESCENTS' FEELINGS ABOUT ADOPTION

As children grow older and become aware subjectively that most children are born to their parents, adopted children will think of many things; they will not restrict their thoughts to what has been said in bedtime stories. They will wonder why their natural parents let other parents have them. Adopted children may wonder what their natural parents were like and whether they had been loved by them. The thought is bound to occur to them that the adoptive parents might have preferred to have children born to them. Adopted children are likely to have envious feelings toward other children who live with their "own" parents and have to face no questions or puzzles about their background.

During adolescence, when children feel a great need to be like others in all possible ways, some of the questions in their minds will suggest answers that may not fit with the picture the parents have tried to give them of adoption. If they begin to think that on even one point the parents have tried to give a picture not exactly true to the facts, serious doubts may begin to trouble them, not only about the parents but about themselves as well. One girl in her teens who was almost frantically seeking information about her natural relatives said, "I can't ask my mother anything. She has always seemed to think that everything about my adoption was so wonderful that I can't let her know about all the things that bother me. Sometimes I think she just doesn't know all the facts of life, or she'd *know* that people are luckier to be born to their own parents and get to grow up where they're born. Either she doesn't know that or she's lied to me all my life!"

Another girl of college age said to her mother, "I wish you would find all the records there are anywhere about my background. I'd like to know whether I'm descended from people who lived to be a hundred and never had anything like cancer or TB—or whether my ancestors all died young! I'd like to know what kinds of work they did and whether they were happy families or not. I'd like to know *all* the things about my aunts and uncles and grandparents that all my friends know about theirs!" This kind of interest in one's own hereditary background is most natural. A wise adoptive parent will accept it and be responsive to such questions.

## Legal rights of adopted children

The question arises as to whether the legal rights of adopted children are being denied when they do not have access to the facts of their biological origins. Is there still a holdover of attitudes toward illegitimate children and the treatment of orphans which guides society in denying the rights of adopted children to know their origins? It is estimated that there are approximately five million adoptees in the United States. Some of the desires of teenagers to know about their biological parents may result from other adolescent problems of growing up, but as people get older there are sound reasons for wanting to know their ancestry. Family medical and hereditary history is asked for when people see a doctor. People should have a right to know whether they have predispositions to certain physical weaknesses due to heredity.

A national organization, Adoptees' Liberty Movement Association, has been formed to help adoptees find their biological parents. This organization, which has chapters in different cities, may cause the development of a new concept of the rights of the adoptee. Possibly, the rights of those who have given children for adoption may have been overemphasized and the rights of the adopted children not been given enough consideration. A compromise might be to require those giving children for adoption to provide a more complete medical and family history. This information could be available to the adoptee upon request.

## Importance of honesty and free communication

Two qualities are absolutely necessary in families in which children, whether adopted or natural, make good emotional growth without turmoil and parent–child conflict. These are honesty between parents and children and keeping lines of communication open so that troublesome feelings and experiences can be talked about. Lack of honesty at any point will block the possibility of free communication. Almost no problem or question need be too upsetting if the children and parents can talk it over with trust and confidence. Parents who try to convince adopted children that everything connected with being adopted is sweetness and joy are setting up a block that may later cause loss of confidence on the part of the children. The truth is that there is sadness for at least one person in the background of every adoption. Regardless

CHILDLESS MARRIAGES AND ADOPTION

of the circumstances of the birth or the release of a child for adoption, someone has experienced disillusionment and sorrow of some sort. But is that unique to an adoptive situation? None of us can ever choose every circumstance in life; we must accept the less-than-ideal along with the delightfully perfect in the circumstances of our lives. Children reared by the parents who gave birth to them may easily look about and see other families into which they might have been more fortunately born, just as adopted children may sometimes wish their situation were different. But a good adjustment to life means accepting circumstances that are not controllable, and making the most of the advantages that do exist in every life.

## Handling questions constructively

If a relationship built on confidence and trust has been firmly established during the early years of childhood, adolescent and teen-aged children will be able to bring out into the open their doubts and seek the reassurance that wise parents can give. We quote here two examples of answers given to children by adoptive parents:

> An 11-year-old boy said, "My parents must have been no good." His adopted mother answered, "I don't know very many specific facts about the people you were born to. But I do know this: No matter what unfortunate thing happened that meant they didn't keep you, there were surely some very fine things about them. I know that, because I know you so well, and a boy like you has some wonderful people among his ancestors. I think you'll be like the best of your ancestors and like the best that we are, too." This mother faced openly the feelings of self-doubt that accompanied the boy's troubled feelings about his natural parents.
>
> A 9-year-old girl asked, "Why did my mother give me up, if mothers love their children?" The answer was, "I don't know all the circumstances. But I do know there was some reason why she couldn't keep you, and she did the best she could under the circumstances so that you could have a better and happier life as our child. I'm sorry that she is missing getting to know you and live with you, but I never could be too sorry about it because I'm so glad that you are our child. Sometimes sad things in life turn into happy things and that's the way it is with us and you. So let's try not to worry too much about how it came about, and just enjoy being together."

Both of these parents answered difficult questions with directness and sincerity. Similar answers would probably help the children feel better about themselves and their background, and also contribute to their sense of being valued and loved for themselves in their adoptive family.

Naturally, parents would prefer, if they could, to eliminate all doubtful thoughts and questions from the mind of their children and give them an altogether happy conception of their origin. But, unfortunately, neither adoptive nor natural parents can control the thoughts of children.

Children will have doubts and questions even as the adoptive parents themselves have. If the parents accept their own and their children's feelings and meet questions with honesty and love, the parent–child relationship will contribute to the security and adequacy of the children. Adopted children, like any other children whose parents can manage to keep lines of communication open throughout childhood and the teens, are better able to cope with difficulties that life offers.

## REVIEW QUESTIONS

1  How common a problem is infertility in marriage?

2  What seems to be an accurate assessment of the partners' responsibility in a sterile marriage?

3  Give some of the most common causes of infertility.

4  What proportion of supposedly sterile marriages may be successfully treated?

5  What is the purpose of the rat hyperemia test?

6  Does a rise in temperature necessarily indicate ovulation? Explain.

7  When could ovulation be expected in a 20-day cycle? a 28-day cycle? a 40-day cycle?

8  What is the legal status of a child conceived by donor artificial insemination?

9  Summarize the progress made in overcoming infertility.

10  In what ways have fluctuations in the birth rate from 1930 to the present been a factor affecting the adoption of children?

11  Discuss the combination of factors affecting the ratio between potential parents and children available for adoption.

12  What are five important questions that prospective adoptive parents should answer before they seriously consider adopting a child?

13  What will be the most important factor in determining how the adopted child develops? What mistake did Mr. and Mrs. A. make when they adopted their second child?

14  Does the adopted child have the legal rights of other children?

15  What are some of the special tasks adoptive parents have that natural parents do not have? How might some of these tasks be handled?

16  Discuss the "dilemma" of the adoptive family.

17  What questions are adopted children likely to raise sooner or later? How might these questions be answered by the parent?

18  Do you think the rights of adopted children are adequately protected? Why? Would people feel as free to adopt children if the children were granted more rights to knowledge of their heredity?

19  What two things are necessary in families if children are to achieve a good emotional growth? Why?

## PROJECTS AND ACTIVITIES

Interview the person in charge of your local welfare agency, or the head of a state or local adoption agency, concerning the present status of adoption in your area. Is there a surplus of homeless children or is there a waiting list of potential parents? What policies are being followed to remedy any discrepancy that exists? Report to the class.

# WHEN CHILDREN COME

# 25

Sometimes husbands and wives who have lived together for two or three years and have worked out satisfactory relationships in all areas are baffled to find, after the first baby arrives, that new and unexpected differences arise, requiring readjustments in their relationship. The arrival of a third person in the home upsets the status quo and the couple must achieve a new working arrangement. The new interaction pattern involves different roles for each.

## OVERROMANTICIZING PARENTHOOD VERSUS SHOCK

The readjustments required by the birth of the first child come as a shock to many parents. They have not been prepared for this aspect of parenthood. For young people in our culture, parenthood, like marriage, has been overromanticized.

The romantic picture of parenthood is reinforced by friends and relatives who usually respond to the prospect of a first baby with much the same kind of enthusiasm they have for a wedding. Showers and gifts are given; there is attentive interest in the names being considered for the coming baby. Thus, in spite of some problems they may meet during the pregnancy, most couples proceed with happy anticipation toward the birth of the first baby.

During the pregnancy they look forward in a way to their "dream child" and are not prepared for the actual appearance of the newborn baby. The oversized head, sometimes appearing pointed or flat for a day or two after birth, the red or mottled-looking face, the unruly hair or bald head, and the unresponsiveness of the newborn infant may come as a shock to some parents.

They may have sudden inner doubts about themselves as parents because of their immediate unresponsiveness to the baby. Mothers, especially, if they have not been prepared for this period of time, may feel disillusioned. A mother may have assumed that she would feel an immediate love for the baby, and if she did not, she would be concerned that such lack of feeling might mean she could not be a "good mother." Many new mothers suffer from feelings of guilt because they do not have the immediate emotional reactions they think they should have.

Such misery could be avoided for most of those who experience it if they were better prepared. For one thing, after a birth the mother is undergoing a major shift in hormone function, which inevitably affects her emotionally. Some mothers are aware of a special sense of well-being at this time and do feel a joyful and loving response to the new baby, but some others have an opposite experience. The feelings of depression and disillusionment that trouble some new mothers may be brief and relatively undisturbing or they may be extreme. The extreme reactions are called "postpartum depression" by the medical profession. Most doctors have encountered this disturbance and qualified doctors will treat it as being serious. The doctor will try to help the mother understand what is happening. He or she will give her support in accepting her emotions and overcoming her feelings of guilt and, if it becomes necessary, will give medication to help her through the troublesome stage.

With some mothers the problem arises not so much from effects of hormone changes as just from the fact that the mother is tired from the birth, and is having to adjust to sudden new responsibilities that may seem overwhelming at the moment. It helps if she can realize that maternal feelings develop differently in different women. Not all mothers respond positively to all stages of infancy and childhood. Some enjoy their babies right away, while others find the early months exhausting and a burden. Some may find the child more enjoyable after he or she begins to walk and talk.

There are many different kinds of "good mothers." It is especially important for new parents to realize this. Some painful emotional experiences would be avoided if parents were aware ahead of time that neither of them can count on feeling a sudden, great wave of loving responsiveness to the baby at the first moment of arrival. If they are not among those who have the happy experience of an immediate positive emotional response to the baby, they should not feel that they are abnormal or lacking in the potential for being good parents.

## PARENTHOOD AS CRISIS

New parents, even those who go easily and happily through the first stage, the first days of a baby's life, will have many adjustments to make as they move into their new parental role. Sociologists who have studied family crises have pointed out that any family crisis results in shock because the "crisis event" forces a reorganization of the family as a social system. Roles must be reassigned, status positions shifted, values re-oriented, and needs met through new channels. E. E. LeMasters theo-rized that if the family is seen as a small social system, it follows that the *adding* of a new member forces a reorganization as drastic as does the *removal* (death or divorce) of a member.[1] He therefore hypothesized that the arrival of the first child must be seen as a critical event or crisis.

LeMasters tested this notion through a study of couples who had had their first child, and he found that 83 percent of the couples reported "extensive" or "severe" crisis in adjusting to changes that accompanied the arrival of the first child. Things the parents reported as especially difficult or unexpected were: loss of sleep and exhaustion, guilt at not being "better" parents, long hours, and a seven-day week in caring for a baby. In addition, mothers listed decline in housekeeping standards and worry over their appearance. Fathers gave decline in sexual response of wife, economic pressure resulting from increased expenses and loss of the wife's income, interference with social life, worry about a possible second pregnancy occurring too soon, and a general disenchantment with the parental role. Both parents found being tied down especially hard. They seriously missed the freedom of the honeymoon stage of marriage. LeMasters suggested that "parenthood (not marriage) marks the final transition to maturity and adult responsibility in our culture. Thus the arrival of the first child forces the young married couple to take the last painful step into the adult world."

LeMasters concluded, "In all fairness to this group of parents, it should be reported that all but a few of them eventually made what seems to be a successful adjustment to parenthood. That does not alter the fact that most of them found the transition difficult." In a restudy that followed LeMasters's work, Dyer found that a large majority (80 percent) of both husbands and wives admitted that things were not as they expected them to be after the child was born. Forty percent of the couples indicated they were still experiencing problems at the time the study was made, which was on the average 12 months after the birth of the baby. Only 24 percent of the mothers and 38 percent of the fathers felt they had largely overcome the "crisis" at the time of the study.[2]

After a time, most couples who have become parents do establish a new interaction pattern. But their adjustments will not remain static. Changes will occur as the child grows and as other babies are born.

In a study similar to those mentioned above, Russell examined the satisfactions as well as the crises which come with parenthood. Listed below are the types of gratification of parenthood reported by 1068 parents in the Russell study:

[1] E. E. LeMasters, "Parenthood as Crisis," *Marriage and Family Living* 19:4 (November 1957), 352.

[2] Everett D. Dyer, "Parenthood as Crisis: A Restudy," *Marriage and Family Living* 25:2 (May 1963), 196–201.

1 Pride in my baby's development.
2 Fewer periods of boredom.
3 Closer relationships with relatives.
4 Increased appreciation for family and religious tradition.
5 Increased contacts with neighbors.
6 More things to talk about with spouse.
7 Feeling "closer" to spouse.
8 Feeling of "fulfillment."
9 New appreciation of my own parents.
10 Fun to play with baby.
11 A purpose for living.
12 Enjoy baby's company.

Approximately 42 percent of both husbands and wives reported the marriage relationship had remained about the same after the arrival of the baby, and only 6 percent reported a deterioration in the relationship. As reported in the studies quoted, the parents mentioned the additional stress which comes with a baby in the home. The Russell study revealed that good adjustment to parenthood was related to having planned the pregnancy and especially to the fact of having conceived after, rather than before, marriage; to a good marital adjustment; to being committed to the parenthood role; to good maternal health; and to having a good, healthy baby.[3]

## REARING CHILDREN—A MARITAL PROBLEM

Studies of marriage adjustment among long-married couples and among people in the early years of marriage agree in finding that training the children ranks high with both groups as a problem in marital adjustment. Our study of 409 marriages of parents of college students revealed that the care and disciplining of the children had ranked next to sex among those problems on which couples had failed to reach satisfactory agreement. In the study of marriages of younger couples, disagreements over child training ranked next to trouble with in-laws and economic difficulties as focal points of friction. The explanation is understandable. When two young people enter marriage, each comes with a vast array of "old wives' tales," superstition, and hearsay, but very little reliable information about child rearing. After the arrival of the first baby, the differences in their attitudes, produced by different family backgrounds, will become evident. An analysis of responses given by different groups of couples who assessed their agreement or disagreement about child rearing shows the highly optimistic view of engaged couples on this point. Responses

[3] Candyce Smith Russell, "Transition to Parenthood: Problems and Gratifications," *Journal of Marriage and the Family* 36:2 (May 1974), 294–301.

WHEN CHILDREN COME

of the different groups are shown in Figure 25-1. In another aspect of the same research, married couples having problems in this area reported they had been married two years or more before they became aware of their differences here. This means, of course, that they became aware of them after they had a child.

When parents differ over child training, both are inclined to react emotionally to their differences. Neither can appreciate the way the other feels. One may believe in "reasoning" with the child, the other may believe in requiring instant obedience. One may believe in a rigid schedule, the other may not. The wife may feel the husband is not applying any principles of psychology to situations, the husband may complain that the wife is too permissive. On all these points there is a conflict in the folk methods that the young people have taken into their marriage. Couples who read together some of the more sensible books on child training are sometimes able to compromise and agree on methods recommended by an outside expert. However, some will not change their ideas. An immature parent may feel he or she has lost face if personal theories are not supported in the literature, and may decide to stick to his or her methods regardless of the consequences. Moreover, rigidity in adhering to individual notions is sometimes motivated by resentments directed at the spouse but having their basis in frustrations arising out of the necessity to adjust to the new roles of parenthood.

A common complaint among the younger couples as well as among the parent generation in our research studies was that one spouse would countermand orders given by the other. That policy is damaging to marital and parental relationships and to the best development of the child. If the mother tells Johnny to stop throwing the ball against the house and the father tells Johnny that it won't hurt anything, it's all right,

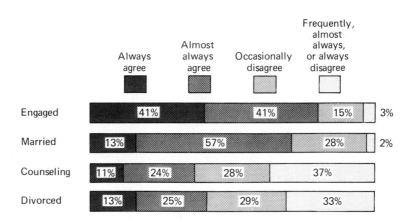

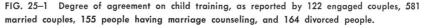

FIG. 25–1 Degree of agreement on child training, as reported by 122 engaged couples, 581 married couples, 155 people having marriage counseling, and 164 divorced people.

Johnny has soon learned to pit one parent against the other in order to do as he pleases. Besides incurring his wife's displeasure and weakening her authority, the husband has also weakened his own future authority with his son.

If discipline is to be effective, parents must present a united front to the children. It is almost impossible for one parent to do anything with the children if the other is issuing different orders. Not only does such variance cause failure with the children, but it creates increasing marital tension between the husband and wife. Parents will differ, but successful parents will discuss these differences and reach compromises when the children are not present.

## PARENTAL ROLES AND FATHER–CHILD RELATIONSHIPS

It has been traditionally assumed that the father's primary responsibility is to support his family, since in our society the family tends to be mother-centered. Too often the father becomes absorbed in his work and is almost unconscious of his other kinds of family responsibilities, or his work may even become a means of escape from the obligation to share in his children's guidance and rearing. If children are to be well reared, the father and the mother must work together.

The division of parental responsibility into distinctly separate categories—the father as the provider and the mother as the nurturer—has unfortunate results for fathers and for children. To many children, the father has little positive significance as a person. He is the man who comes home tired and irritable and whose arrival means that activities must be curbed to make less noise. He is not a person to whom the child can freely go for comfort or for patient response to questions. In papers written by college students, in which they considered their own growing up and the attitudes they had developed as children, we find over and over such statements as: "My father worked hard and seemed to have little time for us children. I felt closer to my mother." "He was sort of the 'Great White Father.' I respected him because my mother always treated him with respect, but things were a lot more comfortable and relaxed around home when he was absent."

This kind of family situation seems to develop over a period of time into a pattern that deprives both fathers and their children of some of the benefits of family life. This pattern is shown also by comments in the students' papers: "When I was older I sometimes wished I could talk to my father but I didn't feel that I knew him very well. I never knew what he really thought about things." "I almost felt sorry for my father. He worked so hard for us all, but he seemed to be on the outside. The good times we had at home didn't really include him. I don't know whether he realized it or not."

It seems that educated young parents should be able to avoid the kind of separation of responsibilities that deprive the father of close and

FIG. 25–2  "I gave him away."
*Ladies' Home Journal*, Sivic

affectionate association with his children. Even in families in which both father and mother have jobs, there is often the tendency for the mother to accept the nurturing role exclusively and the father to be something of an outsider or a distant figure to his children.

The compartmentalization of life by young parents may have its beginnings in the early months of their first baby's life, when the new mother may be understandably absorbed in caring for the baby.

Some new fathers complain that the wife is too anxious about minor details of the baby's life. A husband may begin to feel critical of his wife and her child-care methods because he feels left out or relegated to an unaccustomed second place. Such a reaction is immature, and the father himself may not recognize the real reasons for his feelings. However, his reactions may be a factor impelling them both toward their opposite corners, each one drawing some confidence from a specifically delineated sphere of authority and responsibility.

## FAMILY FACTORS AFFECTING CHILDREN'S HAPPINESS

One hundred and fifty university students made lists of the specific home circumstances they recalled as having brought greatest happiness to them when they were between the ages of 5 and 12. The 15 factors listed most frequently were then arranged in a list for a second group of 2000 students to check. The order in which the second group of students ranked these home circumstances is as follows:

1  Happiness of parents
2  Parental expression of love for me
3  Sense of the family's interest in me
4  Sense of parents' trust
5  Mother a good cook

6   Companionship with parents
7   Family unity and fellowship
8   Meals always on time and house always clean
9   Family able to provide adequate financial means
10  Pride in accomplishments of family
11  Pleasure in doing things together as a family
12  Parents' approval of friends
13  The family's religion
14  Family cooperation
15  Feeling that I had a responsible part in our family

It is interesting that happiness of the parents rated highest. For the parents to be happily married seems to be of primary importance to the happiness of the children. Other studies have shown that the happiness of parents not only contributes to the happiness of the children in the home but also conditions them for later successful family living in their own homes.

Second to happiness of parents, the students named items that emphasize the importance to the children of overt expressions of parental love for them. In many homes the parents take it for granted that their parental care and their efforts to provide for all the needs of their children will be recognized by the children as evidence of love. But to young children, shelter and food are simply part of the environment; they are not necessarily defined in children's thoughts or emotions as expressions of love. Children must be reassured that they are loved through open and free expressions of affection.

It is interesting that young people gave adequate finances ninth place in the list. Apparently, a sense of being loved and trusted and a feeling that there is a companionship with parents are more important to the development of the children than are possessions. Some parents mistakenly think that they have taken care of their children's needs simply because they have given them their material needs. But nothing can be substituted for parental happiness, love, and companionship in the lives of young children.

The same students were asked to list specific factors that they recalled as having caused greatest unhappiness in their lives between the ages of 5 and 12. Their list is as follows:

1   Death and illness in the family
2   Parents' quarreling
3   Conflict with parents' views
4   Quarreling of brothers and sisters
5   Inability of parents to see my point of view
6   Loneliness
7   Misunderstanding in the family

8  Parents' unhappiness

9  Quarreling with parents

10  Feeling of being misunderstood

11  Being compared with other children

12  Parents nagged me

13  Lack of companionship with parents

14  Afraid parents would separate

15  Father hard to get along with

16  Lack of association with those my own age

17  Lack of adequate finances

Illness and death ranked first as a major cause of unhappiness for children. It is understandable that serious illness or death usually represents a family crisis that threatens or destroys the security of the children. The students ranked a quarreling pattern in the home second to illness and death as a source of unhappiness. Quarrels between parents caused greatest unhappiness, but quarrels between siblings also rated high. Not very much can be done to keep children from worrying about illness and death, but families can do something about quarreling. Parents who quarrel easily, without considering their quarrels to be serious, would be shocked to learn the extent of emotional tension it creates for children.

Another source of unhappiness for children has to do with conflicts over points of view between parents and children. A measure of conflict on this score will be inevitable in parent–child relationships. Sometimes it seems impossible to make clear to the children reasons for parental attitudes. Again, parents may make arbitrary rulings with a total lack of understanding of the young people's points of view. Successful parents accept their responsibility for guiding their children. They try to avoid making arbitrary rulings and work for understanding and agreement with their children about desirable or undesirable behavior.

## SELF-APPRAISAL BY CHILDREN FROM HAPPY AND UNHAPPY HOMES

In our study of 3189 college students, those students who thought their parents were happily married, in contrast to those who thought their parents were unhappily married, described themselves as follows: [4]

1  They had closer relationships with both parents.

2  They were more religious.

[4] For a summary of the comparable study of 3000 students in 1952, see Judson T. Landis, "A Comparison of Children From Divorced and Nondivorced Unhappy Marriages," *Family Life Coordinator* 9:3 (July 1962), 61–65; also, Landis, "Dating Maturation of Children From Happy and Unhappy Marriages," *Marriage and Family Living* 25:2 (May 1963).

Parents' marital happiness

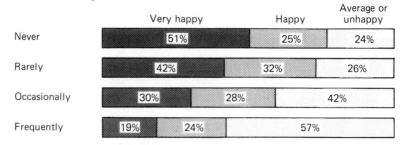

FIG. 25–3 Doubts about their own chances for successful marriage and parental marital happiness, as reported by 3189 students at 18 colleges in 1967.

3   They had received more sex information from their parents.

4   They had developed more desirable attitudes toward the place of sex in life.

5   More of them had refrained from premarital sexual relations.

6   They had dated more people in junior and senior high school.

7   They had less difficulty making friends in early adolescence.

8   They had greater confidence in associating with members of the other sex in college.

9   Fewer of them wished to be of the other sex.

10   They gave themselves a higher than average rating in personality.

11   More of them never doubted their chances for a successful marriage.

It seems that the above list of self-characterizations by children who see their parents' marriages as happy indicates that these young people probably had greater basic security than had people from unhappy

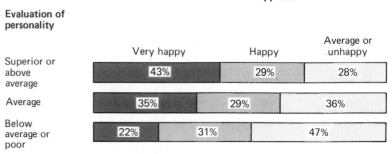

FIG. 25–4 Evaluation of their own personalities in early adolescence and parental marital happiness, as reported by 3189 students at 18 colleges in 1967.

homes, and thus could more easily achieve satisfactory growth and adjustment in the outside world.

## SITUATIONS CAUSING ANXIETIES IN CHILDREN

Even children from happy homes have certain fears and worries that are more or less universal. If the home is happy, these troubles are not permanently serious. If the home is not happy and if the child lacks the inner confidence that comes with family solidarity, childhood problems assume greater importance. A common worry in childhood has to do with physical appearance. A third of all the college students included this item in their free list. Why are children so acutely conscious of physical characteristics that they suffer over their real or imagined defects? The reason often goes back to thoughtless remarks and comments made within the family while the children are young. A parent or relative may remark that Robert has inherited those ears from the other side of the family. Robert may be a handsome, attractive child, but that has nothing to do with his reactions to comments on his ears. He begins to feel that his ears are big and conspicuous. Or while his sister is still a toddler, mother and aunts remark, "It is too bad her hair is so thin." After she hears that a few times, she feels that her hair is a serious handicap to her looks.

Their actual appearance seems to have little to do with whether children worry over how they look. Some children do have features or defects that might be expected to be handicaps; yet, if the matter has been handled well in the family, and if overall emotional needs are met, the children may be entirely unconscious of the characteristics. Individual features are a handicap only if children feel conscious of them and consider them a handicap.

One of the most important gifts a father and mother can give their children is to help them feel self-appreciation and that they are a credit to the family, that they are liked and that the parents are proud of them. Whether they happen to be tall or short, fat or slim, with big ears or small, should be very unimportant as far as family love is concerned.

Other childhood troubles have to do with situations in which the children feel that they have "lost face" before others. If they are punished before others, if parents discuss them and their traits in the presence of others, or if they are forced to dress or act in ways noticeably different from those about them, they will feel embarrassed. Table 25-1 gives a more complete listing of home circumstances causing anxiety in children.

Preparation for marriage and parenthood should include a consideration of these things that affect the happiness and sense of well-being of children. The happiness of the children is important not only to the happiness of the parents; it is also significant because of the influence it will have on the children's future marriages.

TABLE 25-1    Student ranking of specific circumstances that caused anxiety during childhood *

| Physical features | Losing face before others |
|---|---|
| 1 Afraid I would always be homely | 1 Had to wear long stockings or under-wear |
| 2 Crooked teeth | 2 Scoldings before other children |
| 3 Awkwardness | 3 Had to perform for others |
| 4 Too fat or too slim | 4 Parents made me apologize for things |
| 5 Wearing glasses | 5 Parents bragged about me |
| 6 Complexion | 6 Didn't dress as other children did or had to wear hand-me-down clothes |
| 7 Unattractive hair | 7 Teasing |
| 8 Not growing any taller | 8 Being left out of things |
| | 9 Couldn't do things others did |
| | 10 Mother always let everyone know I was the baby |

| Conditioned fears | Desire for security |
|---|---|
| 1 Darkness | 1 That our house would burn |
| 2 Lightning and thunder | 2 That my father would die |
| 3 Animals, snakes, bugs, etc. | 3 That my mother would die |
| 4 Being left alone | 4 That my brothers or sisters would die |
| 5 Fires | 5 That I would die |
| 6 Deep water | 6 That I was adopted |
| 7 Being locked in closet | 7 That my parents would separate |
| 8 Old empty houses | 8 Being kidnaped |
| 9 Fear of not getting to heaven | 9 That the world would come to an end |
| 10 Fear of going to hell | |
| 11 Fear of being punished by God | |
| 12 Ghosts | |

* Three hundred and fifty students listed the specific factors that caused great anxiety in their lives when they were between the ages of 5 and 12. These common fears and worries have been classified under four headings in the above table. In each grouping, the items are listed in descending order, from those mentioned most frequently to least frequently. Some of these fears are quite universally conditioned in small children, others reflect a child's feelings of insecurity in the home, and still others are natural reactions to "losing face" before one's friends.

Parents need to take the long view of their children's growing up. The continuous task is to look beyond immediate problems that may seem baffling and to decide which childish actions or attitudes have significance in determining what kind of men or women their children will eventually be. They need to see in today's fascinating and frustrating 2-year-old the prophecy of tomorrow's 20-year-old. While they are busy coping with specific details of child rearing, they can also have clearly in mind the contribution they can make to the personality development of their children.

Authorities on infant care tend to stress such matters as breast-feeding, toilet training, and methods of weaning as important factors in the development of the basic personality pattern of children. Some young mothers are anxious and insecure because of uncertainties about using the "right" methods of infant care.

In the thirties, "good" mothers put their babies on a three- or four-hour feeding schedule and allowed nothing to interfere with it. They let babies "cry it out" if they attempted to upset the schedule. They weaned babies from the breast or bottle to a cup as early as possible, and felt that toilet training must begin when babies were only a few months old and be completed by a set time. Now, mothers are advised to do the opposite, to let nature take its course in the development of the children lest they create tensions, fears, and frustrations in them that may handicap personality growth.

An investigation of some 644 articles written between 1890 and 1949 on the subject of care of children showed that most of the articles written in 1890 suggested that the mother "loosely schedule"; most of those written in 1920 advocated that she "tightly schedule" and let the babies cry it out; and most in 1949 urged that she permit the infants to "self-regulate."[5] Hence, in this period of about 60 years, there was a swing of the pendulum from one extreme to the other and back again on many matters of infant care.

Sewell attempted to test the importance of the relationship between details of physical care and psychological and emotional growth through a study of the personalities of a group of children and an examination of the methods used in their care as infants. He found few significant relationships between infant-care practices and later personality. He reports, "Such practices as breast-feeding, gradual weaning, demand schedule, and early or late induction to bowel and bladder training . . . were almost barren in terms of relation to personality adjustment as measured in this study."[6]

Sewell's findings mean that specific methods used in the early months of infants' lives are less crucial than are certain other factors affecting personality development. In the years when infant-care practices were characterized by rigidity, and again in the years when the opposite methods were considered best, a great many children still managed to develop well-adjusted and basically secure personalities. That fact alone suggests that successful parenthood goes far beyond following specific "right" or "wrong" methods of infant care.

[5] Clark E. Vincent, "Trends in Infant Care Ideas," *Child Development* 22 (September 1951), 199–209.

[6] William H. Sewell, "Infant Training and the Personality of the Child," *American Journal of Sociology* 58:2 (September 1952), 150–59.

Basic in determining the personality of children is the *quality of the total relationship* between parents and children. This defies examination in even the most carefully devised studies. To illustrate: Mothers may breast-feed their babies because of a strong sense of duty, and may reject the children emotionally and actually may have little understanding of their total needs. Some mothers may not be able to breast-feed their babies or may choose not to for reasons of convenience, but may show greater warmth and affection for the babies than do resentful, nursing mothers. When it was popular to put babies on a schedule and let them "cry it out," there were still a great many babies whose total emotional relationships with their mothers led to their feeling loved and secure. These babies could therefore adjust to the rigid schedules without emotional damage.

Certainly, today's emphasis on a close relationship between mothers and babies from the earliest days of their babies' lives is sound. Other sound practices are the less rigid feeding schedules, and greater flexibility in toilet training and in some matters of discipline. However, no amount of doing things "right" in infant care will ever take the place of the intangible and more important attitudes—really wanting the children, understanding them as individuals, and making them feel valued.

Children may have all their physical needs satisfied from the time they are born until they reach adulthood and yet turn out to be unhappy, maladjusted people, because their emotional needs were never met in the parent–child interaction. Moreover, some mistakes in method will not ruin children if the total parent–child relationship is sound and healthy. We do not accept the theory that children's personalities are absolutely set at a very young age and that early mistakes in method made by parents are inevitably disastrous. Children are amazingly tough, both physically and emotionally; parents who, through lack of experience, knowledge, or understanding, make mistakes with their young children can overcome their mistakes as they themselves mature and gain insight into their children's development. Evidence of this can be seen in adults who may have been handicapped by their early life experiences, but who, with motivation and increased insight, and perhaps aided by counseling, later overcome their handicaps and become flexible, better-qualified personalities.

## REVIEW QUESTIONS

1   In what ways does the coming of the first child fit the definition of a family crisis?

2   What readjustments in husband–wife relationships are often required when the first child is born?

3   What are some factors underlying conflict between husbands and wives over the training and discipline of their children?

WHEN CHILDREN COME

**4**  What are some of the more common differences concerning child training?

**5**  Why is it essential for parents to present a united front in child training?

**6**  Discuss some disadvantages and advantages of a strict division of responsibility between fathers and mothers.

**7**  What home circumstances seem to be important to the happiness of children?

**8**  Cite some home situations that make for the unhappiness of children.

**9**  What are some of the most common fears and worries of children?

**10**  How can children be made to feel that their physical features are not a handicap?

**11**  Name some of the trends in child care during a period of 60 years. What is the trend today?

**12**  What is the relationship between child-care practices and personality?

**13**  What elements are basic in the personality development of the child?

## PROJECTS AND ACTIVITIES

**1**  Examine some widely read magazines for advertisements or illustrations that present the romantic view of parenthood.

**2**  Write a case history of parental conflict over the training and disciplining of children. Bring out the effect of the conflict on the relationship of the parents as well as the reaction of the children to the conflict.

**3**  Write an analysis of your own home, bringing out the circumstances that made for your happiness or unhappiness and the things you worried about as a child.

**4**  *Role playing.*  Jack and Elizabeth have been married ten years. They have three children, aged 2 months, 3 years, and 7 years. Scene: Jack has just spanked John, the 7-year-old, when Elizabeth comes into the room and says to Jack, "You shouldn't spank John. He didn't mean to break the window!"

# BRINGING UP CHILDREN

What is the real task of parents in rearing children? Can people approach parenthood with their goals and purposes clearly defined? Some students of child development speak of the responsibility of parents in terms of the socialization of children, the concept being used rather broadly to include the nurture of children physically and emotionally and the transmitting to them, through life experiences, of the values and expectations of the society in which they live. The concept also implies equipping children to function satisfactorily within the limits of their cultural setting.

A more specifically applied definition states the purpose of child rearing as twofold: (1) to help children achieve a personal state of well-being (mental health), and (2) to help them become productive, well-socialized members of the family of man.[1] These are the broad, long-term goals of rearing children.

## PARENTAL PERSPECTIVE

Few parents formulate for themselves their goals in such terms as those above, but successful parents do become able, early in the lives of their children, to take the long view of their children's growth. They try to help their children develop feelings of security and self-confidence that will enable them to cope with the challenges they meet, and they try to help them understand the requirements a social world will place on them. When young parents can take the long rather than the short view

[1] Calvin F. Settlage, "The Values of Limits in Child Rearing," *Children* 5:5 (September–October 1958).

of their children's development, they find that the necessary decisions and choices do not look so difficult or frightening. They can begin to feel more confident about their own ability to be "good" parents.

In simplest terms, their responsibility is to help their children develop attitudes and characteristics that will enable them to live successfully later without the help of their parents. One aspect of their helping is not to hinder the children's development by letting too many of their own emotional pressures or handicaps dictate their policies with their children. In almost all areas of child rearing, thoughtful parents can recognize tendencies toward some courses of action arising out of their own past experiences. By the time people become parents, emotional pressures have been built into them regarding many subjects, and it is easy to act blindly rather than to make rational choices of policy in dealing with their children. Some of these "inherited" or conditioned attitudes influence parental action in sound and constructive ways; others have a negative effect.

A task of parents is to try to interpret childish behavior in the light of whether an act is a predictable expression of childish nature, or whether it indicates development of an undesirable tendency that has bearing on the adult personality into which the child will grow. Parents without perspective may punish children for getting their clothes dirty at play, for breaking a dish when they are trying to help, or for making too much noise in crowded living quarters, meanwhile overlooking the fact that the children are frequently dishonest, not simply because of pleasure in fantasy but because lying enables them to avoid facing unpleasant facts or situations. The same parents may punish children for trivial acts that are annoying but take no notice if the children are destructive of property belonging to others or cruel in relationships with other children. Such parents are unaware of the relative importance of events. If a pattern of lying or cruelty or destructiveness develops in children's behavior, parents must consider the entire situation, and examine their own responses to their children and their interaction with them. Such behavior may indicate the children are calling for help with feelings and problems with which they cannot cope. Alert parents will try to assess behavior and determine which actions are signals indicating unmet needs and which are merely typical of behavior for children at certain ages.

## DEVELOPMENT OF MARRIAGEABLE INDIVIDUALS

What traits characterize people who are able to function adequately at each stage of life? How can parents help children develop traits that will enable them eventually to become marriageable people? Let us review, from the chapters on marriageability, some of the characteristics of people who have made a success of marriage. The research shows that happily married people tend to have certain traits: [2]

They are optimistic, having the "habit of happiness," rather than being given to moodiness, depression, or wide swings in emotional levels.

They show self-reliance and initiative.

They are responsible and able to apply themselves dependably to work-tasks that life requires of them.

They are inclined to be unselfish and considerate.

They have a sense of proportion about their own rights and the rights of others.

They can live comfortably with the sex mores and social conventions in the culture.

They are reasonably self-confident and secure, as indicated by lack of jealousy and by the ability to assess fairly accurately their own strengths and weaknesses.

They have learned constructive ways to work through problems.

In addition to personal characteristics, some of the life circumstances predictive of successful marriage are also pertinent to our further discussion. These circumstances are: superior happiness of parents, childhood happiness, lack of conflict with mother and father, home discipline that was firm but reasonable and not harshly restrictive, and parental frankness about matters of sex.

It seems clear that the first and probably the most important advantage, next to love, that can be given children is a background of happily married parents. The couple who can apply self-discipline and objectivity to their own marital relationships to work out happy adjustments are not likely to meet insurmountable difficulties in bringing up their children. Happiness in the home and optimistic attitudes toward the circumstances of life strongly influence children. The habit of happiness is learned and practiced, not inherited.

## SELF-RELIANCE AND INITIATIVE

Self-reliance can begin to develop early, when children first show an interest in doing things for themselves. They should be encouraged, but not pushed, in their attempts to dress and feed themselves. It is here that parents often fail, for it is far easier to take over than to wait for the children to make progress at their own pace. But at this point children need the sense of mastery that comes with each new achievement.

[2] Lewis M. Terman, *Psychological Factors in Marital Happiness* (New York: McGraw-Hill Book Company, 1938), pp. 142–66; Ernest W. Burgess and Leonard S. Cottrell, *Predicting Success or Failure in Marriage* (Englewood Cliffs, N.J.: Prentice-Hall, Inc., 1939).

Many parents with their first child do not realize how early a child's urge toward independence may appear. The mother of a 9-month-old boy was struggling through dinner with the baby in his highchair. Each time she offered him food in a spoon, he swung at her hand and frequently succeeded in knocking either the spoon or the food to the floor. She said, "I don't know why Ronald does that. I have a terrible time feeding him." A friend said, "Why don't you just let him go it alone? He may be swinging at the spoon because he'd like to get hold of it and feed himself instead of having you push the food at him." The mother protested that the baby was too young to feed himself, but she began setting his food before him with a spoon beside it and going about her other work. Promptly Ronald tried the handle of the spoon, his fingers, and other methods of getting his food to his mouth, and in a very short time he was feeding himself with no worse spillage than had been occurring when his mother had been trying to feed him. And his great satisfaction in being able to feed himself independently was easily apparent in the enthusiasm with which he welcomed mealtimes. How better can young children be spending their time and energy than in learning, even by hit and miss, to do for themselves? If parents can curb their impatience and allow children to go ahead and learn for themselves with a minimum of interfering help, they will be letting their children progress toward self-reliance. Seemingly unimportant matters such as feeding or dressing themselves provide the beginnings of the concept children acquire of themselves as adequate or inadequate in life situations.

As children grow a little older, they often want to take part in their parents' activities, to "help" with whatever work they see the parents doing. If the father is pounding with a hammer, small children want to pound too. Efforts of children are not always helpful, especially if the father's pounding is a hurried attempt to fix something that has been needing to be fixed for many weeks. A too-frequent result of efforts by the children to help is, "Come get this child out of my hair if you want me to get anything done."

Some children who follow their mothers around wanting to "help" sometimes meet the same kind of rebuff. One mother was washing the kitchen floor when in came her 3-year-old son with a small pan of water and a clean towel from the bathroom. He put down his pan of water with a big splash on the part of the kitchen floor she had just finished cleaning and began scrubbing the floor with a great swishing of the towel and splashing of water. Thinking only of the work to be done over, his mother descended upon him angrily, snatching the pan and towel away from him with a "No, no, naughty boy to get the clean floor all wet again," which sent him crying from the kitchen.

There are undoubtedly too many similar incidents in the background of older children whose mothers complain, "They never show any initiative or willingness to take their share of the responsibility." Wise parents will, from the earliest years, respect and encourage evidence of initiative

FIG. 26–1 Children develop self-reliance and initiative by being encouraged to do things for themselves. Courtesy of Rondal Partridge.

in their children, even if their attempts to help are not always helpful. It remains a matter of taking the long-range view. Which is of more permanent importance, getting the housework or repair work done on schedule or helping little children to feel they are needed by the parents and useful to them, that the ideas and help of the children can make a contribution to the family activities? It is unreasonable to squelch evidences of the initiative of children for years because "they are too little," and then suddenly to assume that "now they are old enough" and expect them to show initiative. Growth and development are not that simple.

## HELPING CHILDREN TO THINK FOR THEMSELVES

As with developing self-reliance, so growth toward independent judgment is gradual. No one certain day or particular age marks the point at which children become old enough to think for themselves. It would be easier for parents if there were such a point. Parents must decide frequently in individual situations, "Does this call for guidance and direction? Is it a decision so entirely beyond the child's experience that it should be decided for her or for him? Is it one of the many cases that in itself is not so important, the important thing being that the child should make the decision independently?"

Some children seem to shrink from making their own decisions and depend on parents too much. These children need to be encouraged toward self-reliance. Here again, parents must be able to be objective. Sometimes parents, perhaps more often mothers, become so wrapped up in the lives of their children that they are too much occupied with making too many decisions for their children. Wise parents will realize that it is better for the children to be given all possible latitude in making decisions, because the time is not far ahead when they will *have* to make their own choices. They will need confidence in their own judgment if they are to take their places with others in the outside world. If children shrink from making their own decisions, parents can help them by talking with them about the possible choices and then encouraging them to feel that they are ready to decide for themselves. Parents can help especially by showing respect for the judgment of their children and by withholding criticism when they make choices that are not exactly the same as ones the parents would make. To make too many decisions for children indicates a basic lack of respect for them as individuals and may destroy their self-confidence.

## RESPONSIBILITY

In considering the ways in which children develop a sense of responsibility and begin to cope with tasks, the subject of handling money arises. The use of money is inevitably tied up with developmental experiences of children in our culture. Parents should evaluate their own attitudes regarding money and the responsibilities and obligations involved in its use. The children's conception of what their responsibility is in the family and in the outside world will be influenced by their early experiences with money. Giving children an allowance and guiding them in spending that allowance are effective teaching devices, whether or not the parents intend it that way.

> In one family, four children, ranging in age from 8 to 15, received allowances sufficient to take care of their needs. They were expected to work out a yearly budget, including their clothing, recreation, books, and expenses except food and shelter. The parents spent many hours assisting them with their budgets.
>
> In another family the two children, 10 and 12 years old, received allowances of one dollar a week. The allowance was paid to them every Saturday morning and the procedure was usually the same. They collected their allowances and rode their bicycles to town in time to be waiting when the variety stores opened. A half-hour later their money was gone. Sometimes they brought home a small toy or gadget, and sometimes they spent their money for things that were gone even before they returned home. The rest of the week, if they saw something they wanted or needed, they "begged mother" for it and—except for the rare occasions when she argued with them—she either bought it for them or gave them the money for it. This mother once said, "We have closets full of junk the children have bought. I have sometimes wanted to give some of it away when the Christmas toy drives have come along, but the children won't let me. They seldom use any of it, but after all it does belong to them; they bought it."

These cases represent two extremes. It is doubtful whether young children should be expected to take as much responsibility as the children in the first case cited. Many adults shrink from struggling with a budget, and it would be unusual children who would enjoy coping with the problem as part of their regular responsibility. Moreover, to have to be so much involved with money management so early might easily cause a distorted view of the importance of money and material things. In the second case, the logical outcome of the policy would be that the children would become irresponsible people in more than money management. Patterns of selfishness and impulsive behavior were being encouraged. Many such incidents could be cited to show how early experiences affect children's sense of responsibility and also help to form the code of ethics that will dominate their dealings with other people.

> A young man who was engaged to be married, with the wedding date set for December, was saving $25 each week in a special fund to pay for the honeymoon. In November he was invited to go on a hunting trip with some friends, and on impulse he spent most of the honeymoon fund for a new deer rifle and an expensive hunting jacket. He felt that his fiancée was unreasonable to be upset over his action, even though it did mean that their long-standing plans for a wedding trip would have to be changed. Her criticism of his action seemed to him unfair, for his pattern had always been to indulge his immediate wants, if possible, regardless of plans for the future and without thought for the effect his actions might have on another person.

Many kinds of experiences can help children learn to be responsible and dependable, if their parents are alert to the importance of these traits and *if the parents are themselves dependable*. Parents handicap their children's development if they make promises and then change their minds without an urgent and unavoidable reason, or if they are capricious instead of consistently reliable in their dealings with their children. Parents can help children to learn by their example and by teaching that it is important to keep promises and to finish tasks undertaken rather than quitting if the going gets rough or boring. A man who had achieved success and fame said, "When I was a little boy I used to help my grandfather in his shoe-repair shop, and he often said to me, 'John, you are a *dependable* boy!' I grew up thinking that it was very important and necessary to be dependable—and I still think so."

## CONSIDERATION FOR OTHERS

The happiest married couples are those who can see situations from another person's viewpoint and are not self-centered in relationships with others. The habit of consideration for others usually was developed in these people long before they married. It begins in the early experiences of children whose parents help them define accurately the limits of personal rights in relation to the rights of other people.

Very young children can understand that sometimes it is necessary to play quietly because their father or mother is tired and needs to rest. They can realize that they should not run and play across the line in the neighbor's yard because they might crush flowers the neighbor has worked hard to raise. Children do not need to be too suppressed or too much inhibited in order to learn to be considerate. They can see that consideration works two ways in their family, *if it does*. Just as they try to let someone else sleep, or not to interrupt when parents are talking, so parents are careful to respect the rights of their children, and do not interrupt them. Parents also respect property of their children; they would not lend or give away their things without consulting them. They show respect; they would not laugh at serious comments or embarrass the children in front of other people. If parents do not treat children with respect and consideration, they cannot expect to succeed in teaching children to show respect and consideration for themselves and for others.

Always in child rearing there must be a balanced share of example and teaching; neither one alone will suffice. Parents may need to point out to a child, "Billy, I would not act to you as you are acting now, and you are not to act that way to me. We owe each other respect." Parents who have been firm but reasonable about such matters are not as likely to be complaining when their children reach adolescence, "They are rude and disrespectful and *talk back* to me."

Many mothers, in their desire to be good mothers, regularly tolerate inconsiderate behavior on the part of their growing children. They are not doing the children a kindness to allow them to develop selfish, demanding attitudes toward life, for such attitudes will make trouble for them in their contacts with other people. Children will be far happier if they learn to think of the wishes and feelings of others.

## SEX ATTITUDES OF CHILDREN

A part of rearing children that involves uncertainty for many parents is what policy to follow with regard to their children's developing sexual nature. How can they help them grow up with wholesome attitudes about sex and a healthy understanding of the place of sex in life? As long ago as 1907 Sigmund Freud wrote, "From the very beginning, everything sexual should be treated like everything else that is worth knowing about." Most educated parents today recognize the truth of that view, but they may still find it difficult to respond appropriately to questions about sex or to situations that may arise in the development of their children as sexual human beings. Problems for most parents arise from certain specific sources:

**Sex is an emotional subject.** First, the subject of sex is an emotionally weighted subject for adults. It is not as easy to talk about with children as the blue sky or the high mountains. Personal experiences of the parents, their urges and impulses, are factors. Moreover, in our culture, despite what may appear to be great freedom to discuss sex and liberal attitudes toward sexual behavior, the subject of sex is loaded with taboos, exaggerations, restrictions, fears, and folklore. It is not easy for average parents to overcome personal and cultural handicaps and respond adequately to questions or behavior of children in the area of sex.

**Parents lack information.** The second basis for the problem is that most parents simply do not have enough accurate information about sex to be able to answer with confidence many of the questions young children ask. Confronted with their own inexact knowledge, they become confused or embarrassed. Many people grow up thinking they know the facts of life and then are shaken, if not overwhelmed, when the questions of their children make them realize that they do not have the words or the specific knowledge to give answers that will stand up under the impact of the children's later knowledge and experience.

**Social patterns have an influence.** A third aspect of the problem arises because parents who may have prepared themselves to answer their children's questions truthfully are likely to realize by the time the children are three or four that *the facts of life are not all sex facts.* The facts of reproduction, which can be discussed on an intellectual level, are one thing. The emotional aspects of sexual drives and functioning are on a different level. The mechanics of reproductive functioning are not half so significant for their children's development as the social values involved and the cultural patterns with which they must live, sexual nature and all. The task of giving sex facts and at the same time preparing their children to live in a complicated and not always consistent social world is a major challenge.

David Mace has speculated that it is possible that the incest taboo, which is a product of human culture and not found in animals, may underlie some of the resistance and inner conflict many parents have in relation to communicating with their children about the emotional aspects of sex. He suggests that if this is true, perhaps parents cannot be expected to help their children in this area and that this part of sex education is rather the responsibility of other institutions in our society.[3] Our society does not accept that responsibility, however, except insofar as it exacts penalties for nonconformity to social norms. Parents are still faced with the necessity of giving their children an adequate measure of guidance in this, as in other phases of socialization.

## PARENTAL POLICY TOWARD QUESTIONS

Many parents are surprised at the very early age at which children may ask questions about sex. By the time children are two or three years old —or as soon as they can talk—they are asking questions about everything, the questions becoming more involved as they grow older. "How do birds fly?" "Why can't I fly?" "How do fathers and mothers make babies?" "What makes apples red?" "How was I born?" "What makes thunder?" "If I swallow this seed will a baby grow in me?"

Young children are curious about every unexplained thing in their world. Sex has no more emotional connotations for them than has any of the other interesting things in the world; they can be objective about sex, more than most parents can be. His parents may feel convinced that Johnny is a budding genius because of some of his questions, but be confused or shocked when he asks others—those about sex—at so young an age.

How parents react to their children's first questions affects the direction their children take in their attitudes about sex. When parents are evasive, the children sense that this is a loaded subject, a subject in some way different from all others. If parents try to get by with a tale about a stork, or about the doctor's bringing babies, or about babies' being sent down from heaven, a step is taken toward losing the children's confidence. Children will, sooner or later, find out that the parents have told them a false story in answer to a serious question.

There is no better way than to answer children's questions about sex as accurately as possible *when the questions are asked,* even if children

---

[3] D. R. Mace, "Some Reflections on the American Family," *Marriage and Family Living* 24:2 (May 1962), 109–12.

start asking as soon as they can talk. To think that the responsibility for giving sex facts can be met in one big facts-of-life session when the children are "old enough to understand" is a delusion. Young children are able to understand, at least in a measure, the answers to whatever questions they are capable of asking about sex.

The realistic viewpoint is to recognize that the alternatives are not whether children should or should not know about sex. The only choice that parents have is between letting their children get garbled information from random outside sources or giving accurate sex information at home, thus providing a more healthy emotional development.

## ANSWERING SPECIFIC QUESTIONS

The most common first question asked by preschool children has to do with the origin of babies. "Where did I come from?" Or "Where did you get me?" When children first ask this question, a satisfactory answer is simply that the baby grew in the mother's body. There is nothing shocking to the child about the answer. He or she may not be much impressed, and the next question may be on some subject far removed, such as why the sky is blue, or why water is wet. He or she may come back three weeks later and again ask where babies come from.

When children first start asking questions, biologically complete answers are not needed, any more than a complete explanation is needed of the functioning of the internal combustion engine the first time the child asks what makes the car go. Some children ask more specific questions that call for more detailed answers. "How does the baby get out?" Children may be told that there is a special place in the mother where the baby grows until it is ready to come out into the world through the passageway that is provided for it. This explanation or a similar one will satisfy many young children. But some will ask more, especially as they get a little older. Whenever they ask specific questions that show they are ready for specific information, children should be given more complete answers and the correct terms should be used for various parts of the reproductive system.

The most emotionally loaded question for parents to answer seems to be about what part the father plays in getting a baby started. Questions about the father's part in reproduction usually come at later ages than the other questions. Table 26-1 summarizes the reports of 581 mothers on the specific questions their children asked and the ages at which different kinds of questions were asked. When children ask about the father's part in conception, the question should be answered accurately, if the parent can do so. The children may be reminded that mothers and fathers are different physically and that the father is constructed with a special organ (the penis) with which to unite his cells with the mother's to start the new baby. This is not hard for children to understand and it will not shock them if the facts are given in a straightforward manner at the time when the question is asked. Average children will already have observed that their father is made differently from their mother and will not be surprised to learn of this reason for the difference.

When children learn this fact later, as preadolescents, and apply it to their parents, sometimes it is shocking to them. It would be better had they known it and accepted it earlier. Asking the questions at an early age is evidence that the children were ready for the answers.

Some parents feel hesitant, even alarmed, at the idea of an eight- or nine-year-old daughter's knowing exactly how babies are conceived. The fear is likely to be: What if she experiments with other children now, or in two or three years when such experimentation could mean trouble? But children do wonder how conception comes about, and the mother whose children ask her the question can only appreciate her children's confidence and go ahead to do her best to give an honest explanation. (We say the mother, here, because she is the parent more often at hand to be asked.) Children who are aware enough to ask the questions and to discuss the answers with their parents will certainly get enough understanding as they grow up to accept what it means to bring a baby

TABLE 26-1

The specific types of questions asked by children about sex and reproduction, as reported by 581 mothers *

| Questions asked | Age of child | Percentage of children who asked | Percentage question was of total asked |
|---|---|---|---|
| Origin and growth | 2–5 | 43 | 20 |
|   Where did I come from? | | | |
|   Where did my brother (sister) come from? | | | |
|   Where did you get me? | | | |
|   Where do babies grow? | | | |
| Body structure and function | 2–5 | 25 | 32 |
|   Why is brother (sister) different from me? | | | |
|   What is that? (referring to genitalia) | | | |
|   What are those? (referring to breasts) | | | |
|   Why do boys and girls look different? | | | |
| Birth of babies | 6–9 | 25 | 25 |
|   How do babies get out? | | | |
|   How are they born? | | | |
|   How do they know when to come out? | | | |
|   Are babies born through the navel? | | | |
| Fertilization and mating | 6–13 | 5 | 22 |
|   How do babies get in? | | | |
|   How does the egg get fertilized? | | | |
|   Where does the sperm come from? | | | |
|   How are babies made? | | | |
|   How is the seed planted? | | | |
|   Do you have to be married to have a baby? | | | |

* Landis, study of 581 couples in 1967. See note 2, p. 5.

into the world and take care of it, to give it a home and the loving care that make life comfortable and happy. In terms of their own family life, children will interpret what is said, and there is little reason to worry about experimentation being dangerous. Without doubt, many young children do experiment, whether or not parents have given accurate answers to their questions. There is no evidence that such experimentation does any serious harm, unless trauma results from the way the situation is handled when the play activities are discovered.

**Vocabulary to use.** One reason for much parental difficulty in keeping lines of communication about sex matters open as children approach adolescence is that the parents do not know what language they should use in discussing sex with their children. They may have used a baby language for bodily functions and parts of the body. Children have been taught to say "hand," "foot," "eyes," "ears," and "stomach," but they have not been given the right names for sex organs or for processes of bodily elimination. In fact, many parents themselves do not use accurate language; all they know is the street language or words they learned as children. Since they would feel uncomfortable using this language with their children, this actually becomes an area in which parents and children cannot converse without great awkwardness. They do not have the vocabulary. If terms such as bowel movement, urinate, penis, and vulva are used appropriately from the beginning, children will accept the terms just as readily as they accept feet, hands, stomach, arms, and legs, and the family will have a language that is understood by all and available when needed.

## KINDS OF INFORMATION PARENTS GIVE

In our study of 3000 students in 11 colleges in 1952 and again in the study of 3189 students in 18 colleges in 1967, the students were asked the source of most of their sex information, and also what specific information their parents had given them. By far the most common source of sex information for boys was other children. For girls, mothers ranked with other children as a source of *most* information. Table 26-2 shows the types of sex information the students in both studies said their parents had given. During this 15-year period some changes in sex attitudes and behavior have occurred, but parents of college students have not changed much in their giving of sex information to their children.

Interesting differences are observable in the types of information parents gave to boys and girls. For example, parents were more likely to tell girls about the difficulty of controlling sexual emotions than to tell boys, and were less likely to give boys information on each subject. One reason for this might be that it is usually the mother who answers questions, and girls are with their mothers more and generally communicate with their mothers on many more subjects than do boys. There may

TABLE 26-2

Specific sex and reproduction information given by parents, as reported by 3189 students from 18 colleges in 1967 and 3000 students from 11 colleges in 1952.

| | Men | | Women | |
| | (N–1056) | (N–1005) | (N–1944) | (N–2185) |
| Information given | 1952 | 1967 | 1952 | 1967 |
| --- | --- | --- | --- | --- |
| Where babies come from | 57.0% | 53.0% | 74.0% | 66.0% |
| Menstruation | 25.0 | 21.0 | 90.0 | 89.0 |
| Venereal disease | 30.0 | 25.0 | 33.0 | 19.0 |
| Difficulty of controlling sexual emotions | 21.0 | 31.0 | 38.0 | 40.0 |
| Coitus (sexual intercourse) | 26.0 | 26.0 | 37.0 | 27.0 |
| Masturbation | 22.0 | 15.0 | 17.0 | 9.0 |
| Sex perversions | 14.0 | 13.0 | 19.0 | 13.0 |
| Pleasure of sexual relations | 13.0 | 14.0 | 23.0 | 19.0 |
| Nocturnal emissions | 22.0 | 17.0 | 15.0 | 10.0 |
| Contraceptives | 13.0 | 15.0 | 21.0 | 12.0 |
| Orgasm | 10.0 | 15.0 | 10.0 | 9.0 |

also be differences between sex curiosity in young boys and in young girls. Boys tend to ask different kinds of questions if they ask, and they are less likely to ask questions at all. This difference has been observed with children and young people of all ages.

An analysis was made of the questions asked by groups of adolescent boys and girls who participated in family life education conferences in which groups of parents also participated.[4] The conclusion after the conferences was that the boys typically felt at first that they "know all about sex," but when given a chance to get correct information without losing face they expressed eagerness to learn and a sense of relief. Parents and sons were generally aware that embarrassment made communication about sex far more difficult for them than parents and daughters found it to be. The adolescent boys' questions showed most concern about their own normality as males and about masturbation and homosexuality. The girls were better informed and had had better communication with parents, especially their mothers. Their questions showed most concern about their understanding of boys: "What do boys think about . . ." "Why do boys . . ." and so on. The report on the conference commented that, while boys are struggling to understand themselves, girls are taking the facts of life for granted and are already involved with trying to understand and relate to boys.

It is clear that, with both boys and girls, the majority of parents do not go beyond the most elementary facts, if they discuss sex at all. They ignore the point of their greatest worry, which is that the young people will not be able to control their sexual emotions during the dating years and as a result may complicate their lives. Granting that parents must

[4] Deryck Calderwood, "Differences in the Sex Questions of Adolescent Boys and Girls," *Marriage and Family Living* 25:4 (November 1963), 492–95.

cope with their own inhibitions, it is still possible for some parents to communicate to their children an appreciation of the sexual drive as a valuable, constructive force that enhances relationships and which needs to be understood in its relevance to all other facets of personality and experience. Many parents who worry about their children's ability to cope with the strong sexual urges that become new to them during adolescence offer only negative warnings and ignore the positive aspects of sexuality in life.

### Facing the subject of sexual deviation

Another subject that few of the parents of the university students in our research had ever discussed with their children is sexual deviation. It is understandable that many parents would avoid the subject, hoping that their children need never know anything about it. But that is not a realistic point of view. A study among 1800 university students revealed that, as children or in their teens, one-third of both men and women had had one or more encounters with sexual deviation.[5] The most common encounters for girls were with exhibitionists or older persons who made improper sexual advances; for boys the most common had been encounters with homosexuals.

Most parents know that such things happen; they would like to make sure that their children are prepared to avoid or resist undesirable experiences, but they do not want to cause children to be fearful and distrusting in their attitudes toward others, nor to be overimpressed with the threatening aspects of sexual behavior in the world. The goal of parents must be first to try to help their children develop normal and healthy attitudes concerning sex; that will constitute an important form of protection. But even as children must know that there are dishonest or unkind people in the world and that part of growing up is learning to cope with whatever kinds of people one encounters, so they ought to know that there are people with unhealthy and warped attitudes about sex, and they should know how to cope with such people if they should encounter them. Frightening or "scare" talk can contribute as much or more to unwholesome attitudes in children as might an encounter with some types of deviates. In fact, the evidence seems to show that much of the trauma following experiences some children may have with the more common types of deviates is caused by the way the matter was handled after it happened. The shock and horror of parents and adults may be more frightening to children in many cases than the experience itself.[6]

[5] Judson T. Landis, "The Non-delinquent Child and the Sexual Deviate," *Research Studies of the State College of Washington, Proceedings of the Pacific Sociological Society* 23:2 (June 1955), 92–101; also, Landis, "Experiences of 500 Children with Adult Sexual Deviation," *The Psychiatric Quarterly Supplement* Part 1 (1956).
[6] Ibid.

One of the best protections children can have is lines of communication that are kept open all along the way. Children who will not hesitate to say to the parent, "Say, I heard a queer thing today, some of the kids were saying . . ." and then go on to tell what it was they had heard and let the parent comment, are not in much danger of having their ideas about sex too distorted by the mistaken ideas or the warped attitudes of others. Similarly, children who have discussed most subjects freely with their parents will not only be more alert to avoid undesirable sexual experiences but can also allow the parents to help protect them from such experiences. A ten-year-old girl went home from school and reported, "On the way home today there was a man sitting in a car when I passed. He opened the door and asked me very politely to come over there because he wanted to ask me a question. He smiled like he was trying to be *so nice*, but the way he looked at me kind of scared me. I wasn't polite. Was it all right just to not answer him and to walk on home as fast as I could?" Even if this man might have been harmless, the mother had an excellent opportunity to discuss the subject of deviation and to help her child think about ways to avoid such people without having to be rude or mistrustful toward strangers.

### Recognizing the social aspects of sex

Always a complicating factor in parental policy in sex education of children is the matter of social values and cultural patterns. When parents talk about sex with their children, the parents are usually aware that, as the children grow up, if they are relatively uninhibited and "natural" in their sexual attitudes, they may get social disapproval that may inhibit them, may go through emotional experiences that handicap them. That is why social norms and the contradictions in social attitudes about sex should be faced as openly within the family as are the social aspects of other areas of living. Parents teach values relative to other phases of life almost from the beginning of their children's lives. They use a variety of situations and incidents in daily living to emphasize with children that people have certain obligations, and that the world expects certain kinds of behavior. But sex attitudes and values tend to be communicated negatively or by default, the result being that children formulate their ideas on the basis of vague implications of taboos and restrictions, rather than receiving any positive interpretations of social values, patterns, and attitudes.

In the average family, some problems arise because sexual activities and attitudes are subject to many outside influences. It may be hard for parents to maintain their objectivity and to handle a situation in such a way that they do good rather than harm when their children become involved with other children in activities that may shock other parents

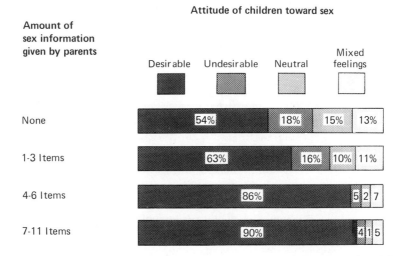

FIG. 26–2 Relationship between children's attitudes toward sex and the amount of sex information given by parents. Attitudes were rated according to responses of 3000 students to a check list of items, such as "Sex is dirty and vulgar." "Sex is for mutual husband and wife enjoyment." (See Table 26–1 for a summary of what sex information was given by parents.)

or observers. If children are discovered undressing at play, eliminating in public, masturbating publicly, or attempting sexual experimentation with other children, parents need to know *why* they feel concern about the actions—that certain things should not be done because of social unacceptability rather than because the acts are bad, unnatural, or shocking in themselves. Parents who have this distinction clear in their own minds can deal with children's acts more appropriately than they can if they just react with emotional shock and feel disgraced by the children's acts. They can help the children begin to distinguish actions that may be thought to be morally wrong from those that are to be avoided because of social unacceptability.

Sometimes children who have been freely told the facts about sex and reproduction create neighborhood friction by telling the neighbors' children things their parents consider them too young to know. Actually, the talking about sex that children do, whether or not their parents approve, is harmless, especially if the children have been given accurate information. In general, parents must have the courage to do what seems best in their children's sex education, as in other matters of child rearing, and not worry too much about "what people think."

For some parents, it may take special courage to deal wisely with masturbation in very young children. Almost all children masturbate at some time, and the practice may begin much earlier than the parents had expected that it might. It may begin when children are as young as six months, at six years of age, or not until later. At one time, almost all parents punished their children for masturbating, believing the folklore that the habit would cause insanity, stunted growth, and other horrible effects.

Even today some people hold such opinions. But students of human development recognize that there are no harmful physical or mental effects of masturbation per se; rather, bodily exploration and manipulation are a normal part of infancy and childhood. Censuring children and making them feel guilty and fearful about masturbation can do emotional damage.

Although masturbation, occurring as an accompaniment of certain phases of development, is not harmful, it is true that it can create problems for children in their social world. Parents are conscious of how others who deal with their children may react when they observe such activity. The children may be censured or ostracized by others, with resulting emotional damage. It is best to take a constructive approach. Parents need to make sure that children are provided with interests and activities that fill their time adequately. They must see that children have the security that comes with knowing that they are appreciated and loved. As children approach and enter adolescence they become secretive about masturbating, just as they try to protect their privacy in other ways. Parents usually cannot discuss concerns about their children's masturbating, nor can the children discuss their concerns about it with the parents. All need to make the effort to relax and to recognize that it may be a part of normal sexual behavior in children and adolescents, and at times, adults.

## Sex attitudes and the whole personality

It is important that children grow up with an appreciation of the fact that healthy sexual development is social and emotional as well as physical and that sex with all its implications is one of the positive forces in personality. Successful parents approach this phase of bringing up their children with the same common sense and affection that is evident in all their other dealings with their children. Clearly, many variables other than how information has been given or who gives the information affect the development of sexual attitudes and behavior.

Sexual delinquency in teenagers is likely to be an indication of other serious problems in their lives and may be an attempt to find a solution to other conflicts. Many delinquent young girls especially feel rejected by their parents, unloved and unwanted; their behavior shows they are striving for a satisfaction of personality needs which have not been met in their relationships at home.

In our culture death has been as taboo a subject as sex. A survey concerning attitudes and experiences relating to death was conducted by a national magazine in 1971. The editors reported that the single biggest surprise in the results was the sheer volume of response. More than 30,000 readers returned the questionnaire, and more than 2000 sent substantial letters with their replies.

The editors commented, "It was almost as though thousands of persons had been waiting for a legitimate occasion to unburden themselves about death . . . for many, the major result of the death questionnaire was that the respondent could remove death from his list of taboo topics. To mention death usually results in embarrassment, evasion or pretense." [7]

One young man wrote, "When I was twelve, my mother died. She was there when I went to bed, and gone when I woke in the morning. My father took my brother and me on his knee and burst into sobs and said, 'Jesus took your mother,' then we never talked about it again. It was too painful." Any answer which suggests to children that Jesus took away the loved one is very hard for them to understand, and such an answer should never be given. In this instance the 12-year-old boy could never comprehend the father's answer and has never forgiven a Jesus that would take away his mother. He has rejected formal religion as an adult.

Many children become aware of death fairly early, and they have fears about their own death or the deaths of their parents. The general philosophy that should be imparted to children when they ask if they will die or if their parents will die is that everyone will die eventually but that they and their parents probably will live a long time, and that when they gradually get old and weak they will not want to continue to live. When pets die, children can see this process, and the death can be explained in the same way. Explanations associated with death that implicate God, or imply that the person has gone on a long trip, or is ill, or is going to the hospital, or has gone to sleep, should be *avoided*. The young child may have unfounded and unnecessary fears about going to sleep, sickness, and hospitals if these are overemphasized. The prayer sometimes used with children, "If I should die before I wake . . .," might be questioned as something which could arouse fears in children. Sometimes the children's first experience with death comes when a loved grandparent dies. In such a case a parent may try to hide his or her own grief from the children, explaining only that Grandma has "gone away" or that Grandpa "went to sleep and is in Heaven." It is always

[7] Edward S. Shneidman, "You and Death," *Psychology Today* 5:1 (June 1971), 43.

damaging to answer children's questions with a lie, or with an explanation that the parents do not honestly believe to be true, whether the questions are about sex, death, or any other serious subject. Children sense hypocrisy and it is upsetting to them. To say one who has died is asleep or gone away can make children fearful about going to sleep, or may cause them to wonder if it was something they did that caused Grandma to go away and leave them. Many children suffer from feelings of personal guilt when a family member dies.

Grieving parents who try to cover their feelings and express no sorrow before the children may increase emotional problems for the children. The children, perceptive of their parents' suffering, become even more frightened and insecure. Psychiatrists have written about "grief work," the painful process a bereaved person must go through as he or she gradually accepts the fact of death and the loss of a loved one. Dr. Stanley Sturges of Menninger Memorial Hospital says, "It is important that grief be allowed to come out. Unless it is expressed, distortion occurs." [8]

Parents who understand children's feelings will try to be honest about their own grief in order to help their children recognize and express their grief, and thus try to reassure the children. Questions should be answered as well as possible. Sometimes it is necessary to say "I don't know," for whatever one's religious belief or philosophy of life, there are still many things about death that are beyond understanding or explaining. Some things we do know. We know that to be born and to die are both part of every life. People live their lives and the time comes to die, just as it does with every living thing in nature. The old must die in order to make room for the new and young, with people just as with plants and animals. Children can accept that this is the way things are. It is like many other facts and concepts they are learning and accepting.

It is better to be open about the fact of death, without overdoing it, all the way along, before children actually have to encounter the death of someone personally. Then when the death of a loved one does occur, the truth can be faced. Grief can be shared and love freely given to the living. Mentally healthy attitudes about death on the part of other family members are important. A seven-year-old in such a family said to the grandmother, "Grandma, I hope you live a *long time* yet. I hope you live for years and years, and when you get through with your life, I hope you have a *happy ending!*"

[8] Stanley G. Sturges, "Understanding Grief," *Menninger Perspective* 1:1 (April–May 1970).

Many of the goals parents hope to achieve with their children will be easier to attain if the family associates together as people who like each other and enjoy one another's companionship. This requires a specific effort in today's world. There is pressure on all members of the family to participate in activities that are specialized for age and sex. Consequently, members of the family do not participate in many of the same groups outside the home. Although many of the organized activities for children and adults are excellent in purpose, they leave little time for family life unless people are intelligent in determining where to draw the line in their participation.

There is no substitute equal to family companionship as a source of happiness and security for the child. To young children it is not important what the activity is, or how much time is occupied with it, as long as all participate and it can be depended upon to have its regular place in the daily or weekly routine. Children gain great pleasure from looking forward to pleasant family activities that they know will take place without fail. The knowledge that the parents will not let them down by allowing unimportant outside interests to displace the family activities is important to children's sense of security.

Some parents who establish the precedent of spending Sunday evenings together when the children are young find to their surprise that even when their children are adolescent and have many outside interests they prefer to save Sunday evenings to spend with the family. Often the children bring their friends, enlarging the circle; such an arrangement adds to the pleasure of family activities as the children grow older. Invariably, children from families who have little or no family life are eager to be welcomed into such activities of other families. It is not always easy or convenient for parents to be consistent about spending time with their children, but parents who make it a practice find that it pays in building good relationships and in keeping open lines of communication. Perhaps the point here is that parents who attach as much importance to their "social obligations" to their children as they do to their social obligations among friends and associates are also the parents who manage to meet their other responsibilities in child rearing.

The findings of a study by Arnold Rose among college students indicate that families maintaining close ties with each other, even into and beyond the children's adolescence, are ones in which the children can accept adult responsibility more adequately and in which the children are sooner "emancipated" from the family circle. In discussing his findings, Rose hypothesized that: (1) family closeness provides the emotional support conducive to "normal" development; (2) parents and older siblings provide good role models for adult responsibility, so that family closeness helps adolescents learn adult roles; and (3) parents who are close to their adolescent children are deliberately and successfully teaching them adult roles.[9]

Family closeness is not suddenly achieved at some point in the children's development when the need for it or the lack of it becomes apparent. Family closeness is developed over the years through consistent habits in family living.

## A SENSE OF HUMOR

No discussion of child rearing would be complete without some attention to the importance of a sense of humor for both parents and children. The best possible tension reliever is laughter. The ability to see the humor inevitably present even in one's own difficulties helps one to face problems and be more effective in discovering solutions. Parents are giving their children an advantage in life if they themselves can keep in mind that some things are better laughed about than wept over or shouted about. They can help their children see the humor in many tension-producing situations in daily life.

Like the habit of happiness, a sense of humor is a learned characteristic, not inherited or presented as a ready-made gift. Even people who are naturally serious-minded and humorless can overcome their handicap if they recognize the value of shared laughter in family life. What laughter can mean in a child's life was expressed by a little boy whose parents had been undergoing a period of unusual strain. He said unexpectedly at dinner one day, "What's the matter with us all? Are we sick? We haven't had a good laugh for a week!"

## THE WORKING MOTHER AND CHILDREN'S DEVELOPMENT

At times throughout this book, references have been made to the fact that in the United States a considerable percentage of married women, including mothers, hold jobs other than as housewives and mothers. Of the college girls reading this book, at least a third will have outside jobs or careers for most of their future years. Does that mean that this large group of educated mothers will not be able to contribute to their children's development in all the ways so far discussed in this chapter? Will the mothers' work outside the home deprive their children of the enriched childhood that a "good" mother hopes to make possible for her children?

Axelson's study of attitudes of husbands toward working wives showed that the husbands of nonworking wives tended to believe that

[9] Arnold M. Rose, "Acceptance of Adult Roles and Separation From Family," *Marriage and Family Living* 21 (May 1959), 120–27.

a mother should not work at an outside job as long as school-age children were at home.[10] Husbands of working wives tended to disagree with that view, although a minority of the husbands of working wives agreed. These responses are fairly representative of general public opinion on the subject of working mothers. Partly because of the force of public opinion, working mothers themselves often have emotional conflict over whether they should be working while children are young. Even if all seems to be going well, even if the children seem to be developing entirely satisfactorily emotionally and physically, the mother who says frankly and with conviction, "I think it's a good thing for our family that I work. The children are doing better than I could hope they would do if I didn't work," has to be strongly independent. The question is always good for debate, and probably will continue to be for some time in the future, because individual cases can easily be found to prove every possible viewpoint about the evils or the advantages to children of mothers' working and leaving their children in child-care centers or with sitters. To find some reliable truth in the welter of views and information, some authorities have reviewed and synthesized available research on the subject. From these careful analyses, one can reach some conclusions about the significance of mothers' working as a factor in the healthy emotional growth of children.

In general, a lot of what "everyone knows" about working mothers and their children is not necessarily true. For example, many working mothers actually spend more time in meaningful activities with their children than do nonworking mothers. The working mothers may make a greater specific effort to plan time for activities in which the children are interested or which enrich the children's lives. The full-time mother may leave the children to play alone outdoors or at a neighbor's for long periods of time, or she may take them along with her when she goes on household errands and on activities that interest her but that are tiring or at best may be boring and unproductive for the child.

Much of the evidence seems to imply that it is better for babies to be with their mothers or in their mothers' care most of the time. But for preschool children, the more important point is how life is organized for the children and what arrangements are made for the hours in their day.[11] Is it better for a three-year-old to be following his or her mother around in a crowded department store while she looks at furniture and talks to salespeople, to be sitting on the floor beside her while she studies patterns in the yard-goods department, or to be in a nursery school with

[10] Leland J. Axelson, "The Marital Adjustment and Marital Role Definitions of Husbands of Working and Non-working Wives," *Journal of Marriage and the Family* 25:2 (May 1963), 189.

[11] Eleanor M. Maccoby, "Children and Working Mothers," *Children* 5 (1958), 83–89.

other children the same age, participating in interesting and challenging activities?

Even when the mother keeps her child at home with her most of the time, life may be difficult for the active preschool child whose days are spent in a small house or apartment with a mother who sees the day's work as getting the cleaning done, finishing a sewing task, laundering, or cooking. Under such circumstances, mothers as well as children become frustrated and discontented. One mother said, "Cooped up all day with my three-year-old son while I'm trying to get my work done drives me wild. Sometimes I realize when night comes that practically all I've said to him all day long is 'No' or 'Stop that' or 'Be quiet.' "

The point to be made here is that the question of the healthy emotional growth of young children is not so simple as whether the mother works or does not work. In research in which the one factor of the mother's working or not working is held constant, no significant differences of healthy emotional growth are found in the children. But analysis shows that differences do appear when children are grouped in another way. When the children are grouped according to how their mothers, whether jobholders or housewives, *feel* about their work, more well-adjusted, happy children are found among the group whose mothers *like what they are doing*, whether it is being a housewife or holding an outside job. More problems are found among the children of mothers who feel discontented with what they are doing, whether at home or at work.[12]

Skard concluded, after studying a wide variety of findings about children and mothers, that "The provisional conclusion from these investigations is that for some women the best thing is to go out to work, for others it is best to stay in the home. But it seems important that the mother have a permanent arrangement. Children develop best and most harmoniously when the mother herself is happy and gay. Whether she has work outside the home or not seems rather unimportant from the child's viewpoint." [13]

## WHAT IS SUCCESSFUL PARENTHOOD?

People who would evaluate their effectiveness as parents must look objectively at their children, not just at their faults or virtues. Are the children generally happy? Are they developing resources within themselves so that they are not too dependent on outside circumstances for contentment? Do they believe that others like and value them? Are they

[12] Marian Rodke Yarrow, "Maternal Employment and Child Rearing," *Children* 8 (November–December 1961), 223–28.

[13] Aase Gruda Skard, "Maternal Deprivation, the Research and Its Implications," *Journal of Marriage and the Family* 27:3 (August 1965), 342–43.

dependable? Are they self-reliant, with self-confidence and ability to cope with life as it comes? A part of their self-confidence is recognition of personal responsibility for their own acts. Can they accept the consequences of their own acts without offering alibis, or blaming other people or circumstances? If the parents are people who do their best but are not afraid to say "I was wrong," children will appreciate the fact that although their parents are not infallible they are able to work things out in spite of mistakes. This realization will help them to have the same attitude toward themselves.

In order to help children develop desirable traits, parents need to be sure of their own attitudes toward their children. They must love them for the individuals they are, and not as a reflection of the parents' own personalities. Objectivity does not come naturally to parents. It must be cultivated. When it is achieved, one's role as a parent is more easily understood. There must be warmth of love, so that from infancy children have the security that comes with a consciousness that they are loved and valued. But this parental love must not be so overwhelming and smothering that it stands as a wall between children and the realities of the world about them.

The ultimate responsibility of all parents is to contribute to their children's physical, mental, and emotional growth, so that in due time they become autonomous individuals able to create and maintain satisfactory relationships with others.

## REVIEW QUESTIONS

1 Explain what is meant by the "socialization" of the child.

2 Define the twofold task of parents in terms of the broad basic purposes to be achieved.

3 List some personality characteristics that parents might keep in mind in training their children which would make the children more marriageable.

4 What home circumstances contribute to the future marriageability of children?

5 Why is it hard for parents to see the behavior of their children in its proper perspective?

6 How can parents help their children develop initiative and self-reliance? Illustrate.

7 Criticize the allowance systems used by the two families described in the text. Did either of these approach the allowance system you had in your family?

8 Why is it difficult for parents to give their children accurate sex information?

9 When are children old enough to receive their first sex information?

10 What are the most common first questions asked by children about sex?

11 Why do many parents fail to use an accurate vocabulary when talking to their children about sex, reproduction, and bodily elimination?

12 How do parents establish rapport with their children in discussing sex and reproduction?

13 How often do children encounter adult sexual deviation? Why is it difficult to prepare the child for such experiences?

14 Will knowledge about sex lead to harmful sex experimentation?

15 Why is it so difficult for parents to have the proper perspective on common sex activities of normal children?

16 Compare the way the facts about sex and about death tend to be handled in our culture.

17 Is it possible for parents to deal with the fact of death in ways that will contribute to the healthy emotional development of their children?

18 Under what conditions or circumstances may a working mother do a better job of child rearing than a nonworking mother?

19 What are some of the considerations that determine positive or negative effects of a mother's having an outside job? Which of these considerations are of equal force in the case of a mother who is a full-time homemaker?

20 How can development of a sense of humor be encouraged?

21 Why is doing things together as a family important to the development of children?

22 What questions might parents ask themselves in deciding whether they are pursuing the right course in training their children?

## PROJECTS AND ACTIVITIES

1 Give a case from your acquaintance in which the parents were careful to discipline their children on unimportant behavior but permitted the children to engage in other reprehensible or significant misbehavior without noticing it.

2 Either from your own family or from a family you know cite how doing things together as a family contributed to the security and happiness of the children.

3 Write your own case history of learning about sex: how it was handled in the home, what you learned from playmates or reading, and your reaction to what you learned.

4 *Role playing.* Steven and Lucy have been married ten years and have four children, ages 2, 4, 6, and 8. (a) John, aged 8, has not shown good judgment in the way he spends his allowance. He received his 50-cents-a-week allowance this morning and at noon was back from town with all the money gone. His mother and father decided to make an issue of it. (b) Mary, aged 4, told Mrs. Smith to go home this morning when Mrs. Smith was talking to Mary's mother. (c) Henry, aged 6, insists on helping his father build things in the shop. The father is annoyed with Henry's taking his tools all the time, getting in the way, and delaying the work. (d) Mary, aged 4, tells the family that a neighbor's child has told her that storks bring babies. She then asks

her mother where babies come from. Other questions follow from all the children after the first one is answered.

5 Interview some mothers in the following groups: (a) full-time jobholders, (b) full-time homemakers, (c) mothers whose children attend nursery school, (d) mothers who disapprove of sending a child to nursery school.

# THE SCOPE OF
# SUCCESSFUL MARRIAGE

Where does successful marriage begin? Not with the wedding. Rather, it begins somewhere in an unending circle made of many parts: childhood experiences and feelings, parents who knew cooperation, learning experiences in youth and adulthood, and attitudes in every area of living.

A backward look at the many topics discussed in this book brings the realization that to build a successful marriage is an accomplishment unlimited in its implications. It goes far beyond the horizons of the two who marry. A good marriage becomes a force having an impact on the lives of other people encountered by either member of the pair in daily living and it reaches into the lives of future generations. It includes romance and responsibility, sacrifice, drudgery, and disappointments, as well as fundamentally rewarding fulfillments—emotional, social, sexual, psychic, and even material.

People who build successful marriages live creatively at each stage of life. During the dating years, they seek to understand themselves and others. As lovers and as newly married people, they try to learn to perceive the needs and feelings of those they love. They learn to bend and adjust in order to develop relationships that give meaning to life. When children come, they are able to grow up to the challenges and responsibilities of parenthood, and yet cherish and nurture the relationship with their mates in such a way that the experience of parenthood enriches the marriage.

Always an essential condition for successful marriage is growth in the two who marry, a continually expanding perception of the needs and feelings of others and an increasing ability and willingness to give acceptance, respect, and cooperation. Those who build successful marriages reject any conception of life or relationships as static; they perceive that people change and that the quality of a relationship is never absolutely set. They discover with the years of living that their interaction has the potential either for growth and improvement or for deterioration and destructiveness. They are aware of the choice in their own hands of determining the direction of their relationships.

People who build successful marriages comprehend that life offers a balance of compensations and disappointments. They accept in the mate weaknesses and the failure to be all that might seem totally desirable with a measure of philosophical equanimity. Each one's confidence that his or her own deficiencies will be overlooked and forgotten and love freely given to him or her anyway, arises in part from that person's willingness to accept and forget the mate's corresponding imperfections. With their acceptance of the contradictions that are inevitably a part of marriage, and their awareness of the balance of joy and pain that life offers, they find that the bonds between them become a settled, irrevocable reality.

As such couples advance in years, they continue to reach new levels of understanding of their mates and themselves. The wisdom gained through the years and the security of a firmly based affection enables them to cope with the new and potentially frustrating physical and emotional conditions in themselves and their mates that come with aging.

In sum, two people who build a successful marriage make the most of their attributes at each stage of life. They live together in such a way that the direction of their dynamic relationship is toward excellence.

# SUGGESTED READINGS

CHAPTER 1

COGSWELL, BETTY E. "Variant Family Forms and Life Styles: Rejection of the Traditional Nuclear Family." *The Family Coordinator* 24:4 (October 1975), 391–406.

CONOVER, PATRICK W. "An Analysis of Communes and Intentional Communities with Particular Attention to Sexual and Genderal Relations." *The Family Coordinator* 24:4 (October 1975), 453–64.

FELDBERG, ROSLYN, and JANET KOHEN. "Family Life in an Anti-Family Setting: A Critique of Marriage and Divorce." *The Family Coordinator* 25:2 (April 1976), 151–59.

GLENN, NORVAL D. "The Contribution of Marriage to the Psychological Well-Being of Males and Females." *Journal of Marriage and the Family* 37:3 (August 1975), 594–600.

GLICK, PAUL C. "A Demographer Looks at American Families." *Journal of Marriage and the Family* 37:1 (February 1975), 15–26.

HOGE, DEAN R. "Changes in College Students' Value Patterns in the 1950's, 1960's, and 1970's." *Sociology of Education* 49:2 (April 1976), 155–63.

KANTER, ROSABETH MOSS, DENNIS JAFFE, and D. KELLY WEISBERG. "Coupling, Parenting, and the Presence of Others: Intimate Relationships in Communal Households." *The Family Coordinator* 24:4 (October 1975), 433–52.

KNAPP, JACQUELYN J. "Some Non-Monogamous Marriage Styles and Related Attitudes and Practices of Marriage Counselors." *The Family Coordinator* 24:4 (October 1975), 505–514.

LaFOLLETTE, PATRICK. "Family Synergy, A Variant Family Organization." *The Family Coordinator* 24:4 (October 1975), 561–62.

LASLETT, BARBARA. "The Family as a Public and Private Institution: An Historical Perspective." *Journal of Marriage and the Family* 35:3 (August 1973), 480–92.

LORBER, JUDITH. "Beyond Equality of the Sexes: The Question of the Children." *The Family Coordinator* 24:4 (October 1975), 465–72.

MARCIANO, TERESA DONATI. "Variant Family Forms in a World Perspective." *The Family Coordinator* 24:4 (October 1975), 407–420.

NYE, F. IVAN. "Emerging and Declining Family Roles." *Journal of Marriage and the Family* 36:2 (May 1974), 238–45.

RAMEY, JAMES W. "Intimate Groups and Networks: Frequent Consequences of Sexually Open Marriage." *The Family Coordinator* 24:4 (October 1975), 515–30.

STRONG, BRYAN. "Toward a History of the Experiential Family: Sex and Incest in the Nineteenth-Century Family." *Journal of Marriage and the Family* 35:3 (August 1973), 457–66.

SUSSMAN, MARVIN B. "The Four F's of Variant Family Forms and Marriage Styles." *The Family Coordinator* 24:4 (October 1974), 563–76.

WEITZMAN, LENORE J. "To Love, Honor, and Obey? Traditional Legal Marriage and Alternative Family Forms." *The Family Coordinator* 24:4 (October 1975), 531–48.

## CHAPTER 2

ASHLEY-MONTAGU, M. F. *The Natural Superiority of Women.* New York: Macmillan Co., 1968.

AXELSON, LELAND J. "The Marital Adjustment and Marital Role Definitions of Husbands of Working and Non-Working Wives." *Marriage and Family Living* 25:2 (May 1963), 189–95.

———. "The Working Wife: Differences in Perception Among Negro and White Males." *Journal of Marriage and the Family* 32:3 (August 1970), 457.

BAHR, STEPHEN J., and BOYD C. ROLLINS. "Crisis and Conjugal Power." *Journal of Marriage and the Family* 33:2 (May 1971), 360.

BART, PAULINE B. "Sexism and Social Science: From the Gilded Cage to the Iron Cage, or, the Perils of Pauline." *Journal of Marriage and the Family* 33:4 (November 1971), 734.

BATTLE-SISTER, ANN. "Conjectures on the Female Culture Question." *Journal of Marriage and the Family* 33:3 (August 1971), 411.

BERNARD, JESSIE. "The Fourth Revolution." In *People as Partners,* edited by Jacqueline P. Wiseman, pp. 17–22. New York: Harper & Row, Publishers, 1971.

BROWN, DANIEL G. "Masculinity–Femininity Development in Children." *Journal of Consulting Psychology* 21:3 (1957), 197–202.

CHESLER, PHYLLIS. "Women as Psychiatric and Psychotherapeutic Patients." *Journal of Marriage and the Family* 33:4 (November 1971), 746.

DOHERTY, EDMUND G., and CATHRYN CULVER. "Sex-Role Identification, Ability, and Achievement Among High School Girls." *Sociology of Education* 49:1 (January 1976), 1–3.

EHRLICH, CAROL. "The Male Sociologist's Burden: The Place of Women in Marriage and Family Texts." *Journal of Marriage and the Family* 33:3 (August 1971), 421.

ETZKOWITZ, HENRY. "The Male Sister: Sexual Separation of Labor in Society." *Journal of Marriage and the Family* 33:3 (August 1971), 431.

FALK, LAURENCE L. "Occupational Satisfaction of Female College Graduates." *Journal of Marriage and the Family* 28:2 (May 1966), 177–85.

FLORA, CORNELIA BUTLER. "The Passive Female: Her Comparative Image by Class and Culture in Women's Magazine Fiction." *Journal of Marriage and the Family* 33:3 (August 1971), 435.

FRIEDAN, BETTY. *The Feminine Mystique.* New York: W. W. Norton & Company, Inc., 1963.

GILLESPIE, DAIR L. "Who Has the Power? The Marital Struggle." *Journal of Marriage and the Family* 33:3 (August 1971), 445.

GORDON, MICHAEL, and PENELOPE J. SHANKWEILER. "Recent Marriage Manuals." *Journal of Marriage and the Family* 33:3 (August 1971), 459.

HOLMSTROM, ENGIN INEL. "Changing Sex Roles in a Developing Country." *Journal of Marriage and the Family* 35:3 (August 1973), 546–53.

JOFFE, CAROLE. "Sex Role Socialization and the Nursery School: As the Twig Is Bent." *Journal of Marriage and the Family* 33:3 (August 1971), 467.

KOMAROVSKY, MIRRA. *Blue-Collar Marriage.* New York: Random House, Inc., 1962.

KOTLAR, S. L. "Middle-Class Marital Role Perceptions and Marital Adjustment." *Sociological and Social Research* 49:3 (April 1965), 283–93.

KRECH, HILDA SIDNEY. "Housewife and Woman? The Best of Both Worlds?" In *People as Partners,* edited by Jacqueline P. Wiseman, pp. 203–15. New York: Harper & Row, Publishers, 1971.

LAWS, JUDITH LONG. "A Feminist Review of the Marital Adjustment Literature: The Rape of the Locke." *Journal of Marriage and the Family* 33:3 (August 1971), 483.

MEAD, MARGARET. *Male and Female.* New York: William Morrow & Co., Inc., 1949.

MILLMAN, MARCIA. "Observations on Sex Role Research." *Journal of Marriage and the Family* 33:4 (November 1971), 772.

NYE, F. IVAN, and LOIS W. HOFFMAN. *The Employed Mother in America.* Skokie, Ill.: Rand McNally & Co., 1963.

OSMOND, MARIE WITHERS, and PATRICIA YANCEY MARTIN. "Sex and Sexism: A Comparison of Male and Female Sex-Role Attitudes." *Journal of Marriage and the Family* 37:4 (November 1975), 744–58.

PAPANEK, HANNA. "Purdah in Pakistan: Seclusion and Modern Occupations for Women." *Journal of Marriage and the Family* 33:3 (August 1971), 517.

PARELIUS, ANN P. "Emerging Sex-Role Attitudes, Expectations, and Strains Among College Women." *Journal of Marriage and the Family* 37:1 (February 1975), 146–53.

POLOMA, MARGARET M., and T. NEAL GARLAND. "The Married Professional

Woman: A Study in the Tolerance of Domestication." *Journal of Marriage and the Family* 33:3 (August 1971), 531.

PRATHER, JANE E. "When the Girls Move In: A Sociological Analysis of the Feminization of the Bank Teller's Job." *Journal of Marriage and the Family* 33:4 (November 1971), 777.

RAPOPORT, RHONA, and ROBERT N. RAPOPORT. "Men, Women, and Equity." *The Family Coordinator* 24:4 (October 1975), 421–32.

ROSEN, RUTH. "Sexism in History or, Writing Women's History Is a Tricky Business." *Journal of Marriage and the Family* 33:3 (August 1971), 541.

SCHEINFELD, AMRAM. *Your Heredity and Environment.* Philadelphia: J. B. Lippincott Company, 1965.

SCHWENDINGER, JULIA and HERMAN SCHWENDINGER. "Sociology's Founding Fathers: Sexists to a Man." *Journal of Marriage and the Family* 33:4 (November 1971), 783.

SPANIER, GRAHAM B. "Measuring Dyadic Adjustment: New Scales for Assessing the Quality of Marriage and Similar Dyads." *Journal of Marriage and the Family* 38:1 (February 1976), 15–28.

WILLIAMS, BRUCE. "Molly Bloom, Archetype or Stereotype." *Journal of Marriage and the Family* 33:3 (August 1971), 545.

## CHAPTER 3

BLOOD, ROBERT O., JR., and SAMUEL O. NICHOLSON. "The Attitudes of American Men and Women Students Toward International Dating." *Marriage and Family Living* 24:1 (February 1962), 35–41.

———. "The Experiences of Foreign Students in Dating American Women." *Marriage and Family Living* 24:3 (August 1962), 241–48.

———. "The International Dating Experiences of American Women Students." *Marriage and Family Living* 24:2 (May 1962), 129–36.

COOMBS, ROBERT H. "Value Consensus and Partner Satisfaction Among Dating Couples." *Journal of Marriage and the Family* 28:2 (May 1966), 166–73.

———, and WILLIAM F. KENKEL. "Sex Differences in Dating Aspirations and Satisfactions with Computer-Selected Partners." *Journal of Marriage and the Family* 28:1 (February 1966), 62–66.

DICKINSON, GEORGE E. "Dating Behavior of Black and White Adolescents Before and After Desegregation." *Journal of Marriage and the Family* 37:3 (August 1975), 602–8.

HUDSON, JOHN W., and LURA HENZE. "Campus Values in Mate Selection: A Replication." In *People as Partners,* edited by Jacqueline P. Wiseman, pp. 73–79. New York: Harper & Row, Publishers, 1971.

KANIN, EUGENE J. "Male Aggression in Dating-Courting Relations. *American Journal of Sociology* 43:2 (September 1957), 197–204.

KIRKPATRICK, CLIFFORD, and EUGENE KANIN. "Male Sex Aggression on a University Campus." *American Sociology Review* 22:1 (February 1957), 52–58.

KLEMER, RICHARD H. "Self-Esteem and College Dating Experiences as Factors in Mate Selection and Marital Happiness: A Longitudinal Study." *Journal of Marriage and the Family* 33:1 (February 1971), 183–87.

KRAIN, MARK. "Communication Among Premarital Couples at Three Stages of Dating." *Journal of Marriage and the Family* 37:3 (August 1975), 609–18.

LANDIS, JUDSON T. "A Comparison of Children from Divorced and Nondivorced Unhappy Marriages." *The Family Life Coordinator* 9:3 (July 1962), 61–65.

———. "Dating Maturation of Children from Happy and Unhappy Marriages." *Marriage and Family Living* 25:3 (August 1963), 351–53.

LEWIS, ROBERT A. "A Longitudinal Test of a Developmental Framework for Premarital Dyadic Formation." *Journal of Marriage and the Family* 35:1 (February 1973), 16–25.

MATHES, EUGENE W. "The Effects of Physical Attractiveness and Anxiety on Heterosexual Attraction over a Series of Five Encounters." *Journal of Marriage and the Family* 37:4 (November 1975), 769–73.

PEARLIN, LEONARD I. "Status Inequality and Stress in Marriage." *American Sociological Review* 40:3 (June 1975), 344–57.

PICKFORD, JOHN H.; EDRO J. SIGNORI; and HENRY REMPEL. "Similar or Related Personality Traits as a Factor in Marital Happiness." *Journal of Marriage and the Family* 28:2 (May 1966a), 190–92.

———. "The Intensity of Personality Traits in Relation to Marital Happiness." *Journal of Marriage and the Family* 28:4 (November 1966b), 458–59.

SCOTT, JOHN F. "Sororities and the Husband Game." In *People as Partners,* edited by Jacqueline P. Wiseman, pp. 64–72. New York: Harper & Row, Publishers, 1971.

SKIPPER, JAMES K., JR., and GILBERT NASS. "Dating Behavior: A Framework for Analysis and an Illustration." *Journal of Marriage and the Family* 28:4 (November 1966), 412–20.

STERRETT, JOYE, and STEPHEN R. BOLLMAN. "Factors Related to Adolescents' Expectation of Marital Roles." *The Family Coordinator* 19:4 (October 1970), 353–56.

STRONG, EMILY, and WARNER WILSON. "Three-Filter Date Selection by Computer." *The Family Coordinator* 18:2 (April 1968), 166–71.

———. "Three-Filter Date Selection by Computer—Phase II. *The Family Coordinator* 18:3 (July 1969), 256–59.

UDRY, J. RICHARD; KARL E. BAUMAN; and CHARLES CHASE. "Skin Color, Status, and Mate Selection." *American Journal of Sociology* 76:4 (January 1971), 722–33.

WEISS, MELFORD S. "Selective Acculturation and the Dating Process: The Patterning of Chinese–Caucasian Interracial Dating." *Journal of Marriage and the Family* 32:2 (May 1970), 273–78.

WITTMAN, JAMES S. "Dating Patterns of Rural and Urban Kentucky Teenagers." *The Family Coordinator* 20:1 (January 1971), 63.

## CHAPTER 4

See suggested readings from Chapter 3.

## CHAPTER 5

DOTY, CAROL M., and RUTH M. HOEFLIN. "A Description of Thirty-Five Unmarried Graduate Women." *Journal of Marriage and Family Living* 26:1 (February 1964), 91–95.

GLENN, NORVAL D. "The Contribution of Marriage to the Psychological Well-Being of Males and Females." *Journal of Marriage and the Family* 37:3 (August 1975), 594–600.

KLEMER, RICHARD H. "Factors of Personality and Experience Which Differentiate Single from Married Women." *Marriage and Family Living* 16:1 (February 1954), 41–44.

RALLINGS, ELISHA M. "Family Situations of Married and Never-Married Males." *Journal of Marriage and the Family* 28:4 (November 1966), 485–90.

SPREITZER, ELMER, and LAWRENCE E. RILEY. "Factors Associated with Singlehood." *Journal of Marriage and the Family* 36:3 (August 1974), 533–42.

STEIN, PETER J. "Singlehood: An Alternative to Marriage." *The Family Coordinator* 24:4 (October 1975), 489–503.

WALLACE, KARL MILES. "An Experiment in Scientific Matchmaking." *Marriage and Family Living* 21:4 (November 1959), 342–48. Also in Robert F. Winch; Robert McGinnis; and Herbert R. Barringer, *Selected Studies in Marriage and the Family.* New York: Holt, Rinehart & Winston, Inc., 1962.

## CHAPTER 6

HALL, EVERETTE, "Ordinal Position and Success, in Engagement and Marriage." *Journal of Individual Psychology* 21:4 (November 1965), 154–58.

HAWKINS, JAMES L., and KATHRYN JOHNSON. "Perception of Behavioral Conformity, Imputation of Consensus, and Marital Satisfaction." *Journal of Marriage and the Family* 31:3 (August 1969), 507–11.

HEISS, JEROLD. "On the Transmission of Marital Instability in Black Families." *American Sociological Review* 37:1 (February 1972), 82–92.

KEMPER, T. D. "Mate Selection and Marital Satisfaction According to Sibling Type of Husband and Wife." *Journal of Marriage and the Family* 28:3 (August 1966), 346–49.

LANDIS, JUDSON T. "Social Correlates of Divorce or Nondivorce Among the Unhappily Married." *Marriage and Family Living* 25:2 (May 1963), 178–80.

————. "A Comparison of Children from Divorced and Nondivorced Unhappy Marriages." *Family Life Coordinator* 9:3 (July 1962), 61–65.

————. "Religiousness, Family Relationships, and Family Values in Protestant, Catholic, and Jewish Families. *Marriage and Family Living* 22:4 (November 1960), 341–47.

————. "The Pattern of Divorce in Three Generations." *Social Forces* 34:3 (March 1956), 213–16.

MURSTEIN, BERNARD K., and VINCENT GLAUDIN. "The Relationship of Marital Adjustment to Personality: A Factor Analysis of the Interpersonal Check List." *Journal of Marriage and the Family* 28:1 (February 1966), 37–43.

———. "Use of Minnesota Multiphasic Personality Inventory in the Determination of Marital Maladjustment." *Journal of Marriage and the Family* 30:4 (November 1968), 651–55.

UDRY, J. RICHARD. "Marital Instability by Race and Income Based on 1960 Census Data." *American Journal of Sociology* 72:2 (May 1967), 673–74.

———. "Marital Instability by Race, Sex, Education, and Occupation Using 1960 Census Data." *American Journal of Sociology* 72:2 (September 1966), 203–9.

## CHAPTER 7

BAUMAN, KARL E. "Relationship Between Age at First Marriage, School Dropout, and Marital Instability, An Analysis of the Glick Effect." *Journal of Marriage and the Family* 29:4 (November 1967), 672–80.

BURCHINAL, LEE G. "Trends and Prospects for Young Marriages in the United States." *Journal of Marriage and the Family* 27:2 (May 1965), 243–54.

———. "Research on Young Marriage: Implications for Family Life Education." *Family Life Coordinator* 9:1–2 (September–December 1960), 6–24.

ESHLEMAN, J. ROSS. "Mental Health and Marital Integration in Young Marriages." *Journal of Marriage and the Family* 27:2 (May 1965), 255–63.

INSELBERG, RACHEL M. "Marital Problems and Satisfaction in High School Marriages." *Marriage and Family Living* 24:1 (February 1962), 74–77.

KAPLAN, HOWARD B., and ALEX D. POKORNY. "Self-Derogation and Childhood Broken Home." *Journal of Marriage and the Family* 33:2 (May 1971), 328–37.

KEMPER, T. D. "Mate Selection and Marital Satisfaction According to Sibling Type of Husband and Wife." *Journal of Marriage and the Family* 28:3 (August 1966), 346–49.

LANDIS, JUDSON T. "High School Student Marriages, School Policy, and Family Life Education in California." *Journal of Marriage and the Family* 27:2 (May 1965), 271–76.

MOSS, J. JOEL. "Teen-Age Marriage: Cross National Trends and Sociological Factors in the Decision of When to Marry." *Journal of Marriage and the Family* 27:2 (May 1965), 230–42.

PORTER, BLAINE. "American Teen-Agers of the 1960's—Our Despair or Hope?" *Journal of Marriage and the Family* 27:2 (May 1965), 139–47.

REINER, BEATRICE S., and RAYMOND L. EDWARDS. "Adolescent Marriage—Social or Therapeutic Problem?" *The Family Coordinator* 23:4 (October 1974), 383–90.

SCHOEN, ROBERT. "California Divorce Rates by Age at First Marriage and Duration of First Marriage." *Journal of Marriage and the Family* 37:3 (August 1975), 548–55.

STINNETT, NICK. "Readiness for Marital Competence and Family, Dating and Personality Factors." *Journal of Home Economics* 61:4 (November 1969), 683–86.

# CHAPTER 8

BEIGEL, HUGO G. "Romantic Love." *American Sociological Review* 16:3 (June 1951), 326–34. Also in Robert F. Winch; Robert McGinnis; and Herbert R. Barringer, *Selected Studies in Marriage and the Family*. New York: Holt, Rinehart & Winston, Inc., 1962.

ENGLAND, R. W., JR. "Images of Love and Courtship in Family-Magazine Fiction." *Marriage and Family Living* 22:2 (May 1960), 162–65.

FROMM, ERICH. *The Art of Loving*. New York: Harper & Row, Publishers, 1956.

———. "The Theory of Love." In *People as Partners*, edited by Jacqueline P. Wiseman, pp. 80–91. New York: Harper & Row, Publishers, 1971.

FROMM, ALLAN. *The Ability to Love*. New York: Farrar, Straus & Giroux, Inc., 1965.

GOODE, WILLIAM J. "The Theoretical Importance of Love." *American Sociological Review* 24:1 (February 1959), 38–47. Also in Robert F. Winch; Robert McGinnis; and Herbert R. Barringer, *Selected Studies in Marriage and the Family*. New York: Holt, Rinehart & Winston, Inc., 1962.

HINKLE, DENNIS E., and MICHAEL J. SPORAKOWSKI. "Attitudes Toward Love: A Reexamination." *Journal of Marriage and the Family* 37:4 (November 1975), 764–67.

KEPHART, WILLIAM M. "Some Correlates of Romantic Love." *Journal of Marriage and the Family* 29:3 (August 1967), 470–74.

MACE, DAVID, and VERA MACE. *Marriage East and West*. New York: Doubleday & Company, Inc., 1960.

WALLER, WILLARD. "The Sentiment of Love." In *The Family*, revised by Reuben Hill. New York: The Dryden Press, 1951.

WILKINSON, MELVIN. "Romantic Love: The Great Equalizer? Sexism in Popular Music." *The Family Coordinator* 25:2 (April 1976), 161–66.

# CHAPTER 9

ADAMS, BERT N. "Structural Factors Affecting Parental Aid to Married Children." *Journal of Marriage and the Family* 26:3 (August 1964), 327–31.

CHILMAN, CATHERINE S., and DONALD L. MEYER. "Single and Married Undergraduates' Measured Personality Needs and Self-Rated Happiness." *Journal of Marriage and the Family* 28:1 (February 1966), 67–76.

CUTLER, BEVERLY R., and WILLIAM G. DYER. "Initial Adjustment Processes in Young Married Couples." *Social Forces* 44:2 (December 1965), 195–201.

ESHLEMAN, J. ROSS, and CHESTER L. HUNT. "Social Class Influences on Family Adjustment Patterns of Married College Students." *Journal of Marriage and the Family* 29:3 (August 1967), 485–91.

FALK, LAURENCE L. "A Comparative Study of Problems of Married and Single Students." *Journal of Marriage and the Family* 26:2 (May 1964), 207–8.

GERSON, WALTER M. "Leisure and Marital Satisfaction of College Married Couples." *Marriage and Family Living* 22:4 (November 1960), 360–61.

HEPKER, WILMA, and JERRY S. CLOYD. "Role Relationships and Role Performances: The Male Married Student." *Journal of Marriage and the Family* 36:4 (November 1974), 688–96.

HURLEY, JOHN R., and DONNA P. PALONEN. "Marital Satisfaction and Child Density Among University Student Parents." *Journal of Marriage and the Family* 29:3 (August 1967), 483–84.

MARSHALL, WILLIAM H., and MARCIA P. KING. "Undergraduate Student Marriage: A Compilation of Research Findings." *Journal of Marriage and the Family* 28:3 (August 1966), 350–59.

NEUBECK, GERHARD, and VIVIAN HEWER. "Time of Marriage and College Attendance." *Journal of Marriage and the Family* 27:4 (November 1965), 522–24.

PECK, BRUCE B., and DIANNE SCHROEDER. "Psychotherapy with the Father-Absent Military Family." *Journal of Marriage and Family Counseling* 2:1 (January 1976), 23–30.

PRICE-BONHAM, SHARON. "Student Husbands Versus Student Couples." *Journal of Marriage and the Family* 35:1 (February 1973), 33–37.

SHANAS, ETHEL. "Family Help Patterns and Social Class in Three Countries." *Journal of Marriage and the Family* 29:2 (May 1967), 257–66.

SUSSMAN, MARVIN B., and LEE BURCHINAL. "Parental Aid to Married Children: Implications for Family Functioning." *Marriage and Family Living* 24:4 (November 1962), 320–32.

## CHAPTER 10

BELL, ROBERT R. "Parent–Child Conflict in Sexual Values." *Journal of Social Issues* 22 (April 1966), 34–44.

———. "American Adolescents in the Mid-Sixties." Special issue of *Journal of Marriage and the Family* 27:2 (May 1965).

———, and JACK V. BUERKLE. "Mother and Daughter Attitudes to Premarital Sexual Behavior." *Marriage and Family Living* 23:4 (November 1961), 390–93.

———; STANLEY TURNER; and LAWRENCE ROSEN. "A Multivariate Analysis of Female Extramarital Coitus." *Journal of Marriage and the Family* 37:2 (May 1975), 375–84.

BERGER, DAVID G., and MORTON G. WENGER. "The Ideology of Virginity." *Journal of Marriage and the Family* 35:4 (November 1973), 666–76.

BURGESS, ERNEST W., and PAUL WALLIN. *Engagement and Marriage*, Ch. 11, "Sex and Engagement," and Ch. 12, "Assessing Premarital Intercourse." Philadelphia: J. B. Lippincott Co., 1953.

CANNON, KENNETH L., and RICHARD LONG. "Premarital Sexual Behavior in the Sixties." *Journal of Marriage and the Family* 33:1 (February 1971), 36.

CENTERS, RICHARD. "Attitude Similarity–Dissimilarity as a Correlate of Heterosexual Attraction and Love." *Journal of Marriage and the Family* 37:2 (May 1975), 305–12.

CHRISTENSEN, HAROLD T., and GEORGE R. CARPENTER. "Timing Patterns in the Development of Sexual Intimacy: An Attitudinal Report on Three Modern

Western Societies." *Marriage and Family Living* 24:1 (February 1962), 30–35.

———. "Value-Behavior Discrepancies Regarding Premarital Coitus." *American Sociological Review* 27:1 (February 1962), 66–74.

HELTSLEY, MARY E., and CARLFRED BRODERICK. "Religiosity and Premarital Sexual Permissiveness: Reexamination of Reiss's Traditionalism Proposition." *Journal of Marriage and the Family* 31:3 (August 1969), 441–43.

HENZE, LURA F., and JOHN W. HUDSON. "Personal and Family Characteristics of Cohabiting and Noncohabiting College Students." *Journal of Marriage and the Family* 36:4 (November 1974), 722–26.

JEDLICKA, DAVOR. "Sequential Analysis of Perceived Commitment to Partners in Premarital Coitus." *Journal of Marriage and the Family* 37:2 (May 1975), 385–90.

JURICH, ANTHONY P., and JULIE A. JURICH. "The Effects of Cognitive Moral Development upon the Selection of Premarital Sexual Standards." *Journal of Marriage and the Family* 36:4 (November 1974), 736–41.

KANIN, EUGENE J. "Premarital Sex Adjustments, Social Class, and Associated Behaviors." *Marriage and Family Living* 22:3 (August 1960), 258–62.

———. "An Examination of Sexual Aggression as a Response to Sexual Frustration." *Journal of Marriage and the Family* 29:3 (August 1967), 428–33.

KINSEY, ALFRED, et al. *Sexual Behavior in the Human Female.* Philadelphia: W. B. Saunders Company, 1953.

———. *Sexual Behavior in the Human Male.* Philadelphia: W. B. Saunders Company, 1948.

LARSEN, KUND S. "An Investigation of Sexual Behavior Among Norwegian College Students: A Motivation Study." *Journal of Marriage and the Family* 33:1 (February 1971), 219.

MOSS, J. JOEL; FRANK APOLONIO; and MARGARET JENSEN. "The Premarital Dyad During the Sixties." *Journal of Marriage and the Family* 33:1 (February 1971), 50.

POFFENBERGER, THOMAS. "Individual Choice in Adolescent Premarital Sex Behavior." *Marriage and Family Living* 22:4 (November 1960), 324–30.

POPE, HALLOWELL, and DEAN D. KNUDSEN. "Premarital Sexual Norms, the Family and Social Change." *Journal of Marriage and the Family* 27:3 (August 1965), 314–23.

REISS, IRA L. "The Scaling of Premarital Sexual Permissiveness." *Journal of Marriage and the Family* 26:2 (May 1964), 188–98.

———. ed. "The Sexual Renaissance in America." Special issue of *The Journal of Social Issues* 22 (April 1966).

———. *The Social Context of Premarital Sexual Permissiveness.* New York: Holt, Rinehart & Winston, Inc., 1967.

———; ALBERT BANWART; and HARRY FOREMAN. "Premarital Contraceptive Usage: A Study and Some Theoretical Explorations." *Journal of Marriage and the Family* 37:3 (August 1975), 619–30.

ROBINSON, IRA E.; KARL KING; and JACK O. BALSWICK. "The Premarital Sexual

Revolution Among College Females." *The Family Coordinator* 21:2 (April 1972), 189–94.

STAPLES, ROBERT. "Research on Black Sexuality: Its Implications for Family Life, Sex Education, and Public Policy." *The Family Coordinator* 21:2 (April 1972), 183–88.

UDRY, J. RICHARD; KARL E. BAUMAN; and NAOMI M. MORRIS. "Changes in Premarital Coital Experience of Recent Decade-of-Birth Cohorts of Urban American Women." *Journal of Marriage and the Family* 37:4 (November 1975), 783–87.

VENER, ARTHUR M., and CYRUS S. STEWART. "Adolescent Sexual Behavior in Middle America Revisited: 1970–1973." *Journal of Marriage and the Family* 36:4 (November 1974), 728–35.

## CHAPTER 11

ALDRIDGE, DELORES P. "The Changing Nature of Interracial Marriage in Georgia: A Research Note." *Journal of Marriage and the Family* 35:4 (November 1973), 641–42.

BABCHUK, NICHOLAS, and HARRY J. CROCKETT, JR. "Change in Religious Affiliation and Family Stability." *Social Forces* 45:4 (June 1967), 551–55.

BARNETT, LARRY D. "Research in Interreligious Dating and Marriage." *Marriage and Family Living* 24:2 (May 1962), 191–94.

———. "Research on International and Interracial Marriages." *Marriage and Family Living* 25:1 (February 1963), 105–7.

———. "Research in Interreligious Dating and Marriage." In *People as Partners*, edited by Jacqueline P. Wiseman, pp. 52–57. New York: Harper & Row, Publishers, 1971.

BEAN, FRANK D., and LINDA H. AIKEN. "Intermarriage and Unwanted Fertility in the United States." *Journal of Marriage and the Family* 38:1 (February 1976), 61–72.

BERNARD, JESSIE. "Note on Educational Homogamy in Negro–White and White–Negro Marriage." *Journal of Marriage and the Family* 28:3 (August 1966), 274–76.

BIGMAN, STANLEY K. *The Jewish Population of Greater Washington in 1956.* Washington, D.C.: The Jewish Community Counsel of Greater Washington, 1957.

CARTER, HUGH, and PAUL GLICK. *Marriage and Divorce: A Social and Economic Study.* Cambridge: Harvard University Press, 1970.

CAVAN, RUTH SHONLE. "Jewish Student Attitudes Toward Interreligious and Intra-Jewish Marriage." *American Journal of Sociology* 76:6 (May 1971), 1064–71.

CHANCELLOR, LOREN E., and THOMAS P. MONAHAN. "Religious Preference and Interreligious Mixtures in Marriages and Divorce in Iowa." *American Journal of Sociology* 61:3 (November 1955), 233–39.

CHRISTENSEN, HAROLD T., and KENNETH E. BARBER. "Interfaith Versus Intrafaith Marriages in Indiana." *Journal of Marriage and the Family* 29:3 (August 1967), 461–69.

FREIND, JACOB, ed. *Jews and Divorce.* New York: KTAV Publishing House, Inc., 1968.

GOLDEN, JOSEPH. "Characteristics of the Negro–White Intermarried in Philadelphia." *American Sociological Review* 18:2 (April 1953), 177–83.

———. "Social Control of Negro–White Intermarriage." *Social Forces* 36 (1958), 267–69. Also in Robert R. Winch; Robert McGinnis; and Herbert R. Barringer, *Selected Studies in Marriage and the Family.* New York: Holt, Rinehart & Winston, Inc., 1962.

HEER, DAVID M. "The Prevalence of Black–White Marriages in the United States, 1960 and 1970." *Journal of Marriage and the Family* 36:2 (May 1974), 246–58.

HEISS, JEROLD S. "Interfaith Marriage and Marital Outcome." *Marriage and Family Living* 23:2 (August 1961), 228–33.

———. Premarital Characteristics of the Religiously Intermarried in an Urban Area." *American Sociological Review* 25:1 (February 1960), 47–55.

HUNT, CHESTER L., and RICHARD W. COLLER. "Intermarriage and Cultural Change: A Study of Philippine–American Marriages." *Social Forces* 35:3 (March 1957), 223–30.

LANDIS, JUDSON T. "Religiousness, Family Relationships and Family Values in Protestant, Catholic, and Jewish Families." *Marriage and Family Living* 22:4 (November 1960), 241–47.

MAYER, JOHN E. *Jewish–Gentile Courtship.* New York: The Free Press, 1961.

MONAHAN, THOMAS P. "Are Interracial Marriages Really Less Stable?" *Social Forces* 48:4 (June 1970), 461–73.

———. "Marriage Across Racial Lines in Indiana." *Journal of Marriage and the Family* 35:4 (November 1973), 632–40.

PEARLIN, LEONARD I. "Status Inequality and Stress in Marriage." *American Sociological Review* 40:3 (June 1975), 344–57.

PRINCE, ALFRED J. "A Study of 194 Cross-Religion Marriages." *Family Life Coordinator* 11:1 (January 1962), 3–6.

ROSENTHAL, ERICH. "Divorce and Religious Intermarriage: The Effect of Previous Marital Status upon Subsequent Marital Behavior." *Journal of Marriage and the Family* 32:3 (August 1970), 435–40.

SLOTKIN, J. S. "Jewish–Gentile Intermarriage in Chicago." *American Sociological Review* 7:1 (February 1942), 34–39.

STRAUSS, ANSELM L. "Strain and Harmony in American–Japanese War-Bride Marriages." *Marriage and Family Living* 16:2 (May 1954), 99–106.

THOMAS, JOHN L. *The American Catholic Family.* Englewood Cliffs, N.J.: Prentice-Hall, Inc., 1956.

WOLF, ROSALIND. "Self-Image of the White Member of an Interracial Couple." In *People as Partners,* edited by Jacqueline P. Wiseman, pp. 58–63. New York: Harper & Row, Publishers, 1971.

## CHAPTER 12

BERGER, MIRIAM E. "Trial Marriage: Harnessing the Trend Constructively." *The Family Coordinator* 20:1 (January 1971), 38.

BOLTON, CHARLES D. "Mate Selection as the Development of a Relationship." *Marriage and Family Living* 23:3 (August 1961), 234–40.

BURGESS, ERNEST W., and PAUL WALLIN. *Engagement and Marriage,* esp. Chs. 5–9. Philadelphia: J. B. Lippincott Co., 1953.

KERCKHOFF, ALLEN, and KEITH E. DAVIS. "Value Consensus and Need Complementary in Mate Selection." *American Sociological Review* 27:3 (June 1962), 295–303.

KIMMEL, PAUL R., and JOHN W. HAVENS. "Game Theory Versus Mutual Identification: Two Criteria for Assessing Marital Relationships." *Journal of Marriage and the Family* 28:4 (November 1966), 460–65.

KRAIN, MARK. "Communication Among Premarital Couples at Three Stages of Dating." *Journal of Marriage and the Family* 37:3 (August 1975), 609–18.

LANDIS, JUDSON T., and MARY G. LANDIS, eds. *Readings in Marriage and the Family:* Part V, Reading 1, "Marriage Adjustment and Engagement Adjustment," Ernest W. Burgess and Paul Wallin; Reading 2, "Personality and Marriage Adjustment," Robert F. Winch; Reading 3, "A Study of 738 Elopements," Paul Popenoe. Part VI, Reading 1, "Of Weddings," Frank H. Ferris; Readings 2 and 3, "A Hindu Marriage in Bengal" and "A Hindu Wife," D. N. Mitra. Englewood Cliffs, N.J.: Prentice-Hall, Inc., 1952.

SCHULMAN, MARION L. "Idealization in Engaged Couples." *Journal of Marriage and the Family* 36:1 (February 1974), 139–46.

SPORAKOWSKI, MICHAEL J. "Marital Preparedness, Prediction and Adjustment." *The Family Coordinator* 17:3 (July 1968), 155–61.

WALLER, WILLARD. *The Family,* revised by Reuben Hill, Ch. 12, "The Engagement." New York: The Dryden Press, 1951.

WELLS, J. GIPSON. "A Critical Look at Personal Marriage Contracts." *The Family Coordinator* 25:1 (January 1976), 33–37.

## CHAPTER 13

ALDRIDGE, DELORES P. "The Changing Nature of Interracial Marriage in Georgia: A Research Note." *Journal of Marriage and the Family* 35:4 (November 1973), 641–42.

BRANDWEIN, RUTH A.; CAROL A. BROWN; and ELIZABETH MAURY FOX. "Women and Children Last: The Social Situation of Divorced Mothers and Their Families." *Journal of Marriage and the Family* 36:3 (August 1974), 498–514.

ELKIN, MEYER. "Conciliation Courts: The Reintegration of Disintegrating Families." *The Family Coordinator* 22:1 (January 1973), 63–71.

HEER, DAVID M. "Negro–White Marriage in the United States." *Journal of Marriage and the Family* 28:3 (August 1966), 262–73.

JACOBSON, PAUL H. *American Marriage and Divorce.* New York: Holt, Rinehart & Winston, Inc., 1959.

JONES, WYATT C.; HENRY J. MEYER; and EDGAR F. BORGATTA. "Social and Psychological Factors in Status Decisions of Unmarried Mothers." *Marriage and Family Living* 24:3 (August 1962), 224–30.

KEPHART, WILLIAM M., and R. B. STROHM. "The Stability of Gretna Green Marriages." *Sociology and Social Research* (May–June 1952), 291–96.

LASLETT, BARBARA. "The Family as a Public and Private Institution: An Historical Perspective." *Journal of Marriage and the Family* 35:3 (August 1973), 480–92.

LITWAK, EUGENE. "Divorce Law as a Social Control." *Social Forces* 34:3 (March 1956), 217–23. Reprinted in Norman W. Bell and Ezra F. Vogel, *A Modern Introduction to the Family.* New York: The Free Press, 1960.

MACKAY, RICHARD V. *Law of Marriage and Divorce.* New York: Oceana Publications, 1959.

MONAHAN, THOMAS P. "When Married Couples Part." *American Sociological Review* 27:5 (October 1962), 625–33.

———. "Marriage Across Racial Lines in Indiana." *Journal of Marriage and the Family* 35:4 (November 1973), 632–40.

PLATERIS, ALEXANDER. "The Impact of the Amendment of Marriage Laws in Mississippi." *Journal of Marriage and the Family* 28:2 (May 1966), 206–12.

STRONG, BRYAN. "Toward a History of the Experiential Family: Sex and Incest in the Nineteenth-Century Family." *Journal of Marriage and the Family* 35:3 (August 1973), 457–66.

VINCENT, CLARK E. "Teen-Age Illegitimacy: A Pisgah Perspective." *Marriage and Family Living* 24:3 (August 1962), 290–92.

WEISBERG, D. KELLY. "Alternative Family Structures and the Law." *The Family Coordinator* 24:4 (October 1975), 549–59.

WEITZMAN, LENORE J. "Legal Regulation of Marriage: Tradition and Change." *California Law Review* 62:4 (July–September 1974), 1169–1288.

## CHAPTER 14

BACH, GEORGE, and PETER WYDEN. *The Intimate Enemy.* New York: William Morrow & Co., Inc., 1969.

BEAN, FRANK D., and ALAN C. KERCKHOFF. "Personality and Person Perception in Husband–Wife Conflicts." *Journal of Marriage and the Family* 33:2 (May 1971), 351.

BERNARD, JESSIE. "The Adjustment of Married Mates." In *Handbook of Marriage and the Family,* edited by Harold T. Christensen, pp. 675–739. Skokie, Ill.: Rand McNally & Co., 1964.

BERNE, ERIC. *Games People Play.* New York: Grove Press, Inc., 1963.

BLAZER, J. A. "Complementary Needs and Marital Happiness." *Marriage and Family Living* 25:1 (February 1963), 89–95.

BURR, WESLEY R. "Satisfaction with Various Aspects of Marriage over the Life Cycle: A Random Middle Class Sample." *Journal of Marriage and the Family* 32:1 (February 1970), 29–37. Also in *People as Partners,* edited by Jacqueline P. Wiseman, pp. 467–80. New York: Harper & Row, Publishers, 1971.

CLEMENTS, WILLIAM H. "Marital Interaction and Marital Stability: A Point of View and a Descriptive Comparison of Stable and Unstable Marriages."

*Journal of Marriage and the Family* 29:4 (November 1967), 697–702.

CROUSE, BRYANT; MARVIN KARLENS; and HAROLD SCHRODER. "Conceptual Complexity and Marital Happiness." *Journal of Marriage and the Family* 30:4 (November 1968), 643–46.

CUTLER, BEVERLY R., and WILLIAM G. DYER. "Initial Adjustment Processes in Young Married Couples." *Social Forces* 44 (December 1965), 195–201. Also in *People as Partners,* edited by Jacqueline P. Wiseman, pp. 184–94. New York: Harper & Row, Publishers, 1971.

DEAN, DWIGHT G. "Emotional Maturity and Marital Adjustment." *Journal of Marriage and the Family* 28:4 (November 1966), 454–57.

DYER, WILLIAM G. "Analyzing Marital Adjustment Using Role Theory." *Marriage and Family Living* 24:4 (November 1962), 371–75.

HAWKINS, JAMES L. "Association Between Companionship, Hostility and Marital Satisfaction." *Journal of Marriage and the Family* 30:4 (November 1968), 647–50.

HURVITZ, NATHAN. "Control Roles, Marital Strain, Role Deviation, and Marital Adjustment." *Journal of Marriage and the Family* 27:1 (February 1965), 29–31.

————. "The Marital Roles Inventory and the Measurement of Marital Adjustment." *Journal of Clinical Psychology* 16 (October 1965a), 29–31.

KIMMEL, PAUL R., and JOHN W. HAVENS. "Game Theory Versus Mutual Identification: Two Criteria for Assessing Marital Relationships." *Journal of Marriage and the Family* 28:4 (November 1966), 460–65.

KOLB, TRUDY M., and MURRAY A. STRAUSS. "Marital Power and Marital Happiness in Relation to Problem-Solving Ability." *Journal of Marriage and the Family* 36:4 (November 1974), 756–66.

KRUPINSKI, JERZY; ELIZABETH MARSHALL; and VALERIE YULE. "Patterns of Marital Problems in Marriage Guidance Clients." *Journal of Marriage and the Family* 32:1 (February 1970), 138–43.

LEMASTERS, E. E. "Holy Deadlock: A Study of Unsuccessful Marriages." *The Midwest Sociologist* 21:1 (July 1959), 86–91.

LEVINGER, GEORGE. "Marital Cohesiveness and Dissolution: An Integrative Review." *Journal of Marriage and the Family* 27:1 (February 1965), 19–28.

LUCKEY, ELEANORE BRAUN. "Numbers of Years Married as Related to Personality Perception and Marital Satisfaction." *Journal of Marriage and the Family* 28:1 (February 1966), 44–48.

————. "Marital Satisfaction and Personality Correlates of Spouse." *Journal of Marriage and the Family* 26:2 (May 1964), 217–20.

————, and JOYCE KOYM BAIN. "Children: A Factor in Marital Satisfaction." *Journal of Marriage and the Family* 32:1 (February 1970), 43–44.

ORTHNER, DENNIS K. "Leisure Activity Patterns and Marital Satisfaction over the Marital Career." *Journal of Marriage and the Family* 37:1 (February 1975), 91–102.

PARIS, BETHEL LOGAN, and ELEANOR B. PARIS. "A Longitudinal Study in Marital Satisfaction." *Sociological and Social Research* 50:2 (January 1966), 212–22.

PATTERSON, GERALD R.; HYMAN HOPS; and ROBERT L. WEISS. "Interpersonal Skills Training for Couples in Early Stages of Conflict." *Journal of Marriage and the Family* 37:2 (May 1975), 295–303.

PINEO, PETER C. "Development Patterns in Marriage." *The Family Coordinator* 18:2 (April 1969), 135.

———. "Disenchantment in the Later Years of Marriage." *Marriage and Family Living* 23:1 (February 1961), 3–11.

RILEY, LAWRENCE E., and ELMER A. SPREITZER. "A Model for the Analysis of Lifetime Marriage Patterns." *Journal of Marriage and the Family* 36:1 (February 1974), 64–70.

ROLLINS, BOYD C., and KENNETH L. CANNON. "Marital Satisfactions over the Family Life Cycle: A Reevaluation." *Journal of Marriage and the Family* 36:2 (May 1974), 271–82.

———, and HAROLD FELDMAN. "Marital Satisfaction over the Family Life Cycle." *Journal of Marriage and the Family* 32:1 (February 1970), 20–27.

SPANIER, GRAHAM B.; ROBERT A. LEWIS; and CHARLES L. COLE. "Marital Adjustment over the Family Life Cycle: The Issue of Curvilinearity." *Journal of Marriage and the Family* 37:2 (May 1975), 263–75.

STRAUSS, MURRAY A. "Leveling, Civility, and Violence in the Family." *Journal of Marriage and the Family* 36:1 (February 1974), 13–29.

## CHAPTER 15

BURGESS, ERNEST W., and PAUL WALLIN. *Engagement and Marriage*, Ch. 20, "The Sex Factor in Marriage." Philadelphia: J. B. Lippincott Co., 1953.

CALDERONE, MARY STEICHEN; PHYLLIS CALDERONE; and ROBERT GOLDMAN. *Release from Sexual Tensions.* New York: Random House, Inc., 1960.

CHRISTENSON, CORNELLA, and JOHN H. GAGNON. "Sexual Behavior in a Group of Older Women." *Journal of Gerontology* (July 1965), 351–56.

CLARK, ALEXANDER L., and PAUL WALLIN. "Women's Sexual Responsiveness and the Duration and Quality of Their Marriages." *American Journal of Sociology* 71:2 (September 1965), 187–96.

DENTLER, ROBERT A., and PETER PINEO. "Sexual Adjustment, Marital Adjustment and Personal Growth of Husbands: A Panel Analysis." *Marriage and Family Living* 22:1 (February 1960), 45–48.

EDWARDS, JOHN N., and ALAN BOOTH. "Sexual Behavior in and out of Marriage: An Assessment of Correlates." *Journal of Marriage and the Family* 38:1 (February 1976), 73–81.

GORDON, MICHAEL, and PENELOPE J. SHANKWEILER. "Recent Marriage Manuals." *Journal of Marriage and the Family* 33:3 (August 1971), 459.

JOHNSON, RALPH E. "Some Correlates of Extramarital Coitus." *Journal of Marriage and the Family* 32:3 (August 1970), 449.

LANDIS, JUDSON T., and THOMAS POFFENBERGER. "The Marital and Sexual Adjustment of 330 Couples Who Chose Vasectomy as a Form of Birth Control." *Journal of Marriage and the Family* 27:1 (February 1965), 57–58.

MASTERS, WILLIAM H., and VIRGINIA E. JOHNSON. *Human Sexual Response.* Boston: Little, Brown and Company, 1966.

RAINWATER, LEE. "Marital Sexuality in Four Cultures of Poverty." *Journal of Marriage and the Family* 26:4 (November 1964), 457–66.

RUSSELL, BERTRAND. "The Place of Sex Among Human Values." In *People as Partners*, edited by Jacqueline P. Wiseman, pp. 94–99. New York: Harper & Row, Publishers, 1971.

SHOPE, DAVID F. "The Orgastic Responsiveness of Selected College Females." *Journal of Sex Research* 4:3 (August 1968), 206–19.

————, and CARLFRED B. BRODERICK. "Level of Sexual Experience and Predicted Adjustment in Marriage." *Journal of Marriage and the Family* 29:3 (August 1967), 424–27.

STONE, HANNAH, and ABRAHAM STONE. *A Marriage Manual.* New York: Simon & Schuster, Inc., 1970.

TRAINER, JOSEPH B. "Sexual Incompatibilities." *Journal of Marriage and Family Counseling* 1:2 (April 1975), 123–34.

WALLIN, PAUL, and ALEXANDER L. CLARK. "Religiosity, Sexual Gratification and Marital Satisfaction in the Middle Years of Marriage." *Social Forces* 42 (March 1964), 303–9.

WHITEHURST, ROBERT M. "Violence Potential in Extramarital Sexual Response." *Journal of Marriage and the Family* 33:4 (November 1971), 683.

WHITLEY, MARILYN PEDDICORD, and SUSAN B. POULSEN. "Assertiveness and Sexual Satisfaction in Employed Professional Women." *Journal of Marriage and the Family* 37:3 (August 1975), 573–81.

## CHAPTER 16

ALDOUS, JOAN. "The Consequences of Intergenerational Continuity." *Journal of Marriage and the Family* 27:4 (November 1965), 462–68.

BABCHUK, NICHOLAS. "Primary Friends and Kin: A Study of the Association of Middle-Class Couples." *Social Forces* 43:4 (May 1965), 483–93.

————, and ALAN P. BATES "The Primary Relations of Middle-Class Couples: A Study in Male Dominance." *American Sociological Review* 28:3 (June 1968), 377–84.

BELLWEG, JOHN A. "Extensions of Meaning and Use for Kinship Terms." *American Anthropologist* 71:1 (February 1969), 84–87.

CROOG, SIDNEY H., and PETER KONG-MING NEW. "Knowledge of Grandfather's Occupation—A Clue to American Kinship Structure." *Journal of Marriage and the Family* 27:1 (February 1965), 69–77.

DRABEK, THOMAS E., and KEITH S. BOGGS. "Families in Disaster: Reactions and Relatives." *Journal of Marriage and the Family* 30:3 (August 1968), 443–51.

DUVALL, EVELYN MILLIS. "In-Laws: Pro and Con." In *People as Partners*, edited by Jacqueline P. Wiseman, pp. 196–202. New York: Harper & Row, Publishers, 1971.

————. *In-Laws: Pro and Con.* New York: Association Press, 1954.

GLASSER, PAUL H., and LOIS N. GLASSER. "Role Reversal and Conflict Between Aged Parents and Their Children." *Marriage and Family Living* 24:1 (February 1962), 46–51.

GOLDSCHNEIDER, CALVIN, and SIDNEY GOLDSTEIN. "Generational Changes in Jewish Family Structure." *Journal of Marriage and the Family* 29:2 (May 1967), 267–76.

HAGSTROM, WARREN O., and JEFFREY K. HADDEN. "Sentiment and Kinship Terminology in American Society." *Journal of Marriage and the Family* 27:3 (August 1965), 324–32.

HAYS, WILLIAM C., and CHARLES H. MINDEL. "Extended Kinship Relations in Black and White Families." *Journal of Marriage and the Family* 35:1 (February 1973), 51–57.

HSU, FRANCIS L. K. "The Effect of Dominant Kinship Relationships on Kin and Non-Kin Behavior: A Hypothesis." *American Anthropologist* 67:3 (June 1965), 638–61.

LEWIS, LIONEL S. "Kinship Terminology for the American Parent." *American Anthropologist* 65:3 (June 1963), 649–52.

LITWAK, EUGENE, and IVAN SZELENYI. "Primary Group Structures and Their Function: Kin, Neighbors and Friends." *American Sociological Review* 34:4 (August 1969), 465–81.

MARRIS, PETER. "Individual Achievement and Family Ties: Some International Comparisons." *Journal of Marriage and the Family* 29:4 (November 1967), 763–71.

SCHNEIDER, DAVID M. *American Kinship: A Cultural Account.* Englewood Cliffs, N.J.: Prentice-Hall, Inc., 1968.

SHULMAN, NORMAN. "Life-Cycle Variations in Patterns of Close Relationships." *Journal of Marriage and the Family* 37:4 (November 1975), 813–21.

STRAUS, MURRAY A. "Social Class and Farm-City Differences in Interaction with Kin in Relation to Societal Modernization." *Rural Sociology* 34:4 (December 1969), 476–95.

WINCH, ROBERT F.; SCOTT GREER; and RAE LESSER BLUMBERG. "Ethnicity and Extended Familism in an Upper Middle Class Suburb." *American Sociological Review* 32:2 (April 1967), 265–72.

## CHAPTER 17

BALLWEG, JOHN A. "Change in Religious Affiliation and Family Stability." *Social Forces* 45:4 (June 1967), 551–55.

BURCHINAL, LEE G., and WILLIAM F. KENKEL. "Religious Identification and Occupational Status of Iowa Grooms, 1953–1957." *American Sociological Review* 27:4 (August 1962), 526–32.

CARDWELL, JERRY D. "The Relationship Between Religious Commitment and Premarital Sexual Permissiveness: A Five-Dimensional Analysis." *Sociological Analysis* 30:2 (Summer 1969), 72–81.

CHANCELLOR, LOREN E., and LEE G. BURCHINAL. "Relations Among Interreligious Marriages, Migratory Marriages and Civil Weddings in Iowa." *Eugenics Quarterly* 9:2 (June 1962), 75–83.

CROCKETT, HARRY J., JR.; NICHOLAS BABCHUK; and JOHN A. BALLWEG. "Change in Religious Affiliation and Family Stability: A Second Study." *Journal of Marriage and the Family* 31:3 (August 1969), 464–68.

GLASNER, SAMUEL. "Family Religion as a Matrix of Personal Growth." *Marriage and Family Living* 23:3 (August 1961), 291–93.

GLOCK, CHARLES Y. "On the Study of Religious Commitment." *Religious Education: Research Supplement* 42 (July–August 1962), 98–110.

GORDON, ALBERT I. *Intermarriage*. Boston: Beacon Press, 1964.

HASTINGS, PHILLIP K., and DEAN R. HOGE. "Religious Change Among College Students over Two Decades." *Social Forces* 49:1 (September 1970), 16–28.

KING, MORTON. "Measuring the Religious Variable: Nine Proposed Dimensions." *Journal for the Scientific Study of Religion* 6:2 (Summer 1967), 173–90.

LANDIS, JUDSON T. "Religiousness, Family Relationships and Family Values in Protestant, Catholic, and Jewish Families." *Marriage and Family Living* 22:4 (November 1960), 341–47.

LAZERWITZ, BERNARD. "Contrasting the Effects of Generation, Class, Sex, and Age on Group Identification in the Jewish and Protestant Communities." *Social Forces* 49:1 (September 1970), 50–59.

MOBERG, DAVID O. "Religion and the Aging Family." *The Family Coordinator* 21:1 (January 1972), 47–60.

## CHAPTER 18

CAVAN, RUTH SHONLE. "Unemployment-Crisis of the Common Man." In *People as Partners*, edited by Jacqueline P. Wiseman, pp. 392–402. New York: Harper & Row, Publishers, 1971.

CUTRIGHT, PHILLIPS. "Income and Family Events: Marital Stability." *Journal of Marriage and the Family* 33:2 (May 1971), 291.

MASTELLER, KENNETH C. *How to Avoid Financial Tangles*. Great Barrington, Mass.: American Institute for Economic Research, 1972.

SCANZONI, JOHN. "Sex Roles, Economic Factors, and Marital Solidarity in Black and White Marriages." *Journal of Marriage and the Family* 37:1 (February 1975), 130–44.

SCHOTTLAND, CHARLES I. "Government Economic Programs and Family Life." *Journal of Marriage and the Family* 29:1 (February 1967), 71–123.

## CHAPTER 19

*Consumer Reports*, "How to Buy Life Insurance," Part I, 32:1 (January 1967), 14–25; "Should Your Policy also Be a Savings Account?" Part II, 32:2 (February 1967), 100–107: "Prices, Options, and Reading the Fine Print," Part III, 32:3 (March 1967), 156–64; "Life Insurance on Campus: Caveat Emptor," 37:1 (January 1972), 50–51.

*Life Insurance from the Buyer's Point of View*. Great Barrington, Mass.: American Institute of Economic Research (latest edition, usually revised annually). One of the best books on the subject from the consumer's point of view.

CHAPTER 20

BAHR, STEPHEN J., and BOYD C. ROLLINS. "Crisis and Conjugal Power." *Journal of Marriage and the Family* 33:2 (May 1971), 360.

BOLTE, G. L. "A Communications Approach to Marital Counseling." *The Family Coordinator* 19:1 (January 1970), 32–40.

BOYER, C. L. "Group Therapy with Married Couples." *Marriage and Family Living* 22:1 (February 1960), 21–24.

BRANDWEIN, RUTH A.; CAROL A. BROWN; and ELIZABETH MAURY FOX. "Women and Children Last: The Social Situation of Divorced Mothers and Their Families." *Journal of Marriage and the Family* 36:3 (August 1974), 498–514.

CHEN, RONALD. "The Dilemma of Divorce: Disaster or Remedy." *The Family Coordinator* 17 (October 1968), 251–54.

DEAN, DWIGHT G. "Alienation and Marital Adjustment." *Sociological Quarterly* 9:2 (Spring 1968), 186–92.

ELKIN, MEYER. "Conciliation Courts: The Reintegration of Disintegrating Families." *The Family Coordinator* 22:1 (January 1973), 63–71.

ENGLAND, J. LYNN, and PHILLIP R. KUNZ. "The Application of Age-Specific Rate to Divorce." *Journal of Marriage and the Family* 37:1 (February 1975), 40–46.

GLASSER, PAUL, and ELIZABETH NAVARRE. "Structural Problems of the One-Parent Family." In *People as Partners,* edited by Jacqueline P. Wiseman, pp. 265–75. New York: Harper & Row, Publishers, 1971.

GLICK, PAUL C., and ARTHUR J. NORTON. "Frequency, Duration, and Probability of Marriage and Divorce." *Journal of Marriage and the Family* 33:1 (February 1971), 307.

GOODE, WILLIAM J. *Women in Divorce.* New York: The Free Press, 1956 and 1965.

KAPLAN, HOWARD B., and ALEX D. POKORNY. "Self-Derogation and Childhood Broken Home." *Journal of Marriage and the Family* 33:2 (May 1971), 328.

KRISHNAN, P., and ASHRAF K. KAYANI. "Estimates of Age Specific Divorce Rates for Females in the United States, 1960–69." *Journal of Marriage and the Family* 36:1 (February 1974), 72–75.

LANDIS, JUDSON T. "Social Correlates of Divorce or Non-Divorce Among the Unhappy Married." *Marriage and Family Living* 25:2 (May 1963), 178–80.

———. "The Trauma of Children When Parents Divorce." In *People as Partners,* edited by Jacqueline P. Wiseman, pp. 438–49. New York: Harper & Row, Publishers, 1971.

LEMASTERS, E. E. "Holy Deadlock: A Study of Unsuccessful Marriages." In *People as Partners,* edited by Jacqueline P. Wiseman, pp. 450–56. New York: Harper & Row, Publishers, 1971.

LEVINGER, GEORGE. "Marital Cohesiveness and Dissolution: An Integrative Review." *Journal of Marriage and the Family* 27:1 (February 1965a), 19–28.

———. "Sources of Marital Dissatisfaction Among Applicants for Divorce." *American Journal of Orthopsychiatry* 36:5 (October 1966), 803–7.

MINDEY, CAROL. *The Divorced Mother*. New York: McGraw-Hill Book Company, 1970.

RENNE, KAREN S. "Correlates of Dissatisfaction in Marriage." *Journal of Marriage and the Family* 32:1 (February 1970), 54–66.

ROBBINS, NORMAN N. "End of Divorce—Beginning of Legal Problems." *The Family Coordinator* 23:2 (April 1974), 185–88.

ROSE, VICKI L., and SHARON PRICE-BONHAM. "Divorce Adjustment: A Woman's Problem?" *The Family Coordinator* 22:3 (July 1973), 291–97.

SCHOEN, ROBERT. "California Divorce Rates by Age at First Marriage and Duration of First Marriage." *Journal of Marriage and the Family* 37:3 (August 1975), 548–55.

SHANAHAN, J. RUE, and LOUISE SHANAHAN. *The Divorced Catholic*. Paramus, N.J.: Paulist Press, 1972.

SPRING, JULIA C. "No-Fault Divorce." *Journal of Marriage and the Family* 37:4 (November 1975), 1046–47.

STETSON, DOROTHY M., and GERALD C. WRIGHT, JR. "The Effects of Laws on Divorce in American States." *Journal of Marriage and the Family* 37:3 (August 1975), 537–47.

## CHAPTER 21

BRANDWEIN, RUTH A.; CAROL A. BROWN; and ELIZABETH MAURY FOX. "Women and Children Last: The Social Situation of Divorced Mothers and Their Families." *Journal of Marriage and the Family* 36:3 (August 1974), 498–514.

COHEN, SARAH BETSY, and JAMES A. SWEET. "The Impact of Marital Disruption and Remarriage on Fertility." *Journal of Marriage and the Family* 36:1 (February 1974), 87–96.

FELDBERG, ROSLYN, and JANET KOHEN. "Family Life in an Anti-Family Setting: A Critique of Marriage and Divorce." *The Family Coordinator* 25:2 (April 1976), 151–59.

GUBRIUM, JABER F. "Marital Desolation and the Evaluation of Everyday Life in Old Age." *Journal of Marriage and the Family* 36:1 (February 1974), 107–13.

HARVEY, CAROL D., and HOWARD M. BAHR. "Widowhood, Morale, and Affiliation." *Journal of Marriage and the Family* 36:1 (February 1974), 97–106.

HUTCHISON, IRA W., III. "The Significance of Marital Status for Morale and Life Satisfaction Among Lower-Income Elderly." *Journal of Marriage and the Family* 37:2 (May 1975), 287–93.

KERCKHOFF, RICHARD K. "Marriage and Middle Age." *The Family Coordinator* 25:1 (January 1976), 5–11.

SPICER, JERRY W., and GARY D. HAMPE. "Kinship Interaction After Divorce." *Journal of Marriage and the Family* 37:1 (February 1975), 113–19.

WILSON, KENNETH L.; LOUIS A. ZURCHER; DIANA CLAIRE McADAMS; and RUSSELL L. CURTIS. "Stepfathers and Stepchildren: An Exploratory Analysis from Two National Surveys." *Journal of Marriage and the Family* 37:3 (August 1975), 526–36.

## CHAPTER 22

DALTON, KATHARINA. *The Menstrual Cycle.* New York: Pantheon Books, Inc. 1971.

EASTMAN, NICHOLAS J. *Expectant Motherhood,* revised edition. Boston: Little, Brown and Company, 1975. A scientific treatment of the prenatal period by a professor of obstetrics at The Johns Hopkins University and Obstetrician-in-Chief to The Johns Hopkins Hospital.

EWY, RODGER, and DONNA EWY. *Preparation for Childbirth: A Lamaze Guide.* Boulder, Colo.: Pruett Publishing Co., 1970.

FARRIS, EDMOND J. *Human Fertility and the Problems of the Male.* White Plains, N.Y.: The Author's Press, Inc., 1950. Laboratory research largely on the human male, but also on the female, to determine the real cause of infertility. Should be of interest to all couples having difficulty conceiving.

FERREIRA, ANTONIO J. "The Pregnant Woman's Emotional Attitude and Its Reflection on the Newborn." *American Journal of Orthopsychiatry* 30:3 (1960), 553–61. Also in Robert F. Winch; Robert McGinnis; and Herbert R. Barringer, *Selected Studies in Marriage and the Family,* pp. 203–12. New York: Holt, Rinehart & Winston, Inc., 1962.

FLANAGAN, GERALDINE LUX. *The First Nine Months of Life.* New York: Simon & Schuster, Inc., 1962. Excellent illustrations.

GENNÉ, WILLIAM H. *Husbands and Pregnancy.* New York: Association Press, 1956.

GOODRICH, FREDERICK W. *Preparation for Childbirth.* Englewood Cliffs, N.J.: Prentice-Hall, Inc., 1966.

HALL, ROBERT E. *Nine Months Reading: A Medical Guide for Pregnant Women,* revised edition. New York: Doubleday & Company, Inc., 1963.

HAZELL, LESTOR DESSEY. *Commonsense Childbirth.* New York: G. P. Putnam's Sons, 1969.

MEYEROWITZ, JOSEPH H. "Satisfaction During Pregnancy." *Journal of Marriage and the Family* 32:1 (February 1970), 38–42.

POFFENBERGER, SHIRLEY; THOMAS POFFENBERGER; and JUDSON T. LANDIS. "Intent Toward Conception and the Pregnancy Experience." *American Sociological Review* 17:5 (October 1952), 616–20.

READ, GRANTLEY DICK. *Childbirth Without Fear.* New York: Harper & Row, Publishers, 1944. The thesis of this book is that by doing away with fear, through knowledge and understanding, childbirth will be the natural, comparatively painless function nature intended it to be.

SCHEINFELD, AMRAM. *Heredity in Humans.* Philadelphia: J. B. Lippincott Co., 1972.


## CHAPTER 23

ANGRIST, SHIRLEY S. "Communication About Birth Control: An Exploratory Study of Freshman Girls' Information and Attitudes." *Journal of Marriage and the Family* 28:3 (August 1966), 284–86.

BALSWICK, JACK O. "Attitudes of Lower Class Males Toward Taking a Male Birth Control Pill." *The Family Coordinator* 21:2 (April 1972), 195–99.

BLAKE, JUDITH. "Abortion and Public Opinion: The 1960–70 Decade." *Science* 171 (12 February 1971).

CUTRIGHT, PHILLIPS. "Timing the First Birth: Does It Matter?" *Journal of Marriage and the Family* 35:4 (November 1973), 585–95.

HALL, ROBERT E. "Abortion: Physician and Hospital Attitudes." *American Journal of Public Health* 61:3 (March 1971).

———. "Induced Abortion in New York City." *American Journal of Obstetrics and Gynecology* 110:5 (July 1971).

HANEY, C. ALLEN; ROBERT MICHIELUTTE; CARL M. COCHRANE; and CLARK E. VINCENT. "Some consequences of Illegitimacy in a Sample of Black Women." *Journal of Marriage and the Family* 37:2 (May 1975), 359–66.

LANDIS, JUDSON T. "Attitudes of Individual California Physicians and Policies of State Medical Societies on Vasectomy for Birth Control." *Journal of Marriage and the Family* 28:3 (August 1966), 277–83.

———, and THOMAS POFFENBERGER. "The Marital and Sexual Adjustment of 300 Couples Who Chose Vasectomy as a Form of Birth Control." *Journal of Marriage and the Family* 27:1 (February 1965), 57–58.

MULLEN, PATRICIA; RICHARD REYNOLDS; PAUL CIGNETTI; and DAVID DORNAN. "A Vasectomy Education Program: Implications from Survey Data." *The Family Coordinator* 22:3 (July 1973), 331–38.

MULLER, CHARLOTTE. "Socio-economic Outcomes of Restricted Access to Abortion." *American Journal of Public Health* 61:3 (March 1971).

OVERSTREET, EDMUND W. "Logistic Problems of Legal Abortion." *American Journal of Public Health* 61:3 (March 1971).

RAINWATER, LEE. *Family Design: Marital Sexuality, Family Size, and Contraception.* Chicago: Adeline Publishing Company, 1965.

ROBERTO, EDUARDO L. "Marital and Family Planning Expectations of Men Regarding Vasectomy." *Journal of Marriage and the Family* 36:4 (November 1974), 698–706.

ROCHAT, ROGER W., et al. "An Epidemiological Analysis of Abortion in Georgia." *American Journal of Public Health* 61:3 (March 1971).

RODGERS, DAVID A; FREDERICK J. ZIEGLER; JOHN ALTROCCHI; and NISSIM LEVY. "A Longitudinal Study of the Psycho-Social Effects of Vasectomy." *Journal of Marriage and the Family* 27:1 (February 1965), 59–64.

THOMPSON, HORACE W., et al. "Therapeutic Abortion: A Two-Year Experience in One Hospital." *Journal of the American Medical Association* 213:6 (August 1970).

TIETZE, CHRISTOPHER, and SARAH LEWIT. "Early Complications of Abortion Under Medical Auspices: A Preliminary Report." *Studies in Family Planning* (July 1971).

VEEVERS, J. E. "The Moral Careers of Voluntarily Childless Wives: Notes on the Defense of a Variant World View." *The Family Coordinator* 24:4 (October 1975), 473–87.

ADAMS, JOHN E., and HYUNG BOK KIM. "A Fresh Look at Intercountry Adoptions." *Children* 18:6 (November–December 1971), 214–21.

CADY, ERNEST, and FRANCES CADY. *How to Adopt a Child.* New York: William Morrow & Co., Inc., 1956.

FARRIS, EDMOND J. *Human Fertility and Problems of the Male.* White Plains, N.Y.: The Author's Press, Inc., 1950.

———. *Human Ovulation and Fertility.* Philadelphia: J. B. Lippincott Co., 1956.

GALLAGHER, URSULA M. "Adoption Resources for Black Children." *Children* 18:2 (March–April 1971).

MURPHY, DOUGLAS P. "Donor Insemination—A Study of 511 Prospective Donors." *Fertility and Sterility* 15:5 (September–October 1964), 528–33.

PRINGLE, M. L. *Adoption—Fact and Fallacies.* London: Longmans, Green & Co., Ltd., 1967.

RAO, S. L. N. "A Comparative Study of Childlessness and Never-Pregnant Status." *Journal of Marriage and the Family* 36:1 (February 1974), 149–57.

ROBERTS, ROBERT W., and DONNELL M. PAPPENFORT. *Maternity Homes: Programs, Services and Physical Plant.* Chicago: Florence Crittenden Association of America, Inc., 1970.

SKEELS, H. M. "Effects of Adoption on Children from Institutions." *Children* 12:1 (January–February 1965).

TORRANO, EDITHA F., and DOUGLAS P. MURPHY. "Cycle Day of Conception by Insemination or Isolated Coitus." *Fertility and Sterility* 13:5 (September–October 1962), 492–94.

TOUSSIENG, PAUL. "Realizing the Potential in Adoptions." *Children* 18:3 (May–June 1971).

VERN, CARROL, ed. *Adoption in Eastern Oceania.* Honolulu: University of Hawaii Press, 1970.

VERNON, GLENN M., and JACK A. BOADWAY. "Attitudes Toward Artificial Insemination and Some Variables Associated Therewith." *Marriage and Family Living* 21:1 (February 1959), 43–47.

VINCENT, CLARK E. "The Adoption Market and the Unwed Mother's Baby." *Marriage and Family Living* 18:2 (May 1956), 124–27.

———. "Unwed Mothers and the Adoption Market: Psychological and Familial Factors." *Marriage and Family Living* 22:2 (May 1960), 112–18.

WITMER, HELEN; ELIZABETH HERZOG; EUGENIE WEINSTEIN; and MARGARET E. SULLIVAN. *Independent Adoptions—A Follow-up Study.* New York: Russell Sage Foundation, 1963.

CHAPTER 25

ALDOUS, JOAN. "Children's Perception of Adult Role Assignments: Father-Absence, Class, Race, and Sex Differences." *Journal of Marriage and the Family* 34:1 (February 1972), 55–65.

BARD, MORTON, and JOSEPH ZACKER. "The Prevention of Family Violence: Dilemmas of Community Intervention." *Journal of Marriage and the Family* 33:4 (November 1971), 677.

DAGER, EDWARD Z. "Socialization and Personality Development in the Child." In *Handbook of Marriage and the Family*, edited by Harold T. Christensen, pp. 740–81. Skokie, Ill.: Rand McNally & Co., 1964.

"Fatherhood." Special issue of *The Family Coordinator* 25, No. 4 (October 1976), entire issue.

GIL, DAVID G. "Violence Against Children." *Journal of Marriage and the Family* 33:4 (November 1971), 637.

GIOVANNONI, JEANNE M. "Parental Mistreatment: Perpetrators and Victims." *Journal of Marriage and the Family* 33:4 (November 1971), 649.

HOBBS, DANIEL F., JR. "Parenthood as Crisis: A Third Study." *Journal of Marriage and the Family* 27:3 (August 1965), 367–72.

LANDIS, JUDSON T. "A Comparison of Children from Divorced and Nondivorced Unhappy Marriages." *Family Life Coordinator* 9:3 (July 1962), 61–65.

———. "A Re-examination of the Role of the Father as an Index of Family Integration." *Marriage and Family Living* 24:2 (May 1962), 122–28.

———. "The Trauma of Children When Parents Divorce." *Marriage and Family Living* 22:1 (February 1960), 7–13.

LEMASTERS, E. E. "The American Father." In *People as Partners*, edited by Jacqueline P. Wiseman, pp. 247–64. New York: Harper & Row, Publishers, 1971.

———. "Parenthood as Crisis." *Crisis and Family Living* 19:4 (November 1957), 352–55.

NYE, F. IVAN. "Child Adjustment in Broken and Unhappy Unbroken Homes." *Marriage and Family Living* 19:4 (November 1957), 356–61.

———, and LOIS WLADIS HOFFMAN. *The Employed Mother in America*, Part II. Skokie, Ill.: Rand McNally & Co., 1963.

OSOFSKY, JOY D. "The Shaping of Mother's Behavior by Children." *Journal of Marriage and the Family* 32:3 (August 1970), 400–406.

RABIN, ALBERT I. "Kibbutz Children—Research Findings to Date." *Children* 5 (1958), 179–84.

ROSSI, ALICE S. "Naming Children in Middle Class Families." *American Sociological Review* 30:4 (August 1965), 499–513.

———. "Transition to Parenthood." *Journal of Marriage and the Family* 30:1 (February 1968), 26–39. Also in *People as Partners*, edited by Jacqueline P. Wiseman, pp. 228–46. New York: Harper & Row, Publishers, 1971.

RUSSELL, CANDYCE SMITH. "Transition to Parenthood: Problems and Gratifications." *Journal of Marriage and the Family* 36:2 (May 1974), 295–301.

SKARD, AASE GRUDA. "Maternal Deprivation: The Research and Its Implications." *Journal of Marriage and the Family* 27:3 (August 1965), 333–43.

SPOCK, BENJAMIN. *The Pocketbook of Baby and Child Care*. New York: Pocket Books, Inc., 1968.

STRAUS, MURRAY. "Some Social Antecedents of Physical Punishment: A Linkage

Theory Interpretation." *Journal of Marriage and the Family* 33:4 (November 1971), 658.

CHAPTER 26

ALEXANDER, JAMES F. "Defensive and Supportive Communications in Family Systems." *Journal of Marriage and the Family* 35:4 (November 1973), 613–17.

AXELSON, LELAND. "Marital Adjustment and Marital Role Definitions of Husbands of Working and Non-Working Wives." *Marriage and Family Living* 25:2 (May 1963), 189–95.

BALSWICK, JACK O. "Effect of Spouse Companionship Support on Employment Success." *Journal of Marriage and the Family* 32:2 (May 1970), 212.

BOSSARD, JAMES H., and ELEANOR S. BOLL. "Family Ritual as an Instrument in Culture Transmission." In *People as Partners,* edited by Jacqueline P. Wiseman, pp. 308–15. New York: Harper & Row, Publishers, 1971.

———. *Ritual in Family Living.* Philadelphia: University of Pennsylvania Press, 1950.

BOWERMAN, CHARLES E., and DONALD P. IRISH. "Some Relationships of Stepchildren to Their Parents." *Marriage and Family Living* 24:2 (May 1962), 109–12.

BRITTON, JOSEPH H., and JEAN O. BRITTON. "Children's Perceptions of Their Parents: A Comparison of Finnish and American Children." *Journal of Marriage and the Family* 33:1 (February 1971), 214.

BURGESS, JANE K. "Single-Parent Family: A Social and Sociological Problem." *The Family Coordinator* 19:2 (April 1970), 137–44.

CALDERONE, MARY S. "Eroticism as a Norm." *The Family Coordinator* 23:4 (October 1974), 337–41.

DUVALL, EVELYN MILLIS. *Faith in Families.* Chicago: Rand McNally & Co., 1970.

GLASSER, PAUL H., and LOIS N. GLASSER. "Role Reversal and Conflict Between Aged Parents and Their Children." *Marriage and Family Living* 24:1 (February 1962), 46–50.

GLENN, NORVAL D. "Psychological Well-Being in the Postparental Stage: Some Evidence from National Surveys." *Journal of Marriage and the Family* 37:1 (February 1975), 105–10.

GOVER, DAVID A. "Socio-Economic Differential in the Relationship Between Marital Adjustment and Wife's Employment Status." *Marriage and Family Living* 25:4 (November 1963), 452–56.

GRAY, ROBERT M., and TED C. SMITH. "Effect of Employment on Sex Differences in Attitudes Toward the Parental Family." *Marriage and Family Living* 22:1 (February 1960), 36–38.

HARRELL, JANET E., and CARL A. RIDLEY. "Substitute Child Care, Maternal Employment and the Quality of Mother–Child Interaction." *Journal of Marriage and the Family* 37:3 (August 1975), 556–64.

JACKSON, JACQUELYNE JOHNSON. "Marital Life Among Aging Blacks." *The Family Coordinator* 21:1 (January 1972), 21–27.

Jacobsen, R. Brooke; Kenneth J. Berry; and Keith F. Olson. "An Empirical Test of the Generation Gap: A Comparative Intrafamily Study." *Journal of Marriage and the Family* 37:4 (November 1975), 841–52.

Kalish, Richard A. "Of Social Values and the Dying: A Defense of Disengagement." *The Family Coordinator* 21:1 (January 1972), 81–94.

Kirkendall, Lester A. *Kirkendall on Sex Education: A Collection of Readings.* Eugene, Ore.: E. C. Brown Center for Family Studies, 1970.

Landis, Judson T. "Experiences of 500 Children with Adult Sexual Deviation." *Psychiatric Quarterly Supplement* 30, Part 1 (1956), 91–109.

————. "The Nondelinquent Child and the Sexual Deviate." *Research Studies of the State College of Washington* 22:1 (March 1955), 92–101.

McKain, Walter C. "A New Look at Older Marriages." *The Family Coordinator* 21:1 (January 1972), 61–69.

Neugarten, Bernice L., and Karol K. Weinstein. "The Changing American Grandparent." *Journal of Marriage and the Family* 26:2 (May 1964), 199–204.

Nye, F. Ivan. "Working Wives and Marriage Happiness." *American Journal of Sociology* 74:4 (January 1969), 392–407.

Silverman, Phyllis R. "Widowhood and Preventive Intervention." *The Family Coordinator* 21:1 (January 1972), 95–102.

Somerville, Rose M. "Family Life and Sex Education in the Turbulent Sixties. *Journal of Marriage and the Family* 33:1 (February 1971), 11.

Streib, Gordon E. "Older Families and Their Troubles: Familial and Social Responses. *The Family Coordinator* 21:1 (January 1972), 5–19.

Troll, Lillian E. "The Family of Later Life: A Decade Review." *Journal of Marriage and the Family* 33:2 (May 1972), 263.

U.S. Department of Labor. *Your Child from One to Six.* Childrens Bureau Publication 30. Washington, D.C.: Government Printing Office, latest revision.

Whiting, Beatrice B., ed. *Six Cultures: Studies of Child Rearing.* New York: John Wiley & Sons, Inc., 1963.

# INDEX

American Board of Obstetrics and Gynecology, 411
American College of Life Underwriters, 351
American Institute for Economic Research, 348
Annulment
  age at marriage and, 219
  Catholics and, 230
  children and, 228, 230–31
  defined, 228
  extent of, 7, 229–30
  grounds for, 228–29
Artificial insemination
  attitudes toward, 452
  legal aspects of, 452
  sperm banks, 439–40
  uses of, 447, 449, 452
Aschheim-Zondek test for pregnancy, 406
AXELSON, LELAND J., 504–5

BACH, GEORGE R., 260
BALSWICK, JACK O., 143
Banns, 222, 223
BABER, RAY E., 256
BARDWICK, JUDITH M., 279
BARRON, MILTON L., 167
BELL, HOWARD M., 164
BELL, ROBERT R., 142, 147, 269
BENEDEK, THERESE, 278
BERNARD, JESSIE, 44, 172, 392
Bigamous marriages, 228, 229, 231
Birth. See Childbirth
Birth certificates
  legitimacy shown on, 231–32, 233–34
  short form of, figure, 231
Birth control. See Contraception
Birth rate
  curbing (see Contraception)
  factors influencing, 431
  teenage pregnancies and, 434
  trends in, 430–31; figure, 431
BLOOD, ROBERT O., JR., 261–62, 289, 297
BOLL, ELEANOR STOKER, 67
Borrowing money, 330–32; table, 332
BOSSARD, JAMES H.S., 67
Budgeting, 320–21
BURCHINAL, LEE G., 104, 124, 162
BURGESS, ERNEST W., 53–54, 80–81, 85–86, 101, 112, 139, 147, 149, 175, 183, 194, 268, 444–45, 485
BUXTON, C.L., 405
Buying
  on credit, 324–27, 332
  housing, 333–35
  intelligence in, 327–30
  life insurance (see Life insurance)

CALDERWOOD, DERYCK, 496
CAPLOW, THEODORE, 188–89
Carnegie Corporation, 351

CARTER, HUGH, 158
CARTER, PRESIDENT JAMES, 12
Catholic-Protestant marriage, 159–61, 162. See also Jewish-Gentile marriages
  children in, 160–61, 165–66
  conflicts in, 164–65
  divorce rate, 162–64, 166
Catholics
  abortion views, 442
  annulment for, 230
  artificial insemination views, 452
  birth control views, 161, 432, 433; table, 433
  birth rate, 431
  homogamy among, 158
Catholic Separation Courts, 290
CERVANTES, LUCIUS F., 164, 168
CHANCELLOR, LOREN E., 162
CHASKES, JAY B., 142, 147
Childbirth
  anaesthetics and, 421–24
  circumcision, 426
  culture and, 421
  death during, 68, 425
  duration of labor, 419, 420, 421, 425
  fear of, and failure to marry, 66
  "natural," 423–25
  pain during, 420–21, 424
  postpartum depression, 468
  rooming-in, 426–27
  sex adjustment after, 415
  stages in, 419–24; figures, 422–24
  training for, 420, 421, 424–25
  Yale University study on, 424–25
Child care. See also Child rearing; Parenthood
  college marrieds and, 122, 124
  in communes, 7, 8
  discussing during engagement, 199
  parental help with, 124
Childlessness. See Adoption; Infertility
Child marriages, 217–19; figure, 218
Child rearing. See also Child care; Parenthood
  agreement on, 470–72; figure, 471
  anxiety-causing situations, 477–78; table, 478
  basic principles of, 480
  consideration for others and, 490–91
  death and, 500–502
  developing desirable personality traits, 484–85
  evaluating success in, 506–7
  factors affecting children's happiness, 473–77, 485
  family companionship in, 503–4
  father-child relationships, 472–73
  goals of, 483
  habit of happiness and, 485
  independent thinking and, 488

education and, 93, 101, 368
engagement and, 193–94; *table,* 58
extent of, 6–7, 360–61; *figures,* 361, 362
  legal changes and, 364–65
  postwar, 365–66
  remarriage and, 382–84, 389, 392; *figure,* 383
extramarital sex and, 269
failure to adjust and, 366–67
family background and, 86–88, 368; *figure,* 88
grounds for, 362–64
health and, 368, 386
in homogamous marriages, 163, 164
in-law relationships and, 290, 301
in interfaith marriages, *figure,* 163
  Catholic-Protestant, 162–64, 166
  Jewish-Gentile, 168–69
in interracial marriages, 172–73
law and, 212, 361–65
moving toward, 366–67
as new hope, 385–86
permanent, 377–78
premarital pregnancy and, 103–4, 442–43; *figure,* 443; *table,* 58
rate (*see* Divorce, extent of)
religion and, 307, 308, 368
remarriage after (*see* Remarriage)
selective factors in, 368
as social adjustment, 365
trauma of, 373–76
years married before, 383–84; *figure,* 240
Dominance, 261–62
DUVALL, EVELYN MILLIS, 289, 290
DYER, EVERETT D., 469

Economic adjustment. *See* Money in marriage
Ecumenical Council, 160
Education
  age at marriage and, 32, 101
  birth rate and, 430, 431
  differences in, and marital success, 174–75
  discussing during engagement, 198
  divorce and, 93, 101, 368
  interracial marriage and, 172
  premarital sex and, 145
  sex (*see* Sex education)
  venereal disease and, 153
  for women, changes in, 11
EHRMANN, WINSTON W., 45, 138
Elopement, 204–5
Emotional maturity. *See* Maturity for marriage
Empathy, 82–83
Engagement
  becoming engaged, 181–82
  broken, 183–92

causes of, 51–52, 184–87; *tables,* 54, 184
  extent of, 183
  methods of, 191
  reactions to, 189–90, 191–92; *table,* 190
  recovering from, 187–91; *figure,* 189; *table,* 188
coitus during
  agreement about, 44, 147–49, 200; *table,* 44
  attitudes toward, 140–41, 145–47; *tables,* 141, 146
  contraception and, 200, 201
  effect on relationship, 147–50; *case studies,* 148–49, 149–50; *table,* 148
  extent of, 138–40; *table,* 139
  limiting, 147–49; *table,* 44
  sex adjustment and, 200, 201–2
  values and, 192–93
confessing the past during, 202–4; *table,* 203
danger signals in, 51–53, 194–97, 249; *case studies,* 195, 196; *table,* 54
financial planning in, 187, 197–98, 321
first and second marriages compared, *table,* 127
informal ("understanding"), 181
  broken, 183–84, 187
  coitus during, 140; *table,* 139
legal status of, 179, 183
length of, marital adjustment and, 193–94; *figure,* 194
length of courtship to, 179–80; *table,* 180
marital adjustment and, 143, 181, 182
living together during, 201
making marriage contracts during, 199
percentage ending in marriage, 183; *figure,* 184
premarital examination, 204
process of, 181–82; *table,* 182
purpose of, 197–99
rituals, 181–82; *table,* 182
self-study outline for, 206–8
social change and, 179, 181, 183
symbols, 182
ENGLE, E.T., 405
Equal Rights Amendment, 12
ESHLEMAN, J. Ross, 121
Eugenic regulations, 212, 214–15, 217
Exploitation
  in dating, 44–46
  by matrimonial agencies, 65
Extramarital affairs, 269, 369

Families. *See also* Children; In-law relationships; Parenthood; Parents
  approval of
    and marital success, 186–87

Marriage adjustment (*cont.*)

discussing differences, 252–54; *figure*, 253

quarreling, 249–52

reactions to pressure, 254–57; *table*, 254–55

state of hostility, 241

personality traits and, 2, 3, 75–78, 80–83

physical differences and, 175

place married and, *figure*, 312

positive feelings and, 255; *table*, 254

pregnancy and, 412–15, 442–43

premarital confidence and, 54, 55, 143; *figure*, 55

premarital sex and, 143–45

preparation for, 138–39

problem solving and, 83–85, 260; *table*, 258

punctuality and, 246, 248

quarreling and, 241, 249–52, 253–54, 260

reactions to pressure and, 254–57; *table*, 254–55

religion and (*see* Religion; Religiousness)

in remarriage, 388–90, 394–96

role attitude and, 11, 21–22, 24, 27

satisfaction with, 245; *figure*, 245

separation and, 129–32

sexual bond and, 239 (*see also* Sex adjustment)

stress and, 257–60; *tables*, 258, 259

tension relievers, 249, 257, 504

testing and, 263

time factor in, 240, 242–45, 248–49, 289; *figures*, 240, 244, 247, 250

tolerance and, 263

"tremendous trifles," 256–57

vasectomy and, 439

in widowed remarriage, 394–96

work and, 245, 246, 248

Marriageability

adaptability and, 80–82

defined, 72

divorce in family and, 86–88; *figure*, 88

empathy and, 82–83

family background and, 79, 85–89; *table*, 87

habit of happiness and, 79

happiness of parents' marriage and, *figure*, 86 (*see also* Family background)

helping children develop, 484–85

husband-wife grievances, 79–80; *table*, 79

for mixed marriage, 176

personality traits and, 75–78, 80

problem solving and, 83–85

for remarriage, 388

self-study outline on, 89–90

of widowed, 392

Marriages involving separation, 129–32

Marry, failure to. *See also* Singleness

reasons for, 66–67, 70

unequal sex ratio and, 64

Martin, Patricia Yancy, 23

Masturbation, 499–500

Maternal mortality, 68, 425

Mate selection

danger signals and, 51–52

dating function and, 31, 39

marital success and, 47, 263–64, 365

reaction to crises and, 259–60

in remarriage, 388; *figure*, 389

sex role attitudes and, 21, 24

Maturity for marriage

age as a factor in, 93, 100–104; *figure*, 103; *table*, 101

broken engagements and, 190–92

divorce and, 93, 102–4; *figure*, 103

education and, 93

emotional, 93–100

emotional dependence and, 187

evaluating, 96

family background and, 96

independent thinking and, 97

in-law relationships and, 297–98, 301

law and, 93, 104

for mixed marriage, 176

objectivity and, 94

philosophy of life and, 95

present desires, future goals and, 98

problem solving and, 96–97

readiness for parenthood and, 122

readiness to sacrifice and, 98–99

realistic conceptions and, 94–95

responsibility for mistakes and, 97–98

second marriage, 128–29

self-assessment and, 96, 100

self-study outline on, 105–6

sex attitudes and, 99

understanding motivations and, 97

Meissner, Hanna H., 442

Men

achievement differences from women, 17, 19

age at marriage and marital adjustment, 101, 102; *table*, 101

biological differences from women, 14–17

broken engagements and, 184, 185, 188, 189

death rates and marital status, 68, 69; *table*, 69

as fathers, 472–73

female equality and, 12–14, 19–20, 24

find joy in housework, 24

grades and college marriage, 119–20

premarital sex and, 139–42, 145, 201; *tables*, 139, 141, 142

reproductive anatomy, 400–401

waiving waiting period for, 223
Premarital requirements, of states, 222, 223–25; *table*, 215–16
Premarital sexual relations
  attitudes toward, 137–38, 140–43, 200; *tables*, 141, 142
  confessing, *table*, 203
  contraception in, 150–51, 201, 434
  in dating, 34, 35, 42–46, 138
  double standard, 43, 138, 141
  education and, 145
  effects on relationship, 147–50; *table*, 148
  in engagement (*see* Engagement)
  exploitative, 44–46
  family background and, 142, 143, 144
  first and second marriages compared, *table*, 127
  guilt feelings and, 145–47
  high school students and, 145
  initiating, 42–43
  limiting, 43–44
  marital adjustment and, 143–45
  postmarital sexual adjustment and, 272, 273
  pregnancy and (*see* Premarital pregnancy)
  prevalence of, 1, 137–40, 142
  reasons against, 142–43; *table*, 142
  religion and, 142, 143, 144, 145
  in remarriage, 387; *table*, 127
  responsibility and, 154–55, 201
  sexual freedom and, 137–38, 154
  venereal disease and, 153–54
Presbyterian Ministers Fund, 351
PRINCE, ALFRED J., 165, 166
Protestants
  artificial insemination views, 452
  birth control views, 432, 433; *table*, 433
  birth rate, 431
  homogamy among, 158
  interfaith marriages (*see* Catholic-Protestant marriages; Jewish-Gentile marriages)
Puberty. *See* Adolescents
Pure Food and Drug Administration
  IUDs and, 438
  on oral contraceptives, 435–36

Quakers, marriage and, 222, 225–26
Quarreling
  avoiding, 257
  as danger signal, 52–53, 249
  happiness of children and, 474, 475
  marital adjustment and, 241, 249–52, 260; *case study*, 250–51
  timing and, 253–54

Rabbinical Assembly of American Jews, on birth control, 432

Race, birth rate and, 431. *See also* Mixed marriages
RAINWATER, LEE, 21
RANDALL, JOHN HERMAN, 310
Rape, statutory, 45
RASCHKE, HELEN JUNE, 384
REED, ROBERT B., 445
REISS, IRA L., 143
Relatives, marriage between, 219–20
Religion
  adult needs and, 311
  artificial insemination views and, 452
  birth control and, 432–33; *table*, 433
  birth rate and, 431
  current expressions of need for, 311–12
  dating reveals importance of, 39
  discussing during engagement, 198
  divorce and, 170, 307, 308, 368
    by affiliation, 162–64; *figure*, 163
  family relationships and, 308–11, 312–13, 319–20
  happiness and, 313
  happiness in marriage and, 312–13, 314; *figure*, 312
  interfaith marriages (*see* Mixed marriages)
  as marital problem area, 239, 243
  marriage ceremony and, 225–26
  marriage license and, 222
  parenthood and, 313–14
  premarital sex and, 142, 143, 144, 145
  self-discipline through, 313
  student views on, 309–10
Religiousness
  divorce and, 170, 307, 308, 368
  family relationships and, 308–11, 312–13, 319–20
  happiness and, 313
  marital success and, 307–8, 310–11, 312–13, 314; *figure*, 312
  student views on, 309–10
Remarriage
  adjustment in, 388–90
  age of spouses in, 382
  approach to, *table*, 127
  attitudes toward, 126–27; *table*, 127
  children and, 128
  courtship for, 386–88, 392–94
  of divorced, 385–91
  divorce rate for, 382–84, 389, 392; *figure*, 383
  experience and, 128–29
  extent of, 212, 381
  factors to consider in, 125–29
  family position on, 126, 127–28
  living together before, 391
  mate selection for, 388; *figure*, 389
  personality traits and, 388, 389
  premarital sex in, 387; *table*, 127
  success in, 382–84; *figure*, 383
  types of, 125, 388–90; *figure*, 389

Remarriage (*cont.*)
    wedding activities, 126, 387; *table,* 126
    of widowed, 391–96
Reproduction. *See also* Childbirth; Pregnancy
    explaining to children, 491–500 (*see also* Sex education)
    female anatomy of, 399–400
    male anatomy of, 400–401
    as marriage function, 7
Rhythm method. *See* Contraception
RILEY, LAWRENCE E., 67, 70, 86
RIOCH, DAVID, 114
ROBBINS, NORMAN N., 363, 370
ROBINSON, IRA E., 143
ROCK, Dr. JOHN, 450
Roles
    adult, learning through family companionship, 503–4
    agreement on needed, 11, 21–22, 24, 27
    attitudes toward, 22–24; *table,* 22
        assessing during engagement, 198–99
    college marriages and, 122, 124
    conflicts in, 25–26
    contracts about, 199
    differences in, sources of, 12–19, 22
    dominance and marital adjustment, 260–62
    flexibility in needed, 19–20, 25–26
    inconsistencies, 26–27
    interdependence of, 19–20
    money and, 319
    in parenthood
        father-child relationships, 472–73
        readjusting, 467, 469
    in poverty cultures, 21
    working wives and, 23–24
Rooming-in, 426–27
ROOSEVELT, THEODORE, 453
ROSE, ARNOLD M., 503–4
ROSEN, LAWRENCE, 269
ROSENBERG, MORRIS, 384
ROSENGREN, WILLIAM R., 413–14
RUBENSTEIN, B.B., 278
RUSSELL, CANDYCE SMITH, 469–70
Russell Sage Foundation, 331
RYDER, NORMAN B., 150

Safe period. *See* Contraception
Salpingectomy, 438–40
Savings bank life insurance. *See* Life insurance
SCHEINFELD, AMRAM, 18, 408, 409
Separation. *See also* Marriages involving separation
    broken engagements and, 184, 185–86
    extent of, 7
    time from wedding to, *figure,* 240
SETTLAGE, CALVIN F., 483
SEWELL, WILLIAM H., 479
Sex adjustment

age at marriage and, 101, 102
agreement and, 269, 272, 273; *figures,* 269, 273
attitudes and, 282
*case study,* 275
conditioning and, 270–71, 272, 273–74
counseling and, 281–82
environmental factors affecting, 280, 281
fatigue and, 280
frequency of coitus and, 280–82
honeymoon and, 205–6, 272, 277–78
importance of, 239, 244–45, 246, 267–68, 281, 283–84
initiating lovemaking, 276–77, 281
knowledge and, 270–71, 282, 283
marital adjustment and, 247, 267–69, 282–83
in marriages involving separation, 130
menstrual cycle and, 278–79
mutuality and, 21, 268, 269–70, 279–80, 281; *figure,* 269
in older marriages, 396
orgasm and, 275–76, 277–78, 279–80; *table,* 277
personality traits and, 269
poor, causes of, 270–71
pregnancy and, 412–13, 414–15; *figure,* 414
premarital coitus and, 200, 201, 272, 273
role segregation and, 21
sex drive differences and, 201, 275–79, 281
suggestions for, 284
time as factor in, 243, 244, 271–73, 277–78; *figure,* 271
vasectomy and, 439
Sex differences
    achievement, 17, 19
    biological, 13, 14–17
    developmental, 16–17
    roles, sources of, 12–19, 22
    sex adjustment and, 269–70, 274–80, 281
    in sex drive, 19, 201, 275–79, 281
    in sexual response, 274–78, 279–80, 281
Sex drive, differences in, 19, 201, 275–79, 281
Sex education
    age for, 492–95; *table,* 494
    attitudes toward sex and, *figure,* 499
    communicating positive aspects, 496–97, 500
    conditioning and, 273–74
    deviation, 497–98
    experimentation and, 273, 274, 494–95, 498–99
    home vs. school, 492
    marital adjustment and, 85, 273–74
    masturbation and, 499–500

misinformation, 270–71, 282
problems in, 491–92
questions asked, 493–94, 495–96; *tables,* 494, 496
answering specific questions, 493–95
parental policy toward, 492–93
vocabulary to use, 495
sources of information, 495
types of information parents give, 495–500; *table,* 496
values and, 491–92, 496–97, 498–500
Sex ratio
at conception, 408
marriage rate and, 64
Sexual attraction, love and, 110, 111, 115
Sexual deviation, 497–98
Sexuality
attitudes toward and maturity for marriage, 99
singleness and, 71
Sexual promiscuity
postmarital sex adjustment and, 273
prevalence of, 138, 140
venereal disease and, 153, 154
Sexual relationships
in communes, 7–8
extramarital, 269, 369
premarital (*see* Premarital sexual relations)
responsibility and, 154–55
role segregation and, 21
Sexual standards, changes in, 137
SHERMAN, JULIA A., 404
SHIPMAN, GORDON, 223
SHNEIDMAN, EDWARD S., 501
SIMON, WILLIAM, 141
Singleness. *See also* Marry, failure to
advantages of, 70, 71
computer dating and, 65–66
death rates and, 68–69; *tables,* 68, 69
disadvantages of, 70–71
of divorced people, 359, 385
family background and, 66–67
happiness and, 71–72
homosexuality and, 67
living a single life, 69–70
meeting others, 64–66
pressures against, 63–64, 69–70
reasons for, 66–67, 70
sex ratio and, 64
SKARD, AASE GRUDA, 506
SKIPPER, J.K., JR., 45
SLOTKIN, J.S., 168
SMITH, TED C., 289, 291
Social change
engagement and, 179, 181, 183
marital adjustment and, 245–46
marriage and, 1–2
SPREITZER, ELMER, 67, 70, 86
Steady dating. *See* Dating
Sterility. *See* Infertility

Sterilization
acceptance of and future of marriage, 7
as birth control method, 438–40
compulsory, 212, 214
STEVENSON, ROBERT LOUIS, 264
STEWART, CYRUS S., 145, 309
STEWART, H.L., 419
STRAUS, MURRAY A., 260
STRAUSS, ANSELM, 4, 5, 6
STRONG, EMILY, 47
STURGES, STANLEY G., 502
Successful marriage. *See also* Happiness in marriage; Marriage adjustment
determining, 3–4, 6, 249
engagement and, 193–94, 197–99; *figure,* 194
extent of in U.S., 6–7
love and, 109–16
marriageability and, 75
mate selection and, 365
pair identity and, 359
personality needs and, 94–95
premarital education and, 365
scope of, 511–12
while in college, 120–21
Supreme Court
on abortion, 441
on contraception, 433
on interracial marriage, 172, 220, 221
on validity of out-of-state divorce, 213
on voluntary sterilization, 440
on women, 12
SUSSMAN, MARVIN B., 124

Teachers Insurance and Annuity Association of America, 351
TEELE, JAMES E., 166
Temporary National Economic Committee, 348
Tension relievers, 257, 504
TERMAN, LEWIS M., 17, 19, 76–80, 85, 101, 137, 174, 277, 278, 307, 444, 485
THOMAS, JOHN L., 289, 290
THOMASON, O. BRUCE, 200, 276, 277
THOMS, HERBERT, 425
TIEN, H. YUAN, 223
TIETZE, CHRISTOPHER, 437
TORRANCE, PAUL, 12
TRILLING, DIANA, 13–14
TURNER, STANLEY, 269

Unwed mothers, 151–52, 154

Validity of marriage, 214, 226
Values
assessing during dating period, 39
discussing during engagement, 198
economic, 318–20
marriage adjustment and, 248; *table,* 6